SYMBOLS TABLE

SYMBOL	RELIGION	DESCRIPTION
	BAHÁ'Í	**Nine Pointed Star –** the number nine has particular significance for Bahá'ís, being known as "the number of Bah". The Arabic letters of the word "Bah", the first part of the title of the founder of the Bahá'í faith, Bahá'u'lláh, add up to nine in the Abjad notation.
	BUDDHISM	**Wheel of Law and Truth –** An eight spoked wheel with the spokes symbolising the eight-fold path, the Middle Way, propounded by the Buddha. By following the Middle Way a Buddhist may obtain Moksha and thus escape the cyclical nature of rebirth.
	CHRISTIANITY	**Cross –** Of prime significance to the Christian Church because of the belief that the crucifixion of Jesus was the ultimate expression of God's love for humanity. Crosses can be found in a variety of forms and may depict the Crucified Christ or may be plain – symbolising the resurrection.
	HINDUISM	**Om (Aum) –** The utmost sacred symbol in Hinduism. Regarded as bija (seed) of all mantras. The three phonetic elements (AUM), connected but remaining distinct are said to represent Shiva, Vishnu and Brahma, respectively the destroyer, the creator and the sustainer.
	ISLAM	**Crescent moon and star –** Introduced as an emblem of the Islamic faith by the Ottomans, the constantly regenerating moon is a reflection of God's everlasting purpose and control. Portrayed with the star the symbol represents divine authority and paradise. Just as the moon and stars are guiding lights so too is Islam.
	JAINISM	**Palm –** The raised hand is a symbol of protection and blessing. In Jain belief there have been twenty-four great teachers called Tirthankaras. Thus the wheel is divided into twenty-four segment. Central to the wheel is the word ahimsa, meaning non-violence and reverence for life, one of the five principles of Jainism.
	JUDAISM	**Menorah –** The Mosaic seven-branched candelabrum which indicates divine presence. According to Josephus the seven branches represent the sun, the moon and the planets and also the seven days of the week. The Star of David, an equilateral hexagram, originally known as the Seal of Solomon, is found on the base of the branches.
	SIKHISM	**Khanda –** The double edged sword in the centre signifies truth, strength, freedom and justice. The circle or chakkar represents the eternal and the two swords (Miri and Piri) represent political and spiritual sovereignty.
	ZOROASTRIANISM	**The Fravashi –** All humans have a Fravashi or the Guardian Spirit of Ahura Mazda. The Fravashi is depicted artistically as half human – half bird and its right hand is always pointed upwards towards heaven while its left hand is always holding the ring of divine sovereignty. Often erroneously the Fravashi is described as an angel as Ahura Mazda, but in practice the Fravashi is seen to represent Ahura Mazda's essence within humans as the "Wisdom of all knowledge".

Symbols take on different meanings for different people. What may be seen as being a "pretty picture" or object for one person may be seen as being something that invokes a feeling of reverence in another, in that it is a symbol that serves a religious purpose to people of a particular community. Religious symbols can be found across all religious communities in their beliefs and practices and their arts and cultures. Indeed some religious communities may share particular symbols but will probably attach a slightly differing meaning to them. Therefore symbols are not and cannot be definitive, in that many symbols have a slight variation of form depending on context in which they appear. In many cases, however, the basic form of certain symbols has become synonymous with particular religions. The religious symbols found on the front cover of the directory come from a wide range of religious symbols and are some of the most common religious representations found among the world religions.

BIBLIOGRAPHY

Bowker, J (ed) *The Oxford Dictionary of World Religions*, Oxford University Press, Oxford and New York, 1997.

Cooper, J C, *An Illustrated Encyclopaedia of Traditional Symbols*, Thames and Hudson Limited, London, 1978.

Giddens, A, *Sociology* (2nd edition), Polity Press, Cambridge, 1993.

Tressider, J, *The Hutchinson Dictionary of Symbols,* Helicon Publishing Ltd, 1997.

RELIGIONS IN THE UK
2007-2010

edited by
Paul Weller

researched by
*Paul Weller, Michele Wolfe
and Eileen Fry*

*Published by the Multi-Faith Centre at the University of Derby
in association with the Faculty of Education, Health and Sciences
of the University of Derby*

This edition of the directory is dedicated to Eileen Fry, to mark her upcoming retirement from being Director of the Multi-Faith Centre at the University of Derby (2001-2007), as well as in recognition of her pivotal role in two (1997 and 2001) of the three previous editions of the directory as Project Research Assistant, 1994-1998 and Project Manager, 1998-2001.

ISBN 978-0-901437-30-3

Published by the Multi-Faith Centre at the University of Derby (Registered Charity number 1087140) in association with the Faculty of Education, Health and Sciences of the University of Derby

The Multi-Faith Centre at the University of Derby, Kedleston Road, Derby, DE22 1GB.

The Faculty of Education, Health and Sciences of the University of Derby, Kedleston Road, Derby, DE22 1GB.

Typeset by Debbie Walkington of the University of Derby Print Unit and Indexed by David Bush.

Printed by Nuffield Press, Abingdon, Oxon.

CONTENTS

Page references for the more detailed sections within each chapter can be found in the left hand column at the start of each major chapter. More detailed page references for sub-sections can be found in the Topic Index.

PREFACE 7

USER'S GUIDE 13

RELIGIOUS LANDSCAPE OF THE UK
The Variety of Religions 21
The Development of a Religiously Plural
   Country 22
The 2001 Census Picture of Religions in
   the UK 26
The Geography and Ethnicity of Religions
   in the UK 29
Religion, Belief, Humanism and Atheism 34
Places of Worship 38
Religions and Inter-Faith Relations 44
Religions in Public Life: The Christian
   Inheritance 48
Religions in Public Life: Evolving Inclusivity 50
Religion, Belief and the Law 56
Religious Communities and Education 62
European Contexts 70
The Challenges of the Future 71
Further Reading 73

INTRODUCING BAHÁ'ÍS IN THE UK
Bahá'ís in the UK 91
Origins and Development of the Bahá'í faith 92
Sources of Bahá'í Beliefs and Practices 93
Key Bahá'í Beliefs 93
Bahá'í Life 94
Traditions in the Bahá'í Faith 96
Bahá'í Worship 96
Bahá'í Places of Worship 97
Bahá'í Calendar and Festivals 98
Baha'i Organisations 99
Further Reading 101

INTRODUCING BUDDHISTS IN THE UK
Buddhists in the UK 103
Origins and Development of Buddhism 104
Sources of Buddhist Beliefs and Practices 106
Key Buddhist Beliefs 108
Traditions in Buddhism 110
Buddhist Life 114
Buddhist Worship 116
Buddhist Places of Worship 116
Buddhist Calendar and Festivals 118
Buddhist Organisations 119
Further Reading 124

INTRODUCING CHRISTIANS IN THE UK
Christians in the UK 127
Origins and Development of Christianity 130
Sources of Christian Beliefs and Practices 131
Key Christian Beliefs 133
Traditions in Christianity 137
Christian Life 141
Christian Worship 144
Christian Places of Worship 146
Christian Calendar and Festivals 148
Christian Organisations 152
Further Reading 165

INTRODUCING HINDUS IN THE UK
Hindus in the UK 169
Origins and Development of Hinduism 170
Sources of Hindu Beliefs and Practices 171
Key Hindu Beliefs 173
Traditions in Hinduism 175
Hindu Life 178
Hindu Worship 181
Hindu Places of Worship 182
Hindu Calendar and Festivals 184
Hindu Organisations 185
Further Reading 189

INTRODUCING JAINS IN THE UK
Jains in the UK 193
Origins and Development of Jainism 193
Sources of Jain Beliefs and Practices 194
Key Jain Beliefs 195
Traditions in Jainism 197
Jain Life 198

Jain Worship   198
Jain Places of Worship   199
Jain Calendar and Festivals   200
Jain Organisations   201
Further Reading   202

INTRODUCING JEWS IN THE UK

Jews in the UK   203
Origins and Development of Judaism   204
Sources of Jewish Beliefs and Practices   205
Key Jewish Beliefs   207
Traditions in Judaism   208
Jewish Life   209
Jewish Worship   212
Jewish Places of Worship   213
Jewish Calendar and Festivals   215
Jewish Organisations   217
Further Reading   219

INTRODUCING MUSLIMS IN THE UK

Muslims in the UK   223
Origins and Development of Islam   224
Sources of Muslim Beliefs and Practices   226
Key Muslim Beliefs   227
Traditions in Islam   228
Muslim Life   230
Muslim Worship   231
Muslim Places of Worship   232
Muslim Calendar and Festivals   233
Muslim Organisations   235
Further Reading   238

INTRODUCING SIKHS IN THE UK

Sikhs in the UK   247
Origins and Development of Sikhism   248
Sources of Sikh Beliefs and Practices   249
Key Sikh Beliefs   250
Sikh Life   252
Traditions in Sikhism   252
Sikh Worship   255
Sikh Places of Worship   256
Sikh Calendar and Festivals   258
Sikh Organisations   259
Further Reading   261

INTRODUCING ZOROASTRIANS IN THE UK

Zoroastrians in the UK   265
Origins and Development of Zoroastrianism 266

Sources of Zoroastrian Beliefs and Practices   267
Key Zoroastrian Beliefs   268
Zoroastrian Life   273
Traditions in Zoroastrianism   276
Zoroastrian Worship   277
Zoroastrian Places of Worship   277
Zoroastrian Calendar and Festivals   278
Zoroastrian Organisations   281
Further Reading   281

SOME OTHER RELIGIOUS COMMUNITIES AND GROUPS

Introduction   283
Brahma Kumaris   287
Christian Scientists   289
Church of Jesus Christ of Latter-Day Saints 291
Jehovah's Witnesses   293
Namdhari Sikh Community   295
Pagans   297
Rastafarians   301
Ravidassia   302
Sant Nirankaris   304
Sathya Sai Service Organisation   305
Valmikis   306

RESOURCES FOR MAKING CONTACT, ORGANISING EVENTS AND FINDING OUT MORE

Introduction   309
Making Contacts and Organising Events   309
Finding Out More   316
General Texts On Religions   318
Directories About Religious Organisations 323
Other Directories   326

ACKNOWLEDGEMENTS

Introduction   329
Consultation Processes and the 2007 Edition 330
Consultants to the 2007 edition   332
Consultants on the Chapter on Some
    Other Religious Communities and
    Groups   333
Collection and Verification of Organisational
    Data   333
Consultants to the 1997 and 2001 Editions 334
Other Acknowledgements   337

INDEXES

Topic Index   339
Significant Word Index   347

PREFACE

Religions in the UK: A Ground-Breaking Project

The 1993 edition of *Religions in the UK* was the first comprehensive directory of national and local religious organisations and places of worship covering the United Kingdom's major faith communities. It was widely welcomed as a new resource for a multi-faith society and was followed by updated and extended editions in 1997 and 2001. Religious organisation representatives, journalists, academics and educators, as well as those working in community relations and service provision, are among the many for whom it has become a standard reference book.

The 2007 Edition

This new edition of the directory, like the first three editions, is designed to facilitate the participation in public life of the religious communities of the UK as well as to assist and encourage the further development of inter-faith contact and dialogue. However, unlike the three previous editions, the 2007 edition does not contain listings of religious organisations in hard copy form, but rather includes them on an enclosed CD-ROM.

The CD-ROM includes material that was developed by the Religions in the UK: On-Line Database of Religious Organisations project that took place in 2005-6, in the context of work that was undertaken for the Office for National Statistics' Neighbourhood Statistics Service, and with funding from the UK Government Home Office. At the same time, the database listings as finalised are the responsibility of the project alone.

The Religions in the UK: On-Line Database project allowed the Multi-Faith Centre both to update the contact information previously contained in the organisational listings sections of the 2001 edition of *Religions in the UK*, but also to complement this by the addition of basic location information on local Christian places of worship that was not included in any of the three previous editions of the directory. The provision of this data in electronic format also means that it can be readily updated by means of the issue, in due course, of new CD-ROMs. It will also be accessible in database format in a more limited way through the website of the Multi-Faith Centre at http://www.multifaithcentre.org.

Finally, the preparation of this new edition has given an opportunity to update the introductions to each religion in the UK to be as accurate as possible at the time of writing, while the previously separate material on visiting places of worship has been integrated into the introductions on each individual religion.

As in previous editions of the directory, work on these chapters has been carried out dialogically, in consultation with a number of key individual consultants from within the faith communities, as well as from among academic specialists on the religions concerned.

These introductory materials on the religions in the UK are therefore the product of a lengthy, extensive and careful process of consultation and debate that has taken place not only in preparation for this edition, but also over a decade and a half of the project's life. This process has involved a wide range of consultants whose names are listed in the "Acknowledgements" chapter.

An important principle of effective inter-faith dialogue is that partners in dialogue should be free to define themselves. The editorial process has tried to take into account as fully as possible the perspectives and sensitivities of adherents from across the spectrum of each of the included religions. At the same time, the drafting process has benefited from the input and advice of academic experts working in the relevant fields, while final responsibility for the contents remains with the editor.

The chapter on "The Religious Landscape of the UK" has been substantially rewritten to reflect developments in the years since the publication of the last edition, including the publication of census data relating to religious affiliation derived from the 2001 decennial

Census in which questions on religious affiliation were, for the first time, asked in all countries of the UK.

This chapter has not been the subject of any consultation with consultants from the religious communities, although there was consultation with academic specialists on the topic areas that it covers. This means that, while the content of all the chapters of the directory is, in the final analysis, the responsibility of the editor, the chapter on "The Religious Landscape of the UK" is written in a different way than the introductions to the various religions.

Therefore, while this chapter does touch upon matters of concern to the religious communities and groups in the UK, it has not sought specifically to reflect the perspectives of these communities and groups, but rather to give a more general and external overview of the religious landscape.

Summary material on inter-faith relations has been incorporated into the chapter on "The Religious Landscape of the UK" rather than, as was the case in previous editions, being covered in a separate chapter. This reflects the increasing integration of inter-faith activity into the "mainstream" of the UK religious landscape. But it also recognises that the Inter Faith Network for the UK (with which the *Religions in the UK* project had been in partnership for over a decade in producing the previous three editions) now publishes a substantial separate volume on inter-faith organisations, *Inter Faith Organisations in the UK: A Directory*.

A fourth, 2007 edition of this is expected soon after the publication of this volume. Users of the present volume are therefore referred to it for more detailed information on inter-faith initiatives. This includes contact information for inter-faith organisations at local, regional and national levels of a kind that was contained in previous editions of *Religions in the UK*, but is not now included in the organisational listings on the CD-ROM that accompanies this volume.

Data from *Religions in the UK* also remains available as part of the *KnowUK's* Internet service at http://www.knowuk.co.uk. This was developed for libraries and public authorities by Proquest. In this and other ways the original Multi-Faith Directory Research Project that lies behind this publication has extended and developed the ways in which directory data is being made available.

The Partnerships Behind the Directory

The current edition of *Religions in the UK* draws on the inheritance of a decade of active partnership between (initially) the Religious Resource and Research Centre of the University of Derby (and later) the Multi-Faith Centre at the University of Derby, together with the Inter Faith Network for the UK. Since its foundation in 1987, the Inter Faith Network for the UK has been a key body in the development of inter-faith relations, and in the developing liaison between religions and the structures of governance in the UK at national, regional and local levels.

The Network's formal association with the project was ended by mutual agreement in 2006. Nevertheless, the directory project remains indebted to the Network both for its initial financial contribution that helped to make the project possible in the first place, as well as for its collaborative work on previous editions. At the same time, the Network carries no responsibility for the contents of the present edition that has been produced in the context of a new partnership between the Multi-Faith Centre at the University of Derby, and the University's Faculty of Education, Health and Sciences.

Having, by agreement with the Inter Faith Network, received all the intellectual property rights in the project, the Multi-Faith Centre has in turn shared these with the Faculty of Education, Health and Sciences of the University of Derby, which has reinvested in the project to enable the publication of this edition, thus re-establishing the University's original partnership in the project.

The Multi-Faith Centre at the University of Derby was opened in 2004 as a purpose-built building, designed by representatives of seven world religious traditions working together to provide a context for the provision of education, dialogue, and awareness raising in the field of inter-faith and multi-faith activities. It now runs a full programme of activities in conjunction with the University and the local community, as well as being engaged in a range of regional, national and international projects.

The Faculty of Education, Health and Sciences, and its predecessors at the University of Derby, have been the base for a number of research projects concerned with the interface between religion and public life: including a Home Office commissioned research project (1999-2001) on Religious Discrimination in England and Wales and, most recently (2005-6), a Review of the Evidence Base on Faith Communities, conducted for the (then) Office of the Deputy Prime Minister (now Department for Communities and Local Government), which particularly examined reasearch on the Hindu, Muslim and Sikh populations in the UK with special reference to ODPM policy areas.

The Challenge of the Task

Describing such a range of religions and traditions within a single volume is a challenging and sensitive task. Similarly, it is a complex and extensive operation to gather data on thousands of their organisations. The project has aimed for the highest level of comprehensiveness and accuracy possible given the constraints of funding and the ever-changing nature of the religious organisational scene. However, it is almost inevitable that a work of this scope will contain omissions and accidental inaccuracies. For any such we apologise. We also ask readers to draw them to our attention so that we can correct them at the earliest opportunity.

It is our hope that *Religions in the UK* might continue to be a standard reference work and resource for building a society that is characterised by mutual understanding and respect. As the significance of religion in public life becomes increasingly recognised at local, national and European levels, it is our hope that this edition of the directory will prove to be of use in across all the sectors of society in which the resources of religious organisations might, in partnership with others, be able to make a contribution of distinctive value to the wider common good.

Paul Weller

Professor of Inter-Religious Relations, University of Derby, and Visiting Fellow of the Centre for Christianity and Culture, Regent's Park College, University of Oxford.

THE MULTI-FAITH CENTRE AT THE UNIVERSITY OF DERBY

Trustees:

The Rt Revd Alastair Redfern (Bishop of Derby, Chairman), Dr M Manazir Ahsan MBE, Mr Raj Kumar Bali, Revd Dr Inderjit Bhogal, Professor Paul Bridges, Mr Kian Golestani, Mr Jogindar Singh Johal, Dr Wendi Momen, Venerable Dr Phrakhru Panyasuddhammawithet, Mr Harindra Punchihewa, Revd Malcolm Weisman OBE, Professor Paul Weller.

Company Secretary:

Mrs Eileen Fry

The gestation of the concept of the Multi-Faith Centre, based at the University of Derby, is almost coextensive with the history of the Directory project. The group within which the idea germinated was a liaison committee between the University and a range of different faith communities, established to provide advice to the University on its policies and procedures, and its teaching and research in Religious Studies (including the Directory project itself). The development of the Multi-Faith Centre thus exemplifies the values that lie at the heart of the Directory.

The Multi-Faith Centre building was opened in 2004, following a fund-raising campaign of several years. The original idea emerged from the grassroots in a group drawn from the local Bahá'í, Buddhist, Christian, Hindu, Jewish, Muslim and Sikh communities alongside the University of Derby. The design brief and fundraising were achievements of inter-faith dialogue.

The Centre exists to promote mutual understanding between people of different faiths and beliefs, and to build respect between people as fellow human beings. The Centre is a shared space where people are invited to speak freely and fearlessly, in the spirit of "Listen to others as you want them to listen to you".

The Centre Trustees have resolved to focus the Centre's main efforts on high profile events, projects, and conferences of regional or national significance. In parallel, a network of local "ambassadors" will strengthen connections with all parts of the local community. The Centre has a small Library of religious/non-religious books and other resources as well as the website www.multifaithcentre.org. The Centre provides space for meetings, pastoral consultations, prayer, worship, meditation and study.

The Centre has been established as a charitable company, limited by guarantee, in a way that ensures that the different communities are genuine stakeholders in the project. The Centre is built on land gifted for 125 years, close to the main entrance to the buildings on the main campus of the University. The Centre's mode of operation makes it an ideal location for the future development of the Directory.

Contact:

Mrs Eileen Fry, Director, Multi-Faith Centre at the University of Derby

Kedleston Road, Derby DE22 1GB

Tel: (01332) 591285 **Fax:** (01332) 591573

Email: mfc@derby.ac.uk   **Website:** www.multifaithcentre.org

UNIVERSITY OF DERBY:
FACULTY OF EDUCATION, HEALTH AND SCIENCES

The University of Derby is a key stakeholder in the nationally important Multi-Faith Centre (MFC) located on site. While the MFC remains governed by an independent charitable trust, the University nominates three of the MFC's Trustees, and also supports the Centre through a service-level agreement.

Within the University, Religious and Philosophical Studies is available as part of the University's access and foundation level provision. The Religious and Philosophical Studies provision there is led by Father Daniel Joseph, who is also Russian Orthodox Chaplain within the Ecumenical Christian Chaplaincy that is part of the University's Religious and Pastoral Services.

At undergraduate level, Sociology offers two undergraduate modules that relate to religion: a level 5 module on "Religion and Society" and a level 6 module on "The Bible in Culture and Society" and is currently developing "Religion and Society" as a subject pathway on a Joint Honours degree to be validated for September 2008 start.

Sociology staff, undertaking research on religion, include:

Dr. Kristin Aune is researching gender and religion, with specific reference to evangelical Christianity. Her publications include *Single Women: Challenge to the Church?* (Paternoster, 2002) and *Women and Religion in the West: Challenging Secularization* (Ashgate, forthcoming).

Professor David Chalcraft is researching the interpretation of the Protestant Ethic and the Spirit of Capitalism and also the role of the Bible in contemporary culture and society. His publications include *Social Scientific Old Testament Criticism* (Continuum, 2006), *Sectarianism in Early Judaism: Sociological Advances* (Equinox, 2007)). Within the Faculty, doctoral scholars are undertaking research in areas related to religion:

- "Competing Realities, Diverse Needs: a Multi-Disciplinary Approach to Religious Contexts of HIV Prevention and Care in Leicester"

- "Maintaining Purity in an Impure World: A Comparative Study of Issues Relating to Purity and Impurity at the Time of Death in Two Gujarati Communities"

- "Female Perceptions of the Annulment of Marriage in the Catholic Church"

- "Complementary Therapy: Teachers' Perceptions of the Therapeutic Value of Hatha Yoga".

Recent contracted research projects related to religion include:

- Religious Discrimination in England and Wales, for the Home Office (1999-2001)

- Religious Group Participation, Inter-Faith Infrastructure and Capacity-Building in Derby, for the Community Empowerment Fund (2003-4)

- Multi-Faith Infrastructure Support: An Investigation Into Activity and Needs in the East Midlands and Government Office, East Midlands, for Engage East Midlands (2004-5)

- Review of the Evidence Base on Faith Communities, with the "Mercia Group" of academics from the Universities of Birmingham, Oxford and Warwick, for the Office of the Deputy Prime Minister (2005-6).

USER'S GUIDE

INTRODUCTION 13

RELIGIONS COVERED BY THE DIRECTORY 13

INTRODUCTIONS TO THE RELIGIONS IN THE UK 13

CALENDARS AND FESTIVALS 14

TRANSLITERATION, TRANSLATION AND DIACRITICAL MARKINGS 15

USING THE ORGANISATIONAL DATA ON THE ACCOMPANYING CD-ROM 15

UNDERSTANDING THE ORGANISATIONAL DATA 16

HOW THE ORGANISATIONAL DATA WERE COMPILED 18

RESOURCES FOR MAKING CONTACT, ORGANISING EVENTS AND FINDING OUT MORE 20

INDEXES 20

FURTHER READING AND HELP 20

INTRODUCTION

This chapter explains the layout of the directory and what the reader will find in its texts and CD-ROM listings.

RELIGIONS COVERED BY THE DIRECTORY

The directory contains basic information about Bahá'ís, Buddhists, Christians, Hindus, Jains, Jews, Muslims, Sikhs and Zoroastrians in the UK, as well as some guidance on how to find out more.

There are many other kinds of formal and informal religious belief and practice in the UK, but it is not possible to be totally comprehensive within the constraints of a single volume. However, the chapter on "Some Other Religious Communities and Groups" provides information on some of these and gives signposts for further information.

For information on New Religious Movements, readers are referred to the specialist information service, INFORM (The Information Network Focus on New Religious Movements, Tel: (020) 7955 7654, Email: inform@les.ac.uk, and Internet at: http://www.inform.ac.uk). There is a full page panel at the end of the chapter on "Some Other Religious Communities and Groups", that gives information on the work of INFORM.

INTRODUCTIONS TO THE RELIGIONS IN THE UK

The materials that introduce each religious tradition have been prepared with the input of religious practitioners and academic specialists to provide a starting place for the interested enquirer. Information on those who have been involved in this process is set out in the "Acknowledgements" chapter at the end of the directory.

More detailed information about each religion and in particular about its communities, groups and organisations in the UK, can be found in the books and articles suggested in the sections on "Further Reading"; from religious organisations themselves; and in the chapter on "Resources for Making Contact, Organising Events, and Finding Out More".

For ease of reference for the general reader, the introductory chapters to the religions generally follow a standard format. Slight variations in approach and internal balance reflect some differences concerning how a specific religion and its tradition can best be presented to the general reader. However, normally, the main sections in each chapter are:

In the UK

Basic historical, ethnic, linguistic and also statistical information.

Origins and Development

The historical origins of the religion in terms of its significant or founding figure or figures and an outline of some of the principal features of its global and its historical development.

Sources of Beliefs and Practices

The teachings, scriptures and religious structures that are seen as authoritative within the religion.

Key Beliefs

The religion's central understandings of the nature of the human and the divine or the ultimate, as well as its basic understandings of the purpose of existence.

Traditions

The principal traditions of interpretation within the religion.

Life

How adherents are initiated into the religion and something of the way in which the religion shapes their everyday life in terms of ethics, family, food and similar matters.

Worship

Outlines of some of the main forms of worship within the religions.

Places of Worship

Information about the buildings in which the religion's worship takes place.

Calendar and Festivals

The dating system of the religion, the rhythm of its year, and its major days of religious observance.

Organisation

Organisational patterns of the religion in the UK and descriptions of the roles of its religious personnel.

Further Reading

Details of a number of useful general introductions to the religion, together with a number of books and articles which particularly focus on the life of that religion in the UK. The references are not comprehensive, but provide signposts to a range of relevant materials.

CALENDARS AND FESTIVALS

The directory cannot list specific dates for every festival since many religious traditions operate according to calendars that differ from that used in public life in the UK. Some do not determine the dates of their festivals far in advance, and many have dates which change from year to year.

A calendar of festivals is produced annually by the Shap Working Party on World Religions in Education. The calendar is available from

Shap at P O Box 38580, London, SW1P 3XF, Tel: (020) 78981494, Fax: (020) 7898 1493, Internet: http://www.shap.org/). There is a full page panel on the resources provided by Shap, which can be found at the end of the chapter on "Resources for Making Contact, Organising Events and Finding Out More". Many religions also publish their own calendars.

In this directory, dates are given as CE (Common Era) rather than AD (Anno Domini), and BCE (Before Common Era) rather than BC (Before Christ), reflecting the increase in this usage. Thus, instead of 2007AD, one will find 2007CE.

TRANSLITERATION, TRANSLATION AND DIACRITICAL MARKINGS

The religious traditions covered in the directory all have scriptures and other important texts that were not originally written in English. For some religions, languages other than English remain the main medium for their religious discourse and practice. In the directory, such terms are given in italics in the original language in a transliterated form, together with an English approximation of their meaning as a translation.

Italics have also been used for English language terms that, although perhaps in more general usage, may have a specific religious meaning or overtone that might not be clear to English speakers from outside the tradition concerned. Personal names are not italicised, but the names of religious titles, of scriptures and of particular books within them are italicised.

Apostrophes, inverted apostrophes, acute, grave and circumflex accents and a number of other markings are used in the transliterations, but other less well known diacritical markings of the kind often used in scholarly texts are generally not used.

In the descriptions of the religions an attempt has been made to ensure consistency of transliteration and translation. However, in the organisational listings found in the accompanying CD-ROM there is variety, since the directory has largely followed the spellings and transliterations supplied by which the organisations are generally known rather than the directory attempting to impose an editorial conformity upon them.

USING THE ORGANISATIONAL DATA ON THE ACCOMPANYING CD-ROM

Contact Details

Accompanying the present volume is a CD-ROM that includes searchable contact and other information on the organisations and places of worship in the UK of the nine religions that form the principal focus of *Religions in the UK*. For all other than Christian religions this includes contact details for UK-wide organisations as well as for organisations that operate on a national level within the four nations of the UK. Local and regional organisations as well as places of worship are also included.

Christian Organisational Data

The Christian organisational data differs from those for other religions due to the sheer number of Christian organisations and places of worship in this country. While there is not comprehensive coverage, relatively full data is provided on a range of key UK-wide Christian organisations, including *ecumenical instruments* as well as on some other groupings of *Churches* that operate at a UK-wide level.

Also included on a similarly more detailed basis, is information on major *Churches* that operate at UK and/or national level within the UK and that are directly or indirectly (through their affiliation to a full member organisation) part of an *ecumenical instrument*, together with some data on a small number of other Christian *Churches*.

This also applies to information Networks, agencies and other bodies that are either directly or indirectly part of an *ecumenical instrument*. Relatively full contact information is also included on Christian regional level organisations, including regional *ecumenical instruments*, and regional structures of the individual Christian Churches. In London, most *Church* regional bodies cover more than one London borough.

For the first time in the CD-ROM accompanying this edition, the project provides information about local Christian places of worship. This had not been included in 1994, 1997 or 2001 editions of *Religions in the UK* partly due to the impracticality of including such a large number of entries in a hard copy publication.

Rather, recognising the more bureaucratically and regionally structured nature of the majority of the Christian church groups as compared with those of other religions, national and regional contact information was provided instead.

The data that is included on Christian places of worship is, however, very basic in comparison with that on other organisations. On this occasion it provides only key address details together, in some cases, with information on the "tradition", "movement" and "denomination" of which the local place of worship is a part. In a number of cases this is a present given as "unspecified".

The national and regional *Church* and *ecumenical instruments* are able to give more detailed information about local Christian organisations and places of worship. The vast majority of Christian *Churches* produce their own national handbooks and directories. Many also have publications covering regional and local areas, as do a number of regional and local *ecumenical instruments*.

In addition to *Churches* and places of worship, there are many hundreds of Christian voluntary organisations. The *UK Christian Handbook* (see further in the chapter on "Resources for Making Contact, Organising Events and Finding Out More") gives information on many that are active in the UK. Details of English and Welsh Christian and other religious buildings certified as places of worship and/or for the solemnisation of marriage can be obtained from the General Register Office of the Office for National Statistics. There are no comparable lists for Scotland and Northern Ireland.

UNDERSTANDING THE ORGANISATIONAL DATA

Every organisation about which information is given in the CD-ROM includes a name and a postal or email address or telephone number for the organisation or place of worship. For most organisations and places of worship there is also additional contact information. Further information given about such matters as activities and the particular traditions, movements, or social groupings within a religion varies according to the detail provided by the organisations.

Data on local Christian places of worship does not include anything more than basic contact address information and at present does not extend to include cover of Northern Ireland. This reflects the relatively new incorporation of this material into the directory project, and the limited resources accessible to the project to undertake (see the section below on "How the Organisational Data Were Compiled") what would be a massive task. Nevertheless, the inclusion of even this basic level of information represents an addition to what was available in the previous editions of the directory. It is also hoped that, if the necessary resources can be secured, then it might in future be possible to build further upon the start that has now been made.

For other than Christian places of worship and organisations about which details are available on the CD-ROM, it is important to note that where the organisations concerned themselves have provided the information, then the data or lack of it in these fields reflects the choices that weremade by listed organisations. Generally speaking, the directory has not imposed information editorially, unless it is quite clear from the other information supplied (for example, where an organisation has, in its title, "Reform Jewish" but did not itself indicate its alignment with "Reform" as a "tradition" within Judaism). With regard to the affiliations field, organisations may have more affiliations than are listed here, but what appears reflects the information prioritised by the organisations themselves.

National organisations have also had the option to add a note on matters that they feel it is particularly important for the directory user to know. Where this opportunity has been taken, then brief self-descriptions follow. The information fields that are used for records other than those of local Christian places of worship are as follows (with the fields also included for Christian places of worship marked with a "+"). Not all fields are searchable, but those which are, are explained on the CD-ROM:

Name (+):
Name of organisation or place of worship.

Address (+):
Normally that of the organisation's offices in a public building or of the place of worship.

Telephone:
Normally that of an organisation's offices in a public building or the place of worship. Some places of worship and organisations do not have an office telephone, or the regular contact person for that organisation is not generally present at the place of worship. In such cases, the entry may well be the home or mobile telephone number of the contact person. If we have been informed of the home or mobile telephone number then this is also given.

Fax:
Normally that of an organisation's office or of a place of worship.

Email:
An email address is given if one is available. Some places of worship and organisations do not have an email address, or the regular contact person for that organisation is not generally present at the place of worship. In such cases, the entry may well be the home email address of the contact person. If we have been informed of the home email address, then this also appears.

Internet:
Where the organisation has a Web site and has supplied information on this, then this Internet address is given.

Contact:
The person or office holder designated as the principal contact to handle incoming enquiries. This may be an individually named person or an office-holder such as a Chairperson, President or Secretary. Office holders may change (sometimes annually) but former officers will usually refer callers to the relevant new person.

Position:
A description of the position that the contact person holds in the organisation such as President or Secretary.

Contact Person's Telephone:
Home or mobile telephone number of the contact person if they are willing for this to be published.

Contact Person's Email:
Email address of the contact person if one is available.

Activities:
For most religions, there is also the heading:

Traditions (+):
The major broad grouping within the religion with which the organisation or place of worship identifies.

For a number of religions, there are also the headings:

Social Groups:
Any particular social group(s) with which the organisation or place of worship most closely identifies.

Movements (+):
Any specific movements with which the organisation or place of worship most closely identifies. Christian places of worship alone also include a field on **denomination (+)**.

Other Languages:
Up to four languages other than English are listed, if spoken by significant numbers within the organisation or at the place of worship. They appear in the order of most widespread use.

Affiliations:
The name of one local or regional body, one national body, and one international body within its own religious tradition to which the organisation or place of worship is affiliated.

Organisation Self-description:
For national organisations up to thirty words of self-description about the organisation.

HOW THE ORGANISATIONAL DATA WAS COMPILED

The dataset provided on the CD-ROM accompanying this volume aims to provide an authoritative and as comprehensive as possible source of data for religious organisations and places of worship covering other than Christian religions in the UK as well as basic address and location details for Christian places of worship.

The dataset builds on information that has been gathered, collated and presented in a project that has developed in an evolutionary way during around fifteen years of developmental work, leading to the publication of the previous 1993, 1997 and 2001 editions of the directory.

These editions were available only in paper format, which limited their usage and accessibility. The electronic database offers the possibility of both a more systematic approach in updating and expanding on the work of the previous directories, as well as of improving the usability and access to the information related to places of worship and religious buildings.

The categories according to which the data has been collected and organised draw upon a careful consultative process undertaken over the years in which the Multi-Faith Directory was developed, the project having benefited from the contributions of over two hundred consultants with academic expertise and/or having community standing in the religions covered by it.

The data collected has been on the basis of free inclusion in the directory, thus ensuring that its coverage is as wide as possible. The variety of information contained in each organisation's entry reflects both the questions asked of organisations in different religious traditions and the choices made by particular organisations about the kind of information that they wished to have published.

To understand the range of information provided in different entries on organisations and places of worship, it is important to explain something of the process by which they came to be included in their present form.

Information was gathered and checked in ways that were intended to construct a grid of interlocking sources to ensure as many organisations and as much information as possible has been included:

The 2001 baseline data that lies behind the present dataset included on the CD-ROM accompanying this directory had itself been cross-checked with assistance from a range of local inter-faith groups in various localities, project consultants from within the religious communities and from higher education institutions and religious organisations.

Draft entries were sent to each organisation that had returned a questionnaire, giving them an opportunity to update and correct its draft entry or to ask for it to be omitted. Wherever possible, prior to publication of the 2001 edition, final telephone checks had been made in respect of organisations that had not returned a questionnaire, but where the project had telephone contact information.

For the creation of the present dataset, resources precluded the conduct of such an extensive range of cross-checking. However, the dataset was created through postal contact being made with each organisation and place of worship that was included in the 2001 edition of *Religions in the UK*, sending them a print out of the information that was held about them, and asking them to amend and update the information, as appropriate, and also to supply any missing information in relation to a list of data fields and descriptors.

Finally, during the course of the project, other published directories and sources of reliable information were used in order to identify additional organisations and places of worship that might have come into being since the 2001 edition of *Religions in the UK*. For these, new questionnaires were despatched for completion and return to the project.

The questionnaires used for this exercise had been developed on the basis of the project's past questionnaire formats (themselves the product of extensive consultative processes and of piloting with religious organisations and places of worship). Thus, the questionnaire used for the present edition incorporated only minimal presentational variations from the format used to collate information for the 2001 edition of *Religions in the UK*.

In the mailings sent both to previously included and to new organisations and places of worship, a copy of the project leaflet was included, explaining that the project was working with the Office for National Statistics' Neighbourhood Statistics Service. A Freepost envelope was provided for reply, including an option for the respondent to reply stating that they did not wish to be included in the directory.

Where organisations or places of worship did not return a questionnaire, but where the project had telephone and/or email contact details, follow-up contact was made.

Those entries that were not confirmed by the organisation or place of worship itself are included on the basis of verification from other reliable sources and/or on the basis of the best judgement of the project.

The process of obtaining data about local Christian places of worship did not, due to lack of resources, extend to postal questionnaires or direct contact with the places of worship concerned, but it was based on the identification of basic contact details from denominational or confessional directories and/or headquarters or other similar listings and websites.

Accuracy

Users will appreciate that not all organisations reply to correspondence and questionnaires, not all are contactable by telephone, and that contact details can and do change with the passage of time. As a result, the absolute accuracy of all entries cannot be guaranteed. But as will be seen, the project has gone to considerable lengths to ensure that the entries are as accurate as possible as at the time the data was collected, in 2006.

Apparent Omissions

We have also sought to respect the wishes of organisations that have requested that we do not include details about their existence, even where this information might be available elsewhere in the public domain. The small number of such requests may be the reason why some organisations known to directory users do not appear on the CD-ROM. Organisations were, in addition, given the opportunity to decline to be included in internet versions.

RESOURCES FOR MAKING CONTACT, ORGANISING EVENTS AND FINDING OUT MORE

The final chapter "Resources for Making Contact, Organising Events and Finding Out More", points the directory user to additional sources of information as well as to a range of organisations that provide information relevant to religions in the UK.

INDEXES

There are two indexes:

The "Topic Index" gives page references for each major section and sub-section of the introductions to each religion and the other descriptive material in the directory. It enables the directory user to find broad topic areas.

The "Significant Word Index" indexes italicised words found throughout the directory.

FURTHER READING AND HELP

At the end of most chapters there is a section on "Further Reading" to assist directory users in following up additional relevant information.

Questions about the directory itself can be directed to the editor, Professor Paul Weller, at the Multi-Faith Directory Research Project, Faculty of Education, Health and Sciences, University of Derby, Kedleston Road Campus, Derby DE22 1GB, Tel: (01332) 591179; EMail: P.G.Weller@derby.ac.uk.

Questions about the directory project more widely and further advice and information about inter-faith relations and making contact with religious communities and their organisations can be obtained from the Multi-Faith Centre at the University of Derby, Kedleston Road, Derby, DE22 1GB, Tel: (01332) 591285; Email: mfc@derby.ac.uk.

Further information about the Multi-Faith Centre and the University of Derby and its Faculty of Education, Health and Sciences can be found in display panels that precede this chapter as well as, respectively, on the internet at www.multifaithcentre.org and www.derby.ac.uk.

RELIGIOUS LANDSCAPE OF THE UK

THE VARIETY OF RELIGIONS   21

THE DEVELOPMENT OF A RELIGIOUSLY PLURAL COUNTRY   22

THE 2001 CENSUS PICTURE OF RELIGIONS IN THE UK   26

THE GEOGRAPHY AND ETHNICITY OF RELIGIONS IN THE UK   29

RELIGION, BELIEF, HUMANISM AND ATHEISM   34

PLACES OF WORSHIP   38

RELIGIONS AND INTER-FAITH RELATIONS   44

RELIGIONS IN PUBLIC LIFE: THE CHRISTIAN INHERITANCE   48

RELIGIONS IN PUBLIC LIFE: EVOLVING INCLUSIVITY   50

RELIGION, BELIEF AND THE LAW   56

RELIGIOUS COMMUNITIES AND EDUCATION   62

EUROPEAN CONTEXTS   70

THE CHALLENGES OF THE FUTURE   71

FURTHER READING   73

THE VARIETY OF RELIGIONS

Inheritance and Change

The United Kingdom (UK) has a Christian inheritance that remains the predominant religious tradition, particularly in Northern Ireland, Scotland and Wales, but also in England. At the same time, as in many other European countries, after Christians, Muslims form the largest religious group.

In the case of the UK, however, there are also relatively large groupings of Hindus, Sikhs and Jews, together with smaller numbers of Buddhists, Bahá'ís, Jains and Zoroastrians. In terms of the range of world religious traditions with significant communities here, this gives the UK a greater degree of religious diversity than is found in any other country of the European Union (EU).

The nature and degree of processes often referred to as "secularisation", together with their effect on personal and social life, are contested. What is clear, however, is that whatever judgement is made about the extent and impact of such secularisation, in general terms religions in the UK continue to exhibit a considerable degree of vigour, while the diversity of religions is a strongly visible part of public life in the UK.

As well as people who have an active involvement in the corporate life of their religious communities, the UK also has significant numbers of people whose religious belief and practice is often described as "folk religion", "implicit religion", or "residual Christianity". Such people may turn to an active involvement in Christian religious life only, or mainly, at times of crisis or personal significance such as birth, marriage and death, or at festivals such as *Christmas*.

Other faith communities also have followers whose religious observances are relatively limited but who feel different degrees of affinity with their religions in terms of cultural inheritance.

In relation to all communities there are, in addition, individuals and groups who acknowledge their connection with a particular tradition but find themselves in conflict with its official representatives over one or other single issue or across a whole range of ways of understanding the significance of their inherited or adopted tradition.

Alongside those who have either a direct or indirect relationship with the major world religions in the UK, there are also those who follow other forms of religious expression. Among these are groups often popularly referred to as "sects" or "cults" but which, in academic usage, have normally come to be described as *New Religious Movements* (NRMs), as well as those who understand themselves as Pagans of various traditions.

Another area of religious life, often described as *New Age* spirituality, is characterised by a concern for personal growth and draws upon spiritual practices and traditions from a variety of sources This is also the case with those who follow *esoteric* teachings and traditions.

There are also those who identify more generally with a concern for "spirituality" and/or an "holistic" approach to life, but not with a particular historic religious tradition. In addition, there are a number of individuals who have a "dual" religious identity, of which Buddhist Quakers would be an example.

THE DEVELOPMENT OF A RELIGIOUSLY PLURAL COUNTRY

History of Christians in the UK

Over the centuries, Christianity in these islands has developed into richly diverse forms. This diversity reflects doctrinal differences and the varied national and religious histories of the different parts of the UK. It also reflects the migration of groups into the UK from other parts of the world, bringing with them their traditions, organisations and forms of practice.

Within the four nations, a range of groups and denominations within Christianity can be found (in ways that are set out in more detail in the chapter on "Introducing Christians in the UK") in varying strengths in different countries, and also in different regional and local areas.

In England, the largest single Christian *Church* is the Church of England, whilst in Scotland it is the Church of Scotland (which is *Presbyterian* in tradition). In Wales, the *Free Churches* collectively are larger than any other Christian tradition, as are the *Protestant Churches* in Northern Ireland, although the *Roman Catholic Church* is the largest single *Church* there.

Throughout England, Scotland and Wales, *Roman Catholic* Christians are predominantly concentrated in urban areas whilst, in rural areas of England, the Church of England has a more widespread presence than any other Christian *Church*. But the UK's historic mix of *Anglicans*, traditional *Free Churches* (*Baptist*, *Methodist*, *Congregationalist* and others) and *Roman Catholics* has been supplemented, especially during the twentieth century, by a further diversification arising from the migration into the UK of significant numbers of Christians from other parts of the world.

For example, migrants from Italy led to the ethnic diversification of the *Roman Catholic* Christian community as well as to its overall numerical growth. More recently, migration movements from Poland following its 2004 accession to the EU, as well as refugee and migration movements from Africa, Latin America, added still further to the size and diversity of the *Roman Catholic* Christian community.

In addition *Orthodox* Christians have arrived here, including groups of people with Cypriot, Serbian, Bulgarian, Romanian and Russian backgrounds. The *Orthodox* Christian population remains numerically small, although in the earlier part of the twentieth century it was strengthened by Russian emigrés following the Bolshevik Revolution in Russia and by economic migration from Greece and refugee migration from Cyprus. In more recent times, it has grown further through the arrival of refugees from the Balkans.

In the 1950s, new settlers in the UK had included people from the Caribbean islands, the majority of whom, in their countries of origin, were Christians and were usually identified with one or other of the historic Christian denominations that had originally developed in the context of UK history.

Some of these Christians, in response to what they often felt was at best a frosty reception, and at worst racism among indigenous Christians, formed independent congregations where they could practise Christianity in ways that could draw upon the integrity of their own Christian experience and leadership, free of the racism they had experienced within the older *ecclesial* communities.

A number of the congregations formed by black Christians have grouped together to form denominations of their own, while others have linked up with international movements based abroad, particularly in the USA. A significant proportion of migrants from African, and especially from West African countries, brought with them forms of indigenous Christian life that were developed in *African Independent Churches*, such as those of the Cherubim and Seraphim traditions.

Thus the migration, settlement and development of new Christian communities has further diversified the profile of Christianity in England beyond even its relatively (as compared with many other European countries) pluralistic Christian inheritance of *Anglican, Presbyterian, Roman Catholic* and *Free Church* traditions.

But also for reasons apart from migration, Christianity has undergone other significant transformations in which new forms of Christian life and organisation have emerged either outside of, or overlapping with, the more traditional Christian *Churches*. This has, for example, occurred in the development of the so-called *Restorationist* or *New Church* movements that seek to recover a more authentic form of Christian life than they feel has been transmitted by the traditional *Churches*, and such congregations are increasingly organised in wider groupings and networks.

As a result, the Christianity of the UK in the early twenty-first century is much more diverse than many could have imagined, even half a century ago, both in terms of its ethnicity and the variety of its traditions, movements, denominations and other forms of organisation and presence.

Beyond Christian Diversity

Pagan traditions were, of course, present in the UK from before the arrival of Christianity. Some aspects of Pagan traditions were incorporated into local Christian practice (as, for example, in the ways and places in which some festivals were celebrated), whilst other aspects were driven underground until the modern era when there has been a serious attempt to revive Pagan religion.

From the time of the Roman conquest onwards, alongside varieties of Christian belief and practice, individuals and groups of people belonging to other religious traditions have come as visitors, or to live here. Thus, a small Jewish presence was established after the Norman conquest in 1066. Initially, the Jewish community in the UK was predominantly *Sephardi*, which refers to those Jews who originally migrated from Spain and Portugal. However, Jews were expelled in 1290 and only re-admitted during the Commonwealth period, following the seventeenth century English Civil War.

As Britain's international role expanded through trade, with the development of colonialism and imperialism, as well as the diversification of the Christian population through migration into the UK, individual Hindus, Muslims, Zororastrians and others came to live here as servants or *ayahs*.

The first Zoroastrians known to have visited Britain came in 1723 and a Zoroastrian family business called Cama and Company was the first Indian business to be launched, being founded in 1855. Zoroastrians were, in fact, the first group with South Asian origins to make an early and significant community impact upon social and political life in the UK. They settled in significant numbers during the nineteenth century and the majority were of Indian origin and known as *Parsees* or *Parsis*. The first three Members of Parliament of Asian ethnic origin were all *Parsis*. The first of these, in 1892, was Dadabhai Naoroji who was elected as a Member of Parliament for the Liberal Party.

During the nineteenth century, people from China with a varied Buddhist, Confucianist and Taoist religious inheritance settled in Britain. Most were seafarers from the southern provinces of China, particularly from Guangdong. However, there was only a small Chinese population in Britain until after the Second World War.

Also during the nineteenth century a significant degree of academic interest in Buddhism developed among indigenous scholars. As a result, Buddhist texts were translated into English, and an increasing number of individuals became interested in Buddhist teaching. The earliest Buddhist missions to the UK were undertaken by indigenous people who became Buddhists when outside of the country and then returned later to lead Buddhist missions.

Bahá'ís have been present in the UK since 1899 and some of the early formative history of the religion took place in London, where Shoghi Effendi (1897-1957), who became *Guardian of the Faith* and *Interpreter of Scripture*, lived for some time.

From 1881 until 1914, *Ashkenazi* Jews seeking betterment through economic migration in the face of restricted social and economic possibilities in Eastern Europe and others seeking to escape the pogroms in the Russian Empire of the time arrived in significant numbers to supplement and further develop the already resident Jewish community.

One of the first Sikhs to live in the UK was the exiled Sikh prince, Dalip Singh, the son of Maharaja Ranjit Singh and who lived on the Elveden Estate in Norfolk. The earliest Muslim presence in the UK was that of individuals who, during the period of expansion of the British Empire, arrived as servants, visitors or settlers. Already during the nineteenth century, significant communities began to emerge in geographically localised areas in particular when Muslim seafarers and traders from the Middle East began to settle around major seaports such as Liverpool and Cardiff, as well as Yemenis in North-East England.

Following the First World War there was further settlement by Muslims and people of other religions from all over the Empire who had been demobilised from the armed forces of the British Empire. Together with the movement of families from the original seaport areas of settlement this led to the establishment of small Muslim communities in a larger number of localities.

Religious Diversification After the Second World War

Prior to the Second World War, although some degree of religious plurality existed in the UK, this was primarily related to the internal diversity within the Christian tradition and the presence of the Jewish and Muslim population. From 1933 onwards, the arrival of escapees from Nazi persecution and the Holocaust in Germany and other Nazi-occupied European countries led to a further strengthening of the Jewish community in the UK, leading to the *Ashkenazi* stream becoming predominant in Jewish life in the UK.

It was also from the middle of the 20th century onwards that the size, distribution and significance of the other religious groups, such as Hindus, Muslims, Sikhs and Jains, grew in importance in the UK. Once again, this occurred initially through the settlement of individuals during the demobilisation of the armed forces of the British Empire, this time following the Second World War.

But it was the labour migration, to work in the mills and the factories during the years of post-war reconstruction and labour shortage that, in the 1950s and 1960s, led to workers of Hindu, Muslim and Sikh backgrounds from the Indo-Pakistani subcontinent becoming a permanent feature of UK life and bringing about the existence here of significant communities of Hindus, Muslims and Sikhs.

Following the passage of the 1962 *Commonwealth Immigrants Act*, the flow of primary migration slowed down, but spouses and children began to join the original, mainly male, migrants. The result of this was that secondary immigration accelerated. As a consequence, the character of what could, by then, properly be called emergent "communities" began to form, as originally migrant minorities started to perceive themselves more in terms of settled groups rather than as a collection of visiting individual workers. Thus, increasing attention began to be paid to building the structures necessary for sustaining and developing an established internal community life and for relating to the wider society, including the creation of religious organisations and places of worship.

Due to the Africanisation policies of the newly independent African states of the former British Empire and Commonwealth, the original migrant groups were, during the later 1960s and early 1970s, supplemented by the arrival from Tanzania, Kenya, Uganda, Zambia and Malawi of a substantial number of people of East African of Asian origins. This especially led to the growth of the Hindu population, together with direct migrants from Fiji, Trinidad and Guyana. However, further significant growth of these populations by means of migration was limited with the passage of the 1981 *Nationality Act* and subsequent ever-tighter immigration regulations.

Those who migrated in the early post-war period focused first on the basic need to find somewhere to live, and on getting a job so that they could send remittances back to their families in their home countries. In this phase of settlement, ethnic associations flourished rather than groups organised on a distinctively religious basis, resulting in forms of organisation centred around groupings based on the country of origin. It is possible that this form of development was based not on internal dynamics alone, but related strongly to the shape at the time of both public funding streams and government policies for relating to diversity, and that was based on "racial" and "ethnic" rather than "religious" categories.

With the tightening up of immigration restrictions between the 1960s and the 1980s, the number of spouses and children joining the original migrants accelerated due to a growing concern that it would become increasingly difficult or impossible to do so later. This phase of migration laid the basis for the development of a range of social, cultural and religious communities and institutions that would maintain and transmit their religious traditions. *Mandirs, gurdwaras* and *mosques* were founded and became an increasingly established part of community life.

The Chinese population in the UK grew from the 1960s onwards, with the migration of ethnic Chinese from Singapore, Malaysia and the rural Territories of Hong Kong. Between the 1960s and the 1980s, refugee settlement further strengthened, in particular: the Buddhist population, following the Chinese take-over of Tibet; the *Orthodox* Christian population following conflict in Cyprus; the Hindu, Jain and Sikh populations by South Asian Hindus, Jains and Sikhs migrating from East African states as a consequence of the Africanisation policies introduced during the early 1960s; and the Bahá'í and Zoroastrian communities in the wake of the Iranian Revolution.

In the 1990s, further diversification occurred with the arrival of new and predominantly Muslim refugee and migrant groups following conflicts in Somalia and other parts of Africa, Bosnia and other parts of the former Yugoslavia, and the Middle East, but also mainly Hindu Tamils fleeing the conflict in Sri Lanka.

In terms of religion, Muslims form the largest minority religious group that became established here based primarily on immigration from the New Commonwealth and Pakistan in the years immediately following the Second World War. Also the Hindu population became more fully established when significant numbers settled from East Africa in the years following the inception there of Africanisation policies, and the outlines of an organised community began to emerge.

This increasing religious diversity was, however, overlaid upon the pre-existing processes of secularisation that emerged from the nineteenth century, in which secular and humanist perspectives came to the fore, the impetus for which had accelerated during the 1960s. Thus, alongside increased religious diversity, there was also increasing secularity in diverse areas of personal, social and institutional life.

At the same time, the twentieth century also saw the growth of a plethora of New Religious Movements. Some of these see their role in unique or original terms, while others understand themselves as being related to one or more of the world religious traditions. Some earlier movements, that developed in late nineteenth and early twentieth century and have often been seen in the wider society as "sects" more than as "New Religious Movements", had a

relationship with the Christian tradition. These include the Jehovah's Witnesses, the Christian Scientists, the Church of Jesus Christ of Latter-day Saints (popularly known as the *Mormons*).

Newer groupings include the Church of Scientology and the Family Federation for World Peace and Unification. The latter was formerly known as the Unification Church, whose followers were therefore known as *Unificationists* (or sometimes more popularly and with derogative overtones were referred to as the "*Moonies*", in a reference to their Korean founder, Revd Sun Myung Moon).

In addition, a growing number of people identify with Pagan religious traditions. Some of these also understand themselves as being, in some sense, heirs to earlier Pagan traditions of these islands. In some regions of England and the UK, the original Pagan traditions remained strong in their own right, even after Christianity gained ascendancy. But in more recent times, this inheritance has also been re-developed through the modern revivals and/or reinterpretations that can be found among the neo-Pagan and "deep ecology" movements.

THE 2001 CENSUS PICTURE OF RELIGIONS IN THE UK

Counting Religion: Christian, Plural and Secular

Until the 2001 decennial Census, with the exception of Northern Ireland (where a religion question had been asked in the Census since the inception of the Northern Ireland state) there had been no generally comparable data available on the size of the various religious groups in the UK. The only previous official Census relating to religion that was conducted in England took place in 1851 and this focused on participation in public worship.

Thus the only extensive surveys of religion in England and the UK had been voluntary surveys such as the English Church Census organised by the Christian organisation, MARC Europe (and later by Christian Research) and also relatively small sample-based studies on such questions as the nature and extent of religious belief, affiliation and practice of a kind that have formed a part of the British Social Attitudes Survey and the European Values Survey.

In the course of considering the range of questions to be included in the 2001 decennial Census, the Office for National Statistics consulted both data users and religious communities on the desirability of including a question on religious identity. In the light of this consultation a question on religious affiliation was included in the 2001 Census for England and Wales. The necessary amending legislation to permit this was passed by the Westminster Parliament. A religion question was also included in the Census in Scotland and the Scottish Parliament passed the relevant legislation for this.

As a result, in the 2001 Census, questions on religious identity were included on a voluntary basis in each of the four nations of the UK. This means that, at least with regard to figures relating to broad community identification, a more solid basis for comparison has been available than was the case when the 1993, 1997 and 2001 editions of this directory were published when, in general, only very broad internal and external estimates could be given.

However, for the various parts of the UK the 2001 Census contained a range of different questions on religion as well as a range of differing pre-set options for response. Therefore, the National Statistics website includes a note of caution on this matter explaining that "Different versions of the religious identity question were asked in England and Wales, in Scotland and in Northern Ireland, to reflect local differences in the requirement for information". Thus, it may be that the use of the word "belonging" in both the Scottish and Northern Irish forms of the religion question encouraged respondents to interpret the question in a "harder-edged" way than the "What is your religion" version of the question in England.

Therefore, although the National Statistics website's own cautionary note concludes that, "…results are comparable across the UK as a whole", the differing questions and responses offered mean that data relating to different parts of the UK may not be entirely comparable. This must therefore be borne in mind when looking at any data presented on a UK-wide basis.

Given that the Office for National Statistics has indicated that it does plan to include a question on religious identity in the 2011 Census, the use of different questions will be an important matter for consideration in the consultation process on this that is now underway, especially in the light of the increasing use of such data in the formation and development of public policy.

Questions About Religious Affiliation

There remain, then, questions about the precise meaning of the Census results on religion, while there are also other datasets – in particular the British Social Attitudes Survey (see the section on "Religion, Belief, Humanism and Atheism" below) – the results of which appear to give a different picture, indicating much lower numbers of people affirming religious belief than might be inferred from the results of the Census.

However, it is important to recognise that the Census questions were to do with religious affiliation in the sense of identification with a religion rather than asking specifically about either religious belief or religious practice. Therefore, in terms of broad identification with a religion, as seen in Table 1, it would seem that religion remains a factor of at least some significance in the self-understanding of almost three-quarters of the population of the UK (45,162,895 people or 76.8% of the population). Among these, Christians are by far the largest group, followed by Muslims; then Hindus and Sikhs; then Jews; then Buddhists; and then Jains, Bahá'ís and Zoroastrians.

In the case of each of these religious traditions, people who identify with them share in common many beliefs and practices. However, within most religious groups there are also significant variations of tradition, organisation, ethnicity and language. In addition to diversity within traditions, in some cases the boundaries between different religious traditions can be somewhat fluid.

Table 1: Religion Responses in the 2001 Census

Religion	England	Scotland	Wales	Northern Ireland	UK Total	UK %
Buddhist	139,046	6,830	5,407	533	151,816	0.3%
Christian	35,251,244	3,294,545	2,087,242	1,446,386	42,079,417	71.6%
Hindu	546,982	5,564	5,439	825	558,810	1.0%
Jewish	257,671	6,448	2,256	365	266,740	0.5%
Muslim	1,524,887	42,557	21,739	1,943	1,591,126	2.7%
Sikh	327,343	6,572	2,015	219	336,149	0.6%
Other Religions+	143,811	26,974	6,909	1,143	178,837	0.3%
Total	38,190,984	3,389,490	2,131,007	1,451,414	45,162,895	76.8%
No religion	7,171,332	1,394,460	537,935	★	9,103,727	15.5%
Not stated	3,776,515	278,061	234,143	★	4,288,719	7.3%
No religion/ Not stated	10,947,847	1,672,521	772,078	233,853	13,626,299	23.2%

Table reproduced from *Inter Faith Update*, 21, p 3, the newsletter of the Inter Faith Network for the UK. Due to rounding, percentages may not total 100%.

★ In Northern Ireland, separate statistics for those of 'No religion' and 'not stated' are not available.

+ The Census Table M275 Religion (Most Detailed Categories) gives breakdowns of the write-in responses coded to these religions and groups that was undertaken by the Office for National Statistics, but only for England and Wales. In relation to the three other world religious traditions with significant communities in the UK that are the main focus of this directory, around 4,374 respondents in England and 271 in Wales gave a write-in response that was coded as Bahá'í; 15,067 in England and 271 in Wales, a response that was coded as Jain; and 3,555 in England and 383 in Wales, a response that that was coded as Zoroastrian.

THE GEOGRAPHY AND ETHNICITY OF RELIGIONS IN THE UK

Geography of Religions in the UK

It is clear that, overall, there has been a significant change in the cultural and religious composition of the UK population as compared to the historic picture in which there was comparatively little religious diversity. Nevertheless, across the UK as a whole Christians still form the largest group. This is, however, now followed by Muslims, Hindus, Sikhs and Jews; then Buddhists; then, Bahá'ís, Jains and Zoroastrians; and, finally, by a range of other communities and groups.

Of the four nations that comprise the UK, England has both the broadest and most numerous variety of religious traditions and communities. In this, 60% of the total population and 77% of the population indicating identification with any religion at all identify with a religion other than Christianity. Among these, Muslims form the largest religious minority followed by Hindus, and then by Sikhs, Jews, "Other Religions" and Buddhists.

In Scotland, as in England, Muslims make up the largest religious minority, although in Scotland this is followed by those using the write-in option for "Other Religions", and then by Buddhists, Jews, Sikhs, and Hindus.

For Wales, as in all other countries in the UK, Muslims form the largest religious minority. As in Scotland, this is followed by "Other Religions", then by Hindus, Buddhists, Jews and Sikhs.

In Northern Ireland, forms of religious believing and belonging that are other than Christian often seem to be relatively invisible. But while both the absolute and relative size of these groups is much smaller than in the rest of the UK, religious diversity does exist. As in other parts of the UK, Muslims constitute the largest religious minority and, as in Wales and Scotland, Muslims are followed by those using the write-in option for "Other Religions", and then by Hindus, Buddhists, Jews and Sikhs.

In addition to these differences between the countries of the UK, because of the differing patterns of migration and settlement some areas within each country are characterised by a more pronounced religious diversity than others. In each nation, the greatest diversity of religions is to be found in cities, metropolitan boroughs and some towns.

Seaports such as Liverpool, Cardiff and London often have the oldest minority religious communities because trade led to the settlement in such places of seafarers from other countries and to the establishment of some degree of community life. Many old industrial towns and cities of the English Midlands and North, such as Leicester and Bradford, have communities that were established as a result of migration from particular areas of Commonwealth countries in response to the invitation to work in British industries during post-World War II labour shortages.

In relative terms the minority faith presence in the English regions is at its greatest in the West Midlands, the North West, Yorkshire and the Humber and the East Midlands. The main concentrations of minority religions are found in the areas of greatest general population density, including London, the West Midlands, the Leicester-Nottingham area, and the conurbations of the Pennines.

The cosmopolitan nature of London means that religious as well as ethnic and linguistic diversity is at its widest there, with only three-fifths of London's population recording their religion as Christian. For all the other religions the highest proportion of their regional populations is to be found in London, with the exception of the Sikhs, whose share of the regional population is at its greatest in the West Midlands.

Both longer-term religious and national history and more recent patterns of migration and settlement have affected the religious composition of each local and regional area. Therefore some areas have a more multi-faith character, and others have concentrations of people of particular religions and/or traditions within these religions.

As a proportion of the total population in local authority areas, the 2001 Census shows that, in England, the greatest percentage share of respondents identifying as Muslims is in the London Boroughs of Tower Hamlets (36.4%) and Newham (24.3%); Blackburn and Darwen (19.4%); Bradford (16.1%) and the London Borough of Waltham Forest (15.1%).

The greatest percentage share of Hindus is in the London Boroughs of Harrow (19.6%) and Brent (17.2%); Leicester (14.7%); and the London Boroughs of Redbridge (7.8%) and Ealing (7.8%). And the greatest percentage share of Sikhs is to be found in the London Boroughs of Slough (9.1%), Hounslow (8.6%) and Ealing (8.5%); Wolverhampton (7.6%) and Sandwell (6.9%).

Among the much more ethnically diverse Buddhist population, the greatest percentage share of Buddhists is in the London Boroughs of Westminster (13%), Camden (13%), Kensington and Chelsea (11%) and Hackney (11%); and Ribble Valley (11%).

With regard to the Jewish presence, in England, the greatest percentage share is in the London Borough of Barnet (14.8%); Hertsmere (11.3%); and the London Boroughs of Harrow (6.3%), Redbridge (6.2%) and Camden (5.6%). Outside of the Greater London area, the largest provincial Jewish populations are found in Manchester, Leeds and Glasgow. There are also other sizeable Jewish communities in Birmingham, Bournemouth, Brighton, Liverpool and Southend.

Among Bahá'ís, until 1939, most activity in the UK centred upon England, but after the Second World War it also spread to the other nations in the UK. Bahá'í *Spiritual Assemblies* and Bahá'í *Groups* can therefore be found scattered throughout the UK rather than having particularly strong regional concentrations. Many Jains live in and around Greater London and in Leicester where the largest Jain Temple in Europe is located. The majority of Zoroastrians live in and around London, and in the Greater Manchester area.

In particular local areas in the UK, members of faith communities may also share ethnic, cultural and linguistic backgrounds. In some cases the bulk of those adhering to a religion may, for example, be Muslims from Pakistan or, in others, Muslims from Bangladesh, or even from particular regions and even villages within these regions. For example, in Preston the Muslim population is largely Gujarati, as are the local Hindus. With greater population mobility, such local homogeneity may begin to diminish in the future, although it is also likely that, at least for the foreseeable future, broad differences will persist.

Religion, Ethnicity and Language

Religion is an important marker of identity for significant numbers of individuals and groups. For some it is the most important. Other aspects of identity are represented by ethnicity and language. These are often linked with religious identity because of the history of when and where religious traditions developed. Thus, for example, the majority of people in the UK with Pakistani antecedents are also Muslim, and nearly all Sikhs have some antecedents in the Punjab.

However, the patterns of overlap between religion and ethnicity are not always straightforward and the majority of the UK's religious communities are ethnically diverse, having origins in various parts of the world. So, for example, the Christian population includes, among others, people of African, African-Caribbean, Chinese, Korean, East and Central European and South Asian backgrounds. Buddhists in the UK are also of very diverse ethnic and national origins.

Similarly, while the largest group of Muslims in the UK have ancestral origins in the Indo-Pakistani subcontinent (coming to Britain either directly or via earlier migrations to East Africa and the Caribbean), the remainder of the Muslim population has ethnic and national origins in countries such as Cyprus, Malaysia, Turkey, Iran and the Arab world, together with the growing numbers of indigenous Britons who have embraced Islam.

Other groups are less diverse. Most Bahá'ís in the UK are of indigenous British ethnic origin and the majority are converts from other religions or former agnostics or atheists. There are, though, also Bahá'ís whose family roots are in Iran, most of whom have arrived since the Iranian Revolution.

Hindus in the UK have ancestral origins as Gujaratis and Punbjabis, and also from other parts of India such as Uttar Pradesh, West Bengal, and the southern Indian states, as well as in countries such as Sri Lanka. Thus the Hindu population is composed of many ethnic and linguistic groups, the most common of which are Gujarati, Punjabi, Bengali and Tamil.

Within the Hindu population as a whole, but especially among Gujaratis, *caste* or *jati* groups have important functions ranging from social

networking to voluntary welfare support. Although, in the UK, such groups do not necessarily correlate with the social, economic or occupational status of individuals and families, within many aspects of internal Hindu community life they remain significant social, cultural and economic networks. Due to differential patterns of settlement, *jati* groups can be found concentrated in specific localities including, for example, a concentration of Mochis in Leeds and Lohanas in Leicester and North London.

The vast majority of Sikhs are of Punjabi ethnic background, while Jains are of South Asian ancestral origin, including Gujaratis, Rajasthanis and Punjabis, the contemporary Zoroastrian community includes both *Parsees* (Pars being a province of Iran and *Parsis* had migrated from Persia to Sanjan in Gujarat, India) and *Irani Zardushtis* or, simply, *Iranis*. The majority of Zoroastrians in the UK are of *Parsi* origin, though in more recent years an *Irani* presence has also developed as a result of refugee movements arising from the Iranian revolution.

The relationship between broad religious identification and ethnic self-identification found in the 2001 Census results for England and Wales is set out in percentage terms in Table 2 below.

Table 2: Percentages of "Religion By Ethnicity" Among 2001 Census Respondents in England and Wales

Ethnic Group	Christian	Buddhist	Hindu	Jewish	Muslim	Sikh	Other	No Religion	Not Stated	All People	Base
White	96.3	38.8	1.3	96.8	11.6	2.1	78.4	94.5	90.9	91.3	47,520,866
Mixed	0.9	3.2	1.0	1.2	4.2	0.8	2.5	2.0	1.9	1.3	661,034
Asian	0.3	9.6	96.6	0.7	73.7	96.2	13.7	0.4	31	4.4	2,273,737
Black or Black British	2.2	1.0	0.5	0.4	6.9	0.2	3.3	1.1	31	2.2	1,139,577
Chinese or Other Ethnic Group	0.3	47.3	0.6	0.9	3.7	0.7	2.0	2.0	10	0.9	446,702

Due to rounding, figures may not total 100%.

Source: Census, April 2001 National Statistics website: www.statistics.gov.uk. Crown copyright, 2004. Crown copyright material is reproduced with the permission of the Controller of HMSO Percentages as shown are calculated by the present author on the basis of the original Census data

While it should be noted that interpreting these data, other than in very broad terms, is not straightforward, it is clear that there can often be a significant overlap between particular religions and particular ethnic groups. At the same time it is also clear that Islam, in particular, has a diverse ethnic profile in England and Wales. Thus, in Table 2, 11.6% of those identified as "Muslim" are also identified as "white"; 4.2% of the "Muslim" population is "mixed"; 73.7% of the "Muslim" population is "Asian"; 6.9% of the "Muslim" population is "Black" or "Black British"; 3.7% of the "Muslim" population is "Chinese or Other Ethnic Group".

However, while the number of "white" adherents to Islam is increasing, some of the 11.6% of "Muslims'" recorded as "white" are likely to include Middle Eastern respondents who opted for the descriptor of "white" in preference to any of the other pre-set categories for response.

There are also regional differences in this regard: since while in northern England and the West Midlands, Muslims are predominantly "Asian" (and mostly of Pakistani and Bangladeshi ancestral origins), in north London Boroughs the "white" Muslim population (including Turks and Turkish Cypriots) outnumbers "Asian" Muslims, while "Black" or "Black-British" Africans also form a substantial part of the Muslim population in some London boroughs.

Conversely, as can be seen from Table 3, in England and Wales the overwhelming majority of those who are recorded as being of "Asian" origins are also recorded as "Muslim", "Hindu" or "Sikh" by religion. Muslims of Bangladeshi origin are, in fact, the most homogeneous religio-ethnic grouping in England, with nearly all having their ancestral origins in the Sylhet District of the north-east of what is today Bangladesh. The Pakistani population of England is also almost entirely Muslim and has origins mainly in the Punjab and the north of Pakistan including,

especially, Pathans and other groups from the Afghan border districts, while there are also people from more diverse areas such as Mirpur.

Nevertheless, it is also the case that as many as 4.1% of all those recorded as "Asians" are also recorded as "Christians". The Indian ethnic group is, in fact, the most religiously diverse, with 45% being Hindu, 29% Sikh and 13% Muslim, while a further 2% belong to other religious groupings including Jains and Parsis. Finally, only 1.4% of all "Asians" indicate "no religion" as compared with a relatively very high 33.7% of "Chinese and Other Ethnic Group" respondents, 15.3% of the "white" population, and 15.5% of the population as a whole.

Finally, shared language can also be an important factor in the relationship between religion and ethnicity. For example, other than English, Punjabi is the common language among most Sikhs. In Wales there are local Christian communities for whom Welsh is the first language of both worship and everyday life and this is also true of Gaelic for smaller numbers of Christians in Scotland.

Demography

There are considerable contrasts in the age and gender structure between the various religious groups. Based on 2001 Census data (it needing to be recognised that, since then, over half a decade has passed), on average, the oldest populations are the Jewish and Christian ones, while the Muslim population is the youngest and most rapidly increasing faith group. The average age of Hindus and Sikhs is substantially greater than that of Muslims. While there are broadly equal numbers of males and females of Sikh religion, among Muslims and Hindus, males outnumber females. Although more than half of the Sikh population was born in the UK, fewer than half of Muslims and only 37.5% of Hindus were born in the UK.

Table 3: Percentages of "Ethnicity By Religion" of the 2001 Census Respondents in England and Wales

Religious Group	White	Mixed	Asian	Black or Black British	Chinese or Other Ethnic Group
Christian	75.7	52.5	4.1	71.1	27.2
Buddhist	0.1	0.7	0.6	0.1	15.3
Hindu	★0.02	0.9	23.5	0.3	0.7
Jewish	0.5	0.5	0.1	0.1	0.5
Muslim	0.4	9.7	50.1	9.3	12.8
Sikh	★0.01	0.4	13.9	0.1	0.5
Other	0.3	0.6	0.9	0.4	0.7
No Religion	15.3	23.3	1.4	7.6	33.7
Not Stated	7.7	11.5	5.5	11.1	8.6
All People	100	100	100	100	100

In this table, in two instances, percentages are shown to two decimal points to allow for comparison between religions since, with rounding up to a single decimal point, the differences between the relatively small proportions of religious groups in some ethnic groups would otherwise be invisible.

Source: Census, April 2001. National Statistics website: www.statistics.gov.uk. Crown copyright, 2004. Crown copyright material is reproduced with the permission of the Controller of HMSO. Percentages as shown are calculated by the present author on the basis of the original Census data.

The overall shape of the Muslim population is typical of a population experiencing rapid increase, with the number of people in an age group increasing when considered in relation to decreasing age bands. This reflects both a relatively high birth rate and also continuing immigration to the UK. Thus, in England, a third of the Muslim population is aged fifteen or under compared with the England average of 20%, while only 5% are aged sixty or over as compared with general average for England of 20%.

Socio-Economic Profiles

As well as demographic differences, there are also significant differences in socio-economic profiles as between groups of people understood with reference to religion. In terms of participation in the formal labour force Muslims are significantly less involved than other religious groups. While in England, the overall average participation rate for those aged twenty-five or above was 67%, for Muslims it was 50% as compared with a 70% and 71% participation rate, respectively, for Sikhs and Hindus.

The Muslim figures for economic participation are very largely due to the low female participation rate in the formal economy. Only 29% of Muslim women aged twenty-five and over were economically active, which is half the overall average (59%)

for women in England, while the economic activity rates for Hindus and Sikhs were just above the average at 62%.

Alongside the data for "economic activity", nearly 18% of Muslims aged sixteen to twenty-four were unemployed and nearly 14% of those aged twenty-five and above. By contrast, the unemployment rate for Hindus aged sixteen to twenty-four and twenty-five and over were, respectively, 7% and 5%.

In terms of occupational profile, among males aged twenty-five and above in England, at 42% Muslims have the lowest proportion of men in the four white-collar major groups of the year 2000 Standard Occupational Classification (SOC) - in other words among managers and senior officials, professionals, associate professionals and technical occupations and administrative and secretarial occupations.

The Muslim position compares with the overall England average of 50%, while 63% of Hindu males and 80% of Jewish males are in these occupations By contrast 34% of Muslim men in England work in semi-skilled and unskilled occupations as compared with 18% among Hindus and 31% among Sikh men.

Muslims have an above average family size and the concentration of Muslim households in flats or terraced homes leads to a higher than average degree of over-crowding. The higher the percentage of children brought up in overcrowded conditions, the poorer the living conditions of a community and the worse their children's life chances.

40% of Muslim children, 20% of Sikh and 30% of Hindu children in England live in overcrowded homes, compared with an all-England average of 10%. Patterns of disadvantage are also reflected in educational attainment as seen by religious group. Thus, among people aged 16-64, 41% of Muslims have no educational qualifications, as compared with less than 30% for all other religious groups.

The degree to which these socio-economic differences are rooted particularly in religious discrimination and disadvantage on the basis of religious identity, or else pertain to pre-existing socio-economic factors shared by people in a particular group, is a matter of some debate. What Census indicators do reveal is a consistent picture in relation to the relative vulnerability of Muslims as compared with people from other religious groups.

The relatively better overall socio-economic position of the Hindu and the Sikh population, as compared to Muslims, arguably owes as much to the position of the forebears of these groups prior to migration to the UK as to what has occurred since their arrival. A significant (though much smaller proportion of the Sikh and the Hindu population) part of both populations had origins among those who fled from East Africa, where they had previously formed a professionalised middle class. In contrast, many among the original Muslim migrants came from a rural peasant background.

Examination of the demographic and socio-economic profiles of the diverse religious groups of the UK is a reminder that, while religious identity, believing and belonging are of great importance, there are also other factors beyond the immediate sphere of religion that play an important role.

RELIGION, BELIEF, HUMANISM AND ATHEISM

Secularisation

Having noted above the diversification and persistent importance of religious identity, communities and groups it is also important to take account of the degree to which the UK can appropriately be characterised as "secular" as well as "Christian" and "religiously plural".

What is marked by the concept of secularisation has clearly brought something distinctively and significantly challenging to all religions. The development of secularity, the origins of which are to be found in the humanism of the Renaissance period, was accelerated by the Industrial Revolution and the urbanisation of life that it brought. As a result of this, a sense grew of humanity becoming increasingly insulated from the mysteries and unpredictabilities of natural life.

The machine became the emblem of progress and its mechanical precision a symbolic ideal. With the loss of mystery, it seemed as though the divine was being banished and the world was becoming explicable solely in terms of itself. Darwinism seemed to offer a new account of human beginnings; anthropology questioned the uniqueness of claims about religious revelation; and with Freud, psychoanalysis began to explain human mysteries in terms of sexuality.

Technology and globalisation began to shrink the world as air travel became ever faster, cheaper and more popular. Communication by satellite and the development of the mass media brought the whole world into the living rooms of ordinary British people. Human beings even left the earth in space flight. The first cosmonaut, Yuri Gagarin of the Soviet Union, declared that when had been in space he had not seen God.

The meanings associated with the concept of secularisation and the extent of the social reality that it attempts both to describe and to interpret are varied and contested. Some approaches see secularisation as a process in which religious thinking, practice and institutions lose social significance. Other definitions see secularisation more as the process by which sectors of society and culture are removed from the domination of religious institutions and symbols.

In both approaches there is a shared analysis of the role that religion plays in the public sphere that do not necessarily depend on any position concerning an absolute decline in religious belief and practice of a kind that,

from the 1960s onwards, has often been popularly associated with the concept of secularisation.

In current debates that have an impact on specific issues of religion and public policy, there is an increasing recognition of the need to try and distinguish between an understanding of the "secular" that is a more "procedural" one, understood as being one way to try to facilitate the inclusion and participation of a range of groups within society and the state, and a different approach which attempts to confine religion to the private sphere alone, on the basis of either politically pragmatic and/or ideological considerations.

People of "No Religion" in the 2001 Census

In the 2001 Census, 9,103,727 people (or 15.5% of the population) across the UK stated that they are of "no religion". These included the phenomenon of 39,127 people in England and Wales (or 0.7% of the population) who identified themselves as "Jedi" or "Jedi Knights", after the key characters in the film series, *Star Wars*. This followed an internet campaign that occurred also in Australia, Canada and New Zealand to encourage people to respond to the Census question on religion in this way, and which led to 2.6% (6,480 people) of the population of Brighton and Hove in England declaring themselves in this way.

In addition, it is also worth noting that Census Table M275 Religion (Most Detailed Categories) - which gives the breakdown (for England and Wales only) of respondents who used the "Other Religions – write in" response to the religion question - also includes some respondents from groups often associated as being of "no religion" or, at least, of philosophical alternatives to religion.

These included 586 Free Thinkers; 8,296 Humanists; 3 Internationalists; 37 Rationalists; 104 Realists; and 11 Secularists. Conversely, the "no religion" headline figures also include 269 people who used the write-in option to give the description of "Heathen" (which can be a form of Pagan religious identity as well as being taken in its more popular sense of meaning generally irreligious).

Alongside those who, in response to the 2001 Census questions on religion stated that they were of "No religion", there were, in addition, 4,288,719 people (or 7.3% of the population) who did not respond to the voluntary question. A significant number of these may also not identify with religion in general and/or any religion in particular.

At the same time, it is possible that some of these may have been respondents who do understand themselves in relation to a religious tradition, but who had religious and/or other conscientious reasons for not responding to a question on religion that some people found inappropriately intrusive in the context of a Government-initiated Census.

Whatever the judgement made about these the non-respondents to the religion questions, according to the Census results, Scotland would seem to be the country of the UK, with the largest share of its population (in fact over a quarter) who stated in the Census that they are of "no religion". By contrast England, often thought to be less religious than the "Celtic Britain", had the smallest proportion of its population who gave this response.

It is possible that at least some aspects of these results reflect differences in the form of the religious affiliation question as asked in Scotland and in England and Wales. This is because, in the case of Scotland the form of the question was concerned with the "harder-edged" notion of "belonging" to a specific religion and/or denomination as compared with the "What is your religion?" form of the question that was asked in England and Wales.

There is some evidence to suggest that respondents in England and Wales may have been making a statement that was as much, or more, to do with ethnic identity as with religious identity. Thus, in contrast with the Census data, it should be noted that, in the British Social Attitudes survey for 2001, only just over half of the population (54%) of Great Britain indicated that they regarded themselves as being Christian (29% per cent being Church of England/Anglican; 11% being Catholic, and 14% being of other Christian denominations), while 4% regarded themselves as belonging to another religion, but as many as 41% said that they belonged to no religion. At the same time, it should be noted that, in contrast to the Census, the BSA survey is based on a very small sample.

Belief and Practice

It is important to recognise that Census results do not necessarily indicate anything about the levels of religious belief and/or practice. In contrast to what is often popularly assumed, belief in God and identification with a religion are not identical.

There are, for example, religions such as Buddhism and Jainism that are not *theistic*. In addition, as the sociologist of religion, Grace Davie, has argued, there is also the complexity that arises from the phenomenon of "believing without belonging" in which religious belief may be considerably wider than either active involvement in, or even a passive identification with, a religious tradition or community. Conversely, in all religious communities there are numbers of people who could be described as "belonging without believing".

Christian orthodoxy has certainly declined. However, it is also arguable that a large proportion of the population continue to share many "folk beliefs" that are related to Christianity and the significance of this should not be underestimated. There is also work on religious experience that argues that religious experiences are more widespread than what is suggested by statistics on religious membership and participation, or by the affirmation of religiously orthodox beliefs. The concepts of "folk religion", "implicit religion" and "residual religion" have been used to indicate these areas of religious life which can still surface even where individuals do not have a very strong connection with a specific religious tradition.

Reflecting something of this complexity, the British Social Attitudes Survey, 1998 showed 21% of respondents saying that, "I know God exists and I have no doubt about it", 23% saying that, "While I have doubts, I feel that I do believe in God" and 14% saying that, "I don't believe in a personal God, but I do believe in a Higher Power of some kind" In addition, 14% of respondents said, "I find myself believing in God some of the time, but not at others", 15% that, "I don't know whether there is a God and I don't believe there is any way to find out" and 10% that, "I don't believe in God" 3% did not respond.

In the 1999-2000, European Values Survey, when asked a "yes" or "no" question about "belief in God", 71.8% of respondents in Great Britain answered "yes" and 28.2% answered "no". When asked "which of these statements comes closest to your beliefs", 31% said "personal God", 40.1% said "spirit or life force", 18.7% said "don't know what to think" and 10.2% said there is "no spirit, God or life force".

When the European Values Survey asked "independently of whether you go to church or not" would you say you are "a religious person", 41.6% of respondents in Great Britain affirmed this, while 53.4% said they were "not a religious person", while only 5% said they were "a convinced atheist".

Whilst atheism and secularism as systematised epistemologies and integrated ways of life were once sponsored by the states and political systems that were controlled by Marxist-Leninist ideology, principled stances of atheism can now be found only among relatively small numbers of people. Thus, the 2001 Home Office Citizenship Survey showed that only 4% of those not affiliated to a faith community stated that not having a religious affiliation was important to their identity. Contemporary affirmations of secular humanism are more often to do with perceptions of the irrelevance of organised religions to the life concerns and perspectives of significant numbers of people than they are to do with explicit ideological conflict.

The kind of secularity in which many of those who are non-religious are indifferent to religion rather than antagonistic towards it, is very much a part of the plurality of contemporary England and the UK. At the same time, there are those who do not identify with any religion and who have deeply felt concerns about allowing too prominent a role for religion in public life. In terms of organised campaigning, these concerns are expressed by the National Secular Society.

However, such concerns are also likely to be considerably more widespread than among "signed up" secularists, especially following the September 11th attacks in the USA and the concerns about religious extremism to which these gave rise. Similar concerns may be held by Humanists (among whom, for example, British Humanist Association offers a value system, philosophical beliefs and rites of passage, while nevertheless seeing itself as non-religious) as well as by "non-religious" members of the general public who may identify themselves explicitly as either Humanists or Secularists.

While those who identify themselves as non-religious are usually indifferent rather than antagonistic towards religion, some do have deeply felt concerns about allowing too prominent a role for religion in public life and certainly about any official privileging of religion in general or any one religion in particular. Thus in the 1999-2000 European Values Survey, in response to the question of whether respondents agree or disagree with the statement that "religious leaders should not influence government decisions", 20.3% of respondents from Great Britain indicated that they "agree strongly" and 44.9% that they "agree". 19.1% said they "neither agree nor disagree", with 12.1% saying they "disagree" and 36% that they "disagree strongly".

From the perspective of religious communities and organisations in the UK, however, it is argued that individuals of religious belief and conviction should be able to play as full a part in public and political life, while remaining true to their religious identity, as do those for whom religion does not play a central part in their lives. Furthermore, it is pointed out that religious organisations and groups play a major role in the voluntary and community sector, with far more people actively involved in religious organisations than are, for example, members of political parties.

Finding an appropriate balance in terms of inclusivity, equity and participation for individuals and groups of both religious and non-religious convictions is likely to prove one of the major challenges of the coming decades in the UK. Alongside and intersecting with this will be the difficulties that will inevitably be involved in negotiating the tensions that can exist between the various equalities and human rights strands in both law and social policy, some of which are explored in the section below on "Religion, Belief and the Law".

PLACES OF WORSHIP

The historical development and present diversity of the religious profile of the UK is mirrored and given expression in its religious architecture. One way in which the religious landscape has quite literally changed is in the presence and range of a variety of different religious buildings. *Church* steeples and towers are a familiar part of both the urban and rural landscape of the UK. *Synagogues* have had a long historical presence, but increasingly *gurdwaras, mandirs, mosques* and *viharas* are also becoming part of the skyline in a significant number of areas.

Places of worship can have an important role as community resources within local neighbourhoods, although some places of worship are not frequented as much by women and young people as by older men. Places of worship incorporate the sources and goals of their religious traditions, thus signifying the established presence and the geographical belonging of these traditions of faith to both national and local society.

Pagan places of worship are to be found in particular landscape locations throughout Britain, some of which were then built upon by Christian church buildings. Church buildings, of course, are a very widespread feature of both the urban and rural landscapes. Apart from pre-Christian Pagan traditions, Christians and Jews were the first to establish places of worship in Britain. The oldest *synagogue* in current use is the Bevis Marks Synagogue in London, which was built in 1701. As other communities began to emerge, places of worship within their traditions also began to be established. For example, the first purpose-built *mosque* was established in Woking in 1889 and the first Sikh *gurdwara* in Putney, London, in 1911.

It was in the wake of the major post-Second World War migrations that the pattern and distribution of places of worship began to change significantly. Gradually, during the 1960s, as migrants decided to settle in the UK and to bring their families rather than just working here, the provision of worship facilities began to emerge as a community concern. People began to look for premises in which to meet. Often lacking the economic means to buy or build new facilities, they either adapted existing private dwellings for religious purposes or, faced with prejudice and misunderstanding from the general population, turned to those Christian places of worship which were sympathetic in order to seek hospitality for their gatherings for worship.

This phase coincided with the continuing numerical decline in attendance at the traditional Christian *Churches* that was resulting in the closure of many Christian buildings, particularly in those inner city areas where traditional Christianity had become weak. As a result, minority religious organisations quite often sought to purchase formerly Christian places of worship. This gave rise to considerable debate among Christians.

For some Christians these developments seemed tangible evidence of Christianity's lessening significance in British life. In addition, for many minority ethnic groups within the Christian *Church*, such sales were met with puzzlement. The *Churches* that have predominantly black Christian membership and leadership often could not understand why such redundant buildings were not either given or sold on favourable terms to them as fellow Christians, since they also needed places of worship and often lacked the economic means to build new ones.

In addition to purchasing redundant *church* buildings, minority religious groups began to convert dwelling-houses and to purchase old warehouses, cinemas and other public buildings and, in a few cases, to construct their own buildings. At this stage, it was often the case that groups which would normally have remained separate on grounds of ethnicity, *caste* or sect found that, in the new situation, and under pressure of smaller total numbers and the consequent limitations of economic resources, they needed to join together to create premises for common use within the community.

In areas with the greatest numerical concentrations, the process of rediversification into sectarian and ethnically based groups has sometimes occurred with relatively increased security and prosperity. Conversely, pressing economic factors have been influential in bringing about a degree of rationalisation and *ecumenical* sharing of buildings among the Christian traditions, especially in the inner urban areas.

There has been a recent growth in the numbers of purpose-built places of worship for minority religious traditions that has led to the need for flexibility on the part of planning authorities in relation to architectural styles that are traditional in the religions concerned.

"Registered" Places of Worship in England and Wales

An indication of numbers of places of worship in various religions that are to be found in England and Wales (no parallel figures are kept for Scotland and Northern Ireland) can be derived from tables found in the *Annual Register of Statistics* of the Registrar General in the Office for National Statistics. The list is not published, but is available for consultation, and contains annual cumulative totals relating to three kinds of buildings.

Buildings of all religious bodies are "registered" as places of worship once the denomination in question (excluding buildings of the Church of England or the Church in Wales, which are all automatically "recorded") has "certified" them, and the Registrar General has considered the recording of this certification. "Recorded" churches and chapels of the Church of England and the Church in Wales.

The categories in which running totals are kept in the *Annual Register of Statistics* do not exactly match the nine world religious traditions with which this directory is principally concerned. For example, there is no separate data for Bahá'í, Buddhist, Hindu, Jain and Zoroastrian places of worship, although there is a collective category of "other (Eastern) bodies" than the Christian, Jewish, Muslim and Sikh categories for which separate data is recorded.

Bearing this in mind, the tables included in this section of the chapter give the total number of places of worship that can be derived from the Office for National Statistics' *Classification of Denominations and Production of Annual Statistics*, as at 30th June 2004 (which, at the time of publication, was the most recent set of figures available).

The legislative framework for "registration" is the *Places of Worship Registration Act* passed in 1855. "Registration" is not compulsory, but has benefits. Provided the worship held in the building is accessible to the general public it can bring exemption from local taxation – an exemption which extends to associated and attached buildings of the place of worship even if used for purposes other than religious worship. It is also the basis for an application to become a place of worship that is "registered" for the solemnisation of marriages.

Before the Registrar General would record "certification" of a place of worship, the Registrar General needs to be satisfied that it is being used predominantly as a place of religious worship. This is done by submitting to the local Superintendent Registrar of Births, Marriages and Deaths two copies of a document signed by an owner, occupier, minister or member of a building's congregation, declaring an intention to use this building for the purposes of worship, and naming the religious tradition concerned.

The Superintendent Registrar forwards this to the Registrar General who, if satisfied that the certified place is to be used "wholly or predominantly" for worship by an identifiable and settled group will, through the Superintendent Registrar, then record the "certification". *Churches* of the *established* Church of England and the *Anglican* Church in Wales do not need to apply to be "certified", since they are automatically "recorded".

Places of worship are not required to "certify" themselves and/or be "recorded" as "registered". Therefore, because house-based places of worship are rarely "certified", the total numbers of those listed in the *Classification of Denominations and Production of Annual Statistic* is not likely to give a completely accurate picture of the actual numbers of places of worship for each tradition. Especially for the earlier years in which records were kept, the number of places of worship that were listed is likely to have reflected an under-reporting. Not all in the minority traditions knew the procedures for "certification" and since many of their early places of worship were house-based, they were less likely to follow this procedure.

In recent years the relationship between the actual numbers of places of worship and the numbers listed in the *Classification of Denominations and Production of Annual Statistics* is likely to have become closer as increasing numbers of buildings in minority religions have "certified" themselves to the Registrar General and have been "registered" as such. However, since there is still likely to be no complete correspondence between the numbers of listed places of worship (see Table 4) and the actual numbers of places of worship, the directory also presents its own figures for the numbers of places of worship in other than Christian traditions (see Table 5).

The number of places of worship included in the CD-ROM accompanying this will differ from the total number indicated by the ONS' *Annual Register of Statistics* because the places of worship for which there are details on the CD-ROM cannot be known with certainty since in their replies to the project, not all organisations have made it clear if they have a place of worship. In addition, some places of worship have specifically asked not to have their details included on the CD-ROM. Thus the figures that are given represent what is an informed judgement of the numbers of places of worship that have details on the CD-ROM.

TABLE 4

Christian (Trinitarian, non-Trinitarian, and Christian "other"), Jewish, Muslim, Sikh and "Other" Places of Worship in England and Wales listed in the *Classification of Denominations and Production of Annual Statistics* on 30th June, 2004 (with 2004 being the latest year for which data is available)

	1972	1975	1980	1985	1990	1995	2000	2004
Christian Churches	47638	47139	45378	45129	44922	44722	44729	44563
Jewish Synagogues	320	348	335	351	355	357	360	367
Muslim Mosques	79	90	193	314	452	535	621	708
Sikh Gurdwaras	40	59	90	129	149	174	182	190
Other (Eastern) Bodies	222	217	219	264	305	342	394	447

The Register does not give separate figures for Bahá'ís, Hindus, Jains and Zoroastrians whose places of worship are included in this overall category of "Other".

TABLE 5

Approximate Numbers of Places of Worship in the UK in the Buddhist, Christian, Hindu, Jain, Jewish, Muslim and Sikh Traditions recorded in the CD-ROM accompanying this volume (data as in 2006)

UK	England	Scotland	Wales	Northern Ireland
Christian	18930	2114	1313	★
Buddhist	84	3	5	2
Hindu	92	4	2	2
Jain	1	0	0	0
Jewish	196	4	2	0
Muslim	656	24	24	1
Sikh	179	9	4	2

★ The CD-ROM does not contain data on local Christian *churches* in Northern Ireland due to the impact of resource constraints on the project. It is however in future hoped to extend coverage to include these. Coverage of Christian *churches* in England, Scotland and Wales is not yet comprehensive, as data collection for these is still ongoing in what is a very substantial task. However, the data that is included on the CD-ROM represents a development on the 2001 edition.

The Buddhist figures include details of centres, *viharas*, monasteries and other publicly accessible Buddhist buildings. The Bahá'ís do not have one of their *Houses of Worship* in the UK, but *Religions in the UK* contains details of a number of Bahá'í centres that are publicly accessible buildings. The Zoroastrians do not have any *Fire Temples* in the UK, although the new Zoroastrian Centre in Harrow contains a dedicated space that is used for worship, as does Zoroastrian House in London.

TABLE 6

Church of England and Church in Wales, other Christian Trinitarian, non–Trinitarian and "other Christian" Places of Worship in England and Wales listed in the *Classification of Denominations and Production of Annual Statistics* **on 30th June, 2004** (with 2004 being the latest year for which data is available)

	1972	1975	1980	1985	1990	1995	2000	2004
Christian	47683	47139	45378	45129	44922	44722	44729	44678
Trinitarian (composed of:)								
Anglican	17046	16901	16721	16614	16563	16529	16481	16447
Roman Catholic	3502	3585	3630	3673	3693	3699	3711	3704
Traditional Free Church	21059	20237	18655	18117	17668	17235	17125	16841
Non-Trinitarian								
Jehovah's Witnesses	652	723	759	809	872	907	921	929
Society of Friends	368	368	355	358	365	363	365	368
Unitarian	192	199	186	186	178	178	180	180
Other								
"Other Christian"	4864	5126	5072	5372	5583	5811	5946	6094

In relation to Christian places of worship in England and Wales, what is presented in Tables 6 as "Trinitarian" Christian figures are derived from the Register's categories of Baptist, Brethren, Methodists, Church in Wales, Church of England, Congregationalist, Methodist, Roman Catholic, Salvation Army and United Reformed Church. The "non-Trinitarian" Christian figures are derived from the Register's categories of Jehovah's Witnesses, Society of Friends and Unitarians. "Christian other" is used for all other Christian organisations.

TABLE 7: Places of Worship by Region in England and Wales listed in the *Classification of Denominations and Production of Annual Statistics* **on 30th June, 2004** (with 2004 being the latest year for which data is available)

	Trinitarian	Non-Trinitarian Christian	Other Christian	Jewish Synagogues	Muslim Mosques	Sikh Gurdwaras	Other (Eastern) Bodies
North East	2162	74	275	10	17	6	10
Yorks and Humb[1]	3309	165	511	15	173	25	33
North West	4035	210	873	63	151	11	60
East Midlands	3385	114	446	5	47	17	46
West Midlands	3123	138	644	9	158	51	57
Eastern	4724	135	525	6	10	14	31
London	2493	125	936	209	112	33	113
South East	3538	222	789	34	46	24	71
South West	5066	179	587	10	7	6	22
Wales	5157	115	508	6	17	3	4
TOTALS	**36994**	**1477**	**6094**	**367**	**738**	**190**	**447**

[1] Yorkshire and Humberside is now the government office region of Yorkshire and the Humber, the county of Yorkshire and Humberside having been abolished.

Trends in Places of Worship

The columns of figures in Tables 4, 6 and 7 present the earliest cumulative figures held by the General Register Office in Southport - namely, those for 1972, and then record figures at five yearly intervals between 1975 and 2000, and finally the latest figures available at the time of publication, which are those for 2004. From these cumulative totals, it is possible to discern certain trends in the provision of places of worship.

Thus from Table 4, it can be seen that the overall (including *Trinitarian*, non-*Trinitarian* and "Christian other") number of registered and recorded Christian *churches* has shown a pattern of decline over the period surveyed. Over the same period, Muslim *mosques*, Sikh *gurdwaras*, and places of worship of "Other Bodies" have more or less consistently increased in number. This is also true of Jewish *synagogues*, perhaps surprisingly in view of the overall slight demographic decline of the Jewish population.

The majority of the changes leading to increased numbers of Muslim and Sikh places of worship are due to the opening of new buildings, while the majority of the decrease in the number of Christian *churches* is due to the closure of buildings. However, some of both changes are due to the buildings of what were formerly Christian places of worship becoming, instead, places of worship in other than Christian traditions.

The overall bald national figures also hide a number of other variations that are more clearly visible in Table 6. For example, the main decline in the numbers of certified and recorded Christian places of worship has been among the *Trinitarian* Christian traditions, with the exception of the *Roman Catholic* tradition which, until the most recent year for which there is data (2004), has seen some small increase over the same period.

The *Unitarians* have, until the most recent figures, also reflected the pattern of decline found among the *Anglican* and traditional *Free*

Churches. However, the Society of Friends has, since 1980, shown some slight upward movements bringing them, in 2004, back to the number of Meeting Houses recorded in 1972 and 1975. However, the number of certified places of worship for the Jehovah's Witnesses has grown significantly, making the overall trend among *non-Trinitarian* Churches one of growth.

The "Other Christian" category has also seen a significant expansion of the number of its certified places of worship. This sector is likely to include *churches* of the *Pentecostalist* and *Independent* movements, as well as the other burgeoning "black-led" or "black-majority" *Churches*. At the same time, it should be noted that there may well be places of worship within the *New Church* movement (networks of Christians not in the traditional denominations, often meeting in private homes or hired public buildings rather than in specially constructed and/or specifically dedicated *church* buildings) which are not certified.

Table 7 illustrates regional variations in the distribution of "recorded" and "registered" places of worship that are of considerable significance because they reflect the geographical concentrations of people within the minority religious traditions. However, in relation to comparison over time it should be noted, as set out in notes below the table concerned, that the basis for classifying and presenting figures has changed from 2000 onwards with respect to the Eastern and South Eastern regions (Essex having been moved from alignment with the South East region to the Eastern region).

Thus the 2004 figures of over 150 *mosques* in each of Yorkshire and Humberside, the North West and the West Midlands, reflect the main concentrations of Muslim settlement. The presence of 209 *synagogues* in the London area underlines the importance of London for the Jewish community in England, while the 63 and 34 *synagogues* in the North West and the South East, respectively, demonstrate the clear provincial centres of the Anglo-Jewry. The 51 *Gurdwaras* in the West Midlands testify to the large Sikh settlement in that area.

As has been noted, the "Other (Eastern) Bodies" category includes all those other traditions that are separately featured in *Religions in the UK* - namely, the Bahá'ís, Buddhists, Hindus, Jains and Zoroastrians, along with other groups - and it is therefore difficult to read much of significance from the regional variations in this category.

RELIGIONS AND INTER-FAITH RELATIONS

Origins and Early Developments of Inter-Faith Initiatives

Alongside the continued role of the Christian Churches, the development of greater religious plurality, and the continued spread of secular perspectives, the emergence of inter-faith initiatives and structures at all levels of society has increasingly become another important dimension of the changing religious landscape of the UK.

Inter-faith initiatives generally began at a more international level such as the World Parliament of Religions held in Chicago in 1893. One of the earliest initiatives in the UK was the Religions of the Empire Conference, organized by Sir Denison Ross and held in conjunction with the British Empire Exhibition in 1924. The explorer and mystic Sir Francis Younghusband took a prominent part in this and in 1936 convened the World Congress of Faiths which established itself that year as an inter faith organisation which still continues its work today.

The colonial and imperial projects of the nineteenth century turned out, in many ways, to have been a significant catalyst for a growth in consciousness about religious diversity and plurality and for engagement

with the challenges brought by this. As has already been noted earlier in this chapter, one of the consequences of colonialism was that substantial numbers of people of other than Christian religions migrated from former colonies to the UK.

In addition, in the earlier period, a significant number of colonial administrators, members of the armed forces and Christian missionaries contributed to the dissemination in the UK of the texts, ideas and beliefs of a variety of religions. A number of these people also became involved in these early inter-religious initiatives.

In the earlier part of the twentieth century, there was a tendency for inter-faith organisations to be perceived either as organisations just for inter-faith "enthusiasts" or else as places where more socially and religiously marginalised religious traditions could find a public platform.

The earliest initiatives tended to be multi-lateral ones involving a wide range of different religions. However, other initiatives and organisations developed, the activity of which focused on relationships between two or three particular religions and, more specifically, relationships between Christianity and one or two other religions. These initiatives generally secured a greater degree of endorsement from the leaderships of the mainstream bodies within their sponsoring religions, a good example of this being in the field of Christian-Jewish relations.

Other than Christianity, Judaism is the world religious tradition that has had the longest settled community presence in the UK. Not surprisingly, among the first of the organised inter-faith initiatives were those specifically concerned with Christian-Jewish relations. An early instance of this was the founding, in 1927, of the London Society for Jews and Christians that continues to hold meetings today and emerged from an initiative of the Social Service Committee of the Liberal Jewish Synagogue.

In 1942, partly as a response to the situation of Jews in Nazi-occupied Europe, a Council of Christians and Jews (CCJ) was formed. As described below, in more recent years as the Muslim population has expanded in the UK there have been further initiatives concerned with relationships between the "Abrahamic faiths" of Judaism, Christianity and Islam, alongside wider multi faith developments.

Inter-Faith Initiatives at a National Level

The challenge of living together in an increasingly religiously plural society has meant that "mainstream" communities have gradually needed to develop ways to interact and co-operate with one another. In addition, of course, the presence and claims of other religions pose profound philosophical and epistemological challenges to all religions. Therefore for both practical and theological/philosophical reasons, religious communities and organisations in the UK have been giving increasing attention to relationships with people from religious traditions other than their own.

For example, Churches Together in Britain and Ireland (CTBI) has a Churches' Commission for Inter-Faith Relations (soon to become a "network" rather than a commission). Its predecessor body, set up more informally under the auspices of the then British Council of Churches, was formed in 1978. A number of CTBI member Churches also have their own committees that focus on inter-faith matters. The Board of Deputies of British Jews has recently appointed an inter-faith officer; and the Muslim Council of Britain has an inter-faith relations committee.

However, alongside initiatives that have been taken from within a single religious tradition, one of the distinctive features of recent decades in the UK has been the emergence of multi-lateral organisational frameworks for dialogue and co-operation between religions.

Among these, one of the most significant developments has been the emergence in 1987 of the Inter Faith Network for the UK. This has provided a major catalyst in the transformation of inter-faith initiatives from what were for the most part, historically, relatively marginal initiatives into a central feature of the contemporary religious landscape of England and the UK. At the time of writing, it links in total over 130 organisations within four different categories of membership.

The organisations affiliated to the Network include representative bodies from within the historic world religious traditions with significant communities in the UK (namely, the Bahá'í, Buddhist, Christian, Muslim, Hindu, Jain, Jewish, Sikh and Zoroastrian traditions); UK-wide, national, regional and other inter-faith organisations; local inter-faith groups and councils; and a number of educational and academic centres that are concerned with the study of religions, including relationships between them.

The Network is primarily a framework for co-operation and communication. It provides information and advice to a wide range of organisations and individuals on inter-faith matters and on how to contact communities at both national and local level. It holds regular national and regional meetings and organises seminars and conferences on a variety of issues and projects and publishes a range of material to help encourage and resource inter faith activity.

In recent years a Faith Communities Forum has been developed within the framework of the Network to provide a mechanism for consultation between faith community representative bodies on matters of mutual concern, including issues on the public agenda as well as the development of inter-faith relations.

There is a wide range of other inter-faith organisations operating at national level, including some, as noted above, with a long history. Some newer national inter-faith organisations focus on a particular bilateral or trilateral relationship, for example the Three Faiths Forum that brings together Jews, Christians and Muslims; Alif Aleph UK and the Joseph Foundation, which focuses on Jewish-Muslim relations; as well as a recently established Christian Muslim Forum. There is also an informal Christian-Hindu dialogue group.

Among the multilateral bodies, some focus on particular aspects of inter-faith relations, for example Religions for Peace (UK), which has a particular concern for issues of international peace and justice. This, like others such as the British Chapter of the International Association for Religious Freedom and the United Religions Initiative (UK), is linked to international inter-faith organisations that operate in many different countries. The organisation Minorities of Europe has an inter-faith programme that focuses particularly on work with young people. The International Interfaith Centre helps to provide a link between a range of international inter-faith organisations which have their headquarters in different countries.

Many of these national organisations are, in principle, UK-wide in their operations. There is now also a Scottish Inter Faith Council, an Inter Faith Council for Wales and a Northern Ireland Inter Faith Forum; and within England regional faith forums have emerged to engage in relationships with the regional structures of Government in their particular regions.

There are also a number of academic institutions which have centres dedicated to work on inter faith matters and which play a national role, such as the Centre for the Study of Islam and Christian-Muslim Relations at the University of Birmingham; in Cambridge the Centre for the Study of Jewish-Christian Relations and for the Study of Jewish-Muslim Relations; and at the University of Glasgow, the Centre for Inter-Faith Studies.

The contribution of multi-faith Religious Education and the work of bodies such as the Religious Education Council for England and Wales, the National Association of SACREs and the Shap Working Party on World Religions in Education has also been a significant resource for inter-faith activity.

As well as a growth in inter-faith bodies across recent years, a number of multi-faith bodies have been established to link religious communities and groups in working on particular issues. For example, the Faith Based Regeneration Network UK was started in 2002 to provide a link between people from various religions who are involved in regeneration and related work.

Local Inter-Faith Initiatives

The development of local inter-faith initiatives has been of particular significance for the contemporary religious landscape of the UK. For some decades the existence of a network of local Councils of Christians and Jews has provided a link between national and international dialogue between Jews and Christians and dialogue at local level. More recent has been the development of groups at local level linked to the Three Faiths Forum bringing together Jews, Christians and Muslims.

Emerging in the last quarter of the twentieth century and spreading more rapidly towards the beginning of the twenty-first century, one of the most significant developments for inter-faith relations has been the development of wider, local inter-faith initiatives and groups in towns and cities throughout the UK. The third, 2006, edition of the Inter Faith Network for the UK's directory of *Inter Faith Organisations in UK* recorded 23 inter-faith organisations operating at UK and/or national level within the UK.

It also included details of 194 local inter-faith groups and initiatives throughout the UK (excluding local groups linked to the Council of Christians and Jews or the Three Faiths

Forum). These local initiatives included 3 in Wales and 10 in Scotland, and 1 – which also operates at the Northern Irish level - in Northern Ireland. In England, details of 180 groups were recorded including 16 in the East of England; 17 in the East Midlands; 33 in London; 7 in the North-East; 30 in the North-West; 26 in the South-East; 14 in the South-West; 17 in the West Midlands; and 20 in Yorkshire and Humberside.

The majority of these local groups are to be found in localities characterised by a high degree of ethnic diversity and visible religious plurality, including groups such as the Harrow Inter-Faith Council, the Leicester Council of Faiths, the Wolverhampton Inter Faith Council and others. However, there are also groups such as the Beaminster One World Fellowship and the West Somerset Inter Faith Group that have been formed to promote greater understanding of religious diversity in geographical areas that are less visibly diverse.

The Inter Faith Network has supported and encouraged the development of local inter-faith structures and it publishes *The Local Inter Faith Guide* that provides advice on the establishment and development of local inter-faith initiatives.

In 2003, the Network carried out a major survey of local inter-faith activity across the UK. As shown in that survey, local inter-faith groups have a variety of histories, self-understandings and methods of working. These can include a desire for better understanding and appreciation of another religious tradition; an objective of social harmony and friendship; a wish on the part of participant groups to secure greater social and religious acceptance; or an imperative within one's own religion to work with others.

In the early days of local inter-faith organisations and initiatives, one of the main needs was simply for information about one another's beliefs and practices and a good deal of inter-faith activity was oriented towards this aim. There remains a continuing need for this, but inter-faith activity has also expanded and developed in a variety of ways with differing goals, participants and forms of organisation as people from various communities of faith have responded to the challenges presented by a multi-faith society.

As local authorities have increasingly sought to engage with, and facilitate, the contribution that religions can make to wider public life, a pattern of local inter-faith initiatives has emerged, the main rationale for which lies in the wish of religious groups to work together in their relationships with local authorities, business and other community groups through mechanisms such as Local Strategic Partnerships.

The varied character of these local groups and the diverse approaches taken by them is often reflected in the terminology used in their organisational names. Some have used the word "group" in their titles, such as the Derby Multi-Faith Group. Such a title can often indicate a more informal style of organisation and an individual basis of membership rather than an attempt to be a more "representative" body.

At the same time, there are those, such as the Birmingham Council of Faiths, that see themselves as more formally structured attempts to achieve a balanced representation from the principal religious traditions. Such bodies tend to see a major part of their work as being concerned with the interface with wider public life and, particularly, with local government. This is also true, from a different angle, of those groups formed specifically for the purpose of addressing this interface, and which are often known as "forums of faiths".

In recent years, emerging trends include a greater focus on women's involvement in local inter faith work, in some cases with inter-faith initiatives being started and run by and for women. A 2006 report on *Women's Inter Faith Initiatives in the UK*, and published by the Inter Faith Network, looks in some depth at these.

RELIGIONS IN PUBLIC LIFE: THE CHRISTIAN INHERITANCE

Religious and Civil Belonging

For much of the history of these islands (as elsewhere in the world) it has been difficult to distinguish between political and religious loyalties. There have, in the past, often been attempts to impose varying degrees of uniformity in the public profession of belief and in religious worship, sometimes through physical force, sometimes through the use of the law, and sometimes through the pressures of social expectations and conventions.

Despite this, as seen above, religious diversity has always been present from pre-Christian times to the present. Among Christians especially, it has developed in indigenous ways arising from the sixteenth century *Reformation* and the diverse forms of Christian believing and belonging that emerged in that context. Nevertheless, prior to the nineteenth century, religious minorities both within and beyond the Christian tradition experienced a variety of civil disabilities, including exclusion from higher education and from local government and a number of offices of state.

During the nineteenth century, there were rapid advances in religious toleration and the abolition of many civil disabilities related to religion. This facilitated both the development and the public visibility of diverse forms of religious life, including an expansion of the influence of *Nonconformist* Christian denominations and the re-emergence of *Roman Catholic* Christianity as a public religion. After centuries of restricted existence *Catholic* Christianity was also strengthened here by the migration from Ireland of many *Catholic* workers to fill jobs, especially in the construction industries.

Religion, State and Society in the UK

Christianity, especially in its *established* forms, still plays a pre-eminent role in the public religious life of the UK. Within this, the established Church of England has a special constitutional position with regard to the UK state as a whole that marks it out from other *Churches*. As an expression of the current relationship between the state and this *Church*, at the time of writing, twenty-four of its *bishops* and its two *archbishops* continue to sit in the House of Lords as of right and the Prime Minister's Office and the monarch are involved in their appointments.

However, despite this special relationship with the state, and in contrast with the national *Churches* of some other European countries, the Church of England is not funded by the state in any direct way. Also, within the constituent nations of the UK there is a range of different arrangements for defining the relationships between religious bodies, the state and society.

In its report published in January 2000, The Royal Commission on the Reform of the House of Lords made proposals to widen the basis of representation for "organised religions" in the second chamber as part of an overall process of reform.

The Government's White Paper of 2001 envisaged retaining a smaller number of Church of England bishops, together with members from other religions, among the appointed section of a reformed second chamber. Its later proposals of February 2007 were for a "hybrid" House, partly elected and partly appointed, including continued representation of the Church of England. However, both Houses subsequently voted in favour of a wholly elected second chamber and at the time of writing it unclear what the outcome of the current political debate will be and when.

Religion, State and Society in England

In England, the Church of England is the form of religion "by law established" and other Christian denominations do not have any formal link with the state. The reigning monarch is its *Supreme Governor* (not, as is sometimes popularly, but incorrectly stated, its "Head").

The monarch has the title *Defender of The Faith*. Although the origins of this title pre-date the *Reformation*, since the *Reformation* it has generally been understood in terms of upholding the particular character and role of the Church of England. Nevertheless some years ago the Prince of Wales made a suggestion that the more general term *Defender of Faith* might be more appropriate given the religiously plural nature of contemporary society.

The Church of England continues to have a special role in public ceremonial on both ordinary occasions (such as the daily prayers offered by an *Anglican Chaplain* in the House of Commons) and special ones (such as the prayers at the Cenotaph on Remembrance Day). Its *ecclesiastical* law is treated as a part of the public law of England, being passed through parliamentary processes and then receiving the Royal Assent. In addition, its ecclesiastical courts currently have the legal power to call as witnesses individuals of any faith or none.

Religion, State and Society in Scotland

Since the 1603 accession of James VI of Scotland to the English Crown as James I and the union of the Parliaments in 1707, Scotland has had close links with England and Wales through a shared monarch and participation in the political system of the UK. But in many ways Scotland remains distinct, especially in its systems of law and education, as well as in relation to matters of religion. The re-establishment of the Scottish Parliament in 1999 has reinforced this distinctiveness.

The *Presbyterian* Church of Scotland (rather than the *Anglican* tradition's Episcopal Church of Scotland) is the *established* Church in Scotland and among *Presbyterians* in Scotland is often understood as the national Church. Prior to the recent devolution of powers from Westminster to the Scottish Parliament, the *Kirk* (as it is known in Scotland), which is governed by a hierarchy of elected clerical and lay *Kirk* Sessions, *Presbyteries* and also the *General Assembly*, was frequently seen as a surrogate Scottish parliament.

The Scottish form of *establishment* differs from that of the Church of England in that it does not place legal restrictions upon the Church of Scotland's self-government, nor does the British Prime Minister, the Secretary of State for Scotland nor the First Minister of the Scottish Executive, have any role in the appointment of its leadership. Similarly, despite its legal status and prominent role within Scottish history, the Church of Scotland has no right, corresponding to that of the Church of England, for its leaders to have seats in the House of Lords. The Church of Scotland does, however, maintain a formal link with the Crown that is symbolised by the Lord High Commissioner's presence at the Church of Scotland's *General Assembly*, which meets each May in Edinburgh.

The re-establishment of the Scottish Parliament has led to the consideration of new and important questions concerning the role of religion in such institutions of state, and the implications of the contemporary religious plurality for such a role. So, for example, in the Westminster Parliament there has been a long tradition of beginning the day with prayers that have traditionally been led by a member of the clergy of the Church of England.

By contrast, the new Scottish Parliament debated whether or not prayers or a time of reflection would be appropriate at all and, if so, which people of what religions should lead such prayers. It concluded that a time of non-denominational reflection should be held each week, and that those leading this should be selected on a basis that broadly reflects the relative size of the various Scottish communities of religion and belief.

In 1998 the Scottish Churches Parliamentary Office was set up with a Parliamentary Officer who provides information and facilitates working relationships between the Scottish Parliament and member *Churches* of Action of Churches Together in Scotland. The *Catholic* and Jewish communities in Scotland have each appointed their own Parliamentary Officers who provide a similar service for their communities.

Religion, State and Society in Wales

Until the recent creation of the Welsh Assembly, Wales had very little modern constitutional distinctiveness, but its culture and language were vigorously revived during the 1960s through the campaigns of *Cymdeithas yr Iaith Gymraeg* (the Welsh Language Society).

Following the 1920 *disestablishment* of the Anglican Church in Wales, there is now no established form of religion in Wales. Unlike in Scotland, in Wales there has not been a predominant single denominational tradition that has acted as a focus for national identity. At the same time, the multiplicity of *Free Churches* has played a significant role in the social, political and cultural life of Wales, including a role in preserving and promoting the use of the Welsh language.

Religion, State and Society in Northern Ireland and the Republic of Ireland

Northern Ireland has a much higher level of professed religious belief and participation than England, Wales and Scotland, as does the Republic of Ireland. However, neither Northern Ireland nor the Republic of Ireland has an officially *established* form of religion. The *episcopal* Church of Ireland (which is part of the global *Anglican* Communion) was *disestablished* in 1871 and the *Northern Ireland Act* specifically proscribed the establishment of any particular religion or religious tradition.

In Northern Ireland, although the *Roman Catholic* population is the largest single denomination, it is outnumbered around 53% to 44% by the combined *Protestant* groupings of which the *Presbyterians* (organised in a number of different denominations) are the largest.

In the Republic of Ireland, the Roman Catholic Church originally had a special position within the 1937 constitution which meant that its teachings had a formative effect upon legislation in the Republic, particularly in areas of personal, social and sexual morality. However, in 1972 its "special position" clause in the Irish Republic's constitution was abolished.

Despite the existence of the political border between Northern Ireland and the Republic of Ireland, nearly all the *Churches* of the island of Ireland are organised on an all-Ireland basis with regional and local bodies existing within a common organisational framework both north and south of the border.

At the same time, religion has undoubtedly been a dimension of the conflict which became known as "The Troubles" and which has resulted in a substantial level of violence, loss of life, injuries and death until the cease-fire of paramilitary organisations and the Good Friday/Belfast agreement of 1998.

The *Roman Catholic* community in the North has been closely identified with broad nationalist aspirations, whilst the continuing demographic decline of Southern *Protestants* has reinforced the concerns of their co-religionists in the North about the minority position of Protestantism in the island of Ireland as a whole.

RELIGIONS IN PUBLIC LIFE: EVOLVING INCLUSIVITY

Religious Diversity and Change

The Christian *Churches* continue to play a significant role in public life in the UK and in its constituent nations. Alongside these, as the religious composition of society continues to change and evolve, the bodies of other religions have been playing an increasingly significant role. As a result of this, patterns of consultation by, and engagement with, Government and other bodies have been evolving accordingly.

This process has been encouraged by bodies such as the Inter Faith Network for the UK which has, since the early 1990s, endeavoured to facilitate the participation of the full range of religious communities in the public life of the UK. It has also encouraged Government Departments and other public bodies to consult religious communities on the development and implementation of policies and programmes that are of particular concern to them.

At local level, inter-faith initiatives have developed that not only engage in promoting good relations between individual religions, but also in facilitating interaction between religions and the wider society in its secular, Christian and religiously plural dimensions.

State Occasions and Religious Observances

The issue of how religions other than Christianity can be represented in events to mark key points in national and local life is a complex one. Because of the particular relationship between the state and the Church of England, this *Church* has had, and continues to have, a special role in many public events at both local and national levels.

During the latter part of the 20th century, other Christian denominations were also given an opportunity to participate in many such events and activities. Increasingly, though, religious groupings other than the Christian *Churches* have also been invited to take part in various ways. For example, for some years there has been a tradition, at the annual Commonwealth Day Observance, held at Westminster Abbey, to include contributions from representatives of other than Christian religions. In the year 2000 representation at the Remembrance Sunday event in London was widened to include representation for the first time from Buddhist, Hindu, Muslim and Sikh traditions.

The Government asks the *Churches* to organise "national services" to mark particularly significant events. In England and Scotland, the lead in the organisation of these events is taken by the *established Churches* of these countries with significant involvement from other major Christian denominations through the ecumenical structures of Churches Together in England and Action of Churches Together in Scotland. In Wales and Northern Ireland, the Christian *ecumenical* structures are invited to take the lead. Churches Together in Britain and Ireland is also involved in discussions about any UK-wide state religious observance.

At the local level, civic services are generally arranged by the *Churches* just as are "national services". They therefore usually take place in *cathedrals* or *churches* and operate within clearly Christian parameters. In the case of the Church of England *canon law* dictates this. *Canon law* is the ecclesiastical law of the Church of England that, because of its established status, is also part of the law of the land. This makes it difficult for anything more than short readings or prayers from other traditions to be included and rules out any readings not compatible with Christian doctrine. In consequence the readers are most often Christian. While representatives of other faiths may well be seated prominently as "honoured guests" they are unlikely to be active participants in the liturgy.

In some contexts, new forms of civic religious events are emerging and it is challenging to develop ones with a structure and content with which all participants are at ease. January 2000 saw the first example of a Government hosted event bringing together leaders and members of the principal faith communities in the UK. This was the Shared Act of Reflection and Commitment held at the Houses of Parliament as part of the official celebrations during the first weekend of the new Millennium and was arranged with the assistance of the Inter Faith Network for the UK. Comparable gatherings happened in different areas of the UK, mirroring the move towards more devolved government. As a result, at the beginning of the new Millennium special services took place in Belfast, Cardiff, Edinburgh, and London.

The Westminster event complemented the "national services" which were held by the Christian *Churches* earlier in the weekend but it was not, in itself, a service of worship in order that no participants needed to feel compromised by being invited to join in prayers or actions with which they might not feel comfortable. The Shared Act of Reflection and Commitment was opened by the Secretary of State for Culture, Media and Sport (the lead agency on the Millennium) and the Archbishop of Canterbury. It included speakers from all the major faith communities, and closed with a speech from the Prime Minister.

Patterns of Public Consultation with Religious Bodies

Because of their presence over a long period in the UK, the Christian and Jewish communities have been able to develop the kind of broadly representative bodies which can facilitate consultation at a variety of local, regional and national levels with Governmental, public and voluntary bodies.

The national bodies of the Christian Churches, together with the Board of Deputies of British Jews, have acted on behalf of their communities in this engagement on a variety of issues. These bodies are professionally staffed and funded by their congregations and by donors from within their traditions. Prior to the 1980s a range of

consultation arrangements were in place with these two communities. For example, the Churches' Main Committee has been used by the Government for consultation on measures relating to the practical aspects of Church life, such as taxation or property matters as distinct from major social issues.

As other religious communities have settled and developed in the UK over the recent decades they have had to engage with the difficult task of developing representative bodies that can find general acceptance within their own communities and can also engage with Government on their behalf.

This has been particularly difficult to achieve at national level since many of these communities naturally had to put their initial energies into establishing places of worship and building up their local organisational capacity. However, organisations have been emerging at national level to cater for the needs of these communities to engage with Government and other public bodies.

There has also been a significant growth in interest on the part of Government and other public bodies in the potential for making use of multi-faith mechanisms as a means of facilitating appropriate consultation with faith communities. One of the earliest initiatives in this regard was the foundation, in 1992, within what is now the Department for Communities and Local Government, of the Inner Cities Religious Council (ICRC).

The ICRC was created as part of the Government's response to the issues raised by the Church of England's *Faith in the City* report. It has offered advice on issues affecting the inner cities from the perspective of the Christian (including black-majority Churches), Hindu, Jewish, Muslim, and Sikh communities.

In more recent years, local authorities have increasingly recognised the potential contributions that can be made by religious groups and inter-faith organisations. For example, it is now not uncommon for a local authority to seek input from the local Council of Faiths with regard to local policies and services. Some local authorities, such as Blackburn with Darwen, played an active role in seeking to establish new local inter-faith initiatives for conversation with local religious communities.

As already noted above, a further stimulus has taken place in the context of Local Strategic Partnerships for economic and social regeneration, the groundwork for which was laid by the ICRC's sponsorship, during the 1990s, of regional and local consultancy to elicit the support of religious groups in urban regeneration.

These developments have both been stimulated by, and given rise to, a range of good practice guides in which the Local Government Association has played a significant role. Thus, for example, in association with the Inner Cities Religious Council, Active Community Unit, the Home Office, and the Inter Faith Network for the UK, the Association produced *Faith and Community: A Good Practice Guide for Local Authorities*.

One of the more recent developments in this regard has been the emergence, alongside the structures for regional governance in England, of a range of regional inter-faith bodies of varied kinds. These have often been created to support religious representation in the Regional Assemblies, but also to connect the religious traditions and communities with the economic and social initiatives of the Regional Development Agencies.

Thus, as well as the range of local inter-faith groups and initiatives already noted, the Inter Faith Network's *Local Inter Faith Organisations* in the UK directory for 2006 includes details of 12 regional bodies in the 9 English regions (3 in London, 2 in the East of England, 2 in the South West, 1 in the East Midlands, North West, South East, West Midlands, Yorkshire and Humberside, and none in the North East).

Towards the end of the 1990s, preparations for marking the new Millennium were undertaken by the so-called Lambeth Group. This worked on a religiously inclusive basis to develop guidelines for religious involvement in the observance of the new Millennium, and provided advice on the planning of the Faith Zone in the Millennium Dome in a way that reflected both the Christian inheritance of the UK and also its religious plurality. The Scottish Parliament also moved in this direction by seeking faith community input on particular policy areas, for example, through the Scottish Inter Faith Council.

Thus, in a whole range of areas, organisations and bodies that had previously only liaised with the Christian and Jewish communities were now beginning to make efforts to consult more widely. At the same time, however, the position was a patchy one and there was some concern among more recently settled religious communities that these developments in the direction of consultation were neither fast enough nor sufficiently widespread. Religious leaders and other representatives of these religious communities still found it hard to gain access to many public and social institutions on the same basis as most Christian leaders and representatives, bearing in mind that this problem could also affect representatives of the smaller Christian denominations.

In the light of this, the Government began to recognise the need for greater co-ordination of its activities in relation to religious communities. Therefore, in 2003 the Religious Issues section of what was then the Home Office Race Equality Unit was reconstituted into the Faith Communities Unit, and the Government initiated a Review of its Interface with Faith Communities.

The outcome of this review was contained in the report, *Working Together: Co-Operation Between Government and Faith Communities*. The aim of the review was to draw on the good practice that already existed, together with the perspectives of faith community representatives, and from this to offer a set of recommendations designed to make these processes both more effective and more widespread across Government.

That review considered the possible need for creating a new national mechanism for consultation with faith communities to act as a single point of reference and consultation across the machinery of Government. At that time, it concluded that the case for this had not yet been demonstrated. However, in 2006 a new Faith Communities Consultative Council was established, bringing together the streams of work of the Inner Cities Religious Council and the Working Together exercise and was jointly serviced by the Home Office and the Office of the Deputy Prime Minister.

With the creation of the Department for Communities and Local Government responsibility for the Council passed to that Department. In addition to representatives of the Bahá'í, Buddhist, Christian, Hindu, Jain, Jewish, Muslim, Sikh and Zoroastrian communities, the Inter Faith Network for the UK and the Faith Based Regeneration Network UK have seats on the Council, as do the Northern Ireland Inter Faith Forum, the Scottish Executive Core Liaison Group and the Inter Faith Council for Wales.

The Government has also recently made much more use of bilateral, rather than multi-lateral, consultation with faith communities, particularly for example, with the Muslim community on issues relating to the agenda on tackling extremism. Thus there remains continuing debate about the right pattern of religious community organisations for the Government to consult.

One aspect of the *Working Together* review was to encourage the establishment of appropriate mechanisms for consultation and liaison between individual Government Departments and faith communities. In some

Departments there has been provision for this for some time. For example, in the case of education there has been regular consultation in a variety of ways.

In the case of the Churches the development of the Joint Churches Education Policy Group has facilitated this engagement. In addition, the establishment some quarter of a century ago of the Religious Education Council for England and Wales has provided a framework for faith communities more generally, including the Churches, to consider together issues on Religious Education and collective worship, and has helped in their engagement with Government on these particular issues.

There has also been consultation between the Department for Education and Science and faith communities on the subject of "faith schools". Furthermore, there have been important developments in Scotland and Wales in arrangements for consultation between the devolved administrations and religious communities there.

The development of the Government's approach to handling equality and discrimination issues has involved extensive consultation on new anti-discrimination legislation and on plans for establishing the new Commission for Equality and Human Rights. One of the strands with which the Commission will be dealing is "religion and belief". A Religion and Belief Consultative Group has been set up to facilitate discussion between faith community representative organisations, the British Humanist Association and the National Secular Society on issues arising in this field. In addition, the new Commission for Equality and Human Rights may itself make arrangements itself for a consultation mechanism with religious communities and other stakeholders.

The issue of engagement with organisations relating to the "non-religious" belief sector, alongside faith communities, is becoming an increasingly significant one, while with the greater development of its own consultation arrangements, the Government is now less reliant on consultation with inter-faith organisations except on issues relating directly to their particular areas of work.

Media and Advertising

In modern societies the mass media play one of the most extensive and significant roles in terms of effects upon public and political attitudes and perceptions. The interface between the media and religion is therefore of great interest to religions and of significance for UK society more broadly, especially at times of crisis in relation to particular religious groups, such as those that, for the Muslim community in the UK, followed the events of 9/11 and 7/7 and the invasions of Afghanistan and Iraq.

UK regulation of television and radio broadcasting on religion differs from that found in the USA and in many other European countries, since the British Broadcasting Corporation (BBC) and the Independent Television Commission (ITV) are required to offer a specific number of hours of religious programming per week, albeit with stricter controls on their content than in many other countries.

Up to the mid 1990s, much religious broadcasting, broadsheet and tabloid coverage of religion (with the notable exception of New Religious Movements) gave relatively scant coverage to religions other than Christianity. The last few years have, however, seen significant change with coverage beginning to reflect more proportionately the religious mix of the UK population. The BBC and ITV continue to make use of the Central Religious Advisory Committee which has members drawn from a number of different religious traditions.

At the same time, people from a range of religious traditions have expressed increasing concern about what has been felt to be the misuse of religious images and symbols in advertising. During the year 2000, this became a pressing concern for some Buddhists who were troubled by the use of images of Buddhist *monks* to sell a range of products. Hindus have also, for example, successfully complained about the use of Hindu related imagery in advertising a chicken sauce.

Under the 1990 *Broadcasting Act* and the 2003 *Communications Act*, religious bodies are able to hold local and national licenses for digital radio and digital terrestrial television. However, they are not allowed to hold licenses for national sound broadcasting license nor a public teletext license.

Chaplaincy and Pastoral Care

The particular relationship of the Church of England and the Church of Scotland to the state is reflected in their pastoral access to, and influence within, social institutions such as hospitals, prisons, schools, and institutions of higher education. This access is sometimes rooted in specific legal aspects of *establishment* and at other times is a matter of long-rooted tradition.

The increase in religious diversity has led to a fresh assessment of what arrangements are now appropriate. For example, a research project carried out at the University of Warwick during 1994-96 looked at the pattern of publicly funded chaplaincy provision in the health and prison services and the role of civic religion. Its focus was on the Church of England and its relationship with other religions in these contexts.

Chaplaincy in public institutions is a rapidly changing area and, in a number of contexts, chaplaincy provision is gradually opening up to include the participation of people from other than Christian religious traditions. A number of hospitals and prisons now have multi-faith chaplaincy teams and the then Department of Health and Social Security initiated a Multi Faith Joint National Consultation in 1997, which worked to a draft guidance document on developing such an approach.

With regard to the prisons, at national level there is now a Muslim adviser to Her Majesty's Prison Service, although it should be noted that this post does not exist on the same legal basis within the Prison Service as that of the Church of England's chaplaincy provision.

In the armed forces, since 2005 there have been Buddhist, Hindu, Muslim and Sikh chaplains, alongside of those of *Anglican*, *Roman Catholic* and *Free Church* Christian traditions, and an honorary officiating Jewish chaplain. Due to the numbers of service people of Buddhist, Hindu, Muslim and Sikh backgrounds, these new chaplains are all civilians rather than being commissioned chaplains, and they serve across the different armed forces. They were appointed on a three-year fixed term contract, with the Muslim chaplain being appointed on a full-time basis, while the others are part-time.

RELIGION, BELIEF AND THE LAW

Religions, Belief and the Legal Systems of the UK

The legal framework for the practice of religion in the UK is clearly of importance to all religious communities since it has a bearing on the degree to which religions can operate in accordance with their own traditions.

In general terms, the legal system for England and Wales differs from that of Scotland, and these differences could well develop still further in the light of political devolution from Westminster. Northern Ireland, in turn, has many provisions that are different from those which exist in the rest of the UK.

Unlike some other European countries, the UK has no formal list of religions officially recognised by the state, although such a list exists for the purpose the recognition of religion within the Prison Service. From time to time, although there are no clear criteria, the courts have to decide whether a particular organisation or movement is a "religion" in order, for example, to interpret a legal provision in relation to charity law.

In the past, indicators of religious status have been taken to include monotheistic belief, but even this cannot be a firm requirement since, for instance, it is clearly problematic with regard to Buddhism. In a 1999 decision of the Charity Commission for England and Wales, the Church of Scientology was held not to fall within the definition of a religion in charity law, and it is not recognised as a religion by the Prison Service.

Recognition and the Legal Protection of Religious Identity: History

The status of religious belief and practice is a complex matter. At times in the UK's history, the law has been used to uphold certain forms of belief and suppress others. For example, the position of the Church of England as the *established* church in England has been buttressed, not only by custom, but also by laws such as the *Corporation* and *Test Acts* of 1661 and 1673, which limited the holding of office under the Crown to communicant members of the Church of England.

Most of the provisions of the *Corporation* and *Test Acts* were repealed in 1828 and 1829, removing important legal restrictions on the participation of *Roman Catholic* and *Non-Conformist* Christians in public life. Many of the legal restrictions on the full participation of Jewish people in wider social and political life, however, were not fully removed until 1858.

A number of restrictions still remain with respect to people within traditions other than *Anglican* Christianity. For example, it is still the case that an heir to the Throne is specifically precluded from marrying a *Roman*

Catholic. In addition, there is legal uncertainty over whether the office of Lord Chancellor can be held by someone who is not a Christian. Although most forms of overt legal religious discrimination have now been lifted, the degree to which the present law accommodates the full practice of all religious traditions is being continually tested.

For example, Sikhs had to engage in a lengthy struggle before being allowed exemption from a 1972 *Road Traffic Act* requirement for motorcyclists to wear safety helmets. The *Road Traffic Act* 1988, re-enacting the *Motor-Cycle Crash Helmets (Religious Exemption) Act* 1976, now exempts a follower of the Sikh religion "while he is wearing a turban" from the crash helmet requirements applicable to others. A similar exemption was granted by the *Employment Act* 1989 to allow turbaned Sikhs to work on construction sites without a helmet or hard hat as required by new safety regulations.

Another example is the exemption that exists for Jewish and Muslim methods of animal slaughter from the general legislation governing the protection of animals at the time of slaughter. A Statutory Instrument of 1995, that implemented the European Community's Directive on this matter, contains provision to allow Jews and Muslims to follow the requirements of their religious traditions with regard to the slaughter of animals for Jewish and Muslim consumption, waiving, for example, the general requirement for pre-stunning of animals prior to slaughter.

Family, marriage and burial law has also been the subject of legal and social debate involving the religious communities, raising questions about the relationship to religious law and practice of social legislation on matters such as marriage, divorce and inheritance. There has also been debate about the extent to which employers can or should provide time and facilities at work for the performance of obligatory prayers and days off for the observance of religious festivals.

Until recently, the response of the legal system to increased religious diversity has generally proceeded on the basis of the historically distinctive approach found in English law of *ad hoc* and pragmatic developments, rather than seeking to provide generally applicable new frameworks for law. It has therefore often been concerned with defining permissible exceptions to generally applicable laws.

However, from the early 1990s onwards there was intensifying debate about the extent to which the law should protect people against forms of direct discrimination connected with religious identity. Much of the previously developed legislation and social policy that was designed to deal with social identities based upon race and ethnicity did not sit easily with the rising importance of religion in the self-definition of individuals and groups that occurred throughout the 1990s, partly as a by product of both domestic and international developments.

Recognition and the Legal Protection of Religious Identity: Developments

For many years, Northern Ireland was the exception in the UK in having legal provisions against religious discrimination in employment and for the prosecution of incitement to religious hatred.

Nevertheless, in the common law tradition of England and Wales, there continued to be some traditional provisions against *blasphemy* and *blasphemous libel*. However, as the testing of these provisions in the courts during the controversy over the book *The Satanic Verses* in the late 1980s and the early 1990s demonstrated, these laws only give protection to the Christian religion and, sometimes, more particularly only to the doctrines and practices of the Church of England.

In England, Scotland and Wales, since the introduction of race relations legislation, there have been provisions against discrimination in relation to a member of an "ethnic group". One of the factors that is taken as indicative of a group being an "ethnic group" is that of a long, shared group history in which a shared religion may be a dimension of this.

Jews have therefore been judged to be an "ethnic group", as have Sikhs, following the case of *Mandla v Dowell Lee* in 1983. Muslims qua Muslims, however, have generally fallen outside the scope of the *Race Relations Act* because they have correctly been viewed as being a religious, and not a racial or ethnic group.

Being members of a community that defines itself in relation to its diversity of ethnic groups, Muslims (as also applies to Buddhists and Christians) have not been viewed as having a shared history linked to a shared ethnicity in the same sense as Jewish or Sikh people have. Thus "indirect" discrimination has been the most that white Muslims, Buddhists or Christians could claim under Race Relations law, by pursuing a case as an Asian or Arab or as a Yemeni or Pakistani, relying on a racial or national identity, and complaining that certain practices or procedures may have had a disproportionately adverse effect because they unjustifiably interfere with their religious observance.

Religion, Belief and Human Rights: New Developments

Newer developments that were potentially significant for religion, discrimination and the law began with the implementation of the *Human Rights Act* 1998 in the year 2000.

This Act introduced into domestic law the provisions of the *European Convention on Human Rights*, including those of Article 9 which states that: "Everyone has the right to freedom of thought, conscience and religion: this right includes freedom to change his belief and freedom, either alone or in community with others and in public or private, to manifest his religion or belief, in worship, teaching, practice and observance",

and also that "Freedom to manifest one's religion or beliefs shall be subject only to such limitations as are prescribed by law and are necessary in a democratic society in the interests of public safety, for the protection of public order, health or morals, or for the protection of the rights or freedom of others".

Under the *Human Rights Act*, Government and all bodies acting as "public authorities" must examine how far their policies, practices and proposals conform with the *Convention*, since individuals are now able directly to appeal to its protection within the UK courts. The precise implications of this are, however, still subject to interpretation while the courts build up a body of case law deriving from the Act.

Religious Discrimination: Evidence and Policy Options

It was, however, the lack, other than in Northern Ireland, of legal protection against discrimination on religious grounds that led to increasing calls for specific legislation to be enacted. In its *Second Review of the Race Relations Act 1976*, published in 1992, the Commission for Racial Equality stated that it considered the present *blasphemy* laws to be unsatisfactory and it recommended that consideration be given to making incitement to religious hatred an offence under English law, as well as to incorporating international obligations against religious discrimination into domestic law, bringing law in the rest of the UK into line with that of Northern Ireland.

In the early 1990s, the Commission for Racial Equality conducted a survey of advice agencies to collect evidence of religious discrimination. Although advice agencies had not generally reported such discrimination, the overwhelming majority of religious organisations that were consulted believed there was a need for legislation to outlaw religious discrimination. However, the

Government of the day felt that there was insufficient hard evidence to act in terms of legislation.

In 1999, the Home Office commissioned research on religious discrimination in England and Wales from the University of Derby's then Religious Resource and Research Centre. The project team conducted questionnaire and fieldwork research in relation to the evidence of religious discrimination, both actual and perceived; the patterns shown by this evidence, including its overall scale, the main victims, the main perpetrators, and the main ways in which discrimination manifests; and the extent to which religious discrimination overlaps with racial discrimination.

The aim of this research was to identify the broad range of policy options available for dealing with religious discrimination. In January 2000, the project issued *Religious Discrimination in England and Wales: An Interim Report* and, in February 2001, the Home Office Research, Development and Statistics Directorate published the project's final, empirical report as Research Study No 220 on *Religious Discrimination in England and Wales*.

The report found that ignorance and indifference towards religion were of generally widespread concern amongst participants from all religious groups. It also found that in institutional settings such ignorance and indifference can contribute to an environment in which discrimination of all kinds, including also institutional discrimination, is able to thrive Education, employment and the media were the areas most often highlighted as contexts for unfair treatment and for discrimination on the basis of religion.

A consistently higher level of unfair treatment was reported by Muslim organisations than by most other religious groups. Such treatment has, among many Muslims and some others, come to be identified in terms of *Islamophobia*. Such unfair treatment was also consistently reported to be frequent rather than occasional. Hindu, and especially Sikh, organisations also reported a relatively high level of unfair treatment. Pagans and people from New Religious Movements frequently complained of open hostility and discrimination.

In terms of policy options for tackling religious discrimination, research participants generally advocated a comprehensive approach in which education, training and a bigger effort in teaching about several religions in schools would all play an important part. The strengths and limitations of the law were recognised and many participants thought the law could help if used appropriately and in conjunction with other approaches.

The Home Office Research, Development and Statistics Directorate also published a parallel report (Research Study No 221) from the University of Cambridge's Faculty of Public Law, entitled *Tackling Religious Discrimination: Practical Implications for Policy Makers and Legislators* and that explored the strengths and weaknesses of various available legal options.

Discrimination in Employment: Religion and Belief

As a response to a European Directive on discrimination in employment that derived from the Amsterdam Treaty of the European Union, in 2003 new legal rights were introduced with regard to employment, religion and belief. In line with the provisions of the *European Convention on Human Rights and Fundamental Freedoms*, the Regulations relate to both "religion" (as generally understood) and "belief" (meaning a settled philosophical system or orientation) governing an individual's life. These new rights are set out in the *Employment Equality (Religion or Belief) Regulations*, 2003.

These regulations, for the first time in England, Wales and Scotland, made discrimination on these grounds illegal. In the context of employment (including vocational training defined to include staff and students of both further and higher education) the Regulations prohibit direct discrimination on grounds of religion or belief (except for genuine and determining occupational requirements) as also, indirect discrimination (except for objective justification that is both appropriate and necessary). Finally, they prohibit harassment, as well as victimisation on grounds of pursuit of issues relating to discrimination or harassment on the grounds of religion or belief.

While the introduction of these Regulations did not make it illegal to discriminate on the grounds of religion or belief in the provision of goods and services (as part 2 of the *Equality Act, 2006* has subsequently done), they marked a significant step forward in the evolution of legal frameworks appropriate to a religiously plural and secular society. In a key area of social life that has a central bearing on the life chances of individuals and communities these Regulations both codify expectations of behaviour and provide individuals with means of redress supported by the possibility of legal proceedings and sanctions.

However, beyond the legal requirements within which they must now operate, many organisations are also now positively trying to take religion into account in developing their equal opportunities policies and practice. To assist in this the Arbitration, Conciliation and Advisory Service (ACAS) has produced a guidance booklet on *Religion or Belief and the Workplace: A Guide for Employers and Employees*.

At the same time, although discrimination in employment was one of the main areas of concern identified in the Religious Discrimination in England and Wales Research Project, the media and education were the other two principal foci for concern. The Regulations do not apply to these except in relation to matters of employment and vocational training.

In Northern Ireland, the *Fair Employment Act* proscribes discrimination on the grounds of religious or political opinion in the area of employment. All public sector employers and all companies with more than ten employees must report each year to the Equality Commission on the religious composition of their workforces, and they must also review their employment practices every three years. Non-compliance can result in criminal penalties and the loss of government contracts.

In addition, the 1998 *Northern Ireland* Act stipulates that all public authorities must show due regard for the need to promote equality of opportunity, including on the basis of religious belief and must report their plans to promote equality to the Equality Commission, which reviews such plans every five years.

Equalities and Human Rights: An Emerging Unified Approach

There have therefore still been areas of social life in England, Scotland and Wales within which it has continued not to be illegal to discriminate on the grounds of religion or belief. Thus there are those who have still been pressing for the introduction of wider legislation on religious discrimination, either parallel to other anti-discrimination legislation or as part of an overall human rights approach.

At the same time, the 2006 *Equality Act* tackled substantial parts of this, by making it illegal to discriminate on the grounds of "religion or belief" or lack of it in the provision of goods, facilities and services, education, the use and disposal of property, and the exercise of public functions. The *Equality Act* also established the Commission for Equality and Human Rights (CEHR), which is to become operational from October 2007.

The establishment of the new Commission reflects the Government's intention to bring together the various so-called "equalities strands" into a more unified structure. The CEHR will take on the previously separate legal roles of the Equal Opportunities Commission, the Commission for Racial Equality and also the Disability Rights Commission, with regard to equalities legislation in the areas of gender, race and disabilities. It will also have responsibilities in relation to equalities and discrimination in relation to religion and belief, sexual orientation and age.

The Equality Review, which reported early in 2007, recommended adoption of a ten-step programme for making Britain a fairer and more equal society and proposed that the CEHR should produce a triennial progress report. This could be subsumed within the CEHR's statutory statutory responsibility, also triennially, to produce a "state of the nation" report across the full range of its responsibilities.

The CEHR's remit with regard to Scotland is different, in that there it covers only human rights matters that are reserved to Westminster, while other human rights matters are to be covered by the Scottish Commission for Human Rights, unless the Scottish Commission agrees that that CEHR should deal with such matters.

In parallel to the Equalities Review, the Department for Trade and Industry and the Cabinet Office had also (in 2005) initiated Discrimination Law Review, the outcome of which is expected at around the time of the publication of this edition of the directory. The Discrimination Law Review is considering the fundamental principles of discrimination legislation and its underlying concepts and its intention is to address concerns about inconsistencies in the current anti-discrimination legislative framework. The Review is working to develop a legal framework that could be clearer and more streamlined, as well as having due regard to "better regulation" principles and being more user-friendly.

Incitement to Religious Hatred

In Northern Ireland, the *Prevention of Incitement to Hatred Act (Northern Ireland)* 1970 made it an offence intentionally to stir up hatred against, or rouse the fear of, any section of the public on the grounds of religious belief, colour, race or ethnic or national origins. This covers the publication or distribution of written or any other matter which is threatening, abusive or insulting as well as the use of words of a similar nature in a public place or in a public meeting. These provisions were further developed in part III of the *Public Order (Northern Ireland) Order,* 1987.

Although these provisions have only rarely been used, their scope is not only concerned with incitement directed to, or against religious groups, but is also concerned with incitement against any group when such incitement is carried out on religious grounds.

In England and Wales, the *Public Order Act, 1986,* did not address incitement to religious hatred, but in part III contained provisions relating to incitement to racial hatred. As in Northern Ireland, this law has only rarely been used over the two decades that it has been in force, with 76 prosecutions taking place, resulting in 44 convictions.

In England and Wales, the notion of a "religiously aggravated offence" was introduced with the *Anti-Terrorism, Crime and Security Act,* 2001. The original Bill, taken to Parliament by the Government in the wake of the disturbances in the northern mill towns in the summer of 2001 and the events of 9/11 in the USA, had also included provision for an offence of "incitement to religious hatred". However, because the measure was rushed it did not find a consensus of support, even among religious groups.

Nevertheless, further attempts to legislate followed with the Private Members' *Religious Offences Bill*, 2002 and in the Government's *Serious Organised Crime and Police Bill*, 2004. Each of these attempts was based on modifications to the existing provisions for incitement to racial hatred found in the *Public Order Act*, 1986.

The attempt to legislate in this area has remained controversial throughout, due to the difficulties involved in trying to balance the freedom of people within religions to live without fear of intimidation and hatred being stirred up against them, and the freedom of people to satirise religious topics and also advance either strong religious convictions or convictions critical of religion.

At the same time, according to the *Racist Incident Monitoring Annual Report* of the Crown Prosecution Service (which covered the period April 2004 to May 2005) for offences under the *Anti-Terrorism, Crime, and Security Act* in England and Wales, twenty-seven of thirty-four defendants were prosecuted for religiously aggravated offences, and in twenty-three of these, the actual or perceived religion of the victim was Islam.

The 2005 Labour Party Manifesto for England and Wales (though not for Scotland) contained a commitment to legislate balancing protection, tolerance and free speech, on the basis of which the Government introduced further measures into Parliament.

Nevertheless, in October 2005, the *Racial and Religious Hatred Bill*, 2005 was defeated in the House of Lords, with amendments from the Lords separating out racial and religious hatred, making the offence refer only to "threatening" words and behaviour and not "threatening, abusive or insulting", and requiring the prosecution to prove an intention to stir up hatred.

In January 2006, the Government attempted to reinstate reference to "abusive and insulting behaviour" and the notion of being "reckless" about stirring up hatred, but suffered its second defeat in the Commons, losing by one vote. The measure was finally passed in an amended form, referring only to England and Wales, and being concerned with "acts intended to stir up hatred" where religious hatred is understood as being hatred against a group of persons defined by reference to religious belief or lack of religious belief.

At the time of writing, these provisions have not yet been brought into force, although an announcement about the timetable for this is expected. Specific explanation was included that the provision of this law should not be read in a way that prohibits or restricts debate, antipathy, dislike or even ridicule or insult of religions, their belief and practices, nor to exclude proselytism. It was also made clear that prosecution of an offence under these provisions can only proceed with the permission of the Attorney General.

RELIGIOUS COMMUNITIES AND EDUCATION

Religion, Education and the Four Nations of the UK

As in other aspects of life in the UK, there are both commonalities and important differences with respect to the relationship between religion and education in the various nations. Schools in both England and Wales share much of the same legislative framework, despite education administration in Wales now being the responsibility of the devolved National Assembly. Education in Scotland is devolved to the Scottish Parliament.

Religiously Based Schools in England and Wales

Religious communities have always had an interest in education. The Church of England became a provider of education before either national or local Government did. When, early in the twentieth century, educational provision generally came under Government administration, the Church of England's denominational schools became part of a national education framework as a result of an agreement between it and the state embodied in the 1902 *Education Act*.

Following the *1944 Education Act*, the continuing *Anglican* denominational schools preserved some degree of autonomy as "voluntary aided" or "voluntary controlled" schools. Both categories of school receive public funding, but a proportion of the financial responsibility for "voluntary aided" schools rests with the sponsoring religious body. These schools also have more autonomy with respect both to admissions policies as well as arrangements for Religious Education and Collective Worship.

"Voluntary controlled" schools are much more fully integrated into the local authority system. Thus, for example, they follow the Agreed Syllabus of the Local Education Authority (except where parents make a request denominational teaching). "Collective worship" in "voluntary controlled" schools is, however, to be in accordance with the foundation trust deed of the school, as in "voluntary aided" schools.

"Voluntary aided" schools can, in their appointment of teachers (but not other staff), include criteria designed to ensure that there is a sufficient proportion of teachers who are related to the religious tradition upon which the school is founded, in order to maintain its fundamental character and ethos.

The *Anglican* and *Roman Catholic* (and to a much lesser extent the *Methodist*) *Churches* now have "voluntary aided" and "voluntary controlled" (nearly all *Anglican*) schools in England and Wales, as has the Jewish community, and as do some of the Christian *Churches* in Northern Ireland.

Within the independent, fee-paying sector, there are a significant number of institutions based on a religious foundation or ethos,

including around sixty Muslim schools. During the 1980s and 1990s, a significant body of opinion among Muslims pressed the Government to grant public funding, as voluntary aided schools, to a number of Muslim schools that applied under Government criteria for recognition.

In this period it was frequently pointed out that, although the Government affirmed that, in principle, there could be Muslim schools alongside Jewish and Christian ones, no applications were successful, leading to a significant concern that discrimination may well have been at work. However, the Government's decision to fund two Muslim primary schools represented a new development that is now being followed by some groups in other religious communities.

Under the provisions for "Foundation Schools" made in the 1998 *School Standards and Framework Act*, such schools receive funding directly from national Government rather than through the Local Education Authority. There remains a body of opinion, however, that the designation of Voluntary School status for Muslim and other faith-based schools is necessary as a signal of parity of esteem with the Christian and Jewish Voluntary Schools.

In 2006, there were in England 6,874 state-funded schools with a religious character, representing around 35% of all the schools in the state sector. These included 4,659 Anglican schools, 2,053 Roman Catholic schools, 1 Greek Orthodox school, and 1 Seventh-day Adventist school, with other Christian denominations accounting for 115 schools. There were 36 Jewish schools, 7 Muslim schools, and 2 Sikh schools.

In February 2005, Stephen Twigg, the then Schools Minister for England, published a list of best practices about how "faith schools" could best contribute to inclusiveness and collaboration. During 2006 a significant controversy developed when, against the background of growing concerns about the potentially negative implications of faith schools for social cohesion, the Government made proposals to implement a quota of children to be taken from outside of the faith community concerned. While a number of faith schools were content with this, the Roman Catholic Church strongly opposed the move, which was eventually dropped.

The majority of children attend what are now known as "Community" schools (often, in the past, referred to as "county" schools) rather than attending religiously based (or "denominational") schools whether these are Foundation Schools, Voluntary Schools or Private Schools. Educators in these schools have therefore had to confront issues arising from the growth of religious diversity in their catchment areas.

Religious Education in England and Wales

In UK schools there are legal requirements for Religious Education and Collective Worship, although parents may withdraw their children from these if they so wish. In England and Wales the 1944 *Education Act* made "Religious Instruction" mandatory and required that syllabuses should be drawn up ("agreed") at a local level. By way of guidance, the Act merely specified that the content of the "instruction" should not be of a "denominational" character, although the unwritten assumption of that time was that the content would be Christian.

However, a gradual shift of approach took place, reflected in a change of subject name to "Religious Education". Increasingly, the task of Religious Education was no longer seen as "instructing" or "nurturing" pupils in a particular religious tradition, but as educating them *about* religion. Its scope also broadened to include learning about religions other than Christianity. With changes in the composition of society and the development of new faith communities, "multi-faith syllabi" were developed which were designed to help children understand the diversity of religious traditions.

By the late 1970s those maintained schools that employed Religious Education specialists were teaching this kind of broader-based Religious Education, but many schools used only Christian content or failed to provide the subject at all. Many "denominational" schools, on the other hand, had also introduced learning about a variety of religions.

The 1988 *Education Reform Act* (which applies to England and Wales but not to Scotland and Northern Ireland) introduced a requirement that any new Religious Education syllabus must "reflect the fact that the religious traditions in Great Britain are in the main Christian whilst taking account of the teaching and practices of the other principal religions represented in Great Britain".

The precise meaning and implications of these new statutory provisions have been widely debated since the 1988 legislation was enacted. In 1994 the Schools Curriculum and Assessment Authority (SCAA) that advised the Government on the content of the school curriculum published "model syllabi" for Religious Education. These do not have statutory force, but are intended as advisory guidance to local authority Agreed Syllabus Conferences. The SCAA model syllabi do not, however, have any standing in Wales since SCAA had only a remit for England.

A variety of religious traditions are represented on every local authority's Agreed Syllabus Conference that has responsibility for drawing up the syllabus of Religious Education to be used by publicly funded schools in the relevant area. Voluntary aided schools do not have to include other religious traditions within their Religious Education syllabi, although they often mirror the local agreed syllabus to a greater or lesser extent.

In early 2000, the Qualifications and Curriculum Authority (QCA), which took over the previous functions of the SCAA, published non-statutory guidance designed to supplement the model syllabi and also released schemes of work. These were not intended to displace existing local syllabi but to exemplify work in schools that can fulfil locally determined requirements. These were later updated in its 2004 *Non-statutory National Framework for Religious Education.*

In Wales, Religious Education has been included in a curriculum review undertaken by the Welsh Assembly Government and the non-statutory document called, *The National Exemplar Framework for Religious Education* (DELLS) is under consultation with an implementation date set for September 2008.

The National Exemplar Framework for Religious Education follows the same principles as documents for other curriculum subjects in terms of shared philosophy and layout, and will be supported by exemplification material. As with the QCA's *Non-statutory National Framework for Religious Education* in England, *The National Exemplar Framework for Religious Education* covers the full-age range from Foundation Phase to Post-16.

The QCA has also published guidance for schools on the new requirements for citizenship education and, in its Religious Education document, noted the role that Religious Education can play in preparing pupils "for life as citizens in a plural society".

It pointed out that Religious Education promotes the values and attitudes needed for citizenship in a democratic society and suggested that "pupils can understand how believers in different religious traditions may interact with each other, not just historically, but in contemporary ways, nationally and locally". The schemes of work include units dealing with inter-faith issues.

All Agreed Syllabi now have to be reviewed on a five yearly basis. Local religious groups (including, in England, the Church of England and representation from other Christian *Churches* and other religions) are also represented, alongside teacher and local authority representatives, on SACREs (Standing Advisory Councils for Religious Education). These have a statutory role in monitoring the delivery of Religious Education and collective worship within the publicly funded sector of education in their area. Agreed Syllabus Conferences are often constituted from the membership of the local SACRE.

In Wales SACREs have only three constituent Committees, with the Church in Wales being part of a single Committee along with other Christian denominations and other religious groups, as compared with the position in England where the Church of England has its own Committee. In both England and in Wales there are National Associations of SACREs. In Wales there is also a National Advisory Panel for Religious Education (NAPfRE).

While parents have a statutory right to withdraw their children, many within the minority religious communities have been concerned that the emphasis given to Christianity in Religious Education and collective worship in recent legislation and non-statutory guidance has shifted the balance back from the broader approaches that had been developing during the 1970s and 1980s.

At the same time the evidence of OFSTED (Office for Standards in Education and Training) inspections in England suggest that breadth and rigour are growing in Religious Education, with the possible exception of the earlier years in secondary school. Religious Education may be negatively affected by the general weakness of educational provision in some urban areas. However, in both England and Wales, recent years have seen an unanticipated rise in the number of students taking the subject for both General Certificate of Secondary Education (GCSE) and Advanced Level qualifications. In Wales there has been a clear shift in popularity of option choices at examination level, with ethics, philosophy, and "Eastern religions" proving particularly popular.

Evidence of inspections undertaken by Estyn in Wales suggest that Religious Education has performed well when compared with national curriculum subjects, and that there has been an overall increase in good and very good standards at all key stages. In Wales, the Qualifications, Curriculum and Assessment Authority for Wales (ACCAC); the Department for Education, Lifelong Learning and Skill (DELLS); and Estyn carry similar responsibilities, respectively, to the SCAA, QCA and OFSTED in England.

Collective Worship in England and Wales

The 1988 *Education Reform Act* included complex provisions on school collective worship in England and Wales. In recent years many schools had moved away from exclusively Christian acts of worship seeing these as being inappropriate for a plural school community containing children with different religious commitments and with none.

The 1988 legislation requires that the majority of acts of "collective worship" should be "wholly or mainly of a broadly Christian character". As in Religious Education, the existing right of parents to withdraw their children from collective worship was maintained and fresh provisions were introduced under which what is known as a "determination" might be issued by a local authority to allow alternative arrangements for whole school collective worship to take place.

In January 1994 the then Department for Education issued a circular on *Religious Education and Collective Worship* setting out the provisions of the 1988 Act (and also supplementary provisions enacted in 1993) and giving guidance on their application. Many educators and religious community leaders expressed considerable concern that,

with regard to collective worship, the circular went beyond legislative requirements.

Such concern related to whether the requirements provided for an appropriate balance between the need to respect the integrity of pupils from different faith backgrounds and those without any religious commitment. It is also related to the need to encourage the development, in an inclusive way, of the whole school as a community, as well as to the capacity of schools to meet the current requirements for collective worship. Debates on the issues involved have continued.

In 1997, the Religious Education Council for England and Wales, the National Association of SACREs, and the Inter Faith Network co-sponsored a consultative process that explored the degree to which any consensus might exist or emerge concerning educationally appropriate provision for collective worship in schools in modern Britain. However, this did not reach agreed conclusions and neither did the Government accept its recommendation that the existing provisions needed review.

Religion and Education in Scotland

From the years of the *Reformation* in Scotland until 1872, two approaches to school education evolved. In rural areas, the *established* Church of Scotland shared responsibility for education with the civic authorities. This partnership underpinned the 1696 *Education Act's* requirement that there should be a school established, and a schoolmaster appointed, in every parish "by advice of the Heritor and Minister of the Parish".

These schools were, in effect, *Presbyterian* in outlook. But eventually, during the first half of the 19th century, the Scottish Episcopal Church and the Roman Catholic Church established their own denominational schools. In the burghs, a variety of schools developed. By the nineteenth century these included denominational schools established by the Scottish Episcopal Church, the Roman Catholic Church and the Free Church.

The 1872 *Education (Scotland) Act* aimed to transfer responsibility for education in Scotland wholly to the state. However, the right to continue religious instruction was secured in a Preamble to this Act, subject to the operation of a conscience clause that gave "liberty to parents, without forfeiting any other of the advantages of the schools, to elect that their children should not receive such instruction".

Under the 1918 *Education (Scotland) Act*, *Roman Catholic* schools, which had not been transferred in 1872, became part of the state system, thus establishing in Scotland a system of denominational schools that continues to be fully publicly funded.

Historically, therefore, it has been the custom for religion to be practised and instruction in religion to be provided in Scottish schools, together with some form of religious observance or practice. This tradition has been reflected in recent *Education Acts* that allow education authorities to continue this provision. Indeed, it is unlawful for an education authority to discontinue religious observance or instruction unless the proposal to do so has been the subject of a poll of the local government electors in the area concerned and has been approved by the majority of those voters.

Every school run by the education authority must be open to pupils of all denominations and faiths, and the law continues to provide a "conscience clause" whereby parents may withdraw their children from any instruction in religious subjects and from any religious observance in the school. It also continues to be laid down that no pupils must be placed at a disadvantage as regards their secular education at the school, either because they have been withdrawn from such classes or because of the denomination to which they or their parents belong.

Guidance on the provision of Religious and Moral Education and Religious Observance in both primary and secondary schools has been consolidated in the 5-14 initiative of the 1990s and in the current revision of the Scottish curriculum entitled, *A Curriculum for Excellence*.

This curriculum revision confirms that Christianity, historically the main religious tradition in Scotland, is an essential component of Religious Education. But the syllabus should also take account of the teaching and practices of other religions Religious Education should enable the individual to explore questions concerning the meaning of life. It should aim to promote understanding and respect for the belief of others, which is recognised as being particularly important in schools where there are significant numbers of children from faiths other than Christianity.

Government guidelines indicate that religious observance in non-denominational schools should be based on the Christian tradition in Scotland. The form that it takes varies very much from school to school, but it should take account of the presence of the pupils of different faiths and of none.

There is one publicly funded Jewish primary school in Scotland, but denominational schools are mainly *Roman Catholic* and provide their own particular form of worship. The devolved Scottish Executive has so far not made any change to guidance on denominational schools. Some Muslim groups in Glasgow have lobbied to establish a state-funded Muslim school in the city, but so far they have been unsuccessful.

Religion and Education in Northern Ireland

In Northern Ireland, more than 90% of students attend schools in which the pupil body is predominantly of *Catholic* or *Protestant* background. "Integrated" schools serve approximately 5% of school-age children. All pupils who apply to an existing integrated school gain admittance. However, in surveys, parents generally express the view that more integrated provision should be available.

In the sense that *Catholic* schools are religious schools, there are only a few *Protestant* religious schools in Northern Ireland. Generally speaking, what were *Protestant* schools are now state schools. Such schools are, in principle, open to pupils of any religious persuasion or none, although traditionally, most of them provide broadly Christian assemblies and collectively celebrate the festivals of Harvest, Christmas and Easter. Other school activities and pastoral support programmes normally do not reflect or commend specifically religious values or beliefs.

In this regard state schools contrast with *Catholic* schools, which have an overtly confessional orientation and ethos, and in relation to which the *Roman Catholic* Church has a significant measure of control. Since 1993, and in contrast with the funding for equivalent *Church* schools in other parts of the United Kingdom, in Northern Ireland both the capital and maintenance costs of *Roman Catholic* schools have been met entirely by the state

The Education Reform (Northern Ireland) Order of 1989 made provision for a common Core Syllabus of Religious Education in Northern Ireland to be taught in all schools. Those Protestant Churches, who had transferred their schools to the state system in 1930, namely the *Presbyterian*, Church of Ireland and *Methodist* churches, were invited along with the Roman Catholic Church to draw up the new statutory Syllabus.

This historic achievement provided a commonly agreed programme of Religious Education from across both sides of the traditional *Catholic-Protestant* divide. At the same time, it was characterised by an exclusively Christian content. While schools were free to include teaching relating to religions other than Christianity within their total Religious Education programme this has not, in practice, been very widespread.

Proposals for a revision of the Northern Ireland curriculum were supported by the Council for Curriculum Examinations and Assessment (CCEA) in its published advice to the Minister of Education (April 1999) suggesting that in the new schools' curriculum there should also be "a shift in the emphasis of religious education towards understanding of major world religions, in particular Islam, as well as other Christian denominations within Northern Ireland".

In February 2002, following a request by Martin McGuinness, then Minister of Education, the Church of Ireland, *Methodist*, *Presbyterian*, and *Roman Catholic Church* Leaders established a Steering Group and Working Party to undertake a review of the Agreed Core Syllabus for Religious Education.

As part of the review the Department of Education asked the *Church* Leaders to consider, as an integral part of the Core Syllabus, the inclusion of the study of other world religions (and also the implications of recent equality and human rights legislation).

An advisory sub-group on World Faiths was also established. Proposals by the Working Party (which includes the requirement of a short study of Judaism and Islam to be conducted during the first three years of secondary-level education) went to Public Consultation in September 2003, some 400 responses were received, most of which were positive.

The Department of Education received the Churches' final advice in January 2005 and submitted their proposals to a full Equality Impact Assessment (as required by Section 75(1) of the *Northern Ireland Act*, 1998): the Equality Assessment has now been concluded and the proposals of the Churches' Working Party have been officially endorsed by the Department of Education.

Critical voices, however, have been raised. For example, Northern Ireland Inter Faith Forum, which involves other than Christian religious minorities in Northern Ireland (about 0.3% of the population), has expressed its disappointment that the Churches have not adopted a multi-faith model of Religious Education or endorsed the teaching of non-Christian religions at every stage of the pupils' school experience.

Higher Education and Religious Identity

There has been a steady growth in the religious diversity of the student population of the United Kingdom. During 1998, a project carried out by Dr Sophie Gilliat-Ray of Cardiff University gathered information on university/college policies on student religious identity.

It also examined how institutions are developing structures for relating to the various religious groups on campus; the provision of worship facilities by higher education institutions, how chaplaincy arrangements are being developed in multi-faith contexts to respond to the pastoral needs of students of the various faiths; the emergence of inter-faith organisations on campus; and how faith communities are developing national structures to respond to the religious needs of their students.

A short report, *Higher Education and Student Religious Identity* was published in 1999 and circulated to all institutions of higher education to enable sharing of good practice and a chance for developing strategies appropriate to multi-faith campuses. More recently, at the time of writing, a study of multi-faith chaplaincy initiatives is currently being conducted under the aegis of the Church of England's Board of Education.

A number of higher education institutions have become sites of considerable conflict between student groups, with some minorities feeling that radicalised groups from other religious minorities were developing an atmosphere of intimidation in a number of campuses. In 2005, and in the context of debates on incitement to hatred and to terrorism, Universities UK published guidance for Universities on *Promoting Good Campus Relations: Dealing with Hate Crimes and Intolerance*.

Following the events of 9/11 and 7/7, Government and police concern has developed about what is perceived to be the potential for terrorist and extremist recruitment on University campuses. Research and consultation is at present being carried out by the Markfield Institute for Higher Education in Leicester, on the teaching of Islam in higher education, as well as on the place of student religious societies and pastoral support provided by Muslim chaplaincy.

Most recently of all, a number of student Christian bodies have initiated legal action in relation to Student Unions that have prevented them from meeting on campus due to their refusal to abjure positions and activities deemed by the Student Unions concerned to be homophobic, but which are seen by the Christian Unions concerned as examples of their right to free speech in accordance with the protection offered to the expression of religious convictions under human rights legislation.

Immigration Regulations and Ministers of Religion

In 2004, new immigration regulations came into force that required visa applicants who wish to enter the country as ministers of religion to obtain Level Four competence within the International English Language Testing System (IELTS), although visa adjudicators can, on a discretionary basis, waive the testing requirement where other evidence of English competence can be provided from applicants in English-speaking countries.

Under the new regulations, Ministers of religion are also required to have worked as such for at least one year in the last five years. Ministers of religion applying for visas must also either have one year of full-time experience or two years of part-time training following their ordination for faiths where ordination is the only route for entering the Ministry.

EUROPEAN CONTEXTS

Religion and the Wider Europe

Since the accession of the UK to the EU there has been an increasing need to set domestic debates about religion, equity, discrimination and participation in a wider than UK setting. In particular, there is a need to take account of the impact of the economic, social and political project of the EU.

In the wider Europe, from the Atlantic to the Urals, the context of the Council of Europe will also be important as an arena for questions related to religion in the maintenance and promotion of international standards of human rights. Thus the Council of Europe has, for many years, carried out work in the area of freedom of religion and belief that has been especially important in the context of the post-Soviet states and societies of Central and Eastern Europe.

There is also, of course, the ongoing role of the European Court of Human Rights and the *European Convention on Human Rights and Fundamental Freedoms* that, as we have seen, through its incorporation in domestic law via the *Human Rights Act*, 1998, now frames all legislative developments relating to religion by reference to the principles of treating "religion" and "belief" equally.

Religion and Belief in the European Union

In contrast to the situation in many other EU member states, in the UK the majority of the religious minorities with roots in recent migrations who settled here either had, or were entitled to take up, British citizenship. There does, however, remain a gap between this formal, legal position and the personal and social experiences of discrimination and disadvantage found among the minority communities.

Nevertheless, the formal and legal position of the minority religious communities in the UK offers a stronger basis for organisational and community development than in some other European countries where their second or third generation counterparts still retain the status of migrants rather than citizens, with all of its accompanying legal and psychological consequences.

The increasing religious diversity of UK society continues to raise new questions and possibilities. Such questions need increasingly to be considered within a wider international context. In terms of the EU, the role of religion will increasingly need consideration as part of the widening agenda of political as well as economic integration.

Although the UK's legal and constitutional arrangments is a key factor in how newer communities develop their structures, the political significance of the EU is becoming increasingly important for the future development of both law and social policy in the UK. In the past, there have been attempts in the European Parliament to legislate, for example, in relation to the activities of New Religious Movements without taking full account of the complex issues involved.

More recently, it is significant that debates over the EU constitution included a heated discussion about whether the Preamble to the constitution should contain an explicit reference to Christianity. This debate has also been connected with the question of whether it will be possible, at some point in the future, for Turkey – as a country in which Muslims numerically predominate - to become a full member of the European Union.

More immediately, though, as we have seen in the development of UK law on religion, belief and employment, under Article 13 of the *Amsterdam Treaty* of the EU, it is now the case that when there is unanimity in the European Council of Ministers, acting on a proposal of the European Commission, and after consulting the European Parliament, the competence of the EU extends to taking appropriate action against discrimination on the basis of "racial or ethnic origin, religion or belief, disability, age or sexual orientation". In March 2007, the EU established a Fundamental Rights Agency.

THE CHALLENGES OF THE FUTURE

Whither "Multi-Culturalism"?

In the UK, since the mid-1960s, the ideal of multi-culturalism has been the basis of a general political consensus underlying the equal opportunity policies of central and local government and other significant social institutions. On the basis of this policy, significant political and social institutions have engaged in concerted attempts at positive action to address the needs of those citizens widely referred to as "ethnic minorities".

At the outset, religion was only rarely considered in terms of the implications of the new plurality. As this chapter has indicated, there has been a more recent change in this regard, reflecting a greater recognition of the increasing differentiation of personal and social identities on the basis of religion.

In a cultural milieu in which ethnicity, nationality, class and lifestyle have been seen as the major determining factors of individual and corporate identity, for people and organisations to define themselves primarily in terms of their religious identity and values represented a significant challenge to the prevailing social ethos. In this context,

questions have begun to be asked about how far pluralist societies can and should go in accommodating difference and to what degree.

Most recently these questions have been focussed through debates concerning the wearing by Muslim women of full head coverings that obscure the face, except for the eyes. For some in British society, including Government ministers who have previously been identified with the defence of Muslims against religious discrimination, this has been seen as a step too far. Others have questioned the reason why, at this point in time, issues of dress that had previously been dealt with through local agreement have now been highlighted and made into matters of political and media controversy.

Whatever the immediate reasons for the emergence of this debate, it is undoubtedly the case that recent years have seen an increasing questioning of, if not challenge to, the broad multi-cultural consensus. This has occurred partly as a result of the impact of events such as the decade long Satanic Verses controversy, which brought into focus the potentially serious conflicts of values that can emerge in a complex "three-dimensional" society characterised by Christian, secular and religiously plural heritages.

The new Commission for Equality and Human Rights is likely to have a major role in dealing with such tensions and conflicts in the coming years. An example of such tensions can be seen in what occurred around the implications for religious people and organisations of the introduction of Sexual Orientation Regulations, where aspects of these were seen as coming into tension, if not actual conflict, with the positions of a substantial number of religious groups and, in particular, with the position and work of Roman Catholic adoption agencies.

The Challenges of Terrorism and Social Cohesion

However, the major challenge to the consensus has come about in the period following the 9/11 attack on the World Trade Centre in New York and the Pentagon, as well as the Madrid train bombing of March 2004 and, most close to home, the 7/7 London Transport bombings of July 2005.

As a consequence of the kind of violence that has been visited by a small number of those who understand themselves as Muslims upon the civilian populations of those states and societies that, in their military actions are seen as embodying a violent and Islamophobic foreign policy in relation to Afghanistan, Iraq, Iran, and Palestine, some Muslim religious groups, activities and organisations have become the focus of counter-terrorist suspicions and measures.

There have also been political initiatives aimed at promoting social cohesion and challenging religious extremism. Thus, in the wake of the London Transport bombings of 7/7, the Government launched a "Preventing Extremism Together" initiative and created joint "Task Forces" together with members of the Muslim communities in order to address these issues within that community.

Religious communities and individuals stand at the intersection between the global and the local in a world that is both increasingly globalising and localising. They are simultaneously part of transnational communities of information and solidarity, while sharing in the civic society of the state of which they are citizens and being rooted firmly within their wider local communities.

In the UK, as elsewhere in the world, religious communities have great potential to contribute to the common good, but they can also become sources of fragmentation and conflict. The challenge facing both religious communities and the wider societies in which they are set is that of encouraging the common visions and structures necessary for sustaining an integrated but richly diverse community, but avoiding both assimilation and fragmentation.

It is now, more than ever, recognised that societies and states need to respond in positive ways to the challenges and opportunities presented by increasing religious diversity. At the same time, it is equally evident that the religious communities themselves will need to develop still further their own responsibilities within the civil societies of which they are a part and, at all levels of their organisation and activity, to intensify their commitment to positive inter-faith relations.

It is such challenges that, following a 2006 Cabinet reshuffle, led to the Government establishing a Race, Cohesion and Faiths Directorate in the newly created Department for Communities and Local Government, the Department which also in 2006 set up a Commission on Integration and Cohesion. The new Directorate continues the work initiated by the former Faith Communities Unit in the Home Office, but connects this with the wider agendas of race and cohesion.

This Unit is responsible for tackling racism, extremism, and hate, as well as for promoting interfaith activity in England and Wales. It also engages with faith communities to ensure government policies and services are delivered appropriately and in equitable ways.

The report of Commission on Integration and Cohesion (which is due to be published at around the time of publication of this volume) is likely to be highly significant for the direction of Government policy on ethnic and religious diversity. Because of this, it will be of considerable importance whether the report itself, and the debate which it will stimulate, will issue in a reaffirmation of the previously hard won consensus around a vision of multi-culturalism which, for all its failings, has given the UK what is in many ways a more richly diverse society than is found in many other European countries, or whether it will provide justification for a retreat from that vision.

As the international community passes through turbulent times of upheaval and challenge to international law and human rights; and as the devolution of power to the constituent nations and regions of the UK accelerates in the context of an increasingly integrating EU; then the shape of our common future in the UK will increasingly depend upon whether the religious communities, the wider civic society and the state can rise to the challenge of living equitably in diversity and distinctiveness, while accepting a shared responsibility to work for the common good.

FURTHER READING

Details follow of a number of general overviews relating to key sections of the "Religious Landscape of the UK" chapter. The references are primarily to materials that deal specifically with religion, rather than with the more general topic areas of ethnicity, migration, law, the media and education that form a significant part of the backcloth to the chapter. It should also be noted that the references that are included are not comprehensive, but provide signposts to a range of relevant materials.

Abbas, T, "The impact of religio-cultural norms and values on the education of young South Asian women", in *British Journal of Sociology of Education*, Volume 24, no 4, 2003, pp 411–428.

Abrams, M, Gerard, D and Timms, N (eds), *Values and Social Change in Britain*, MacMillan, London, 1985.

Ahmed, I, et al, "Bradford: between co-existence and dialogue", in *World Faiths Encounter*, No 1, March 1992, pp 32–42.

Ahmed, R and Salter, J, *Ethnic and Faith Community Development*, Community Relations Section, Royal Borough of Kensington and Chelsea, 1999.

Ahmed, R, Finneron, D, Miller, S, and Singh, H, *Tools for Regeneration: A Holistic Approach for Faith Communities*, Faith Based Regeneration Network UK, London, 2006 (revised and expanded edition).

Alexander, C, *The Asian Gang: Ethnicity, Identity, Masculinity*, Berg, London, 2000.

Alibhai-Brown, Y, *After Multiculturalism*, Foreign Policy Centre, London, 2000.

Allen, C and Nielsen, J, *Summary Report on Islamophobia in the EU after 11 September 2001*, European Monitoring Centre on Racism and Xenophobia, Vienna, 2002.

Amin, K, "Ethnic Minorities and Religious Affiliations: Their Size and Impact on Social Work", in N Patel, D Naik, and B Humphries (eds), *Visions of Reality: Religion and Ethnicity in Social Work*, Central Council for Education and Training in Social Work, London, 1998, pp 20-41.

Andrews, A, "The inter-faith movement in the UK", in *The Indo-British Review: A Journal of History*, Volume 20, No 1, nd, pp 123-130.

Annette, J, *Faith Communities, Social Capital and Education for Citizenship*, Institute for Community Development, Middlesex University, nd.

Anonymous, 'The AWWAZ Group', in N Patel, D Naik, and B Humphries (eds), *Visions of Reality: Religion and Ethnicity in Social Work*, Central Council for Education and Training in Social Work, London, 1998, pp 52-69.

Arbitration, Conciliation and Advisory Service, *Religion or Belief and the Workplace: A Guide for Employers and Employees*, ACAS, London, 2003.

Archbishops' Commission, *Church and State 1970*, (reprinted), Church Information Office, London, 1985.

Archbishop's Commission on Urban Priority Areas, *Faith in the City: A Call for Action by Church and Nation – The Report of the Archbishop of Canterbury's Commission on Urban Priority Areas*, Church House, London, 1985.

Avis, P (ed), *Public Faith? The State of Religious Belief and Practice in Britain*, SPCK, London, 2003.

Badham, P, "Religious Pluralism in Modern Britain", in S Gilley and W Sheils (eds), *A History of Religion in Britain: Practice and Belief from Pre-Roman Times to the Present*, Blackwell, Oxford, 1984, pp 488-502.

Badham, P (ed), *Religion, State and Society in Modern Britain*, Edwin Mellen Press, Lampeter, 1989.

Badham, P, "The Contribution of Religion to the Conflict in Northern Ireland", in Cohn-Sherbok, (ed), *The Canterbury Papers: Essays on Religion and Society*, Bellew, London, 1990, pp 119-128.

Bailey, E (ed), *The Secular Quest for Meaning in Life: Denton Papers in Implicit Religion*, Edwin Mellen, Lampeter, 2002.

Ball, W and Beckford, J, "Religion, Education and City Politics: A Case Study of Community Mobilisation", in N Jewson and S MacGregor (eds), *Transforming Cities: Contested Governance and New Spatial Divisions*, Routledge, London, 1997, pp 193-204.

Ballard, R, "Migration and Kinship: The Differential Effects of Marriage Rules on the Process of Punjabi Migration to Britain," in C Clarke, C Peach and S Vertovec, *South Asians Overseas: Migration and Ethnicity*, Cambridge University Press, Cambridge, 1990, pp 219-249.

Ballard, R (ed), *Desh Pardesh: The South Asian Presence in Britain*, Hurst and Co, London, 1994.

Ballard, R, "The Emergence of Desh Pardesh", in R Ballard (ed), *Desh Pardesh: The South Asian Presence in Britain*, Hurst and Co, London, 1994, pp 1-34.

Ballard, R, "The Growth and Changing Character of the Sikh Presence in Britain", in H Coward, J Hinnells and R Williams (eds), *The South Asian Religious Diaspora in Britain, Canada and the United States*, State University of New York Press, New York, 2000, pp 127-144.

Ballard, R and Kalra, V, *The Ethnic Dimensions of the 1991 Census*, Manchester University Press, Manchester, 1994.

Barker, D, Holman, L and Vloet, A, *The European Values Study, 1981-1990: Summary Report*, Gordon Cook Foundation, Aberdeen, 1992.

Barker, E, *New Religious Movements: A Practical Introduction*, HMSO, London, 1989.

Barley, C, Field, C, Kosmin, B and Nielsen, J, *Religion: Reviews of United Kingdom Statistical Sources, Volume 20*, Pergamon Press, Oxford, 1987.

Barnes, P, "Reforming Religious Education in Northern Ireland: A Critical Review", in *British Journal of Religious Education*, Volume 19, No 2, 1997, pp 73-82.

Barnes, P, "World Religions in the Northern Ireland Curriculum", in *Journal of Beliefs and Values*, Volume 23, No 1, 2002, pp 19-32.

Barnes, P, "Religion, Education and Conflict in Northern Ireland", in *Journal of Beliefs and Values*, Volume 26, No 2, 2005, pp 123-138.

Barnes, P, "Was the Northern Ireland Conflict Religious?", in *Journal of Contemporary Religion*, Volume 20, No 1, 2005, pp 53-67.

Barot, R (ed), *Religion and Ethnicity: Minorities and Social Change in the Metropolis*, Kok Pharos, Kampen, 1993.

Barot, R, "Religion, Ethnicity and Social Change: An Introduction", in R Barot, (ed), *Religion and Ethnicity: Minorities and Social Change in the Metropolis*, Kok Pharos, Kampen, 1993, pp 1-16.

Barrett, D, *World Christian Encyclopaedia: A Comparative Survey of Churches and Religions*, 2nd edition, Oxford University Press, Oxford, 2000.

Bates, J and Collishaw, S, *FaithinDerbyshire: Working Towards a Better Derbyshire: Faith Based Contribution*, Derby Diocesan Council for Social Responsibility, Derby, 2006.

Bauman, G, *Contesting Cultures: Discourses of Identity in Multi-Ethnic Britain*, Cambridge University Press, Cambridge, 1996.

Bauman, G, *The Multicultural Riddle: Rethinking National, Ethnic and Religious Identities*, Routledge, London, 1999.

Bayfield, T and Braybrooke, M, *Dialogue With a Difference: The Manor House Group Experience*, SCM Press, London, 1992.

Beales, C, "Partnerships for a change: the Inner Cities Religious Council", in *World Faiths Encounter*, No 8, July 1994, pp 41-46.

Beattie, A, Mortimore, C, and Pencavel, H, *Faith in Action in the South West: A Survey of Social and Community Action by Faith Groups in the South West of England*, Faithnet Southwest, Bristol and Newton Abbot, nd.

Beckerlegge, G, "The Followers of 'Mohammed, Kalee and Dada Nanute': The Presence of Islam and South Asian Religions in Victorian Britain", in J Wolffe (ed), *Religion in Victorian Britain, Volume 5, Culture and Empire*, Manchester University Press, Manchester, 1997, pp 221-270.

Beckford, J, "Three paradoxes in the relations between religion and politics in an English city", in *Review of Religious Research*, Volume 39, No 4, 1998, pp 363-378.

Beckford, J, "Social Justice and Minority Religions in Prison: The Case of England and Wales", in J Richardson (ed), *Regulating Religion Case Studies from around the Globe*, Kluwer/Plenum, New York, 2004, pp 237-245.

Beckford, J; Gale, R; Owen, D; Peach, C; Weller, P, *Review of the Evidence Base on Faith Communities*, Office of the Deputy Prime Minister, London, 2006.

Beckford, J and Gilliat, S, *The Church of England and Other Faiths in a Multi-Faith Society*, Warwick Working Papers in Sociology, University of Warwick, Coventry, 1996.

Beckford, J and Gilliat, S, *The Church of England and Other Faiths in a Multi-Faith Society, Volume I & Volume II*, Department of Sociology, University of Warwick, Coventry, 1996.

Beckford, J and Gilliat, S, *The Church of England and Other Faiths in a Multi-Faith Society: Summary Report*, Department of Sociology, University of Warwick, Coventry, 1996.

Beckford, J and Gilliat, S, *Religion in Prison: Equal Rites in a Multi-Faith Society*, Cambridge University Press, Cambridge, 1998.

Beclett, C, and Macey, M, "Race, gender and sexuality: the oppression of multiculturalism", in *Women's Studies International Forum*, Volume 24, No 3-4, 2001, pp 309-319.

Bennett, C, "Within God's gracious purposes: a review of fifteen years of ecumenical interfaith collaboration in Britain, 1977-1992", in *Discernment: A Christian Journal of Inter-Religious Encounter*, Volume 6, No 3, 1993, pp 3-16.

Bennett, C, "How can religious values impact on shared citizenship", in *Interface: Religion and Public Policy in the UK*, Volume 1, No 1, Spring 2005, pp 50-52.

Berman, D, *A History of Atheism in Britain: From Hobbes to Russell*, Croom Helm, London, 1988.

Beverluis, J (ed), *A Sourcebook for the Community of Religions*, The Council for a Parliament of the World's Religions, Chicago, 1993.

Birmingham City Council, *A Pathway to Greater Inclusion: Birmingham and its Faith Communities*, Birmingham City Council, Birmingham, 2002.

Bishop, P, "Victorian Values? Some Antecedents of a Religiously Plural Society", in R Hooker and J Sargant (eds), *Belonging to Britain: Christian Perspectives on a Plural Society*, Council of Churches for Britain and Ireland, London, nd, pp 31-52.

Bradley, I, *Celtic Christianity, Making Myths and Dreaming Dreams*, Edinburgh University Press, Edinburgh, 1991.

Bradley, I, *God Save the Queen: The Spiritual Dimensions of Monarchy*, Darton, Longman and Todd, London, 2002.

Bradley, I, *Believing in Britain: The Spiritual Identity of Britishness*, I.B Tauris, London, 2007.

Bradney, A, "Separate schools, ethnic minorities and the law", in *New Community*, Volume 13, No 3, Spring 1987, pp 412–420.

Bradney, A, *Religions, Rights and Laws*, Leicester University Press, Leicester, 1993.

Brierley, P, *'Christian' England: What the English Church Census Reveals*, MARC Europe, London, 1991.

Braybrooke, M, *Inter-Faith Organisations, 1893-1979: An Historical Directory*, Edwin Mellen Press, Lampeter, 1980.

Braybrooke, M, *Children of One God: A History of the Council of Christians and Jews*, Valentine Mitchell, London, 1991.

Braybrooke, M, *Pilgrimage of Hope: One Hundred Years of Global Interfaith Dialogue*, SCM Press, London, 1992.

Braybrooke, M, "Interfaith Developments in Europe", in S Gill, G D'Costa and U King (eds), *Religion in Europe: Contemporary Perspectives*, Kok Pharos, Kampen 1994, pp 201-213.

Braybrooke, M, *Faith in a Global Age: The Interfaith Movement's Offer of Hope to a World in Agony: A Personal Perspective*, Braybrooke Press, Oxford, 1995.

Braybrooke, M, *A Wider Vision: A History of the World Congress of Faiths*, One World, Oxford, 1996.

Brierley, P, *Religious Trends No 2, 2000/01 Millennium Edition*, Christian Research Association, London, 2000.

Brierley, P, "Religion", in Halsey, A and Webb, J, *British Social Trends 2000*, Macmillan, Basingstoke, 2000.

Bristol City Council, *Demand for a Muslim School in Bristol Final Report*, Bristol City Council, Bristol, 2004.

Brown, A, *Festivals in World Religions*, Longmans, Essex, 1986.

Brown, C, *The Death of Christian Britain: Understanding Secularisation 1880-2001*, Routledge, London, 2001.

Brown, M, "Religion and economic activity in the South Asian population", in *Ethnic and Racial Studies*, volume 23, no 6, 2000, pp 1035-1061.

Bruce, S, *Religion in Modern Britain*, Oxford University Press, Oxford, 1995.

Buchanan, C, *Cut the Connection: Disestablishment and the Church of England*, Darton, Longman and Todd, London, 1994.

Cairns, J and Gardner, A (eds), *Faith Schools: Conflict or Consensus?*, Kogan Page, London, 2004.

Carrette, J and King, R, *Selling Spirituality: The Silent Takeover of Religion*, Routledge, Abingdon, 2005.

Chalke, S, *Faithworks: Actions Speak Louder Than Words*, Kingsway Publications, Eastbourne, 2001.

Chambers, P, "Religion, Identity and Change in Contemporary Wales", in S Coleman and P Collins (eds), *Religion, Identity and Change: Perspectives on Global Transformations*, Ashgate, Aldershot, 2004, pp 69-83.

Charlton, R and Kay, R, "The politics of religious slaughter: an ethno-religious case study", in *New Community*, Volume 12, No 3, Winter 1985-86, pp 409-503.

Chryssides, G, "Britain's Changing Faiths: Adaptation in a New Environment", in G Parsons (ed), *The Growth of Religious Diversity: Britain From 1945, Volume II Issues*, Routledge, London, 1994, pp 55-84.

Churches Regional Commission in Yorkshire and Humberside, *The Churches and Regional Development in Yorkshire and the Humber*, The Churches Regional Commission, Leeds, 1998.

Cohn-Sherbok, D and McClellan, D (eds), *Religion in Public Life*, Macmillan, London, 1992.

Coleman, D and Salt, J, *Ethnicity in the 1991 Census of Population*, HMSO, London, 1996.

Coleman, S with Collins, P (eds), *Religion, Identity and Change: Perspectives on Global Transformations*, Ashgate, Aldershot, 2004.

Comerford, R, Cullen, M and Hill, J, *Religion, Conflict and Coexistence in Ireland*, Gill and Macmillan, London, 1990.

Commission for Racial Equality, *Britain a Plural Society: Report of a Seminar*, Commission for Racial Equality, London, 1990.

Commission for Racial Equality, *Schools of Faith: Religious Schools in a Multi-Cultural Society*, Commission for Racial Equality, London, 1990.

Commission for Racial Equality, *Religious Discrimination: Your Rights*, Commission for Racial Equality, London, 1997.

Commission on the Future of Multi-Ethnic Britain, *The Future of Multi-Ethnic Britain*, Profile Books, London, 2000.

Commission on British Muslims and Islamophobia, *Addressing the Challenge of Islamophobia*, Commission on British Muslims and Islamophobia, London, 2001.

Copley, T, *Teaching Religion: Fifty Years of Religious Education in England and Wales*, Exeter University Press, Exeter, 1997.

Council for Voluntary Action Research, *The Establishment of a Regional Faith Forum for the West Midlands*, Centre for Voluntary Action Research, Aston Business School, Birmingham, 2002.

Council of Europe, *Religion and the Integration of Migrants*, Council of Europe, Strasbourg, 1999.

Coward, H, Hinnells, J and Williams, R, *The South Asian Religious Diaspora in Britain, Canada and the United States*, State University of New York Press, Albany, 2000.

Cranmer, F, Lucas, J and Morris, B, *Church and State: A Mapping Exercise*, The Constitution Unit, University College London, London, 2006.

Cumper, P, "Religious Discrimination in Britain: New Opportunities and Fresh Challenges Within Employment", in N Ghanea (ed), *The Challenge of Religious Discrimination at the Dawn of the New Millennium*, Martinus Nijhoff Publishers, Leiden, 2003, pp 157-184.

Cumper, P, "Inciting Religious Hatred: Balancing Free Speech and Religious Sensibilities in a Multi-Faith Society", in N Ghanea, A Stephens and R Walden (eds), *Does God Believe in Human Rights?: Essays on Religion and Human Rights*, Martinus Nijhoff Publishers, Leiden, 2007, pp 233-258.

Davie, G, *Religion in Britain Since 1945: Believing Without Belonging*, Blackwell, Oxford, 1994.

Davie, G, *Religion in Modern Europe: A Memory Mutates*, Oxford University Press, Oxford, 2000.

Dusche, M, "Multiculturalism, Communit-arianism and Liberal Pluralism", in J Malik and H Reifeld (eds), *Religious Pluralism in South Asia and Europe*, Oxford University Press, New Delhi, 2005, pp 120-144.

Eade, J, "Nationalism, Community and the Islamization of Space in London", in B Metcalf (ed), *Making Muslim Space in North America and Europe*, University of California Press, Berkley, 1996, pp 217-233.

Eade, J, "Identity, Nation and Religion", in J Eade (ed), *Living the Global City: Globalization as a Local Process*, Routledge, London, 1997, pp 146-62.

Eberle, C, *Religious Conviction in Liberal Politics*, Cambridge University Press, Cambridge, 2002.

Edge, P, "The European Court of Human Rights and Religious Beliefs", in *International Comparative Law Quarterly*, No 47, 1998, pp 680-687.

Edge, P, "The construction of sacred places in English law'", in *Journal of Environmental Law,* Volume 14, No 2, 2002, pp 161-183.

Edge, P, *Religion and Law: An Introduction*, Ashgate, Aldershot, 2006.

Edge, P and Harvey, G (eds), *Law and Religion in Contemporary Society: Communities, Individualism and the State*, Ashgate, Aldershot, 2000.

Edwards, D, "A Brief History of the Concept of Toleration in Britain", in J Horton and H Crabtree (eds), *Toleration and Integrity in a Multi-Faith Society*, University of York, Department of Politics, York, 1992, pp 41-49.

Evans, C, *Freedom of Religion Under the European Convention on Human Rights*, Oxford University Press, London, 2001.

Evans, M, *Religious Liberty and International Law in Europe*, Cambridge University Press, Cambridge, 1997.

Fane, R, "Is Self-Assigned Religious Affiliation Socially Significant?" in L Francis (ed), *Sociology, Theology and the Curriculum*, London, 1999, pp 113-124.

Farnell, R, Furbey, R, Al-Haqq Hill, S, Macey, M and Smith, G, *'Faith' in Urban Regeneration? Engaging Faith Communities in Urban Regeneration*, Policy Press, Bristol, 2003

Favell, A, *Philosophies of Integration: Immigration and the Idea of Citizenship in France and Britain*, Macmillan, Basingstoke, 1998.

Fergusson, D, *Church, State and Civil Society*, Cambridge University Press, Cambridge, 2005.

Finneron, D and Dinham, A, *Building on Faith: Faith Buildings in Neighbourhood Renewal*, The Church Urban Fund, London, nd.

Forrester, D, *Beliefs, Values and Policies*, Oxford University Press, Oxford, 1990.

Fowler, J, *Humanism: Beliefs and Practices*, Sussex Academic Press, Brighton, 1999.

Francis, L, "The relationship between personal prayer and purpose in life among churchgoing and non-churchgoing 12-15 year olds in the UK", in *Religious Education*, No 9, 1996, pp 9-21.

Francis, L, "The impact of personality and religion on attitude towards substance abuse among 13-15 year olds", in *Drug and Alcohol Dependence*, No 44, 1997, pp 95-103.

Francis, L, "Religion and Social Capital: The Flaw in the 2001 Census in England and Wales", in P Avis (ed), *Public Faith? The State of Religious Belief and Practice in Britain*, SPCK, London, 2003, pp 45-64.

Francis, L and Katz, Y (eds), *Joining and Leaving Religion: Research Perspectives*, Gracewing, Leominster, 2000.

Francis, L and Kay, W, *Teenage Religion and Values*, Gracewing, Leominster, 1995.

Froh, M, *Roots of the Future: Ethnic Diversity in the Making of Britain*, Commission for Racial Equality, London, 1996.

Fryer, P, *Staying Power: The History of Black People in Britain*, Pluto, London, 1984.

Furbey, R, Dinham, A, Farnell, R, Finneron, D, Wilkinson, G, with Howarth, C, Hussain, D, and Palmer, S, *Faith as Social Capital: Connecting or Dividing?*, Policy Press, Bristol, 2006.

Furbey, R and Macey, M, "Religion and urban regeneration: a place for faith?", in *Policy and Politics*, Volume 33, No1, 2005, pp 95-116.

Gale, R, *Pride of Place and Places: South Asian Religious Groups and the City Planning Authority in Leicester*, Papers in Planning Research 172, University of Wales, Department of City and Regional Planning, Cardiff, 1999.

Gale, R, *The Impact of Urban Planning Law and Procedure upon Religious Groups amongst the South Asian Diaspora in Britain*, DPhil Thesis, University of Oxford, 2004.

Gale, R, "The multicultural city and the politics of religious architecture: urban planning, mosques and meaning-making in Birmingham, UK", in *Built Environment*, Volume 30, No 1, 2004, pp 18-32.

Gale, R, "Representing the city: mosques and the planning process in Birmingham, UK", in *Journal of Ethnic and Migration Studies,* Volume 1, No 6, 2005, pp 1161-1179.

Gale, R and Naylor, S, "Religion, planning and the city: the spatial politics of ethnic minority expression in British cities and towns," in *Ethnicities,* Volume 2, No 3, 2002, pp 389-411.

Gay, J, *The Geography of Religion in England,* Duckworth, London, 1971.

Ghanea, N, Stephens, A, and Walden, R (eds), *Does God Believe in Human Rights?: Essays on Religion and Human Rights,* Martinus Nijhoff Publishers, Leiden, 2007.

Gilbert, A D, *The Making of Post-Christian Britain: A History of the Secularization of Modern Society,* Longman, Essex, 1980.

Gill, S, D'Costa, G and King, U (eds), *Religion in Europe: Contemporary Perspectives,* Kok Pharos, Kampen, 1994.

Gilley, S and Sheils, W (eds), *A History of Religion in Britain: Practice and Belief from Pre-Roman Times to the Present,* Blackwell, Oxford, 1994.

Gilliat-Ray, S, *Higher Education and Student Religious Identity,* Department of Sociology, University of Exeter, Exeter, in association with the Inter Faith Network for the United Kingdom, London, 1999.

Gilliat-Ray, S, *Religion in Higher Education: The Politics of the Multi-Faith Campus,* Ashgate, Aldershot, 2000.

Gilliat, Ray, S, "The trouble with 'inclusion': a case study of the Faith Zone at the Millennium Dome", in *The Sociological Review,* Volume 52, No 4, 2004, pp 459-477.

Gilliat-Ray, S, "The use of 'sacred' space in public institutions: a case study of worship facilities at the Millennium Dome", in *Culture and Religion,* Volume 6, No 2, 2005, pp 281-302.

Gilliat Ray, S, " 'Sacralising' sacred space in public institutions: a case study of the prayer space at the Millennium Dome", in *Journal of Contemporary Religion,* Volume 20, No 3, 2005, pp 357-372.

Graham, D and Waterman, S, "Underenumeration of the Jewish population in the UK 2001 Census", in *Population, Space and Place,* Volume 11, No 2, 2005, pp 89-102.

Greater London Authority, *The Greater London Authority Faith Equality Scheme,* Greater London Authority, London, 2005.

Guessous, F, Hopper, N and Moorthy, U, "Religion in prisons 1999 and 2000", in *Home Office Statistical Bulletin,* 15/01, National Statistics, London, 2000.

Gunter, B and Viney, R, *Seeing Is Believing: Religion and Television in the 1990s,* John Libbey and Co, London, 1994.

Haberlin, M, "Historical Roots of Plurality in Europe", in J Malik and H Reifeld (eds), *Religious Pluralism in South Asia and Europe,* Oxford University Press, New Delhi, 2005, pp 23-41.

Haines, W, "Identity and authority in citizenship education and religious education", in *Interface: Religion and Public Policy in the UK,* Volume 1, No 1, Spring 2005, pp 13-33.

Halman, L, *The European Values Study: A Third Wave Sourcebook of 1999/2000 European Values Study Survey,* WORC Tilburg University, Tilburg, 2001.

Halstead, M, *The Case for Muslim Voluntary-Aided Schools: Some Philosophical Reflections,* Islamic Academy, Cambridge, 1986.

Harding, S, Phillips, D and Fogarty, M, *Contrasting Values in Western Europe,* Macmillan, Basingstoke, 1986.

Hare, W (ed), *Religions of the Empire: A Conference of Some Living Religions Within the Empire,* Duckworth, London, 1925.

Harrison, P, *'Religion' and the Religions in the English Enlightenment*, Cambridge University Press, Cambridge, 1990.

Hastings, A, *Church and State: The English Experience The Prideux Lectures for 1990*, University of Exeter, Exeter, 1991.

Heelas, P and Woodhead, L, et al, *The Spiritual Revolution: Why Religion is Giving Way to Spirituality*, Blackwell, Oxford, 2005.

Hepple, B and Choudhary, T, *Tackling Religious Discrimination: Practical Implications for Policy Makers and Legislators*, Home Office Research Study 221, Home Office Research, Development and Statistics Directorate, London, 2001.

Herbert, D, *Religion and Civil Society: Rethinking Religion in the Contemporary World*, Ashgate, Aldershot, 2003.

Herne, R, "The challenge of Paganism within inter faith work", in *World Faiths Encounter*, No 23, July 1999, pp 32-37.

Hewer, C, "Schools for Muslims", in *Oxford Review of Education*, Volume 27, No 4, 2001, pp 515-27.

Hodgins, H, "Planning permission for mosques – the Birmingham experience", in *Research Papers – Muslims in Europe*, no 9, 1981, pp 11-27.

Home Office, *Building Cohesive Communities: A Report of the Ministerial Group Chaired by John Denham*, Home Office, London, 2001.

Home Office, *Community Cohesion: Report of the Independent Review Team Chaired by Ted Cantle*, Home Office, London, 2001.

Home Office Faith Communities Unit, The *Working Together: Co-Operation Between Government and Faith Communities Recommendations of the Steering Group Reviewing Patterns of Engagement Between Government and Faith Communities in England*, Faith Communities Unit, The Home Office, London, February 2004.

Hooker, R, and Sargant, J (eds), *Belonging to Britain: Christian Perspectives on a Plural Society*, Council of Churches for Britain and Ireland, London, nd.

Horton, J, "Religion and Toleration: Some Problems and Possibilities", in J Horton and H Crabtree (eds), *Toleration and Integrity in a Multi-Faith Society*, University of York Department of Politics, York, 1992, pp 62-70.

Horton, J (ed), *Liberalism, Multiculturalism and Toleration*, Macmillan, London, 1993.

Horton, J and Crabtree, H (eds), *Toleration and Integrity in a Multi-Faith Society*, University of York Department of Politics, York, 1992.

Husband, C, "The Political Context of Muslim Communities' Participation in British Society", in B Lewis and D Schnapper (eds), *Muslims in Europe*, Pinter, London, 1994, pp 79-97.

Husbands, C, " 'They Must Obey our Laws and Customs!' Political Debate About Muslim Assimilability in Great Britain, France and the Netherlands", in A Hargreaves and J Leaman (eds), *Racism, Ethnicity and Politics in Contemporary Europe*, Edward Elgar, Aldershot, 1995, pp 115-130.

Hulmes, E, *Education and Cultural Diversity*, Longman, Harlow, 1989.

Inter Faith Network for the UK, *Statement on Inter-Religious Relations*, Inter Faith Network for the UK, London, 1991.

Inter Faith Network for the UK, *Building Good Relations Between People of Different Faiths and Beliefs*, Inter Faith Network for the UK, London, 1993.

Inter Faith Network for the UK, *Mission, Dialogue and Inter-Religious Encounter*, Inter-Faith Network for the UK, London, 1993.

Inter Faith Network for the UK, *Places of Worship: The Practicalities and Politics of Sacred Space in Multi-Faith Britain*, Inter Faith Network for the UK, London, 1995.

Inter Faith Network for the UK, *Britain's Faith Communities: Equal Citizens?*, Inter Faith Network for the UK, London, 1996.

Inter Faith Network for the United Kingdom, *The Quest for Common Values: Conference Report*, Inter Faith Network for the United Kingdom, London, 1997.

Inter Faith Network for the United Kingdom, *The Local Inter Faith Guide: Faith Community Cooperation in Action*, Inter Faith Network for the UK in association with the Inner Cities Religious Council of the Department for the Environment, Transport and the Regions, London, 1999.

Inter Faith Network for the UK, *Local Inter Faith Activity in the UK: A Survey*, Inter Faith Network for the UK, London, 2003.

Inter Faith Network for the UK, *Partnership for the Common Good: Inter Faith Structures and Local Government*, Inter Faith Network for the UK, London, 2003.

Inter Faith Network for the UK, *Inter Faith Organisations in the UK: A Directory*, 3rd edition, Inter Faith Network for the United Kingdom, London, 2006.

Inter Faith Network for the UK and Commission for Racial Equality, *Law, Blasphemy and the Multi-Faith Society*, Commission for Racial Equality, London, 1990.

Inter Faith Network for the UK/Inner Cities Religious Council, *The Local Inter Faith Guide: Faith Community Co-Operation in Action*, Inter Faith Network for the United Kingdom in association with the Inner Cities Religious Council of the Department for the Environment, Transport and the Regions, London, 1999.

Ipgrave, M, " 'Fidei Defensor' Revisited: Church and State in a Religiously Plural Society," in N Ghanea (ed), *The Challenge of Religious Discrimination at the Dawn of the New Millennium*, Martinus Nijhoff, Leiden, 2003, pp 207-222.

Jack, H A, *A History of the World Conference on Religion and Peace*, New York, 1993.

Jackson, M and Kimberlee, R, *Daily Service: How Faith Communities Contribute to Neighbourhood Renewal and Regeneration in the South West of England. Final Report to the Government Office for the South West and the South West Council of Faiths*, Government Office for the South West, Bristol, 2004.

Jackson, M and Kimberlee, R, *Daily Service: How Faith Communities Contribute to Neighbourhood Renewal and Regeneration in the South West of England. Case Studies Prepared for the Government Office for the South West and the South West Council of Faiths*, Government Office for the South West, Bristol, 2004.

Jackson, R, *International Perspectives on Citizenship, Education and Religious Diversity*, Routledge Falmer, London, 2003.

Jackson, R, "Citizenship, Religious and Cultural Diversity and Education", in R Jackson (ed), *International Perspectives on Citizenship, Education and Religious Diversity*, Routledge Falmer, London, 2003, pp 1-28.

Jackson, R, "Should the state fund faith-based schools? A review of the arguments", in *British Journal of Religious Education*, Volume 25, No 2, 2003, pp 89-102.

Jacobsen, K and Kumar, P (eds), *South Asians in the Diaspora: Histories and Religious Traditions*, E J Brill, Leiden, 2004.

Jones, T, *Britain's Ethnic Minorities*, Policy Studies Institute, London, 1993.

Judge, H, "Faith-based schools and state funding: a partial argument", in *Oxford Review of Education*, Volume 27, No 4, 2001, pp 463-474.

Kaye, "The politics of religious slaughter of animals: Strategies for ethno-religious political action", in *New Community*, Volume 19, No 2, 1993, pp 235-250.

Kerr, D (ed), *Religion, State and Ethnic Groups*, Dartmouth Publishing Company, Aldershot, 1992.

Kerr, D, "Religion, State and Ethnic Identity", in D Kerr (ed), *Religion, State and Ethnic Groups*, Dartmouth Publishing Company, Aldershot, 1992, pp 1-26.

Knott, K, "Women and Religion in Post-War Britain", in G Parsons (ed), *The Growth of Religious Diversity: Britain From 1945, Volume II Issues*, Routledge, London, 1994, pp 199-230.

Knott, K, "The Religions of South Asian Communities in Britain," in J Hinnells (ed), *The New Handbook of Living Religions*, Oxford: Blackwell, 1996, pp 756-774.

Knott, K "Britain's changing religious landscape: drowning or waving?", in *Beriche zur deutschen Landeskunde*, Volume 78, No 2, 2004, pp 213-229.

Knott, K, *The Location of Religion: A Spatial Analysis*, Equinox, London, 2005.

Knott, K, "Researching Local and National Pluralism: Britain's New Religious Landscape", in M Baumann and S Behloul (eds), *Religioser Pluralismus: Empirische Studien und Analytische Perspektiven*, Transcript Verlag, Bielefeld, 2005, pp 45-68.

Knott, K and Francis, M, *Leeds Pilot Faiths Consultation Exercise on Restorative Justice and the Rehabilitation of Young Male Ex-Offenders*, Community Religions Project, University of Leeds, Leeds, 2004.

Küng, H and Kuschel, K-J (eds), *A Global Ethic: The Declaration of the Parliament of the World's Religions*, SCM Press, London, 1993.

Lamont, S, *Church and State: Uneasy Alliances*, Bodley Head, London, 1989.

Land Registry, HM, *Cultural Diversity, A Resource Booklet on Religious and Cultural Observance, Belief, Language and Naming Systems*, HM Land Registry, Diversity and Equal Opportunities Team, London, 2002.

Larsen, T, *Friends of Religious Equality: Nonconformist Politics in Mid-Victorian England*, The Boydell Press, Woodbridge, 1999.

Lewis, J and Randolph-Horn, E, *Faiths, Hope and Participation: Celebrating Faith Groups' Role in Neighbourhood Renewal*, New Economics Foundation and Church Urban Fund, London, 2001.

Lewis, S, *Beyond Belief? Faith at Work in the Community: A Report by the South East of England Faith Forum about Faith Based Regeneration Activities*, South East of England Faith Forum, 2004.

Lindley, J "Race or religion? The impact of religion on the employment and earnings of Britain's ethnic communities", in *Journal of Ethnic and Migration Studies*, Volume 28, no 3, 2002, pp 427-442.

Local Government Association, *Faith and Community: A Good Practice Guide*, Local Government Association Publications, London, 2002.

London Churches Group for Social Action and Greater London Enterprise, *Regenerating London: Faith Communities and Social Action*, London Churches Group for Social Action and Greater London Enterprise, 2002.

London Fire and Emergency Planning Authority, *Review of Faith and Diversity - Meeting the Spiritual Needs and Pastoral Needs of Employees*, London Fire and Emergency Planning Authority, London, 2003.

Lovatt, R, Lyall-Grant, F, Morris, Z, and Whitehead, C, *Faith in Action: A Report on Faith Communities and Social Capital in the East of England for the East of England Faiths Leadership Conference*, East of England Development Agency, East of England Faiths Council, and University of Cambridge, 2003.

Lynch, J, "Cultural Pluralism, Structural Pluralism and the United Kingdom", in Commission for Racial Equality, *Britain a Plural Society: Report of a Seminar*, Commission for Racial Equality, London, 1990, pp 29-43.

McKinney, S.J, "Symbol or stigma? The place of Catholic schools in Scotland", in *The Catalyst*, No. 7, January 2007, an online publication of the Commission for Racial Equality.

Mason, D (ed), *Religion in Leeds: A Centenary Volume*, Sutton Press, 1994.

Millard, D (ed), *Faiths and Fellowship: The Proceedings of the World Congress of Faiths*, held in London, July 3rd-17th, 1936, J M Watkins, London, 1937.

Mitchell, C, *Religion, Identity and Politics in Northern Ireland: Boundaries of Belief and Belonging*, Ashgate, Aldershot, 2006.

Modood, T, "Religious anger and minority rights", in *The Political Quarterly*, Volume 40, July-September, 1989, pp 280-285.

Modood, T, "British Asian Muslims and the Rushdie affair", in *The Political Quarterly*, Volume 61, No 2, 1990, pp 143-160.

Modood, T, *Not Easy Being British: Colour, Culture and Citizenship*, Trentham Books, Stoke-on-Trent, 1992.

Modood, T, "Minorities, faith and citizenship", in *Discernment: A Christian Journal for Inter-Religious Encounter*, Volume 6, No 2, 1992, pp 58-60.

Modood, T, (ed) *Church, State and Religious Minorities*, Policy Studies Institute, London, 1997.

Modood, T, "Introduction: Establishment, Reform and Multiculturalism", in T Modood, (ed), *Church, State and Religious Minorities*, Policy Studies Institute, London, 1997, pp 3-15.

Modood, T, "Anti-essentialism, multiculturalism and the 'recognition' of religious groups", in *Journal of Political Philosophy*, Volume 4, no 4, 1998, pp 378-399.

Modood, T, *Multicultural Politics*, Edinburgh University Press, Edinburgh, 2005.

Modood, T, Beishon, S and Virdee, S, *Changing Ethnic Identities*, Policy Studies Institute, London, 1994.

Modood, T, Berthoud, R, et al, *Ethnic Minorities in Britain: Diversity and Disadvantage*, Policy Studies Institute, London, 1997.

Modood, T, Triandafyllidou, A, and Zapata-Barrero, R (eds), *Multiculturalism, Muslims and Citizenship: A European Approach*, Routledge, Abingdon, 2006.

Modood, T and Werbner, P (eds), *The Politics of Multiculturalism in the New Europe: Racism, Identity and Community*, Zed Books, London, 1997.

Modood, T and Werbner, P (eds), *Debating Cultural Hybridity: Multi-Cultural Identities and the Politics of Anti-Racism*, Zed Books, London, 1997.

Morris, Z, Maguire, K and Kartupelis, J, *Faith in Action: A Report on Faith Communities and Social Capital in the East of England*, East of England Faiths Leadership Conference, Cambridge, 2003.

Moyser, G (ed), *Church and Politics Today: The Role of the Church of England in Contemporary Politics*, T & T Clark, Edinburgh, 1985.

Mubarak, F, *Women's Inter Faith Initiatives in the UK: A Survey*, Inter Faith Network for the UK, London, 2006.

Murphy, T, "Toleration and the Law", in J Horton and H Crabtree (eds), *Toleration and Integrity in a Multi-Faith Society*, University of York Department of Politics, York, 1992, pp 50-61.

Nasser, N, "South Asian ethnoscapes: the changing cultural landscapes of British cities", in *Global Built Environment Review*, Volume 3, No 2, 2003, pp 26-39.

Nesbitt, E, *Intercultural Education: Ethnographic and Religious Approaches*, Sussex Academic Press, Brighton, 2004.

Nesbitt, E and Arweck, E, "Researching a new interface between religions and publicly funded schools in the UK", in *International Journal for Children's Spirituality*, Volume 8, No 3, 2003, pp 239-254.

Nesbitt, E, Arweck, E, and Jackson, R, "Common values for the common school? using two values education programmes to promote 'Spiritual and Moral Development', in *Journal of Moral Education*, Volume 34, No 3, 2005, pp 325-342.

Nielsen, J, *Islamic Law: Its Significance for the Situation of Muslim Minorities in Europe*, Research Papers on Muslims in Europe, No 35, September 1987.

Northwest Development Agency, *Faith in England's Northwest: The Contribution Made by Faith Communities to Civil Society in the Region*, Northwest Development Agency, Warrington, 2003.

Northwest Regional Development Agency, *Faith in England's Northwest: Economic Impact Assessment*, Northwest Regional Development Agency, Warrington, 2005.

Nye, M, *Multiculturalism and Minority Religions in Britain – Krishna Consciousness, Religious Freedom and the Politics of Location*, Curzon Press, Richmond, 2001.

O'Beirne, M, *Religion in England and Wales: findings from the 2001 Home Office Citizenship Survey*, Home Office Research Study 274, Home Office, London, 2004.

Office for National Statistics, *Britain 2001: The Official Yearbook of the United Kingdom*, The Stationery Office, London, 2001.

Office for National Statistics, *Social Trends 31: 2001 Edition*, The Stationery Office, London, 2001.

Pan, L, *The Encyclopaedia of the Chinese Overseas*, Curzon Press, Richmond, 1998.

Parekh, B, "Britain and the Social Logic of Pluralism", in Commission for Racial Equality, *Britain a Plural Society: Report of a Seminar*, Commission for Racial Equality, London, 1990, pp 58-78.

Parekh, B, *Rethinking Multiculturalism: Cultural Diversity and Political Theory*, Macmillan, Basingstoke, 2000.

Parker-Jenkins, M, "Equal access to state funding: the case of Muslim schools in Britain", in *Race, Ethnicity and Education*, Volume 5, No 3, 2002, pp 273-289.

Parker-Jenkins, M and Hartas, D et al, *In Good Faith: Schools, Religion and Public Funding*, Ashgate, Aldershot, 2004.

Parsons, G (ed), *The Growth of Religious Diversity: Britain From 1945, Volume I: Traditions*, Routledge/Open University, London, 1993.

Parsons, G (ed), *The Growth of Religious Diversity: Britain From 1945, Volume II: Issues*, Routledge/Open University, London, 1994.

Patel, N, Naik, D and Humphries, B (eds), *Visions of Reality: Religion and Ethnicity in Social Work*, Central Council for Education and Training in Social Work, London, 1998.

Pearl, D, *Family Law and the Immigrant Communities*, Jordan's, London, 1986.

Peach, C, "Islam, ethnicity and South Asian religions in the London 2001 census", in *Transactions of the Institute of British Geographers*, ns No 31, 2006, pp 353-370.

Peach, C and Gale, R, "Muslims, Hindus and Sikhs in the new religious landscape of England", in *The Geographical Review*, Volume 93, No 4, 2003, pp 469-490.

Penoyre and Prasad Architects with Audley English Associates, Matrix Feminist Co-Op, Elsie Owusu Architects and Safe Neighbourhoods Unit, *Accommodating Diversity: The Design of Housing for Minority Ethnic, Religious and Cultural Groups*, National Federation of Housing Associations and North Housing Trust, London, 1993.

Poulter, S, *English Law and Ethnic Minority Customs*, Butterworth's, London, 1986.

Poulter, S, *Asian Traditions and English Law: A Handbook*, Trentham Books, Stoke-on-Trent, 1990.

Poulter, S, "Cultural Pluralism and its Limits: a Legal Perspective", in Commission for Racial Equality, *Britain a Plural Society: Report of a Seminar*, Commission for Racial Equality, London, 1990, pp 3-28.

Poulter, S, *Ethnicity, Law and Human Rights: The English Experience*, Clarendon Press, Oxford, 1998.

Ratcliffe, P (ed), *Ethnicity in the 1991 Census: Social Geography and Ethnicity in Britain*, Volume 3, HMSO, London, 1996.

Ravat, R, *Enabling the Present: Planning for the Future: Social Action by the Faith Communities of Leicester*, Leicester Faiths Regeneration Project, Leicester, 2004.

Rex, J, *The Concept of a Multi-Cultural Society*, University of Warwick Centre for Research in Ethnic Relations, Coventry, 1985.

Rex, J, "Religion and Ethnicity in the Metropolis", in R Barot (ed), *Religion and Ethnicity: Minorities and Social Change in the Metropolis*, Kok Pharos, Kampen, 1993, pp 17-26.

Rex, J, *Ethnic Minorities in the Modern Nation State: Working Papers in the Theory of Multi-Culturalism and Political Integration*, Macmillan Press, Basingstoke, 1996.

Rhys, G, "The Divine Economy and the Political Economy: the Theology of Welsh Nationalism", in R Hooker and J Sargant (eds), *Belonging to Britain: Christian Perspectives on a Plural Society*, Council of Churches for Britain and Ireland, London, nd, pp 55-74.

Richardson, N, *A Tapestry of Beliefs: Christian Traditions in Northern Ireland*, Blankstaff Press, Belfast, 1999.

Robilliard, St John, *Religion and the Law: Religious Liberty in Modern English Law*, Manchester University Press, Manchester, 1984.

Robinson, V, "Boom and Gloom: The Success and Failure of South Asians in Britain", in C Clarke, C Peach and S Vertovec (eds), *South Asians Overseas: Migration and Ethnicity*, Cambridge University Press, Cambridge, 1990, pp 251-267.

Royal Commission on Reform of the House of Lords, *Reform of A House for the Future: A Summary*, Royal Commission on Reform of the House of Lords, London, 1999.

Runnymede Trust, The, *A Very Light Sleeper: The Persistence and Dangers of Antisemitism*, Runnymede Trust, London, 1994.

Runnymede Trust, The, *Islamophobia: A Challenge for Us All*, Runnymede Trust, London, 1997.

Ryan, M, *Another Ireland: An Introduction to Ireland's Ethnic-Religious Minority Communities*, Stranmillis University College, Belfast, 1996.

Sacks, J, *The Persistence of Faith*, Weidenfeld and Nicholson, London, 1991.

Saghal, G and Yuval-Davis, N (eds), *Refocusing Holy Orders: Women and Fundamentalism in Britain*, Virago Press, London, 1992.

Schmool, M and Cohen, F, *A Profile of British Jewry*, Board of Deputies of British Jews, London, 1998.

Scottish Office, The, *Ethnic Minorities in Scotland*, HMSO, London, 1991.

Sheils, W (eds), *A History of Religion in Britain: Belief and Practice from Pre-Roman Times to the Present*, Blackwell, Oxford, 1994, pp 363-380.

Simpson, B and Weyl, R, *The International Council of Christians and Jews*, International Council of Christians and Jews, Heppenheim, Germany, 1988.

Smart, N, "Church, Party and State" in P Badham (ed), *Religion, State and Society in Modern Britain*, Edwin Mellen Press, Lampeter, 1989, pp 381-395.

Smith, G, *Faith in the Voluntary Sector: A Common or Distinctive Experience of Religious Organisations*, Working Papers in Applied Social Research, No 25, Department of Sociology, University of Manchester, Manchester, 2003.

Smith, G, "Faith in community and communities of faith? Government rhetoric and religious identity in urban Britain", in *Journal of Contemporary Religion*, Volume 19, No 2, 2004, pp 185-204.

Smith, K, *Faith in the North East: Social Action by Faith Communities in the Region, Churches' Regional Commission for the North East*, Durham City, 2004.

Social Policy Group of the British Council of Churches Committee on Relations with People of Other Faiths and the Race Relations Unit, "Religiously-based voluntary schools", in *Discernment: A Christian Journal of Inter-Religious Encounter*, Volume 6, No 2, 1992, pp 32-40.

Sutcliffe, S, "Unfinished Business – Devolving Scotland/Devolving Religion", in S Coleman and P Collins (eds), *Religion, Identity and Change: Perspectives on Global Transformations*, Ashgate, Aldershot, 2004, pp 84-106.

Thomas, P, *Candle in the Darkness: Celtic Spirituality in Wales*, Gomer, Lladysul, 1993.

Thomas, T (ed), *The British: Their Religious Beliefs and Practices*, Routledge, London, 1988.

Taylor, C, *Multiculturalism and the Politics of Recognition*, Princeton University Press, Princeton, 1992.

Trigg, R, *Religion in Public Life: Must Faith be Privatized?*, Oxford University Press, Oxford, 2007.

Verma, G, "Pluralism: Some Theoretical and Practical Considerations", in Commission for Racial Equality, *Britain a Plural Society: Report of a Seminar*, Commission for Racial Equality, London, 1990, pp 44-57.

Vertovec, S (ed), *Aspects of the South Asian Diaspora, Volume II, part 2: Papers on India*, Oxford University Press, Delhi, 1991.

Vertovec, S, "Multi-cultural, multi-Asian, multi-Muslim Leicester: dimensions of social complexity, ethnic organisation and Local Government interface", in *Innovation: European Journal of Social Sciences*, Volume 7, No 3, 1994, pp 259-276.

Viney, R, "Religious Broadcasting on UK Television: policy, public perception and programmes", in *Cultural Trends*, 36, 1999.

Visram, R, *Ayahs, Lascars and Princes: The Story of Indians in Britain 1700-1947*, Pluto Press, London, 1986.

Voas, D, "Is Britain a Christian Country?", in P Avis (ed), *Public Faith: The State of Religious Belief and Practice in Britain*, SPCK, London, 2003, pp 92-105.

Voas, D and Bruce, S, "The 2001 Census and Christian Identification in Britain", in *Journal of Contemporary Religion*, Volume 19, No 1, 2004, pp 23-28.

Watson, B, "Integrity and Affirmation: an Inclusivist Approach to National Identity", in R Hooker and J Sargant (ed), *Belonging to Britain: Christian Perspectives on a Plural Society*, Council of Churches for Britain and Ireland, London, nd, pp 135-148.

Weigel, G, *The Cube and the Cathedral: Europe, America and Politics Without God*, Gracewing, Leominster, 2005.

Weller, P, "'Inheritors together': the Inter Faith Network for the United Kingdom", in *Discernment: A Christian Journal of Inter-Religious Encounter*, Volume 3, No 2, Autumn, 1988, pp 30-34.

Weller, P, "Integrating religious, social and political values in a multi-cultural society", in *Current Dialogue*, June, 1990, pp 39-44.

Weller, P, "The Rushdie affair, plurality of values and the ideal of a multi-cultural society", in *National Association for Values in Education and Training Working Papers*, Volume 2, October 1990, pp 1-9.

Weller, P, "Religion and equal opportunities in Higher Education", in *Cutting Edge*, No 2, 1991, pp 26-36.

Weller, P, "Inter-Faith roots and shoots: an outlook for the 1990s", in *World Faiths Encounter*, No 1, March, 1992, pp 48-57.

Weller, P, "Religion and equal opportunities in Higher Education", in *The Journal of International Education*, Volume 3, November, 1992, pp 53-64.

Weller, P, "Integrating social, political and religious values in a multi-faith society", in *World Faiths Encounter*, No 12, November, 1994, pp 28-37.

Weller, P, "The Inter Faith Network for the United Kingdom", in *Indo-British Review: A Journal of History*, Volume 20, No 1, 1994, pp 20-6.

Weller, P, "Values, visions and religions: pluralist problematics in a secular and multi-faith context", in *Cutting Edge*, No 9, February 1994, pp 15-17.

Weller, P, "The Changing Patterns of Worship Space Provision in Britain", in the Inter Faith Network for the United Kingdom, *Places of Worship: The Practicalities and Politics of Sacred Space in Multi-Faith Britain*, Inter Faith Network for the UK, London, 1995, pp 4-16.

Weller, P, "Equity, Inclusivity and Participation in a Plural Society: Challenging the Establishment of the Church of England", in P Edge and G Harvey (eds), *Law and Religion in Contemporary Societies: Communities, Individualism and the State*, Ashgate, Aldershot, 2000, pp 53-67.

Weller, P, "Insiders or Outsiders?: Propositions for European Religions, States and Societies", in A Race and I Shafer (eds), *Religions in Dialogue: From Theocracy to Democracy*, Ashgate, Aldershot, 2002, pp 193-208.

Weller, P, "What We Might Think and How we Might Act: Diplomacy, Challenge and Exploration in Multi-Faith Britain", in D Hart (ed), *Multi-Faith Britain: An Experiment in Worship*, O Books, Alresford, pp 127-139.

Weller, P, "The Dimensions and Dynamics of Religious Discrimination: Findings and Analysis from the UK", in N Ghanea (ed), *The Challenge of Religious Discrimination at the Dawn of the New Millennium*, Martinus Nijhoff Publishers, Leiden, 2003, pp 57-81.

Weller, P, "Unfair Treatment Between Religions: Findings of a Research Project in England and Wales", in *Interreligious Insight*, Volume 1, No 2, 2003, pp 62-71.

Weller, P, "Identity, Politics and the Future(s) of Religion in the UK: The Case of the Religion Questions in the 2001 Decennial Census", in *Journal of Contemporary Religion*, Volume 19, No 1, 2004, pp 3-21.

Weller, P, "Hindus and Sikhs: Community Development and Religious Discrimination in England and Wales", in K Jacobsen and P Kumar (eds), *South Asians in the Diaspora: Histories and Religious Traditions*, Brill, Leiden, 2004, pp 454-497.

Weller, P, *Time for a Change: Reconfiguring Religion, State and Society*, T & T Clark, London, 2005.

Weller, P, "Religions and social capital: theses on religion(s), state(s) and society(ies): with particular reference to the United Kingdom and the European Union", in *The Journal of International Migration and Integration*, Volume 9, No 2, 2005, pp 271-289.

Weller, P, "Addressing religious discrimination and Islamophobia: Muslims and liberal democracies. The case of the United Kingdom", in *The Journal of Islamic Studies*, Volume 17, No. 3, September 2006, pp 295-325.

Weller, P, " 'Human rights', 'religion' and the 'secular': variant configurations of religion(s), state(s) and society(ies)", in *Religion and Human Rights: An International Journal*, Volume 1, No 1, 2006, pp 17-39.

Weller, P, " 'Human Rights', 'Religion' and the 'Secular': Variant Configurations of Religion(s), State(s) and Society(ies)", in N Ghanea, A Stephens and R Walden (eds), *Does God Believe in Human Rights?: Essays on Religion and Human Rights*, Martinus Nijhoff Publishers, Leiden, 2007, pp 147-179.

Weller, P and Andrews, A, *Religions and Statistics Research Project: Report of a Pilot Phase (March 1994-March 1995)*, 1996, University of Derby, Derby.

Weller, P and Andrews, A, "Counting religion: religion, statistics and the 2001 census", in *World Faiths Encounter*, No 21, November, 1998, pp 23-34.

Weller, P and Beale, D, *Multi-Faith Infrastructure Support in the East Midlands: An Investigation Into Activity and Needs in the East Midlands*, University of Derby, Derby, 2004.

Weller, P, Feldman, A and Purdam, K, *Religious Discrimination in England and Wales*, Home Office Research Study 220, Home Office Research, Development and Statistics Directorate, London, 2001.

Weller, P and Purdam, K, et al, *Religious Discrimination in England and Wales: Interim Report*, University of Derby, Derby, 2000.

Weller, P and Wolfe, M, *Involving Religions: A Project Report on Religious Group Participation, Inter-Faith Infrastructure, and Capacity-Building in Derby*, School of Education, Health and Sciences, University of Derby, Derby, 2004.

Werbner, P, "Islamophobia: incitement to religious hatred – legislating for a new fear?", in *Anthropology Today*, Volume 21, No 1, 2005, pp 5-9.

West Midlands Faiths Forum, *Believing in the West Midlands: Report of the First Conference of the West Midlands Faiths Forum*, Held March 2005, West Midlands Faiths Forum, 2005.

Williams, G, *The Welsh and Their Religion*, University of Wales Press, Cardiff, 1991.

Wilson, B, "Old Laws and New Religions", in D Cohn-Sherbok (ed), *The Canterbury Papers: Essays on Religion and Society*, Bellew Publishing, London, 1990, pp 210-224.

Wohlrab-Sahr, M, "Invisible Religion between Individualization and Cultural Defense", in J Malik and H Reifeld (eds), *Religious Pluralism in South Asia and Europe*, Oxford University Press, New Delhi, 2005, pp 170-183.

Wolffe, J (ed), *The Growth of Religious Diversity: Britain From 1945 A Reader*, Hodder and Stoughton, Sevenoaks, 1993.

Wolffe, J, "Religions of the silent majority", in G Parsons (ed), *The Growth of Religious Diversity: Britain from 1945 Volume I: Traditions*, Routledge, London, 1993, pp 305-346.

Wolffe, J, *God and Greater Britain: Religion and National Life in Britain and Ireland, 1843-1945*, Routledge, London, 1994.

Wolffe, J, "And there's another country': religion, the state and British identities", in G Parsons (ed), *The Growth of Religious Diversity: Britain From 1945 Volume II, Issues*, Routledge, London, 1994, pp 85-159.

Wolverhampton Inter Faith Group, *30 Years of Dialogue and Community Cohesion: Reflections on the Past, Visions for the Future. Review of the Past and Spirations for the Next 30 Years*, Wolverhampton Inter Faith Group, Wolverhampton, 2006.

Wood, M, "Kinship Identity and Noncoformative Spiritual Seekership", in S Coleman and P Collins (eds), *Religion, Identity and Change: Perspectives on Global Transformations*, Ashgate, Aldershot, 2004, pp 191–206.

Wraight, H (ed), *UK Christian Handbook: 2007/2008*, Christian Research, London, 2007.

Yarrow, S, *Religious and Political Discrimination in the Workplace*, Policy Studies Institute, London, 1997.

Yilmaz, I, "Law as chameleon: the question of incorporation of Muslim personal law into the English law", in *Journal of Muslim Minority Affairs*, Volume 21, no 2, 2001, pp 297–308.

Yilmaz, I, "The challenge of post-modern legality and Muslim legal pluralism in England", in *Journal of Ethnic and Migration Studies*, Volume 28, no 2, 2002, pp 343–354.

York, M, *The Emerging Network: A Sociology of New Age and Neo-Pagan Movements*, Rowman and Littlewood, London, 1995.

Yorkshire and Humber Assembly, *Religious Literacy: A Practical Guide to the Region's Faith Communities*, Yorkshire and Humber Assembly, Wakefield, 2002.

Yuval-Davis, N, "Fundamentalism, Multi-culturalism and Women in Britain", in J Donald and A Rattansi (eds) *'Race' Culture and Difference*, Sage, London, 1992, pp 278–291.

INTRODUCING BAHÁ'ÍS IN THE UK

BAHÁ'ÍS IN THE UK 91

ORIGINS AND DEVELOPMENT OF THE BAHÁ'Í FAITH 92

SOURCES OF BAHÁ'Í BELIEFS AND PRACTICES 93

KEY BAHÁ'Í BELIEFS 93

BAHÁ'Í LIFE 94

TRADITIONS IN THE BAHÁ'Í FAITH 96

BAHÁ'Í WORSHIP 96

BAHÁ'Í PLACES OF WORSHIP 97

BAHÁ'Í CALENDAR AND FESTIVALS 98

BAHÁ'Í ORGANISATIONS 99

FURTHER READING 101

BAHÁ'ÍS IN THE UK

History in the UK

Bahá'ís have been present in the UK since 1898, when Miriam Thornburgh-Cropper, the first Bahá'í to live in London, started to attract others to this new faith. She had been inspired by her visit to the Holy Land to meet 'Abdu'l-Bahá, eldest son and successor of Bahá'u'lláh, the founder of the Faith.

The growth of the faith was greatly stimulated by the visits of 'Abdu'l-Bahá to a number of cities in England and Scotland during 1911-13. By then groups of Bahá'ís were holding regular meetings in London, Bournemouth and Manchester.

Up until 1939 most Bahá'í activity was centred in England, but in the years following the Second World War the Bahá'í Faith was also established in Scotland, Wales and Ireland.

Populations

Worldwide, the Bahá'í Universal House of Justice (see below) estimates that there are around 5,000,000 Bahá'ís. In the UK, the 2001 decennial Census questions on religion did not offer to respondents the category of "Bahá'í" as a pre-set category of response.

However, the specially commissioned Census Table M275 Religion (Most Detailed Categories) provides the breakdown of responses for England and Wales of respondents ticking the "Other Religions - please write in" box in the Census question on religious affiliation. From an analysis of this table, there were 4,374 Bahá'í respondents in England and 271 in Wales. Across the UK as a whole, the Bahá'í Community itself estimates its membership as between 5,500 and 6,000.

Ethnicity

Most Bahá'ís in the UK are of indigenous ethnic origin and the majority are converts from other religions or are former agnostics or atheists. There are, though, also Bahá'ís whose family roots are in Iran, most of whom have arrived since the Iranian Revolution. Most Bahá'ís in the UK pray and read their scriptures in English. Some of Iranian descent use also Persian and Arabic. A number of Bahá'ís in the UK community are of South Asian, Chinese, African, African-Caribbean and other ethnic origins.

ORIGINS AND DEVELOPMENT OF THE BAHÁ'Í FAITH

The Báb

The Bahá'í Faith began in Persia on 23rd May 1844, with the declaration of a new religion, distinctive from the *Shi'a* Islam found there. Four people were central to the development of the Bahá'í Faith: the *Báb, Bahá'u'lláh, 'Abdu'l-Bahá* and Shoghi Effendi.

The person known to Bahá'ís by the title of the *Báb* (the *Gate* or *Door*, 1819-1850) was born in Shiraz, Persia. The *Báb* was originally known by the personal name of Ali-Muhammad and was a descendant of the Prophet Muhammad. In 1844 the *Báb* proclaimed himself the *Messenger* of God and heralded the coming of *One Whom God Shall Make Manifest*, and who would bring a new age of civilisation characterised by world peace. He was executed in Persia on 9th July 1850 under the charge of heresy against Islam. Many of his early followers, known as *Bábis*, were also persecuted after his death.

Bahá'u'lláh

Husayn Ali (1817-1892), known to Bahá'ís by the title of *Bahá'u'lláh* (the *Glory of God*) was born in Tehran, Persia. In 1863, he claimed to be the *One Whom God Shall Make Manifest*, and of whose coming the *Báb* had foretold. He said he was the bringer of divine revelation who was to fulfil the promises made by the previous *Messengers* of other religions. *Bahá'u'lláh* was banished from Persia in 1853, and later exiled to Palestine by the Ottoman Turkish authorities in 1868. He died in 1892 at Bahji, a mansion on the outskirts of Akka, where he is buried. His burial place is the holiest shrine of the Bahá'í world and provides a physical focus for its global unity.

'Abdu'l-Bahá

After the death of *Bahá'u'lláh*, his son *'Abdu'l-Bahá* (*Servant of the Glory* - also known among Bahá'ís as the *Master*) was appointed in *Bahá'u'lláh's Will* (known as the *Book of the Covenant*) to be the head of the Bahá'í Community, and as the authorised interpreter of Bahá'í teachings. *'Abdu'l-Bahá* was born in 1844 and died in Haifa in 1921.

Shoghi Effendi

On the death of *'Abdu'l-Bahá*, and as appointed in his *Will*, his grandson Shoghi Effendi (1897-1957), became the *Guardian of the Faith* and *Interpreter of Scripture*. Shoghi Effendi died whilst he was on a private visit to London, where there was already an established community of Bahá'ís. With his death, authority passed temporarily to an appointed group of distinguished believers called the *Hands of the Cause of God*. This was a group of twenty-seven people appointed by Shoghi Effendi to be the *Chief Stewards of the Faith*.

Universal House of Justice

In 1963 the *Universal House of Justice* was established as a supreme governing body for the Bahá'í community. It is based at the Bahá'í World Centre in Haifa in Israel and is re-elected every five years.

Recent Decades

Over the past thirty years, the Bahá'í Faith has experienced major expansion, especially in India, Africa, South America, the Pacific and more recently in Eastern Europe.

SOURCES OF BAHÁ'Í BELIEFS AND PRACTICES

Bahá'í Scriptures

Bahá'ís believe their scriptures to be the revealed message of God. These scriptures consist of the *Writings* of the three central figures of the Bahá'í Faith: the *Báb*, *Bahá'u'lláh*, and *'Abdu'l-Bahá*.

They include all documents hand-written by them; all documents signed by them; and records of their spoken words, authenticated either directly or indirectly by the speakers. The *Kitáb-i Iqán* (*The Book of Certitude*) contains the key doctrinal beliefs and *Bahá'u'lláh's Hidden Words* is a frequently used collection of ethical aphorisms.

Most of the *Writings* of *Bahá'u'lláh* and *'Abdu'l-Bahá* are in the form of letters known as *Tablets* and are written in Persian or Arabic. The collection and classification of Bahá'í sacred *Writings* and also of their authoritative interpretations by Shoghi Effendi still continues today.

There are now over 60,000 original documents or copies kept at the Bahá'í World Centre in Haifa and the Bahá'í scriptures have been translated into over 820 languages. Foremost among these scriptures is *Bahá'u'lláh's* 1873 *Kitáb-i-Aqdas* (*Most Holy Book*) which is considered the basis for Bahá'í laws, moral principles and institutions.

KEY BAHÁ'Í BELIEFS

A Summary

A summary of key Bahá'í beliefs can be found in the various collections of the talks which *'Abdu'l-Bahá* gave in America. The key Bahá'í beliefs are belief in one God; the unity of mankind; independent investigation of truth; the common foundation of all religions; progressive revelation; the essential harmony of science and religion; key social teachings, including equality of opportunity for men and women; elimination of prejudice of all kinds; universal compulsory education; a universal auxiliary language; abolition of extremities of poverty and wealth through international legislation; the establishment of universal peace by world government which will have international courts of justice and an international military force; and the establishment of an ever-advancing civilisation based on spiritual principles.

Progressive Revelation

Unity and its establishment in the world is a central theme of the Bahá'í religion. Its followers share a conviction that there has only ever been one religion and one God though people have called God by different names. This conviction was continually emphasised by *'Abdu'l-Bahá*.

God is seen as being beyond gender and as infinite and unknowable in Divine Essence, yet revealed to humanity through a series of *Messengers* sent to different places at different times. Moses, Krishna, Zoroaster, *Buddha*, *Christ* and Muhammad are all believed by Bahá'ís to be *Messengers* from God and are described by *Bahá'u'lláh* as *Manifestations* of God. Bahá'ís believe that every people on earth have, at some point in their history, been recipients of a Divine *Manifestation* or *Prophet*.

There is therefore a progressive view of revelation in which each recognised *Messenger* is believed to have passed on divine law informing society how to live and behave. All *Messengers* are also believed to have promised a time when a great *Messenger* would come and bring peace to the world. Bahá'ís believe that *Bahá'u'lláh* was that *Messenger*.

Oneness of Humankind

Bahá'ís believe that the future of the world lies in a new civilisation based on justice and existing for the benefit of everyone regardless of race, religion, class or gender. This will involve the abolition of prejudices; equality for men and women; abolition of the extremes of wealth and poverty; universal compulsory education; and a world commonwealth with a world parliament.

It is within this context that the Bahá'í commitment to a universal auxiliary language, to be taught in schools alongside one's own language, should be understood. This does not entail a commitment to any particular language to serve this purpose - the choice of such a language is to be left to the people of the world to choose, through their representatives. But its introduction and use is seen as both an aid to practical communication and as a force to help develop even further the world unity that is seen as necessary for the survival and prosperity of humanity.

It is believed that once the unity of humankind has been firmly established world peace will follow. The establishment of Bahá'í communities and groups throughout the world is seen as contributing to this process and, indeed, as modelling a new world order.

Nature and Goal of Human Life

Bahá'ís believe that the basic purposes of human life are to know and worship God, developing spiritual qualities that enable individuals to fulfil their God-given potential and to become better people.

Bahá'ís believe that each human being has a separate rational soul that is related to, but also distinct from, the human body and persists after death. The world is understood as a place where this soul can develop. The analogy is often used of the world as a womb, in which the foetus is growing arms, legs, eyes and other organs whose purpose will only become clear when it moves into the next phase of existence by being born into the world. Similarly, human beings, in this life, are seen as developing positive spiritual

qualities, the true importance of which will only be appreciated in the next world. To the extent that spiritual qualities have been developed in this world, to that extent will the soul to able to progress in the next world.

Heaven is seen as a state of nearness to God and hell as being remoteness from God, each of which follows as a consequence of efforts, or the lack of them, to develop spiritually. The Bahá'í teachings emphasise that death is a "messenger of joy" and deal with the subject of the life to come in great depth. *Bahá'u'lláh* states that there are many worlds of God through which our souls will pass on their journey towards Him.

Education and Spirituality

The importance of education is a central theme in the Bahá'í understanding of one's place in the world. There is no dichotomy between what are often called the secular and the spiritual dimensions of life. Religion and science are viewed as being complementary ways of discovering truth: science through investigation and religion through revelation.

Ethics and Spirituality

Bahá'í ethics are understood as being both individual and social. As already indicated in terms of the analogy of the womb, the development of positive spiritual qualities is seen as the individual task of every human being. At the same time, humankind is understood to be social with the relationships between individuals also being part of the task of spiritual development. Hence Bahá'í ethics include both individual and social dimensions, as explained in the following section.

BAHÁ'Í LIFE

Joining the Community

A Bahá'í is a person who accepts *Bahá'u'lláh* as the *Manifestation of God* for the present day. When someone feels moved to accept

Bahá'u'lláh they make a declaration of faith. This can be in private or it can be made verbally or in writing to any other Bahá'í individual or institution. Often new Bahá'ís will wish to make this declaration to the person who has been teaching them, but individuals are free to make their own decision about this.

The Bahá'í to whom the declaration is made, or the *Local Spiritual Assembly* (see below), will ensure that the new declarant is basically informed about the central figures of the Bahá'í faith, about the existence of laws that should be followed, and about the Bahá'í administrative institutions, whose decisions and guidance should be obeyed.

A person becomes a member of the Bahá'í community by application to a Bahá'í administrative body such as a *Local Spiritual Assembly* (see the section on "Bahá'í Organisations" below). An *Assembly* will accept them if it is satisfied that they truly believe the tenets of the Bahá'í Faith and are basically informed about the central figures of the Faith, the existence of laws they must follow, as well as the administrative system with which they must live in conformity. Being a part of the Bahá'í worldwide *Administrative Order* gives individual Bahá'ís confidence that they can contribute in the best way to the goals of the Bahá'í religion.

Once a person has declared, he or she can register as a member of the Bahá'í community by giving their contact details to an individual Bahá'í or to one of the Bahá'í administrative bodies, typically their *Local Spiritual Assembly*. Registering as Bahá'ís allows them to exercise their vote in Bahá'í elections, donate to Bahá'í funds, attend the *Nineteen Day Feast*, and play a full role in the life of the Bahá'í community.

The Covenant

By declaring faith and enrolling in the community, a Bahá'í accepts the terms of what is known as *The Covenant*, which is central to the unity of the Bahá'í community. By its terms, set out in *The Will and Testament of Bahá'u'lláh*, in the *Kitáb-i-Ahd* (the *Book of His Covenant*), and in the *Will and Testament* of *'Abdu'l-Bahá*, Bahá'ís accept the authority of *Bahá'u'lláh* as the *Manifestation of God*, of the revealed text, of *'Abdu'l-Bahá* as the *Centre* of the *Covenant* of *Bahá'u'lláh*, of *Shoghi Effendi* as the *Guardian* of the Bahá'í Faith, and of the *Universal House of Justice* as the Bahá'í community's world governing council, as set out in the writings of *Bahá'u'lláh*.

Teaching and Pioneering

Bahá'ís are forbidden to proselytise in the sense of holding out the promise of reward or the threat of punishment (whether material or spiritual) in order to make converts. However, Bahá'ís are always eager to share their vision and beliefs with enquirers and hold out a welcome to people who wish to join the Bahá'í community. This sharing of vision and belief is known among Bahá'ís as *teaching*. Many are also involved in what is known as *pioneering*, which is spreading the Faith by means of moving where there are currently few or no Bahá'ís.

Core Activities

Bahá'ís in the UK are part of a culture change that is going on throughout the worldwide Bahá'í community. The aim is to establish a culture of learning and an outward orientation by focussing on four activities that are open to all, whether Bahá'í or not.

These activities are: devotional gatherings; small groups which study the Bahá'í scriptures and teachings; spiritual and moral classes for children; and work with young people in the 11-14 age group, using specially designed learning materials.

The study groups use materials originally developed in Colombia in South America, and which are now adopted worldwide. By inviting their family, friends, neighbours and work colleagues to take part in these activities, Bahá'ís are developing a growing community of interest, some of whom are joining the Bahá'í community.

Women and Men

Men and women have equal status in the Bahá'í community. Any distinctions in gender roles are culture-specific rather than religious and *'Abdu'l-Bahá* specified that both men and women should receive education of equal standard. *Bahá'u'lláh* stated that, if for any reason education is not available to all, then women, as the first educators of the next generation, should have priority.

Diet

There are no specific dietary laws in the Bahá'í Faith, although vegetarianism is commended as a healthier and more natural lifestyle and one that it is anticipated will become the norm for human beings in the future. However, the consumption of alcohol is strictly forbidden (including its use in cooking and sauces) as is the taking of habit-forming drugs, and smoking is discouraged.

Voluntary Sharing

Bahá'u'lláh advocated voluntary sharing rather than an externally imposed equalisation of wealth. Sharing is a matter of free choice and therefore is seen as more desirable.

TRADITIONS IN THE BAHÁ'Í FAITH

The Bahá'í community is well structured and organised. At each stage in the development of the Bahá'í religion there have been those who have split off from the community because they disputed the succession and leadership set out in the *Wills* of *Bahá'u'lláh* and *'Abdu'l-Bahá*, and who have tried to establish an alternative movement under the Bahá'í name.

These groups are referred to by Bahá'ís as *Covenant-breakers*, since the *Covenant* that binds Bahá'ís together is seen to consist of the unity of the line of authority from *Bahá'u'lláh* through to the *Universal House of Justice*. The consequence of such *Covenant-breaking* is expulsion.

Covenant-breaking is understood by Bahá'ís to be fundamentally different from simply leaving the religion or behaving in a way that falls short of Bahá'í ideals, since it is seen as disobeying the *Wills* of *Bahá'u'lláh* and *'Abdu'l-Bahá*.

Bahá'ís are forbidden to have social relationships with those who have attempted to establish alternative authorities and groups. None of the groups that are viewed as *Covenant-breakers* have gained a major following and some of the people involved in them have subsequently gone on to practise other religions or philosophies.

Bahá'ís are not organised into any identifiably distinct traditions of interpretation or practice. It is a part of the Bahá'í self-understanding that their religion is unique among the world's religions in that it has not only survived a century and a half without splitting into sects, but it is believed that it will continue to be united in the future.

BAHÁ'Í WORSHIP

Individual Daily Prayers

Every Bahá'í over the age of fifteen must recite daily one of three prayers known as the "obligatory" prayers. These three prayers differ in length and must be recited in differing ways. The three prayers are: a short prayer which should be recited once every twenty-four hours between noon and sunset; a medium length prayer which should be recited three times in a day - morning, noon and evening; and a long prayer which should be recited once every twenty-four hours.

In addition to reciting one of these obligatory prayers, Bahá'ís are required to read extracts from the scriptures every morning and evening. When praying, Bahá'ís turn in the direction of Bahji, near Akka in Israel, which is the burial place of *Bahá'u'lláh*.

Bahá'í Collective Worship

The Bahá'í religion has no set worship services and no ordained priesthood. Devotional programmes are simple and consist of prayers, meditations, and the reading of sections from the sacred scriptures of the Faith and of other world religions.

At present, worship takes place mainly in Bahá'í homes, although in some cities Bahá'í centres can be found. Music is generally encouraged in Bahá'í worship. In *Houses of Worship* (see section on "Bahá'í Places of Worship" below) an unaccompanied choir provides the music.

Small regular meetings for discussion and that take place in homes are known as *Firesides*. *Firesides* sometimes begin and end with prayers and include information and discussion. Those interested in learning more about the Bahá'í faith may attend *Study Circles*, which provide systematic courses of study. Other meetings, for example *Nineteen-Day Feasts* (see section on "Bahá'í Calendar and Festivals" below), may be held in local Bahá'í Centres.

A *Unity Feast* is an informal gathering of Bahá'ís and their friends. It often begins with devotional readings, prayers or songs. Visitors may join in or not, according to their wish. During prayers, a reverent silence is requested. There is no sacred food or sacrament. The *Feast* closes with a period during which people meet each other and share refreshments.

BAHÁ'Í PLACES OF WORSHIP

Buildings

There are no formal buildings for Bahá'í worship in the UK. Therefore Bahá'í places of worship and devotional practice are not recorded as a separate category in the running totals of certified places of worship in England and Wales kept by the Registrar General.

Gatherings are held at the Bahá'í Centre in London and various regional Bahá'í centres. Most Bahá'í gatherings, however, including those of the *Local Spiritual Assemblies* (see section on "Bahá'í Organisations" below), take place in members' homes or in hired meeting rooms.

Houses of Worship

Across the world there are seven, purpose-built, *Houses of Worship*. These are in Sydney, Australia; in Wilmette, near Chicago, the USA; in Frankfurt, Germany; in Panama City, Central America; in New Delhi, India; in Apia, Western Samoa; and in Kampala, Uganda). *Houses of Worship* are at present of continental rather than national or local significance.

There are regular services at the *Houses of Worship* that are open to all. The oldest surviving *House of Worship* is the one at Wilmette, otherwise known as the *Mother Temple of the West*, which was dedicated in 1953. A new *House of Worship* for South America is currently under construction in Santiago, Chile.

A considerable number of sites for the development of future *Houses of Worship* have been purchased. The *Houses of Worship* have been built at the request of *Bahá'u'lláh*, who gave them the name *Mashriqu'l-Adhkar* (*Dawning Place of God's Praise*), and they are built to *'Abdu'l-Bahá's* specifications. Each is nine sided and surmounted by a dome, standing in large gardens with fountains, trees and flowers.

In addition to the place of worship itself, there are also buildings for educational, charitable and social purposes, for example old people's homes and orphanages. *Bahá'u'lláh* believed that this would ensure that Bahá'í worship would always be closely associated with the beauty of nature and art as well as with practical work for the amelioration of poor social conditions, the promotion of general education and the conduct of administration.

Visitors to Bahá'í Worship

Most Bahá'í gatherings and meetings – and particularly study circles, devotional meetings, children's classes, and programmes for juniors, youth and women – are open to people of any faith or none. Anyone is welcome to attend the devotional gatherings that Bahá'í local communities, families and individuals organise in their Bahá'í centres (where there is one), in a hired venue, or in their homes. These gatherings are one of the four *Core Activities*, and are open to all, as are the *Holy Day* celebrations.

Firesides (informal discussion meetings), organised by Bahá'í individuals or families, are also often open to anyone who wishes to attend, although some may be by invitation only. The *Nineteen Day Feast* is for Bahá'ís only. However, visitors who are not Bahá'ís will not be asked to leave, but the consultative part of the Feast will be omitted and the Feast will be termed a *Unity Feast*.

There are no special clothing requirements, although it is appropriate to dress tidily and modestly. On entering a Bahá'í meeting, visitors may find a place wherever they feel comfortable.

Those wishing to attend a Bahá'í meeting should contact the host or the secretary of the *Local Assembly* or one of the *Cluster Co-Ordinators*, to make suitable arrangements.

BAHÁ'Í CALENDAR AND FESTIVALS

Calendar

Bahá'ís follow a solar calendar that was inaugurated by the *Báb* and consists of nineteen months each containing nineteen days. The Bahá'í era (denoted by the letters "BE") dates from the declaration of the *Báb* in 1844. Thus, 2006-7 CE is 162 BE.

The *Báb* named the months after what he considered to be God's attributes. For example, the first two months of the Bahá'í year as translated into English are called *Splendour* and *Glory*. Each day begins at sunset. *Nineteen-Day Feasts* are held on the first day of each Bahá'í month. The year is fixed and begins at the March equinox.

Festivals

The following are nine holy days on which Bahá'ís suspend work (dates are given according to their location in the Gregorian calendar):

Feast of Naw–Rúz (21st March)
This is the Bahá'í New Year and the first of the nine Bahá'í holy days. On this day the nineteen day fast of the month of 'Alá (see below) finishes. This is a particularly joyful time of celebration.

Feast of Ridván (21st April – 2nd May)
This is the most important day in the Bahá'í calendar, described by *Bahá'u'lláh* as *"the Lord of Feasts"*. It commemorates *Bahá'u'lláh's Declaration* of his mission. Celebrations take place and the feast commemorates the twelve days Bahá'u'lláh spent in the Ridván garden before leaving Baghdad and during which his *Declaration* took place. On the first day of Ridván the *Local Spiritual Assemblies* are elected in Bahá'í communities.

Ninth Day of Ridván (see above).

Twelfth Day of Ridván (see above).

Anniversary of the Declaration of the Báb (23rd May)
This date also coincides with the birthday of *Abdu'l-Bahá*, which is not commemorated. Celebrations take place relating to the *Báb's* revelation of his mission to his first disciple, Mulla Husayn, in 1844.

Anniversary of the Ascension of Bahá'u'lláh (29th May)
A day of solemn commemoration of *Bahá'u'lláh's* passing away, in 1892, at Bahji, near Akka.

Martyrdom of the Báb (9th July)
A day of solemn commemoration of the *Báb's* death by firing squad.

Anniversary of the Birth of the Báb (20th October)
The *Báb* was born in Shiraz, Persia, in 1819.

Anniversary of the Birth of Bahá'u'lláh (12th November)
Bahá'u'lláh was born in Tehran, Persia, in 1817.

Bahá'ís also mark the following days, but do not suspend work on them:

Day of the Covenant (26th November)
This day is dedicated to *'Abdu'l-Bahá*.

Ascension of Abdu'l-Bahá (28th November)
A day on which to mark the *Ascension* of *'Abdu'l-Bahá*.

Intercalary Days (Ayyam-i-Ha)
(26th February - 1st March)
These days, in preparation for *The Fast* (see below) are days of celebration, gift-giving, charity hospitality, and parties.

Period of the Fast (2nd - 21st March)
This is the Bahá'í month of 'Alá, in which Bahá'ís abstain from food and drink from sunrise to sunset. *The Fast* is not applicable to children under fifteen years or binding on adults over seventy, or for travellers or those who are too old or too weak (for example because of illness or giving birth). It is considered a time for reflection on spiritual progress and for detachment from material desires.

The Nineteen-Day Feast
The *Nineteen Day Feast*, which is rooted in a spirit of hospitality and conviviality, has three parts: devotional (recitation of prayers and readings), business (consultation on the affairs of the community) and a social time for fellowship and refreshment. Only Bahá'ís may attend the *Nineteen Day Feast*, but if a non-Bahá'í appears he or she is welcomed and the consultative part can be omitted.

BAHÁ'Í ORGANISATIONS

Organisational Listings

The CD-ROM accompanying this volume contains contact details for a range of Bahá'í organisations working at UK and for *Local Spiritual Assemblies*, all of which are affiliated to the *National Spiritual Assembly* in the UK.

In total, the CD-ROM has details of 4 Bahá'í organisations operating on a UK level, as well as on 3 Scottish, 1 Welsh and Northern Irish organisations. Also included are details of 114 *Local Spiritual Assemblies* (of which 96 are in England, 7 in Scotland, 3 in Wales, and 8 in Northern Ireland).

Local Spiritual Assemblies

The key Bahá'í organisations are administrative bodies called *Spiritual Assemblies*, which are to be found throughout the world at local and national levels, and whose members are elected by and from among the Bahá'ís in their areas of jurisdiction. Each *Spiritual Assembly*, whether local or national, has nine members and elects officers to help conduct its affairs. This pattern was laid down by *'Abdu'l-Bahá* and developed by *Shoghi Effendi* based on guidance in *Bahá'u'lláh's* writings.

Local Spiritual Assemblies have responsibility for deciding on all matters of common action on the part of the local community, such as arranging the *Nineteen Day Feast* and other kinds of meetings, engaging in projects of social and economic development, of humanitarian service, and in organising activities to promote the Bahá'í teachings. They undertake external affairs activities, often in partnership with local government and non-governmental organisations, in order to influence processes towards world peace.

A Bahá'í community must have a minimum of nine members aged twenty-one or older before it can form its *Local Spiritual Assembly*. Each year, on the first day of Ridván, nine people (including both men and women) are elected to serve on the *Local Assembly*. All Bahá'ís of twenty-one years or more who reside in the *Assembly's* area of jurisdiction have the right to vote and to serve on the *Assembly* if elected. There are no prior candidatures or nominations and canvassing is forbidden. Strict secrecy in the personal duty of election is understood to be Divinely ordained even amongst members of the same family

Local Groups

A Bahá'í *Local Group* is formed where there are not sufficient numbers to meet the criteria for forming a *Local Spiritual Assembly*.

Regional Level

In some countries, where the circumstances warrant this, there are bodies known as *Regional Bahá'í Councils*. These nine-member bodies have a considerable degree of autonomy and are elected annually by the members of the *Local Spiritual Assemblies* in the *Bahá'í Council's* area of jurisdiction.

There are four such bodies in the UK, one each in England, Northern Ireland, Scotland and Wales. They are responsible for planning regional-level activities, for developing the functional capacities of the *Local Spiritual Assemblies* in their region and for regional external affairs (other than the Bahá'í Council for England), especially in relation to the devolved governments, the Scottish Parliament and the Northern Ireland and Welsh Assemblies.

National Spiritual Assemblies

Each national Bahá'í community that has a significant numerical presence and a well established network of *Local Spiritual Assemblies* elects a *National Spiritual Assembly* as its national governing council. In the year 2006 there were 182 of these bodies worldwide. These bodies have authority over all the Bahá'í activities and agencies in their area of jurisdiction and play a central role in promoting the Bahá'í teachings, social and economic development, and external relations with government and other non-governmental organisations. Most have their own headquarters building known as the *HazÌratu'l-Quds* (the *Sacred Fold*).

The *National Spiritual Assembly* of the British Isles was first elected in 1923 and was one of the earliest to be established anywhere in the world. It became the National Spiritual Assembly of the Bahá'ís of the United Kingdom in 1972, when a separate *National Spiritual Assembly* was established in the Republic of Ireland.

The *National Assembly* appoints volunteer agencies and committees for specialist work and also employs a number of administrative and executive staff for its Secretariat and various Offices, such as those for External Affairs, the Advancement of Women, and Religious Education. Bahá'í Books UK sells Bahá'í literature. This agency was established in 1937, under its original name of the Bahá'í Publishing Trust.

International Level

The *Universal House of Justice*, based in Haifa, Israel, is the international governing council of the Bahá'ís. Ordained in *Bahá'u'lláh's* writings, the *House of Justice* was first elected in 1963 and published its formal constitution in 1972. It has authority over all other Bahá'í institutions.

The nine members of the *Universal House of Justice* are elected every five years by secret ballot and without candidature or canvassing from among all the adult male Bahá'ís in the world. The electors are the members of the *National Spiritual Assemblies* acting as delegates on behalf of their Bahá'í communities. This is the only Bahá'í institution whose membership is restricted to men.

The *Universal House of Justice* appoints the members of a parallel institution known as the *International Teaching Centre*. This body, whose members, men and women alike, are known as *International Counsellors*, monitors Bahá'í activity and progress throughout the world and advises the *Universal House of Justice*. It also oversees the working of *Continental Boards of Counsellors*, whose members are appointed by the *House of Justice* and which work closely with the *National Spiritual Assemblies* and with the *Regional Bahá'í Councils* in their respective continents, advising, guiding and sharing information between countries.

The *Continental Boards of Counsellors*, which came into existence in 1968, appoint members to *Auxiliary Boards*. The *Auxiliary Board* members work in an advisory and partially pastoral capacity with *Local Spiritual Assemblies* and individuals in sub-national territories; they also appoint assistants to help them with their work.

In 1948 the *Bahá'í International Community* was established as the international Bahá'í non-governmental organisation linked to the United Nations. All *National Spiritual Assemblies* are affiliated and it has offices in New York and Geneva.

It acts under the supervision of the *Universal House of Justice* to participate in international conferences on a wide range of issues, such as human rights, social development, economic development, and the status of women; it also advises *National Spiritual Assemblies* and provides training and support for national external affairs work.

The Bahá'í International Community gained consultative status with the United Nations Economic and Social Council in 1970 and with UNICEF in 1976. It undertakes projects in a number of countries in partnership with UN and government agencies as well as with other non-governmental organisations. In the year 2000 the Community's Principal Representative to the United Nations was one of the co-chairs of the Millennium NGO Forum that took place in New York in the run-up to the UN Millennium Summit of Heads of State and Government.

The Consultative Principle

All Bahá'í organisations work on the basis of the principle of consultation. This entails gathering information from a wide range of sources and perspectives; being frank but courteous about one's views; owning as the idea of the group an idea put forward by an individual; and striving for unanimity. However, if unanimity cannot be achieved then a majority vote may be taken although, in this case, all must be united behind the final decision of the majority.

Personnel

Bahá'ís have no priesthood or clergy, professional or volunteer. Contact with Bahá'í communities and organisations can be made at local level through the secretaries of the *Local Spiritual Assemblies* and at national level through the Secretary of the *National Spiritual Assembly*.

FURTHER READING

Details follow of a number of useful general introductions to the Bahá'í faith, together with books and articles that provide some focus on Bahá'ís and Bahá'í organisations the UK. The references are not comprehensive, but provide signposts to a range of relevant materials.

Bahá'í International Community, *The Bahá'ís: A Profile of the Bahá'í Faith and its Worldwide Community*, Bahá'í International Community, New York, 1992.

Bahá'í Publishing Trust, *Bahá'í Prayers*, Bahá'í Publishing Trust, London, 1975.

Bahá'í Publishing Trust, *Principles of Bahá'í Administration*, Bahá'í Publishing Trust, London, (4th edition), 1976.

Balyuzi, H, *Baha'u'llah: The King of Glory*, George Ronald, Oxford, 1963.

Balyuzi, H, *Abdu'l-Bahá*, George Ronald, Oxford, 1971.

Balyuzi, H, *The Báb*, George Ronald, Oxford, 1973.

Collins, W, *Bibliography of English-Language Works on the Bábi and Bahá'í Faiths, 1844-1985*, George Ronald, London, 1990.

Finch, T, "Unclipping the wings: a survey of secondary Bahá'í literature in English on Bahá'í perspectives on women", in *The Bahá'í Studies Review*, Volume 4, No 1, 1994, pp 9-26.

Gouvion, C and Jouvion, P, *The Gardeners of God An Encounter with Five Million Bahá'ís*, One World, Oxford, 1995.

Hainsworth, P, *Bahá'í Focus on Human Rights*, Bahá'í Publishing Trust, London, 1985.

Hainsworth, P, *Bahá'í Focus on Peace*, Bahá'í Publishing Trust, London, 1986.

Hatcher, W and Martin, J, *The Bahá'í Faith: The Emerging Global Religion*, Harper and Row, San Francisco, 1984.

Leith, B, "A More Constructive Encounter: A Bahá'í View of Religion and Human Rights", in N Ghanea, A Stephens and R Walden (eds), *Does God Believe in Human Rights?: Essays on Religion and Human Rights*, Martinus Nijhoff Publishers, Leiden, 2007, pp 121-144.

MacEoin, D, *Rituals in Babism and Baha'ism*, I B Tauris, London, 1995.

Momen, M, *A Short Introduction to the Bahá'í Faith*, Oneworld, Oxford, 1997.

Momen, M, *The Bábi and Bahá'í Religions, 1844-1944: Some Contemporary Western Accounts*, George Ronald, Oxford, 1981.

Momen, W and Momen, M, *Understanding the Bahá'í Faith*, Dunedin Academic Press, Edinburgh, 2005.

Smith, P, *The Bábi and Bahá'í Religions: From Messianic Shi'ism to a World Religion*, Cambridge University Press, 1987.

Smith, P, *A Short History of the Bahá'í Faith*, Oneworld, Oxford, 1996.

Smith, P, *A Concise Encylopaedia of the Bahá'í Faith*, Oneworld, Oxford, 2000.

Smith, P and Momen, M, "The Bahá'í Faith 1957-1988: a survey of contemporary developments", in *Religion*, Volume 19, 1989, pp 63-91.

Walbridge, J, *Sacred Arts, Sacred Space, Sacred Time*, George Ronald, Oxford, 1996.

INTRODUCING BUDDHISTS IN THE UK

BUDDHISTS IN THE UK 103

ORIGINS AND DEVELOPMENT OF BUDDHISM 104

SOURCES OF BUDDHIST BELIEFS AND PRACTICES 106

KEY BUDDHIST BELIEFS 108

TRADITIONS IN BUDDHISM 110

BUDDHIST LIFE 114

BUDDHIST WORSHIP 116

BUDDHIST PLACES OF WORSHIP 116

BUDDHIST CALENDAR AND FESTIVALS 118

BUDDHIST ORGANISATIONS 119

FURTHER READING 124

BUDDHISTS IN THE UK

History in the UK

A wide variety of Buddhist organisations, *viharas*, *monasteries*, temples, centres and more informal groups are to be found in the UK today. They reflect both the variety of ethnic groups and the different schools of Buddhism found among UK Buddhists.

The late nineteenth century saw the development of the western academic study of Buddhism. As scholars produced an increasing number of English translations of Buddhist texts, some people developed an interest in Buddhism as a philosophy, a way of life, and a religion. One of the foremost was Edwin Arnold, whose account of the life and teaching of the *Buddha*, the best-selling and often reprinted, *The Light of Asia*, was first published in 1879.

In 1881 T W Rhys founded the Pali Text Society which fostered this development. In 1899, Gordon Douglas, the first English person to be ordained as a Buddhist monk, took his vows in Colombo, Sri Lanka and became Bhikkhu Asoka. He did not, however, return to Britain. In 1898 another Englishman, Alan Bennett, went to study Buddhism in Sri Lanka. In 1901, whilst in Burma, he was ordained as a *monk*, taking the name Ananda Metteyya.

In 1907, a Buddhist Society of Great Britain and Ireland was formed to receive a Buddhist mission that eventually arrived in 1908, led by Ananda Metteyya. The Society did not, however, become firmly established and in 1924 Christmas Humphreys founded the Buddhist Centre of the Theosophical Society that incorporated its remnants. In 1926, this new foundation became the Buddhist Lodge of the Theosophical Society. In 1943, it was constituted as a new and independent organisation, known as The Buddhist Society. Christmas Humphreys remained its President until his death in 1983.

In 1926, Humphreys had welcomed the Sinhalese Anagarika Dharmapala, who had previously visited Britain in 1893, 1896, and again in 1904 on a mission. Subsequently, a branch of the Maha Bodhi Society was founded in London, followed, in 1928, by the first *monastery* for Sinhalese *monks*.

Until the 1960s Western engagement with Buddhism was often of an individual, and sometimes rather theoretical, kind. In recent times, however, increasing numbers of Westerners have begun to practise Buddhist meditation and apply Buddhist ethical norms, seeing them as vehicles for bringing about change in their lives and ultimate awakening.

Throughout the twentieth century, individuals and small groups of migrants with Buddhist beliefs also arrived from Sri Lanka, Thailand and Burma. Indian (mostly *Ambedkarite* - see below) Buddhists and the Hong Kong Chinese came mainly with the New Commonwealth migrations of the 1950s and 1960s. The number of Buddhists in the UK has been further expanded by refugees, including those following the *Dalai Lama's* 1959 flight from Tibet; then by Vietnamese Buddhist refugees, who arrived in the late 1960s and early 1970s; and more recently by refugees from the Sri Lankan civil war.

Global and UK Populations

Worldwide, there are an estimated 359,982,000 Buddhists. In the UK, the 2001 decennial Census questions on religion yielded 151,816 (or 0.3% of the total UK population) Buddhist respondents. This is also 0.3% of the population that identifies itself with any specific religion at all. Of these 151,816, a total of 139,046 were in England, 5,407 in Wales, 6,830 in Scotland, and 533 in Northern Ireland.

As a proportion of the population in local authority areas, the 2001 Census shows that in England the greatest proportion of respondents identifying themselves as Buddhist was found in the London Boroughs of Westminster (1.3%), Camden (1.3%), Kensington and Chelsea (1.1%) and Hackney (1.1%); and in the Ribble Valley (1.1%).

Ethnicity in England and Wales

According to the 2001 Census, 47.3% of the Buddhist population of England and Wales gave their ethnicity as "Chinese or Other Ethnic Group", 38.8% as "White", 9.6% as "Asian", 3.2% as "Mixed", and 1.0% as "Black or Black British". Considered in terms of the ethnicity of respondents, 15.3% of all those recorded as "Chinese or other Ethnic Group" also identified as Buddhist, along with 0.7% of "Mixed" respondents, 0.6% of "Asian", 0.1% of "Black or Black British", and 0.1% of those recorded as "White".

Buddhists in the UK are of very diverse ethnic and national origins. However, while many languages are in use among Buddhists, most Buddhist teaching in the UK is conducted in English. The Buddhist scriptures are preserved in *Pali* (in the case of the *Southern Canon*, which forms the basis of the *Theravada* tradition - see section on "Buddhist Traditions" below) and Chinese, Japanese, Sanskrit and Tibetan (in the case of the *Mahayana* scriptures - see section on "Buddhist Traditions" below).

ORIGINS AND DEVELOPMENT OF BUDDHISM

Gautama Buddha/Gotama Buddha

Buddhism does not teach belief in a personal deity. It makes no claims to possess a divinely revealed book and it also has no central organisational authority. The teachings of Buddhism are the inheritance of Siddhartha Gautama/Siddhattha Gotama's search for truth (here, and in the text that follows, after being introduced in both their Sanskrit and Pali forms, only the Sanskrit form of key words and titles is used in the main body of the text, except in relation to the term *sangha*, where only this form is used).

According to Buddhist tradition, Siddhartha Gautama (Gautama being the family name and Siddhartha the personal name, while Shakya, as in his title *Shakyamuni*, was the clan name) was born in Lumbini. This was early in the fifth century BCE (traditional, although not uncontested, estimates suggest around 563BCE), in what is today Nepal. He then grew up nearby in Kapilavatthu.

There is no canonical life of the *Buddha*. The earliest, surviving continuous narratives date from the third century CE onwards. They draw upon biographical fragments that introduced the discourses of the *Buddha* which were preserved initially by oral transmission, though may also have made use of other materials now no longer available.

Traditionally, it is said that Siddhartha Gautama's father was the ruler of Kapilavastu and that, on his birth, it was prophesied that Siddhartha would either become a great king or someone who renounced the world in search of *Enlightenment*. In order to try to ensure the former, it is said that his father surrounded the young prince with a life of luxury.

However, this had an effect opposite to that intended by his father because, when he got his charioteer to take him to see life in the city, what he encountered made a dramatic impact on his life. On the first occasion he encountered an old man; on the second, a diseased man; on the third, a dead man; and, finally, he encountered a *mendicant* (a man who had renounced the world).

These experiences awakened in him a wish to understand and alleviate suffering. So, at the age of twenty-nine, he began a spiritual search which lasted for six years until it reached its culmination in his *Enlightenment* under a pipal tree (now known as the *Bodhi Tree*), at the place in North India now called as Bodh Gaya.

During Gautama's period of searching, he studied with two important teachers of his time, but he was still dissatisfied and decided to continue alone. Adopting contemporary ascetic practices, he underwent extremes of self-denial and self-mortification. Since these, too, did not answer his purposes, he finally decided on a less extreme approach and ate some food to regain his strength.

At this point five *ascetics* who had previously joined up with him left him in disapproval. He then sat down under the *Bodhi Tree* in a determined attempt to break through to that which he was seeking. It is said that on the night of the full moon in May he finally attained the state of *nirvana/nibbana* (see section on "Key Buddhist Beliefs" below). He then sought out the five *ascetics* who had previously been with him and convinced them of the validity of his *Enlightenment*. With them as his first followers, the *sangha* (the Buddhist monastic community) was initiated, in the Deer Park near Varanasi.

Traditionally, it is thought that it was around 483BCE, and on his eightieth birthday, that he passed away at Kushinagara and entered into what Buddhists describe as his *parinirvana/parinibbana* (final entry to *nirvana*). The last words attributed to him were "Work out your own salvation with diligence", which underlines the insistence of Buddhism on the personal responsibility of each individual for what they do, say and believe.

Transmission

The form of the Buddhism that spread south is known as the *Theravada* (see below) tradition. It was brought to Sri Lanka in 250BCE and, early in the second millennium CE, spread to those countries now known as Thailand, Cambodia, Laos and Myanmar, as well as to the southern part of Vietnam.

Between the first and seventh centuries of the Common Era Buddhism spread slowly north-eastwards into Central Asia and into what is now China, Korea, Japan, the northern part of Vietnam and (from the seventh and eighth centuries) northwards into Nepal, Tibet, Mongolia and adjacent parts of what is now Siberia.

Islam has now replaced Buddhism in Afghanistan, Kashmir and much of Central Asia where it was once strongly represented. In Indonesia, however, there is a strong native Indonesian Buddhist influence. Significant Buddhist communities can also be found in Singapore and Malaysia, largely among people of Chinese ethnic origins.

The forms of Buddhism traditionally associated with these countries are therefore often known as the *Northern Transmission*, or the *Mahayana* (see below) tradition. In India itself, after the first millennium CE Buddhism almost died out (apart from in what is now Bangladesh) until its revival in the twentieth century.

Initially this revival was through the activities of Anagarika Dhammapala's Maha Bodhi Society and then, following Indian independence, through the attraction of the *Ambedkarite* (named after the Indian social reformer Dr Ambedkar) movement for the Indian *scheduled castes* and tribal peoples, once popularly referred to as *untouchables* and now more often known by their self-chosen name of *dalits*.

SOURCES OF BUDDHIST BELIEFS AND PRACTICES

The Buddha

The historical *Buddha* is revered as the uncoverer of the *dharma/dhamma* (teachings) that exist independently of him. He himself claimed only to have rediscovered "an ancient way leading to an ancient city". Therefore, the emphasis is upon the *dharma* and upon the *Buddha* as exemplar of the teaching. Strictly speaking, therefore, Gautama is not viewed as a religious founder, but as the teacher and as the latest in a succession of revealers of the *dharma*.

Buddhists are those who claim to have found these teachings to be valid for themselves. In the early stages of Buddhist training one can learn the details of the teachings, but in the end every individual must discover truth in their own experience and not simply as what they have been taught.

The Three Refuges

Buddhists speak of "going for refuge" or "taking refuge" in the *triratna/tiratana* (*Three Jewels*). This is an affirmation of their commitment as Buddhists and to the sources of Buddhist life: "I take refuge in the *Buddha*; I take refuge in the *dharma* (the *Buddha's* teachings); I take refuge in the *sangha* (the *Buddha's* community)."

Buddha

Siddhartha Gautama was acknowledged by his followers to be a *Buddha* or *Awakened* or *Enlightened* one (from *bodhi* meaning to awaken). In the *Mahayana* Buddhist tradition, Siddhartha Gautama is generally known as *Shakyamuni/Sakyamuni* (the sage of the Shakya/Sakya clan) in order to distinguish him from the pantheons of *celestial Buddhas*. In the *Theravada* tradition references to the *Buddha* are usually to the historical figure of Gautama, who is the one who initiated the transmission of the teaching in the current era.

Both the *Mahayana* and *Theravada* traditions also assume the existence of numerous *Buddhas* before and after him. The *Mahayana* also believe in multiple worlds, in which innumerable *Buddhas* can simultaneously appear. Going to the *Buddha* for refuge not only means accepting the *Buddha* as the ultimate spiritual guide and example for one's life, but also appreciating one's own potential for *enlightenment*, which some *Mahayanists* call one's *Buddha-nature*. Many Buddhist homes and temples contain *rupas* (statues) or pictures of the *Buddha* as reminders of the teaching and as aids to devotion and meditation.

Dharma

Dharma has several meanings according to context. It refers to "the way things are in reality" and also to the Buddhist teaching about this. This is expressed in the so-called *Four Noble Truths* (see section below on "Key Buddhist Beliefs"). Going for refuge to the *dharma* is understood to involve focusing one's energies to understand, practise and realise in one's own life what has been taught by the *Buddha*, thus bringing about understanding of the mutual dependence of all living beings and expressing goodwill towards them.

Sangha

Historically, for many Buddhists, *sangha* has been understood as the community of celibate Buddhist *monks* and *nuns*, although it has also been seen as including lay practitioners who adhered to the *Five Precepts* (see below) and who were known as *upasaka* (males) and *upasika* (females).

Some *Tibetan* schools have married *lamas* and married *priests* officiate in temples of the *Pure Land* (see below) tradition in *Japanese* lineage. In the UK, there are lay orders such as the Western Buddhist Order, founded in 1968 and the Amida Order, founded in 1998. The Order of Buddhist Contemplatives, founded in 1978, has lay ministers as well as male and female *monastics*.

Among other Buddhists in the *Mahayana* tradition, and particularly in some parts of western Buddhism, the term *sangha* is understood primarily as the totality of followers of the *Buddha* who have formally taken refuge. However, for some Buddhists, the meaning of the *sangha* can be taken to embrace all who possess the *Buddha-nature*, in other words all sentient beings.

The Pali Canon

Several *canons* of scripture help explain the *dharma*. Most were eventually committed to writing from an original oral transmission. The Pali language *canon* (sometimes called *The Southern Transmission*) contains some of the oldest material that is ascribed to the *Buddha* and his disciples.

This *canon* is also known as the *Tipitaka*, meaning the *Three Baskets*, perhaps because its palm leaf manuscripts were originally kept in three different containers or baskets – the *Vinaya-pitaka* (*Basket of [Monastic] Discipline*); the *Sutta-pitaka* (*Basket of Discourses*); and the *Abhidhamma-pitaka* (*Basket of Further Teachings*).

These are probably the common heritage of early Buddhism and are the only scriptures accepted by the *Theravada* school as being *canonical*. They are, in general, acceptable to all Buddhist schools, though the *canon* is not much known in large parts of the *Mahayana* traditions, which also reject the *Abhidhamma* as inauthentic.

The Mahayana Canon

The *Mahayana canon* is extensive. Its wide variety of texts include many that were originally written down in Sanskrit or other Indian languages and then translated into Tibetan and Chinese, plus some which were originally written in these languages. Some texts, known in the Far East as the *Agama*, are held in common with the *Pali canon*. The term *sutra/sutta* is used of the texts and refers to the idea of a single "thread" running through the discourse.

Among the more widely known *Mahayana sutras* are the *Saddharma-pundarika* (*Lotus of the True Dharma*), the vast collection of the *Prajna-paramita sutras* (*Perfection of Wisdom*), the long *Mahayana Parinirvana Sutra*, and the compilation known as the *Avatamsaka Sutra* (*Flower Ornament*).

These *sutras* were enormously important in the development of East Asian Buddhism and were gathered into canonical collections of writings. The *Chinese canon* is known as the *Ta-ts'ang-ching* (*Great Scripture Store*) and its standard modern edition consists of fifty-five volumes with forty-five supplementary volumes. In Japan, this standard compilation is known as *Taizokyo*. The equally vast *Tibetan canon* consists of the *bKa'gyur* (pronounced "Kangjur" and meaning "*The Translated Words of the Buddha*") which is ninety-eight volumes in length, and the *bsTan'gyur* (pronounced "Tengjur" and meaning "*The Translated Treatises*"). This, in its Beijing edition, is in two hundred and twenty-four volumes and it can also be found in Japan in its original wood-block print copies.

Jataka Stories

Within the *Sutta-pitaka* of the *Pali canon*, is a collection of over five hundred *Jataka* stories which are said to have been told to his followers by the *Buddha*, and are about his former lives. Among them can be found the earliest collection of animal fables in the world. They form the basis of much popular teaching and reflection in both *Theravada* and *Mahayana* traditions and are often used in teaching children.

KEY BUDDHIST BELIEFS

Four Noble Truths

The *Catur Aryasatya/Cattari Ariyasaccani* (Four Noble Truths) are at the heart of Buddhism. The four truths concern: *duhkha/dukkha* (suffering or unsatisfactoriness), *samudaya* (the origin of suffering or unsatisfactoriness), *nirodha* (the cessation of suffering or unsatisfactoriness) and *marga/magga* (the way leading to the cessation of suffering or unsatisfactoriness).

Duhkha (Suffering or Unsatisfactoriness)

The literal meaning of *duhkha* is "suffering". However, the *Buddha* extended its meaning to cover other uncomfortable mental states and in subjective terms it might be better understood as "unsatisfactoriness".

In his first teaching, the *Buddha* said: "Birth is *duhkha*, ageing is *duhkha*, sickness is *duhkha*, death is *duhkha*; sorrow, lamentation, pain, grief and despair are *duhkha*; association with

what one dislikes is *duhkha*; separation from what one likes is *duhkha*; not to get what one wants is *duhkha*." Elsewhere, the *Buddha* comments that, as well as the physical and mental suffering arising from these, there are more subtle states of unease occasioned by our reactions to change and challenge to what constitutes our ego.

Duhkha is one of the *Three Signs of Being* or characteristics of existence, the other two are *anitya/anicca* (impermanence), and *anatman/anatta* (not-self). One cannot expect to find permanent happiness from impermanent causes. Investigation and reflection reveal that all conditioned phenomena and our experience of them are impermanent and are for ever "coming to be and ceasing to be". Change is a constant characteristic of all things.

Anatman is the teaching that there is ultimately no permanent or immortal self. An "everyday self" is recognised but it is understood to be a composite of the five *skandhas/khandhas* (aggregates) that are themselves forever in flux. They are: *rupa* (material form), *vedana* (feelings), *samjna/sañña* (perceptions and discriminations), *samskaras/sankharas* (volitions), and *vijnana/viññana* (consciousness).

Samudaya (Origin of Suffering or Unsatisfactoriness)

The origin of *duhkha* is seen by Buddhists to lie in *trishna/tanha*. Literally used, the word means "thirsting" or "craving". This craving, of its very nature, can never be satisfied and goes on reproducing itself. It manifests itself as greed and desire for, and attachment to, material things and mental objects. It also includes a thirst for continued existence and an opposite desire for non-existence.

Such craving or thirst results in *duhkha* and in behaviour that will lead to *rebirth*. This *rebirth* is not understood as the transmigration of a soul or reincarnation, which would be inconsistent with the teaching of *anatman*. Rather, the habits that are reinforced by craving bring about a "rebecoming" rather than transmission of a discrete soul.

Nirvana (Cessation of duhkha)

The transcendence of *trishna* (craving) leads to the cessation of *duhkha* and is known as *nirvana*. The full meaning of *nirvana* cannot adequately be described. In literal terms it means the "quenching" or "extinction" of the thirst and craving that results in *duhkha*.

It does not therefore mean, as it has often been misunderstood to mean, a state of annihilation. Rather, the "quenching" and "extinction" to which it refers is that of the fires of the greed, hatred, ignorance and craving which cause *duhkha*. It is seen as deliverance from *samsara* (see below), which is the world in which *duhkha* holds sway. Buddhists affirm that this deliverance can be realised in this life, as in the case of Gautama *Buddha* himself.

Marga (The Way)

The first three *Noble Truths* analyse the human condition and affirm the possibility of transcending *duhkha*. The fourth, more fully known as the *Arya Ashtanga Marga/Ariya Atthangika Magga* (The Noble Eightfold Path – see section below on "Buddhist Life"), is a way of training, the diligent practice of which leads one out of *samsara*. This path is often known as the *Middle Way*, the course between and beyond the excesses of self-indulgence and self-denial.

Paticca Samuppada/Pratitya Samutpada (Dependent Origination)

Dependent origination is a sequence or consequence according to which all phenomena arise in dependence upon their interrelated causes. In relation to sentient beings, it explains the rebirth process and is often seen in terms of a chain with twelve links, each link/cause depending upon the previous one and leading to the next.

Karma and Vipaka

Karma/Kamma (literally meaning "deed") is understood in Buddhism as a law of consequences inherent in the nature of things. Technically, *karma* is the deed and *vipaka* the consequence, but popularly *karma* refers to both deeds and consequences. All deliberate actions have their consequences and whether a particular action has useful or negative *karmic/kammic* effects depends predominantly upon the intention.

Samsara

Samsara (the cycle or wheel of birth and death) is not the *reincarnation* or *transmigration* of a soul since, as has been noted, Buddhism does not posit the continuing existence of such a substantial or permanent selfhood. This is because the individual is understood to be a cluster of various aggregates held together by desire. Buddhists therefore usually speak of a *"rebirth"* or *"rebecoming"* of these aggregates rather than of the *transmigration* of an entity.

This *rebirth* is possible on a number of levels (not just the human) and throughout aeons. In the popular Tibetan diagram, the "wheel" of birth and death is divided into six realms or states illustrative of these possibilities. Depending on the *karma* accumulated in one lifetime, the *rebirth* or *rebecoming* will be of different kinds. The principal concern is ultimately not to gain a better future *rebirth*, but to escape altogether from this wheel of rebirth and death and to attain *nirvana*.

Being born as a human being is viewed as a precious opportunity since it is believed that deliverance can best be achieved from the human state. In *Mahayana* Buddhism, having escaped from the wheel of birth and death, the *enlightened* being may compassionately return to the world, without being *karmically* bound to it, in order to assist others to awaken.

Shunyata/Suññata

Shunyata (Voidness or Emptiness) is a concept of ultimate reality that is of great importance in the *Mahayana* tradition, where the idea of *anatman* or no-self has undergone further development. All that exists is seen as being devoid of any abiding essence, and "empty" of any ultimate characteristics. To understand this is to recognise the ultimately fluid and inter-connected nature of all phenomena. It is to understand the true nature of *samsara*. The deep realisation of *shunyata* is believed to end the fear and the craving which is seen as keeping beings bound to the wheel of rebirth.

Bodhi

Bodhi literally means "awakening" and refers to *Enlightenment*. This is the state of *Buddhahood* or spiritual perfection that is the goal of the Buddhist spiritual life. It comes about with the perfection and bringing into balance of *prajna/pañña* (wisdom) and *karuna* (compassion). It brings a complete seeing into the ultimate nature of existence and a spontaneously self-less and compassionate response to all beings and situations.

TRADITIONS IN BUDDHISM

Main Branches

The central teachings are common to all the traditions and schools, but they contain differences in emphasis, as well as some differences in practice. The principal traditions are the *Theravada* (*Way of the Elders*) or the *Southern Transmission*, also sometimes referred to as *Pali Buddhism*, and found principally in South-East Asia, and the *Mahayana* (often translated as the *Great Vehicle* - from *maha* meaning "great" and *yana* meaning "vehicle") or *Northern Transmission*, with its two main branches of *Far Eastern* and *Tibetan* Buddhism.

In the sections that follow, more space is devoted to *Mahayana* Buddhism than to the *Theravada*. This not to be understood as in any way reflecting an evaluation of their relative importance. Rather, it is out of recognition that the *Mahayana* contains much more diversity and will be encountered in these various forms that need some explanation in relation to their difference, while the *Theravada* has much that is held in common among all Buddhists.

Within *Tibetan* Buddhism, there is a tendency to refer to three "vehicles" or transmissions, namely, the *Theravada*, the *Bodhisattvayana* and the *Vajrayana*. In some books on Buddhism the *Theravada* is occasionally referred to as the *Hinayana* (*Lesser Vehicle*). However, the origins of the term *Hinayana* are to be found in an unfavourable contrast with the *Mahayana* (Great Vehicle).

Another designation sometimes found for *Theravada* is *Shravakayana* (*Vehicle of the Disciples*). More properly, *Theravada* relates to the body of teaching introduced to Sri Lanka in the third century BCE.

What is now called the *Mahayana* appeared around the beginning of the Common Era. Fundamentally the *Theravada* accepts the validity of the *Mahayana* and vica versa. The *Vajrayana* (or "*Diamond Vehicle*"), often involving *tantric* practices that can be secret, is to be understood as "skilful means" to achieve the goals of the *Mahayana*.

Within each of the major traditions there are also many different schools that emphasise particular beliefs and practices. In the West there are, also, newer developments that do not fully identify with any one traditional branch of Buddhism. Some of these are working to evolve new western styles of Buddhism. For example, the development of a Network of Engaged Buddhists, concerned with practical action to relieve suffering and distress, has led some to talk of a "Fourth *Yana*".

Although this can also be seen as a contemporary extension of the *Bodhisattva* ideal (to embrace compassionate action as well as leading beings to *Enlightenment*), Buddhists of all traditions are increasingly engaged in such activity. The practice of engaged compassion may therefore develop as an inclusive vehicle of the Buddhist path.

Theravada

The ideal of the *Theravada* tradition is that of the *arahat*, a perfected individual who has found release from the cycle of birth and death as a *sravaka*, following the teaching of the *Buddha*. Its hallmarks are renunciation, self-reliance and a focus upon the historical *Buddha*.

This tradition is based upon the *Pali canon* and is today mainly represented in the Buddhism of the South-East Asian countries of Sri Lanka, Myanmar, Laos, Kampuchea and Thailand (and the monasteries in other countries that are dependent upon these for teaching) as well as pockets in other countries of the region.

It is therefore sometimes known by the name of *Southern Transmission*. Variations within the *Theravada* tradition reflect the different cultural contexts in which the tradition has taken shape rather than the existence of distinctive schools as such. Within these countries, however, there are also monastic groupings (*nikaya*) that are based on different interpretations of their codes of discipline.

Mahayana

In addition to the concept of *shunyata* and a belief in many simultaneously present *Buddhas*, the particular characteristics of the *Mahayana* tradition include an emphasis on the ideal of the *Bodhisattva* (literally meaning "*Enlightenment being*"). A *Bodhisattva* among humans is one who vows to practise the Buddhist path totally in order to help and liberate all beings as well as themselves.

There are also cosmic *Boddhisattvas* who are seen as embodying various facets of *Enlightenment*. These include Avalokiteshvara (the Tibetan Chenrezig, the Chinese Kuan Yin and the Japanese Kanzeon), as well as Manjushri (the Tibetan Jampelyang, Chinese Wenshu and Japanese Monju).

Bodhisattva-Mahasattvas are fully perfected *Bodhisattvas*, greater than any other being except *Buddhas*. They live permanently in the realm of "transcendence" and from this position strive constantly for the welfare of others. The *Theravada* also accepts the taking of the *Bodhisattva* or *Bodhisatta* (Pali) vow as one method of training, albeit primarily seen in the *Jataka* stories about Siddhatha's previous lives.

Mahayana is a generic name for a wide movement embracing many different groups in the northern countries of China, Japan, Vietnam, Korea, Mongolia and Tibet. It is sometimes known as the *Northern Transmission* because it was first transmitted via the Northern Silk Road.

All have in common the same basic principles, but each grouping has developed in a different cultural setting or is often associated with one or more of the great *sutras* and has thus evolved variations in practice.

Due to repeated persecutions most of these groups became extinct in China by the fifteenth century, but many were introduced to Korea and Japan and some are still extant there as the *Tendai*, *Pure Land*, *Shingon* and *Zen* schools, with one temple of the *Kegon* school. In China itself, an amalgamation of the groups took place within the broader *Ch'an* tradition (see below) and this process was broadly replicated in Vietnam and Korea.

Tibetan Buddhism

Buddhism was established in Tibet during the reign of Trisong Detsen (755-797CE) through the activities of the Indian sages Shantarakshita and Songsten Gampo (618-650CE) and then Padmasambhava (meaning "*Lotus-Born*"). Distinctively, the *Tibetan* traditions use *tantric* rituals and *visualisation* to accelerate inward transformation. The goal of "diamond-like" clarity and indestructible unity of wisdom and compassion, gives it the name *Vajrayana* (or "Diamond Vehicle'). *Tantric* practices are regarded as very powerful. Certain advanced practices (such as those known as "protection practices") are regarded as spiritually/psychologically dangerous in the wrong hands.

Some claim that the *Vajrayana* reaches back to esoteric practices taught by *Shakyamuni Buddha*, which were passed down from teacher to teacher. *Tibetan* Schools are very conscious of their *lineages*, which are recited in rituals and displayed in lineage trees, linking present-day teachers to the "founders" of the particular school. The relation of the *guru* and the *lama* to the disciple is a very important one.

Shakyamuni himself is no longer accessible, but the *Mahayana* tradition offers access to "transcendent support", notably from *Maha-Bodhisattvas*, such as Avalokiteshvara and Dolma (or Tara), the *Bodhisattva* embodying aspects of compassion and Jamelyang or Manjushri, the *Bodhisattva* embodying aspects of wisdom. These have postponed *nirvana* and vowed to work for the *Enlightenment* of all beings (practising *bodhicitta*).

There are four main schools of *Tibetan* Buddhism. The *Nyingma* (*Old School*) originated in Tibet with the arrival of successive Indian sages, including Padmasambhava (Guru Rinpoche), but it traces its lineage back to an emanation of the *Primordial Buddha*.

The famous so-called *Bardo Thodol* (more popularly known as the *Tibetan Book of the Dead*) originated in this school as a hidden teaching (or *terma*) of Guru Rinpoche. It describes how to control the journey from death to *rebirth* through the various *bardo* states. This process is visualised during a *Bardo Retreat* lasting forty-nine days in total darkness and isolation.

The *Kagyu* ("Teaching Lineage") traces its origins to the Indian sage, Tilopa (988-1069CE), said to have received teachings from *Vajradhara*, an emanation of the *Buddha's*

"*Enjoyment Body*". Emphasis is placed on direct experience as, for example, in the *mahamudra* solitary retreat of three years and three months.

The lineage continues via Naropa to Marpa, the first Tibetan master, and thence to Milarepa and Gampopa, from which the main sub-schools derive, e.g. the *Karma Kagyu*, headed by the first *Karmapa*. While recognised by the Chinese authorities (though, it should be noted, not by some *Tibetan* Buddhists, see below), His Holiness the seventeenth *Gyalwa Karmapa*, Ogyen Trinley Dorje, fled Tibet in the year 2000 and was given refugee status in India in the following year.

The *Sakya* lineage begins with the Indian master, Virupa (1034-1102CE), and owes its name ("Grey Earth") to the site of the monastery built by Gonchok Gyalpo (in 1073CE). The most recent school, the *Gelug* (*System of Virtue*), was created by Je Tsong Khapa Losang Drakpa (1357-1419CE). He built the Ganden monastery in 1410CE, and reformed the *Kadampa* tradition, founded by the Indian master, Atisha (982-1054CE).

The different schools have sometimes had turbulent relationships in Tibetan history, though leading figures have practised under masters from different schools. The nineteenth century saw the rise of an eclectic non-sectarian movement (*Rimé*) associated with Jamgon Kongtrul (1811-1899CE). There are also mixed lineage groups appearing in the West, such as the Dechen Community (*Sakya, Karma Kagyu*) and the Longchen Foundation (*Kagyu, Nyingma*).

Tibetan Buddhism has evolved a unique institutional interpretation of *reincarnation*, whereby high *lamas* may decide to be "reborn" to continue their work. The first person to be recognised as a reincarnate lama (or *tulku*) was Karma Pakshi (1204-1283CE), the second *Karmapa*. The discovery, recognition and education of reincarnate *lamas* (or *tulkus*) allows a celibate lineage to preserve continuity.

However, because recognition of a *tulku* is connected with power and authority, their recognition has sometimes been connected with controversy. Thus, within the *Kagyu* school, some *lamas* claim that the seventeenth *Karmapa* is Thinle Thaye Dorje and that His Holiness the *Dalai Lama* had no right to recognise Ogyen Trinley Dorje in this role.

The most well-known of the reincarnate *lamas* is Tenzin Gyatso, His Holiness the Fourteenth *Dalai Lama* (meaning "Ocean of Wisdom", a title bestowed on his sixteenth century predecessor by the Mongol Emperor Altan Khan). The Fifth *Dalai Lama* used inherited alliances in order to consolidate his power, and that of the *Gelug* school, over the whole of Tibet by 1640, thus establishing the *Dalai Lamas* as both religious and political leaders.

The second highest *lama* in the school is the *Panchen Lama*, whose recent *reincarnation* is a matter of dispute between the *Dalai Lama* and the Chinese authorities. This has long-term implications for *Tibetan* Buddhist religious structures, since it is the *Panchen Lama* who should oversee the discovery of the next *Dalai Lama*.

Recently, a controversy has also developed in relation to a practice involving the propitiation of Dorje Shugden. In popular culture, Shugden is seen as a "worldly deity", bringing good luck and success in enterprise. Those in the *New Kadampa Tradition* (NKT) believe that they experience Shudgen as a supra-mundane deity, able to strengthen their inner resolve to keep the *dharma*.

The controversy developed when the *Dalai Lama* declared that Shugden was an "evil force", harmful both to himself and to the cause of the Tibetan people. He noted that the origins of the propitiation of Dorje Shugden lay in a conflict with the Fifth *Dalai Lama*, and he saw it as being associated with "sectarianism". Members of the NKT took part in highly-publicised demonstrations against the *Dalai Lama*. This campaign has now finished, but tensions from this complex controversy continue to be present.

Ch'an, Zen, Thien and Son Buddhism

Ch'an is an abbreviated form of the Chinese word *Ch'an-na*, which is derived from the Sanskrit term *dhyana* that refers to the state of mind during meditation in which the distinctions between subject and object are transcended. *Zen* is a shortened form of *zenna*, which derives from a Japanese pronounciation of the word *Ch'an-na*. *Son* is the Korean equivalent, and the *Thien* the Vietnamese.

Although meditation is important in all Buddhist schools, *Zen* stresses the practice of *zazen* (sitting meditation) in developing awareness. Zen affirms that direct insight into true reality is possible through this practice, hence the Japanese name of *satori* or *kensho*, meaning "seeing into one's true nature".

In the sixth century BCE, the Indian monk Bodhidharma introduced his iconoclastic emphasis on the simple practice of meditation. What was to become *Soto Zen* was introduced into Japan in the thirteenth century century by Dogen Rishi (1200-1253CE).

The *Rinzai Zen* lineage found its way to Japan in the twelfth century CE through the monk Eisai (1141-1215CE). *Soto Zen* emphasises *Shikantaza* (or "just sitting"), which is sometimes known as *Serene Reflection Meditation*. In the *Rinzai* tradition, *zazen* is combined with the use of *koan*. These are questions employed by a *Zen Master* designed to engender and test genuine insight and are used, through the shock of facilitating sudden insight, to prise one free from illusions.

Pure Land Buddhism

Pure Land Buddhists are devoted to Amitabha, a cosmic *Buddha* who vowed to bring those reborn in his *Pure Land* to liberation. In *Japanese* Buddhism (where

Amitabha is known as Amida) the school has two main branches - the *Jodo Shu* (*Pure Land* school) and the *Jodo Shinshu* (*True Pure Land* school, often simply known as *Shin*).

Both schools are products of an emphasis in Buddhist teaching on adaptation of the *dharma* to the world in forms that are most suitable for ordinary people. They therefore offer a path which they can follow in difficult times, teaching dependence upon the infinite merit of *Amida Buddha*.

The difference between the *Jodo Shu* and the *Jodo Shinshu* is that the latter emphasises the complete abandonment of all *jiriki* (self-effort) and strong faith in the efficacy of Amitibha's vow to save all those who call on his name. As a central part of their practice, Pure Land schools recite the *Nembutsu*, which is an invocation of the *mantra Namu-Amida-butsu* (Hail to Amida *Buddha*), as well as its equivalents in *Chinese Buddhism* and *Vietnamese Buddhism*. This is believed to bring about a strong connection with Amida that enables rebirth in the *Pure Land*.

Nichiren Buddhism

The *Nichiren* traditions (see section on "Some Other Japanese Groups", below) draw upon the teachings of the Japanese teacher Nichiren (1222-1282CE), who saw the *Lotus Sutra* as the highest form of Buddhist teaching, the essence of which could be found in its title. Nichiren taught that recitation of the *sutra's* name was all that was necessary for liberation.

Recitation of the *mantra* having the name of the *sutra, Namu myoho renge-kyo* (Veneration to the Lotus of the Good Law), was therefore introduced as a key practice within this tradition. Some schools of the tradition have been closely connected with peace activities.

BUDDHIST LIFE

The Five Precepts

The *Five Precepts* (or *Panca Silani*) are the basic rules of living for lay Buddhists. They express the intention to refrain from: harming living beings; taking what is not given; sexual misconduct; harmful speech; and the recreational use of drink or drugs which cloud the mind. For the lay Buddhist this is the basis of *samyakkarmanta/samma kammanta* (Right Action), which is one factor in the *Noble Eightfold Path*. Buddhists who are *ordained* take additional vows (see section below on "Buddhist Organisations").

Noble Eightfold Path

In Buddhist teaching the *Noble Eightfold Path* (*Arya Astangika Marga*) is the fourth of the *Four Noble Truths* and is the way to overcome *duhkha*. The eight factors of the Path are traditionally grouped into three. The first two factors are concerned with wisdom, the next three with morality, and the final three with forms of mental discipline. All aspects of the *Eightfold Path* are, however, interdependent.

Right Understanding or Right View

Samyagdrishti/samma ditthi (meaning right understanding or right view) means correct understanding of the teachings of the *Buddha*, and especially of the *Four Noble Truths*. This includes realisation that actions have consequences now and in the future (the law of *karma*) and that rites and rituals alone have no efficacy.

Right Intention

Samyaksamkalpa/samma sankappa (right intention) is the changed motivation that develops with corrected vision. It is expressed in behaviour that is informed by *ahimsa* (or harmlessness), *karuna* (compassion), and *nekhamma* (renunciation of self-interested action).

Right Speech

Samyagvac/samma vaca (right speech) emerges from right understanding and intention and causes no injury to oneself or others and thus avoids lying, abuse, slander and gossip.

Right Action

Samyakkarmanta/samma kammanta (right action) consists of refraining from what is harmful and involves, among other things, cultivating the *Five Precepts* and practising what is beneficial for oneself and others.

Right Livelihood

Samyagajiva/samma ajiva (right livelihood) includes right daily conduct and not earning one's living in ways inconsistent with the *Five Precepts* and the *Noble Eightfold Path*.

Right Effort

Samyagvyayama/samma vayama (right effort) requires constant attentiveness and effort to sustain and generate good dispositions, as well as to refrain from what are harmful states of mind.

Right Mindfulness

Samyaksmriti/samma sati (right mindfulness) is a state of awareness rooted in four things: in the body and its activity; feelings; states of mind; and mental contents. The practice of *mindfulness* leads ultimately to the realisation that all conditioned things are impermanent, unsatisfactory, and devoid of any lasting quality.

Right Concentration

Samyaksamadhi/samma samadhi (meaning right concentration) is nurtured through meditation practices that centre the mind upon a single object.

Paramita

Paramita is usually translated as "perfections". In the *Theravada* tradition, the main emphasis is on the *Four Noble Truths* and the practice of the *Noble Eightfold Path*, though the moral perfections are illustrated in the *Jataka* stories.

In *Mahayana* the stress is on the *paramitas* of the *Bodhissattvas*. The *Theravada* enumerates ten of these, while *Mahayana* schools generally focus on six. These include generosity; keeping the moral precepts; forebearance; courage; meditation (see below) and wisdom (the genuine insight which results from this practice and has compassion as its natural accompaniment).

Meditation

Meditation or, perhaps more correctly, *bhavana* (meaning, "cultivation") plays a central role in Buddhist practice. Through such meditation, faith (as confidence), concentration, mindfulness, energy and wisdom are cultivated as the five foundations or powers of the developing spiritual life. Meditation is also a form of right action.

There are numerous methods of meditation within the various branches of Buddhism and they all require training and practice. There are, however, two basic forms that underlie the variety of methods. These are *shamatha/samatha* (concentration practices or tranquillity meditation) and *vipashyana/vipassana* (insight meditation).

Concentration disciplines the mind by centring it on a single point and promotes states of mind characterised by calm, joyful confidence and mindfulness in order to integrate the emotions and develop positive energies. Common forms of *shamatha* meditation are awareness or mindfulness of breathing and the practice of positive good will, radiating "loving-kindness" to all beings.

Vipassana meditation is concerned with the clarity of seeing things as they really are and in realising the *Three Signs of Being* (see under the *Four Noble Truths*). This realisation is seen as breaking the bondage of *samsara* and thus as bringing liberation from *duhkha*.

There is a variety of ways in which meditation may be aided. For *Theravadins*, the *Rupas* (material forms or images) of Gautama *Buddha* are a reminder of his life and teaching. *Mahayana* traditions have a rich artistic heritage and teach visualisation of many *Buddhas* and *Bodhisattva*s. They are often accompanied by *mantras*, verbal formulae which, when chanted, are believed to resonate in ways that have a deep efficacy and bring one into a relationship with that with which they are associated. *Mandalas* are sacred diagrams in the shape of circles, squares or angular designs that depict symbolically the teachings of Buddhism.

In *Tibetan* Buddhism *mandalas* are either permanently constructed, such as those painted on *thang-ka* (scroll or wall-hanging) or are temporarily made from different coloured sands or other such materials. *Mudras* are hand gestures that, like *mantras*, are believed to have a spiritual effect and are employed during the chanting of scriptures or other formulae.

In *Zen* Buddhism great attention is paid to sitting meditation as well as to practice of the *precepts* and meditation applied to daily life. The state of mind cultivated is known as "empty heart", which is not a state of thoughtlessness, but of an "at-one-ness" which has passed beyond the distinction of subject and object. When practised this state prevails not only when sitting in meditation but also in the day-to-day activities of life, including all kinds of work.

Vegetarianism

Buddhists emphasise the avoidance of intentional killing. However, there is a variety of practice with regard to the eating of meat. Many *Tibetan* Buddhists do eat meat and, in *Theravada* Buddhism, *monks* and *nuns* are allowed to eat meat if they have not seen, heard or suspected that the animal has been specifically killed for them. In particular they are able to accept meat if it is offered to them as alms, which is the only way in which the monastic discipline permits them to obtain food.

Chinese Zen has become strictly vegetarian, whereas in *Japanese Zen* the same rules apply as in *Theravada*, although meat is never served in *monasteries*. In general, even where Buddhists are not fully vegetarian, what are perceived as the higher forms of life are often avoided. In *Chinese* forms of Buddhism garlic and onions are also avoided since they are thought to heat the blood and so make meditation more difficult. The precept of right livelihood certainly excludes the "trade in flesh" entailed in being a butcher, hunter or fisher.

BUDDHIST WORSHIP

Devotional Practice

Alongside various forms of meditation (as discussed in the section on "Buddhist Life" above) most Buddhists also practise *Puja*. Devotional practices are also considered as *bhavana*. These involve the offering of food, flowers, incense and water, together with chanting, and are carried out by all schools within Buddhism as an observance alongside meditation, although taking different forms in each school. Such observance expresses *shraddha/saddha* (trust or confidence) in the *Buddha*. It is not blind faith that should be the aim here, but confidence based on the efficacy of the *Buddha's* teachings when put into practice.

BUDDHIST PLACES OF WORSHIP

Buildings for Devotional Practice

Buddhist places of worship and devotional practice are not recorded under a separate Buddhist category in the running totals of certified places in England and Wales kept by the Registrar General. However, the CD-ROM accompanying this directory contains contact details for around 94 Buddhist centres and monasteries of worship in the UK, of which around 84 are in England, 5 are in Wales, 3 are in Scotland, and 2 are in Northern Ireland.

Buddhist places of devotion vary considerably in style and practice and various types can be found in the UK reflecting the different traditions, schools and ethnic groupings of the Buddhists who use them. Styles range from the stark simplicity of meditation halls to the elaborate ornateness of some temples.

Such places may be a part of a *vihara* (a place where *monks* live), or may be found in a general centre. In either case, the actual place of devotion is the *shrine room* which is primarily a place for meditation and teaching.

The *shrine room* may also, though, contain a statue or image of a *Buddha* or, in some Buddhist traditions, of a *Bodhisattva*. These will be in a central position, commonly with an incense holder, flowers and candles by its side, since the *shrine room* is also a place for the performance of *puja*, which is a way of expressing one's devotion by means of offerings and chanting.

The offering of incense is symbolic of the importance of diligent action. Candles symbolise the light that the *Buddha's* teaching brings to the world. There are vases of cut flowers as a reminder of impermanence and sometimes a Buddhist text wrapped in silk represents the teaching.

Tibetan Buddhists offer bowls of water to represent water for bathing, washing the feet, rinsing the mouth and drinking, as well as food, flowers, incense and light. In the *Zen* tradition, offerings of fruit, tea and water are made.

If a temple is influenced by Chinese tradition (in other words is Vietnamese, Korean or Japanese) there will be a funerary memorial chapel set outside the main place of worship, where memorials of a family's dead are kept.

Shrines and Buddharupas

Other places of devotion may be in converted houses or even private homes in which a room is set aside as the central shrine or meditation space. Yet others are purpose-built constructions on extensive sites such as the Temple at the Samye Ling Tibetan Centre in Scotland, the Dhammatalaka Pagoda in Birmingham, and the *Theravada* Thai Buddhapadipa Temple in Wimbledon, while some are relatively small structures such as the Nipponzan Myohoji (a Japanese *Nichiren* movement) Peace Pagodas in Milton Keynes and Battersea Park in London.

Despite this variety there are a number of common features. A Buddhist temple or *vihara* (or *monastery*) usually contains at least a *Buddharupa* (statue of the *Buddha*) and a *stupa/thupa*, which is a characteristic form of Buddhist architecture. *Stupas* were originally burial mounds built over relics of the *Buddha* or other saints or other holy objects and are reminders of the *Buddha* and his teachings.

The temple is commonly a place where teaching, religious observance and meditation takes place, and it may have adjacent accommodation for resident *monks* or *nuns*. It can thus physically focus the three refuges of Buddhism - the *Buddha*, the *dharma* and the *sangha*.

Most Buddhists have a small shrine somewhere in their homes. The *Buddharupa* is usually found in a central position within the shrine area, in front of which there will usually be an incense holder, flowers and candles.

Visitors to a Buddhist Temple

When visiting a Buddhist temple there are no particular requirements with regard to clothing except that it should be modest. For reasons of practicality it is best if clothing is loose fitting because of the normal practice of sitting on the floor. Because of the need to remove shoes, clean and presentable socks, stockings or tights are a good idea.

Before entering the *shrine room*, shoes should be removed as a mark of respect. Inside the room, seating is generally on the floor and it is appropriate to adopt a quiet and meditative demeanour. One may see Buddhists, on entering a temple or *shrine room*, prostrating themselves three times (representing body, speech and mind, or the *Three Refuges*) before the shrine, or else bowing with hands in the *anjali* (hands together) position. There is no expectation that visitors will do this, although they may do so, if they wish.

In some traditions it is considered disrespectful to sit with one's legs or feet pointed in the direction of the shrine, or with one's back turned to the *Buddha*.

BUDDHIST CALENDAR AND FESTIVALS

Calendar

Buddhist religious festivals are based on the lunar calendars of the countries concerned. However the actual festivals and their dates and meanings vary according to Buddhist tradition and the national/ethnic origins of the group concerned. Because of these national/ethnic variations and the lunar cycle, individuals cannot easily predict the exact dates of particular festivals.

Some, as in Japan, have fixed dates by the Western calendar. But many other Buddhists rely for moon dates on printed calendars, such as the one produced at the Tibetan Medical Centre in Dharamsala, India, which is consulted by *Tibetan* Buddhists all over the world. Many festivals also incorporate pre-Buddhist customs and, in the West, large-scale celebrations often take place on the weekend nearest to the festival.

Festivals

Uposatha Days

Uposatha Days are observed at full moon and new moon and also on the days half-way through the lunar fortnight. The full moon and new moon observances are the most important. On these days *monks*, *nuns*, and devout lay Buddhists engage in more intense religious activities. The way in which these days are observed varies considerably among Buddhists, but their observance usually includes a visit to a *monastery* to make offerings of food to the *monks* and *nuns*, to pay one's respect to *Buddha* images and shrines, and to listen to a *Dharma* talk.

Parinirvana (early February)
Far Eastern Mahayana Buddhists mark the final passing away of *Shakyamuni Buddha* at Kushinagara, India, at the age of eighty.

Buddha's Birthday (8th April in Japan)
Far Eastern Mahayana Buddhists celebrate this as a festival of flowers, reflecting the *Buddha's* birth in a garden. Sweet tea or water is ceremonially poured over a statue of the infant *Buddha*.

Wesak or Buddha Day (May)
Known variously as *Wesak*, *Vaisakha Puja* and *Buddha Jayanti* in *Theravada Buddhism*, this festival generally occurs on the full moon day in May. It commemorates the *Birth*, *Enlightenment* and *Parinirvana* (passing away) of the *Buddha*, all of which, according to the *Theravada* tradition, occurred on the full moon day in the Indian lunar calendar month equivalent to May. *Far Eastern Mahayana* Buddhists celebrate these three events on different dates (see above). In the West, the day is generally known as *Buddha Day* and it is usually observed in common by Buddhists of all schools.

Poson (June)
Poson is the Sri Lankan name for the month and the festival that marks the conversion of Sri Lanka to Buddhism through the Venerable Mahinda, son of the Indian Emperor Asoka, who brought the *dharma* to what is now Sri Lanka in c.250BCE.

The Rains Retreat (June/July –September/October)
The retreat is known in South Asian countries as *Vassa* and is an annual feature of the *Theravada monastic* calendar which *monks* and *nuns* observe for three months. During this period *monks* and *nuns* should remain in one place except for emergencies. In the *Northern Transmission* and in the West, dates vary in accordance with the climate. The *Zen* school has two such retreats each year, each one for three months. Special services are held on the opening and closing days.

Asalha (Dhammachakka Day) (July/August)
This is the anniversary of the *Buddha's* first sermon to the five ascetics at what is now Sarnath, a suburb of the Indian holy city of Varanasi. It is celebrated by *Theravadins* and the Friends of the Western Buddhist Order. The *sutra's* name is *The Discourse on the Turning of the Wheel of the Dharma*, the last phrase of which is, in Pali, the meaning of *Dhammachakka*. The day also marks the beginning of the *Rains Retreat*.

Kathina Day (October/November)
This is celebrated by *Theravadins* and follows the *Rains Retreat* either on its final day or within one month. On this day, the laity present *monks* and *nuns* with a cloth which is supposed to be made into a robe for a *monk* on the same day (although nowadays it is often ready-made). The precise date of its observance varies according to the end of the rainy season in the various countries.

Sangha Day (November)
This is celebrated by the Friends of the Western Buddhist Order and sometimes by other Western Buddhists as an expression of the spiritual community of all Buddhists.

Enlightenment Day (8th December)
This is celebrated by *Far Eastern Mahayana Buddhists*. In India, *Mahayana* Buddhists observe this by celebrating under the *Bodhi Tree* in Bodh Gaya.

New Year
Although it is generally celebrated in Buddhist countries as a major festival, apart from the incorporation of some elements of Buddhist practice into its observance, *New Year* is not a specifically religious festival for Buddhists. The Sri Lankan, Burmese and Thai New Years fall in mid-April, and in Thai tradition, New Year also involves a water festival. It is of greater importance in the *Mahayana* countries with their colder and darker winters. The Chinese New Year (also marked by Vietnamese and Tibetans) falls at the end of January or the beginning of February. In Japan, the western New Year date has been adopted.

Padmasambhava Day
There is a *Padmasambhava Day* in every Tibetan Lunar month; it is celebrated among *Tibetan* Buddhists in order to honour Padmasambhava as a founder of Buddhism in Tibet.

Some *Mahayana* Buddhists also have festival days for various *Bodhisattvas* and for the founders of particular *temples* and *monasteries*. In the Far East, the Spring and Autumn equinoxes are celebrated as times of change and for remembrance of the dead.

BUDDHIST ORGANISATIONS

Buddhist Organisational Listings

The CD-ROM includes contact details for a variety of forms of Buddhist local organisations that are referred to in this directory, including *vihara*s, where *monks* and nuns live; centres that have residential Buddhist communities, lay and/or monastic; as well as groups which meet in the homes of members or in hired premises. A number of these centres and groups may be based in one geographical location, but they also have a more wide-ranging regional, and sometimes national, function.

Overall, then, the CD-ROM includes details of around 70 Buddhist organisations working at a UK level and as well as around 1 Buddhist organisation working at each of the English, Scottish, Irish and Welsh levels. It also includes details of around 422 Buddhist local organisations (including 364 in England, 30 in Wales, 23 in Scotland and 5 in Northern Ireland).

The CD-ROM also contains contact details of a number of Buddhist bodies that operate beyond local boundaries, including around 30 monasteries or centres, including 29 in England and 1 in Wales that have a regional role as points of reference for wider national networks that look to them for guidance and support.

"Umbrella" Organisations

The Buddhist Society is the oldest Buddhist organisation in Europe. It provides a central source of information about Buddhism, running a series of educational courses and publishing a widely-read journal. In 1992 the Network of Buddhist Organisations was formed and now links 35 member bodies and groups, with a further 10 in associate membership.

These include some of the Britain's largest and oldest Buddhist groups, but also a range of small and more locally based groups. It provides a forum for discussion and a point of contact for information and advice. There is also a United Kingdom Association of Buddhist Studies (UKABS) that brings together scholars, insiders and outsiders, and publishes its own journal.

Theravada Organisations

Followers of the *Theravada* tradition in the UK include many who are ethnically European. There are also substantial groups of people with personal or ancestral roots in the traditional *Theravada* countries such as Sri Lanka, Burma and Thailand. Another group are the *Ambedkarites*, who are followers of Dr Ambedkar, who led a social movement in India among low and "scheduled *caste*"

Indians, many of whom converted to Buddhism from Hinduism. Around a further half million, including many in the UK, converted in 2006 on the fiftieth anniversary of Dr Ambedkar's death.

A Sri Lankan *vihara* that opened in London in 1928 operated until 1940. In 1954, the London Buddhist Vihara was established with Sri Lankan teachers. A Thai Buddhist *vihara* of the traditional Thai style, known as the Buddhapadipa Temple, was opened in South West London in 1966 by the King and Queen of Thailand. Ananda Metteyya's mission had been funded by Burmese Buddhists who gave substantial assistance to the Buddhist Society.

In 1978, the West Midlands Buddhist Centre was opened as a joint *Theravada/Karma Kagyu* development. In due course, the Birmingham Buddhist Vihara Trust was separately set up and oversaw the building (with Burmese co-operation) of the Dhammatalaka Pagoda, opened in 1998. A monastery and a teaching hall have since been built on the same site.

In 1956 the English Sangha Trust was set up to establish a Western Theravada Sangha and in 1962 it founded the Hampstead Buddhist Vihara. That then relocated when, in 1979, the Venerable Sumedho, an American-born *monk*, moved from there to found the Chithurst Forest Monastery with a group of western *monks* and *nuns* trained in the Thai forest tradition.

This now has branches that opened in Northumberland in 1981; in Devon in 1984; while in 1985, the Amaravati Buddhist Monastery was established near Hemel Hempstead. This Western Theravada Sangha should be distinguished from the Friends of the Western Buddhist Order (see below).

Mahayana Organisations

The *Mahayana* traditions in Britain are represented by diverse religious and ethnic groups.

Tibetan Buddhist Organisations

In 1959 there was a great diaspora of Tibetan *Lamas* following the Lhasa uprising against Chinese rule and the flight into exile of the *Dalai Lama*. European Buddhists offered help to Tibetan refugees such as Chogyam Trungpa, a one time Abbot of the Surmang group of monasteries in Tibet, who came to Oxford in 1963.

In 1967 he and Akong Rinpoche, the former Abbot of the Drolma Lhakhang Monastery, founded the first Tibetan Buddhist Centre in the West at Johnstone House in Dumfriesshire. Opened in 1988, it was named Samye Ling, after the first Buddhist monastery in Tibet. There are now many other *Tibetan Buddhist* centres in the UK.

The *Kagyupa* and *Gelugpa* schools are numerically the strongest *Tibetan* Buddhist traditions in Britain. The *Kagyupa* temple in the grounds of the Samye Ling monastery in Eskdalemuir, Scotland is built in traditional Tibetan style. The Jamyang Centre in London, begun in 1978 by pupils of Lama Thubten Yeshe and the *Lam Rim* centres in Bristol and Wales are examples of *Gelugpa* centres in converted premises.

The *New Kadampa* tradition emerged from the *Gelugpa* school and has centres and groups throughout the UK under the leadership of Geshe Kelsang Gyatso.

Four *Sakya* centres have been established with the *Dechen* community directed by the English Lama Nyakpa Jampa Thaye.

Zen Buddhist Organisations

The Japanese Buddhist Dr D T Suzuki attended the 1936 World Congress of Faiths in London. Although some of his work was concerned with *Pure Land* and other forms of *Mahayana* Buddhism, he is considered to have introduced *Zen* to the West, and specifically the *Rinzai* school.

Both the *Rinzai* and *Soto* schools can be found in Britain together with the Korean *Son*, the Vietnamese *Thien* and the Chinese *Ch'an*. Most notably, these include the Fo Guang Shan temples, which are in the *Linji* tradition. The followers of Thich Nhat Hanh in the Community of Interbeing are an example of the *Thien* (the Vietnamese form of *Zen*) tradition, while the Vietnamese-founded Tu Dam Tu in Birmingham is an example of a large-scale *Thien* temple in traditional style.

Rinzai Zen is practised at The Buddhist Society and at Shobo-an, a training temple founded in 1984 in North London by the Venerable Myokyo-ni. There are other *Zen* organisations in London and in the rest of the country, the largest of which is the Throssel Hole Priory, founded in Northumberland in 1972 by Revd Master Jiy-Kensett, a training monastery and retreat centre, which practises *Soto Zen*.

Pure Land Buddhist Organisations

Shin Buddhism has been the most influential *Pure Land* school in Britain. The Shin Buddhist Association of Great Britain was founded in 1976 and the Pure Land Buddhist Fellowship in 1977.

Shingon Mahayana Buddhism

Shingon is a Sino-Japanese form of esoteric Buddhism based on the *Mahavairocara* (*Great Sun*) *Sutra* and the *Kongocho* (*Diamond Peak*) *sutra*. The first Shingon Association in the west was founded in 1958 and the Kongoryuji Temple in Norfolk is a centre for *Shingon* Buddhism.

Some Other Japanese Buddhist Groups

A range of similar Japanese groups tend to have a lay orientation and non-ascetic approach to Buddhist practice. *Soka Gakkai* (The Value Creation Society) is one such movement that was founded in 1930 as a lay association within the *Nichiren Shoshu* sect, and eventually spread globally. This was, in the end, excommunicated by the Japanese ecclesiastical leadership. But now known as Sokka Gakkai International (SGI), it exists independently, having arrived in Britain during the 1980s.

Sokka Gakkai is based on: faith in the power of the *mantra Nam-myoho-renge-kyo* (as distinct from the *Namu-myoho-renge-kyo mantra* of some other schools); on study of Buddhist teaching as presented by Nichiren and his successors; and on the twice daily practice of reciting the *mantra*, which is the Japanese name of the *Lotus Sutra*, in front of the *Gohonzon* (a scroll on which the *mantra* is written).

Other Japanese groups include Rissho Kosei-Kai (Society for Righteousness and Friendship), which is another *Nichiren* lay offshoot, founded in 1938. There is also the Nipponzan Myohoji Order, which is well-known for its campaign for peace and the Peace Pagodas it built in Milton Keynes (1980) and Battersea in London (1985), the opening of which was attended by the founder of the order, the Most Venerable Nichidatsu Fujii (1885-1985CE). Their practice is based on the recitation of the *mantra, Namu-myoho-renge-kyo*.

Friends of the Western Buddhist Order

In 1967, the Venerable Sangharakshita, an Englishman who was ordained into the three major traditions of Buddhism while living in India, returned to the UK and established the Western Buddhist Order later supported by the Friends of the Western Buddhist Order (FWBO). This is a new Buddhist movement that draws upon all the traditions of Eastern Buddhism whilst maintaining a strong engagement with Western culture.

It seeks to find new ways of living out the basic principles of Buddhism through the commitment of its members to the *Three Jewels* shared by all Buddhists. Many people involved in the FWBO live in single-sex, residential communities and work in co-operative right-livelihood businesses, but there are also those who live quasi-monastic lives in retreat centres and others who have ordinary jobs.

Non-Aligned Buddhist Groups

There are a number of non-aligned Buddhist organisations, set up for the study and practice of Buddhism, such as the Gaia House in Devon, founded by Christina Feldman and Christopher Titmus; and the Sharpham Centre, founded by Stephen and Martine Batchelor.

Political and Social Engagement

A number of Buddhist groups have emerged in recent years to address social issues from the perspective of Buddhism. These include the Network of Engaged Buddhists and groups with specific foci such as the Buddhist Hospice Trust. Angulimala, the Buddhist Prison Chaplaincy Organisation, was formed in 1984 to provide and train Buddhist chaplains for prison work.

There is now also a Buddhist Chaplain to H M Forces, as well as a number of Buddhist chaplains to local police forces, in institutions of further and higher education, and in other social institutions. Buddhists have served as hospital chaplains for many years and a body to regulate and accredit their work is in process of formation. In the field of education, a small Dharma School opened in 1994 in the Brighton area and currently caters for seventy young children.

Personnel

Bhikshu and Bhikshuni

The *sangha* or community of *monks* and *nuns* is central in traditional Buddhism. *Monks* are known as *bhikshu/bhikkhus* and *nuns* as *bhikshuni/bhikkhunis*, which literally means "almsmen" and "almswomen", reflecting the originally mendicant lifestyle of the *sangha*. The original role of the *sangha* was to work for their own spiritual development and to share the *dharma* with others, but Buddhist *monks* have often also called upon them to officiate in *priest*-like ways at rites of passage, and they have also often become involved in tasks related to education and health care.

The *Theravada sangha* can be recognised by their shaved heads and saffron (orange or ochre) robes. They do not personally possess money and do not eat after mid-day. They do not take vows of obedience and need not necessarily stay in the order for life. Indeed, among Thai and Burmese Buddhists it is typical for young men temporarily to take on the *shramanera* (novice) *ordination* as a kind of rite of passage into adulthood.

Those who take the novice *ordination* are called upon to live by the *Ten Precepts*. These include the *Five Precepts* together, but the third against sexual misconduct, is extended to total chastity. In addition, they entail refraining from eating at unseasonable times (that is, between midday and sunrise the following morning); dancing, singing and visiting musical shows; wearing garlands, perfumes and unguents, finery and adornments; the use of high or luxurious beds and seats; and the handling of gold, silver or money in general.

After *upasampada* (higher) *ordination*, *monks* and *nuns* live according to the full *monastic* code, known as the *vinaya*. This entails extensive additional obligations set out in the 227 disciplinary rules for *monks* and 348 for *nuns*. The *ordination* of women as *nuns* was, in the Buddha's day, a revolutionary innovation and the *Buddha* only instituted the *bhikshuni* order after the pleading of his widowed foster mother and at the request of the *monk* Ananda.

The *order* was founded on the basis that the *nuns* followed additional special rules, intended for their protection. Generally, Buddhism argues for the equality of men and women in their spiritual potential and on several occasions Gautama defended the equality of the sexes in this regard. In the highest realms of *rebirth* a person or entity is not conceived of as having any gender.

The *bhikshuni* order survived only in *Northern Buddhism* and, specifically, in the Chinese-derived tradition. In *Tibetan* Buddhism there was controversy over the validity of their *ordination*, which did not come from the Indian line but was introduced in the twelfth century. This was resolved late in the twentieth century by *Gelugpa nuns* obtaining female ordination from *Far Eastern* Orders that had an unbroken line of ordination that was believed to date back to the *Buddha*. In other *Mahayana* schools, the spiritual equality of women and men is recognised and women receive full *ordination*.

In the *Theravada* tradition, the ordination link was broken and therefore only ordination as a *novice* was allowed for women. In Myanmar, which has the highest number of Buddhist *monasteries* in the world relative to its population, nuns (of lower *ordination*) outnumber men. In the wake of the highly publicised mass *ordinations* of women, especially those held at Bodh Gaya, the total number of fully ordained *nuns* worldwide has, in all traditions, been increasing. In the West, a *Theravada* nuns' *sangha* has been re-established, with some *Theravada* women taking full *ordination* from the *Far Eastern* (*Mahayana*) orders, although this still remains controversial and is resisted in traditional circles.

Lamas

In the *Tibetan* tradition a *Lama* (spiritual teacher or *guru*) can be of either sex and does not necessarily have to belong to a *monastic* order. There are lay people who are skilful teachers and are revered as *Lamas*.

In the *Far Eastern Mahayana* schools, except for the *Pure Land School*, both *monks* and *nuns* shave their heads at first *ordination* and live in monastic communities. Robes, rules and practices differ from school to school, but all are dedicated to the *Bodhisattva Way*, wishing to be of benefit to all living beings.

In the *Mahayana* tradition, a layperson of either gender can take on a *Bodhisattva* commitment and may then be recognised as being of higher spiritual attainment than either a *monk* or a *nun*.

Teachers and Priests

In the *Japanese* schools, the teachers are generally *monks* and *nuns* or *ministers*, although in Britain there are also a number of *lay ministers* who have a limited role in teaching.

In the *Rinzai* school, *koans* are only taught by teachers authorised to do so. In all *Japanese* schools a *priesthood* – as distinct from *monks* and *nuns* – was introduced after the Meiji Restoration of 1868, when the Japanese Government of the time encouraged temple incumbents/*abbots* to marry (although *nuns* remained celibate). Today, there are training monasteries with celibate *monks* or *nuns* and a celibate *Zen Master*, and temples with *ordained priests* who may be married and train *postulants* for entry into a *monastery*.

Dharmacharis and Dharmacharinis

In the Western Buddhist Order members are ordained either as *Dharmacharis* (males) or as *Dharmacharinis* (females). Some members of the Order live monastic lifestyles whilst others have families. Within the Order these differences in lifestyle are not seen as being differences in status. All members of the Order follow *Ten Precepts* (a different list from the ten *samanera precepts* of the *Theravada monastic* tradition) that lay down basic ethical principles governing actions of body, speech and mind.

FURTHER READING

Details follow of a number of general introductions to Buddhism, together with books and articles that provide some focus on Buddhists and Buddhist organisations in the UK. The references are not comprehensive, but provide signposts to a range of relevant materials.

Almond, P C, *The British Discovery of Buddhism*, Cambridge University Press, Cambridge, 1988.

Armstrong, K, *Buddha*, Weidenfeld and Nicholson, London, 2000.

Batchelor, S, *The Awakening of the West: The Encounter of Buddhism and Western Culture*, Aquarian Press, London, 1994.

Batchelor, S, "Buddhism and European Culture", in S Gill, G D'Costa and U King (eds), *Religion in Europe: Contemporary Perspectives*, Kok Pharos, Kampen, 1994, pp 86–104.

Bechert, H and Gombrich, R, *The World of Buddhism*, Thames and Hudson, London, 1984.

Bluck, R, *British Buddhism: Teachings, Practice and Development*, Routledge, Abingdon, 2006.

Buddhist Society, The, *The Buddhist Directory*, The Buddhist Society, London, 2006.

Burton, S, *Buddhism, Knowledge and Liberation: A Philosophical Study*, Ashgate, Aldershot, 2004.

Connolly, P and Erricker, C, *The Presence and Practice of Buddhism*, West Sussex Institute of Higher Education, 1985.

Conze, E, *A Short History of Buddhism*, Allen and Unwin, 1980.

Conze, E, Horner, I, Snellgrove, D and Waley, A, *Buddhist Texts Through the Ages*, Oneworld, Oxford, 1995.

Cousins, L, "Buddhism in Britain", in Dhammakaya Foundation, *Buddhism into the Year 2000*, Bangkok, 1995, pp 141–150.

Cousins, L, "Buddhism", in J. Hinnells (ed), *The New Penguin Handbook of Living Religions*, 2nd edition, Penguin, London, 1997.

Dalai Lama, H H, *The World of Tibetan Buddhism*, Wisdom Publications, Boston, 1995.

Deegalle, M, "Sri Lankan Theravada Buddhism in London: Communal Activities of a Diaspora Community", in K Jacobsen and P Kumar (eds), *South Asians in the Diaspora: Histories and Religious Traditions*, E J Brill, Leiden, 2004, pp 52–73.

Gethin, R, *The Foundations of Buddhism*, Oxford University Press, Oxford, 1998.

Gombrich, R, *Theravada Buddhism: A Social History from Ancient Benares to Modern Colombo*, Routledge and Kegan Paul, London, 1988.

Green, D, "Buddhism in Britain: Skilful Means or Selling Out?", in P Badham (ed), *Religion, State and Society in Modern Britain*, Edwin Mellen Press, Lampeter, 1989, pp 277-291.

Gross, R, *Soaring and Settling: Buddhist Perspectives on Contemporary Social and Religious Issues*, Continuum, New York, 1998.

Harris, E, *What Buddhists Believe*, Oneworld, Oxford, 1998.

Harris, E, *Theravada Buddhism and the British Encounter*, Routledge, London, 2006.

Harvey, P, *An Introduction to Buddhism: Teachings, History, and Practices*, Cambridge University Press, Cambridge, 1990.

Harvey, P, *The Selfless Mind: Personality, Consciousness and Nirvana in Early Buddhism*, Curzon Press, London, 1995.

Harvey, P, *An Introduction to Buddhist Ethics: Foundations, Values and Issues*, Cambridge University Press, Cambridge, 2000.

Hawkins, B, *Buddhism*, Routledge, London, 1999.

Humphreys, C, *The Development of Buddhism in England*, The Buddhist Lodge, London, 1937.

Humphreys, C, *Sixty Years of Buddhism in England 1907-1967: A History and a Survey*, The Buddhist Society, London, 1968.

James, S, *Zen Buddhism and Environmental Ethics*, Ashgate, Aldershot, 2004.

Kasulis, T, *Zen Action, Zen Person*, UPH, 1981.

Kay, D, "The New Kadampa Tradition and the continuity of Tibetan Buddhism in transition", in *Journal of Contemporary Religion*, Volume 12, No 3, October 1997, pp 277-293.

Kay, D, *Tibetan and Zen Buddhism in Britain: Transplantation, Development and Adaptation*, Routledge Curzon, London, 2004.

Keown, D, *Buddhism: A Very Short Introduction*, Oxford University Press, Oxford, 2000.

Keown, D, *Buddhist Ethics: A Very Short Introduction*, Oxford University Press, Oxford, 2005.

Keown, D and Prebish, C, *Encyclopaedia of Buddhism*, Routledge, London, 2007.

Kiblinger, K, *Buddhist Inclusivism: Attitudes Towards Religious Others*, Ashgate, Aldershot, 2005.

King, R, *Indian Philosophy: An Introduction to Hindu and Buddhist Thought*, Edinburgh University Press, Edinburgh, 1999.

Lopez, D, *Prisoners of Shangri-La: Tibetan Buddhism and the West*, University of Chicago Press, Chicago, 1999.

Myokyo-ni, *The Zen Way*, The Zen Centre, London, 1978.

Myokyo-ni, *Gentling the Bull*, The Zen Centre, London, nd.

Pauling, C, *Introducing Buddhism*, Windhorse Publications, Glasgow, 1993.

Powell, A, *Living Buddhism*, British Museum, London, 1989.

Powers, J, *Introduction to Tibetan Buddhism*, Snow Lion, Ithaca, New York, 1995.

Queen, C, *Engaged Buddhism in the West*, Wisdom Publications, Boston, 2000.

Robinson, R; Johnson, W and Thanissaro, *Buddhist Religion*, 5th edition, Wadsworth, 2005.

Saddhatissa, Venerable H, *The Buddha's Way*, Allen and Unwin, London, 1971.

Sangharakshita, Venerable, *New Currents in Western Buddhism*, Windhorse Publications, Glasgow, 1990.

Smith, S, "Western Buddhism: tradition and modernity", in *Religion*, Volume 26, 1996, pp 311-321.

Snelling, J, *The Elements of Buddhism*, Element Books, Dorset, 1990.

Subhuti, *Buddhism for Today*, Element Books, London, 1983.

Suzuki, Shunryu, *Zen Mind, Beginner's Mind*, Weatherhill, New York, 1970.

Walpola, R, *What the Buddha Taught*, Oneworld, Oxford, 1998.

Waterhouse, H, *Buddhism in Bath: Adaptation and Authority*, University of Leeds Community Religions Project, Leeds, 1997.

Williams, P, *Mahayana Buddhism: The Doctrinal Foundations*, Routledge and Kegan Paul, London, 1989.

Williams, P and Tribe, A, *Buddhist Thought*, Routledge, London, 2000.

Wisdom Publications, *The International Buddhist Directory*, Wisdom Publications, London, 1984.

INTRODUCING CHRISTIANS IN THE UK

CHRISTIANS IN THE UK 127

ORIGINS AND DEVELOPMENT OF CHRISTIANITY 130

SOURCES OF CHRISTIAN BELIEFS AND PRACTICES 131

KEY CHRISTIAN BELIEFS 133

TRADITIONS IN CHRISTIANITY 137

CHRISTIAN LIFE 141

CHRISTIAN WORSHIP 144

CHRISTIAN PLACES OF WORSHIP 146

CHRISTIAN CALENDAR AND FESTIVALS 148

CHRISTIAN ORGANISATIONS 152

FURTHER READING 165

CHRISTIANS IN THE UK

History in the UK

Christianity is the largest and longest established of the world religious traditions in the UK. In its various forms, it has shaped the past and present life of these islands and has helped mould legal structures, public institutions, and the social and intellectual tradition.

Christianity was introduced into Britain from continental Europe when some of its Celtic inhabitants were converted during the early centuries of the Common Era. *Celtic* Christianity developed in Ireland and North-West Scotland, with some influence from the Egyptian Desert Fathers, and spread from there to other parts of northern England, Scotland and Wales. This spread began in the seventh century. Christian life also developed in the south of England during Roman times.

The ethos and structures of *Celtic* Christianity were influenced by its tribal society, and were independent of the organisational structures of the rest of *Western Christendom* that had developed around the *Bishop of Rome* (the *Pope*), on lines reflecting a more ordered, imperial society.

In 597 CE, Augustine, an emissary of *Pope* Gregory the Great of Rome, arrived in Kent. Canterbury became the base for his *missionary* work. He became *Archbishop of Canterbury* and was given authority by the *Pope* over the *bishops* in the rest of Britain, an authority which they acknowledged at the Synod of Whitby in 664 CE.

The *Catholic* form of Christianity gradually displaced *Celtic* Christianity, although in Wales and Ireland *Celtic* forms of Christianity continued independently for some centuries. Western Christianity gradually became consolidated under the jurisdiction of the *Pope*, and Christians in the different parts of these islands remained part of what was known as the *Catholic* (meaning universal) tradition.

This tradition played a substantial and ongoing role in the development of European history following the fall of the Roman Empire. It provided a conduit for culture and scholarship. Through its use of the Latin language and the development of its *Canon Law*, it provided a focus for a wider unity that went beyond the competing claims of local rulers. Through its variety of religious *Orders* and diversity of spiritual disciplines, it enabled a rich diversity within unity of Christian life and organisational forms.

At the same time, the organised forms of the tradition were susceptible to corruption and abuse. In the context of these failings, and in the light the new learning of the Renaissance coupled with the increased translation of the scriptures into vernacular languages, popular and theological discontent developed in relation to a range of practices and teachings that had developed within the *Catholic* Church during the late Middle Ages. This discontent eventually issued into the fracture of Western *Christendom* known generally to history as the *Protestant Reformation*.

Protestant Reformation

During the sixteenth and seventeenth centuries *Western Christendom* underwent major religious and political upheavals. This period is referred to as the *Reformation*, because of the attempts made by *Protestants* (initially those reformers within the *Catholic Church* who protested against certain of its doctrines and practices in the *Catholic Church*) to remodel the Christian *Church* in a way which, they believed, reflected more truly the earliest forms of Christianity to which the *New Testament* scriptures witnessed. Key reformers in continental Europe included Martin Luther and John Calvin.

In England and Wales, various changes took place in the *Church* which reflected these movements. After King Henry VIII's political break with the *Papacy*, the Church of England was recognised as the *established* form of religion in England. The Church of Scotland, embodying a *Calvinist, Presbyterian* (see below) form of *Church* government, became the *established* religion in Scotland. In Ireland, *Presbyterianism* spread with the influence of settlers from Scotland, whilst the adherence of the majority of the population to *Catholic* Christianity also became a dimension of resistance to English attempts to establish control over Ireland.

At the same time, there was a continuing presence of *Roman Catholics* in England and Scotland. Nevertheless, during the sixteenth and seventeenth centuries Christians of various traditions were persecuted depending upon the balance of power at the time. This persecution owed as much to political pressures as to theological differences.

The *Roman Church* and other countries with *Catholic* rulers were seen as powers hostile to English and Welsh interest, and under the *Protestant* monarchs, individual *Roman Catholics* were often seen as being potentially disloyal citizens. These perceptions took a long time to overcome, with *Roman Catholic* Christians remaining subject to legal disabilities and penalties until into the nineteenth century.

In addition to the Churches of England and Scotland, other forms of *Protestant* Christianity developed during the sixteenth, seventeenth and eighteenth centuries. These movements are often known as *Nonconformist* because of their refusal to conform to ways of worship and organisation required in the *Churches* established by law. Like *Roman Catholics*, they were subjected to numerous civil and religious restrictions and penalties until the nineteenth century.

Global and UK Populations

Worldwide, there are an estimated 1,999,564,200 Christians. In the UK, the 2001 decennial Census questions on religion yielded 42,079,417 (or 71.6% of the total

UK population) respondents identifying themselves as Christian. This is 93.2% of the population that identifies itself with any specific religion at all. Of these 42,079.417, a total of 35,251,244 were in England; 2,087,242 in Wales; 3,294,545 in Scotland; and 1,446,386 in Northern Ireland.

There is, of course, a question about the extent to which those responding as "Christian" in the religion questions of the 2001 Census were making a broad statement about their cultural identity rather than a specifically religious one.

As noted in the directory chapter on "Religious Landscape of the UK, the data for England and Wales may be particularly reflective of a broadly cultural response, given the very broad form of religion question asked there, as compared with the questions as asked in Scotland and Northern Ireland, both of which asked current religious "belonging" and also about the religion in which respondents were "brought up".

Nevertheless, whatever the debate about the nature and extent of the population's active identification with Christianity, it is clear that in broad cultural terms, Christianity remains a substantial feature of the UK religious landscape.

Ethnicity among Christians in the UK

Groups of Christian immigrants have brought their own distinctive traditions with them. Over the centuries, these have included the French *Reformed Huguenots*, Irish *Roman Catholics* and, more recently, Greek, Russian and other *Eastern Orthodox* (see below) Christians, as well as members of the *Pentecostal*, *Holiness* and *Spiritual Churches* of mainly African-Caribbean membership.

In recent years, all the historic Churches of the UK have experienced diversification through the arrival of migrants of various ethnic backgrounds. These have included people from Africa, Asia and Latin America, who now form a growing and increasingly significant proportion among practising Christians, especially in England. There are also groupings of Chinese Christians with origins in Hong Kong and of other Asian Christians with ethnic origins in the Indian sub-continent, Korea and elsewhere. Most recently of all, the expansion of the European Union to include Poland has seen the arrival of a substantial number of Poles of *Roman Catholic* background.

According to the 2001 Census results for England and Wales, in terms of the categories used for classification of responses to the religion and ethnic questions, 96.3% of respondents identifying as Christian, are "White", 2.2% are "Black or Black British", 0.9% are "mixed", 0.3% are "Asian" and 0.3% are of "Chinese or Other Ethnic Group".

Considered in relation to ethnicity, this means that 75.7% of all those classified as "White" identified as Christian, along with 71.1% of "Black or Black British" respondents, 52.5% of "Mixed", 27.2% of "Chinese or Other Ethnic Group", and 4.1% of those recorded as "Asian".

Traditions in the UK

A breakdown into Census data by denominational tradition within Christianity is not available for the UK as a whole. This is because, while the forms of the census question on religious affiliation used in Scotland and in Northern Ireland did ask about both original denominational background and current affiliation, the form of the question as asked in England and Wales did not do so. However, Christian Research's *UK Christian Handbook: Religious Trends,* provides broad estimates for "community membership".

"Community membership" is a way of understanding the relationship of individuals, families and groups to a religion that indicates a broader rather than a more specific (such as "church membership", see below) form of identification. Arguably, it therefore most closely aligns with the kind of information about religion that the Census data produces.

In terms of "community membership", based on Christian Research estimates for the year 2000, out of an overall total of 41,000,000, the following can be calculated as a proportion of Christian "community membership" in the UK:

- 67.5% (or 28,300,000) were *Anglicans*
- 13.8% (or 5,800,000) were *Catholics*
- 6.9% (or 2,900,000) were *Presbyterians*
- 3.3% (or 1,400,000) were "All Other Churches"
- 3.1% (or 1,300,000) were *Methodists*
- 1.2% (or 500,000) were *Baptist*
- 1.2% (or 500,000) were *Orthodox*
- 1.0% (or 400,000) were *Independent*
- 1.0% (or 400,000) were *New Churches*
- 1.0% (or 400,000) were *Pentecostal*

However, when taking the more restrictive notion of "Church membership" (which in the Christian Research definition includes adult members/adherents), and based on Christian Research estimates for the year 2001, out of an overall total of 5,903,267 the following can be calculated as a proportion of Christian "Church membership" in the UK:

- *Roman Catholics* at 29.6% (or 1,745,652)
- *Anglicans* at 28.3% (or 1,668,025)
- *Presbyterians* at 16.2% (or 958,268)
- *Methodists* at 5.2% (343,696)
- *Orthodox* at 4.3% (or 255,308)
- *Pentecostal* at 4.3% (or 253,722)
- *Baptist* at 3.6% (or 215,062)
- *Independent* at 3.2% (or 187,497)
- Other *Churches* (including, for example, *Christian Brethren, Congregationalists, Lutherans, Moravians* and *Salvationists*) at 2.4% (or 139,983)
- *New Churches* at 2.3% (or 136,054)

ORIGINS AND DEVELOPMENT OF CHRISTIANITY

Early Years

The historical origins of Christianity are to be found in what is now the territory of Israel/Palestine around two thousand years ago as a radical renewal movement within Judaism. It is rooted in the life and teaching of Jesus of Nazareth. The early Jesus movements were linked strongly to Jewish life, but as the tradition spread throughout the Middle East and beyond it came to include also *Gentiles*, or those of a non-Jewish background. It developed a separate life but retained a complex and often problematic link to the Jewish tradition.

For a long period Christians suffered localised opposition, coupled with sporadically intense persecution throughout the Roman Empire, especially under the Emperors Nero, Decius and Diocletian. However, Christianity gradually gained a wider following and, following the conversion of the Roman Emperor Constantine in the early fourth century CE, it eventually became the official religion of the Roman Empire.

The Roman Empire became divided into Eastern and Western parts which followed distinct Christian traditions. Although the *Churches* in the East and the West had much in common, differences of doctrine and practice began to emerge within the different jurisdictions. Following the *Great Schism* between these *Churches* in 1054, by the twelfth century these differences had resulted in the distinctive forms of *Eastern* and *Western Christendom* which underlie, on the one hand, the various forms of *Eastern Orthodoxy* and on the other the varied forms of *Catholic* and *Protestant Churches* in the West.

Eastern and Western Christendom and Protestant Reformation

After the rise of Islam in the seventh century CE, the *Churches of Eastern Christendom* in the Middle East and in North Africa became separate religious minorities. By contrast, in *Western Christendom*, Christianity was the dominant religious tradition, largely supplanting indigenous *pagan* traditions. In the Middle Ages, *Western Christendom* was commonly understood as a socio–political unity with two poles of authority: the state power of the *Holy Roman Emperor* or an individual country's monarch, and the ecclesiastical and spiritual authority of the *Pope* (the *Bishop of Rome*, the senior *bishop* of the *Western Church*).

There was a continued tension between these secular and spiritual poles until, in the sixteenth century, *Western Christendom* fragmented, with many territories becoming *Protestant* and no longer acknowledging *papal* jurisdiction in the spiritual or political sphere. Many *Protestant Churches* developed as national *Churches* having a close relationship with the states in which they were set.

The Protestant Reformation and the Missionary Movement

With growing European awareness of the world beyond Europe, both *Protestant* and *Roman Catholic* Christians increasingly became convinced of a need to spread the message of Christianity to the countries where European colonies were being established. The *missionary* movement began with the *Roman Catholic* missions of the sixteenth and seventeenth centuries to China, Goa, Japan and the New World. It reached its peak during the latter part of the nineteenth century and the first half of the twentieth century, with the development of the *Protestant* and *Anglican* Christian missions.

Many of the *missionary societies* had a background in the *Evangelical Revival*. These *missions*, in turn, led to Christian *Churches* of many denominations being established in

many parts of the globe. This process then in turn contributed to the development of the *ecumenical* movement (see below) towards unity in faith, prayer and action among the Christian *Churches* of the world.

Many individual Christian *missionaries* were undoubtedly motivated by genuine Christian convictions about their responsibility for spreading the Christian message, but the relationship between the *missionary* movement and European colonialism and imperialism has, with hindsight, been criticised by the more recently founded *Churches* in other continents and by many of the European *Churches* themselves. However, the *missionaries* made a significant impact, and today the global focus of Christianity has shifted significantly from Europe and North America to Africa and Latin America.

SOURCES OF CHRISTIAN BELIEFS AND PRACTICES

Scriptures

The Christian *scriptures* comprise what Christians have traditionally called the *Old Testament* and the *New Testament* (*testament* meaning *covenant*). Together they form what is known among Christians as the *Bible*.

From the earliest years of Christianity Christians have believed that one God speaks through both the Jewish *Torah*, the *prophets* and the writings as recorded in the *Hebrew Scriptures* (commonly known among Christians as the *Old Testament*), and through Jesus as testified to in the *Gospels*, *Epistles* and other writings (which collectively came to be known among Christians as the *New Testament*).

The Christian *Old Testament* is similar in content to the Jewish *Tanakh* (see chapter on "Introducing Jews in the UK"), though different in its internal order after the first five books. The *New Testament* is a collection of texts dating from the first and early second centuries which describe the impact of Jesus upon his followers who became known as *"Christians"*, together with beliefs about him, the story of the formation of early Christian communities, and the elaboration of the ethical implications of Christian belief.

The *canon* (normative contents) of the Christian *New Testament* emerged out of a process of debate concerning the authenticity and authority of a wider range of writings which were in circulation among the early Christian communities. The *canon* was finalised by a *Church Council* held in Carthage in 397 CE, although there remains some difference among Christians today concerning the place of a number of Greek texts collectively known as the *Apocrypha* (literally, "the hidden things") which are not included in the Hebrew language version of the *Old Testament*.

Roman Catholics and some other Christians understand these books to be fully a part of the scriptures, whilst others see their religious value as of less centrality. The status of these texts is, however, different from that of texts which emerged much later in history, such as the forged *Gospel of Barnabas*, which is not accepted by Christians as authentic in any sense.

In the *New Testament* the four *Gospels* (the English term from the Saxon word *Godspell*, meaning *Good News*) tell the story and describe how Christians understand the significance of Jesus, emphasising particularly his public life, death and *resurrection*. They are named after four early followers of Jesus: *Matthew, Mark, Luke* and *John* (who are traditionally held to have been their authors, or at least, editors).

They are followed by the *Book of the Acts of the Apostles* (by the same writer as the *Gospel According to Luke*) which describes the spread of early Christianity; the *Epistles*, in which the leaders of the early *Church* address problems and issues arising in the Christian communities; and finally the *Book of Revelation*, which records a series of visions.

The scriptures are central to the life of all Christians. Some Christians understand them as being the literal words of God without error or human distortion, whilst others see them as human testimony, guided by the Spirit of God in all central matters of belief and practice, and bearing witness to Jesus as the revelation of God in human nature.

Therefore Christians vary considerably in their view of how the scriptures should be interpreted and in what way they are authoritative in decisions over belief and life. However, all Christians agree that the scriptures must be taken seriously as a key source of guidance and reference-point for Christian living.

The Creeds

Creeds (from the Latin *Credo*, meaning "I believe") are summary statements of orthodox beliefs hammered out during vigorous controversies throughout the first centuries of CE. The most commonly used and important are the *Apostles' Creed* and the *Nicene Creed*. There are, however, some Christian denominations which dislike the use of *credal* formulae, notably some *Baptists* and members of the Society of Friends, often more widely known as *Quakers*.

Tradition

For *Orthodox, Roman Catholic* and *Anglican* Christians, *Tradition* is the second key source of belief and practice. *Tradition* is understood to embrace the authoritative understandings and interpretations of basic Christian beliefs contained in the scriptures and the *creeds* of the *Church*.

The texts of the *Patristic* period (the period of the early *Church Fathers*) are of great importance for many Christians, and particularly, although not exclusively, for those within the *Orthodox Churches*, as authoritative interpretations of scripture.

These texts form the common heritage of Christians before even the schism between

Eastern and *Western* forms of Christianity. Also important for belief and practice, although less authoritative, are the writings of the great Christian *saints* (see below).

Reason, Conscience and Experience

Human reason, individual conscience and religious experience are also recognised sources of belief and practice when exercised in the context of the scriptures, the *creeds*, *Tradition* and the teaching of the *denomination* or the local *church*. In the *Methodist* tradition, as part of the so-called *Wesleyan Quadrilateral* of scripture, Tradition, reason and experience, there has, historically, been a particular emphasis on the latter.

However, Christians differ on the scope for individual interpretation since it is commonly held that while human beings reflect the "image" of God, that image is marred and distorted by *sin*, the human tendency to depart from God's way. Therefore reason and conscience alone are not always reliable in the interpretation of religious experience in an imperfect world.

The Church

On the basis of its scriptures, and for many *Churches* also drawing on *Tradition*, the *Church* provides guidance to Christian individuals and Christian communities. The community of those who follow Jesus is known as the *Church* (from the Greek, *kuriakon*, meaning "belonging to the Lord").

The Greek word *ekklesia* (translated as *Church*) originally referred to the whole community of believers and is still used today with reference to the totality of the global Christian community. Nevertheless, the English word *Church* has also come to be used in a variety of other ways.

Sometimes (usually when it begins with a capital letter) it is used to refer to particular national bodies or world communions such as the Russian Orthodox Church. At other times it refers to the buildings in which

Christian worship takes place (as when people refer to "the *church* on the corner of the street" or the local Christian group which is found there). In these latter instances, the word usually begins with a small "c".

KEY CHRISTIAN BELIEFS

Jesus

The common focus of Christianity is upon the person of Jesus of Nazareth. Christian groups differ to some extent in their interpretations of his teaching, life, death and *resurrection* (being raised from the dead), but these matters are at the heart of the teaching and way of life of all of them.

The earliest Christian confession of faith appears to have been the expression "Jesus is *Lord*". In other words, he was seen as the criterion by which all of life was to be evaluated, and not simply as the *Saviour* of those who followed him. By this title of *Lord*, used also in Jewish tradition of God, the universal significance of Jesus is asserted.

The name "Christians" was originally a nickname given to the early followers of Jesus, who confessed him to be the *Christ*. The English word *Christ* comes from the Greek *Christos* which is, in turn, a translation of the Hebrew *Mashiach*.

Although this word often appears together with Jesus as if Jesus Christ is a personal name, Jesus is the personal name and *Christ* is a title given to him by the early Christians, who believed that Jesus fulfilled the expectations of the Jewish people for the *Messiah* (the *Anointed One* - understood as a coming deliverer).

Other titles used of Jesus in the *New Testament* scriptures include *Son of Man*, *Son of God*, *Saviour* and *Word of God*. More figurative titles, such as the *Good Shepherd*, the *True Vine* and the *Head of the Church* are also used.

Christians turn to the four *Gospels* and the *Book of the Acts of the Apostles* for an account and explanation of the origins of Christianity, the history of Jesus and its significance.

These documents indicate that Jesus was born in Bethlehem, approximately two thousand years ago; that he grew up in the town of Nazareth in the region known as Galilee; that when he was about thirty years old he began to teach, heal and travel through Judaea, Samaria and Galilee with a group of *disciples* (learners) from among whom he chose twelve *apostles* (*messengers* – from the Greek *apostoloi*); that in his work, as well as associating with the ordinary people of his nation, he deliberately also associated with the disreputable and with social and religious outcasts, in order to demonstrate the love of God for all kinds of people.

The *Gospels* also indicate that Jesus called people to turn to God, *repent* (literally, to turn their backs on) their sins and receive forgiveness, teaching that the self-righteous are actually those who cut themselves off from God rather than the outcasts. They indicate that although Jesus was a faithful Jew, he also came into conflict with the Jewish authorities of his day and was put to death by the Roman occupiers of the country through *crucifixion*, (a form of execution usually applied to slaves and political rebels, which entailed hanging its victims upon a *cross* made of wood until death by asphyxiation).

The *Gospels* recount that three days later his tomb was found empty; that he was met by one of his women followers and his disciples reported meeting with him, talking with him and eating with him. They eventually arrived at the firm conviction that he had been *resurrected* from the dead and, after a further forty days, had *ascended* to be with God the *Father*.

The *Acts of the Apostles* describe the early Christians' experience of the *Holy Spirit* being sent down on gathered followers and also give an account of the spread of the new faith. These texts and the *Epistles* (from the Greek *epistole*, meaning "letter") reveal the significance of Jesus for the earliest Christians

and show something of Christianity's development in a variety of different geographical locations throughout the eastern Mediterranean area. The *Epistles*, in particular, portray Jesus as the key to God's activity in the world, and they attempt to apply his teaching to daily life.

God, Incarnation and Revelation

Christians are most appropriately considered as *monotheists*, although this is nuanced by their belief in God as *Trinity* or *Tri-unity*. The belief is that there is one God who has been revealed as *Father* and as the *Creator*, *Sustainer* and *Redeemer* (or, restorer) of all that is. It is also believed that while this one God has been manifested in many different places and times, and in particular through the history and faith of the Jewish people, God's nature has been shown most clearly in the person, life, teaching, death and *resurrection* of Jesus of Nazareth.

Indeed, the core belief of Christianity is that God the *Son* (see section below on the *Holy Trinity*) became a human being, the *Word* of God made flesh in Jesus, born as a Jew, and that in and through Jesus, God became fully human. This is called the *incarnation* (from the Latin for "enfleshed"). The classical *credal* definition of this at the 451CE Council of Chalcedon contains the affirmation that Jesus was both fully human and fully divine. This expresses the belief that Jesus was fully human in all respects, except for sin (understood as falling short of the will of God).

It is because of belief in the *incarnation* that, in Christian understanding, Jesus' teachings, such as the well-known *Sermon on the Mount*, cannot ultimately be separated from his life, death and *resurrection* as the embodiment and expression of the nature of God. Through Jesus, understood as God made flesh, the nature of God is pre-eminently seen as being that of self-giving love (signified by the use of the Greek word *agape*, one of three Greek words rendered in English by the word "love").

Salvation

Jesus is therefore seen as the pivotal historical locus of God's activity. This activity is first of all seen as creative. God is recognised and worshipped as the origin of all things, both seen and unseen, which were created as good. But God's activity is also seen as *salvific* (putting right that which has gone wrong), because the world and human beings within it are understood to have become fundamentally flawed and to be in need of God's healing. This flawedness has been understood in a variety of ways within Christianity from the effect of original sin passed down the generations from the sins of the first humans, Adam and Eve, to the falling away from God of each individual human.

Whatever the cause, humans are believed by Christians to fall short of God's intention for them. Human beings are created in the image of God, but the image in each has become clouded over or damaged and is in need of restoration, so that they can come back into right relationship with God. It is believed by Christians that God takes the initiative in this restorative forgiveness and acceptance and this activity of God is known as *grace*.

God's healing *salvific* activity is understood by Christians to be most fully demonstrated in Jesus' life and teaching, which serves as a pattern for human life, and in God's participation in Jesus' death and *resurrection*.

The *Gospels* show the death of Jesus as the inevitable consequence of his faithful announcement of the message of the coming *Kingdom of God*. They proclaim his death and *resurrection* in terms of a sacrifice on behalf of human sin, the purpose of which was to bring about an *atoned* ("at-oned") and restored relationship with God.

It is also believed that in the *crucifixion* of Jesus God plumbed the depths of human experience: death itself, the last enemy of human life. Death was then conquered in the *resurrection* and it is this conquest that Christians celebrate at *Easter*. In traditional belief, because of Jesus' conquest of death, no lesser powers can bind or enslave any who put their trust in him, and death itself will be overcome after this life by those who partake, through faith, in his *resurrection*.

Many Christians also hold to the traditional biblical idea that Jesus will return a second time to judge humanity and bring about a complete renewal of all creation: not just of human beings. For some *Evangelical* Christian groups, this idea of a *Second Coming* is connected with a belief that it is possible to interpret world events in the light of such biblical texts as the *Book of Revelation* in order to discern when Jesus will come again.

Judgement and Eternal Life

Christians believe that human beings have only one life and that they will be judged on how they have lived this life. The exact shape of beliefs about judgement has varied over time, but some biblical texts describe a *Last Judgement* which will be followed by immortal union with God or by punishment.

In parts of the *Catholic* tradition, a state called *Purgatory*, or the place where sins are purged, has been seen as preparatory for entry to heaven. Generally speaking, contemporary Christianity focuses more on the importance of Christian faith and love in this world and the positive promise of life in the world to come, while focusing less on the penal aspect of the afterlife than was often the case in earlier centuries.

The Holy Trinity

Jesus is seen as the most complete expression and revelation of God, expressed in traditional language as the *Son of God* made flesh. However, the Christian vision and experience of God does not focus on the person of Jesus alone. The Christian conviction about the ultimately unfathomable nature of God came to be expressed as in the Christian doctrine or *Mystery* of the *Holy Trinity*, as the best possible reflection of the nature of the Christian experience of God as *Father*, *Son* and *Spirit*.

The Christian doctrine of the *Trinity* should not be understood as *tritheism* (belief in three individual gods) since the oneness of God is emphatically affirmed by Christians. Rather, it is intended to express belief in a dynamic interrelationship of community, inter-dependence and unity within the nature of the one God. God's nature and activity are said to be expressed in what the original Greek doctrine referred to as three *hypostases* (often, somewhat misleadingly, translated into English as three "*persons*", although *hypostasis* does not refer to an independent individual in the modern sense of the word "person").

Although expressed in highly complex language in its doctrinally developed form, by this doctrine Christians give expression to their experience that it is by the *Holy Spirit* of God within them, in and through God revealed and active in Jesus, that they worship God as *Father*.

The Virgin Mary

The *Virgin Mary*, the *Mother of Jesus*, is a focus of devotion for millions of Christians. However, Christians have varying views about the place which Mary has within Christian life and doctrine.

Most Christians believe that Jesus had no human father but was conceived by the *Virgin Mary* through the *Holy Spirit*; therefore she is to be honoured for her role of being the mother of Jesus and the first and best example of Christian faith and obedience.

The *Roman Catholic, Orthodox* and *Anglo-Catholic* traditions, however, emphasise this unique role more than do the *Protestant Churches*. Hundreds of *church* buildings within the *Roman Catholic, Anglican* and *Orthodox* traditions are named after her.

Orthodox and *Roman Catholic* tradition calls Mary by the title of *Theotokos* (Greek for "God-bearer") since it is through her that the *incarnation* is believed to have taken place. She is therefore held to have a special role as a link between the spiritual and material worlds. Among *Roman Catholics* Mary is known primarily as the *Mother of God* and of the *Church*, and sometimes as the *Queen of Heaven*.

In both the *Orthodox* and *Roman Catholic* traditions, Christian believers address petitions to Mary, asking her to intercede with Jesus on behalf of those who ask. Mary is not considered to answer prayers in her own right, but to share in, and so assist, the believer's prayer to God through her closeness to her son, Jesus.

Some in the *Anglican* tradition also share in the veneration of Mary as the most honoured of human beings. Very few *Protestant* Christians address petitions to Mary. The official teaching of the Roman Catholic Church proclaims a belief that Mary, by the singular *grace* of God and through the merits of Christ's saving work, was conceived without *Original Sin*. This is known as the doctrine of the *Immaculate Conception* (not to be confused with the miraculous conception of Jesus expressed in the doctrine of the *Virgin Birth*). It is also maintained by the Roman Catholic Church that Mary was assumed body and soul into heaven, a doctrine that is known as the *Assumption of the Blessed Virgin Mary*.

The Saints

In the early Christian *Church*, the scriptures referred to all Christian believers as the *saints* as distinct from the more specialised and restrictive use of the term which developed in the course of *Church* history. Thus, today, in some branches of Christianity, individual Christian men and women who have led particularly holy and exemplary lives manifesting the grace and power of God are venerated as *saints* (from the Latin *sanctus*, meaning "holy" and "set apart") and are looked to for help and support.

This veneration of the *saints* is particularly true of both *Orthodox* and *Roman Catholic* Christianity where it underlines the universal

Christian sense that the *Church* is composed of all Christian people, both present and past. Many *Church* buildings are named after individual *saints* who are also often associated with particular places of Christian pilgrimage.

TRADITIONS IN CHRISTIANITY

Main Branches

Globally, the largest Christian traditions are the *Roman Catholic, Orthodox, Protestant* and *Pentecostal*. The *Anglican* tradition of Christianity understands itself as being both *Reformed* and *Catholic* in tradition. These traditions share many of the key beliefs described above, but they also have their own distinctive teachings, ethos and emphases.

Roman Catholic

The Roman Catholic (the epithet "Roman" in general applied by those who are not members of that *Church*) Church embraces around half the Christians in the world. It understands itself as "one, holy, *catholic* and *apostolic*"; that is to say, as one united *Church* which is sanctified by God, which is universal in scope (*Catholic* from the Greek, *katholos*), and in an authentic and unbroken line of transmission of the Christian faith from the earliest *apostles* until the present time.

Its *bishops* are believed to be in direct *apostolic* line of succession from the *Apostles* of the *Church* (the twelve appointed by Jesus together with the *Apostles* Paul and Barnabas). The *Pope* is understood by *Roman Catholics* to be Peter's successor by virtue of his office as the *Bishop of Rome*.

The *bishops* are nominated by the *Pope* and consecrated by other *bishops* who are in communion with the *Pope*. They are responsible for the teaching and discipline of the *Church* as well as for ordaining *priests* and *deacons* to serve local Christian communities, and thus for maintaining what is known as the *Apostolicity* of the *Church*.

In *Roman Catholic* teaching the scriptures, as interpreted according to tradition, are given the supreme authority within the *Church*. But it is believed that the teaching authority of the *Church*, known as the *magisterium*, resides in the collective role of all the *bishops* gathered in *Ecumenical Councils* such as were held in the early centuries of Christianity and during the Middle Ages (the *ecumenical* nature of these later Councils being contested by *Orthodox* Christians).

Since the time of the *Reformation, Roman Catholics* have recognised three further *Ecumenical Councils* - the Council of Trent (1545-1563), Vatican I (1870) and Vatican II (1962-65). At the same time, a supreme authority is given to the *Pope* as the *Bishop of Rome* and the head of the *College of Bishops*, and the right, under strictly defined conditions, to make infallible declarations on matters of faith and morals.

The *Roman Catholic* commitment to *Catholicity* refers to the universality and the unity-in-diversity of that *Church* in all geographical contexts and also throughout space and time. There is therefore a great sense of belonging to a living tradition reflecting the diversity of humanity and yet kept in unity particularly by celebration of the *Eucharist* (see below under "Christian Places of Worship" and "Worship") as the focus of unity.

Participation in sacramental *Communion* at the *Mass* generally requires full initiation into the Roman Catholic Church in the sense of being in *communion* with the *bishops* and the *Pope*, who are seen as maintaining the *Church's Apostolicity*.

Orthodox

The *Churches* of the *Orthodox* tradition of Christianity understand themselves to be representing the tradition and practice of the undivided *Church* before the separation of *Eastern* and *Western Christendom*. *Orthodoxy* thus claims to represent a more original form of Christianity than others.

The *Orthodox* give central importance to the doctrine of the *Holy Trinity*. Differing interpretations around the origination of the Spirit led to the so called *filioque* controversy between *Orthodoxy* and *Western Christendom*. This is the debate over whether, within the *creeds* of the *Church*, it should be said with reference to *Trinitarian* doctrine that, the Spirit proceeds "from the *Father*", the source of all Godhead (which is the *Orthodox credal* form) or "from the *Father* and the *Son*" which is the *Western credal* form).

The *Western* formulation expresses the understanding that the *Spirit of God* is always manifested in terms of the character and person of Jesus. The *Orthodox* are concerned that such a formulation may subordinate the role of the *Spirit* to that of Jesus. They also see the *Western* addition, made without the authority of an *Ecumenical Council*, as an illegitimate act by one section of the *Church*.

The *Orthodox* tradition places a great emphasis on prayer, on spirituality and on celebration of the *Liturgy*. In *Church* government, the *Orthodox* tradition has what are known as *autocephalous* (Greek, meaning "independently governed") *Churches* with their own *patriarchs* (senior *bishops*) or *Archbishops*, although all *Orthodox Churches* recognise the *Patriarch of Constantinople* as the *Ecumenical Patriarch* who is first in order of seniority. In global terms, the numerical strength of the *Orthodox Churches* is to be found primarily in Eastern Europe, the Mediterranean, the Middle East and North Africa.

Protestant

Protestant is the name given to the Christian groupings whose particular character derives from the sixteenth and seventeenth century division in the *Church* in Europe generally referred to as the *Reformation* (see above).

In general, the *Protestant* tradition declares the supremacy and authority of the *scriptures* in matters of belief and *Church* government. However, it also emphasises the role of the individual believer, under the guidance of the *Holy Spirit*, in reading and interpreting the text of the *Bible*. It places emphasis upon personal faith in Jesus as the means to *salvation*.

In some *Protestant* traditions, such as *Methodism*, this has also been supplemented by a focus on the need for a strong personal experience of *conversion*, understood as a complete change of life orientation and issuing in "social holiness".

Most *Protestant Churches* also place particular emphasis upon *preaching* (the proclamation of the *Word of God* believed to be revealed in *scripture*). Through this, God is understood to offer eternal life in Christ and by the *Holy Spirit* to enable Christian hearers to deepen their faith and live in a more Christlike way.

Protestant Churches vary in belief and practice particularly with regard to *Church* organisation and government. There are also differences between those *Protestant* Christian traditions that have seen a close relationship with the state and/or the nation in a positive light (for example, in Scotland the Church of Scotland, which is in the *Reformed* tradition) and those traditions, generally known as the *Free Churches*, which have advocated the separation of the *Church* and the state.

Anglican

The *Anglican* tradition is a worldwide Christian tradition composed of autonomous *Churches* which look to the *Archbishop of Canterbury* for their international leadership. Like the Church of England, and as a consequence of the distinctive course of events of the *Reformation* in England and Wales, these *Churches* understand themselves as being both *Reformed* and *Catholic* in tradition.

The *Catholic* element is part of the *Anglican* emphasis on its continuity with the past and in *apostolic succession* to the earliest *Church*. The *Protestant* element was rooted in the correction of matters which, at the time of the *Reformation*, were judged to be abuses and distortions of *Catholic* Christianity.

Anglicanism classically seeks a balance between the opposing poles of many debates within Christianity. In doctrine, this has traditionally been expressed by affirming *scripture*, *Tradition* and reason as God-given instruments for interpreting revelation. In more recent years, experience has also been added.

In matters of authority, reason is seen as a necessary interpreter of *scripture* and *Tradition*, and in matters of church order individual and *parochial* (the level of the local *parish*) freedom is combined with an *episcopal* (the order of *bishops*) *Church* structure. Over recent decades most *Anglican Churches* have developed *synodical* democratic structures where key issues in the life of the *Church* are debated by both lay and ordained elected representatives.

There is also an attempt to balance a developed liturgical life and private devotion with a focus on scripture and social responsibility. There is concern, too, for comprehensiveness, which is envisaged as embracing a breadth of Christian belief and practice containing several identifiable theological and *liturgical* streams of life. These streams are known as the *Evangelical* (sometimes called *Low Church*), the *Anglo-Catholic* (sometimes called *High Church*), the *Liberal* (or *Broad Church*) and the *Charismatic* (see below for an explanation of these terms).

Pentecostal

The *Pentecostal* tradition has historical roots in *Protestantism* but there are also good reasons for regarding it as a distinctive tradition of Christianity that has come to global prominence in the course of the twentieth century. The *Pentecostal* tradition shares with the wider *Protestant* tradition a commitment to the primacy of the scriptures for individual and *Church* life, as well as the necessity of personal faith in, and commitment to, Jesus.

However, the tradition of *Pentecostalism* goes further to assert that the immediacy of the power of God, that was available to the first Christian believers as recorded in the scriptural book of the *Acts of the Apostles*, is still available to Christians today.

Pentecostalists emphasise the necessity of actually experiencing this power and love as well as believing in it. An event which they describe as the experience of *baptism in the Spirit* is seen as the occasion in and through which individuals can gain access to the spiritual gifts of God.

In classical *Pentecostal* practice, one key outward sign of this *baptism in the Spirit* has been seen as the ability to engage in *glossolalia* (or "speaking in tongues"). This involves the individual producing sounds, directed in praise and worship to God, which are not the words of the person's day-to-day language. However, although this has become particularly identified with *Pentecostalism*, the tradition's own emphasis is upon all the spiritual gifts of God, including the gifts of prophecy and healing, although these *charismatic* elements are also now to be found in all the main Christian traditions and movements.

Restorationist and House Church Movements

During the 1970s and 1980s, European Christianity has seen the growth of the so-called *Restorationist* and *House Church* movements, organised separately from the traditional Christian *denominations*. Christians in these movements often feel that the older *Churches* have stifled the real spirit of Christianity in outmoded structures. They therefore seek to develop forms of organisation and networking which they believe to be more consistent with those that were found among the earliest Christian communities.

Quakers and Unitarians

As well as the traditions outlined above, there are also some groups which do not fit neatly into any of these categories but which have historical roots in *Protestant* Christianity. Among these are the *Quakers* (officially known as the Religious Society of Friends) and the *Unitarian and Free Christian Churches*. Both are non-*credal* traditions, believing that *credal* statements about orthodoxies of belief or *church* order are restrictive of true religion.

In the case of *Quakers* this reflects the conviction from their beginnings in the seventeenth century that the "inward light of Christ" is available to all whether or not they use *Christian* terms to describe it. To be faithful is to act in accordance with its guidance not simply to hold the right beliefs about it.

A number of members of the *Unitarian* traditions and some *Quakers* do not wish to be identified as specifically Christian in any way which they believe implies separation from people of other religions or, sometimes, also from humanists.

Churchmanship

Within many of these major traditions of Christianity there are streams or tendencies of what often used to be called *churchmanship*, which refer to Christians in all the major traditions who have particular emphases within their Christian understanding and life.

Among the principal tendencies are the following, although it should be noted that some of these terms have subtly differing meanings when applied to one's own group or to one of which one does not feel a part, and that many of them can be used in polemical, as well as descriptive, ways:

Anglo-Catholic

Anglo-Catholics are *Anglican* Christians who emphasise the *Catholic* inheritance of the *Anglican* tradition in various aspects of theology, doctrine and worship.

Charismatic

Charismatic Christianity is a movement that is historically related to the *Pentecostal* branch of Christianity, but which is now present in all other major branches of Christianity. It is characterised by an emphasis on the direct experience of the *Holy Spirit* being available to Christian believers today, including the possibility that the *Holy Spirit* can produce miraculous works in the contemporary world. *Charismatic* Christians do not, however, necessarily adopt particular items of *Pentecostal* theology or practice, such as the emphasis on *speaking with tongues* as a necessary evidence of *baptism in the Spirit*.

Evangelical

Evangelicals are Christians who draw upon the inheritance of the *Protestant Reformation* particularly as it developed in the eighteenth and nineteenth centuries, especially through the so-called *Evangelical Revival*. They try to live according to the Christian scriptures viewed as the supreme authority for Christian life, and understood as revealed and inspired without human error or distortion.

Because their personal decision to follow Jesus is so central, they feel strongly called to bring others into the Christian *Church* by means of *evangelism* (meaning sharing of *Good News* – from the Greek word *euangelizo*). *Evangelism* means sharing the good news of what Christians believe God has done in and through Jesus. Whilst *Evangelical* Christians are centrally concerned with this, other Christians also engage in *evangelism*, since bearing witness to Jesus is understood to be obligatory for all Christians (see section on "Christian Life" below).

Liberal

Liberal Christians are those Christians in all traditions and denominations who emphasise the importance of understanding and practicing Christianity in a contextualised way and believe that rationality and contemporary relevance are crucial for the meaning and communication of the Christian message.

The Ecumenical Movement

Particularly during the twentieth century, the *Ecumenical Movement* (from the Greek *oikumene*, meaning "the whole inhabited earth") has developed. This represents a commitment among Christians of all traditions to fulfil the prayer of Jesus for the unity of the *Church* and so to build a universal Christian fellowship which transcends or embraces all divisions and boundaries and shares resources for witness and ministry.

This global movement has sometimes found expression in the search for common and unified *Church* structures and organisations in attempts to form united *Churches* out of two or more formerly separate *Churches* as, for example, the United Reformed Church (see below). Among others, it has found expression in agreements, such as that achieved by the work of International Anglican-Roman Catholic Commission for Unity and Mission's statement on *Growing Together in Mission and Unity: Building Together on 40 Years of Anglican-Roman Catholic Dialogue*.

More recently, the organised *Ecumenical Movement* has also sought to achieve closer co-operation and working relationships in common projects between Christians who remain in separate *Churches*, as in the work of Churches Together in Britain and Ireland. At the European level many *Protestant* and *Orthodox* Churches belong within the Conference of European Churches (CEC). At an international level many *Anglican*, *Protestant* and *Orthodox Churches* belong to the World Council of Churches (WCC) and

Roman Catholics participate fully in its Faith and Order Commission.

CHRISTIAN LIFE

The Pattern of Jesus

Jesus commanded his disciples to "love one another as I have loved you", and so Christian believers are called upon to live according to the pattern of Jesus' life which was characterised by sacrificial and self-giving love or *agape* (the Greek word for this form of love).

Sin and Grace

Without the assistance of the power of God, Christianity sees human beings as being gripped by self-centredness and powers beyond their control, a condition described as enslavement to *sin*. The liberation which believers experience when they put their trust in God through Jesus is known as *salvation*. This means a progressive liberation from all that enslaves human beings in terms of self-centredness.

In the Christian life there is a dynamic tension between the belief that one is already, in principle, freed from the power and guilt of *sin*, whilst in this life never being entirely free from it. This is expressed in the Christian scriptures by the concept of *salvation* appearing in all three tenses: past, present and future.

The characteristic by which God is believed to draw people into God's purposes is referred to as *grace*. This is a word that expresses dependence upon the free and unmerited gift of God's power in contrast to reliance upon human goodness or self-sufficiency, and Christians are called to put their trust in God's name.

This trust is described by the word *faith*, which is understood to be evoked and sustained through the power of the *Holy Spirit* at work in and among believers. Christians believe that they can work within this power of God through their practice of prayer, and they are supported in this by participation in fellowship with other Christian believers within the *Church*.

Baptism

The rite of *baptism* (from the Greek *baptizo*, meaning to dip or immerse) in water accompanied by prayer and conducted in the name of the *Holy Trinity* marks a person's entry into the Christian *Church*. In many older *church* buildings the *baptismal font* (usually a standing receptacle which holds the water used in *baptism*) is near the door of the *Church*, to show symbolic entry. The waters of *baptism* are understood as a sign of the remission of *sins* and entry into new life in Jesus.

In the *Anglican, Methodist, Roman Catholic, Reformed*, and *Orthodox Churches* the *baptismal* rite is generally administered to babies or infants. They are presented for *baptism* by their parents who, together with friends or relatives designated as *godparents*, make promises on behalf of the infant. In the *Anglican, Roman Catholic* and *Reformed Churches*, a small amount of water is usually poured on the child's head. Some then anoint with *chrism* oil. In the *Orthodox Churches*, the baby is immersed three times in the *baptismal* waters and is then *chrismated* (anointed with oil) and admitted to full *Communion*.

In other Christian traditions, such as the *Baptist* and *Pentecostal* movements, it is believed that *baptism* should only be administered to those (generally teenagers and adults) who are capable of a personal confession of Christian faith. In these traditions *baptism* is also generally by complete immersion in the *baptismal* waters. Such *Churches* usually have specially constructed sunken *baptistries* (tanks) designed for this purpose.

There are a few Christian traditions, such as the Society of Friends and the Salvation Army, which do not practise water *baptism*.

Their emphasis is on a spiritual and inner *baptism* rather than on outward signs such as the rite of *baptism*.

In some traditions infant *baptism* is popularly known as *christening*, a word which derives from the ancient practice of giving candidates for *baptism* a Christian name to indicate their new identity as believers and members of the *Church*.

Confirmation and Membership

In the *Roman Catholic* tradition, *confirmation* with *Holy Communion* completes initiation into the *Church* by means of believers affirming their faith and making their own the promises that were originally made on their behalf at *baptism*. The Christian believer bears public witness to Jesus and is believed to receive the *Holy Spirit* of God in a special way. Such an understanding of *confirmation* can also be found in the *Anglican* tradition and in some parts of the *Protestant* tradition. Among those who have grown up within the *Church, confirmation* often takes place in the early teenage years.

In *episcopal Churches, confirmation* is usually administered by a *bishop* by the *laying-on of hands* on the head of the candidates, accompanied by prayer. In the *Roman Catholic* tradition, and among many *Anglicans*, renewal of baptismal promises and anointing with *chrism* also takes place. In the *Orthodox* tradition, the *chrismation* with oil blessed by the *bishop*, which immediately follows after *baptism*, is the equivalent of *confirmation*.

In *Churches* that are in the *Reformed* tradition *confirmation* or what is sometimes otherwise known as *reception into membership* is usually administered by the *minister*. This is done within a solemn service at which *baptised* individuals (usually at least in their mid-teens) confess their own personal faith and commitment and are welcomed as full members of the world–wide *Church* and of the local worshipping community. Thereafter, those who have been welcomed play their part in the decision-making processes within their *Church*, their names being entered on the roll, or list, of *Church* members.

Christian Witness

The *Gospel According to Matthew* records that Jesus' last command was to preach the *Gospel* and make *disciples*. The commitment to spread the message of Christianity is undergirded by the conviction that the Christian message is (as *euangelion*, the Greek of the word *Gospel* suggests) *Good News* to announce to people, concerning which it would be selfish to remain quiet.

Some Christians see their responsibility to bear *witness* in terms of participating in organised *evangelistic* activities known as missions, or in belonging to *missionary* organisations that are specifically concerned with presenting the claims of the Christian message, both in this country and in other parts of the world.

Other Christians see the call to *witness* more in terms of the way in which they attempt to go about their day-to-day activities in conformity with the life and teaching of Jesus. In practice this is a difference of emphasis rather than of principle: all Christians would agree that both dimensions of *witness* are necessary.

Ethics and Discipleship

Discipleship, for Christians, involves following the example or "way" of Jesus. For all Christians, the example of Jesus and the teachings of the *Bible* are key sources for decision and practice. In this context, the *Decalogue* or *Ten Commandments* (shared with Judaism) have been key point of reference in Christian ethical understanding, as have Jesus' *Beatitudes* and the rest of his *Sermon on the Mount*.

For Christians in the *Protestant* tradition, individual conscience is also particularly important in deciding how to apply the teachings of the *Bible*. In the *Roman Catholic* tradition, the role of conscience is affirmed although there is a strong emphasis on informing the individual conscience by the scriptures and the corporate teaching of the *Church*.

This teaching is expressed, in particular, through its *bishops* and, supremely, through the *Ecumenical* and other *Councils* of the *Church* and the official pronouncements of the *Pope* (some of which are known as *Encyclicals*). These are often very specific in the guidance they give to individual believers and some aspects of this guidance are reinforced through the application of measures of *Church* discipline.

Christianity has a strong tradition of social concern. Jesus reinforced the *Old Testament* command to love one's neighbour as oneself and he enjoined his disciples to "love as I have loved you". In his teaching concerning the *Last Judgement* of human beings he pointed out that in serving or neglecting the hungry, the sick and the imprisoned, his followers would be serving or neglecting Jesus himself.

In the light of such teaching, Christians have been behind the foundation of many philanthropic and educational initiatives in the UK. But in the twentieth century, alongside a commitment to charitable works, the Christian *Churches* have also increasingly come to understand that they have a calling to oppose structural and institutionalised injustice.

Dietary Issues

Christians do not have any universally agreed dietary regulations, though there are also some, especially those within the *Protestant* traditions, who refrain, on principle, from drinking alcohol.

Fasting

Many Christians observe, in various ways, the discipline of abstaining from certain foods during the season of *Lent* (see the section on

"Calendar and Festivals"). Some Christians also *fast* at other, individually chosen times, in order to focus on prayer or as an act of solidarity with the poor, donating the money which they would have otherwise spent on food to a Christian justice and development charity such as Christian Aid, Tear Fund or the Catholic Agency For Overseas Development (CAFOD).

Monks, Nuns and Religious

The majority of Christians lead ordinary lives at work in the world and within family life, but from the earliest years of Christianity some have felt called to form special groups in which they could aim to share a more complete devotion to Jesus, and to the pattern of his life and work. Some groups are known as *Orders*, and those within them, generally called *monks* (men) and *nuns* (women), have taken what are known as "solemn vows" of poverty, chastity and obedience.

There are also *Congregations* whose members are known as *Religious*. There are also *Religious Brothers* who are not necessarily *monks*, but make vows to live in community. *Monks*, *nuns* and *Religious* can be found in the contemporary *Roman Catholic*, *Orthodox* and *Anglican Churches*. The particular pattern of life of a group of *monks*, *nuns* or *Religious* varies according to the self-understanding of the *Order* or *Congregation* of which they are a part. This, in turn, is based upon the life and teachings of its founder. Some emphasise prayer and meditation and retreat from the world, whilst for others practical service in the world is basic to their calling.

Among the more well-known *Orders* that have grown up in *Western Christianity* are the Society of Jesus (*Jesuits*, founded by St. Ignatius of Loyola and noted for teaching and missionary work); the *Benedictines* (founded by St. Benedict and with an emphasis on prayer, work and the reading of holy books); the *Dominicans* (after the spirit of St Dominic,

and who are known for intellectual study and rigour); the *Carmelites* (known for silent prayer and meditation); and the *Franciscans* (who follow the rule of St Francis of Assisi).

Many other organisations and groups exist within and with the blessing of the *Churches*, having developed as responses to particular contemporary needs or in order to strengthen and renew Christian life. These include *ecumenical* communities such as Iona in Scotland and Lee Abbey in Devon, England, and the L'Arche Communities around the world.

CHRISTIAN WORSHIP

Prayer

In both public and private prayer the *Lord's Prayer* is important. It is the prayer which Jesus is recorded in the *Gospels* as having taught his first *disciples*, and is therefore a pattern for all Christian prayer. In addition to participating in corporate prayer and in worship, many individual Christians have private and personal disciplines of prayer, scriptural study and meditation. There is also a contemplative and mystical tradition of Christian prayer that is associated with such figures as Lady Julian of Norwich, St John of the Cross, and St Teresa of Avila, as well as in the tradition of the so-called *Jesus Prayer*, found in *Orthodox* Christianity.

Eucharistic Worship

Holy Communion is the most characteristic and central act of Christian worship. Some Christians, such as the Religious Society of Friends (the *Quakers*) and the Salvation Army, do not celebrate *Holy Communion*.

Communion means sharing (from the Latin *communio*) and refers to the sharing of bread and wine and of the life of the *Christ*. The *Gospels* record *communion* as having been instituted by Jesus himself at what is known as the *Last Supper* when he blessed, or gave thanks, over bread and wine, declaring it to be his body and his blood and then shared this with his disciples before his *crucifixion*.

Holy Communion is also known as the *Eucharist* (from the Greek word *eucharistia*, meaning "thanksgiving"); among *Roman Catholics* as the *Mass* (probably originating from Latin words spoken at the end of the service *ite, missa est*, the meaning of which has variously been translated as "It is offered" or "Go, you are sent forth"); among the *Orthodox Churches* as the *Divine Liturgy* (from the Greek word *leitourgia*, meaning service); and among some *Protestant Churches* as the *Sacrament of the Lord's Supper* or the *Breaking of Bread*.

The content, interpretation and frequency of this event vary considerably among Christians of different traditions. *Roman Catholic* churches celebrate the *Mass* daily, as do some *Anglican churches* (especially those in the *Anglo-Catholic* tradition), whilst others have one or more weekly celebrations. Some *Protestant Churches* have only monthly or quarterly celebrations, using other forms of worship at other times.

The elements of the *Eucharist* also differ from *Church* to *Church*. *Roman Catholics* normally use a flat wafer of unleavened bread. This is also an *Anglican* practice, although in a number of *Anglican* churches ordinary bread is used. *Anglicans* normally receive wine also, whereas in *Roman Catholic* churches there is a variety of practice, with some offering *Holy Communion* under the form of both bread and wine and also under one element only. *Orthodox* Christians receive a small piece of bread dipped in wine from a long spoon.

In some *Protestant churches* pieces of bread are taken from a single loaf and each individual receives an individual cup of wine (which may be non-alcoholic). In most *Churches*, however, the wine is alcoholic and is drunk from a common cup.

In *Roman Catholic*, *Orthodox* and *Anglican Churches* the *congregation* usually go up to the front of the *church* to receive *communion* either from the *priest* or, in the *Anglican* and *Roman Catholic Churches*, also from a *deacon* or lay *eucharistic* ministers of *Holy Communion*, who are authorised to assist the *priest* and *deacon* in the distribution of the *sacrament*. In some *Protestant Churches* the bread and wine are taken out to the *congregation* by lay officers of the *church* or are passed from member to member.

For all Christians, Jesus' words at the *Last Supper* are of central significance. However, the *Protestant* traditions have generally seen *Holy Communion* more as a remembrance (increasingly this is seen in a stronger sense of "re-presenting" rather than in the weaker and more general useage of "remembrance") of Jesus' death and *resurrection* in obedience to his command to do so in remembrance of him, as recorded in the *New Testament*, with God's act of *atonement* in Jesus being symbolised by the bread and wine which represent Jesus' body and blood.

There is also an emphasis on the spiritual nourishment that is received by believers, individually and collectively, with a sense of reliance upon the indwelling *Spirit of God* expressed by the idea of spiritually feeding on *Christ* by faith.

Among *Roman Catholics*, the *Orthodox* and many *Anglicans* within the *Anglo-Catholic* tradition, the elements of the bread and wine are professed to, in a real sense, become the body and blood of Christ so that, by sharing in them, the faithful can actually have *communion* with the risen Jesus. The *Eucharist* is understood as the memorial or making present of Christ's sacrifice in his saving death and *resurrection*, so that by taking part in the celebration, the faithful are united with Christ's once-for-all work of *salvation*. Among *Roman Catholics*, and in some *Anglican churches*, *First Communion* is usually received by children after a period of preparation at around the age of seven or eight and is of great personal and family significance and is increasingly happening among *Anglicans*.

Preaching

All the Christian *denominations* in the UK give an important place to *preaching* or expounding the *scriptures* within worship. But among the *Churches* of the *Reformation* and among *Churches* founded following the *Evangelical Revival* of the seventeenth and eighteenth centuries, the *preaching* of the *Word* is often given greater prominence than the celebration of the *sacrament* of *Holy Communion*.

Preaching is normally a special responsibility of *ordained ministers*, but most *Churches* in addition authorise appropriately trained and designated *lay preachers* to share in the leading of worship, including the ministry of *preaching* based upon the *scriptures*. In the *Roman Catholic* Church, only *bishops*, *priests* and *deacons* may normally preach at *Mass*.

CHRISTIAN PLACES OF WORSHIP

Church Buildings

The strong history, presence and influence of Christianity in these islands is reflected in the number of Christian places of worship that can be found in all parts of the country.

The Registrar General's list of certified places of worship for 2004 (which is the most recent available at the time of publication) includes details of 16,447 "recorded" (which applies only to buildings of the Church of England and of the Church in Wales) and 29,828 "certified" (which applies to all other Christian groupings) Christian places of worship in England and in Wales.

This includes 15,012 *Anglican* places of worship in England and 1,435 in Wales; 3,459 *Roman Catholic* places of worship in England and 245 in Wales; and 13,364 traditional *Free Church* places of worship in England and 3,477 in Wales. It also includes 357 *Quaker* places of worship in England and 11 in Wales, as well as 156 *Unitarian* places of worship in England, and 24 in Wales, together with 5,586 "Other" Christian places of worship in England, and 508 in Wales.

The CD-ROM accompanying this volume includes basic contact details of 21,817 *churches* and *chapels* (see below) in the UK of which 18,390 are in England, 2,114 in Scotland and 1,313 in Wales.

Most Christian buildings for worship are referred to as *churches*, but in some *Protestant* branches of Christianity, especially among the *Free Churches*, the word "*Church*" is generally reserved for describing the people who make up the community of the *Church*. In these cases, in England and Wales (though not generally in Scotland or Ireland) the word *chapel* may be used to describe the building, instead of *church*.

However, the word *chapel* is also used among *Roman Catholics* and *Anglicans* to denote a small *church* without a *parish* building or a small part of a larger building. Some *Nonconformist* places of worship, such as those of the *Quakers*, are called *meeting houses*. These are not *consecrated* buildings, thus underlining the belief that it is the people who are the *Church* and the place where they meet for worship does not confer sanctity on the proceedings. For the same reason, and especially with regard to Quaker *meeting houses*, they are usually without religious decoration or symbols of any kind.

Some Christians do not meet in recognisably religious buildings but in private homes or in hired public meeting places such as schools, as with the *House Church* or *Restorationist* movement which is a growing form of Christian life in the UK.

From the outside, Christian places of worship vary in appearance. Many old *churches*, however, have a range of recognisable features such as a tower or spire which makes them landmarks in both town and countryside. Very old buildings of this kind are, in England and Wales, generally now of the *Anglican* Christian tradition, and a large number of them pre-date the *Reformation*. By contrast, other Christian places of worship may have the external appearance of a simple square or rectangular hall. Many *churches* of all kinds have stained glass windows frequently depicting scriptural characters, stories or events.

Once inside a building there is again a very wide variety in terms of what might be found. At one end of the spectrum, some *Baptist* or *Methodist chapels* may have an interior bare of religious symbols except perhaps for a wooden *cross* on the wall, although a number of local *churches* now have colourful banners hanging from their walls.

In many *Protestant* buildings, attention is focused on the *pulpit* (the raised enclosed platform, usually at one end of the building, from which the *preacher* addresses the *congregation*) with a simple table in front of it from which the service of *Holy Communion* (see above) is led, but in others, the *pulpit* is no longer used even if it remains in the building.

In most *Protestant* and *Catholic churches* there are seats for the worshippers, but in *Orthodox Churches* most of the *congregation* stand during the service. A place of worship in the *Orthodox* tradition may have brightly coloured frescoes and also many religious pictures called *icons*, whose purpose is to bring close to the worshipper the spiritual realities which they depict in *iconographic* form.

As well as an elevated *pulpit*, there may be a modest *lectern* (reading desk). Instead of a simple table for *Communion*, an *Orthodox church* will have an *altar* which is hidden from general view behind a screen known as an *iconostasis*. This is a screen which is covered in *icons* and has doors in the middle through which the *priest* passes to bring out the bread and wine from the *altar* to the *congregation*.

In *Roman Catholic* and *Anglican churches* in the *Catholic* tradition the main focal point is the *altar*. Another focal point is the *tabernacle*, a secure container in which is placed the consecrated bread from the *Eucharist*. The presence of the consecrated bread is indicated by a lightened lamp or candle. There will also be statues of the *Virgin Mary* and perhaps of *saints* as well. These statues help the worshippers to focus their devotion. They are not, in themselves, objects of worship.

In *Orthodox*, *Roman Catholic* and *Anglo-Catholic Anglican church* buildings, services of worship may be accompanied by the use of incense. Organs and often other musical instruments, sometimes including guitars, are used to accompany singing in *Anglican*, *Protestant* and *Roman Catholic churches*, but not in *Orthodox churches*. *Choirs* are to be found in most Christian traditions, but vary greatly in style between the traditional and formal *Cathedral choirs* and the more informal and contemporary *Gospel choirs* of the *Pentecostal* tradition.

The main church building of *Anglican*, *Roman Catholic* and *Orthodox Dioceses* is known as a *Cathedral*. Such buildings act as focal points for their respective *Dioceses* since they are where the *bishop* has his *cathedra* or seat. Church of England *Cathedrals*, in particular, are very often also seen as places where events of civic and social importance are held, as well as being important parts of the country's architectural and spiritual heritage and thus also as tourist attractions.

Visitors to a Christian Church

There is a wide variation in practice between different types of *churches*, but as a general rule it is wise to dress tidily and avoid particularly revealing clothing. This is perhaps most strongly true in *Orthodox* as well as conservative *Catholic* and *Protestant churches*. Men traditionally remove their hats when entering *church*. It is a courtesy for any male visitors of other religious traditions who normally keep their head covered for religious reasons, to explain this fact to their hosts and no offence will be caused. In some very conservative Christian *churches* women are expected to cover their heads.

Most *churches* have *pews* (benches with raised backs) or rows of seats, although in *Orthodox churches* people generally stand for worship. Where there are *pews* or seats, find a seat and sit quietly. Christians will not generally expect visitors to bow or show other forms of special outward respect to the *altar* (or to any of the statues or *icons* that may be found respectively in *Catholic* or *Orthodox churches*). In some *Orthodox* and *Eastern Catholic churches*, women sit on the left and men on the right.

Visitors are generally welcome to join in the prayers and hymns of the service if they wish. During services, the congregation may kneel, stand or sit depending on the part of the service. Visitors who are not Christians usually sit and stand with the rest of the congregation and kneel if they feel comfortable doing so. Visitors attending a *Eucharist/Mass/Communion* service and who are not *communicant* Christians will not be expected to receive *communion* (and in many *churches*, may not be allowed to do so).

In certain *Protestant churches* the bread and wine of the *Communion* service is passed around the seated congregation. In this case, visitors of other faiths would let the plate and cup pass by to the person next to them. Visitors to a *church* where people are going up to the *altar* to receive *Communion* should simply remain in their seats at this time unless non-communicants are invited to come forward and receive a *blessing* from the *priest*, when it is optional to do so.

No visitors need feel obliged to participate in any action of worship with which they are uncomfortable, especially in going forward for *communion* rather than *blessing*. It is quite acceptable to remain in one's place in prayer or thought.

If a visitor chooses to go forward to receive a *blessing*, rather than remain seated, they should stand or kneel with head bowed, and hands kept folded together or holding a book or service paper so that the priest can see a *blessing* is sought rather than *Communion*. It is important to be aware that the form of any *blessing* is very likely to be specifically Christian, including the invocation of the name of Jesus, or of God the *Son*.

CHRISTIAN CALENDAR AND FESTIVALS

The Christian Calendar

The Christian calendar dates world history in relation to what was believed to have been the year of the birth of Jesus, although it is now generally accepted that this took place a number of years earlier than was originally thought. The *Millennium* which has just begun is the third *Millennium* for Christians.

Because of the Christian belief in the *Incarnation*, the birth of Jesus is seen as being the pivotal point of world history. It is in this context that the letters "AD" (from the first letters of the Latin words *Anno Domini*, meaning "In the Year of our Lord") and "BC" (for "Before Christ") came to be used for dating world history, although outside of internal Christian usage this notation is more generally being replaced, as in this directory, by the letters "CE" (for Common Era) and "BCE" (for Before the Common Era).

Sunday

Christianity inherited its seven day week from Judaism. Sunday (the first day of the Jewish week) is usually observed as the day of assembly for Christian worship because, as it was the day of the week on which Jesus is believed to have been raised from death, it marks *resurrection* and new beginning. However, the so-called *Sabbatarian* or *Seventh Day Churches* believe that the commandment to the Jews to keep the seventh day (Saturday) holy is still binding on Christians after the coming of Jesus.

The understanding of Sunday observance varies considerably among Christians. Many *Roman Catholics* attend *Vigil Sunday Mass* on Saturday evening since, following the Biblical tradition, the day is seen as commencing the previous evening. Some *Protestants* refrain from employment or secular recreation throughout Sunday, concentrating on participation in morning and evening worship.

The Church Year and Festivals

The Christian *liturgical year* begins with *Advent* around the end of November. The *liturgical* year marks key events and commemorates figures connected with the Christian story and it is particularly important for *Roman Catholics*, the *Orthodox* and *Anglicans*. Most *Protestant Churches* of the *Reformed* and *Congregational* traditions observe only Sundays, *Advent, Christmas, Holy Week, Easter* and *Pentecost* (see section on "Christian Calendar and Festivals" below), while some do observe *Lent* and *Epiphany*.

In some small Christian groupings even these days are seen as, at best, of marginal importance. At worst they are seen as a corruption of pure Christianity, introduced largely to incorporate some elements of pre-Christian tradition in order to wean Christians away from the traditional celebrations at these times of year.

There are three cycles of festivals within the Christian *liturgical* year. The *Christmas* cycle has dates which are fixed within the *Gregorian* calendar. Then come Sundays in *Ordinary Time* during *Lent*; and then the *Easter* cycle, the dates of which vary for reasons explained below under *Easter*. Finally, there is a third cycle of festivals and commemorations of *saints* and *martyrs* of the *Church*, which are observed on fixed dates. A number of *Orthodox Churches* follow the so-called *Julian* calendar which, in the present century, is thirteen days behind the date of the calendar which is in common social use in the UK.

Those who observe the liturgical calendar understand it as unfolding the whole mystery of *Christ* and the *Church's* belief in his saving work, from his *incarnation* to his *second coming*. Once a year at *Easter*, the *passion* and *resurrection* of Jesus is celebrated with the utmost solemnity.

In *Anglican, Orthodox* and *Roman Catholic churches*, each week on a Sunday, understood as the day of the *Lord's* resurrection, the *eucharist* is celebrated, as also in the *Roman Catholic* tradition and among some *Anglicans* (especially those in the *Anglo-Catholic* tradition), on a daily basis.

The season of *Lent* is understood as a time of preparation for the celebration of *Easter*, by means of prayer and penitential practices. The joy of *Easter* is celebrated in the *Easter* season which culminates with *Pentecost*, the fiftieth day, which recalls the descent of *Holy Spirit* on the first *apostles* of the Christian *Church*. During the season of *Advent* and *Christmas* the manifestation of the Lord both in his first coming in the *incarnation* and in his *Second Coming* at the end of time is celebrated in a special way.

Accompanying the celebration of the mystery of *Christ* in this yearly cycle, the *Orthodox* and *Roman Catholic* traditions, together with significant numbers of *Anglican* Christians, also venerate with a particular love Mary, the *Mother of God* and, on specifically appointed days, set before the devotion of the faithful the memory of the Christian *martyrs* and other *saints*.

Advent (November-December)
Advent means "coming" and it refers to the coming of Jesus into the world and to his *Second Coming* at the end of time. The season is observed by *Western* Christians as a solemn preparatory season for *Christmas*, traditionally beginning on the fourth Sunday before *Christmas*.

Immaculate Conception of the Blessed Virgin Mary (8th December)

Roman Catholics celebrate the belief that Mary the Mother of Jesus was herself, by virtue of Christ's redeeming work, conceived free of original sin in order that she might be sinless for the bearing of Jesus.

Christmas (25th December)

Celebrates the birth of Jesus, the precise date of which is unknown, but the Catholic Church fixed on 25th December which coincides with the pre-Christian winter solstice. Some Orthodox Churches keep to the pre-Gregorian calendar date of either 6th or 7th January celebrating the birth of Jesus. For the other Churches, the 6th January is the twelfth night of Christmas, which closes the Christmas season with the festival of Epiphany.

Epiphany (6th January)

The word Epiphany is Greek meaning "manifestation". In the Orthodox Churches, this refers to the manifestation of Jesus at his baptism as the Son of God. In the Western Churches, Epiphany celebrates also the adoration of Jesus by the Magi or Wise Men, and thus his being revealed to the Gentiles (non-Jews). It is sometimes referred to as the Twelfth Night as it is twelve days after Christmas.

Shrove Tuesday (February/March)

This is a popular folk festival marking the day before the start of Lent, and has a number of traditional and popular cultural customs attached to it. The name comes from the Middle English word shriven which referred to the practice of making confession before the beginning of Lent. The popular custom of making pancakes arose from the need to use up eggs before Lent, a period of fasting. The same day is sometimes known by the French title Mardi Gras (fat Tuesday) which refers to the using up of all the fats before Lent.

Ash Wednesday (February/March)

This is the first day of Lent and is so called because in some churches the priest marks the forehead of believers with ash as a sign of mortality and of penitence before God. In the Roman Catholic Church and in Anglican churches of Catholic tradition, it is a day of fasting and abstinence.

Lent (February-March/April)

This is a period of forty days, not counting Sundays, between Ash Wednesday and the Saturday before Easter. It is a preparation for Easter. Its roots can be found the early Church's tradition of a season of preparation for those hoping, during the season of Easter, to be admitted in baptism or restored to membership of the Church. It has also become associated with Gospel stories of Jesus being tempted for forty days in the wilderness prior to the beginning of his public ministry. In the Orthodox tradition it is known as the Great Fast and starts on the Monday (known as Clean Monday) before the first Sunday of Lent rather than on the Wednesday as in the Western Churches. In all traditions it has become associated with a season of penitence and preparation in which many Christians abstain from some foods and/or luxuries and commit themselves to prayer, study and almsgiving.

The Annunciation to the Blessed Virgin Mary (25th March)

This celebrates the announcement by the Angel Gabriel to Mary that she was to give birth to a son to be called Jesus, and her assent to this. It is celebrated nine months prior to Christmas Day.

Mothering Sunday (March)

This is the fourth Sunday in Lent and is widely known as Mother's Day. Though it may have begun with the idea of Mother Church or of Jerusalem as the "mother of us all", it has become a more popular occasion upon which to recognise and thank mothers for all that they do.

Passion Sunday (March)
This is the fifth Sunday in *Lent* when Christians begin to concentrate their thoughts on the significance of the *Passion* (or suffering) of Jesus, in preparation for recalling the events of *Holy Week*.

Palm Sunday (March/April)
This is the first day of *Holy Week*. On this day Christians are often given pieces of palm leaf in the form of a cross to recall the *Gospel* accounts of how Jesus was greeted by crowds waving palm leaves as he entered into Jerusalem a few days before his *crucifixion*.

Holy Week (March/April)
The last week of *Lent*, which is dedicated to remembering the suffering and death of Jesus.

Maundy Thursday (March/April)
The Thursday in *Holy Week* which commemorates the day on which, at his *Last Supper* with his disciples, Jesus instituted the *Holy Eucharist*. It was also the occasion of Jesus' command to his disciples to wash one another's feet as a sign of mutual humility and service. A *foot washing* ceremony is held on this day in some *churches*. It is also the day on which Jesus gave his *disciples* the commandment to love one another, and prayed for their unity. The name *Maundy Thursday* comes from the Latin of the beginning of the *Gospel of John* chapter 13 verse 34, where Jesus is recorded as giving the *disciples* a new commandment (*Mandatum novum*). In *churches* in the *Catholic* tradition the *altars* are generally stripped bare at the end of this day.

Good Friday (March/April)
The Friday of *Holy Week* which commemorates the *crucifixion* of Jesus is generally an austere and solemn day, but is called "Good" because Christians believe *salvation* to be effected through the *crucifixion*. In the *Roman Catholic* Church and in *Anglican churches* of *Catholic* tradition, it is a day of *fasting* and abstinence. In many *churches*

a service with meditations upon Jesus' words from the *cross* is held between noon and three o'clock in the afternoon. The symbolism of the *cross* of Jesus lies behind the traditional practice of eating buns marked with a *cross* on this day.

Holy Saturday (March/April)
This is a day of prayerful waiting and preparation for *Easter*. In the *Roman Catholic* and *Orthodox* traditions and among *Anglo-Catholic Anglicans*, a special night service takes place (the *Easter Vigil*) as the main celebration of *Easter*. This involves the biblical story of creation, the solemn proclamation of the *resurrection* of Jesus, the lighting of the *Paschal* candle and the renewal of *baptismal* vows. Among *Roman Catholics*, it is the service at which adults are *baptised* into the *Church*.

Easter (March/April)
Easter commemorates the *resurrection* of Jesus. It is the central Christian festival and is full of joy. It was traditionally the main time for *baptism*. In the *Western* Christian tradition it is celebrated on the first Sunday following the first full moon after the spring equinox. The date therefore varies within the solar calendar adopted by western countries. The *Orthodox* calculate *Easter* in a different way and their celebration of the season also continues, in total, for fifty days until *Pentecost*, and therefore also includes *Ascension Day*. The name *Easter* derives from the old English *eostre* which was the name for a pre-Christian Spring festival. The giving of *Easter* eggs, symbolising new life, appears to be a survival of an ancient fertility custom.

Ascension Day (May/June)
This is celebrated on the fortieth day after *Easter* and commemorates the last earthly appearance of the Risen Christ to his first disciples which is recorded in the scriptures. His *ascension* marks his transcending of all earthly limitations and the celebration of his kingly rule. It is always celebrated on a Thursday.

Pentecost (May/June)

The name derives from the Greek *pentecoste*, meaning fiftieth day and it is celebrated on the seventh Sunday after *Easter*. *Pentecost* (or the *Feast of Weeks*) is a Jewish harvest festival which has been given a different meaning by the *Church*. For Christians, it marks the outpouring of the *Holy Spirit* upon the followers of Jesus, and the commencement of the *Church's* mission to spread the message about Jesus throughout the world. It is sometimes known as *Whitsun* (*White Sunday*), from the custom of converts presenting themselves on this day for *baptism* dressed in white clothes.

Trinity Sunday (June)

This is celebrated in the *West* on the Sunday following *Pentecost*. The *Orthodox Churches* celebrate *All Saints* on this day. *Trinity Sunday* is devoted to contemplation of the mystery of God, which Christians see as an indivisible unity and yet revealed in the inter-related communion of God the *Father*, *Son* and *Holy Spirit*.

Corpus Christi (on a Sunday following *Trinity Sunday*, therefore usually in June)

This is particularly a *Roman Catholic* festival and celebrates belief in the presence of Jesus in the *Eucharist* in a more joyful way than is appropriate on *Maundy Thursday*. The festival is also observed by some *Anglicans* as a thanksgiving for the institution of the *Holy Communion* or *Eucharist*.

Transfiguration (6th August)

This recalls the scriptural account of the shining of Jesus' face and clothes on the so-called Mount of Transfiguration, when his heavenly glory is believed to have been revealed to his disciples.

Assumption of the Blessed Virgin Mary (15th August)

Roman Catholics, *Anglicans* in the *Catholic* tradition, and *Orthodox* (who call it the *Dormition* - the falling asleep of the *Mother of God*) celebrate the belief that Mary, body and soul, was *assumed*, or taken up into heaven.

St. Michael and All Angels (29th September)

This day celebrates the Archangel Michael, the adversary of Satan. Sometimes known as *Michaelmas*, this is a season of the *Western Church's* year in which the *ordination* of *priests* and *deacons* may take place, though many *ordinations* also occur on *Trinity Sunday* and, in the *Anglican* tradition, at *Petertide* (at the end of June).

Harvest Festival (September/October)

Although it is not an official part of any *Church* year, the observance of a *harvest* festival has become a regular event in many *churches*. It celebrates the bounty of God in creation. Such festivals became common from the Middle Ages onwards and were revived in the nineteenth century. Displays of foodstuffs are often made in church and these are then distributed to the needy after the festival is over. Increasingly, this is linked with justice issues.

All Saints Day (1st November)

Since the names of every *saint* cannot be known, this festival commemorates all the *saint*s. In many *churches* there is a focus upon the sense of fellowship of Christians today with those from past times and other parts of the world.

All Souls Day (2nd November)

Is a day upon which to remember all those who have died and are within the so-called *Communion of Saints* - the unity in Jesus of all believers, past, present and future.

CHRISTIAN ORGANISATIONS

Organisational Listings

In the UK there are numerous Christian *Churches* belonging to the principal Christian traditions described earlier. In what follows, attention is focused on these *Church* bodies as such (often described as *ecclesiastical* bodies – from the Greek word *ecclesia* meaning *Church*). There are, in addition, very many Christian organisations with particular foci for their work, some of which are *Church*-sponsored, others of which are voluntary associations of Christians with various foci for their work, such as the Christian Ecology Group, the Christian Socialist Movement and many others. Details of many of these organisations can be found in the *UK Christian Handbook*.

Due to the large number of Christian places of worship and local organisations, in the CD-ROM accompanying this volume detailed information is given only on UK, national and regional levels of organisation, in relation to which details are included of around 81 Christian organisations working at a UK level as well as around 5 working at an English level, 13 at a Scottish level, 13 at a Northern Irish level/Irish Republic level, and 17 at a Welsh level.

There are other details of around 327 Christian organisations working at a regional level, of which 227 are in England, 48 in Scotland, 28 in Northern Ireland and 24 in Wales. At the same time, basic contact details are given for (the first time, as these could not be accommodated within the paper-based editions of the directory in 1993, 1997 and 2001) local Christian places of worship, including basic address details of around 21,817 local *churches* (including around 18,390 in England, 1,313 in Wales, and 2,114 in Scotland).

Christian Traditions and Churches in the UK

The principal characteristics of the *Churches* in the UK reflect the wider, global Christian traditions of which they are a part and which were outlined in the section above on "Traditions in Christianity".

However, by reason of history and contemporary circumstances these traditions are to be found in different proportions within the UK and its various nations than is the case internationally.

Also, as a result of the specific history of Christianity in the UK, it is more common to use the categories of *established Churches* (the Church of England and the Church of Scotland), the Roman Catholic Church, the *Orthodox Churches*, and the *Free Churches* than the categories which are more common globally of *Roman Catholic*, *Protestant*, *Orthodox*, *Anglican* and *Pentecostal*.

The principal *Protestant Churches* in the UK, and which are also *Free Churches*, include the Methodist Church, the United Reformed Church and *Baptist churches*, but now also *Churches* with a majority of black members and with a predominantly black leadership. The *Anglican Churches* regard themselves as drawing upon both the *Catholic* and the *Protestant* traditions.

The variations in the pattern of *Churches* in the UK are closely related to the diverse but connected national histories of these islands. In particular, the contemporary patterns of Christian organisation reflect the various national outworkings of the events of the *Reformation* as outlined below. As a religious movement which had political dimensions, the *Reformation* affected different parts of these islands in different ways.

Christian Traditions and Churches in England

In England, the *Reformation* led to the establishment of what is now called the Church of England through the 1534 *Act of Supremacy* of King Henry VIII, who initially styled himself *Head of the Church*. This title was later modified under Queen Elizabeth I to *Supreme Governor*. Thus the *Church* in England became independent of the jurisdiction of Rome, but closely identified with the monarchy.

In the period which followed in England, Christians who maintained allegiance to the

Roman Catholic Church were persecuted under King Edward VI (1549-53). Under the *Catholic* Queen Mary (1553-58), *Protestants* were persecuted. Under Queen Elizabeth I, the position was again reversed.

The Church of England preserved many of the characteristics of *Catholic* Christianity, but also embraced certain *Protestant* features, such as a stress on the availability of the Christian scriptures to be read and studied in the everyday language of ordinary believers rather than in Latin since Latin was accessible only to *priests*, scholars and others who had received a formal education and, in any case, had not been the original language of the scriptures.

By the end of the sixteenth century, *Congregationalists* (whose origins lay in the conviction that the *Church* consists of committed believers and who argued that therefore spiritual authority resides in the local congregation rather than in supra-local *Church* structures) were emerging, followed during the seventeenth century by *Baptists* and *Quakers*.

After the period of political and religious upheaval which followed the English civil war and the restoration of the monarchy, the 1662 *Act of Uniformity* led to over one thousand *clergy* being ejected from their parishes in England due to their refusal to be bound by its provisions which made the *Book of Common Prayer* compulsory.

This strengthened the *Presbyterian Independent* and *Congregationalist* movements as they were joined by many *Anglican clergy* who did not wish to conform to these requirements. From this non-conforming stance, the name for such Christian traditions of *"Nonconformists"*.

Since King Henry VIII's break with the *Papacy*, and the start of the English *Reformation*, the Church of England has generally held a predominant place in English Christian life. Nevertheless, towards the end of the nineteenth century, and in the first part of the twentieth century, the *Free Churches* came to occupy a prominent place in public and religious life, while in the latter part of the twentieth century and the beginning of the twenty-first, *Roman Catholic* Christianity has strongly re-emerged, strengthened by successive migrations of *Roman Catholic* Christians from around the globe, including from Africa and Latin America, and also from Poland when the latter's accession to the European Union brought with it unrestricted travel and settlement rights to Poles.

The Census question as asked in England (and Wales) did not (unlike the form of the question as asked in Scotland and in Northern Ireland) differentiate between denominational traditions of Christianity. However, based on Christian Research estimates for "community membership" in the year 2000, in relation to an overall total of 34,100,000 the following can be calculated as a proportion of Christian "community membership" in England:

- *Anglicans* at 79.8% (or 27,200,000) of the Christian community of England
- *Roman Catholics* at 12.0% (or 4,100,000)
- *Methodists* at 3.2% (or 1,100,000)
- Other *Churches* at 2.3% (or 800,000)
- *Orthodox* at 1.5% (500,000)
- *Baptist* at 0.9% (or 300,000)
- *Presbyterian* at 0.3% (or 100,000)

By contrast, based on Christian Research estimates in relation to the narrower concept of "Church Membership" for the year 2001 out of an overall total of 3,716,816, the following can be calculated as a proportion of Christian "Church Membership" in England:

- *Anglicans* at 37.1% (or 1,377,085)
- *Roman Catholics* at 26.1% (or 971,172)
- *Methodists* at 8.3% (or 308,319)
- *Pentecostals* at 6.1% (or 225,686)
- *Orthodox* at 6.1% (or 225,503)
- *Baptists* at 4.4% (or 164,771)
- *New Churches* at 3.4% (or 127,624)
- *Independents* at 2.9% (or 106,964)

- *Other Churches* at 2.3% (124,387)
- *Presbyterians* at 2.3% (85,305)

In relation to the more limited category of "Church attendance" and based on Christian Research estimates for the year 2000, out of an overall total of 3,533,700, the following can be calculated as a proportion of Christian "*Church* attendance in England":

- *Anglicans* at 29.9% (or 1,063,300)
- *Roman Catholics* at 27.9% (or 990,400)
- *Methodists* at 10.5% (or 372,600)
- *Baptists* at 7.9% (or 280,000)
- *Pentecostals* at 6.1% (216,400)
- *Independent* at 4.2% (or 150,200)
- *New Churches* at 7.0% (or 248,400)
- *United Reformed* at 3.2% (or 112,000)
- Other *Churches* at 3.2% (or 94,800)
- *Orthodox* at 0.7% (or 25,600)

Christian Traditions and Churches in Scotland

It was in Scotland that the Christian *Reformation* tradition of *Calvinism* had its greatest impact within the UK. In 1560 the Church of Scotland was reformed along *Calvinist* principles, with a *Presbyterian* form of *Church* government based upon a collective of local *church* leadership of both *clergy* and non–clerical *elders*. Known as the *presbytery* (from the Greek *presbuteros* meaning *elder*), it is not to be confused with the residence of a *Roman Catholic parish priest*, usually also known as a *presbytery*.

Following the 1603 accession of James Stuart to the English Crown as James I of England, the Church of Scotland played a significant role in the national identity of Scotland. Attempts made to introduce an *episcopalian* (from the Greek *episcope*, meaning oversight) model of *church* government into Scotland, centred upon *bishops* (*episcopoi*) operating at the regional level, were unsuccessful, with the minority who supported an *Episcopalian* model forming the Scottish Episcopal Church.

The dominant *Presbyterian* form of Christianity continued to be recognised as the Church of Scotland which is the *established* Church in Scotland and is generally understood by *Presbyterians* as the national *Church*. Indeed, at times, this identification has been so that, at various points in Scottish history, to be *Episcopalian* was to be seen as English, while to be *Roman Catholic* was often to be seen as Irish.

Against this background, sectarianism has played a role in Scottish life to the extent that it was, in part, a recognition of the need to tackle sectarian issues that led to the form of the 2001 Census question on religion as it was asked in Scotland asking, like that in Northern Ireland, both about current and historic familial identification with particular Christian traditions. Thus from the results of 2001 Census questions on religion, of the total respondents in Scotland who identified themselves as Christian, 65.1% indicated they were *Presbyterian*, 24.4% *Roman Catholic*, and 10.5% other Christian.

In terms of "Church attendance", based on Christian Research estimates for the year 2000, out of an overall total of 602,400 the following can be calculated as a proportion of Christian "*church* attendance" in Scotland:

- *Presbyterian* at 45.1% (or 271,200), of whom 41.3% or 248,600 were Church of Scotland, and the remainder were "other *Presbyterian*".
- *Roman Catholic* at 35.1% (or 211, 200)
- *Independent* at 7.5% (or 45,000)
- Other *Churches* at 5.1% (or 30,700)
- *Baptist* at 4.1% (or 24,800)
- *Episcopalians* at 3.2% (or 19,500)

Christian Traditions and Churches in Wales

In Wales, the Church also shared the *Reformation* history of England in terms of the impact of the 1534 *Act of Supremacy* of King Henry VIII becoming, as in England, independent of the jurisdiction of Rome, but being closely identified with the monarchy. During the sixteenth and early seventeenth centuries the *Bible* and the *Book of Common Prayer* (containing prescribed orders of worship of the Church of England) were translated into Welsh and were quickly accepted into common use among Christians in Wales.

In Wales, the substantial majority of the *Churches* which were formed as a result of these developments worshipped and conducted their congregational and individual Christian life in the Welsh language. Today in Wales, the Union of Welsh Independents, the majority of *congregations* in the Baptist Union of Wales and the Presbyterian Church of Wales, and all *churches* within the Cymru District of the Methodist Church, continue to conduct their worship and *congregational* life in Welsh, as do some *Anglican churches* and several *Unitarian chapels*.

The Census question as asked in Wales (and England) did not (unlike the form of the question as asked in Scotland and in Northern Ireland) differentiate between denominational traditions of Christianity. Unlike in Scotland, in Wales there has not been a single predominant religious tradition that has acted as a focus for national identity, although the multiplicity of *Non-Conformist Free Churches* have played a significant role in the social, political and cultural life of Wales, and played a significant historic role in preserving and promoting the use of the Welsh language.

In terms of "*church* attendance", based on Christian Research estimates for the year 2000, out of an overall total of 223,800 the following can be calculated as a proportion of Christian "church attendance" in Wales:

- *Anglicans* (of the Church in Wales) at 28.2% (or 63,000)
- *Roman Catholics* at 19.6% (or 43,800)
- Other *Churches* at 17.7% (or 39,500)
- *Presbyterians* (of the Presbyterian Church of Wales) at 10.6% (or 23,800)
- *Baptists* at 10.1% (or 22,5000)
- *Independents* (of the Union of Welsh Independents) at 7.3% (or 16,300)
- *Methodists* at 7.0% (or 15,600)

Christian Traditions and Churches in Northern Ireland

In Northern Ireland, as in Wales, there is no officially established form of religion, with the *Episcopalian* Church of Ireland having been disestablished as long ago as 1871. In addition, the *Northern Ireland Act* specifically proscribed the establishment of any particular religion or religious tradition, although the *Presbyterian* tradition which came to Ireland from Scotland is now the largest *Protestant* Christian tradition in Northern Ireland.

The form of the 2001 Census question on religion as asked in Northern Ireland (as also in Scotland) asked about both original and current identification with particular Christian traditions. From responses to this, it would appear that, of those identifying themselves as Christians in response to the religion questions in the 2001 Census in Northern Ireland, out of a total of 1,446,386 responding in this way, the following can be calculated as a proportion of Christian *church* attendance:

- *Roman Catholics* at 46.9% (or 678,462)
- *Presbyterians* (of the Presbyterian Church of Ireland) at 24.1% (or 348,742)
- *Anglicans* (of the Church of Ireland) at 17.8% (or 257,788)
- Other *Christians* at 7.1% (or 59,173)
- *Methodists* (of the Methodist Church in Ireland) at 4.1% (or 59,173)

Anglican Churches

There are four autonomous *Anglican Churches* in these islands which correspond to its main nations. The Church of England, the Scottish Episcopal Church, the Church in Wales, and the Church of Ireland (which operates in both Northern Ireland and the Republic of Ireland.)

In England, in 2004 (which is the most recent year for which data is available), there were 15,012 *Anglican* places of worship recorded with the General Register Office in 2003, with 1,435 in Wales.

At the regional level, the *Churches* of the *Anglican* tradition are organised into *Provinces* and *dioceses*. At the local level, they are organised into *parishes* (the neighbourhood area) and *deaneries* (groupings of *parishes*). In England, Church of England *parishes* are legal entities and taken together cover the whole country, so that there is no area which is not understood as being in a Church of England *parish*.

The Church of England is the *established Church* in England. Its special constitutional position in the UK state is currently reflected by twenty-six of its senior *bishops* having reserved places in the House of Lords. The Church of England has two *Provinces* (of Canterbury and York) and forty-four *dioceses* in all (42 in England and 1 in the Isle of Man) and also one in Europe.

Although an *episcopal* Church (led by *bishops* who have oversight of their *dioceses*), the Church of England is governed by the *General Synod* which includes three categories of *diocesan* representatives: *laity*, *clergy* and *bishops*, with similar *synods* operating at *diocesan* and *deanery* levels. These *synods* have various committees which deal with different aspects of the *Church's* work.

The *Anglican* Churches in Scotland, Wales and Ireland are not *established Churches*. The Scottish Episcopal Church has seven *dioceses*. It is the smallest of the *Anglican Churches* in these islands.

The Church of Ireland has two *Provinces* (Dublin and Armagh). The *Province* of Dublin is almost entirely in the Irish Republic whilst that of Armagh is mostly in Northern Ireland. The *disestablishment* of the Church of England in Wales led, in 1920, to the formation of the Church in Wales that is one *Province*. The *Province* has six *dioceses* and is a bi-lingual *Church*.

Roman Catholic Church

There is a continuity in the English *Roman Catholic* tradition with Christianity before King Henry VIII's repudiation of *Papal* authority.

However, the Roman Catholic Church's contemporary strength in England and Wales is mainly due to the nineteenth and early twentieth century immigration of *Roman Catholics* from Ireland as well as, more recently, migrations to Britain of *Roman Catholics* from other parts of Europe (especially Poland) and the wider world.

In England, in 2004, there were 3,459 places of *Roman Catholic* worship in England, certified as such with the Registrar General, and 245 in Wales.

In Scotland in 1560 there was an attempt to suppress *Roman Catholic* Christianity and *Papal* authority by law. However, the *Catholic* tradition survived in the south-west and in the highlands and islands of the north-west of Scotland.

Immigration from Ireland and Italy also increased the *Catholic* population, which is concentrated around Glasgow. In Ireland as a whole the Roman Catholic Church is by far the largest Christian tradition. It is also numerically the largest single *Church* in Northern Ireland.

In these islands the Roman Catholic Church has three national *Bishops' Conferences*: the Bishops' Conference for England and Wales, another for Scotland, and another for Ireland. Roman Catholic life is focussed upon *parish* and *diocesan*, rather than intermediate or national levels.

At regional level, the *Roman Catholic* Church is organised into *dioceses* and *Provinces*. There are twenty-two *dioceses* in England and Wales and eight *dioceses* in Scotland. There are currently seven *Provinces* in Great Britain, each of which has an *Archbishop*.

The *Archdioceses* of Birmingham, Liverpool and Westminster are the seats of the *Roman Catholic Archbishops* for England, while Edinburgh, Glasgow and St Andrew's are for Scotland, and Cardiff for Wales. The *Archbishops* often give a personal focus to leadership of the *Roman Catholic* Church in these countries. In respect of Northern Ireland, the Archdiocese of Armagh provides a focus for *Roman Catholics* both north and south of the border, since the *Church* is organised, as most other *Churches* on the island of Ireland, on an all-Ireland basis.

Orthodox Churches

In the UK the *Orthodox Churches* as such are a relatively recent presence apart from a number of individuals who settled in the UK from the seventeenth century onwards. The Registrar General's list of places of worship for England and Wales does not keep a running total for a separate category of *Orthodox churches*.

Larger numbers resulted from the arrival of significant emigré groups of Russians after the Russian revolution, and the post-Second World War migrations of Greeks, Serbs and other ethnic groups which have a traditionally close relationship with *Orthodox* Christianity. The *Orthodox Churches* in the UK are, in fact, still related to these older national and ethnic *Orthodox Churches*.

The Greek Orthodox Church is numerically the largest, principally due to immigration from Cyprus. There are also, however, numbers of individuals from other ethnic and national backgrounds who have joined *Orthodox Churches*.

There are now also a growing number of Churches of the *Oriental Orthodox* tradition including the Armenian, Coptic, Ethiopian, Indian and Syrian *Orthodox*, and there is a Council of Oriental Orthodox Churches which seeks to group these *Churches* together co-operatively. Some Rastafarians are also baptised into the Ethiopian Orthodox Church. Because the *Orthodox* in general are not numerically strong and their members are geographically scattered, there is usually only one *diocese* for each *Church*, covering the whole of the UK.

The Registrar General's list for England and Wales does not keep separate cumulative totals of *Orthodox* Christian places of worship.

Protestant Churches

Reformed Churches

The largest non–*Anglican Protestant* tradition in the British Isles is the *Reformed* tradition, within which *Presbyterianism* is the biggest strand. The word *Presbyterian* comes from the Greek word *presbuteros*, meaning *elder* and it refers to the local leadership of a Christian community. *Presbyterianism* is so called because of its emphasis on the local and collective leadership of such *elders*.

The Registrar General's 2004 list of places of worship gives 1,578 certified places of worship for the United Reformed Church in England, and 132 in Wales.

The main *Reformed* Churches of the UK are the Church of Scotland, the Presbyterian Church in Ireland, the Presbyterian Church of Wales and the United Reformed Church (which also includes the *Churches of Christ* and *Congregational* traditions, having been formed initially in 1972 through the uniting of the Presbyterian Church of England and the Congregational Church, formerly the Congregational Union).

There are also a number of smaller *Presbyterian* bodies – the Free Church of Scotland, the Free Presbyterian Church of Scotland, the Reformed Presbyterian Church of Scotland and the United Free Church of Scotland.

In Ireland smaller *Presbyterian* church bodies include the Reformed Presbyterian Church of Ireland, the Evangelical Presbyterian Church, the Non-Subscribing Presbyterian

Church of Ireland, and the Free Presbyterian Church of Ulster.

Methodism

There are 6,939 *Methodist* places of worship recorded in the Registrar General's 2004 list of certified places of worship for England, and 473 in Wales.

Methodism is one of the most numerous *Protestant* denominations in the UK and is in the *Free Church* stream of Christianity. Its origins go back to the *Evangelical Revival* of the eighteenth century and specifically to the religious movement led by John Wesley, aided by his brother, the hymn writer Charles Wesley.

The word *Methodist* describes the systematic and methodical approaches to Christian conduct and training that were adopted by its founders, John and Charles Wesley within their Society, which began as a fellowship within the Church of England.

The Methodist Church of Great Britain covering England, Scotland and Wales is the largest *Methodist* body. Smaller *Methodist* bodies are the Methodist Church in Ireland, the Free Methodist Church, the Wesleyan Reform Union, and the Independent Methodist Connexion. *Methodist* numerical strength is concentrated in England, especially in the South West and the northern counties.

Methodism is organised on the basis of local *congregations* grouped together into what are known as *circuits*, each with a *Superintendent Minister*. These *circuits* are then part of regional bodies known as *Districts*.

Each *District* is overseen by a *Chair*, who is a senior ordained *presbyter*, and all are governed by the national *Conference*, which annually appoints a senior ordained *presbyter* as *President* of the Methodist Conference and a senior lay person as *Vice-President*.

Methodists are noted for their emphasis upon pastoral care by *lay* people; for the large proportion of worship services led by *lay Local Preachers*; for the use of *hymns* to express their faith, and for emphasising that the Christian *Gospel* is for all people and have a strong concern for social responsibility and social justice.

Baptist Movement

The *Baptist* movement emerged at the beginning of the sixteenth century. The Registrar General's 2004 list includes 2,485 certified *Baptist* places of worship in England, and 830 in Wales.

The word *Baptist* is used because of this tradition's practice of reserving *baptism* as a rite of Christian initiation for those who have confessed personal Christian faith rather than administering it to infants. Other than in exceptional circumstances (such as on medical grounds), *baptism* is generally administered in *Baptist congregations* by complete immersion in water.

Today *Baptists* are organised into four main *Unions* of *churches* with some overlap of membership: these are the Baptist Union of Great Britain (the largest), the Baptist Union of Scotland, the Baptist Union of Wales, and the Baptist Union of Ireland.

There are, however, also smaller groups of *Seventh Day* and *Strict Baptists*. Though distributed nationally, there are concentrations in the counties to the north of London and around the Bristol Channel, as well as to some extent in the rest of south-east England.

The individual congregation is the basic unit of *Baptist church* life. The Baptist Union of Great Britain has thirteen *Associations* each of which is led by a regional *Association* team headed by a *Senior Regional Minister*. *Congregations* are also grouped informally into *Clusters* which may vary from three or four *congregations* up to twenty. The main purpose of such groupings is to engage together in *mission*.

Each of the national *Unions* has a governing *Council* and holds an annual *Assembly*. The *Unions,* together with the Baptist Missionary Society, constitute the Federation of British Baptists, an umbrella body which exists to promote consultation and cooperation, though it does not have powers itself.

Congregationalism

Congregationalism goes back to the early *Puritan Separatists* from the Elizabethan *Church*. It grew with the imposition of the *Book of Common Prayer* in 1662, following the Restoration of the Monarchy following the Commonwealth and the Protectorate. In Ireland, the Congregational Union of Ireland is the main representative of this *Congregational* tradition.

Congregationalists accounted for around seventy per cent of the membership of the United Reformed Church at its formation in 1972. The United Reformed Church, which has *congregations* in England, Wales and Scotland, combines elements of both *Congregational* and *Presbyterian* patterns of Church government as well as those of the Churches of Christ.

Local *congregations* are grouped into *Districts*, and *Districts* into twelve *Provinces*, each with a *Provincial Moderator*.

The Registrar General's 2004 list for England and Wales gives a total number of 576 certified *Congregationalist* places of worship in England, and 793 in Wales.

Continuing *Congregational* groups which did not join the United Reformed Church include the Union of Welsh Independents, the Scottish Congregational Church, the Congregational Federation (in England) and also the Evangelical Fellowship of Congregational Churches.

In addition, there are a number of totally un-affiliated *Congregational* congregations which, at the time of the formation of the United Reformed Church, stated that they would not join any other body, with their local structures being similar to those of the *Baptists*.

Salvation Army

The Salvation Army was founded in 1878 by William Booth who tried to respond to both the social and the spiritual needs of the industrial working class.

The Registrar General's 2004 list for England and Wales gives a total of 844 certified Salvation Army places of worship in England, and 76 in Wales.

Its members can be recognised by their distinctive uniforms and its officers have military-style ranks. It is well known for its social service projects among the poor and homeless.

The Salvation Army is organised into local *corps*, which are then grouped into regional level *Divisions* overseen by its National Headquarters. It does not administer the *sacraments* of *baptism* or the *eucharist* but is firmly within the *Evangelical* Christian tradition.

Lutheran

Compared with continental Europe, the *Lutheran* Christian tradition is very small in the UK. Its origins were in the continental *Reformation* and, specifically, the work of the reformer, Martin Luther, from whose surname the tradition takes its name.

The Registrar General's list for England and Wales does not keep separate cumulative totals of certified *Lutheran* places of worship. Most *Lutheran congregations* in the UK have a significant proportion of members who are of German or Scandinavian descent.

Moravian

The *Moravian* tradition, which traces its origins to 1457 in what is now the Czech Republic, has a small presence in the UK and Ireland. The Registrar General's list for England and Wales does not keep separate cumulative totals of *Moravian* places of worship.

The Moravian Church is *Free Church* and *Evangelical* in orientation while having an *episcopal* form of *Church* government. Local *churches* are grouped into *Districts* and *Districts* which together form the British Moravian Church Province. The *Unity* (International) *Synod* meets every seven years.

Brethren

The *Brethren* movement was formed in the nineteenth century with Plymouth as an important geographical centre. The Registrar General's 2004 list for England and Wales gives 687 certified *Brethren* places of worship in England, and 53 in Wales.

The popular name of "Plymouth Brethren" is derived from the movement's place of origin, although its members have never accepted this designation, preferring the terminology of *Christian Brethren.*

There are also other *Brethren* groups, such as those known as the *Exclusive Brethren* and the Churches of God in the British Isles and Overseas. *Churches* of the *Brethren* tradition are local, independent *congregations* following what they understand to be the pattern of Christianity found in the *New Testament.*

Pentecostal Churches

Pentecostal Churches include the Assemblies of God, the Elim Pentecostal Church, the Apostolic Church and a significant number of black-majority *Churches*, many of which have roots in Caribbean, North American and African forms of Christianity.

The Registrar General's list of certified places of worship in England and Wales does not keep a separate running total of churches under the category of *Pentecostalist.*

Black-Majority Churches

The black-majority Churches are a fast-growing and increasingly significant section of the Christian population of the UK. These *Churches* are very diverse in terms of their doctrines, practices and forms of *Church* organisation. They range from *Pentecostal* and *Holiness churches*, through to those of *Sabbatarian* and other traditions.

The Registrar General's list of certified places of worship in England and Wales does not keep a separate running total of *churches* under the category of *Black-majority churches.* In the CD-ROM that accompanies the directory there are basic address details of a range of these very diverse *churches.*

Some of these *churches*, such as the New Testament Church of God or the Church of God of Prophecy, are becoming numerically significant.

Others are quite local and consist of only one or two *congregations*, although they quite often co-operate with other larger groups within the framework of co-ordinating organisations such as the International Ministerial Council of Great Britain and the Council of African and Afro-Caribbean Churches.

Other Ethnically and/or Linguistically-Related Christian Groups

In addition to those *churches* that are of predominantly African and African-Caribbean membership and leadership, there are now also a growing number of other groupings organised in relation to shared ethnicity and/or language including, among others, Chinese Christian Fellowships and Asian Christian Fellowships.

New Churches and House Churches

Over the past quarter of a century, a new stream of Christian life has developed under local leaderships which have gradually built patterns of wider networking and of association. Some of these *New Churches* began in the homes of their members, leading to the description of *House Churches*.

Others have developed through meeting for worship in public buildings that are sometimes hired for the purpose. The Registrar General's list of certified places of worship in England and Wales does not record a total of churches under the category of *New Churches* or *House Churches*.

Quakers

The Religious Society of Friends was founded out of the sixteenth century life and work of George Fox. Today, two discernible strands have emerged: the primarily Christian, and the *Universalist*. The latter has attracted some members of other faiths and humanists into membership of the Society of Friends.

Quakers do not use *creed*s, have no *ordained* ministers, embrace pacifism and have a distinctive style of worship rooted in shared silence and decision-making which aims at unity based on the leadings of the *Holy Spirit*.

Quakers meet in local *Meetings* and also at a national level in a *Britain Yearly Meeting* which covers England, Wales and Scotland. A separate *Yearly Meeting* covers the whole of Ireland.

Those local *Quaker* groups which have their own buildings often open these up for wider use by a range of both religious and secular groups concerned with justice, peace and reconciliation.

The Registrar General's 2004 list of certified places of worship records 357 *Quaker* meeting places in England, and 11 in Wales.

Unitarian and Free Christian Churches

Unitarian Churches had their British origins in the seventeenth century, when they rejected the *Trinitarian* and *Christological* creedal formulations of the then predominant Christian traditions and *Churches*, and upheld religious freedom. In the nineteenth and twentieth centuries there has been a strong influence from the Unitarian Universalist Association of North America.

The Registrar General's 2004 list gives 156 certified *Unitarian* places of worship in England, and 24 in Wales. The General Assembly of Unitarian and Free Christian Churches is not a member of Churches Together in Britain and Ireland.

Ecumenical Structures

Churches Together in Britain and Ireland (CTBI) was set up in 1990 under the original name of the Council of Churches for Britain and Ireland (CCBI), as a result of the *Inter-Church Process*.

This broadened the range of Christian traditions participating in the previous *ecumenical* structure known as the British Council of Churches (BCC). Amongst its thirty members are some of the largest *Churches*, including the *Roman Catholic Church* in England and Wales and in Scotland which as well as a number of smaller *Churches*, had not been part of the BCC.

The CTBI relates to a number of *ecumenical* networks and organisations in Britain and Ireland and, as in the case of the other similar bodies operating at the levels of the four individual nations, it is known as an *ecumenical instrument*.

The CTBI is at present reviewing its structure, but currently works largely through a series of *Networks*, *Agencies* and *Commissions* (see the Christian organisational listings in the accompanying CD-ROM).

The national *ecumenical instruments* are: Churches Together in England (CTE), Action of Churches Together in Scotland (ACTS), Churches Together in Wales (CYTUN), the Irish Council of Churches (ICC) and Irish Inter-Church Meeting (IICM).

The Free Churches Group in Churches Together in England represents the interests that were formerly embodied in the Free Churches Council, including the specifically *Free Church* interests in education and in chaplaincies.

At a local level, many individual *congregations* and *parishes* co-operate in what are known as local Councils of Churches or local *Churches Together* groups or in what were originally called *Local Ecumenical Projects* and are now known as *Local Ecumenical Partnerships* (LEPs).

Member Churches of Churches Together in England are also working closely together in so-called *Intermediate Bodies*. These operate at a level that approximates to a county and are serviced by a full or part-time *ecumenical officer*.

Other Interdenominational Networks

In addition to the *Churches* involved in these structures, there are also networks which link together other national bodies and local *congregations* which have an understanding of their commitment to *Evangelical* Christian tradition that requires them not to be directly involved in these formal *ecumenical* structures.

There is, for example, the Evangelical Alliance which links *churches* and other Christian bodies which assent to its basis of faith and belief, and also a Fellowship of Independent Evangelical Churches (FIEC).

Other Christian Organisations

There are a vast range of Christian based organisations existing alongside the Christian Churches and *Religious Orders* and working at local, regional, national and international levels. The current directory does not attempt to give comprehensive details of this large sector of organisations, fuller details of which can be found in the *UK Christian Handbook*.

These organisations operate in most fields, from social welfare to education. Some are formally sponsored by and receive significant support from national *Churches* while others are supported primarily by the donations of time or money of individual Christians.

Some organisations are aligned with a particular tradition and/or *"Churchmanship"* of Christianity, whilst others – perhaps the majority – are explicitly *ecumenical* or *interdenominational* in character. Details of a selection of these organisations are included in this directory, but for a fuller and more comprehensive range, readers are directed to the *UK Christian Handbook*.

Personnel

Local Leadership

Members of the *Church* who are not *ordained* are generally known as the *laity* (from the Greek word *laos*, meaning people). In some *Protestant Churches* the *laity* can, in principle at least, conduct all the ceremonies, rites and functions of the *Church*, even if in practice these are usually carried out by designated leaders.

Ordained Leadership

The names and functions of the designated religious leadership of various Christian *Churches* vary according to their tradition. Nevertheless, broad categories of personnel can be discerned among *ordained* (set apart and recognised) leaders of the *Roman Catholic, Anglican, Orthodox* and *Protestant churches*.

Among some of the *Churches* which have a shorter history in the UK, and which have geographical origins in Africa and the Caribbean, an even wider variety of titles and functions can be found. For example, among a number of the *African Churches* there is a specific office of *prophet* or *prophetess* and another of *apostle*.

Other Christian groups within the *House Church* and *Restorationist* movements recognise leaders who have wider than local ministries and special gifts of ministry as *apostles* (a word which other Christians generally reserve for the first *disciples* of Jesus who are believed to have had a uniquely special role within the wider Christian community).

In the *Roman Catholic, Anglican* and *Orthodox* traditions, *ordained* leadership at the local level is provided by religious leaders and functionaries who are known as *priests*. In the Western *Roman Catholic* tradition *priests* are not allowed to marry, although some married former *Anglican priests* have recently been *ordained*, or conditionally *ordained*, as *Roman Catholic priests*. In the *Anglican* tradition *priests* may marry; in the *Orthodox* tradition, married men may be ordained *priests* (but may not be *bishops*). In these traditions, presiding at the *Eucharist* is reserved for *priests*.

Priests are also authorised to *baptise* and to *preach*. In these traditions, *priests* are seen both as representing the people to God and also as representing Christ to the *congregation*, as the focal points through whom God cares for the Christian community. This is especially believed to be the case in the *Eucharist*.

In the *Anglican* tradition authorised lay people, known as *Readers*, can *preach*. There are parallel offices in many other traditions, including the *Lay Preachers of Methodism*, who provide much of that *Church's* authorised ministry. There is also an *ordained* order of *ministry* known as *deacons* or the *diaconate* (from the Greek word - *diakonos*, meaning "servant"). This is technically an order in its own right, although *priests*-to-be are first of all *ordained deacon* as a stage on the way to full *ordination* to the *priesthood*. The *diaconate* exists in other Christian traditions, too, sometimes as a permanent order of *ministry*.

Protestant Churches generally have a more functional view of their local *ordained* leadership. In many *Protestant Churches ordained* local leaders are known as *ministers* (*Baptist*, United Reformed Church, Church of Scotland as well as other *Reformed churches*), as *presbyters* (*Methodist*), or as *pastors* (*Christian Brethren*, many branches of the *Pentecostal* movement, and some *Baptist churches*). *Methodism* recognises two orders of ministry, the *presbyteral* and the *diaconal*.

In the *Roman Catholic* and *Orthodox* traditions the *priesthood* is not open to women. Women are now able to be ordained as *priests* in the *Churches* of the *Anglican* tradition in England, Ireland, Scotland and Wales and, in Scotland only, as *bishops*. For many years there have been divided convictions on this issue even though there have been women *priests* in other parts of the worldwide *Anglican* tradition.

Tensions still remain within the *Churches* which have ordained women as *priests*. Specific provision is made, for example in the Church of England, to recognise the position of those who oppose for reasons of conscience, the *ordination* of women as *priests*. In the *Protestant Churches* women are generally able to serve as local *ministers* and some have also assumed responsibilities in regional and national leadership.

Pastoral Care

In all *Churches*, local *clergy* have a role in the pastoral care of the *congregation* as well as in *preaching* and administering the *sacraments*. In the understanding of the *established* Church of England, the *priest's* duty of pastoral care, shared with *lay* people, extends to everyone within the geographical area of the *parish*, regardless of whether or not they are *Anglican* or even *Christian*. A similar duty applies to ministers of the *established* Church of Scotland. In many *Churches* designated lay Christians also share in the pastoral ministry of the *Church*.

Regional, National and International Leadership

In the *Orthodox*, *Roman Catholic* and *Anglican* traditions the focus of unity of the *Church's* leadership is vested in the *bishop*. *Bishops* are senior *clergy* who are responsible for the geographical and ecclesiastical areas known as *dioceses*. *Roman Catholic* bishops and *priests* do not marry. *Anglican* bishops may be married, but whilst *Orthodox priests* may marry before *ordination* as *priests*, the office of *bishop* in the *Orthodox Churches* is open only to *monks* and therefore only to *priests* who are not married or who have become widowers.

In the *Protestant Churches* regional leaders are known by a wide variety of titles such as *Provincial Moderator* (United Reformed Church), *Area Superintendent* (*Baptists*), and *District Chair* (Methodist Church). The Church of England has two *Archbishops*, namely, the Archbishop of Canterbury and the Archbishop of York. The Archbishop of Canterbury is the Church of England's senior *bishop* and is also recognised as having a special seniority in the worldwide *Anglican* communion.

In the *Protestant Churches* national leaders usually have more functional titles such as *General Secretary* (Baptist Union of Great Britain), *Moderator of the General Assembly* (Church of Scotland) or *President of the Conference* (Methodist Church). These indicate the different kinds of roles in each of the *Churches*. In general, *General Secretaryships* are stipendiary posts which are held for several years, whilst the offices of *Moderators of Assembly* and those of *Presidents* tend to be honorary officers, appointed annually.

In the *Orthodox Churches*, senior *Archbishops* are known by the title of *Patriarch* and they may have responsibilities which extend across national boundaries. In the *Roman Catholic* Church in some parts of the world there are also *Patriarchs*. A group of senior *Bishops* and *Archbishops* from all over the world are members of the *College of Cardinals*. Cardinals under eighty years of age at the time of an election choose the *Pope* (meaning "Father") who is installed as *Bishop of Rome* and is recognised as the chief pastor of the *Roman Catholic* Church throughout the world. He is often referred to by *Roman Catholics* as the *Holy Father*.

Among *Protestant Churches*, the international leadership, like the national leadership, has a variety of more functional titles. In keeping with the military imagery used by the Salvation Army, the leader of the Salvation Army worldwide is known as *General*. The World Alliance of Reformed Churches, the Lutheran World Federation and the Baptist World Alliance all have *General Secretaries*. Each of these bodies has a mainly co-ordinating and consultative role in contrast to the more integrated and hierarchical structure of the Salvation Army.

FURTHER READING

Details follow of a number of general introductions to Christianity, together with books and articles that provide some focus on Christians and Christian organisations in the UK. The references are not comprehensive, but provide signposts to a range of relevant materials.

Adogame, A, *Celestial Church of Christ: The Politics of Cultural Identity in a West African Prophetic-Charismatic Movement*, Studies in the Intercultural History of Christianity 115, Peter Lang, Frankfurt, 1991.

Attwater, D, *A Dictionary of Mary*, P J Kennedy, Longmans, 1957.

Ballard, P and Jones, D (eds), *This Land and People: Y Wlad a'r Bobl Hyn: A Symposium on Christian and Welsh National Identity*, Collegiate Centre of Theology, University College, Cardiff (revised edition) 1980.

Barraclough, G (ed), *The Christian World*, Abrams, London, 1981.

Barrett, D, *The World Christian Encyclopaedia: A Comparative Study of Churches and Religions* in the Modern World, AD1900-2000, Oxford University Press, Oxford, 1982.

Bebbington, D, The Nonconformist Conscience, Chapel and Politics, 1870-1914, George Allen and Unwin, 1982.

Bettenson, H, Documents of the Christian Church, Oxford University Press, London, 1975.

Bisset, P, The Kirk and Her Scotland, Handsel Press, Edinburgh, 1986.

Bonk, J (ed), Encyclopaedia of Missions and Missionaries, Routledge, Abingdon, 2007.

Bowden, J, Dictionary of Christian Theology, SCM Press, London, 1983.

Bowie, F and Davies, O (eds), Celtic Christianity Spirituality: Medieval and Modern, SPCK, London, 1995.

Braybrooke, M, The Explorer's Guide to Christianity, Hodder and Stoughton, London, 1998.

Brierley, P, Irish Christian Handbook, 1995-96, Christian Research Association, London, 1994.

Brierley, P and Macdonald, F, Prospects for Scotland 2000, Christian Research Association, London, 1995.

Burgess, S, McGee, G and Alexander, P (eds), Dictionary of Pentecostal and Charismatic Movements, Zondervan Publishing House, Grand Rapids, Michigan, 1988.

Burgess, S (ed), Encyclopaedia of Pentecostal and Charismatic Christianity, Routledge, Abingdon, 2006.

Cameron, H, Davies, D, Richter, P, and Ward, F (eds), Studying Local Churches: A Handbook, SCM Press, London, 2005.

Catholic Bishops' Conference of England and Wales, What Are We to Teach?, Catholic Education Service, London, 1994.

Catholic Church, Catechism of the Catholic Church, Geoffrey Chapman, London, 1994.

Chadwick, O, The History of Christianity, Weidenfeld and Nicolson, London, 1995.

Childs, J F, and Macquarrie, J (eds), A New Dictionary of Christian Ethics, SCM, London, (2nd edition) 1987.

Churches' Commission for Inter Faith Relations, Religious Discrimination: A Christian Response. A Discussion Document from the Churches' Commission for Inter Faith Relations, Churches Together in Britain and Ireland, London, 2001.

Churches Regional Commission in Yorkshire and Humberside, The Churches and Regional Development in Yorkshire and the Humber, The Churches Regional Commission, Leeds, 1998.

Chryssides, G, The Elements of Unitarianism, Element Books, Dorset, 1998.

Coggins, R, and Houlden, J, A Dictionary of Biblical Interpretation, SCM, London, 1990.

Cross, F, and Livingstone, E (eds), Oxford Dictionary of the Christian Church, Oxford University Press, London, (3rd revised edition) 1997.

Davies, H, Worship and Theology in England (Volume I: From Cranmer to Baxter and Fox, 1534-1690; Volume II: From Watts and Wesley to Martineau, 1690-1900; Volume III: The Ecumenical Century, 1900 to the Present), Eerdmans, 1996.

Davies, J, A New Dictionary of Liturgy and Worship, SCM, London, 1986.

Dickens, A, The English Reformation, Collins, London, 1967.

Dupre, L, and Saliers, D (eds), Christian Spirituality: Reformation and Modern, SCM, London, 1989.

Edwards, D, Christian England, Collins, London, 1985.

Furlong, M, C of E: The State It's In, Hodder and Stoughton, London, 2000

Gerloff, R, *A Plea for British Black Theologies: The Black Church Movement in Britain in its Transatlantic Cultural and Theological Interaction, Parts I and II*, Peter Lang, Frankfurt am Main, Germany, 1992.

Gill, S, *Women and the Church of England, From the Eighteenth Century to the Present*, SPCK, London, 1994.

Gill, S, *The Lesbian and Gay Christian Movement: Campaigning for Justice, Truth and Love*, Cassell, London, 1998.

Guest, M, Tusting, K, and Woodhead, L (eds), *Congregational Studies in the UK: Christianity in a Post-Christian Context*, Ashgate, Aldershot, 2004.

Hastings, A, *A History of English Christianity, 1920-1985*, Collins, London, 1986.

Hastings, A, *Church and State: The English Experience. The Prideux Lectures for 1990*, University of Exeter, Exeter, 1991.

Hastings, A et al (eds), *The Oxford Companion to Christian Thought*, Oxford, 2000.

Howard, V, *A Report on Afro-Caribbean Christianity in Britain*, Community Religions Project, University of Leeds, Leeds, 1987.

Keeley, R (ed), *The Lion Handbook of Christian Belief*, Lion Publishing, Tring, 1982.

King, U, *Christian Mystics. The Spiritual Heart of the Christian Tradition*, Batsford, London, 1998.

Latourette, K, *A History of Christianity*, (2 volumes), Harper and Row, London, 1975.

Lossky, N, Bonino, M, Pobee, J, Stransky, T, Wainwright G and Webb, P, *Dictionary of the Ecumenical Movement*, World Council of Churches, Geneva, 1991.

Marthaler, B, *The Creed*, Twenty-Third Publications, 1993 (revised edition).

McAdoo, H, *Anglican Heritage*, Canterbury Press, Norwich, 1991.

McBrien, R, *Catholicism*, Chapman, 1980.

McGinn, B and Meyendorff, J (eds), *Christian Spirituality: Origins to the Twelfth Century*, SCM, London, 1986.

McKenzie, P, *The Christians: Their Practices and Beliefs*, SPCK, London, 1988.

McManners, J (ed), *The Oxford Illustrated History of Christianity*, Oxford University Press, Oxford, 1990.

Nesbitt, E, "The Transmission of Christian Tradition in an Ethnically Diverse Society", in R Barot (ed), *Religion and Ethnicity: Minorities and Social Change in the Metropolis*, Kok Pharos, Kampen, 1993, pp 156-169.

Parrinder, G, *A Concise Encyclopaedia of Christianity*, One World, Oxford, 1998.

Radcliffe, T, *What is the Point of Being a Christian?*, Burns and Oates, London, 2006.

Raitt, J (ed), *Christian Spirituality: High Middle Ages and Reformation*, SCM, London, 1987.

Smart, N, *The Phenomenon of Christianity*, Collins, London, 1979.

Smith, M (ed), *Prospects for the Unitarian Movement*, Lindsey Press, London, 2002.

Smith, N (ed), *Journal of George Fox*, Penguin Classics, 2000.

Strange, R, *The Catholic Faith*, Oxford University Press, 1985.

ter Haar, G, *Halfway to Paradise: African Christians in Europe*, Cardiff Academic Press, Cardiff, 1998.

Toulis, N, *Believing Identity: Pentecostalism and the Mediation of Jamaican Ethnicity and Gender in England*, Berg, Oxford, 1997.

Vickers, A (ed), *A Dictionary of Methodism in Britain and Ireland*, Epworth, Peterborough, 2000.

Voas, D and Bruce, S, "The 2001 Census and Christian identification in Britain", in *Journal of Contemporary Religion*, volume 19, No 1, 2004, pp 23-28.

Wakefield, G, *A Dictionary of Christian Spirituality*, SCM, London, 1983.

Walker, A, *Restoring the Kingdom: The Radical Christianity of the House Church Movement*, Hodder and Stoughton, London, 1988.

Ware, K, *The Orthodox Way*, Mowbray, London, 1987.

Williams, R "South Asian Christians in Britain, Canada and the United States", in H Coward, J Hinnells and R Williams (eds), *The South Asian Religious Diaspora in Britain, Canada and the United States*, State University of New York Press, New York, 2000, pp 13-33.

Wraight, H (ed), *UK Christian Handbook 2007-2008*, Christian Research Association, London, 2006.

Wright, T, *Simply Christian: Why Christianity Makes Sense*, Harper Collins, New York, 2006.

Yearly Meeting of the Religious Society of Friends in Britain, *Quaker Faiths and Practice: The Book of Christian Discipline of the Religious Society of Friends (Quakers) in Britain (2nd edition)*, London, 1999.

Yorkshire Churches, *Angels and Advocates: Church Social Action in Yorkshire and the Humber*, The Churches Regional Commission for Yorkshire and the Humber, Leeds, 2002.

INTRODUCING HINDUS IN THE UK

HINDUS IN THE UK 169

ORIGINS AND DEVELOPMENT OF THE HINDU TRADITION 170

SOURCES OF HINDU BELIEFS AND PRACTICES 171

KEY HINDU BELIEFS 173

TRADITIONS IN HINDUISM 175

HINDU LIFE 178

HINDU WORSHIP 181

HINDU PLACES OF WORSHIP 182

HINDU CALENDAR AND FESTIVALS 184

HINDU ORGANISATIONS 185

FURTHER READING 189

HINDUS IN THE UK

History in the UK

Small numbers of Hindus have visited and worked in the United Kingdom for centuries and the number of students and professionals increased greatly from the late nineteenth century onwards. However, it was not until the 1950s and 1960s that significant numbers of Hindus settled here.

Some came to Britain directly from India. With the development of Africanisation policies in the newly independent African states, others came from the countries to which their foreparents had previously migrated, such as Kenya, Tanzania, Uganda, Zambia, and Malawi. Between 1962 and 1972 some of these came as economic migrants and others, especially those from Uganda, came seeking refuge from persecution. Hindu migrants also came from Nepal, Fiji, and from Trinidad and other Caribbean islands. Since the 1980s, Tamil Hindus have also come to the UK from Sri Lanka in significant numbers.

Global and UK Hindu Populations

Worldwide, there are an estimated 811,366,000 Hindus. The 2001 decennial Census questions on religion yielded 558,810 (or 1.2% of the total population of the UK) Hindu respondents. This is 1.0% of the population that identifies itself with any specific religion at all. Of these 558,810, a total of 546,982 were in England, 5,439 in Wales, 5,564 in Scotland, and 825 in Northern Ireland.

As a proportion of the population in local authority areas, the 2001 Census shows that, in England, the greatest concentration of respondents identifying themselves as Hindus is to be found in the London Boroughs of Harrow (19.6%) and Brent (17.2%); Leicester (14.7%); and the London Boroughs of Redbridge (7.8%) and Ealing (7.8%).

Ethnicity in England and Wales

According to 2001 Census, 96.6% of the Hindu population of England and Wales gave their ethnicity as "Asian", 1.3% as "White", 1% as "Mixed", 0.6% as "Chinese or Other Ethnic Group", and 0.5% as "Black". Considered in terms of the ethnicity of respondents, 23.5% of all those recorded as "Asian" also identified as Hindu, along with 0.9% of "Mixed" respondents, 0.7% of "Chinese and Other Ethnic Group", 0.3% of "Black or Black British", and 0.02% of those recorded as "White".

Between 55% and 70% of Hindus in the UK are thought to be Gujarati (including those from the Northern Kutch region) and between 15% and 20% Punjabi, with the remainder having their ancestral origins in other parts of India such as Kashmir, Uttar Pradesh, West Bengal, and the Southern states, as well as in other countries such as Sri Lanka.

Even where a family has lived for generations in another part of India, or outside India, its members often maintain links with their ancestral region and often speak their ancestral language among themselves. Thus the Hindu population is constituted of many ethnic groups, each of which was originally often based in a particular geographical region of India.

In addition to English, Hindus in the UK often speak one or more other languages. The most common are Gujarati, Hindi, Punjabi, Bengali and Tamil. They mostly use the ancient language Sanskrit in their worship, and the majority of the sacred texts are in this language. Most of the Indian words and names used below are Sanskrit. However, Sanskrit words are adapted in form and pronunciation to the different regional languages, and this accounts for some variations in the transliteration of such words: eg. Siva or Shiv; Rama or Ram.

ORIGINS AND DEVELOPMENT OF THE HINDU TRADITION

Origins

The term "Hindu" is related to the Sanskrit word Sindhu that is the name of the river that in English is called the Indus. In Iranian languages such as Persian, this river was called "Hindu", and the name "Hindu" was applied also to the country adjoining the river, and to its people. The name "Hindusthan" was also applied to the whole of North India, and sometimes to the whole of India. These names became current in India through usage by Persian-speaking people from Afghanistan.

Some Hindus refer to the origin of the terms "Hindu" and "Hindusthan" as being found in the scripture known as the *Brihaspati Agama*. The term "Hinduism" became current in English during the nineteenth century. The Hindu way of life is referred to as *Dharma* or sometimes as the *Sanatana Dharma* (eternal way of life), and many Hindus prefer this description to the word "Hinduism".

The Indus Valley civilisation flourished in north-west India in the third and second millennia BCE, but is known only from archaeological finds. *Sanatana Dharma* is a tradition that is believed by many Hindus to go beyond time and space. It has no precisely traceable beginning, nor a single founder or teacher. Modern historians, including many who are themselves Hindus, point to some formative periods in Indian religious history.

Other Hindus do not accept the position of such modern historians and believe that key events such as the birth of Krishna and the Battle of Kurukshetra (see section on the *Mahabharata*, below) can be dated to a period around 3100BCE by utilising interpretations of astrological data in the *Vedas*. What many identify as the *Vedic* period (considered by some to be between around 1500-500BCE) has left a large body of literature.

The time of the *Buddha* (c.450BCE) was a period of great social and political change. Since then, the tradition has undergone further transformations (see section below on "Traditions in Hinduism") and developed into richly diverse ways of life and thought. Some of the famous figures in this development who are given prominence by many Hindus are: Shankara (seventh century CE), Ramanuja (eleventh century CE), Madhva (eleventh to twelfth century CE), Nimbarka (twelfth century CE), Chaitanya (fifteenth to sixteenth century CE), Vallabha (fifteenth to sixteenth century CE) and Sahajananda (eighteenth to nineteenth century CE).

Some Hindus reject the notion of an historical development of the tradition since it conflicts with the idea of degenerative time (see *Yuga* below), according to which past ages were more glorious and closer to the eternal truth than this one. However, many Hindus see Hinduism as evolving and as coming to fresh understandings throughout time in ways that do not conflict with the idea of an eternal *dharma*.

Commonality and Variety

There are three broad commonalities generally found among Hindus: acceptance of the authority of the *Vedas* (see below); a relationship to India as a common motherland, often referred to as *Bharat desha*; and Sanskrit as a common religious language, with perhaps the greatest commonality being around acceptance of the authority of the *Vedas* (see below).

However, both because of its ancient origins and its understanding of truth as inclusive, the Hindu traditions embrace a very wide range of belief and practices, with regional, linguistic, and doctrinal variations. Within the Hindu traditions various schools of thought, a whole range of philosophical positions, religious practices and devotional foci are accepted.

The Hindu traditions are often described as more a way of life than a religion based upon commonality of belief. However, within this diversity there are a number of beliefs and practices that are more commonly accepted, and the diverse systems of thought have themselves been tested, codified and accepted throughout the centuries.

SOURCES OF HINDU BELIEFS AND PRACTICES

Sacred Texts

Hindus hold a number of texts to be sacred and at the root of their beliefs and practices. Many of them are in Sanskrit or in languages derived from Sanskrit, and fall into two broad categories: *shruti* (that which is heard) and *smriti* (that which is remembered).

The four *Vedas* (see below) are *shruti*. Some Hindus believe that *smriti* such as the *Puranas* and the *Ramayana* are less authoritative than the *shruti*, although others stress that *smriti* texts are extensions of the truths hidden in the *shruti*, made accessible through story and simple language. For example, many *Vaishnavas* (see below) consider the *shruti* and the *smriti* to be on the same level, and call the *Bhagavata Purana* (or *Shrimad Bhagavatam*) the "fifth *Veda*". The text known as the *Mahabharata* also is often considered to be the "fifth *Veda*".

Sacred texts are treated with great respect. They are often wrapped in silk or cotton cloth and devout Hindus will avoid placing them on the floor and touching them with feet or with dirty hands. Prayers are often recited before reading from such texts.

Shruti

Oral Tradition

For Hindus, sacred texts are essentially spoken rather than written. This is why the *Vedas*, the most ancient sacred texts, are referred to as *shruti* (that which is heard). Some Hindus believe that the original revelations were given in what is known as *Dev Vak* (the language of God) and that Sanskrit later emerged from this, modifying and adapting the original language of revelation in order to make it understandable to human beings. Some Hindus believe that there are some revelations that have, until now, been kept as unwritten secrets that are only orally passed on to those qualified to receive them.

The Four Vedas

The sacred texts known as the *Vedas* (meaning "knowledge") are believed to be eternal. Tradition says that there was originally one *Veda*, but it was divided into four at the beginning of the third age of the world (see *Yuga* below), and learnt by the four *rishis* (sages): Paila, Jaimini, Vaishampayana and Sumantu.

They are then believed to have been transmitted by word of mouth by the people of that age who possessed remarkable memories until the beginning of the *Kali-Yuga* (3102 BCE, see below), which is the present age. After that it became necessary to commit the teachings to writing in the form of the four books in which they are known today.

The four *Vedas* are: the *Rig Veda*, which contains *mantras* (verses) spoken in worship; the *Sama Veda*, containing sung *mantras* with their tunes; the *Yajur Veda*, containing further *mantras*, and instructions for the actions (*karma*) used in worship; and the *Atharva Veda*, containing *mantras* for particular purposes such as cure of diseases. There are altogether over 20,000 *mantras* in the *Vedas*, including *mantras* which deal with matters of physics, astronomy and mathematics.

According to some traditions, there are also five main *Upavedas* (sub-branches of the *Vedas*). The *Upavedas* are: *Ayurveda*, which is related to the *Rig Veda*, and is concerned with medical knowledge; the *Gandharvaveda*, which is related to the *Sama Veda*, and is

concerned with expertise in music, dance and drama; the *Dhanurveda*, which is related to the *Yajur Veda*, and is concerned with military science; the *Arthaveda*, which is related to the *Artharva Veda*, and is concerned with the practice of government; and the *Shilpaveda*, which deals with architecture.

Each of the four *Vedas* consists of four parts: the *Samhitas*, the *Brahmanas*, the *Aranyakas* and the *Upanishads*. The *Samhitas* contain *mantras* for recitation; the *Brahmanas* are concerned with ritual and sacrifice, the purpose of which is material prosperity on earth, *moksha* (release from the cycle of birth and death); the *Aranyakas* reflect on the cosmic role of *Vedic* rituals; and the *Upanishads* contain more philosophical and meditative material and discuss the knowledge about *atman* (see below) through which one is liberated from ignorance and finds self-realisation.

Smriti

The *smriti* consist of six categories: *Itihasa*, *Purana*, *Grihya Sutra*, *Vedanga*, *Dharma Shastra* and *Prasthana Vakya*. The *Itihasas* (histories) consist of the two epics: the *Ramayana* (written by Valmiki) and the *Mahabharata*, which includes the *Bhagavad Gita*.

The *Ramayana* and *Mahabharata* are believed by some Hindus to be historical, whilst others see them in more symbolic terms. They contain accounts of the *Lilas* (pastimes) of the divine manifested in human form, as Rama and Krishna. Some Hindus believe that it is Vishnu who was manifested in this way (for further information on Rama, Krishna and Vishnu see section below on "Key Hindu Beliefs").

The *Ramayana* and the *Mahabharata* illustrate Hindu concepts of divinity, of human nature and of *dharma* (see below). They deal with the morality that can guide personal life and protect the social order. Both epics illustrate and inspire perseverance and detachment in dealing with adverse circumstances.

Ramayana

The *Ramayana* is set in ancient India and tells the story of how King Rama fought against the forces of evil headed by Ravana. For many Hindus, Rama and his wife Sita are the epitome of right action and righteousness. Rama acts as the dutiful son, obeying his father's every wish, whilst Sita is seen as the perfect wife. *Rama Rajya*, the reign of Rama as King of ancient Bharat (India), is considered an ideal example of social and political leadership.

Mahabharata

The *Mahabharata* is also set in ancient India. It contains the *Bhagavad Gita* or the *Song of the Blessed Lord* that is a discourse between Krishna and his devotee Prince Arjuna. The *Mahabharata* tells a story which culminates in the battle of Kurukshetra, which marks the beginning of the present age, the *Kali Yuga*.

Immediately before the war, Prince Arjuna, who is called upon to fight, is perplexed at a situation in which he might have to kill his relatives in the enemy's army. Responding to Arjuna's questions, Krishna (who is in human form as Arjuna's charioteer) speaks to Arjuna and teaches him that the essence of *dharma* is to discharge all duties without selfishness or attachment to their rewards and in dedication to the *dharma*.

The *Bhagavad Gita* is one of the most important scriptures for many Hindus throughout the world because of its teachings about *dharma* and about the different ways of reaching the divine, including through right action. In this respect it is closely connected with the *Vedas*. Through the characters of the *Mahabharata*, a code of conduct and a social and ethical philosophy of human relations and problems are presented.

Puranas

The *Puranas* contain stories about the deities Brahma, Vishnu and Shiva and stories about the great sages of Hindu tradition, together with expositions of Hindu theology and religious practice. Whilst many Hindus see these as historical, some understand them as allegory to be interpreted in symbolic terms. There are traditionally eighteen principal *Puranas*, the most widely used of which is the *Bhagavata Purana*, which tells of the activities of Vishnu and some of the famous stories about Krishna.

Other Texts

The *Grihya Sutras* are instructions for domestic rituals, including a special emphasis upon the fire sacrifice and the rites of passage through life.

There are six *Vedangas* (literally limbs of the *Vedas*). These are: *Shiksa*, dealing with phonetics; *Vyakarana*, dealing with Sanskrit grammar; *Nirukti*, dealing with Sanskrit etymology; *Chandas*, dealing with the rules of metre; *Jyotisha*, dealing with astrology and astronomy; and *Kalpa*, setting out regulations for ritual.

The *Dharma Shastras* (law books), the most famous of which is the *Manusmriti* (see also below under "Gender Roles") or *Laws of Manu* (the ancestor of humankind), contain codes of conduct.

The *Prasthana-vakyas* is a generic title for a wide range of literature, much of which is often specific to particular traditions found among Hindus. The most significant of these are the *Vedanta-Sutras* that summarise the key aspects of *Vedic* philosophy and the *Tantras*, which are esoteric texts related to Shiva or to Shakti (the Goddess).

KEY HINDU BELIEFS

One and Many

Some non-Hindus have perceived Hindu belief as *polytheistic* because of its multiplicity of forms and representations of the divine and of *devas* and *devis* (see below – often inadequately rendered into English as gods and goddesses). The *Vedas* describe 33 *koti* (classes) of divine qualities in human beings. These are often misinterpreted to mean that there are 330 million gods and goddesses.

The Hindu traditions allow the use of a variety of symbols, names, terms and images which enable people to discover the divine in ways which are appropriate to them. Within the Hindu *dharma* there are both *monotheists* (believers in one God, and for whom there is a clear distinction between God and the world) as well as *monists* who argue that it is not contradictory to believe that the divine is simultaneously both one and many.

Most Hindus in the UK adhere either to a philosophy of *Advaita*, a form of *monism*, or to a philosophy of *Dvaita*, which is *monotheistic* (For both *Advaita* and *Dvaita* see section below on "Traditions in Hinduism"). Both schools accept the existence of the One Supreme. This is understood either impersonally as the all-pervading *Brahman* (the *Advaita* position) or as a Supreme Person (the *Dvaita* position).

The divine is often represented in a threefold form as *trimurti*. This consists of Brahma with his consort, Saraswati; Vishnu with his consort, Lakshmi; and Shiva with his consort, Parvati (also known by many other names, eg Durga or Shakti).

Simultaneously with accepting the One Supreme in either understanding outlined above, the Hindu traditions also refer to many other beings. Among the best known of these *devas* and *devis* are: Indra (god of lightening), Surya (sun god), Chandra (moon god), Ganesha (remover of obstacles), Yama (god of death), Sarasvati (goddess of learning), Lakshmi (goddess of wealth), Hanuman, the ardent devotee of Rama (who is believed to have assumed the monkey-form to fulfil the prophecy of Nandi whom Ravana called "monkey-face") and also Murugan (with Ganesha, one of the two sons of Shiva and Parvati).

Some Hindus see these as manifestations of different powers and functions of the divine, whilst others accept them as distinctly existing beings.

The Hindu tradition recognises a female principle as a form, and in some cases as the highest form, of the divine. The universal energy of existence is referred to as Shakti, the consort of Shiva, who is considered as the personification of the material energy or Mother Nature. She has various forms, some gentle and nurturing and others fierce and terrible. These go by different names such as Devi, Amba, Parvati, Durga and Kali. She is often referred to simply as *Mata* (meaning "mother").

Atman

Atman is understood to be the spirit that is present in all life and not just human life. It is the energy that activates the body and fills it with consciousness and is distinct from the material body, which consists of *prakriti* (inert matter).

Prakriti is understood to be composed of three *gunas* (qualities) namely: *sattva* (goodness), *rajas* (passion) and *tamas* (ignorance). These affect the make-up of each individual human being according to the proportions in which they are found.

The *atman* is eternal, but is repeatedly embodied, so that it goes through a cycle of birth and death. At death the *atman* is believed to leave the body and, in accordance with the law of *karma* (see below), its actions in one life are believed to determine the nature and circumstances of its future lives.

Moksha

Hindus understand the ultimate goal of all living beings to gain release from *samsara* (the cycle of birth and death). This is known as *moksha* (liberation). The goal of Hindu practice is to realise union between *atman* and *Brahman*. In the *Advaita* perspective this is understood as the *atman* recognising its identity with *Brahman*, the Supreme Spirit. In the *Dvaita* view (also see below), union is understood as serving God eternally and the union is a qualitative rather than a quantitative one. In either case it is believed that it can take many lives to reach this goal.

Dharma

The concept of *dharma* is central to the Hindu traditions. It has no exact English equivalent, although it is often loosely translated as "religion", "law", "duty" or "righteousness". Its linguistic root is the Sanskrit *dhr* meaning "to sustain" or "hold together". Its meaning is therefore approximately "that which sustains", "that which upholds" or "the intrinsic property of something". Thus, for example, the *dharma* of water is its wetness. Following one's *dharma* is essential to achieving *moksha*.

Karma

For Hindus, *karma* is the universal principle of actions and their consequences. While one is free to act, all actions have consequences - good, bad or mixed, depending upon the nature of the act and the intention behind its performance. Because of the relationship between actions and consequences, the results shape one's destiny, whether in the present or in a future life. Whilst one remains ignorant of the principle of *karma*, it leads to *janma* (birth), resulting in *dukkha* (unsatisfactoriness).

Hindu teaching advises that, in order to be released from *karma*, every action should be carried out from a holy sense of duty and dedication, shunning attachment to its results. The law of *karma* applies relentlessly and thus one cannot, for example, escape the results of one's bad actions simply by seeking forgiveness.

Maya

Maya (sometimes explained as meaning "that which is not") is the state of illusion that comes about through ignorance of the *Sanatana Dharma* (the eternal truth). Many Hindus speak more of "ignorance" and

"knowledge" than of "evil" and "good". The illusion of *maya* and our dependence upon the world of appearances decreases as our knowledge increases.

Yuga

Hindus use *Maha Yugas* (4.32 million years) as a measure of counting time from the beginning of what is seen as the current cycle of creation that, in itself, is believed to last for 1,000 *Maha Yugas*. Each *Maha Yuga* consists of four Yugas or ages, which are known as *satya*, *treat*, *dwarpa* and *kali*.

This present age is known as the *Kali Yuga* (Kali in this context is not to be confused with the name of the goddess Kali) or "dark age". It is believed to have begun with the departure of Krishna after the destruction of the *Mahabharata* war, in 3102BCE. At the end of the *Kali Yuga* some Hindus believe that the divine will appear in human form in order to eradicate all evil from the world and clear the way for the return of the next cycle of four ages, beginning with the perfect age.

TRADITIONS IN HINDUISM

The Six Darshanas

Classically, among Hindus there are six *Darshana Shashtras* (schools of philosophy). These are the *Purva Mimamsa* (also called *Mimamsa* for short), *Nyaya*, *Vaisheshika*, *Samkhya*, *Yoga* and *Vedanta* (otherwise known as the *Uttara Mimamsa*).

They are each concerned with different aspects of knowledge: *Mimamsa* is concerned with action and with responsibility; *Nyaya* with logic; *Vaisesika* with the analysis of matter in terms of its atomic structure; *Samkhya* with the analysis of matter in terms of its functioning; *Yoga* with training of the mind and body; and *Vedanta* with knowledge of ultimate reality.

The six different systems developed at different points in time and exist side by side in the Hindu tradition, resulting in a variety of philosophies ranging from *monistic* to *dualistic* (there is also an atheistic school, called *Charraka*). Despite their differences, in most of these systems the common theme is that the goal of human existence is liberation of the *atman* from the cycle of birth and death.

There is also a commitment to the idea that the spiritual life consists of four principal paths: *karma yoga* (way of action), *jnana yoga* (way of knowledge), *raja yoga* (way of self-control) and *bhakti yoga* (way of devotion). The systems do not exclude one another; for instance, a person who follows the *Vedanta* as the way to liberation may also use *Purva Mimamsa* as a guide to ritual practice, *Nyaya* as a system for conducting arguments, and *Yoga* as a means of self-discipline.

Vedanta: Dvaita and Advaita

Many Hindus today subscribe to the *Vedanta* system in one form or another, which seeks to understand the teaching of the *Upanishads*. *Vedanta* literally means "the conclusion of all knowledge". It is concerned with three ultimate entities: God, the *atman* (spirit) and *prakriti* (matter). Within *Vedanta* there are different views of the relation between these three. However, there are two main tendencies - the *dvaita* (*dualist*) and the *advaita* (*monist*).

Dvaita

The term *dvaita* refers to *personalist monotheism*, in which the nature of God is that of an unlimited supreme personality. In this tendency, the *atman* and *prakriti* are seen as eternally distinct from God, and the *atman* depends upon God for its liberation. *Dvaitins* believe that some deities are *avataras* (manifestations and descents) of God. Besides these, it is also believed that there are numerous *devas* and *devis*, each of whom has specific functions within the material sphere.

Advaita

The *Advaita* or *monist* tendency insists that the *atman* and *prakriti* have no existence of their own, but depend for their existence on God, often called *Brahman*. *Brahman* is not a personal name, since God has no name or gender and is seen more in terms of Supreme Intelligence, Supreme Bliss, and Permeative Energy, rather than personality. The *atman* that is the eternal spirit in each conscious being is a manifestation of *Brahman*. Most humans are seen as being unaware of this identity, and think that they exist as separate beings. *Moksha* (salvation) is reached when this limited outlook is overcome and identity with *Brahman* is realised.

Brahman is believed to have manifested in a variety of different times and places and is personified in many different forms. Because of this, *Advaitins* believe that union with *Brahman* can be attained through the worship of any deity that is chosen as one's personal object of devotion.

In the *Advaita* view, *Brahman* can be seen as the underlying principle behind the universe from which is manifested the trinity of creative force (personified as Brahma), preservative force (personified as Vishnu) and dissolving force (personified as Shiva). Everything is therefore seen as being part of an eternal cycle in which is created, maintained for some time, and then destroyed.

Dvaita and *Advaita*, as summarised above, represent two poles of thought within the *Vedanta*. Between these poles can be found a range of subtly varied schools of thought associated with famous Hindu teachers and philosophers. These include the following:

Advaita Vedanta

Non-dualist Vedanta, a philosophy that was propounded by Shankara (7th-8th century CE), in which it is believed that the *atman* or *jiva* (living entity) is identical with God and this has simply to be realised. Only the divine is absolutely real, and everything else is *maya* (illusion or provisional), being real only in a relative and limited sense.

Vishishta–Advaita

A qualified *non-dualism* propounded by Ramanuja (c.1017-1137CE), which holds that there is a difference between God, the living entities, and *prakriti* (nature). Nevertheless, the *atman* and *prakriti* are God, in rather the same way as a person's body is that person: it is God who permeates them and gives them purpose and meaning. Ramanuja identified God as Vishnu.

Navya Vishishta–Advaita

A qualified *non-dualism*, propounded by Sahajananda (c.1781-1830CE). Five eternal realities are distinguished: *jivas* (living entities that are infinite in number); Ishwara or the Lord (cosmic self-omniscience); *maya* (matter in both manifested and unmanifested forms); Akshar Brahman (supreme divine abode of God); and Parabrahman (Supreme Godhead).

Shuddha–Dvaita

A pure *dualism* propounded by Madhva (c.1239-1319CE), also known as *Swaminarayan* (see section on "Spiritual Movements" below), in which God (seen as Vishnu), the living entities and the material world (*prakriti*) are eternally distinct. Madhva maintained even more strongly than Ramanuja the distinctness of these three, and particularly the distinction between the individual soul and God.

Dvaita–Advaita

A philosophy of oneness and difference propounded by Nimbarka (thirteenth or fourteenth century CE), a worshipper of Krishna.

Shuddha–Advaita

A purified *monism* taught by Vishnuswami and his successor Vallabha (c.1479-1531BCE) (see "Spiritual Movements" below), who rejected the doctrine of *maya*.

Achintya–Bhedha–Abheda

A doctrine of inconceivable simultaneous oneness and difference, propounded by Chaitanya (c.1486-1534CE) and by his successors, including Bhaktivedanta Swami Prabhupada (1896-1977) (see "Spiritual Movements" below). It holds that God (identified as Krishna), the living entities and *prakriti* are both one and different at the same time, in a way that cannot be conceived by the human mind.

Shaiva Siddhanta

The system of the worshippers of Shiva, codified in the twelfth to fourteenth centuries CE. This system teaches that there are innumerable living entities, trapped in the world of *rebirth*, but enabled to escape from it by the grace of Shiva.

Sampradaya

The above are the doctrines of some of the many *sampradayas* (traditions) that can be encountered among Hindus in the UK. Each *sampradaya* has its set of doctrines and its form of worship, usually directed to a particular personal form of God, flourishing in a particular region of India and passed down through a succession of *gurus*. *Gurus* are spiritual leaders who are seen by their followers as providing great insight and guidance in spiritual matters. (See further "Spiritual Movements" below.)

Not all Hindus are members of *sampradayas*. However, many Hindus worship a particular form of God, called their *ishta-deva* (chosen deity). On the basis of the form of God which they chiefly worship, they can be classed as *Vaishnavas*, *Shaivas* and *Shaktas*.

Over the centuries, there have been many reform movements, such as the Arya Samaj, the Ramakrishna Mission, and others (see section below on "Hindu Organisations").

Vaishnavas, Shaivas and Shaktas

The term *Vaishnava* is applied to worshippers of Vishnu who understand the Divine and its relationship with humanity in the *Dvaita* way, seeing Vishnu as the supreme divine personal reality and also to those who see Krishna as the divine personal reality. Many British Hindus belong to one or another of the *Vaishnava sampradayas*.

Shaivas are worshippers of Shiva, and *Shaktas* are worshippers of Shakti or the Goddess (also known by other names including Durga and Parvati) and sometimes seen as the consort of Shiva. Some see Shiva and Shakti as being alternative and complementary manifestations of Brahman, understood as supra-personal in the *Advaita* manner.

HINDU LIFE

The Four Aims

The traditional Hindu view of human life is characterised by the four *purusharthas* (aims for human existence). These are: *dharma* (religious life) as a foundation for everything else; *artha* (economic development) as a necessity for life; *kama* (sense gratification) in order to maintain a healthy body and mind, sensual desires being restricted through self-regulation; and *moksha* (liberation, salvation) from the cycle of birth and death.

Most Hindus consider liberation to be the ultimate goal, but among *Vaishnavas* some would say that *bhakti* (devotion to the divine) is a fifth and final goal and that *prema* (love of God) and selfless devotion is higher than liberation (which for the devotees comes by means of the *grace* of God and not just by personal efforts).

Values

There are a number of core ideals and values that are shared by most Hindus, although in practice they are subject to different interpretations that result in varying degrees of observance. These ideals and values include: respect for parents and elders; reverence for teachers; regard for guests; a general adoption of vegetarianism; *ahimsa* (non-violence); tolerance of all races and religions; controlled relations between the sexes in which marriage is considered sacred and divorce, and pre-marital or extra-marital sexual relationships are strongly discouraged; sacredness of the cow whose milk sustains human life; and an appreciation of the equality of all living beings and the sanctity of life.

Hindus seek to promote the *Sanatana Dharma* among all people although, in general, they do not engage in activity aimed at converting non-Hindus to Hindu practice. Nevertheless, individuals are generally welcome to embrace the Hindu way.

Varnashrama Dharma

An understanding of one's personal and social role within the cosmic order of things is at the centre of Hindu life. Understanding *sva-dharma* (literally, "one's own *dharma*") in its relationship to *varna* (social position, or class) and *ashrama* (meaning "stage in life" or "spiritual order") is very important. *Dharma*, understood as a whole, is the morality by which righteousness and religious codes and duties are protected.

The mutual obligations involved in this system are symbolised for many by the ceremony of Rakshabandhan, which involves the tying of a thread (*rakhi*) by sisters around the wrist of their brothers, by students around the wrist of their teachers, and by people in general around the wrist of their leaders. This symbolises the vow to protect *dharma* and promote unity within society.

Various *dharmas* correspond with particular *varnas* and *ashramas* (see below) of which, in each case, there are believed to be four. As already noted (see *dharma* above), *dharma* can mean "intrinsic property", which is different for different things. Similarly, there are different *dharmas* for different people. Among the factors that differentiate people are the four *varnas* and four *ashramas* described below.

The Four Varnas

In the Hindu ideal, everyone's aptitude determines their affiliation to one of the four *varnas*. The *varnas* have, traditionally, come to be perceived as having separate and distinct social roles. These are defined in a well-known *Vedic* hymn, the *Purusha Sukta* (*Rig-Veda*, book 10, hymn 90), in which the whole of society is seen as one person and the *varnas* as interdependent parts of the one social body. A person's *varna* traditionally indicates his or her status and responsibility, and thus the kind of duty which he or she must execute to transmigrate into a higher existence.

According to some interpretations of the scriptures, the system of the four *varnas* is not wholly applicable in this age (*Kali Yuga*). Some Hindus say that it was only after the *Vedic* period that this social system became rigidly hereditary, whereas others maintain that it was always so. According to the *Bhagavad Gita* an individual's *varna* should be understood according to the person's qualities and the tendency towards a particular kind of work. The traditional *varnas* consist of:

Brahmins
These are intelligentsia and priests who are characterised by austerity, knowledge, self-control, honesty and cleanliness and who seek to promote these more widely.

Kshatriyas
These are administrators and military characterised by power, courage and leadership whose purpose in life is to defend the community, society and nation and to establish peace and prosperity.

Vaishyas
These are agriculturalists and merchants whose work is in producing and trading, being responsible for the generation and distribution of material wealth.

Sudras
These are workers who provide labour and service.

The four-fold differentiation of *varnas* is no longer rigidly followed among contemporary Hindus. However it does reflect the broad outlines of a division of labour and responsibilities that are found in many historical and contemporary societies.

Jati
The ideal division of society into four *varnas* is an important concept in *dharma*. But in practice a person tends to identify himself or herself with an hereditary group called a *jati* that is associated with one of the *varnas*. These groups are often referred to in English as *castes* or *sub-castes*. This should not be taken as implying any inherent differences between groups.

While the system of four *varnas* is known throughout India, the pattern of *jatis* varies from region to region. In each region there are dozens of *jatis*, many of them unknown even by name in other regions, and in India as a whole there are thousands.

Many *jatis* are traditionally linked to specific occupations, although their members do not necessarily practise them. *Jati* remains a significant social, cultural and economic factor for many aspects of Hindu life in the UK; for instance, many Hindus marry within their *jati*.

Examples of *jatis* the following include: *Patidars* (traditionally, traders), *Mochis* (traditionally, shoemakers), *Lohanas* (traditionally, traders), *Anavil Brahmins* (traditionally, agriculturalists), *Khattris* and *Aroras* (both traditionally warriors and traders), *Balmikis* (traditionally, manual workers), *Ravidasis* (traditionally, shoemakers), *Rarhi Brahmins* (traditionally, priests) and *Vaidyas* (traditionally, physicians).

Certain *jatis*, generally associated with what are viewed as polluting occupations, have historically been identified as *"outcastes"* and "*untouchables*", and have often suffered social discrimination as a result. The official term used in India to describe this group of people is the "*scheduled castes*". After independence, the Indian Government granted a special status to this group with the intention of achieving social equity.

Many of the present leaders of this group now prefer the self-designation of *Dalit* (oppressed). The majority contemporary Hindu position is that *untouchability* has no sanction within the Hindu *dharma*. The Hindu leader *Mahatma* (Great Soul) Gandhi called such people *Harijans* (children of God) and a number of Hindu groups are today working to eradicate the social injustices experienced by this group.

Gender Roles

The Hindu tradition has advocated equality of worth between women and men but with differentiation of social roles. These are set out in the *Manusmriti* (the *Law of Manu*), where a woman's role is defined primarily as that of an educator of children and housekeeper, with a man's role being one of overall authority coupled with financial responsibility for the family.

Views as to how far the *Manusmriti* applies in the circumstances of contemporary society vary within different sections of the Hindu population and, in the UK, specific gender roles vary from family to family. In spiritual terms, many Hindu women point to the strength and dignity that they derive from the Hindu tradition's representation of the divine in female as well as male forms.

Ashramas

The *ashramas* are the four stages that have traditionally and ideally been followed in the course of one's life. In this ideal sequence one first becomes a *brahmacharin* (student) living a celibate life of study under a *guru*.

Next, one becomes a *grihastha* or *grihini* (householder). In this stage, marriage, family and the bringing up and educating of children, together with hospitality for guests and care for the elderly and disabled, are the main focus of responsibility.

The third stage is that of a *vanaprastha* (hermit who has retired to the forest). This stage can only be entered after the completion of social obligations through the marriage of all one's daughters and preferably also of one's sons, and the handing over to them of all business affairs. This *ashrama* is traditionally a time in which there are increasing periods of withdrawal from society to enable more concentration on the spiritual dimension of life.

The fourth and final stage that may be undertaken is that of the *sannyasin*, who has renounced all earthly ties and looks to the whole world as a family rather than to an immediate biologically-related unit. When a husband becomes a *sannyasin*, the husband and wife part, with the husband going to live in an *ashram* and the wife coming under the care of her sons. This stage is followed only very rarely in conventional society.

Traditionally, *brahmins* go through all four *ashramas*, *kshatriyas* never directly take *sannyasa*, and *vaishyas* do not take *vanaprastha* or *sannyasa*, with *sudras* only accepting the householder *ashrama*. Some early Hindu texts allow for the possibility of becoming a *sannyasi* soon after completing the *brahmacharin* stage.

Whilst the *ashrama* system has not been fully operative since medieval times, a sequence of study followed by familial responsibilities and finally withdrawal from the world remains a powerful ideal for many Hindus, including those in the UK, since these stages are seen as based on a natural progression through life.

Guru-Disciple Relationship

For many Hindus, the *Guru Shishya* (Guru-disciple) relationship (*parampara*) is of great importance. *Gurus* are revered as those who have attained a spiritual perfection and as embodiments of the divine. The guidance and grace of a *guru* is therefore often seen as being essential for those who aspire to liberation.

Vegetarianism

Within the Hindu tradition there is a variety of views on the permissibility of a range of foods and drinks. Whilst Hindus recognise that every living organism depends upon others for food, many Hindus are vegetarians and even those who eat meat abstain from beef. Hindu vegetarianism arises from a belief in the principle of *ahimsa* (non-harming) and thus generally precludes the eating of meat, fish or eggs. Sometimes onions and garlic are also not eaten.

However, as well as the principle of *ahimsa*, there is also a positive conviction concerning the effect of food upon human development, especially for those who practise spiritual disciplines. Milk, yoghurt, butter, ghee (clarified butter) and fruits are considered to be wholesome foods that promote *sattva* (purity and harmony). When preparing their own food, many Hindus offer their food to a deity before eating it, and keep aside a portion for animals.

Products that have been cooked in, or contain, by-products from slaughtered animals would not be acceptable to strict Hindu vegetarians. For example, neither conventional ice cream (which may contain animal fats) nor cheese that contains rennet (extracted from the pancreas of the cow), nor chips which have been cooked in animal fats, would be acceptable. Hindus may also refrain from intoxicating drinks such as alcohol, and in some cases from tea and coffee too.

Fasting

Many Hindus (and especially women) observe *fasts* or *vrats* (vows) as devotion to a deity and on behalf of the well-being of themselves and their family. These vows – which are seen as strengthening willpower and faith - entail the avoidance of certain foods at certain times, such as on particular days of the week, of the lunar month, and of the year.

HINDU WORSHIP

Domestic Worship:

The practice of domestic worship is widespread. In their own homes, most Hindus have a shrine or small area for worship (*ghar mandir*, "house temple") containing pictures and/or *murtis* (see below) of favourite deities and the women of the household have an important role in the religious devotions centred on these shrines. In addition to private worship some fairly large gatherings for worship may also take place in private homes. *Havan* (the rite of the sacred fire) may also be performed at home on important occasions.

Corporate Devotional Activity

Corporate devotional activities include *bhajan* and *kirtan* (singing songs and *mantras*); *pravachan* (sermon); *havan* (the sacred fire ceremony); and the *arti* ceremony (see below). Private devotions, in the temple and at home, include *japa* (*mantra* meditation), prayer, *puja* (worship of the *murti*) and the study of sacred texts.

Arti Ceremony

In the *arti* ceremony, performed several times a day in the Hindu temple or *mandir*, the priest offers articles of worship, representing the five physical elements of life (earth, air, fire, water and space) to the deity including lighted ghee lamps, incense, water for bathing, coconut, flowers and grains. During this, worshippers play musical instruments, sing *bhajans,* and clap their hands in rhythm.

Havan

A fire is lit and Sanskrit mantras are recited, while offerings are made to the holy fire. The worshippers offer their obeisance, through the sacred fire, to the formless God. The practice emphasises the quality of selflessness. No Hindu sacraments, especially weddings, are complete without it.

HINDU PLACES OF WORSHIP

Mandirs

Hindu places of worship are not recorded as a separate category in the running totals of certified places of worship in England and Wales kept by the Registrar General. The CD-ROM accompanying this volume records around 100 Hindu places of worship in the UK, of which around 92 are in England, 4 in Scotland, 2 in Wales, and 2 in Northern Ireland.

At present most *mandirs* (temples) in the UK are converted public or religious buildings and private houses, with only a few purpose-built buildings. One such is the Shri Swaminarayan Mandir in Neasden, North West London. This was the first ever traditional *mandir* carved in white marble stone to be built in Europe and was opened in August 1995.

There is now also the Sri Murugan Temple in Newham, London, which opened in 2006 and serves mainly Tamil Hindu, as well as the new Balaji Temple in Birmingham, opened in 2006 as a purpose-built *mandir* on a twelve acre site.

Within individual *mandirs*, one may see different *murtis* (sacred images or figures that represent deities) and pictures of holy people. This variety can reflect the range of *sampradayas* (see above) that use the temple. *Mandirs* are more likely than in India to cater for a variety of *sampradayas*.

This may partly be because of the minority position of Hindus in the UK and the financial constraints within which they must operate. But it is also made possible by the inclusive approach of the Hindu traditions with respect to the commonalities shared by different deities. As well as the hall for worship, *mandirs* may also have other facilities on their premises, such as social, cultural, educational, and administrative rooms.

Many Hindus also attend a place of worship to associate with saintly persons from whom they can learn about spiritual topics. In a land in which Hindus are in a minority, worship at the *mandir* (see below) also fulfils an important social function, providing an opportunity to engage in community and cultural activities and consolidate faith together.

Murtis

Inside the *mandir*, there is usually a main hall with a shrine where the *murtis* of the *mandir* are installed. There may also be other side shrines. For those who are outsiders to the Hindu tradition, it is sometimes difficult to gain an accurate understanding of the nature of *murtis*. They are more than purely symbolic representations of deities being understood as full of divine energy and yet Hindus also do not believe that the reality of a deity is limited to a particular *murti* in a particular place.

Murtis are installed following several days of ritual. Once dedicated, they are venerated as deities, being dressed in the finest fabrics and decorated with ornaments, jewellery and garlands of flowers. This is in order to foster a mood of *seva* (sacrifice and selfless service) by centring people's devotion on the deity.

The *murtis* are usually made of marble, but can also be made of other kinds of stone, wood or metal. For the believer, the presence of a particular deity is manifested by *murtis* that have specific characteristics. For example, Ganesha is represented by an elephant-headed *murti* with four arms; Krishna is represented as a cowherd seen standing with one leg crossing the other at the ankles, playing a flute, and accompanied by his favourite devotee, a *gopi* (cowherd girl) Radha.

Deities are often accompanied by *murtis* of their *vahana* (a vehicle, the animal or bird on which they ride). For example, Shiva rides on the bull, Nandi. Brightly coloured and sweet-smelling flowers are laid before the *murtis* or hung over them as garlands. The *murtis* may be housed in a *garbha-griha* (inner sanctum), which only the *priest* is permitted to enter.

Other Temple Features

In the main hall there may also be one or more *vyasasanas*. These are decorated thrones on which *swamis* (religious teachers) sit when they deliver discourses to religious gatherings. In a *mandir* it is also likely that there will be incense to purify the air and create a spiritual atmosphere; the *AUM* (or *OM*) symbol to symbolise the primaeval sound representing God in the simplest form; and the *swastika*. This is not to be confused with the *swastika* of Nazism. The original Hindu form of this symbol is a sign of auspiciousness. Hindus feel a sense of outrage at the Nazi co-option and distortion of such a sacred symbol, and also at the use of *OM* on some hallucinogenic drugs.

One might also find a conch shell, the sound of which assists concentration on worship; a *trishul*, which is the trident weapon of Shiva and represents God, the soul and the ignorance through which the soul is held in bondage; a coconut, which is believed to represent the three-eyed Shiva and is symbolic of life by being hard on the outside but sweet on the inside; images of the *lotus*, which is an ancient symbol of the cosmos, of wisdom and of humanity; and a *kalasha*, which is a pot representing the human body.

The mouth of a *kalasha* is considered as Vishnu; its base as Brahma; and its middle as Shiva. The water within it stands for purity and love of the divine. It also relates to the *Pancha Mahabhuta* (the five physical elements).

When visiting a *mandir*, it is customary for Hindus to take some kind of offering for the deity, such as fruit, milk, money or flowers, *haldi* (turmeric) and *kumkum* (red powder). Anyone entering a *mandir* for any purpose must remove their shoes. A bell may be hung for worshippers to ring on entering, to invite the presence of the gods and to ward off evil spirits.

The worshipper then comes face to face with the *murti*. This is called taking *darshan* (sight) of the deity, which is understood as a blissful experience. The worshipper offers respect to the deity/deities by folding hands or by bowing down, and may then offer prayers and a gift, or respectfully sip a few drops of *charnamrita* (holy water used to bathe the deity). The worship of the *murti* with offering of gifts is called *puja*. More formal *puja* is performed by the temple *priest*.

Prior to *arti*, food is offered to the deity and is blessed for later distribution. Food that has been offered to a deity is said to be sanctified and is known as *prasad* or *prasadam*.

Visitors to a Hindu Mandir

Almost all Hindu *mandirs* welcome people from all religions to visit them and, if they wish, to take part in the worship. Clothing should be modest for both men and women, with shoes being removed and put on the racks provided before going into the *mandir*. Clean and presentable socks, stockings, or tights are therefore a good idea. Sometimes women are requested to cover their heads and some Hindu women do not go to the *mandir* during menstruation.

Visitors should walk in quietly and find a place to sit on the floor (usually carpeted) and since the floor is used for seating, women should avoid wearing short dresses and skirts. In some *mandirs* men and boys sit on one side of the room and women and girls on the other. One should sit with crossed legs or with legs pointing to one side as it can be considered disrespectful to sit with legs forward with the feet pointing towards the sacred area at the front of the *mandir*. In some *mandirs* guests may be expected to stand as a sign of respect during *arti*.

There is no expectation that visitors join in the formal prayer and worship unless they wish to do so. As mentioned above, when Hindus go to the *mandir*, they usually take an offering such as food or money to give to the deities. For a visitor who is not a Hindu, this would not be expected, although it would be welcomed.

If food is offered, then it should not be cooked food and especially not if it violates the principle of *ahimsa* (not-harming). Fresh fruit or nuts would be appropriate. Food becomes sacred when given to the deity, usually prior to the ceremony called *arti*. After it becomes sacred it is called *prasada*.

Often the blessed food takes the form of sweets or fruit offered on a tray. Visitors are likely to be offered one piece that they can either eat or take home. If taking a piece, hold it in cupped hands with the right hand uppermost. A visitor who is uncomfortable for religious reasons about being given some of this sacred food to eat, should let the person offering the food know with a quiet "No thank you". If possible, it should be explained to the hosts in advance that any such action would be taken for personal religious reasons, and not out of any disrespect.

HINDU CALENDAR AND FESTIVALS

Calendar

Hindus use both the solar and the lunar cycle calendars, but most religious festivals are based on the lunar calendar, counting days based on the waxing and waning of the moon. Since it consists normally of twelve lunar months, it is ten days shorter than it is in the *Gregorian* calendar year. Approximately once every three years an extra month is added to bring the lunar year in phase with the solar year. Popular Hindu calendars are

the *Vikram*, *Shalivana* and *Yugabda*. The best known of these is the *Vikram Samvat*, which started in the year 57BCE.

Hindu seasons and festival dates do not remain the same each year within the framework of the *Gregorian* calendar, except for a few which are timed by the sun and not the moon. The Hindu calendar is set out in *panchang* (*almanacs*) that provide information on the dates of festivals and other rituals to be followed by various Hindu groups.

Festivals

There are many Hindu festivals, but the following are some of the principal ones. The approximate time of their occurrence indicated below refers to the *Gregorian* calendar in common use in the UK:

Shivaratri or Mahashivaratri
(February/March)
Worship dedicated to Lord Shiva. Devotees spend the night at the temple chanting singing, and contemplating. Milk is poured continuously, as an offering, on to the *linga*, the symbolic form of Lord Shiva. Among some families, there is also a tradition of *fasting*.

Holi (February/March)
This festival of colours to welcome the spring season is associated with many stories of Vishnu and his devotees, and with that of the half-man, half-lion incarnation, Narasimha or Narasingha, and Prahlada, a devotee of Krishna. In India, traditionally, liquid dyes, coloured powders and water are liberally sprinkled on the participants as fun. In the UK the inclement climate, and the fact that it could easily be misunderstood by the wider society, can curtail this traditional practice, but many British Hindus enjoy the bonfire that is another traditional feature of *Holi*.

Yugadi or Gudi Parva (March–April)
For many Hindus, this festival marks the beginning of the New Year in the *Vikram* and

Shalivan calendars. *Puja*, feasting and greetings are common. A special mixture of neem leaves and jaggery is eaten to symbolise acceptance of both bitter and happy things in life.

Rama Navami/Hari Jayanti (March/April)
Celebrates the birth of Lord Rama at Ayodhya in India. Devotees fast, and the Ramayana, which contains the story of Rama and Sita, is read aloud in temples. Devotees of *Lord Swaminaryan* also celebrate his birth on this day singing, *bhajans* and listening to discourses about him.

Janmashtami (August/September)
Marks the birth of Lord Krishna who is believed to have appeared in human form in the fourth century BCE, or in traditional chronology five thousand years ago shortly before the *Kali Yuga*, in the district of Mathura, India, in order to deliver the pious, destroy miscreants and establish the principles of the *Sanatana Dharma*. Devotees perform *puja* and sing *bhajans*. For this festival, a special *puja* is held in the *mandirs* at midnight.

Navaratri (September/October)
Navaratri means "nine nights". It is celebrated with dancing and is held in honour of Lakshmi, Durga and Sarasvati, as well as other goddesses worshipped in this season. It ends with *Dussehra* or *Vijayadashami*, the tenth day, a time of celebration of the victory of good over evil.

Diwali or Deepawali (October/November)
According to some Hindu groups, this festival marks the beginning of a new year in the Hindu calendar. It celebrates the victory of light over darkness and knowledge over ignorance. The festival is also a time when Hindus worship the Goddess Lakshmi (Goddess of prosperity) and is known as the "festival of lights" because of the lighting everywhere of *dipas* or *divas* (small oil lamps). These are lit to celebrate the return of Rama (as the incarnation of Vishnu) and Sita (as his consort, Lakshmi, the goddess of prosperity) to Rama's kingdom of Ayodhya after fourteen years of exile.

Annakuta or Nutan Varsh
(October/November)
This is the day after *Diwali*. Large quantities of sweets and other foodstuffs are brought to the temple to be offered to the deities in celebration of a story from Krishna's childhood and concerned with Mount Govardhan.

Pilgrimages

Pilgrimages also form an important part of Hindu religious observance. Visits to holy places in India may be undertaken with special intentions in mind, such as cure of disease or blessing for the family.

In the *Advaita* Hindu tradition, the most holy of all places of pilgrimage is Varanasi (also known as Benares or Kashi). This is situated on the sacred River Ganga (Ganges) and is especially sacred to those Hindus who venerate Shiva and Rama. Pilgrims who have visited the River Ganga often bring home bottles of water from the river to place in their family shrines. Dying people may request to sip Ganges water and also to have their ashes spread in the river.

In the *Vaishnava* Hindu tradition, Vrindavan and Nathdwar are of special importance because of their connections with Krishna. Ayodhya, Badrinath, Kedaranath, Mathura, Tirupathi and Vaishnodevi, Kashmir, Dwarka are other important places of pilgrimage. There are also some more recently evolved centres of pilgrimage such as Akshardham, in Gandhinagar, Gujarat, a memorial to *Lord Swaminarayan*.

HINDU ORGANISATIONS

Hindu Organisational Listings

The first Hindu organisations in the UK were set up in the late 1950s. Since then a number of different kinds of organisations have developed, many of which serve multiple functions, including lobbying and campaigning groups, youth activities, language classes, women's groups, trust funds, education and propagation of Hindu culture, besides activities that are specifically religious. Some of the local and national groupings are part of international organisations mainly based in, or have ideological links with, India.

The CD-ROM that accompanies this volume includes contact details for head offices of organisations that have branches throughout the country as well as for organisations that aspire to serve the Hindu community on a UK-wide basis. The CD-ROM accompanying this volume records around 75 Hindu organisations with a UK scope.

Details of various Hindu local organisations are also included in the CD-ROM. Among these are *mandirs*, many of which are in buildings adapted from other original uses, but increasing numbers of which are purpose-built. Also included are *caste* groups and other organisations that often meet either in hired premises or in the homes of their members.

The CD-ROM records around 702 local organisations (including around 683 in England, 9 in Wales, 5 in Scotland and 5 in Northern Ireland). Finally, it includes around 15 organisations working at a regional level in England, as well as around 2 in Scotland and 1 in Wales.

Representative Groups

The oldest Hindu organisations operating at a national level, and with branches in various cities in the UK and in Europe more widely include the Hindu Swayamsevak Sangh, established in 1965, and the Vishwa Hindu Parishad UK, established in 1966 as a part of the global Vishwa Hindu Parishad (World Hindu Council).

Another national organisation – the National Council of Hindu Temples – played a significant role in the formation of the Hindu Council of the UK. More recently, the National Hindu Students Forum UK, and the Hindu Forum of Britain, with 275 organisations affiliated to it, has been established.

A number of local and regional areas have seen the development of representative groups such as the Hindu Council (Brent), the Hindu Council of Birmingham, the Leicester Gujarat Hindu Association, the Hindu Council of the North, the Hindu Council of Nottingham, and the Hindu Resource Centre (Croydon).

Jati (Community) Associations

Although *jatis* may be historically associated in India with particular occupations, in the UK they do not generally correlate with one's social, economic or occupational status. *Jati* groups do, however, remain a significant social, cultural and economic factor for many aspects of internal Hindu community life in the UK. Different patterns of settlement have influenced organisational development and therefore *jati* groups are concentrated in particular localities in the UK. For example, there has been a concentration of *Mochis* in Leeds, and of *Lohanas* in Leicester and North London.

Jati associations exist at both national and local levels. They have functions ranging from social networking through to voluntary welfare support and provision. Local organisations may be affiliated to a national organisation. As one example, the Gujarati Federation of Anavil Samaj is an organisation representing members of the *Anavil jati* and has local branches in various parts of the country.

National *jati* organisations are much more characteristic of Gujarati Hindus than Punjabi Hindus and they co-ordinate joint events between local groups and provide a networking function across the country. National *jati* organisations often produce annual directories of members of the local *jati* groups affiliated to them, although these are not readily available to the general public.

Jati associations are sometimes recognisable from the *jati* name in their title, for example, the National Association of Patidar Samaj (*Patidar*), the Shri Kutch Leva Patel Samaj (members of the *Leva Patel jati* from the Kutch region of the state of Gujarat), or Brahma Samaj (*Brahmin*). The Brahma Samaj is a Gujarati *Brahmin* association and should not be confused with the Brahmo Samaj, which is a religious society founded in Calcutta in 1828.

Spiritual Movements

Another form of organisation, often with a regional base in India, is the *sampradaya* or spiritual tradition (see above). A number of *sampradayas*, some relatively modern, have a strong presence in the UK.

Swaminaryans
Swaminarayan Hindus in the UK are predominantly of Gujarati origin and follow teachers in the line of Sahajananda Swami (1781-1830), also called *Swaminarayan*, who is believed to have been an incarnation of the Supreme Lord. *Swaminarayanis* combine traditional Hindu practices with specific customs of their own, including the strict separation of men and women in the temple.

There are various *Swaminarayan* groupings in the UK, reflecting different views concerning the proper line of succession to Sahajananda Swami. The largest in the UK is the Akshar Purushottam Sanstha (the Swaminarayan Hindu Mission) that looks to the leadership of Pramukh Swami, and main UK centre of which is the purpose-built and classically constructed temple in Neasden, London. Another is the group that looks for leadership to Acharya Tejendraprasad Pande and whose main UK centre is in Willesden Lane, London.

Pushtimargis
Other devotional groups include the *Pushtimarg* or *Vallabha sampradaya* (founded in the sixteenth century). Its members, who are largely *Lohana* by *jati*, follow the teachings of Vallabha (c.1479-1531CE) and worship Krishna, particularly in the form of Srinathji and as the infant Krishna.

Krishna Consciousness
There is also the International Society for Krishna Consciousness (ISKCON) whose devotees follow the teachings propounded by A C Bhaktivedanta Swami Prabhupada (1896-1977) in the Chaitanya Vaishnava tradition which flourishes in Bengal. The first ISKCON temple in the UK was opened in 1969 in central London. Later, George Harrison (one of the Beatles) donated Bhaktivedanta Manor in Hertfordshire where, every year, a festival involving thousands of Hindus from all over the UK has been held to celebrate *Krishna-Janmashtami*. A long-running planning dispute that threatened this temple with closure for public worship was settled in 1996.

Arya Samajis
Members of the Arya Samaj follow the teachings of Swami Dayanand Saraswati (1824-1883CE) who rejected the concept of *jati* and the worship of *murtis*. Hindus in the Arya Samaj, who are mainly Punjabis, stress belief in, and the purity of, the *Vedas* and reject those parts of post-*Vedic* Hindu teachings that they believe do not conform to the *Vedic* revelation, including parts of the *Puranas* and *Tantras*.

Ramakrishna Mission
The Ramakrishna Mission was founded by the Bengali Swami Vivekananda (1863-1902CE) in the name of his master Ramakrishna (1836-1886). It teaches *Advaita Vedanta*, and is headed by a highly disciplined and organised body of *sannyasins*.

Hindu–Related Groups

There are also many Hindu-related movements and groups which practise the disciplines of *Yoga*. Some of these focus purely on the more physical exercises of *Hatha Yoga* whilst others seek to present a complete religious approach through *Raja Yoga*. From among those responding to the 2001 decennial Census questions on religion and using the "Other religions – please write in " option, an analysis of Table M275 Religion (Most Detailed Categories) shows that 253 respondents in England and 8 in Wales gave their response as "Raja Yoga".

Some *Yoga* groups are closely connected with the wider Hindu tradition, whilst others have recruitment and management from a cross section of the wider community. These include the Divine Life Mission (18 respondents recorded for England and 3 for Wales, based on an analysis of Table M275 Religion (Most Detailed Categories), the Transcendental Meditation movement and others such as Eckankar (253 respondents recorded for England and 9 for Wales).

Educational Organisations

A number of Hindu educational groups and organisations have emerged, an example of which is the Vivekanada Centre in London. The Swaminarayan Hindu Mission in London has started an independent Hindu school where, in addition to the National Curriculum, students are taught about moral and ethical values and Hindu religion, culture and music. There are also many supplementary schools that teach Indian languages and Hindu religion and culture out of school hours. One such example is the Academy for Indian Culture and Education in Manchester.

Regional/Linguistic Groups

Some groups are organised on the basis of a specific shared regional or linguistic background. Punjabis or Gujaratis or Bengalis have often joined together to form associations. Such groups can sometimes be recognised by the inclusion of regional names in their organisational titles, as in for example, the Preston Gujarat Hindu Society.

Personnel

A Hindu *priest* is often referred to as *pandit, swami*, or *maharaj*. A *priest* whose function is to perform *puja* in a temple is called a *pujari*. One who performs life-cycle rituals for families in their homes is called a *purohit*. Traditionally, these roles have been restricted to those of the Brahmin *varna*. However (as explained in the section on *varna* above), the term *Brahmin* can be understood in a qualitative sense, so that anyone who is knowledgeable and shows *Brahmin*-like qualities can be a *priest*.

Priests are usually male, but can also be female. In some other temples, the wives of *priests* act as *pujari* when their husbands are away. *Priests* may be resident in the *mandir*, and may be appointed and paid by the congregation. Their role is to conduct religious ceremonies and to care for the holy shrines. Many learned Hindus, who have professional jobs, act as *pujaris/purohits*. They usually do this on a voluntary basis in their spare time, in order to help conduct religious ceremonies. Vishwa Hindu Parishad UK and the National Council of Hindu Temples UK both offer *purohit* services to the wider Hindu community.

The *mandir* is usually governed by a managing committee including the offices of temple president and a secretary. Many *pujaris* are from India, staying only for a temporary period before returning home. As such, they will not necessarily speak English, although this situation is changing and developing all the time. However, when wishing to visit a *mandir* it may be preferable to contact the secretary or president of the *mandir*.

Swamis or *gurus* are religious teachers, and they are venerated by Hindus because they are learned in the scriptures, know the methods of worship and have renounced all worldly attachments. Some have authority in relation to particular *sampradayas*, but they also receive respect from non-members.

FURTHER READING

Details follow of a number of general introductions to Hinduism together with books and articles that provide some focus on Hindus and Hindu organisations in the UK. The references are not comprehensive, but provide signposts to a range of relevant materials.

Ballard, R (ed), *Desh Pardesh: The South Asian Presence in Britain*, C Hurst and Co, London, 1994.

Barot, R, *The Social Organisation of a Swaminaryan Sect in Britain*, School of Oriental and African Studies, University of London, PhD thesis, 1980.

Barot, R, "Caste and Sect in the Swaminarayan Movement", in R Burghart (ed), *Hinduism in Great Britain: The Perpetuation of Religion in an Alien Milieu*, Tavistock Publications, London, 1987, pp 67-80.

Barot, R, "Hindus and Hinduism in Europe", in S Gill, G D'Costa and U King (eds), *Religion in Europe: Contemporary Perspectives*, Kok Pharos, Kampen, 1994, pp 68-85.

Becher, H and Husain, F, *Supporting Minority Ethnic Families. South Asian Hindus and Muslims in Britain: Developments in Family Support*, NFPI, London, 2003.

Bharatiya Vidya Bhavan, *Hindu Dharma: The Universal Way of Life*, Bharatiya Vidya Bhavan, London, nd.

Bowen, D (ed), *Hinduism in England*, Faculty of Contemporary Studies, Bradford College, Bradford, 1986.

Bowen, D, *The Sathya Sai Baba Community in Bradford: Its Origin and Development, Religious Beliefs and Practices*, Community Religions Project Monograph, University of Leeds, Leeds, 1988.

Brockington, J L, *The Sacred Thread: Hinduism in Its Continuity and Diversity*, Edinburgh University Press, Edinburgh, 1981.

Bryant, E and Ekstrand, M (eds), *The Hare Krishna Movement: The Post-Charismatic Fate of a Religious Transplant, Columbia University Press*, New York, 2004.

Burghart, R (ed), *Hinduism in Great Britain: The Perpetuation of Religion in an Alien Milieu*, Tavistock, London, 1987.

Carey, S, "The Hare Krishna movement and Hindus in Britain", in *New Community*, Volume 20, Spring 1983, pp 477-486.

Chandrashekharendra Sarasvati Swami, His Holiness, *Hindu Dharma: The Universal Way of Life*, Bharatiya Vidya Bhavan, Bombay, 1995.

Chohan, S, "Punjabi Religion Amongst the South Asian Diaspora in Britain. The Role of the Baba," in K Jacobsen and P Kumar (eds), *South Asians in the Diaspora: Histories and Religious Traditions*, E J Brill, Leiden, 2004, pp 393-414.

Cole, O and Kanitkar, V, *Hinduism*, Hodder and Stoughton, London, 2003.

Cush, D and Robinson, C (eds), *Encyclopaedia of Hinduism*, Routledge, London, 2007.

DeMichaelis, E, "Contemporary Hatha Yoga in the West", in *Journal of Contemporary Religion*, Volume 10, No 2, 1995, pp 193-195.

DeMichaelis, E, "Some comments on the contemporary practice of Yoga in the UK, with particular reference to British Hatha Yoga schools", in *Journal of Contemporary Religion*, Volume 10, No 2, 1995, pp 243-255.

DeMichaelis, E, *A History of Modern Yoga: Patanjali and Western Esotericism*, Continuum, London, 2004.

Dwyer, R, "Caste, Religion and Sect in Gujarat: Followers of Vallabhacharya and Swaminarayan" in R Ballard (ed), *Desh Pardesh: The South Asian Presence in Britain*, C. Hurst and Co, London, 1994, pp 165-190.

Elgood, H, *Hinduism and the Religious Arts*, Cassells, London, 1998.

Firth, S, *Death, Dying and Bereavement in a British Hindu Community*, Kok Pharos, Kampen, 1997.

Flood, G, *An Introduction to Hinduism*, Cambridge University Press, Cambridge, 1996.

Flood, G (ed), *The Blackwell Companion to Hinduism*, Oxford, Blackwell, 2003.

Fowler, J, *Hinduism: Beliefs and Practices*, Sussex Academic Press, Brighton, 1997.

Fowler, J, *Perspectives of Reality: An Introduction to the Philosophy of Hinduism*, Sussex Academic Press, Brighton, 2002.

Henley, A, *Caring for Hindus and Their Families: Religious Aspects of Care*, National Extension College, Cambridge, 1983.

Jackson, R, "Holi in North India and in an English city: some adaptations and anomalies", in *New Community*, Volume 5, 1976, pp 203-209.

Jackson, R and Killingley, D, *Approaches to Hinduism*, John Murray, London, 1988.

Jackson, R and Killingley, D, *Moral Issues in the Hindu Tradition*, Trentham Books, Stoke-on-Trent, 1991.

Jackson, R and Nesbitt, E, *Listening to Hindus*, Unwin Hyman, London, 1990.

Jackson, R and Nesbitt, E, *Hindu Children in Britain*, Trentham Books, Stoke-on-Trent, 1993.

Kamal, Z and Loewenthal, K, "Suicide beliefs and behaviour among young Muslims and Hindus in the UK", in *Mental Health, Religion and Culture*, Volume 5, No 2, 2002, pp 111-118.

Kanitkar, H, "Upanayana Ritual and Hindu Identity in Essex", in R Barot (ed), *Religion and Ethnicity: Minorities and Social Change in the Metropolis*, Kok Pharos, Kampen, 1993, pp 110-122.

Kanitkar, H and Cole, O, *Teach Yourself Hinduism*, Hodder, 1995.

Killingley, D (ed), *A Handbook of Hinduism for Teachers*, Grevatt & Grevatt, Newcastle-upon-Tyne, 1984.

Killingley, D, Menski, D and Firth, S, *Hindu Ritual and Society*, S Y Killingley, Newcastle-upon-Tyne, 1991.

King, R, *Indian Philosophy: An Introduction to Hindu and Buddhist Thought*, Edinburgh University Press, Edinburgh, 1999.

King, U, *A Report on Hinduism in Britain*, Community Religions Project Research Papers, No 2, University of Leeds Department of Theology and Religious Studies, Leeds, 1984.

Klostermaier, K, *A Short Introduction to Hinduism*, Oneworld, Oxford, 1998.

Knott, K, *My Sweet Lord: The Hare Krishna Movement*, Aquarian Press, Wellingborough, 1986.

Knott, K, *Hinduism in Leeds: A Study of Religious Practice in the Indian Hindu Community and in Hindu-Related Groups*, Community Religions Project Monograph, University of Leeds, 1986 (reprinted, 1994).

Knott, K, "Hindu Temple Rituals in Britain: The Reinterpretation of Tradition," in R Burghart (ed), *Hinduism in Great Britain: The Perpetuation of Religion in An Alien Cultural Milieu*, 1987, pp 157-179.

Knott, K, "Hindu Communities in Britain", in R Badham (ed), *Religion, State and Society in Modern Britain*, Edwin Mellen Press, Lampeter, 1989, pp 243-257.

Knott, K, "The Gujarati Mochis in Leeds: From Leather Stockings to Surgical Boots and Beyond", in R Ballard (ed), *Desh Pardesh: The South Asian Presence in Britain*, C. Hurst and Co, London, 1994, pp 213-230.

Knott, K, "Insider and outsider perceptions of Prabhupada", in *Journal of Vaisnava Studies*, Volume 6, No 2, 1998, pp 72-91.

Knott, K, *Hinduism: A Very Short Introduction*, Oxford University Press, Oxford, 2000.

Knott, K, "Hinduism in Britain", in H Coward, J Hinnells and R Williams, *The South Asian Religious Diaspora in Britain, Canada and the United States*, State University of New York Press, New York, 2000, pp 89-107.

Law, J, *The Religious Beliefs and Practices of Hindus in Derby*, Community Religions Project Papers (new series), University of Leeds, Leeds, 1991.

Lipner, J, *Hindus: Their Religious Beliefs and Practices*, Routledge, London, 1994.

Logan, P, "Practising religion: British Hindu children and the Navraratri festival", in *British Journal of Religious Education*, Volume 20, No 3, pp 160-169.

Marshall, P (ed), *The British Discovery of Hinduism in the Eighteenth Century*, Cambridge University Press, Cambridge, 1970.

Michaelson, M, "The relevance of caste among East African Gujaratis in Britain", in *New Community*, Volume 7, pp 350-360.

National Council of Hindu Temples, *Hinduism*, National Council of Hindu Temples, 1983.

Nesbitt, E, *My Dad's Hindu, My Mum's Side Are Sikhs: Studies in Religious Identity*, Arts, Culture and Education Research Papers, National Foundation for Arts Education, University of Warwick, Coventry, 1991.

Nesbitt, E, "Gender and religious traditions: the role learning of British Hindu children", in *Gender and Education*, Volume 5, No 1, 1993, pp 81-91.

Nesbitt, E, "Being Religious Shows in Your Food: Young British Hindus and Vegetarianism", in T Rukmani (ed), *Hindu Diaspora: Global Perspectives*, Concordia University, Montreal, 1999, pp 397-426.

Nesbitt, E, "I'm a Gujarati Lohana and a Vaishnav as Well: Religious Identity Formation Among Young Coventrian Punjabis and Gujaratis", in S Coleman and S Collins (eds), *Religion, Identity and Change: Perspectives on Global Transformations*, Ashgate, Aldershot, 2004, pp 174-190.

Nye, M, "Temple congregations and communities: Hindu constructions in Edinburgh", in *New Community*, Volume 29, 1993, pp 201-215.

Nye, M, "A Place for our Gods: Tradition and Change Among Hindus in Edinburgh", in R Barot (ed), *Religion and Ethnicity: Minorities and Social Change in the Metropolis*, Kok Pharos, Kampen, 1993, pp 123-137.

Nye, M, *A Place for Our Gods: The Construction of a Hindu Temple Community in Edinburgh*, Curzon Press, London, 1995.

Nye, M, "Minority religious groups and religious freedom in England: the ISKCON Temple at Bhaktivedanta Manor," in *Journal of Church and State*, Volume 40, No 2, 1998, pp 411-436.

Nye, M, *Multiculturalism and Minority Religions in Britain − Krishna Consciousness, Religious Freedom and the Politics of Location*, Curzon Press, Richmond, 2001.

O'Keefe, B, *Hindu Family Life in East London*, London School of Economics and Political Science, University of London, PhD thesis, 1980.

Pandey, R, *Hindu Samskaras*, Motilal Banarsidass, Delhi, 1993.

Pearson, A, *"Because It Gives Me Peace of Mind": Ritual Fasts in the Religious Lives of Hindu Women*, State University of New York Press, New York, 1996.

Pocock, D, "Preservation of the religious life: Hindu immigrants in England", in *Contributions to Indian Sociology*, ns Volume 10, No 2, 1976, pp 342-365.

Prabhu, P, *Hindu Social Organization: A Study in Psychosocial and Ideological Foundations*, Popular Prakashan, Bombay, 1988.

Prabhupada, A C Bhaktivedanta Swami, *Bhagavad-Gita As It Is*, Bhaktivedanta Book Trust, London, 1986.

Radhakrishnan, S, *Indian Religions*, Vision Books, Delhi, 1983.

Raj, D, " 'Who the hell do you think you are?': Promoting religious identity among young Hindus in Britain", in *Ethnic and Racial Studies*, Volume 23, No 3, 2000, pp 535-558.

Renard, J, *Responses to 101 Questions on Hinduism*, Paulist Press, New York, 1999.

Shattuck, S, *Hinduism*, Routledge, London, 1999.

Stutley, M, *Hinduism: The Eternal Law*, Crucible, Wellingborough, 1985.

Stutley, M and J, *A Dictionary of Hinduism*, Routledge and Kegan Paul, London, 1987.

Subramaniyaswami, Satguru Sivaya, *Dancing with Siva: Hinduism's Contemporary Catechism*, Himalayan Academy Publications, Hawaii, 1993.

Teifion, M, *A Way to God: Hindu Beliefs in Leicester and Leicestershire*, unpublished MPhil thesis University of Leicester, Leicester, 1982.

Thomas, T, "Hindu Dharma in Dispersion", in G Parsons (ed), *The Growth of Religious Diversity: Britain from 1945, Volume I: Traditions*, Routledge, 1993, pp 173-204.

Vertovec, S (ed), *Aspects of the South Asian Diaspora*, Oxford University Press, Delhi, 1991.

Vertovec, S, "Community and congregation in London Hindu Temples: divergent trends", in *New Community*, Volume 8, No 2, 1992, pp 251-264.

Vertovec, S, "Caught in an Ethnic Quandary: Indo-Caribbean Hindus in London", in R Ballard (ed), *Desh Pardesh: The South Asian Presence in Britain*, C Hurst and Co, London, 1994, pp 272-290.

Vertovec, S, "On the reproduction and representation of Hinduism in Britain", in T Ranger, O Stuart, and Y Samad (eds), *Culture, Identity and Politics*, Avebury, Aldershot, 1996, pp 77-89.

Vertovec, S, *The Hindu Diaspora – Comparative Patterns*, Routledge, London, 2000.

Vishwa Hindu Parishad, *Explaining Hindu Dharma: A Guide for Teachers*, Chansitor Publications, 1996.

Warrier, Shrikala, "Gujarati Prajapatis in London: Family Roles and Sociability Networks", in R Ballard (ed), *Desh Pardesh: The South Asian Presence in Britain*, C. Hurst and Co, London, 1994, pp 191-212.

Weller, P, "Hindus and Sikhs: Community Development and Religious Discrimination in England and Wales", in K Jacobsen and P Kumar (eds), *South Asians in the Diaspora: Histories and Religious Traditions*, Brill, Leiden, 2004, pp 454-497.

Werner, K, *A Popular Dictionary of Hinduism*, Curzon Press, Richmond, 1997.

Wilkinson, S, *Young British Hindu Women's Interpretations of the Images of Womanhood in Hinduism*, unpublished doctoral thesis, University of Leeds, Leeds, 1994.

Williams, R B, *A New Face of Hinduism: The Swaminarayan Religion*, Cambridge University Press, Cambridge, 1984.

Zaehner, R C (ed), *Hindu Scriptures*, J M Dent and Sons, London, 1986.

INTRODUCING JAINS IN THE UK

JAINS IN THE UK   193

ORIGINS AND DEVELOPMENT OF JAINISM 193

SOURCES OF JAIN BELIEFS AND PRACTICES   194

KEY JAIN BELIEFS   195

TRADITIONS IN JAINISM   197

JAIN LIFE   198

JAIN WORSHIP   198

JAIN PLACES OF WORSHIP   199

JAIN CALENDAR AND FESTIVALS   200

JAIN ORGANISATIONS   201

FURTHER READING   202

JAINS IN THE UK

History in the UK

Most Jains now living in the United Kingdom can trace their historical and ethnic origins back to the Gujarat and Rajasthan areas of India. Some migrated directly from India in the 1950s; others came in the 1960s and 1970s from the East African countries in which they or their forebears had previously settled, such as Kenya, Uganda and Tanzania.

Global and UK Populations

Jains estimate that there are around 4,250,000 Jains worldwide. In the 2001 decennial Census questions on religion, the category of "Jain" was not offered as a pre-set category for respondents to tick. However, the specially commissioned Census Table M275 Religion (Most Detailed Categories) provides a breakdown of responses for England and Wales of respondents ticking the "Other religions, please write in" box in the Census question on religious affiliation. From an analysis of this table, there were 15,067 Jain respondents in England and 65 in Wales.

Many of the Jains in the UK live in and around the Greater London area and in Leicester. Jain communities are also found in Coventry, Luton, Manchester, Northampton and Wellingborough. Jains have long been engaged in business and finance. In the UK, they are well-represented in the professions of accountancy, medicine and pharmacy.

ORIGINS AND DEVELOPMENT OF JAINISM

The Tirthankaras

The precise origins of Jainism cannot be traced, but it began in India. The term *Jain* means a follower of the *Jinas* (Spiritual Victors), a line of human teachers who are believed to have existed from time immemorial and to have attained *kevalajnana* (infinite knowledge) and perfect purity through their own spiritual efforts. The *Jinas* are also known as *Tirthankaras*, literally meaning *Ford-Makers*, those who help others to cross over the floods of *samsara* (the cycle of birth and death). Jains believe that in the present cosmic cycle there have been twenty-four *Tirthankaras* who have taught others the tenets of Jainism.

Mahavira

The twenty-fourth *Tirthankara*, Vardhamana, usually called *Mahavira* (the Great Hero), is traditionally said to have been born in 599 BCE into a *kshatriya* (noble) family in the area of what is now Bihar, in India, although some modern scholars have suggested a rather later date.

When he was thirty years old, with the permission of his family he left home on a spiritual quest. Jains affirm that after twelve years he attained *kevalajnana* (omniscience). Shortly after this, eleven learned men came to the place where *Mahavira* was in order to challenge him, but when he answered their doubts they became his disciples and later on the *Ganadharas* (leaders) of the fourfold order of *monks* and *nuns*, laymen and laywomen which he founded.

During the next thirty years, it is thought that his followers within this order grew to about 14,000 *sadhus* (male *ascetics*) and 36,000 *sadhvis* (female *ascetics*). There were also approximately 500,000 *shravakas* (lay men) and *shravikas* (lay women) associated with the order. At the age of seventy-two, *Mahavira* died at Pavapuri (Bihar) and is believed to have attained *moksha* or *nirvana*, the state of perfection beyond the cycle of birth and death.

Jainism in India

At first, Jainism flourished throughout the Ganges valley area of India. After the fall of the Mauryan dynasty of Emperor Ashoka (c200 BCE) many Jains, together with their *mendicant* leaders, migrated west to the city of Mathura on the Yamuna River. Others migrated further west to Rajasthan and Gujarat, and south to Maharashtra and Karnataka, where Jainism rapidly grew in popularity.

SOURCES OF JAIN BELIEFS AND PRACTICES

Scriptures

Jain scriptures are known as the *Shruta*, *Agamas* or *Siddhanta* (doctrine) which comprise the canonical literature containing the teachings of *Mahavira* and other *Tirthankaras*. This literature consists of some sixty texts and is divided into three main groups of writings. These three groups are the *Purvas* (Older Texts); the *Angas* (Limbs); and the *Angabahyas* (Subsidiary Canon). A majority of these texts are written in Ardhamagadhi, an ancient language of Maghadha.

Purvas

The *Purvas* are believed to constitute the teachings of the former *Tirthankaras* as handed down in oral tradition. Jains in the *Shvetambara* tradition (see below under "Jain Traditions") believe that all this material was lost. Jains in the *Digambara* tradition (see below) claim that some of the material from these oral teachings is the basis for their early treatise, *Shat Khanda-Agama* (the Scripture in Six Parts).

Angas

The *Angas* consist of twelve books including such major texts as the *Acharanga Sutra*, which is the oldest, and the *Bhagavati Sutra*, which is the largest. Based on the teachings of *Mahavira*, they were compiled by the *Ganadharas* and contain materials about doctrinal matters, rules of discipline for *monks* and *nuns*, Jain cosmology, ecclesiastical law, and narratives for the instruction of the laity.

Digambaras have traditionally maintained that these texts are no longer extant in their original form.

Angabahya

The *Angabahya* (Subsidiary Canon) texts were composed in a later period by *mendicant* authors. They mainly elucidate the material found in the *Angas*. The most well-known and popular of these is the *Kalpa Sutra* of the *Shvetambaras*, which contains the biography of *Mahavira* and also of other *Tirthankaras*.

Other Texts

In addition to the *canon* itself, there are extensive Sanskrit commentaries and independent treatises written in both prose and verse forms. The *Tattvartha Sutra*, written in the second century BCE by Acharya Umasvati, belongs to this group of texts. This text, together with its several commentaries, was the first significant Jain text written in Sanskrit and is viewed by contemporary Jains as being a fundamental text which provides the basis for Jain education. Its content summarises the key aspects of the whole of Jain teaching, including ethics, metaphysics, epistemology and cosmology.

KEY JAIN BELIEFS

Ahimsa

The cardinal principle of Jainism is *ahimsa*, generally translated as non-violence, although it goes far beyond that to encompass the avoidance of all physical or even mental harm to any living being, including the tiniest. Although they recognise that a completely harmless life is humanly impossible, Jains strive to the best of their ability to obey the precept of *ahimsa*.

Reality in Jain Perspective

Jainism is a religion without a belief in a creator god. According to its scriptures, there is *akasha* (infinite space) within which there is a finite area called *loka* (the universe). Within this universe there are an infinite number of *jiva* or *atmas* (sentient beings). There are also what are called *pudgalas* (non-sentient material atoms) endowed with the qualities of palpability, such as softness/hardness, lightness/heaviness, as well as of taste, smell and colour.

In addition to matter and space, other *ajiva* (non-sentient existents) include the principles of *dharma* (motion), *adharma* (rest) and *kala* (time). These *dravyas* (existents) are all, like the universe itself, viewed as being uncreated, beginningless and eternal. It is only their appearances and surface attributes that are in a state of change, and these appearances and attributes are known as *paryayas* (modifications).

The attribution of two apparently opposite characteristics to the same entity (for example, eternal substance and changing modes) reflects the distinctive Jain view of *anekantavada* (the multi-faceted or pluralist nature of reality). According to this principle, Jains believe that all aspects of reality must be taken into account for a complete and true understanding of its nature. The study of the totality of these aspects, when considered in the context of *dravya* (existents), *kshetra* (place), *kala* (time) and *bhava* (condition), produces *naya* (a correct view of reality).

The idea of *syadvada* (qualified assertion) further underlines the Jain approach of *anekantavada* and is illustrated by the use of the term *syat* (literally, "in some specific sense only") that is employed in Jain discourses on reality as describing only one aspect of the totality.

Sentient Beings

Consciousness is understood as that which distinguishes *jiva* or *atmas* (sentient beings or souls) from all other existents, including material atoms. During the state of embodiment, this consciousness manifests through the senses and the mind, resulting in what is understood by sentient beings as knowledge of objects. The ability to know is understood as varying almost infinitely from one being to another. However, Jains broadly categorise all forms of sentient life in a hierarchy based upon the number of senses they possess.

The lowest forms of life are believed to have only the sense of touch through which they experience pleasure and pain. These forms of life include, for example, algae and plants. Next are those beings with two, three and four senses, for example, insects. Higher than these are animals with five senses and a mind that exhibits some developed means of rational thinking. The most highly developed are seen as being the "hell beings", the "heavenly beings" and humans.

In Jain cosmology, the heavens and hells are temporary abodes and are located, respectively, in the upper and lower parts of the universe. Human beings and animals that have five senses occupy the smallest area of the universe between the heavens and the hells. It should be noted, however, that in Jain thought human beings are distinguished from all other forms of life because of their capacity for a high degree of spiritual progress. Jains believe that it is only from the human state that *moksha* (release from the cycle of birth and death) is possible.

Karma

The variety of life-forms, like life itself, is seen as having no beginning. There is no original form of life from which the others have evolved. Jains believe that, in its transmigration from one body to another, it is likely that one soul will have gone through a wide variety of life-forms. Such variety in embodiment and levels of consciousness is explained by means of the doctrine of *karma*. The doctrine of *karma* maintains that the kind of body a soul may inhabit in its next life is determined primarily by the activities it undertakes in the present life.

Unwholesome volitions, accompanied by attachment and aversion, necessarily produce evil acts such as hurting and lying, whilst wholesome volitions, accompanied by equanimity and friendliness, generate acts of charity and kindness. The strength of the volition of the *soul* at the time of a given action is considered to be the most significant factor in shaping future lives and in perpetuating the cycle of birth and death.

In Jain understanding, all volitional acts attract a certain amount of a very subtle form of matter. This is drawn to the soul and binds with the already existing layer of *karmic* matter in a process known as *bandha* (bondage). An analogy used for this is of dust settling on a wet mirror. Just as a mirror's capacity to reflect perfectly is obstructed by accumulated dust, so the *soul's* capacity for *jnana* (knowledge) and *sukha* (the experience of happiness) is understood as being affected by varieties of *karmic* matter.

Jains categorise this *karmic* matter into eight main varieties according to their effects on the soul. The first four are seen as destructive to the nature of the *soul*. Of these, the first two are those that obscure the qualities of knowledge and perception. The next two are the *karmas* that obstruct the practice of right conduct and limit the energy required for that conduct. The remaining four *karmas* affect body structure, longevity of the body, social environment and, most importantly, the feeling of happiness and unhappiness that is experienced in proportion to one's past good and evil acts.

As understood by Jains, the doctrine of *karma*, far from being pessimistic as is sometimes alleged, is a spur to endeavour: the individual soul is seen as responsible for its own spiritual progress.

Jain Path to Moksha

The beginningless bondage of the soul to *karmic* matter and the soul's ensuing embodiment is, however, not seen as being necessarily endless. Jains affirm that a *soul* can terminate this bondage by gaining *samyak-darshana* (true faith in the nature of reality as taught by the *Jinas*), by *samyak-jnana* (knowing thoroughly the distinction between the soul and *karmic* matter), and by *samyak-caritra* (following proper conduct as exemplified in the lives of the *Jinas*).

Right faith, right knowledge and right conduct are known collectively as *The Three Jewels of Jainism*. Together they constitute the Jain path to *moksha*. Right conduct involves refraining from evil actions, speech and thoughts that prevent the influx of new *karmic* matter. This development is gradual, the initial stages of which are viewed as being applicable to lay people and the advanced stages as being applicable to *mendicants*.

Through renunciation and the constant endeavour to follow their life-long vows (see below), a *mendicant monk* or *nun* effectively blocks the influx of all new *karmas* that will mature and, in the course of time, produce new births for the *soul*. The *mendicant* engages in *tapas* (austerities), mainly in the form of fasting and *dhyana* (sustained meditation), which are believed to bring about *nirjara* (exhaustion) of the mass of *karma* that has accumulated from the past.

It is believed that if one follows such a holy life over a long period of time, indeed over very many lifetimes, a *soul* may attain total emancipation from all destructive *karmic* matter and thus be freed from rebirth forever. Such a person is, at this stage, called an *arhat* (worthy of worship) or a *kevalin* (one who has attained omniscience), being a *soul* that has attained freedom from all residual *karmic* matter. At the end of life, such a *soul* rises instantaneously to the summit of the universe where, motionless, it abides forever in its omniscient glory and is called a *Siddha* (Perfected Being), being now free from all *karmic* matter.

TRADITIONS IN JAINISM

Main Branches

There are two main *monastic* groupings within Jainism, the *Shvetambara* and the *Digambara*. These terms are also used derivatively to describe their lay followers. The majority of Jains worldwide, and in the UK, are *Shvetambara*. The two groups, which emerged in the third and fifth centuries CE, differ in some of their beliefs and practices, but agree in their basic philosophy.

Shvetambara

The *Shvetambara* (white-robed) *monks* and *nuns* wear three pieces of white clothing and carry a set of begging bowls and a *rajoharana* (small woollen whisk-broom) used to avoid harm to insects. They travel on foot, do not stay in one place for more than five days except during the monsoon, and do not keep money or material possessions other than a walking stick and a blanket.

It is estimated that there are over 2,500 *Shvetambara monks* and 5,000 *Shvetambara nuns* living in India today. A group of the *Shvetambara*, known as the *Sthanakvasi*s, and a sub-group of the latter called *Terapanthi*s, additionally wear a *muhpatti* (piece of cloth) over the mouth to avoid harming minute living beings in the air when they breathe.

Mendicant leaders of the *Terapanthi* community have introduced a practice of new renunciants spending a few years in training to teach the Jain religion. These young novices, called *samanas* (male novices) and *samanis* (female novices) are, prior to their full initiation as *mendicants*, permitted to use transport for the purpose of visiting Jain communities in India and overseas. In recent years they have been very active in educational work.

Digambara

The *Digambara* (sky-clad) *monks* renounce all forms of property including clothes and begging bowls. They are allowed to carry only a peacock-feather whisk-broom and a gourd for washing water. *Digambara nuns* are clothed in a white sari. In all other matters the *nuns* obey the same regulations as *monks*, including eating and drinking only once a day in the home of a Jain lay person. Due to the severity of their *mendicant* rules there are probably no more than a few hundred *Digambara monks* and *nuns* living in India today. Because of the restrictions on travel for these *ascetics*, the day-to-day leadership of the *Digambara* community in India and abroad rests upon lay scholars and advanced laymen.

JAIN LIFE

Anuvratas

A layperson who undertakes to refrain from all forms of intentional violence expresses this by assuming the *anuvratas* (five life-long minor vows).

As has been explained, the vow of *ahimsa* (not harming) is the cardinal principle of Jainism. It includes not hurting sentient beings, and is therefore expressed in a strictly vegetarian diet. Jain scriptures permit the consumption of dairy products such as milk, curds and ghee (clarified butter), but prohibit the eating of meat, eggs and honey (the latter because of the harm to bees which gathering honey involves).

They also prohibit the consumption of certain vegetables that grow underground and produce numerous sprouts, such as potatoes, or fruits with many seeds such as figs, as well as fermented products such as alcohol.

Some lay people, as well as all *mendicants*, observe the restriction of not eating after sunset or before sunrise, an ancient practice that was designed to avoid unintentional harm to insects that appear after dark.

The principle of *ahimsa* also underlies the remaining vows of *satya* (truthfulness), *asteya*

(not stealing), *brahmacharya* (refraining from sexual activity outside of marriage) and *aparigraha* (placing limits on one's possessions). Employment is also restricted to occupations where there is only a minimal likelihood of harm to human or animal life.

Mahavratas

Jains consider that the true path of emancipation does not begin until one renounces the household altogether in order to lead the celibate life of a *sadhu* (male *mendicant*) or *sadhvi* (female *mendicant*) by taking the *mahavratas* (the great vows). The vows taken by a *mendicant* are the same as those taken by a lay person, but are much more restrictive.

For example, for *mendicants*, the vow of *ahimsa* includes not harming even the most minute of one-sense beings. The vow of *brahmacharya* means complete celibacy and *aparigraha* means renouncing all possessions except the few items deemed necessary to support a *mendicant* life.

A *mendicant*, therefore, subsists on the voluntary support of the lay people. Giving food and providing necessities to *mendicants* are considered to be the most meritorious acts. The initiation (*diksha*) of a new *monk* or *nun* is accompanied by much ceremony and rejoicing. The *mendicants* are treated with great respect and play an important part in the religious instruction of the laity.

JAIN WORSHIP

Personal Puja

Nearly all Jain houses have non-*consecrated* images or picture of *Tirthankaras* to act as a focus of devotion. Jains may offer *puja* (worship) at their home shrines three times a day, before dawn, at sunset and, at night, by chanting *mantras* (litanies). The most important of these mantras is the *Panca-namaskara-mantra* saying, "I pay homage to the *Arhats* (the living omniscient beings),

Siddhas (the perfected beings), *Acharyas* (the Jain *mendicant* leaders), *Upadhyayas* (Jain *mendicant* teachers) and the *Sadhus* (all other Jain *ascetics*)". The second important ritual is *pratikramana*, a confession of transgressions against one's religious vows committed knowingly or unknowingly.

JAIN PLACES OF WORSHIP

Mandirs

Jain places of worship are not recorded as a separate category in the running totals of certified places of worship in England and Wales kept by the Registrar General. The CD-ROM accompanying this volume gives details of 3 Jain places of worship in the UK, which is in England. Leicester is home to the only purpose built Jain Temple catering for all the major traditions outside of India the Jain Centre.

Jains have *mandirs* that are *consecrated* and also those that are non-*consecrated*. In *mandirs* that are consecrated, the images go through a sacred process of conception, birth, renunciation, becoming omniscient, and liberation, as conducted by a Jain *alaya* (spiritual leader). Such images may become the focus of worship and have to have daily rituals as set out in the Jain scriptures. Strict devotees worship only at *consecrated mandirs* and images.

There are, at present, three *consecrated mandirs* in the UK. These are the Jain Centre in Leicester; the Oshwal Jain Temple in Northaw, Hertfordshire; and the Shree Digamber Jain Temple in Harrow, Middlesex. There are also non-*consecrated* Jain mandirs, including the Mahavir Foundation, in Harrow, Middlesex; the Manchester Jain Samaj Community Centre; and the Oshwal Mahajanwadi, in Croydon, Surrey.

In areas of the country where there is no temple, Jains meet in homes and halls. In addition to worshipping in their home shrines, many Jains also worship at *Shvetambara* or *Digambara mandirs* (temples). These *mandirs* contain images of one or more *Tirthankaras* depicted in meditation, either standing or seated in the lotus posture. Devotion to the *Jinas* represented by these images inspires Jains to engage in meritorious activities.

Before coming into a place of worship Jains purify themselves with a bath. Shoes and all leather objects are left outside. At the entrance to the *mandir*, a worshipper puts sandalwood paste-mark on his or her brow to signify their intention to live a life according to the teachings of *Jina*. Using rice grains, a *swastika* design (not to be confused with the Nazi *swastika*) is made on a low table indicating a desire to be liberated from the four destinies of the world cycle. To the chant of *mantras*, worshippers bathe the images of the *Tirthankaras*, offer flowers and incense, and wave *arati* (lamps) in front of them.

While all *Digamabaras* and the majority of the *Shvetambaras* worship in *mandirs*, the *Shvetambara* groups called the *Sthanakvasis* and the *Terapanthis* do not participate in these temple rituals. Instead, they emphasise *bhava puja* (mental worship) and perform their religious rites in *upashraya* (meditation halls).

In India, *Shvetambaras* and *Digambaras* worship in separate *mandirs*, but in Leicester there is a purpose-built Jain *mandir* that provides places of worship for all Jains. Within this *mandir*, in addition to the main *Shvetambara* shrine, there is a also a *Digambara* shrine and a *Sthanakvasi upashraya* for *pratikramana* (the ritual of confession), as well as a meditation room dedicated to Shrimad Rajachandra (1868-1901), a great spiritual leader and counsellor to *Mahatma* Gandhi on religious matters. The *mandir* also contains a museum that displays the history, philosophy, architecture and way of life of the Jains. The Oshwal Centre in North London has a *mandir* located in a separate building from its community hall.

Visitors to a Jain Temple

For visitors to a Jain temple, clothing should be modest for both men and women, but need not be formal. Jain women will be expected not to enter the temple during menstruation. Head coverings are not necessary for either sex. Shoes should be removed before going into the temple and put on the racks provided. Clean and presentable socks, stockings, or tights are therefore a good idea. All leather objects should be left outside.

No eating or chewing is allowed in the temple area. When Jains enter the temple they bow to the image in the temple and chant a *mantra*. This will not be expected of a visitor, from whom a reverent silence is appropriate. Visitors should therefore enter quietly and find a place to sit on the (usually carpeted) floor, sitting with crossed legs, or with legs pointing to one side. It is considered disrespectful to sit with legs forward with the feet pointing towards the sacred area at the front of the temple or to stand or sit with one's back to the image. There is no expectation that visitors will join in the prayer unless they particularly wish to do so, and there is no custom of offering sacred food to devotees or visitors.

JAIN CALENDAR AND FESTIVALS

Calendar

Jains date the era of *Mahavira*, known as the *Vira-nirvana-samvat*, from the year of his death in 527 BCE. However, except for special events in Jain history, they have traditionally used the *Vikramasamvat* calendar that is also used among Hindus. Both calendars are lunar.

Festivals

The following are the most significant Jain festivals:

Mahavira Jayanti (March/April)
Marks the anniversary of the birth of *Mahavira*.

Akshaya-tritiya (April/May)
Means "Immortal Third" and celebrates the first time that alms were given to Jina Rishabha, the first *Tirthankara* of this cosmic cycle.

Shruta-pancami (May/June)
Or *Guru-pancami*, meaning "Teacher's Fifth", is celebrated by the *Digambaras* on the fifth (*pancami*) day of May/June. Among the *Shvetambaras* this day is known as *Jnana-pancami* (Knowledge-Fifth) and is observed in October/November. It commemorates the day on which the Jain scriptures were first written down. At this time, copies of the scriptures are displayed in Jain *mandirs*. *Paryushana-parva* (August/September).

It is a period of eight to ten days which marks the most important religious period during the four months of the rainy season in India. At this time, Jain *monks* and *nuns* find a fixed place of residence instead of moving from place to place as they do at other times of the year. During this time, lay people often observe special vows of eating only one meal or of *fasting* from sunrise to sunrise. Among *Shvetambaras*, the portion of the sacred *Kalpa Sutra* that contains the life of *Mahavira* is recited.

The *Digambaras* call this season *Dasha-lakshana-parva*, meaning "the Period of Cultivating the Ten Virtues" which are asceticism, forgiveness, humility, honesty, purity, truthfulness, self-restraint, study, detachment, and celibacy. During the festival, each day is devoted to a discourse on one of these virtues. The final day is the holiest in the year and is marked by the celebration of *Samvatsari-pratikramana*. This is an annual ceremony of confession in which all Jains participate, requesting forgiveness from relatives and friends for offences of thought, word or deed by uttering the words *micchami dukkadam* (meaning "may my transgressions be forgiven").

Vira-Nirvana (November)
This coincides with the Indian festival of *Diwali*, when Jains mark the death and *nirvana* of *Mahavira*.

Karttika-purnima (December)
Is the day on which the rainy season retreat for *monks* and *nuns* comes to an end, and they resume their travels on foot. This marks the end of the Jain religious year.

JAIN ORGANISATIONS

Jain Organisational Listings

The CD-ROM accompanying this volume includes contact details of the head offices of organisations with branches throughout the United Kingdom and of organisations that aspire to serve the Jain community at a UK-wide level.

The Jain Academy, Jain Samaj Europe and the Institute of Jainology are three organisations that are concerned with the promotion of Jainism and Jain principles at both national and international levels. Many individual UK Jains and local Jain organizations identify with either Jain Samaj Europe or the Institute of Jainology.

At local level, while the CD-ROM accompanying this volume provides contact details for only three Jain temples, there are also a number of organisations which operate from premises that are either owned or hired, whilst other groups are run from and/or meet in the homes of members. In the Greater London area, quite a number of Jain organisations work at a geographical level beyond local or Borough boundaries.

In total, the CD-ROM accompanying this directory include details of 1 regional Jain organisation (which is in England) and around 28 local Jain organisations (all of which are in England).

The majority of Jains in the UK are *Shvetambara*, but the *Digambara* have the Digambar Jain Visa Mewada Association of the UK as a national organisation.

The Young Jains organisation is concerned with spreading the principles of Jainism among younger people, including the presentation of the relevance of Jain values to non-Jains. It does this, for example, amongst other things, through its promotion of vegetarianism.

Jain organisations in the UK are known by such common Indian terms as *mandal* (the Hindi word literally meaning "circle"), *samaj* (the Hindi word meaning "society") and *sangh* (the Hindi word for "group" or "gathering").

Some Jain groupings at both national and local levels have membership that is specific to particular social groupings within the community, popularly known as *castes*. These include the *Oshwal* and *Navnat* who were originally Indian trading communities and are grouped in organisations such as the Navnat Vanik Association of the UK, representing Vaniks. There are also special interest groups that deal with issues of particular concern to Jains including, for example, the Young Indian Vegetarians.

Personnel

As explained earlier, the Jain community is composed of four groups of people: sadhus (male *ascetics* or *monks*), sadhvis (female *ascetics* or *nuns*), shravakas (lay men) and shravikas (lay women). *Sadhus* and *sadhvis* both dedicate themselves exclusively to the pursuit of *moksha*. They renounce their family and all their possessions and take the *mahavratas* (Five Great Vows) at an initiation ceremony known as *diksha*. Jainism has no priesthood, although at the *mandirs* there are sometimes designated laymen (*pujaris*) who perform the religious rituals.

FURTHER READING

Details follow of a number of general introductions to Jainism together with some books and articles that provide some focus on Jains and Jain organisations in the UK. The references are not comprehensive, but provide signposts to a range of relevant materials.

Acharya Bhuvanbhanusoorishwarji, *Handbook of Jainology*, Sri Vishvakalyan Prakashan Trust, Mehsana, 1987.

Banerjee, S R, *Chhotelal Jain's Jaina Bibliography* (2 volumes), Vir Sewa Mandir, New Delhi, 1982.

Banks, M, *Organising Jainism in India and England*, Clarendon Press, Oxford, 1992.

Banks, M, "Jain Ways of Being", in R Ballard (ed), *Desh Pardesh: The South Asian Presence in Britain*, Hurst and Co., London, 1994, pp 231-250.

Bhargava, D, *Jain Ethics*, Motilal Banarsidass, Delhi, 1968.

Bhattacharya, B C, *The Jaina Iconography*, Motilal Banarsidass, Delhi, (2nd edition), 1974.

Bhattacharyya, N, *Jain Philosophy: Historical Outline*, Munshiram Manohalal, New Delhi, 1976.

Dundas, P, *The Jains*, Routledge, London, 1992.

Ghosh, A, *Jain Art and Architecture* (3 volumes), Bharatiya Jnanapith, New Delhi, 1974-1975.

Jain, J P, *Religion and Culture of the Jains*, Bharatiya Jnanapith, New Delhi, 1975.

Jain, M U K, *Jain Sects and Schools*, Concept Publishing, Delhi, 1975.

Jain Samaj Europe, *Mahavira Darshan and Rituals: Special Issue of The Jain*, April 1992.

Jaini, P S, *The Jaina Path of Purification*, University of California Press, Berkeley, 1979.

Jaini, P S, *Gender and Salvation: Jaina Debates on the Spiritual Liberation of Women*, University of California Press, Berkeley, California, 1991.

Johnson, W J, *Harmless Souls: Karmic Bondage and Religious Change in Early Jainism*, Motilal Banarsidass, Delhi, 1985.

Kapashi, V, *In Search of the Ultimate*, V K Publications, Harrow, 1984.

Laidlow, J, *Riches and Renunciation: Religion, Economy and Society among the Jains*, Clarendon Press, Oxford, 1995.

Marett, P, *Jainism Explained*, Jain Samaj Europe Publications, Leicester, 1985.

Nahar, P and Ghosh, J, *Encyclopaedia of Jainism*, Sri Satguru Publications, Delhi, 1986.

Sangave, V, *Jaina Community: A Social Survey* (2nd edition), Popular Prakashan, Bombay, 1980.

Satyaprakash (ed), *Jainism: A Select Bibliography*, Indian Documentation Service, Gurgaon, 1984.

Shah, S, "Who are the Jains?", in *New Community*, Volume 7, 1979, pp 369-75.

Sogani, K, *Ethical Doctrines in Jainism*, Jaina Samskrita Samrakshaka Sangha, Sholapur, 1967.

Umasvati/Umasvami, *Tattvartha Sutra: That Which Is*, translated by Nathmal Tatia, The Institute of Jainology, International Sacred Literature Trust Series, Harper Collins, London, 1994.

INTRODUCING JEWS IN THE UK

JEWS IN THE UK   203

ORIGINS AND
DEVELOPMENT OF JUDAISM   204

SOURCES OF JEWISH
BELIEFS AND PRACTICES   205

KEY JEWISH BELIEFS   207

TRADITIONS IN JUDAISM   208

JEWISH LIFE   209

JEWISH WORSHIP   212

JEWISH PLACES OF
WORSHIP   213

JEWISH CALENDAR AND
FESTIVALS   215

JEWISH ORGANISATIONS   217

FURTHER READING   219

JEWS IN THE UK

History in the UK

Jewish people have been present for many centuries in the territories that today make up the United Kingdom. The first recorded settlers came after the Norman conquest but their descendants were expelled in 1290 by Edward I. Following the English Civil War, Menasseh ben Israel of Amsterdam successfully campaigned for their readmission.

Sephardi and Ashkenazi

The Jewish population in the UK is composed of both *Sephardi* and *Ashkenazi* Jews. *Sephardi* is the name given to Jews who came originally from Spain, Portugal and the Middle East. *Sephardi* Jews have the longest continuous communal history here, having been present in an organised form since the mid-seventeenth century.

However, the majority of Jews in the UK today are descendants of two waves of immigration by *Ashkenazi* Jews. *Ashkenazi* is the name given to the Jews of Central and East European origins. *Ashkenazi* Jews migrated to England in large numbers for economic reasons or fled from persecution in the Russian Empire between 1881-1914, and from 1933 onwards during the Nazi persecution in Germany and other European countries. Since 1956 small numbers of Jewish immigrants have arrived from Arab and East European countries. There is also a significant Israeli Jewish community in the UK.

Global and UK Populations

Worldwide, there are an estimated 14,434,000 Jews. In the UK, the 2001 Census included voluntary questions on religion that yielded 266,740 (or 0.5% of the total UK population) Jewish respondents. This is 0.6% of the population that identifies itself with any specific religion at all. Of these 266,740 a total of 257,651 were in England, 2,256 in Wales, 6,448 in Scotland, and 365 in Northern Ireland.

As a proportion of the total population in local authority areas, the 2001 Census shows that, in England, the greatest concentration of respondents identifying themselves as Jews is to be found in the London Borough of Barnet (14.8%); Hertsmere (11.3%); and the London Boroughs of Harrow (6.3%), Redbridge (6.2%) and Camden (5.6%). Outside of the Greater London area, the largest provincial Jewish populations are found in Manchester, Leeds and Glasgow. There are also other sizeable Jewish communities in Birmingham, Bournemouth, Brighton, Liverpool and Southend.

Ethnicity in England and Wales

According to the 2001 Census, 96.8 % of the Jewish population of England and Wales gave their ethnicity as "White", 1.2% as "Mixed", 0.9% as "Chinese or Other Ethnic Group", 0.7% as "Asian", and 0.4% as "Black or Black British". Considered in terms of the ethnicity of respondents, 0.5% of all those recorded as "White", as "Mixed" and as "Chinese and Other Ethic Group" also identified as Jewish, along with 0.1% of "Black or Black British" and of those recorded as "Asian".

English is used among UK Jews as the normal language for communication, but Hebrew is often used in religious contexts and Yiddish can also be found. Ladino was the lingua franca of *Sephardi* Jews of Spanish origin and is based on Castilian Spanish. Judaeo-Arabic is spoken among some Jews originally from Arabic lands.

Hebrew is the language of the Bible, of prayer, and of modern Israel. It is the universal language that binds together all Jews in the *Diaspora*. It is the main language of worship and many children learn it in *Cheder* (*synagogue*-based religious instruction) or in Jewish day schools.

Yiddish is a Jewish language of Eastern European origin that was originally a Judaeo-German dialect with a number of Slavic and Hebrew words. Yiddish is used conversationally among a number of the *Haredim* (see "Traditions in Judaism" below). The majority of Jews cannot, however, conduct conversations in Yiddish and in modern Jewish circles it is generally spoken only amongst the older generation of *Ashkenazi* Jews. More recently, though, there has been a concern to prevent the language dying out and organisations have been set up to propagate Yiddish language and literature.

ORIGINS AND DEVELOPMENT OF JUDAISM

Patriarchs

The origins of Judaism are set out in the *Tanach* or Hebrew *Bible*. It is believed that God entered into a *Brit* (a *covenant* forming a permanent relationship) with the Jewish community, first through Abraham and then through Moses at Mount Sinai.

Where an idea of "chosenness" appears within Judaism, it is a reference to the belief that the Jews have been "chosen" for a particular task and to live within a *covenantal* relationship with God and its implications for living. Jews believe that this *covenantal* relationship gives them no advantage above others, but rather an extra responsibility to live in accordance with God's laws and to contribute to the world's moral order.

Abraham is traditionally considered to be the first of three *avot* (forefathers) of the kinship group who are seen as ancestors of the Jewish people. When Abraham died, the leadership of this growing community was passed on to his son Isaac who, in turn, passed it on to his son Jacob. The name Israel (meaning "one who struggles with God"), which was given to Jacob, is also used to describe the Jewish people as a whole.

Moses and the Israelites

Judaism centres on faith in one God and the belief that God made fundamental revelations to the Jewish people through Moses at Mount Sinai around 1300 BCE, after Moses had led them out of enslavement to the Pharaohs in Egypt. Following the death of Moses, Joshua became leader and led the conquest of the land of Canaan that the Israelites believed had been promised to them by God.

After the conquest the land was divided into twelve areas for the twelve tribes of Israel descended from the sons and grandsons of Jacob (Reuben, Simeon, Judah, Issachar, Zebulun, Benjamin, Dan, Naphtali, Gad, Asher, Ephraim, and Menasseh). The tribe of Levi did not have a territory since their inheritance was to be that of worship in the Temple. The terms "Jew" and "Judaism" derive from the name Judah, one of the twelve sons of Jacob.

Kingdoms and Exile

In approximately 1030 BCE Saul was appointed to be King. He was later succeeded by King David. David was then followed by King Solomon, who erected the great Temple in Jerusalem. In time, two kingdoms developed, the Southern Kingdom of Judah with Jerusalem as its capital and the Northern Kingdom of Israel. Both Kingdoms were eventually defeated and occupied by invading armies.

In 586 BCE the Temple was destroyed during the Babylonian invasion and many Jews were exiled to Babylon. Eventually, some of the Jews returned to Jerusalem and rebuilt the Temple but it was again destroyed by the Romans in 70 CE.

A new *Torah* centre was set up at Yavneh, near Jerusalem, and the foundations were laid for the *rabbinic* form of Judaism, not dependent upon the continuation of the *Temple* rituals. The classical texts of *rabbinic* Judaism, such as the *Mishnah* (see below), were originally produced in the first to third century CE. These were then taken up in the Jewish academies of Babylonia (contemporary Iraq) and Palestine where, by the sixth century, the *Talmud* (see below) was completed.

Rabbinic law, commentary and *Biblical* interpretation have been enriched in every generation. From philosophy to mysticism and religious poetry, a rich and diverse cultural tradition has been created and its development still continues in the contemporary world.

Diaspora, Holocaust and Israel

Jewish communities outside of Israel are collectively known as the *diaspora*, and UK Jews are thus one of the many *diaspora* communities. Jewish communities were in *diaspora* throughout the Roman and Parthian Empires before the Common Era. Today there are Jewish communities in many countries. Following the *Holocaust* of European Jewry in which six million Jews were systematically killed by the Nazis and those who collaborated with them, the modern State of Israel was founded in 1948.

SOURCES OF JEWISH BELIEFS AND PRACTICES

Tenakh

Judaism is derived from the Jewish scriptures as interpreted by the *rabbis* (teachers) past and present. These scriptures, traditionally referred to by Christians as the *Old Testament*, are known among Jews as the *Tanach*. This is an acronym of the names of the initials of its three constituent sections: *Torah*, *Nevi'im* and *Ketuvim*.

The *Torah* (teaching) is referred to among Jews as the *Humash* (from the Hebrew word meaning five) because it consists of the five books of Moses (*Genesis*, *Exodus*, *Leviticus*, *Numbers* and *Deuteronomy*). These contain what are believed to be God's revelation to Moses on Mount Sinai. From the *Torah* and later commentaries there are, in total, six hundred and thirteen commandments dealing with questions of ethics, spirituality, diet, ritual and all other aspects of communal and social life.

The *Nevi'im* (plural of *navi* meaning prophet) consist of the books of the prophets, namely *Isaiah, Jeremiah, Ezekiel* and the twelve minor prophets, together with the related historical books of *Joshua, Judges, Samuel* and *Kings* covering the period up to the Babylonian exile.

The *Ketuvim* (writings) include such texts as the books of *Ruth* and *Esther*, as well as the *Psalms* and the *Song of Songs,* major sources of Jewish liturgy and spiritual expression.

Talmud

The *Tenakh* is complemented by the *Talmud* (from the Hebrew root meaning "to study") that was compiled by *rabbinic* scholars in the centuries following the destruction of the second Temple by the Romans in 70CE.

Orthodox Jews believe that it includes material that was revealed at Sinai at the same time as the *Torah*, but which was then transmitted by oral tradition down the generations. The *Talmud* (which means "learning") has two components: the *Mishnah* (meaning "repetition") and the *Gemara* (from the Aramaic meaning "completion").

The *Mishnah* is primarily a summary of religious and civil law. It is divided into six *sedarim* (orders), each of which contains a varying number of volumes or tractates: *zera'im* (seeds), which contains materials on prayers and agricultural laws; *mo'ed* (festivals), which deals with matters related to the *Shabbat* or *Sabbath* (see below) and festivals; *nashim* (women), which includes laws on marriage and divorce; *nezikin* (damages), which contains civil and criminal law; *kodashim* (holy things), which includes laws of sacrifice and *Temple* ritual; and *tohorot* (purification), which contains laws relating to personal and religious purity.

The *Gemara* is a commentary on, and discussion of, the *Mishnah*. It comprises analysis, debate and clarification of legal source material. The text is an edited record of the argumentation and discussions of the scholars, retaining the thrust and parry of the *rabbinic* colleges. The *Gemara* also contains a wide range of narrative material, including historical anecdote, allegory, prayer, religious discussion and ethical guidance.

The non-legal material in the *Talmud* is known as the *Aggadah* (an Aramaic word derived from the Hebrew word for narrative). The legal material is known as *Halakhah* (see below), from a Hebrew root meaning "to go". *Halakhah* is the practice or "way" of the tradition.

Midrash

Another important literary genre of Jewish religious tradition is *Midrash*. The *Midrash* consists of *rabbinic* interpretation of the *Bible* and includes moral teachings, legends and parables from a variety of great *rabbi*s. The earliest texts date perhaps from 400-500 CE, but they reflect generations of literary development. The latest collections are from 1100-1200 CE and major anthologies were made between 1200-1500 CE. Some modern Jewish writers on the Bible use the *Midrash* form for their *exegesis*.

Halakhah

The life of the Jewish community is focused around the interpretation and practice of the *Halakhah* (Jewish law). The wealth of texts used as a basis for legal decisions include the *Talmud*, Moses Maimonides' twelfth century *Code* and the sixteenth century *Shulhan Arukh* of Joseph Caro together with numerous commentaries from all periods including the present.

A *Beth Din* is a court of law that rules according to *Halakhah*. Members of the Jewish community approach it for rulings on issues in personal and social life such as divorce and conversion to Judaism.

KEY JEWISH BELIEFS

Shema

The *Shema* (hear) is a reading composed of three passages in the *Torah*. It contains the basic affirmation of the Jewish faith. It is said daily and its first line is a clear injunction to absolute *monotheism*, stating that the Eternal is one God (Deuteronomy 6 v4).

The one God created the world, extending justice, compassion and love to all women and men. Whilst God's ways can be known, God is also awe-inspiring in God's transcendence and God's ultimate essence lies beyond human cognition. God is seen as both King and Father, worshipped in awe, yet is close to the people of God in intimacy and devotion.

Torah and Mitzvot

The *Torah* is the revelation of God's will that includes the *mitzvot* (commandments) which encompass every aspect of life. The *mitzvot* enable men and women to sanctify their daily lives and bring holiness into the world. Jews emphasise the obligations of love and reverence for God who created heaven and earth. Study of the *Torah* is a passionate and sacred task that is central in the religious life.

Prayer is of great significance and the weekly *Shabbat* and festivals are set aside for celebration and devotion. *Torah*, daily prayer, the weekly *Shabbat* and festivals infuse the mundane with the transcendent and the eternal.

Humanity

The world is understood to be a creation of God and must be treated accordingly. Humanity is made in the Divine image and love of one's neighbour (Jewish and non-Jewish alike) is the great principle of social life and the founding inspiration of the Jewish community. Justice and compassion

are Divine attributes that Jewish people are obliged to realise in all aspects of their lives. There are daily prayers for the forgiveness of *sins*. The *High Holy Days* of the Jewish year are devoted to penitence, prayer, and putting right what has been wrong, but also to charity and forgiveness, since the compassion of God can restore broken relationships.

Kingdom of God

Jews have traditionally looked towards the establishment of God's kingdom on earth. Also, traditionally, this has been connected with a belief in a *Mashiach* (Anointed One), or *Messiah*. There are a variety of different Jewish understandings of the concept of *Mashiach*. In the original sense of *"anointed one"*, the term covers Jewish kings such as David and Solomon as well as *High Priests*.

The traditional belief is that a special person will reveal himself and the Jewish community will be gathered from its exile around the world and re-establish itself in the ancient land; the *Temple* will be rebuilt and never again be destroyed; and the *Kingdom of God* will be established on earth for everyone.

Another perspective, often found among *Progressive* Jews, is that there will be no individual *Mashiach* but rather a new *Messianic* era without war and conflict. Life after death is interpreted by many in terms of the continuity of the soul, rather than bodily *resurrection*. In either case, the coming of the Kingdom of God, even if it includes bodily *resurrection*, is understood in a thoroughly this-worldly way.

Eretz Yisrael, Zionism and Attitudes Towards Israel

For the Jewish people as a whole, the land of Israel is of great importance. For centuries, Israel has been viewed by the Jewish people as the eternal homeland promised by God at the beginning of history. After centuries of exile, the foundation of the modern state of

Israel has created a focus of Jewish life that is both religious and ethnic in its aspirations.

Jews everywhere tend to feel a common destiny with the Jews of Israel as well as with the *diaspora* throughout the world. For the great majority of Jewish people, with the exception of some *Haredim* (or *Ultra-Orthodox* see below), the modern state of Israel is an important part of their identity. Therefore attempts to deny its right to exist are often seen as veiled anti-semitism and there are few issues around which Jews unite as much as the defence and survival of Israel.

The term *Zionism* comes from Zion, another biblical name for Jerusalem and, by extension, for Israel. The concept of *Zionism* is found in both a religious and political sense. As a political movement, most Jews understand *Zionism* in terms of having been a liberation movement of the Jewish people that was intended to end the centuries of exile and to secure a Jewish homeland. Theodor Herzl convened the first Zionist conference at Basel in 1897 and founded the World Zionist Organisation, now based in Israel.

Some *Haredim* (mainly in Israel itself) oppose political *Zionism* on the basis of denying that a secular state can have religious significance. By contrast, religious *Zionists* see redemptive significance in the development of the State of Israel and view the ingathering of the Jewish exiles as a manifestation of Divine providence.

TRADITIONS IN JUDAISM

Main Branches

There are a number of different Jewish traditions present in the UK. Many Jews have moved between traditions. Some people brought up in *Orthodox* communities join *Progressive synagogues* in later life and vice versa.

Orthodox

The *Orthodox* Jewish tradition accords the *Bible* and its *rabbinical* interpretations full authority in determining law, life and religious practice. It believes both the *Torah* and the oral law contained in the *Talmud* to have been revealed by God and to contain God's unchanging words. *Orthodoxy* understands itself as representing the mainstream of Judaism in historical continuity with the Jewish inheritance.

Hasidic

Within the orbit of *Orthodoxy* is the *Hasidic* movement. The word *Hasidic* comes from *Hasid,* which literally means "pious". *Hasidic* groups originated in the *shtetls* (villages) of Central and Eastern Europe during the eighteenth and nineteenth centuries. They followed the teachings of Israel ben Eliezer also known as the Baal Shem Tov who lived in the eighteenth century in Poland, and took a mystical approach to Judaism. Today the term *Hasidic* generally refers to those *Orthodox* whose theology is influenced more by mystic spirituality than by an intellectual orientation.

Haredim

The *Haredim* (often popularly referred to by people outside this group as the *Ultra-Orthodox*), include many *Hasidic* Jews, although not all *Haredim* are *Hasidic*. The distinction between *Haredim*, whether *Hasidic* or not, and the more mainstream *Orthodox* is that the *Haredim* seek to exclude some aspects of modern culture from their lives and tend to reproduce in minute detail the cultural ways of previous generations.

Some groupings are influenced by the body of Jewish mystical philosophy known as the *Kabbalah* that consists of teachings that were transmitted within select circles of disciples. The most important *Kabbalistic* text is the *Zohar*, which is a commentary on the *Humash* and was composed in thirteenth century Spain.

Progressive

Progressive (which includes both *Liberal* and *Reform* Jews, see section on "Jewish Organisations" below) Jews believe that the *Torah* was inspired by God, but written down by humans according to God's will. Thus they see it as open to challenge and revision and subject to the need of reinterpretation. Revelation is viewed as progressive because God's will is seen to be constantly unfolding.

Progressive Jews make a distinction between those parts of Judaism that have eternal significance and absolute value, for example, the *Shabbat* and the pursuit of justice, and those seen as temporary and relative, such as gender distinctions in Jewish law.

The *Reform* movement began in the early nineteenth century as an attempt to create a Judaism consistent with the modern world. The *Liberal* movement was first established in Germany. Liberal Judaism as it developed in the UK was founded by Claude Montefiore and Liby Montagu in 1909. Adherents of these traditions generally consider sincerity of heart to be paramount in Judaism and therefore see rituals as less important. Because of this, in the light of modern knowledge and circumstances they reformed the *synagogue* services, as well as belief and practice. However, in modern times, there has been a return to many of the traditional rituals.

Masorti (Conservative)

Established at the beginning of the twentieth century, what is known as *Masorti* in the UK and as *Conservative Judaism* in the United States, is sometimes characterised as half-way between *Orthodox* Judaism and *Progressive* Judaism. *Masorti* Jews wish to maintain a commitment to the *Halakhah* whilst taking an historically contextual approach to its application. So, for example, the *Shabbat* liturgy may be very similar to that used in *Orthodox* congregations, but men and women may sit together in the *synagogue* during services.

Masorti Jews attempt to comply with as much of the *Torah* as is practicable in modern society, but they may accept the inevitability, for example, of driving to *synagogue* on the Sabbath now that members may live further away.

JEWISH LIFE

Jewishness

In *Orthodox*, *Masorti* and *Reform* Judaism a Jew is traditionally understood to be any person born of a Jewish mother or a person who has converted to the Jewish faith. In *Liberal* Judaism and *Reform* Judaism in the United States, having a Jewish father may also be considered to qualify a child for membership of the community if the child has had a Jewish upbringing.

Circumcision

A number of ceremonies mark transitional points in Jewish life. As a sign of God's *covenant*, Abraham was required to *circumcise* himself and his two sons (Isaac and Ishmael). Because of this, Jewish law asserts that a male Jew should normally be *circumcised* on the eighth day of his life.

This requirement is known as *Brit Milah* and is carried out by a trained *Mohel* (*circumciser*) usually in the home with family and friends present. There is no equivalent requirement for girls, although in some communities a baby-naming ceremony for babies of either gender takes place and they may be blessed in the *synagogue* and, in recent years, there has been the development of a *covenant naming* ceremony for daughters.

Barmitzvah and Batmitzvah

Before the age of thirteen, male Jews are not expected to carry responsibility for *mitzvot* (the *commandments*), but at thirteen years old they take up a new position within the community. The ceremony that marks this is called *Bar Mitzvah* (son of commandment) and it involves the young man reading in Hebrew from the weekly portion of the *Torah* scroll, usually during the Saturday morning service in the *synagogue*.

After the service the family of the boy who has become *Bar Mitzvah* may provide *Kiddush* (see below under "Jewish Worship and Places of Worship") for the congregation, presents are given to the boy, and some families may have a party for family and friends.

In *Progressive* Judaism there is also a *Bat Mitzvah* (daughter of commandment ceremony) for thirteen year-old females that is in the same form as the *Bar Mitzvah* ceremony. In some *Orthodox* circles girls celebrate a *Bat Mitzvah* at the age of twelve, the traditional coming of age for females, whereas others may participate in a communal *Bat Hayil* ceremony. This ceremony often takes place on a Sunday and involves the recitation of *Psalms* and special readings.

In *Progressive* Judaism there is also a confirmation ceremony called *Kabbalat Torah*, which takes place at the age of sixteen and marks the completion of some further religious education by the young students.

Shabbat

The *Shabbat* (or *Sabbath*) is central to the rhythm of Jewish individual, family and communal life. It is observed as a day of worship, rest and peace. Friday night, and Saturday, the day on which it is observed, is believed to correspond to the seventh day of the creation on which God rested from creating the earth.

Shabbat begins about half an hour before sunset on the Friday evening and ends at nightfall on the Saturday night because the description of creation in the scriptural *Book of Genesis* refers to "evening and morning", implying that a day is deemed to begin on its preceding night. The times therefore vary from week to week, starting later in summer and earlier in winter and differ in various parts of the UK. Exact times are available in the Jewish press.

Shabbat is concluded with *Havdalah*, which is a ceremony of separation marking the transition from the *Shabbat* to the working week, and is performed at home after the last *Shabbat* services.

During *Shabbat* it is forbidden for Jews to engage in any activities that are considered as work. This general rule has been variously interpreted by different Jewish traditions. For example, *Orthodox* Jews may not drive their cars on *Shabbat* as this entails making a spark in the engine. This is seen as synonymous with starting a fire that, in turn, is considered to be work. *Progressive* Jews, however, do not deem this as work and therefore do drive. The general exception to these *Shabbat* rules, as in other areas of Jewish life, is where there is danger to life, in which case the laws of the *Shabbat* are set aside and precedence is given to saving lives.

Kashrut

Judaism has a series of important food regulations which are known as *kashrut* (meaning "fitness"). Animals, birds and fish might be either *kosher* (permitted) or *treif* (forbidden). *Treif* is derived from the Hebrew *terephah*, which refers to an animal torn by a wild beast.

Acceptable animals for consumption are all those with split hooves which chew the cud, such as sheep, cows and deer. Pigs, rabbits and horses are unacceptable, as are birds of prey. Other birds are acceptable provided that there is a tradition that the bird is *kosher*. For example, chicken is acceptable but hawk is not. Eggs are considered *kosher* if they are from *kosher* fowl. Only fish that have both fins and scales are acceptable. So, for example, cod is acceptable but prawns are not.

Provided that they are clear of all insects, fruit and vegetables are all acceptable and are also considered *parve*, which means that they are neither milk nor meat products and can be eaten with both (see below). Food that contains, or has been cooked in, products from non-acceptable animals is also unacceptable. Thus, for example, chips cooked in non-*kosher* animal fat are not acceptable, nor foods containing gelatin.

For meat to be *kosher* it must have been humanely slaughtered by a *shochet* (a qualified slaughterer) working under the supervision of the *Beth Din* (religious court). *Shechitah* (which is slaughter according to Jewish law) involves the draining of blood from the animal by slitting its throat.

Once killed, the meat from the animal must then be *kashered*. This involves the meat being soaked and salted or, in certain cases such as liver, broiled, in order to remove excess blood. The biblical prohibition against consuming blood reflects the conviction, based on a biblical statement, that blood represents life. So, for example, eggs with blood spots may also not be eaten.

Jewish law prohibits the mixing of milk foods with meat foods. This derives from *biblical* prohibitions against boiling a kid in its mother's milk. Separate sets of kitchen utensils are used for the two types of food and a time lapse is observed between eating one type of food and the other. Glass (although not pyrex) can be used for both types of food. Fish may be served with milk but then it would not be eaten at the same meal as meat. The extent to which Jewish people are observant of these food laws varies from person to person. If intending to provide food for Jewish guests it is wise to check first about any requirements.

Israel

The majority of Jews identify with Israel and many become involved with its life in several ways. For many Jews, their identity revolves much more around Israel than around the *synagogue* and other "religious" matters. The means of identification and involvement include: taking regular holidays there; taking an interest in Israeli news, politics and culture; becoming involved in and/or giving money to Israeli charities; eating Israeli food, and so on.

Many Jews view Israel as their "spiritual homeland". It is a common practice amongst Jewish teenagers to participate in an Israel experience "tour" or "gap year" following their final examinations in order to learn Hebrew. These tours are often a key factor in developing a Jewish identity.

Women

Women, and especially mothers, are seen as having a key role in Jewish life because of their role in the family which is at the centre of the practice of Judaism and, in particular, of many of its festivals and celebrations.

In *Progressive* Judaism the gender role distinctions specified in Jewish law are no longer recognised as binding. They are, however, still upheld in *Orthodox* Judaism. For example, when a marriage breaks down, in the *Orthodox* and *Reform* traditions a woman may not remarry in a *synagogue* until she has been given a *get* (religious divorce) by her husband. A man normally cannot remarry until a woman has accepted a *get* from him.

Halachically, a woman is believed to become ritually unclean through the process of menstruation. According to *Halachah*, before marriage, after menstruation, and after childbirth, women should visit a *mikveh* or ritual bath. Married women in the *Orthodox* tradition observe this tradition, but many *Progressive* Jews view the practice of visiting the *mikveh* as an option rather than as obligatory.

In *Progressive* Judaism both women and men can form a *minyan* (see section on "Jewish Worship and Places of Worship"), carry the *Torah*, and become rabbis. In the *Orthodox* sector women do not to take on these roles, but many *Orthodox synagogues* employ women as teachers and elect women to positions of *synagogal* and organisational management.

JEWISH WORSHIP

Keeping the Commandments

A *mezuzah* (literally meaning "door post") is a parchment scroll containing two sections of scripture (Deuteronomy 6 v. 4-9 and Deuteronomy 11 v. 13-21) that constitute the first paragraphs of the *Shema*, placed in a small, hollow box. These may be found on the doors of *synagogue* buildings and are also found on the doorposts of most Jewish homes. They are placed slanting in the top third of the right hand doorpost of every room except the toilet and the bathroom and they signify the sanctity of home and communal life.

Clothing and Prayer

Traditionally, during worship (whether at home or in the *synagogue*) all males and married women cover their heads out of modesty when addressing God although some *Progressive* Jewish communities do not observe this practice. Some Jews keep their heads covered at all times in recognition of the continual presence of God. The traditional means for doing this is, for Jewish men, the small cap known as a *kippah* (in Hebrew) or a *yarmulkah* (in Yiddish). Among *Orthodox* Jews, many married women cover their heads at all times with a hat or a *sheitel* (wig). In principle, any form of headcovering is acceptable for either sex.

Tephilin (*phylacteries*) are worn on the forehead and left arm by male *Orthodox* Jews who are over thirteen years of age. They consist of two strap-on leather boxes that enclose parchment sections of the scriptures, the wearing of which is believed by the *Orthodox* to be in accordance with scriptural commandment. *Tephilin* are worn for weekday morning prayers, but not for *Shabbat* or festival prayers.

Tallitot (the singular being *tallit* or *tallis*) are traditional prayer shawls, often with black or blue stripes. *Tzitzit* are the fringes that are attached to the four corners and they act as a reminder of the commandments. Traditional style prayer shawls are usually made of wool.

Some *Orthodox* Jewish men may wear the fringes, known as *Arba Kanfot* (meaning "four corners"), at all times on a vest under their clothes. In *Progressive* Jewish communities women are often encouraged to wear a prayer shawl if they take a leading role in corporate worship, but they are not obliged to do so.

Shabbat Worship

Shabbat is the key occasion for Jewish communal worship. The most regular and well-attended forms of communal worship on *Shabbat* are *Kabbalat Shabbat* (the first *Shabbat* service at dusk on Friday evening) and *Maariv* (the evening service said every day including Friday night), as well as *Shaharit* and *Musaf* on Saturday morning. In *Progressive synagogues* the Saturday morning service usually lasts one to two hours and in *Orthodox synagogues* for between two and three hours.

In the *Orthodox* tradition the entire service, except the *rabbi's* sermon and the prayer for the Royal Family, is conducted in Hebrew. *Progressive* Jewish *congregations* often say other prayers in English, although the extent of English usage varies from *congregation* to *congregation*. In *Progressive synagogues*, the *Shabbat* service may be accompanied by musical instruments. In *Orthodox synagogues* there is no instrumental accompaniment although there may be unaccompanied singing by a male choir.

During the *Shabbat* morning service a portion of the *Torah* is read. The *Torah* is divided into the weekly *Sidrah* or *Parashah* (fifty-four weekly portions) to be read each consecutive Saturday in the *synagogue*. In an *Orthodox synagogue* a minimum of seven men are called to the reading of the *Torah*. Following this reading, the *Haftarah* (an excerpt from the *Nevi'im* which has some connection with the *Torah* portion) is read.

In many *congregation*s, either regularly every week or occasionally, *Kiddush* is recited after the service in an adjoining room or hall. This is the prayer proclaiming the holiness of the *Shabbat* and festivals and on those days it is recited before meals over a cup of *kosher* wine. The congregation usually stays for biscuits, cake and a chat.

Other Communal Worship

Three daily prayers are stipulated. These are the *Shaharit* (morning service), *Minhah* (afternoon prayers) and *Maariv* (evening prayers). In the *Orthodox* tradition, formal communal prayers can only be said when a *minyan* (group of ten or more Jewish males) has been convened. Communal worship can take place anywhere. An example of this is where collective prayers are said at the home of a bereaved person during the seven days of mourning immediately after a death. This is known as *"sitting Shivah"*. It is not necessary for a *rabbi* to officiate at communal prayers and any person familiar with them may lead them.

The *Siddur* (prayer book - derived from the Hebrew word meaning "order") contains prayers for communal services, for private prayer, for special occasions and for travellers. The various Jewish traditions have different authorised prayer books for use in their *synagogues*. Prayers are mainly in Hebrew with the English translation given in prayer books on the opposite page. As with all Hebrew texts, prayer books open from right to left, since Hebrew is written from right to left. There are special prayer books for the *Pilgrim Festivals* and for the *High Holy Days*, known as *Mahzorim* (from the Hebrew word meaning cycle).

Special services for children are held in many larger *synagogues* to encourage them to be able to take an active role in the service when they are older. Above all, *Shabbat* is a family-orientated time with special meals and time for the whole family.

JEWISH PLACES OF WORSHIP

Synagogues

The principal place of Jewish communal worship is the *synagogue*, which *Ashkenazi* Jews usually refer to by the Yiddish word *shul*. The Registrar General's list of certified places of worship for 2004 (which is the most recent year for which data is available) records a total of 361 Jewish places of worship in England and 6 in Wales, while the CD-ROM accompanying this volume includes details of around 201 *synagogues* in the UK of which around 196 are in England, 3 are in Scotland, and 2 are in Wales.

A majority of Jews who are affiliated to a *synagogue* belong to *Orthodox* (see below) *synagogues* and a minority to the *Progressive* sector (see below) of *Reform* and *Liberal* *synagogues*, with a much smaller number being aligned with *synagogues* in the *Masorti* and *Sephardi* traditions.

Due to the *Orthodox* rule of walking to the *synagogue* on *Shabbat* and festivals, *Orthodox* *synagogue* buildings have moved from inner city areas, where Jews first settled, to the suburbs of towns and cities where the main Jewish communities are now established.

The *synagogue* is a building where worship takes place, but it is also a central place of administration, cultural and social activities and education programmes. *Synagogues* are self-financing and may have a *Heder* (room) that is a part-time (usually taking place on Sundays) school for Jewish education where children can gain religious knowledge and learn Hebrew. The *synagogue* might also offer adult Jewish education. In the larger *synagogues* services are held every morning and evening.

In *Orthodox synagogues* men and women are separated for reasons of propriety and women usually sit in a gallery above the section where the men conduct the service. Sometimes, where there is no gallery, the women are seated behind the men with a short curtain or partition separating the two. In some very small house *synagogues*, women and men worship in different rooms.

Inside the *synagogue*, a range of symbols and objects may be seen. The *Magen David* (Shield of David) is a six-pointed star that is a Jewish symbol of no particular religious significance. The *Menorah* is a seven-branched candlestick of a type dating back to the *Temple* in Jerusalem prior to its destruction by the Romans.

The *Bimah* is a raised platform, usually in the centre of the *synagogue*, from which the *Torah* is read. Most *synagogues* also have a pulpit from which the sermon is preached. A *Chazzan* (see section on "Personnel") leads *congregational* prayer.

The *Aron Kodesh* (*Holy Ark*) is an alcove or cupboard with wooden or ornate door panels that contains the *Torah* scrolls. In Western countries it is usually on the East wall of the *synagogue* that is the direction of Jerusalem. It has an embroidered curtain across it, which is known as a *Parochet*. A *Ner Tamid* (everlasting light) is a lamp hung in front of the *Aron Kodesh*, reminding the congregation of the eternal presence of God.

The *Sefer Torah* is a hand-written scroll of the *Torah*. In *Orthodox* synagogues, it is read four times a week, on Monday and Thursday mornings, Saturday mornings and Saturday afternoons. It is also read on other distinctive days such as the holy days.

The *Torah* scroll is kept inside a velvet cover and is usually decorated with metal breastplates and adornments. It has an honoured place in Jewish worship, especially at the festival of *Simchat Torah* (see below). The sanctity of the *Sefer Torah* is underlined by the use of a *Yad* that is a long pointer in the shape of a hand used by the reader so that the place may be kept without touching the parchment.

Visitors to a Jewish Synagogue

When visiting a *synagogue*, dress should be modest, with arms and legs covered, but need not be formal. In a *synagogue* that is *Orthodox*, women should wear a skirt or dress of reasonable length and not trousers and married women should cover their heads. Men and boys should cover their heads when visiting any *synagogue*.

Non-*kosher* food must not be brought into a *synagogue*. If the community is standing quietly in prayer, then visitors should wait at the back until the prayer has finished since this prayer should not be interrupted. *Sabbath* services in *Orthodox synagogues* can be up to two to three hours long, so visitors are advised to take this into account when planning for their arrivals and departures.

There is no expectation that visitors join in the worship unless they particularly wish to do so. *Orthodox* services, and many *Masorti* services, are conducted in Hebrew, but prayer books with translations are generally available in bookcases at the back of the *synagogue*. *Reform* services have a high proportion of English, and *Liberal* services are mostly in English. Visitors will not be expected to make particular gestures of respect toward any objects.

No sacred food is distributed during the service. However, *kiddush* (the Hebrew for *sanctification*) may take place after the service and visitors will be invited to join in the *blessing* that is said or sung over food and drink that is distributed in order to give thanks to God and in which visitors are invited to share as a sign of hospitality, although there is no sense of obligation to participate.

In *Orthodox synagogues*, this food and drink will consist of wine and biscuits or crisps, while in other *synagogues* bread accompanies the wine (in *Orthodox synagogues* bread is not shared at *kiddush*, because this would require the ritual washing of hands). Young children are usually given fruit juice instead of wine.

JEWISH CALENDAR AND FESTIVALS

Calendar

According to the Jewish calendar, which counts from what is traditionally believed to have been the year of the world's creation, the *Common Era* year 2007 is the Jewish year 5767. The relevant year appears on Jewish legal documents such as marriage certificates, on Jewish periodicals and on gravestones.

Jews use a combined lunar and solar calendar, where each month is equivalent to twenty-nine or thirty days, and a year is usually three hundred and fifty-four days. In a nineteen solar year cycle an extra month is inserted into years three, six, eight, eleven, fourteen, seventeen and nineteen, and this reconciles the Jewish calendar with the Gregorian calendar that is in common use in the UK.

Festivals

Because months are based on the moon, no fixed date for Jewish festivals can be given in the *Gregorian* calendar. With regard to the festivals mentioned below, the period of duration given is that followed by *Orthodox* Jews. *Progressive* Jews may celebrate the main festivals for a day less. The reason for this is that prior to mathematical calculation of the new moon, festivals were originally given an extra day in order to ensure their observance on the correct date, since a new moon could fall on one of two days.

Progressive Jews believe that now the new moon can accurately be calculated the addition of an extra day is no longer needed and this has always been the practice in the State of Israel, except in the case of *Rosh Hashanah* (see below) that is observed for two days.

Jewish festivals always begin in the evening and are grouped into three types. These are: the *Yamim Noraim* (Days of Awe); the *Shalosh Regalim* (Hebrew literally meaning "three foot festivals") which are the three festivals that have an agricultural and historical significance and in which it was traditional for every Jew to go to Jerusalem; and the minor festivals.

The Yamim Noraim

Rosh Hashanah (September/October)

Rosh Hashanah is the Jewish New Year. It involves two days of judgement and penitence. The *Shofar* (ram's horn) is blown (except on *Shabbat*) in the *synagogue* to remind people of their sins and to call them to spiritual awareness. It begins the Jewish year and the ten days of repentance that culminate in *Yom Kippur*. *Rosh Hashanah* and *Yom Kippur* are days during which no work may be done.

Yom Kippur (Day of Atonement)

A twenty-five hour *fast* devoted to prayer and worship, recollecting the sins of the past year and seeking forgiveness for them from one another and from God.

The Shalosh Regalim

Sukkot (September/October)

This is the festival of *Tabernacles* that commemorates the wandering of the children of Israel between Egypt and Canaan and God's protection during this period. There is a practice of building *sukkot* (temporary huts) onto the sides of houses or in gardens. This practice is intended to recall how the Israelite ancestors lived in the wilderness. Normally, the UK climate prevents Jews living in *sukkot* for the entirety of the festival, but Jewish families may have their meals in them. *Sukkot* can often be seen on the sides of *synagogue* and Jewish communal buildings.

The festival has a *harvest* connection that is acknowledged by taking four types of plant that are carried in procession around the *synagogue*: a *lulav* (palm branch), an *etrog* (citron), two *aravot* (willow branches) and three *hadassim* (myrtle branches). In *Orthodox synagogues* in the *diaspora*, *Sukkot* is a nine-day period with the first two and last two days as festival days. The final day is *Simchat Torah*.

Simchat Torah (The Rejoicing of the Torah)
This is a day of great festivities to celebrate the completion and recommencement of the annual cycle of readings from the *Torah* in the *synagogue*.

Pesach (March/April)
Pesach (often known in the English language as *Passover*) occurs at a time when the first fruits of barley would have been offered as sacrifice in the *Temple* when the barley harvest was gathered. It is an eight-day period of which the first two and last two days are celebrated as festivals. It commemorates the *Exodus* from Egypt and God's *redemption* of the Hebrew people.

As a reminder that the Hebrews had no time to wait for bread to rise before they had to leave Egypt, no *hametz* (leavened products) are consumed at this time. Such foods must be removed from the home, either by eating them beforehand or by giving them away. Prior to the festival the house is scrupulously cleaned in order to remove any crumbs of *hametz*. *Matzah* (meaning unleavened bread) is consumed during the festival period. A spare set of kitchen utensils, cutlery and crockery are usually used for the duration of the festival.

The home ceremony centres around the *seder* meal which, in the *diaspora*, among the *Orthodox*, takes place on the first two nights of the festival, and among *Progressives* on the first night. The order of service surrounding this meal is found in the *Haggadah* (*Seder* service book) that utilises verses from the *Torah* and from *Midrashic* commentaries in order to tell the story of the *Exodus*. The *Seder* is an important family occasion, in which all present, including young children, are encouraged to participate.

Shavuot (Pentecost) (May/June)
This festival commemorates the Israelites' reception of the *Torah* at Mount Sinai and their pledging of allegiance to God. On the first night before the festival many Jews stay awake all night studying the *Torah* in preparation for the anniversary of the revelation on the next day. The *Book of Ruth* is read during *Shavuot*. This festival lasts for two days and is the festival of the wheat harvest of the Mediterranean and of first fruits such as olives, dates, grapes, and figs. Traditionally, dairy foods are eaten on *Shavuot*.

Minor festivals and additional fast days

There are other festivals which form a part of Jewish life but which are without restrictions on work:

Hanukah (December)
This festival commemorates the rededication of the *Second Temple* in Jerusalem by the Maccabees in 168 BCE after it had been desecrated by the Syrian and the Greek armies. *Rabbinic* legend recounts that only one jar of oil with the *High Priest's* seal on it was found which was fit for use to light the Temple *menorah* (seven-branched candlestick), but by a miracle the little jar lasted for eight whole days until fresh oil could be obtained.

Hanukah lasts for eight days, and for each day one addiitional candle on the *Hanukiah* (a nine-branched candelabrum) is lit at home and in the synagogue. It has a lamp for each of the eight days with an additional serving light. Sometimes large *Hanukiyyot* are erected outside the *synagogue* and in city squares. Some families give gifts to children at this time.

Purim (February/March)
Is the day that commemorates the story found in the *Book of Esther* about the saving of the Jews of the Persian empire from the evil government minister Haman. On this day children dress up and the *synagogue*

services include the reading of the *Book of Esther*, with the worshippers booing and hissing whenever Haman's name is mentioned. Presents are given to friends as well as gifts to the poor. It is a time marked by fancy dress parties and general merry-making.

Yom Hashoa (April/May)
Holocaust Remembrance Day, marked by the lighting of candles and by communal services or meetings to commemorate the murder of six million Jews by the Nazis in the middle of the twentieth century.

Yom Haatzma'ut (May)
Israeli Independence day is celebrated by a service in many *synagogues*.

Tishah Be-Av (July/August)
This day commemorates the destruction of the *First Temple* in 586BCE and the *Second Temple* in 70CE as well as other calamities affecting the Jewish people. It is widely observed as a fast day.

There are also a number of other fasts that are observed by Jews to varying degrees. For example, the day before *Purim* is the *Fast of Esther*.

JEWISH ORGANISATIONS

Organisational Listings

Across the Jewish community as a whole, there has been a dynamic expansion of organisational development servicing every aspect of community life, at national, regional and local levels. The CD-ROM that accompanies this volume contains contact details of an extensive range of organisations operating at a UK level. Priority for inclusion was accorded to those organisations having a specifically religious focus or basis, although a number of more broadly communal organisations are also included.

The CD-ROM also has contact details for a range of differing kinds of local Jewish organisations, including synagogues; welfare bodies; representative bodies; student societies and houses; *yeshivot*; and other educational institutions with the general exception of Jewish schools.

Thus, overall, the CD-ROM accompanying this volume includes details of around 174 Jewish organisations working at a UK level, as well as around 6 working at a Scottish level and 1 at a Welsh level. In addition, it records details of around 333 local Jewish organisations (including around 327 in England, 4 in Scotland, and 2 in Wales). Finally it also includes details of around 6 regional level organisations in England, as well as 1 in Northern Ireland and 1 in Scotland.

There are many more Jewish organisations than those whose details are recorded on the CD-ROM, details of which can be found in *The Jewish Yearbook*.

Representative Organisations

The main national representative organisation for British Jews is the Board of Deputies of British Jews that was founded in 1760. Every *synagogue* and national communal organisation is entitled to elect delegates to the Board that meets most months.

The Board deals with secular matters affecting the status and rights of British Jews including such topics as communal defence, group relations, inter-faith matters, education, relations with Israel and foreign affairs. It also has a Community Research Unit and a Jewish Community Information helpline.

In major local and regional areas of Jewish population, so called Jewish Representative Councils were established to represent and reflect the breadth of the community.

General National Organisations

There are a range of other national representative organisations that are more specific in nature, such as the League of Jewish Women and the Anglo-Jewish Association. In terms of specifically religious organisations, there are national *synagogue* groupings which have local *synagogues* affiliated to them and are described below. There are also other national religious organisations of a more specific nature, for example the Initiation Society that trains and authorises people to *circumcise* in the *Orthodox* tradition, and the National Council of Shechita Boards that deals with issues concerning *shechita*. In addition there are many local religious organisations including local *shechita* boards and *kosher* meals-on-wheels services.

There is a range of national and local organisations that are particular to the Jewish community but do not as such serve a religious function. These include various welfare organisations such as Jewish Care and the Jewish Marriage Guidance Council. There are political organisations and also *Zionist* cultural groups and charitable refugee support groups.

There are several communal educational organisations and *Yeshivot* (plural of *Yeshiva*, a place of advanced Jewish learning, primarily concerned with *Talmudic* study). Whilst *Yeshivot* offer ordination to those studying within them who wish to serve in the *Rabbinate*, there are also academic Colleges that specifically serve this need. In *Orthodox* Judaism there is the London School of Jewish Studies and the Montefiore Kollel, while in *Progressive* Judaism, there is the Leo Baeck College.

In addition, there are many local and national organisations promoting Jewish education and culture in general, including historical societies, musical groups, youth groups and Holocaust remembrance organisations.

There is a whole range of international Jewish organisations that are based in the UK. For example, there is a Conference of European Rabbis to which all *Orthodox rabbis* are entitled to belong. The Reform Synagogues of Great Britain and the Union of Liberal and Progressive Synagogues are constituent members of the World Union of Progressive Judaism that aims to foster the growth and practice of *Progressive* Judaism.

Orthodox Organisations

There are a number of organised groupings of *Orthodox synagogues*, the largest of which is the United Synagogue, established in 1870. The spiritual leader of many *Orthodox Ashkenazi* Jews is known as the Chief Rabbi of the Hebrew Congregations of the Commonwealth. He is appointed by the Chief Rabbinate Council consisting of representatives of the *Orthodox* United Synagogue and of *Orthodox synagogues* from outside London. Other *Orthodox* groupings include the smaller Federation of Synagogues and the Union of Orthodox Hebrew Congregations. There are also Spanish and Portuguese *Sephardi* congregations. The oldest *Orthodox synagogue* still in use in the UK is the Bevis Marks Sephardi synagogue in London, which was built in 1701.

The best-known *Hasidic* group in Britain is part of a world movement known as *Lubavich* (also known as *Chabad*). The *Lubavich* feel a particular obligation to persuade Jewish people to become religiously observant and to prevent the assimilation of Jews into secular culture. *Hasidic* Jews are concentrated in London and Greater Manchester with smaller numbers in other places where there are large Jewish communities.

Reform and Liberal Organisations

There are two *Progressive* Jewish traditions in the UK: *Reform* Judaism and *Liberal* Judaism. *Reform* Judaism is the larger of the two traditions and originally the *Liberal* movement was more radically different from the *Orthodox* community than was *Reform* Judaism. Now, however, the initial distinction between *Liberal* and *Reform* Judaism has diminished and the communities have, to a significant degree, converged in their practice. *Rabbis* for both communities are given the same training at Leo Baeck College in London. Most UK *Progressive* Jews live in London, the South of England, Manchester and Leeds.

The *Reform* movement has its own *Beth Din* (established in 1948), cemeteries, day school and a major cultural centre in North London and was organised nationally as the Reform Synagogues of Great Britain. Now it is known as the Movement for Reform Judaism or, simply, as Reform. The first *Reform synagogue* in the UK was the West London Synagogue opened in 1840.

The *Liberal* movement began in the UK in 1902 with the foundation of the Jewish Religious Union. The first *Liberal* Jewish congregation was set up in 1910 in London and was called the Liberal Jewish Synagogue. From 1944 the name of the national representative organisation of the *Liberal* movement was the Union of Liberal and Progressive Synagogues. Now it is known simply as Liberal Judaism.

Masorti

The *Masorti* grouping is a relatively small one, whose congregations are affiliated to the Assembly of Masorti Synagogues that was founded in 1985.

Independent Synagogues

In addition to the formal groupings, there are a number of independent *synagogues* of both *Orthodox* and *Progressive* traditions.

Personnel

The *rabbi's* role within the Jewish community is to teach and to preach, to take on pastoral duties and to advise on Jewish law. All *rabbis*

in the *Orthodox* sector are male whilst the *Progressive* sector has both male and female *rabbi*s. *Rabbis* are often, but not always, salaried by the congregation. A *synagogue minister* can sometimes be referred to as *Reverend*, a courtesy title that often implies that the minister does not have *rabbinic* ordination. *Hasidic* groupings are led by *Rebbes*. The *Rebbe* is a charismatic spiritual leader. The office of *Rebbe* is hereditary, often, but not always, being passed down to the eldest son.

A *Hazzan/Cantor* is a singer who leads the *synagogue* services and, in *Orthodox synagogues*, is male. *Progressive synagogues* tend not to have *Hazzanim* (plural of *Hazzan*), preferring to have a choir to assist the rabbi during services. A *sofer* (scribe) is a person who writes *Torah* scrolls, *tephillin*, and *mezuzot* by hand, using a quill pen on parchments.

A *dayan* is a judge in Jewish law who serves on the *Beth Din* and administers Jewish law in the cases brought before it. In an *Orthodox Beth Din*, *dayanim* are permanent salaried members, whilst in the *Reform Beth Din*, *rabbis* serve in rotation as *dayanim*. The *Hevra Kaddisha* (holy society) is a Jewish burial society responsible for washing and shrouding Jewish corpses and for looking after the needs of the bereaved.

Many *synagogues* have a committee structure. Some medium sized *synagogues* have part-time Secretaries or Administrators, and some large *synagogues* have full time Secretaries or Executive Directors who can be approached as a first point of contact with the community.

FURTHER READING

Details follow of a number of general introductions to Judaism together with books and articles that provide some focus on Jews and Jewish organisations in the UK. The references are not comprehensive, but provide signposts to a range of relevant materials.

Alexander, P S (ed), *Textual Sources for the Study of Judaism*, Manchester University Press, Manchester, 1987.

Avineri, S, *The Making of Modern Zionism: The Intellectual Origins of the Jewish State*, Weidenfeld and Nicholson, London, 1981.

Close, B, *Judaism*, Hodder and Stoughton, London, 1991.

Cohn-Sherbok, D, *The Jewish Heritage*, Blackwell, Oxford, 1988.

Cohn-Sherbok, D, "Judaism in Modern Britain: A New Orientation", in P Badham (ed), *Religion, State and Society in Modern Britain*, Edwin Mellen Press, Lampeter, 1989, pp 209-224.

Cohn-Sherbok, D and Cohn-Sherbok, L, *A Short History of Judaism*, Oneworld, Oxford, 1994.

Cohn-Sherbok, D, *The Future of Judaism*, T & T Clark, London, 1994.

Cohn-Sherbok, D, *Jewish Mysticism*, Oneworld, Oxford, 1995.

Cohn-Sherbok, D and Cohn-Sherbok, L, *A Short Introduction to Judaism*, Oneworld, Oxford, 1997.

Commission on Representation of the Interests of the British Jewish Community, *A Community of Communities: Report of the Commission on Representation of the Interests of the British Jewish Community*, Institute for Jewish Policy Research, London, 2000.

Cooper, H and Morrison, P, *A Sense of Belonging: Dilemmas of British Jewish Identity*, Weidenfeld and Nicolson, London, 1991.

Englander, D, "Integrated But Insecure: A Portrait of Anglo-Jewry at the Close of the Twentieth Century", in G Parsons (ed), *The Growth of Religious Diversity: Britain from 1945, Volume 1, Traditions*, Routledge, London, 1993, pp 95-132.

Friesel, E, *Atlas of Modern Jewish History*, Oxford University Press, Oxford, 1990.

Gilbert, M, *Jewish History Atlas*, Weidenfeld and Nicholson, London, 1969.

Gilbert, M, *Holocaust Atlas*, Board of Deputies of British Jews, London, 1978.

Glatzer, N (ed), *The Judaic Tradition*, Behrman, New York, 1969.

Goldberg, D and Rayner, J, *The Jewish People*, Viking Penguin, 1989.

Goodkin, J and Citran, J, *Women in the Jewish Community: Review and Recommendations*, Women in the Community, London, 1994.

Graham, D and Waterman, S, "Underenumeration of the Jewish population in the UK 2001 Census", in *Population, Space and Place*, Volume 11, No 2, 2005, pp 89-102.

Gubbay, L and Levy A, *Ages of Man: A Plain Guide to Traditional Jewish Custom, Practice and Belief in Modern Times*, DLT, London 1985.

Halfpenny, P and Reid, M, *The Financial Resources of the UK Jewish Voluntary Sector*, Institute for Jewish Policy Research, London, 2000.

Holmes, C, *Anti-Semitism in British Society, 1876-1939*, Edward Arnold, London, 1979.

Jacobs, L, *The Jewish Religion: A Companion*, Oxford University Press, Oxford, 1995.

Katz, R, *Pastoral Care and the Jewish Tradition*, Fortress Press, Philadelphia, 1985.

Kushner, T (ed), *The Jewish Heritage in British History: Englishness and Jewishness*, Frank Cass and Company, London, 1992.

de Lange, N, *Judaism*, Oxford University Press, Oxford, 1987.

Lawton, C, *The Jewish People: Some Questions Answered*, Board of Deputies of British Jews Central Jewish Lecture and Information Centre, London, 1983.

Leaman, O, *Evil and Suffering in Jewish Philosophy*, Cambridge University Press, Cambridge, 1995.

Leaman, O (ed), *The Jewish Philosophy Reader*, Routledge, London, 2001.

Magonet, J, *The Explorer's Guide to Judaism*, Holder and Stoughton, London, 1998.

Massil, S (ed), *The Jewish Year Book*, Vallentine Mitchell, London, 2006.

Neusner, J, *Between Time and Eternity: The Essentials of Judaism*, Dickenson Publishing Company, Californnia, 1975.

Pearl, C and Brookes, R, *A Guide to Jewish Knowledge*, Jewish Chronicle Publications. London, 1965.

Pilkington, C, *Teach Yourself Judaism*, Hodder, 1995.

Reform Synagogues of Great Britain, *Faith and Practice: A Guide to Reform Judaism*, Reform Synagogues of Great Britain, London, 1991.

Runnymede Trust, The, *A Very Light Sleeper: The Persistence and Dangers of Antisemitism*, Runnymede Trust, London, 1994.

Schmool, M and Cohen, F, *British Synagogue Membership in 1990*, Board of Deputies of British Jews (Community Research Unit), London, 1991.

Schmool, M and Cohen, F, *A Profile of British Jewry: Patterns and Trends at the Turn of the Century*, Board of Deputies of British Jews, London 1998.

Schmool, M and Miller, S, *Women in the Jewish Community: Survey Report*, Women in the Community, Boar od Deputies of British Jews, London, 1994.

Scholefield, L, "Bagels, schnitzel and McDonald's – 'fuzzy frontiers' of Jewish identity in an English secondary school", in *British Journal of Religious Education*, Volume 26, No 3, 2004, pp 237-248.

Seltzer, R M, *Jewish People, Jewish Thought*, Collier Macmillan, London, 1980.

Slesinger, E, *Creating Community and Accumulating Social Capital: Jews Associating With Other Jews in Manchester*, Institute for Jewish Policy Research, London, 2003.

Solomon, N, *A Very Short Introduction to Judaism*, Oxford University Press, Oxford, 1996.

Stratton, J, *Coming Out Jewish*, Routledge, London, 2000.

Turner, R, *Jewish Living*, Jewish Chronicle Publications, London, 1982.

Union of Liberal and Progressive Synagogues, *Affirmations of Liberal Judaism*, London, 1992.

Unterman, A, *The Wisdom of the Jewish Mystics*, Sheldon Press, London, 1976.

Valins, O, "Stubborn identities and the construction of socio-spatial boundaries: ultra-orthodox Jews living in contemporary Britain", in *Transations of the Institute of British Geographers*, Volume 28, No 2, 2003, pp 158-175.

Vincent, P and Warf, B, "Talmudic places in a postmodern world", in *Transactions of the Institute of British Geographers*, Volume 27, No 1, 2002, pp 30-51.

Waterman, S and Kosmin, B, *British Jewry in the Eighties*, Board of Deputies of British Jews (Community Research Unit), London, 1986.

Webber, J (ed), *Jewish Identities in the New Europe*, Littman Library, London, 1994.

Williams, B, *The Making of Manchester Jewry: 1740-1875*, Manchester University Press, Manchester, 1976.

INTRODUCING MUSLIMS IN THE UK

MUSLIMS IN THE UK   223

**ORIGINS AND
DEVELOPMENT OF ISLAM**   224

**SOURCES OF MUSLIM
BELIEFS AND PRACTICES**   226

KEY MUSLIM BELIEFS   227

TRADITIONS IN ISLAM   228

MUSLIM LIFE   230

MUSLIM WORSHIP   231

**MUSLIM PLACES OF
WORSHIP**   232

**MUSLIM CALENDAR AND
FESTIVALS**   233

MUSLIM ORGANISATIONS   235

FURTHER READING   238

MUSLIMS IN THE UK

History in the UK

There has been a significant Muslim presence in the United Kingdom since the early nineteenth century when Muslim seamen and traders from the Middle East and the Indian subcontinent began to settle around major ports.

For example, Yemeni Muslims settled in South Shields and established a Muslim community there and similar communities grew up around the ports of Liverpool and Cardiff. Some of the seamen later moved inland after failing to secure employment in the ports or on the ships and the pattern of settlement thus widened.

After the First World War there was further settlement by Muslims who had been demobilised from military service in the British army.

The size of the Muslim population increased significantly with the arrival in the 1950s and 1960s of workers from the Indo-Pakistani subcontinent who had been recruited for, or were seeking employment, in the mills and factories due to a shortage of workers in the aftermath of the Second World War.

As a direct result of the implementation of Africanisation policies in the newly independent African states, the early 1970's saw the arrival from Kenya and Uganda of a large number of Muslims of Asian ethnic origins. Recently, some Muslim refugees have arrived from countries such as Somalia and Bosnia.

Global and UK Populations

Worldwide, there are an estimated 1,188,243,000 Muslims. In the UK, the 2001 decennial Census questions on religion yielded 1,591,126 (or 2.7% of the total UK population) Muslim respondents. This is 3.5% of the population that identifies itself with any specific religion at all. Of these

1,591,126, at total of 1,524,887 were in England, 21,739 in Wales, 42,557 in Scotland, and 1,943 in Northern Ireland.

As a proportion of the total population in local authority areas, the 2001 Census shows that, in England, the greatest concentration of respondents identifying themselves as Muslims is to be found in the London Boroughs of Tower Hamlets (36.4%) and Newham (24.3%); Blackburn and Darwen (19.4%); Bradford (16.1%); and the London Borough of Waltham Forest (15.1%).

Ethnicity in England and Wales

According to the 2001 Census, 73.7% of the Muslim population of England and Wales gave their ethnicity as "Asian", 11.6% as "White", 6.9% as "Black or Black British", 4.2% as "Mixed" and 3.7% as "Chinese or Other Ethnic Group". Considered in terms of the ethnicity of respondents, 50.1% of all those recorded as "Asian" also identified as Muslim, along with 12.8% of "Chinese and Other Ethic Group", 9.7% of "Mixed", 9.3% of "Black or Black British", and 0.4% of those recorded as "White".

The largest group of the Muslims in the UK have ancestral origins in the Indo-Pakistani subcontinent, coming to Britain either directly or via earlier migrations to East Africa and the Caribbean. The vast majority of the remaining Muslim populations have ethnic and national origins in countries such as Cyprus, Malaysia, Turkey, Iran and the Arab world. There are also growing numbers of indigenous Britons who have embraced Islam.

Because the ethnic background of the UK Muslim population is quite diverse, a number of different languages are spoken in addition to English. Arabic, Bengali, Farsi, Gujarati, Hausa, Malay, Punjabi, Pushto, Turkish, and Urdu are among the most commonly used of these. Among Muslims, a reading knowledge of Arabic is considered very important since this is the language of the *Qur'an* (see below).

ORIGINS AND DEVELOPMENT OF ISLAM

Revelation

According to Muslim belief, the final *Prophet* of Islam was the *Prophet* Muhammad (570-632CE), in relation to whom Muslims generally add, "peace be upon him" or "pbuh". He was born in the city of Makka (in the Arabian peninsula) and from the age of forty received a series of revelations from God (in Arabic, Allah). The revelations are believed to have come to Muhammad through the Angel Jibreel (Gabriel) over a period of twenty-three years.

It is stressed by Muslims that Muhammad did not bring a new faith. As the "seal of the *prophets*" he is understood to complete the succession of *prophets*, renewing and completing the teachings of Abraham, Moses and Jesus who are seen as being among the greatest of the *prophets*.

Muslims believe that essentially the same message, guiding people to the right path, was communicated by God through all the *prophets*. Because people kept disobeying and corrupting the code of guidance which the *prophets* preached, other *prophets* were sent to restate the original message.

Muslims therefore affirm the *Torah* brought by Moses and the *Gospel* or *Injil* of Jesus, although they believe that these have been corrupted from their original purity. Muhammad is thus seen as the last of the *prophets*, correcting error and calling people back to Islam and submission to the ways of God.

The Prophet Muhammad and the 'Umma

All those who believed in Muhammad as the last of the *prophets* and in the revelation to him which forms the *Qur'an*, were welcomed into the 'Umma (world Muslim community) irrespective of their place of origin, language or colour of skin. With this newly established Muslim community, in 622CE Muhammad migrated from Makka to Madina, five hundred kilometres away.

This migration is known as the *Hijra*. The formative significance of this event in Islamic history can be seen from the fact that the Muslim dating system begins from the *Hijra* and that therefore, in English, dates in the Muslim calendar are expressed as "AH" (after *Hijra*).

Caliphate and Imamate

After the death of the Prophet Muhammad, the *Caliphate* (from *khalifa* meaning viceroy) was established to provide leadership for the Muslim community. Among *Sunni* Muslims (see below) Abu Bakr, 'Umar, 'Uthman and 'Ali are recognised as the first four *Caliphs* and are often called *al-khulafa ar-rashidun* (the rightly guided *Caliphs*) because their exemplary lives are viewed as role models for the community.

However, following the death of Muhammad there was a serious dispute within the Muslim community concerning the location of authority. This led to the development of the distinctive *Sunni* and *Shi'a* traditions of Islam (see below), with a different line of authority emerging within the *Shi'a* tradition. The word *Sunni* comes from "one who adheres to the *sunna*", the *sunna* (see below) being one of the four sources of Islamic law which relates to the actions and sayings of the *Prophet* Muhammad. The name *Shi'ite* comes from *shiat 'Ali* (the follower of 'Ali).

The *Shi'a* advocated the appointment of 'Ali ibn Abi Talib as successor to the *Prophet* instead of Abu Bakr. After 'Umar's death and following his appointment by Abu Bakr, 'Ali the son-in-law of the Prophet Muhammad was offered the *Caliphate* on certain conditions, but an arbiter awarded the function to 'Uthman.

After 'Uthman's assassination 'Ali was elected as the Fourth *Caliph*, but was then himself assassinated. Following a series of disputes and a civil war, his son Hasan was elected *Caliph* but gave up the office for the sake of reconciliation.

Following Hasan's death and that of *Amir* Muaviya, Hasan's brother Husayn led a revolt because he thought that the terms of the agreement had not been kept by the appointment of Yazid as *Caliph*. Husayn was betrayed and killed at Karbala in confrontation with the armies of Yazid. This event became the foundation of the developing themes of suffering and persecution to be found in the *Shi'a* tradition of Islam.

Therefore Husayn is seen by *Shi'a* Muslims as an inspiration to all who suffer and struggle against injustice. Reverence for 'Ali and his successors led to the development of the *Shi'a* idea of the *Imamate* in which descendants of Ali have a special sanctity and role in the spiritual leadership of the community.

In *Sunni* Islam, the idea of the *Caliphate* continued under a succession of Muslim dynasties, beginning with the Umayyad dynasty (661-750CE), centred upon the geographical region known today as Syria. Following the Abbasid dynasty centred upon Baghdad, a rival centre was established with Cordoba, Spain, where a second Umayyad ruled dynasty from 929CE seeing themselves as *Amirs*, while Cairo become the capital of the Fatimid dynasty from 969CE. The concept of the *Caliphate* survived into modern times with the Ottoman Empire, finally ending in 1924 through the secularising policies of Mustapha Kemal Ataturk of Turkey.

Development and Diversity

From its origins in Arabia, Islam spread towards the Indian sub-continent after 750CE, and also into Africa and Europe. In Europe the history of Islam is at its longest in the Balkans, Sicily and Spain. In Spain, Islam was initially established by military force through the arrival of the final *Amir* (prince) of the Umayyad dynasty in Damascus (Abdul Rahman, the First) in the early eighth century, Islamic culture spread through the land influencing many aspects of life and thought, developing peacefully alongside Christian and Jewish culture, until the Muslims were finally expelled by the Christian monarchs of the early sixteenth century.

During the Moghul empire (1516-1707CE) Islam made deep inroads into India, from where it spread to Malaysia, Indonesia and the Philippines. The partition of the Indian sub-continent in 1947, following the end of British colonial rule, resulted in the creation of the Muslim majority state of Pakistan. Following a civil war, in 1971 the eastern part of Pakistan became the independent country of Bangladesh.

SOURCES OF MUSLIM BELIEFS AND PRACTICES

Qur'an

The *Qur'an* is the fundamental source of guidance for Muslims. They regard it as the pre-eminent "sign" or "miracle" of God and as the final and ultimate source of guidance which is for all places and all times. It can be applied in each age in the way most suitable to the conditions of that age and is a guide to ethics, human relationships, social justice, political principles, law, trade and commerce.

The text of the *Qur'an* is divided into *surahs* (or chapters) which are of varying lengths and are not in chronological order but are believed to be in this order under divine instruction. The opening *surah*, called the *Fatiha*, is a key prayer of Muslims and a summary of Islamic belief which must be read in Arabic during the observance of every *salah* (Muslim daily prayers – see below).

Because the *surahs* of the *Qur'an* are viewed as the actual words of God, the learning and

recitation of the *Qur'an* is a central duty and joy for believers. The language in which the *Qur'an* was revealed was Arabic, and an understanding of this is therefore seen as essential for penetrating its true meaning. It is thus considered preferable to read it in its original Arabic version, which is considered to be a form of worship, although translations (or more strictly, in Islamic understanding, interpretations) are available in English and many other languages.

Shari'a

The framework within which Muslim life has evolved is the *Shari'a* (law). The sources of *Shari'ah* are the *Qur'an*, the *Sunna*, *Ijma*, *Ijtihad* and *Qiyas*.

The *Sunna* is the example of the *Prophet* and his way of life which acts as a model for Muslims to emulate. It is whatever the *Prophet* said, did or approved of. It therefore also includes the *Hadith*. The *Hadith* are the traditions which contain accounts of the words and actions of Muhammad and his companions and they have been gathered in the form of books at different times and by different authors into generally recognised collections of material, some of which are considered to be more accurate than others.

Ijma is the practice of reaching consensus of approval for particular aspects of *Shar'ia*. Where Islamic legislation is unclear about a situation, experts who are knowledgeable about the holy texts propose clarifications which must gain their consensus agreement for it to become an accepted principle.

'Ijtihad (Sunni term) or *'aql* (Shi'a term) is the concept of independent reasoning or intelligence. Rational discussion and debate is very much at the heart of Islam. One form of reasoning which is often employed is that of *Qiyas* (or analogy).

In the use of *Qiyas*, analogies are drawn between situations in the *Qur'an*, *Sunna* (including the *Hadith*) and contemporary circumstances in order to determine the application of the *Shar'ia* to novel situations. However, among *Sunni* Muslims many have argued that, following the development of classical Islamic jurisprudence, the "gates of *ijtihad*" became closed in the tenth century CE. However, *ijtihad* and *ijma*, however strong, cannot override a *Qur'anic* rule or an established *Hadith*.

Schools

Among the *Sunni* Muslims there are four recognised *madhahib* or *madhhabs* (schools of law) whose scholars have the task of discerning the way of applying the *Shar'iah* in various contexts. These are named after their founders: the *Hanafi*, the *Hanbali*, the *Maliki* and the *Shafi'i* schools. They are all recognised as having developed out of the *usul al-fiqh* (the principles of Islamic jurisprudence), and each school therefore recognises the other as being truly Muslim.

Different schools have come to predominate in various areas of the world. The *Hanafi* school is predominant in India and most parts of the former Ottoman Empire, the *Maliki* school in West Africa and the Arab West, and the *Shafi'i* in Indonesia, Malaysia and the Philippines. The *Shafi'i* is also important in Egypt where the first two schools can also be found. The *Hanbali* school is found in Saudi Arabia and Qatar. Muslims in Britain with ethnic or ancestral backgrounds in these various areas of the world might therefore be expected to follow the relevant predominant school in the land of their ethnic origin.

The *Shi'a* tradition of Islam also has a number of schools, the most widespread of which is the *Ja'fari* school of the *Twelvers* (see below).

KEY MUSLIM BELIEFS

The Key Beliefs and Five Pillars of Islam

Islam rests upon six basic beliefs. It affirms the oneness of God (*Allah*), the books revealed by God, belief in the *prophets*, the angels, the *Day of Judgement* and life after death. The essentials of Muslim practice are summarised in the *Five Pillars of Islam*. The five pillars are:

Shahada

The declaration of faith which states that there is no god except God and Muhammad is his messenger.

Salah

Ritual prayer carried out five times a day (see section on "Muslim Places of Worship and Worship" below).

Zakat

A welfare due which should consist of two and a half per cent of a Muslim's untouched annual savings over a specified amount in order to help the service of the needy. An additional charity is due at the end of *Sawm* (fasting) during the month of *Ramadan*, and this is known as *Sadaqa ul-Fitr*.

Ramadan

A month of fasting and spiritual discipline (for details see section on "Muslim Calendar and Festivals").

Hajj

This is the Pilgrimage to Makka which involves visiting the *Ka'ba* (the *House of God*), believed to have been built around four thousand years ago by Abraham, and performing certain prescribed rituals in and around Makka. For those who can afford it, the *Hajj* is a requirement at least once in a lifetime.

Monotheism

Islam is strictly *monotheistic*. God, *Allah*, is believed to be one and unique and is spoken of in masculine terms although the Divine Reality is affirmed as being beyond the limitations of human gender. He is merciful and powerful, omniscient and omnipresent. He is in control of events in history and of the *Day of Judgement*. He created the universe and sustains it and has prescribed Islam (submission to God) as the correct way of life for the people he has created. It is also believed that, although humans have a choice as to whether they follow this way or not, all will eventually return to God to whom they will be accountable for their deeds in this world.

Goal and Purpose of Human Life

The purpose of human life is to exercise *khilafa* (authority and trust) to manage the world in a responsible way and to live in accordance with God's creative will. Human beings are called back to a life in submission to God's will as expressed in the revelations of *Torah*, *Injil* (*Gospel* of Jesus), of all the other *prophets* of God and, finally, through the revelation of the *Qur'an*. How each person individually responds to the will and revelation of God is believed to determine their eternal destiny.

Belief in the *Day of Judgement*, when an individual's actions will be placed on the scales of good and evil, acts as a powerful reinforcement for the personal responsibility of each human being.

TRADITIONS IN ISLAM

Main Branches

There are two principal traditions within Islam - *Sunni* and *Shi'a*. There is also an aspect of Islam known as *Sufism* (see below) which either *Sunni* or *Shi'a* Muslims might embrace.

Sunni

Ninety per cent of the world's Muslims are *Sunni*. They recognise the first four "rightly guided" *Caliphs* and understand the *Qur'an*, *Sunna*, *Ijma* and *Qiyas* to be the four sources of the law.

Within the *Sunni* branch of Islam there are a range of movements and groupings which have particular emphases or concerns. They are not, however, as organisationally clear-cut as, for example, Christian denominations and there may well be cross-membership of the various tendencies. In the UK, the majority of these groupings are of South Asian origin and are organised in a variety of *Sunni* Muslim traditions:

Barelwis

Barelwi is the term commonly used to denote a devotional style of Islam found among some groups of Muslims with origins in the Indian subcontinent. It holds in high esteem the teachings of Maulana Ahmad Raza Khan (1856-1921) of Bareilly, Uttar Pradesh, in India who was a member of the *Qadiri Sufi* order and a great *Mufti* (Jurist) of the *Hanafi* school of interpretation.

Barelwis celebrate the *milad* (birthday) of the *Prophet* Muhammad as a major festival, giving a particularly high respect to the person of the *Prophet* Muhammad as a model and inspiration for Muslim life but also affirming that he had access to knowledge of "the unseen". A key concept of *Barelwi* thought is that the *Divine Light* which existed from the beginning of time can be seen in Muhammad.

They look to *sayyids* (descendants of the Prophet) and to *pirs* (spiritual guides) for spiritual authority, teaching, guidance and intercession with God and they defend the Islamic legitimacy of popular devotional practice at the shrines of *pirs*.

Deobandis

The *Deobandi* movement was founded in India by Maulana Muhammad Qasim. It is named after a *darul 'ulum* (training college) for Indian Muslim religious scholars founded in 1867 in the Indian town of Deoband. Established in the context of British colonial power in India its scholars were concerned to defend a clear Islamic identity against the influence of non-Islamic ideas.

Its curriculum, and that of the many colleges which came to be modelled upon it, promotes an interpretation of Islam in which the emphasis is on textual scholarship, with pre-eminence given to study of the *Qur'an*, *Hadith* and *Shari'a* (interpreted through the *Hanafi* school). Although its scholars were, like the *Barelwi* movement, within the *Sufi* tradition, the *Deobandi* movement emphasised the role of spiritual guides as exemplars, not accepting the legitimacy of any intercessory role for *pirs*.

Tablighi Jamaat

Tablighi Jamaat was founded in India in 1927 by *Maulana* Muhammad Ilyas (1885-1944), a *Sufi* and a student of *Deoband*. The movement is broadly within the *Deobandi* tradition and is usually non-political. It attempts to encourage other Muslims to practise the ritual aspects of Islam on a more fervent and regular basis and its committed members travel widely to spread its message.

Ahl-e-Hadith

Ahl-e-Hadith is a movement whose followers accept only the teachings of the *Qur'an* itself and the earliest teachings in the *Hadith*. It rejects any regulations which are not from these sources. This movement is sometimes known as *ghayr muqallidun* (not attached to any school of thought).

Jamaat-i-Islami

Jamaat-i-Islami operates as a religious movement in India and Sri Lanka, but as a religio-political party in Pakistan and Bangladesh. It was founded in India in 1941 by Sayyid Abul A'la Mawdudi (1903-1979). It favours a return to the following of traditional Muslim doctrine in the face of the secular influences of Western civilisation and, more specifically, is committed to seeing Islamic ideology enshrined in an Islamic state.

Shi'a

About ten per cent of Muslims worldwide are *Shi'a*, an Arabic word which literally means follower or associate. The *Shi'a* believe that Muhammad instituted from within his family (the descendants of Ali and Fatima, the Prophet's youngest daughter) a succession of individual *Imams* (spiritual leaders) to guide the community. The *Shi'a* concept of the *Imam* should not be confused with the general use of the term by Muslims to describe their local prayer leaders (see section below on "Personnel").

In common with other Muslims, *Shi'as* believe that the process of revelation was completed with the coming of Muhammad, but they differ from other Muslims in believing that *Imams* or *Hujja* (*Proofs of God*) are specially selected by God and have the authority to interpret the *Qur'an* and to provide guidance to believers.

Shi'as observe more festivals than *Sunnis* (see section on festivals). In addition, they value pilgrimages to the shrines of their *Imams* and saints – in particular those of *Imam* 'Ali (in Najaf) and *Imam* Husayn (in Karbala) in Southern Iraq.

Twelvers and Seveners

All *Shi'a* Muslims agree that Ali was the first *Imam*, but thereafter there are differences of view concerning the succession. A minority are known as the *Seveners*, whilst the majority are known as the *Twelvers* (or *'Ithna Asherites*). The *Twelvers* believe in a series of twelve *Imams*, the last of whom, Muhammad Al-Muntazar, was last seen in 873CE and is believed to have been the *Mahdi* (*Guided One*). He is believed to be still alive but is now hidden and waiting for God's command to reappear.

Isma'ilis are a *Shi'a* Muslim group who accept the leadership of the first six *Imams*, but thereafter claim the primacy of the elder son of the sixth *Imam*, Isma'il and therefore are known as *Seveners*. Among the *Isma'ilis* are the *Nizaris* who are also known as the *Agha Khanis*. They believe in the *Aga Khan* as their living *Imam* and expect that he will, in turn, choose a member of his family to succeed him. The *Nizari* and the *Musta'lian Isma'ilis* disagreed over two opposing claimants to the *Imamate*. The *Bohras* are a group which emerged out of the *Musta'lian Isma'ilis*.

Tasawwuf

Tasawwuf (Sufism) is the name for the mystical strand of Islam which can be found in both the *Sunni* and *Shi'a* traditions of Islam. The word is thought to derive from the Arabic *suf* (wool) which characterised the simple clothing worn by early *ascetics*. *Sufism* traces its origins back through *silsilah* (lines of spiritual initiation) and is led by spiritual authorities known as *shaykhs* or *pirs* who advise the initiates of the *Sufi Orders* in their quest for an intimately spiritual relationship with God.

Sufism involves a commitment to the practical and readily accessible aspects of Islam based on the *Shar'ia*, but also emphasises the inner or *esoteric* aspects of Islam. As aids to their spiritual development, the members of *Sufi Orders* may engage in various practices such as meditation, chanting the names of God, or ritual dancing. There are many worldwide *Sufi Orders* including, for example, the *Naqshbandi*, the *Qadiri*, the *Chishti* and the *Suhrawardi*.

MUSLIM LIFE

Becoming a Muslim

In order to become a Muslim a person must accept and declare that there is "no god except God" and that "Muhammad is his *messenger*" (*Shi'a* Muslims adding "and Ali is the seal on the will of the *Prophet*"). This declaration of faith is known as the *Shahada*.

Shari'a

The basic Muslim beliefs are put into practice by means of the way of life given by God, revealed through the *Prophet* Muhammad, and known as the *Shari'ah* (pathway). The *Shari'ah* is concerned not only with prayer and ritual matters but also governs and regulates conduct of all kinds, for example attitudes to economics, family life, and the behaviour of rulers, thus codifying Islamic values as they apply to the whole of life.

Jihad

Jihad, the striving to protect, promote and live by the message of the *Qur'an* through words and actions, is central to Islam. It involves *da'wa*, which is the task of spreading the message of Islam through invitation issued by means of words and deeds; creating satisfactory social conditions for Islam to be practised freely; increasing the self-discipline of people who are already Muslims so that they become better Muslims; and, in limited circumstances, defending Islam by force of arms if necessary.

This last aspect is only one dimension of *jihad* although outside the Muslim community *jihad* is often mistakenly assumed to mean only this. *Jihad* does not include imposing Islam by force on non-Muslims because the *Qur'an* forbids compulsion in matters of religion.

Halal

The term *halal* simply means permitted, and refers to a wide range of things which are allowed to Muslims. In popular usage in the UK, however, it is often identified with food laws which are also an important part of Muslim values and ethics.

The *Qur'an* does not allow consumption of the meat of pigs and carnivorous animals. This includes pork products and foods which contain the by-products of pigs or carnivorous animals. They are *haram* (unlawful). Other meats are also *haram* unless the animal has been ritually slaughtered. Ritual slaughter involves prayers during slaughter, and a method of butchery which allows the blood to flow from the animal's body. Fish is permitted.

When *halal* meat is not available for consumption by Muslims, *kosher* meat (slaughtered according to the Jewish *shechita* method) is permissible for *Sunni* Muslims (although not for *Shi'a Ithna 'Asherites*) or a vegetarian meal will suffice. Foods which contain the by-products of non-*halal* meat are also generally considered unlawful, for example cheese which contains an animal product such as rennet. Also unlawful for Muslims is any food or drink perceived by Muslims to have been offered to an idol or to a false god. Alcohol is also prohibited under Islamic law and any drinks or foods which contain alcohol in any amount are unacceptable, except as part of medicine.

Gender and Family

According to Muslim understanding the *Shari'a* confers equal dignity on both women and men. Men and women generally have the same religious duties, and in most cases the same legal rights, as in the possibility of owning property in their own right. However, women are not obliged to participate in congregational prayers. There are also gender differentiations of rights and responsibilities with regard to social and legal roles, some of which are believed by many Muslims to have been divinely revealed in the *Qur'an*.

In Islam, marriage and procreation are viewed very positively and celibacy is discouraged. Traditionally, the role of a man is believed to involve financial support of his wife and family (irrespective of his wife's wealth and inheritance), and the protection of female family members including wife, daughters and, if his father is deceased, his mother as well.

Muslims believe that it is a duty to marry, and the ideal family structure is based on *monogamy* which is generally the normal practice among Muslims in the UK. However, under the terms of the *Shari'a*, *polygamy* (although not *polyandry*) is considered lawful in certain circumstances. These include infertility of the first wife, or permanent physical or mental infirmity of the first wife.

Under Islamic law a man may take up to four wives at any one time, although the regulations regarding such marriages are such that *polygamy* is often a practical impossibility. These regulations include that a man must have the means to provide for each wife and that he must treat each wife absolutely equally, in both financial and social terms. The contracting of a *polygamous* marriage is not allowed in law in this country, but recognition can be accorded to *polygamous* marriages that have been contracted in overseas countries where this is permitted.

Modesty is an important concept in Islam. For men, modest dress should cover, at a minimum, the area from the navel to the knees. For women, it involves covering the full body and this is interpreted variously. Traditionally, in most Islamic societies this has involved the wearing of a *hijab* or veil of varying kinds.

In some Islamic societies, including a number from which people have come to the UK, there may be an expectation that women will cover their faces from the sight of men other than their husbands and family members and avoid the company of such men by remaining primarily within the home and in female company. This practice is referred to as *purdah*. In mixed contexts it can take the form of the two sexes sitting separately.

MUSLIM WORSHIP

Salah

The main form of *'ibada* (worship) is that of *salah* (Arabic for the five times a day obligatory prayers) or *namaz* (Urdu). The exact times at which prayer takes place vary throughout the year due to the fact that daylight hours are much shorter during the winter than during the summer. Prayer time-tables are published with details of the times, and can often be found on display in *mosques*. Generally speaking, prayer takes place at around the following periods of the day: *Fajr* (dawn), *Zuhr* (midday), *'Asr* (late afternoon), *Maghrib* (after sunset), and *'Isha* (late evening).

Prayers are obligatory from puberty onwards, except for women who are menstruating or in the post-natal period. People who are not fully conscious are also exempted from prayers. Friday is the day for congregational prayers. Most male Muslims attend the *mosque* for this *Salat al-Jumu'a* which is mandatory for them. *Wudu* (ablutions or ritual washing) must take place prior to all prayers. This includes washing hands, face, hair, mouth, nose, arms (up to the elbows), and the feet (up to the ankles).

During prayer, worshippers face Makka, the *qiblah* (direction) of which is marked by the *mihrab*, a small niche in the wall of the *mosque*. In the UK, this direction is towards the south-east. A Muslim can pray in any clean place and use a prayer mat if he or she cannot reasonably attend a *mosque*. Muslim employees, school children and students should have the opportunity to conduct their obligatory prayers while at work or in school or college.

MUSLIM PLACES OF WORSHIP

Mosques

The English word *mosque* comes from the Arabic word *masjid*, meaning a place of prostration. Within the Muslim community *mosques* are known by a number of terms, the most common being *masjid. Jami'* is used to refer to the "central *mosque*". The first *mosques* in the UK were established in Liverpool and Woking around the end of the nineteenth century.

The Registrar General's list for 2004 (with 2004 being the latest year for which data is available) records 721 *mosques* in England that are certified as places of worship, and 17 in Wales, while the CD-ROM accompanying this volume includes records of around 715 Muslim places of worship in the UK of which around 656 are in England, 24 in Scotland, 24 in Wales and 1 in Northern Ireland.

The first *mosques* in the UK were established and financed by the personal efforts of individuals living in the area. For example, the first *mosque* in Birmingham was established in 1941 by two Yemeni Muslims who were concerned to make arrangements for Muslim prayers, burial rites, and religious education for children.

At present many *mosques* are buildings which were formerly private residences, or even rooms in houses which are still used as private residences. Others are in public buildings which had former uses, for example as warehouses or, occasionally, as Christian *churches*. Recently, however, a number of purpose built *mosques* have been constructed.

No images, paintings or decorations which represent living beings are to be found inside *mosques*. In some *mosques*, however, Arabic calligraphy may be observed on the walls and perhaps some geometrical patterns. There are no seats in a *mosque* but the floor is carpeted.

Music is not played although in some *mosques* there may be congregational chanting. There is a *minbar* (*pulpit* or raised steps) to one side of the *mihrab* from which the *imam* delivers sermons on Fridays and at festival times. There may also be a symbol of the crescent moon and star which has come to be associated with Islam.

Although every *mosque* is, in principle, open to all Muslims, the management committees of particular *mosques* may, in practice, reflect specific Muslim tendencies or national or regional groupings. As a result, specific dominant languages are used for instruction and general communication, although the language of the prayers themselves is always Arabic. *Mosques* of different types do, however, sometimes join together to form councils of *mosques*, such as the Bradford Council of Mosques.

Mosques provide a number of services like the channelling of *Zakat* to the poor; providing *imams* to visit Muslims who are sick in hospital or who are inmates in prison; offering educational facilities (see below) and instruction in Arabic and in community mother-tongue languages, as appropriate. In addition to this, many *mosques* are now registered for the solemnisation of marriages, and some *mosques* have installed morgues ensuring that Muslims can perform Islamic burial rites for their fellow Muslims.

Attendance at the *mosque* is not obligatory for Muslim women and, in practice, many *mosques* do not cater for their attendance. Muslim women are expected not to come to the *mosque* during their menstrual period. *Mosque* attendance by Muslim women can vary both according to the Muslim culture and tradition concerned, and the specific local *mosque*. In some cases women are discouraged from worshipping in *mosques* and are only expected to attend for cultural events and special occasions.

Where provision is made for women to pray at the same time as men they usually sit separately, for example in a room upstairs which is also considered as part of the *mosque*, although in some *mosques* women worship behind the men on the same floor.

Visitors to a Mosque

When visiting a mosque, clothing should be modest for both men and women. For women this means an ankle length skirt or trousers, which should not be tight or transparent, together with a long sleeved and high necked top. A headscarf is usually essential for women. Shoes are removed before going into the prayer hall and put on the racks provided. Clean and presentable socks, stockings, or tights are therefore a good idea.

Where women attend the *mosque*, men and women usually enter the prayer hall by separate entrances. Visitors may be greeted by the Arabic greeting *"Assalaam-u-'alaikum"*, which means "Peace be upon you." The answer, if the visitor would like to use it, is *"Wa 'alaikum-us-salaam"*, or "Peace be upon you too." Visitors should not offer, or expect, to shake hands with people of the opposite sex.

Before entering the prayer hall or prayer room in order to pray, Muslim men and women perform *wudu* or ablutions if they have not already done so earlier. This is not necessary for the non-Muslim visitor who will not be joining in the prayer.

On entering the prayer hall of the mosque, visitors should enter quietly and sit on the floor. If arriving when *salah* (Arabic) or *namaz* (Persian/Urdu), one of the five daily prayers is in progress, non-Muslim visitors are welcomed but simply to observe rather than to join in. At such a time, find a place near the rear or side walls and sit quietly observing the prayer. No sacred or blessed food will be offered, nor will visitors be expected to make any physical gesture of respect to holy objects (except removing their shoes and acting respectfully in the prayer hall).

MUSLIM CALENDAR AND FESTIVALS

Calendar

The Muslim calendar is a lunar one, with each year composed of twelve months and each month of twenty-nine or thirty days. As such, the Muslim year is eleven days shorter than a solar year. This means that festival dates move through the solar year and cannot be conclusively dated a long way in advance since they depend upon the sighting of the new moon for the start of a new month.

Al Hijrah

The first day of the Muslim year is the anniversary of the *Hijra* with which the

Muslim calendar begins. This marks the *Prophet* Muhammad's original migration from Makka to Madina which led to the creation of the Muslim community. The year 2007CE is therefore, according to the Muslim calendar, the year 1427/1428AH.

'Ashura

Is a *Shi'a* commemoration marking the martyrdom of *Imam* Husayn, the grandson of the *Prophet* Muhammad. This is the tenth day of the month of Muharram in the Islamic calendar. It is the occasion for "passion plays" and ritual mourning through which *Shi'as,* express their sense of identity with the suffering of Husayn's martyrdom. Some *Sunni* Muslims also celebrate this but for other reasons.

Milad al-Nabi

Is a celebration of the birthday of the *Prophet* on the twelfth day of Rabi' al-Awwal, the third month of the Muslim calendar. It is particularly important among *Barelwis* in view of their special veneration of the *Prophet.*

Lailat al-Baraat

Takes place fifteen days before *Ramadan* and celebrates the popular belief that on this night the fate of humankind is ordained for the next year.

Ramadan

Ramadan is the name of the ninth month (which is either twenty-nine or thirty days long) of the lunar year. During this time Muslims should abstain, from before dawn to sunset, from eating, drinking and sexual intercourse. These daylight abstentions are deemed by Muslims to reflect devotion to God as the person abstains for God alone. *Fasting* is also seen as increasing self-discipline and patience, decreasing selfishness and lending a sense of solidarity between Muslims and equality before God.

There are, however, some categories of people who can be exempt from the requirements of *fasting*. These include children who are below the age of puberty and people who are mentally unfit. They do not have to *fast* nor do they have to compensate in any way for missing the *fast*. People travelling long distances may temporarily break the *fast* but should make up for this by *fasting* at another time for each day they have missed. People whose health would be adversely affected by *fasting* may *fast* in compensation at another point in the year for an equivalent length of time.

Those who will not recover from the risk of ill health or are very old may offer a poor Muslim a meal or, if they can afford it, the financial equivalent for each day of *fasting* missed. Menstruating women, pregnant women, and women who are breast feeding, are also not bound to *fast*. However, they must make up for each day they do not fast by *fasting* at another point in the year.

Lailat al-Qadr (Night of Power)

This marks the time when it is believed that the *Qur'an* began its descent to earth and was first revealed to the *Prophet* Muhammad. It occurs as one of the odd numbered nights of *fasting* in the last third of the month of *Ramadan*. The *Shi'as* regard *Lailat al-Qadr* as being the twenty third night of *fasting* in *Ramadan*. *Sunnis* look for it in the last ten nights of *fasting*, especially on the odd-numbered nights. The night belongs to the day following it, rather than to the one preceeding it.

Eid al-Fitr

This a festival marking the breaking of the *Ramadan fast* which occurs on the first day of the following month, Shawwal. It is one of the major festivals in the Muslim calendar. Between one and two days leave from work is usually taken to participate in this festival. Presents are given and charitable donations are encouraged.

The festival emphasises unity and togetherness. An atmosphere of celebration is promoted, with gatherings held at *mosques* that often overflow outside. Special congregational prayer is offered in *mosques* after sunrise and enough money to pay for a meal for the poor is offered.

Eid al-Adha

This is the *Festival of Sacrifice* which is a three day festival that marks the end of the *Hajj* to Makka and occurs on the tenth day of the Dhu'l Hijjah month. It celebrates the supreme example of sacrifice and submission exhibited by Abraham and his son Ishmael. It is celebrated not just in Makka but throughout the Muslim world. In Muslim countries all Muslim families who can afford to do so sacrifice an animal as Abraham is believed to have done in substitution for his son, Ishmael. To mark the festival a third of this meat is then distributed to the poor, with the other two-thirds being shared out, or which one third goes to charity, one third to family and one third to friends. In the UK this slaughter is usually carried out centrally on behalf of the community rather than by individuals.

MUSLIM ORGANISATIONS

Organisational Listings

The CD-ROM that accompanies this volume includes contact details of national organisations that have head offices and branches throughout the country, as well as of other organisations that aspire to serve the Muslim community on a UK-wide level.

At local level, a variety of forms of Muslim regional and local organisation are listed in this directory. These include *mosques*, schools, welfare bodies and student societies. In some cases, on the accompanying CD-ROM there are separate entries at the same address where a welfare association owns a *mosque* but receives a separate entry because its objectives and activities are wider than the *mosque* activities alone.

There are also some entries that reflect where a number of organisations with a particular sectoral remit, such as women's or youth work, are based at the same address and are sometimes different parts of the same organisation.

Overall, the CD-ROM includes details of around 125 Muslim organisations that operate on a UK basis as well as around 2 that operate on a Welsh level. The directory also includes details of around 1,153 local Muslim organisations (of which around 1,074 are in England, 36 in Wales, and 43 in Scotland).

"Umbrella" Organisations

Over the past decade a number of organizations have attempted to provide a broad representative voice for Muslims of various traditions, movements and ethnic/national groups at a national level within the UK.

For a long time no single organisation established itself as a generally accepted and authoritative national council, although in recent times the development of the Muslim Council of Great Britain (MCB) has emerged as a body which has evidenced both organisational stability and broad representation, although more recently there have been questions about how broadly based this is.

The MCB was formally launched in 1997 following a number of years of preparatory consultation across the community and includes a wide range of Islamic organisations and *mosques* and it seeks to represent the Muslim community as a whole in its contact with Government, other public bodies, and the media.

There are a number of other federations and councils of Islamic organisations at both regional, local, national and European levels. Such bodies can often have a degree of overlap in terms of membership. At the European level there is the European Council of Fatwa and Research, which acts as a point of reference for many European Muslims.

Nationally, there is the Imams and Mosques Council; the Union of Muslim Organisations (established in 1970); the Muslim Parliament of Great Britain; the British Muslim Forum; the Shariah Council, which acts in relation to matters of Muslim family law; and then there is relatively newly emerged Sufi Muslim Council.

Regionally, "umbrella" bodies include the Lancashire Council of Mosques, the West Midlands Council of Mosques, and the Federation of Muslim Organisations in Leicestershire.

At city or county levels there are a number of Islamic federations and councils of mosques such the Bradford Council of Mosques, the Lancashire Council of Mosques and the Federation of Muslim Organisations in Leicestershire.

Movements

The composition of the Muslim population in the UK is varied and can be considered from a number of different perspectives including groupings with an ethnic/national component and movements within the two main traditions within Islam, the *Sunni* and the *Shi'a*.

Individual Muslims can identify themselves with one or more of these groupings at the same time. The *Barelwis*, *Deobandis* and *Tablighi Jamaat* are numerically the strongest of the Muslim movements in the UK and there is some overlap between them. The general background to the various Muslim movements has already been described in the earlier section on "Traditions in Islam".

Barelwi

This tendency is particularly numerous amongst communities with rural origins. Two national organisations linked to the *Barelwi* movement are the Jamaat Ahl-e-Sunnat and the World Islamic Mission.

Deobandi

In the UK, the *Deobandi* movement is found in many areas, but it is at its strongest in Lancashire, West Yorkshire and the Midlands. Two organisations with links to this movement are the Jamiat-e-Ulama of Britain and Dar-ul-Uloom seminary in Bury.

Tablighi Jamaat

The *Tablighi Jamaat* movement in the UK is centred in Dewsbury but is also very active elsewhere in West Yorkshire, Lancashire and the Midlands. Its organisations can also be found elsewhere in Britain. The movement is closely related to the *Deobandi* movement.

Ahl-e-Hadith

Within the UK this movement is mainly concentrated in Birmingham and London.

Jamaat-i-Islami

There are several organisations which have a relationship to the idealist, thinker and founder of *Jamaat-i-Islami*, Abul A'la Mawdudi (1903-1979). Such organisations include the UK Islamic Mission, which has several branches throughout the UK. The movement was originally found mainly amongst migrants from Pakistan. After the emergence of Bangladesh, Bengali Muslims established their own *Dawat-ul-Islam* movement in 1976. Later, the Islamic Forum of Europe was also formed by young Bangladeshis to serve the intellectual needs of Bangladeshi youth throughout Europe.

Sufi Orders

Sufi Orders have branches in most UK towns and cities with a substantial Muslim presence. There are also a number of *Sufi* centres associated with specific *Orders*. These *Orders* are generally *Sunni* rather than *Shi'a*. There are also a number of western *Sufi* organisations. Recently a British Sufi Muslim Council has been formed and has attracted some considerable profile and coverage in the media, as well as interest on the part of Government.

Other National Organisations

In addition to "umbrella" organisations and those that are related to particular movements within Islam, there a number of Muslim organisations were formed to campaign on specific concerns for the Muslims. For example, the UK Action Committee on Islamic Affairs was formed in 1988 in the wake of the controversy over Salman Rushdie's book, *The Satanic Verses*.

The Islamic Society of Britain was formed in 1990 with the aim of projecting Islam's image in the UK not as an "immigrant religion", but as a global tradition developing appropriate national traditions, priorities and policies to meet the challenges facing Islam and Muslims in the West.

Educational Organisations

There is a range of educational bodies which operate on a national level and serve a variety of functions. For example, there is the Muslim College in London, which trains *imams*; the Islamic Foundation in Leicester, which is an educational, research and training organisation founded in 1973 that produces literature and runs courses on Muslim belief and practice for non-Muslim professionals working in a multi-cultural context; the Muslim Community Studies Institute in Leicester, which carries out research and produces publications on Muslim life in both Muslim societies and Western Societies; the Muslim Education Co-ordinating Council UK in London, which monitors and advises on the teaching of Muslim children in local education authority schools; the Muslim Educational Trust, which caters for the educational needs of Muslim children; and the Islamic Academy in Cambridge, which is an educational research organisation.

Madrasas are *Qur'anic* schools which are local in nature and are usually attached to a *mosque* and many Muslim children attend them during the weekends or in the evening after day school. Both boys and girls (usually on separate evenings) attend such lessons where they read and learn sections of the *Qur'an* which in turn necessitates the learning of Arabic. They also learn the rituals and practices of Islam. There are also a few private Muslim day schools which provide a full time educational service for Muslim children. Three Muslim schools have been granted voluntary aided status.

Dawah Organisations

Dawah literally means invitation – the invitation to people to embrace Islam. There are a number of organised *da'wa* initiatives which aim to spread the message of Islam throughout the UK. Some are local independent organisations. Others are affiliates of national organisations such as the UK Islamic Mission, which has branches and affiliated *mosques* throughout the UK. Some *missionary* groups aim to spread the word of Islam to non-Muslims, whilst others focus on drawing back Muslims who have drifted away from their faith.

Youth Groups

Muslim youth organisations include local independent groups of Muslims and local groups affiliated to national organisations such as Young Muslims UK and the Federation of Student Islamic Societies (FOSIS), both of which organise workshops and "camps" for Muslim youth.

Radical Groups

In recent times radical groups such as Hizb ut-Tahrir and Al-Muhajiroun have been active in many institutions of higher education. In the wake of the September 11th attacks on the World Trade Centre and the Pentagon, and the 7/7 attacks on the London Transport System they attracted a substantial amount of media and other attention, disproportionate to their actual size and influence. At the same time, they represent a strand of thinking and organising among Muslims that Muslims who have a deep sense of injustice about the treatment of Muslims throughout the world.

Women's Groups

Muslim women's groups have begun to emerge in various localities, both to represent the experience and to address the needs of Muslim women. The Muslim women's organisation An-Nisa provides a service of this kind. Other Muslim women's groups are being established and developing at all levels, from local through to national. Muslim women's groups have often found successful ways of negotiating ?? and yet also postively through the ?? that can exist for observant Muslims in a non-Muslim society.

Community Groups

Local Muslim community groups are usually attached to the *mosque* and are also normally loosely related to particular Muslim movements, or are composed of a group with the same ethnic origins and languages, such as the various Pakistan Muslim Welfare Associations. They have a welfare and cultural role and may be eclectic with sub-groups for certain sectors of the Muslim population, for example youth groups and women's groups.

Media Organisations

Recent years have seen the development and establishment in the wider society of a range of Muslim media organisations, including Muslim News and Q-News, as well as other media outlets.

Political Organisations

On a national level in recent years some Muslims within the UK began to form explicitly political organisations, an example of which is the Islamic Party of Britain that was launched, in July 1989, by a group of mainly indigenous followers of Islam. Their declared aim was to work for a better future for Islam in the UK and for a radical change to economic injustice in society.

International Organisations

Several organisations with an international membership have a presence in the UK, such as the Muslim World League, which was established in Makka in 1962 and has an office, library and prayer hall in London.

Personnel

Individual *mosques* are usually controlled by *mosque* committees which generally include the offices of president and secretary. Committee membership elections are normally held annually. The *mosque* committee co-ordinates funding for the *mosque* and Muslim organisations connected with *mosques* and is also responsible for appointing an *imam*.

The *imam* is the leader of the prayers. *Imam* is an Arabic word meaning "the one who stands in front". In principle, this can be any Muslim who is most well versed in the *Qur'an* and the requisite knowledge necessary for communal prayers. There is no hierarchy of ordained clergy although the *imam* may act as a spokesperson for the community.

Although *imams* are now being trained in the UK, frequently they will have arrived in adulthood from an area of the world where the majority of the members of a *mosque* community have their ethnic origins, and may therefore only have a poor command of the English language. In these circumstances, the chairperson or secretary of the *mosque* Committee might more usually represent the community to the outside world.

Fuqaha are experts in Islamic law. *Pirs* or *shaykhs* are spiritual guides from the *Sufi* orders. *'Ulama* is a term denoting religious scholars in general.

FURTHER READING

Details follow of a number of general introductions to Islam together with books and articles that provide some focus on

Muslims and Muslim organisations in the UK. The references are not comprehensive, but provide signposts to a range of relevant materials.

Abbas, T (ed), *Muslim Britain: Communities Under Pressure*, Zed Books, London, 2005.

Abdalati, H, *Islam in Focus*, American Trust Publications, Indianapolis, 1975.

Abul-Fadl, M, *Introducing Islam from Within*, Islamic Foundation, Leicester, 1991.

Afkhami, M (ed), *Faith and Freedom: Women's Human Rights in the Muslim World*, IB Tauris, London, 1995.

Afshar, H, "Education: hopes, expectations and achievement of Muslim women in West Yorkshire", in *Gender and Education*, Volume 1, No 3, 1989, pp 261-271.

Afshar, H, "Schools and Muslim Girs: Gateway to a Prosperous Future or Quagmire of Racism", in R Barot (ed), *Religion and Ethnicity: Minorities and Social Change in the Metropolis*, Kok Pharos, Kampen, 1993, pp 56-67.

Ahmad, F, "Modern traditions? British Muslim women and academic achievement", *Gender and Education*, Volume 13, No 2, 2001, pp 137-152.

Ahmad, K, *Family Life in Islam*, Islamic Foundation, Leicester, 1981.

Ahsan, M, "Islam and Muslims in Britain", in H Mutalib and T Hashmi (eds), *Islam, Muslims and the Modern State*, Macmillan, Basingstoke, 1994, pp 339-361.

Ahsan, M and Kidwai, A (eds), *Sacrilege Versus Civility: Muslim Perspectives on The Satanic Verses Affair*, Islamic Foundation, Leicester, 1993 (revised and enlarged edition).

Alexander, C, "Re-imagining the Muslim community", in *Innovation*, Volume 11, No 4, 1998, pp 439-450.

Andrews, A, "Sociological Analysis of Jamaat-i-Islami in the United Kingdom", in R Barot (ed), *Religion and Ethnicity: Ethnic Minorities and Social Change in the Metropolis*, Kok Pharos, Kampen, The Netherlands, 1993, pp 68-79.

Andrews, A, "The concept of sect and denomination in Islam", in *Religion Today*, Volume 9, No 2, 1994, pp 6-12.

Andrews, A, "Muslim attitudes towards political activity in the United Kingdom: a case study of Leicester", in W Shadid and S Van Koningsveld (eds), *Political Participation and Identities of Muslims in Non-Muslim States*, Kok Pharos, Kampen, 1996, pp 115-28.

Ansari, H, *Muslims in Britain*, Minority Rights Group International, 2000.

Ansari, H, "Processes of Institutionalisation of Islam in England and Wales: 1830s-1930s", in J Malik (ed), *Muslim Minority Societies in Europe*, LIT Verlag, Münster, 2004, pp. 35-48.

Ansari, H, *The 'Infidel' Within: Muslims in Britain since 1880*, Hurst, London, 2004.

Ansari, H, "The Legal Status of Muslims in the UK", in R Aliuffi Beck-Pecoz and G Zincone (eds), *The Legal Treatment of Islamic Minorities in Europe*, Peeters, 2004, pp 255-287.

Antes, P, "Islam in Europe", in S Gill, G D'Costa and U King (eds), *Religion in Europe: Contemporary Perspectives*, Kok Pharos, Kampen, 1994, pp 46-67.

Anwar, M, *Muslims in Britain: 1991 Census and Other Statistical Sources*, Centre for the Study of Islam and Christian-Muslim Relations, Selly Oak Colleges, Birmingham, 1993.

Anwar, M, *Young Muslims in a Multicultural Society – Their Educational Needs and Policy Implications: The British Case*, The Islamic Foundation, Leicester, 1994.

Anwar, M, *Young Muslims in Britain: Attitudes, Educational Needs and Policy Implications*, Islamic Foundation, Leicester, 1994.

Anwar, M, "Muslims in Britain", in S Abedin and Z Sardar (eds), *Muslim Minorities in the West*, Grey Seal, London, 1995, pp 37–50.

Anwar, M and Bakhsh, Q, *British Muslims and State Policies*, University of Warwick, Centre for Research in Ethnic Relations, Coventry, 2003.

Awan, B A, "Islam", in Tiptaft, N, *Religion in Birmingham*, Norman Tiptaft Ltd, Warley, 1972.

Badawi, Z, *Islam in Britain*, Ta-Ha Publishers Ltd, London, 1981.

Barton, S W, *The Bengali Muslims of Bradford*, Community Religions Project, University of Leeds, Leeds, 1986.

Becher, H and Husain, F, *Supporting Minority Ethnic Families. South Asian Hindus and Muslims in Britain: Developments in family Support*, NFPI, London, 2003.

Boase, R, *Islam and Global Dialogue: Religious Pluralism and the Pursuit of Peace*, Ashgate, Aldershot, 2005.

Bowker, J, *Voices of Islam*, Oneworld, Oxford, 1995.

Bowker, J, *What Muslims Believe*, Oneworld, Oxford, 1998.

Bunting, M (ed), *Islam, Race and Being British*, Barrow Cadbury Trust, London, 2005.

Choudhary, T, "The situation of Muslims in the UK", in The Open Society Institute, *Monitoring the EU Accession Process: Minority Protection Volume II. Case Studies in Selected Member States*, Open Society Institute, Budapest, 2002, pp 361–447.

Choudhary, T (ed), *Muslims in the UK: Policies for Engaged Citizens*, Open Society Institute, Budapest, 2005.

Commission on British Muslims and Islamophobia, *Addressing the challenge of Islamophobia*, Commission on British Muslims and Islamophobia, London, 2001.

Coulson, N, *A History of Islamic Law*, Edinburgh University Press, Edinburgh, 1964.

Daftari, F, *The Ismailis: Their History and Doctrine*, Cambridge University Press, Cambridge, 1990.

Darsh, S M, *Muslims in Europe*, Ta-Ha Publishers, London, 1987.

Dean, H and Khan, Z, "Muslim perspectives on welfare", in *Journal of Social Policy*, Volume 26, No 2, 1997, pp 193–209.

Dwyer, P, *British Muslims, welfare citizenship and conditionality: some empirical findings*, 'Race' and Public Policy Research Unit, University of Leeds, Leeds, 2000.

Eade, J, "The Political Articulation of Community and The Islamisation of Space in London", in R Barot (ed), *Religion and Ethnicity: Minorities and Social Change in the Metropolis*, Kok Pharos, Kampen, 1993, pp 27–41.

Eade, J, "Nationalism, community and the Islamization of Space in London", in B Metcalf (ed), *Making Muslim Space in North America and Europe*, University of California Press, Berkley, 1996, pp 217–233.

Esak, F, *The Qur'an, Liberation and Religious Pluralism*, Oneworld, Oxford, 1997.

Esposito, J (ed), *The Oxford History of Islam*, Oxford University Press, Oxford, 1999.

Franks, M, "Crossing the borders of whiteness? White Muslim women who wear the *hijab* in Britain today", in *Ethnic and Racial Studies*, Volume 23, No 5, 2000, pp 917–929.

Gale, R, "The multicultural city and the politics of religious architecture: urban planning, mosques and meaning-making in Birmingham, UK", in *Built Environment*, Volume 30, No1, 2004, pp 18–32.

Gale, R, "Representing the city: mosques and the planning process in Birmingham, UK", in *Journal of Ethnic and Migration Studies,* Volume 31, No 6, 2005, pp 1161-1179.

Gardner, K, "Death, burial and bereavement amongst Bengali Muslims in Tower Hamlets, East London", in *Journal of Ethnic and Migration Studies,* Volume 24, No 3, 1998, pp 507-521.

Geaves, R, *Muslims in Leeds*, Community Religions Project, University of Leeds, Leeds, 1995.

Geaves, R, "The Reproduction of Jamaat-i-Islami in Britain", in *Journal for the Study of Islam and Christian-Muslim Relations*, Volume 6, No 2, 1995, pp 187-210.

Geaves, R, "Cult, charisma, community: the arrival of Sufi Pirs and their impact on Muslims in Britain", in *Journal for the Institute of Muslim Minority Affairs*, Volume 16, No 2, 1996, pp 169-192.

Geaves, R, *Sectarian Influences within Islam in Britain: with Reference to the Concepts of 'Ummah' and 'Community'*, Community Religions Project Monograph Series, Department of Theology and Religious Studies, University of Leeds, Leeds, 1996.

Geaves, R, *The Sufis of Britain*, Cardiff Academic Press, Cardiff, 2000.

Geaves, R, Gabriel, T, Haddad, Y, and Smith, J, *Islam and the West Post 9/11*, Ashgate, Aldershot, 2004.

Geaves, R, *Aspects of Islam*, Darton, Longman and Todd, London, 2005.

Geaves, R, "Negotiating British Citizenship and Muslim Identity post 9/11", in T Abbas (ed), *Muslim Britain: Communities Under Pressure*, Zed Books, London, 2005, pp 66-77.

Gilliat-Ray, "Muslim youth organisations in Britain: a descriptive analysis", in the *American Journal of Islamic Social Sciences*, No 14, March 1997, pp 99-111.

Gilliat-Ray, S, " 'No place called home': re-imagining Muslim identity and belonging", in *Muslim World Book Review,* Volume 22, No 4, 2003, pp 5-15.

Gilliat-Ray, S, "Closed worlds: (not) accessing Deobandi *dar-ul-uloom* in Britain", in *Fieldwork in Religion,* Volume 1, No 1, 2005, pp 7-33.

Glassé, C, *The Concise Encylopaedia of Islam*, Stacey International, London, (2nd edition), 1991.

Halliday, F, *Arabs in Exile: Yemeni Migrants in Urban Britain*, I B Tauris, London, 1995.

Halstead, J, "British Muslims and education", in T Choudhary (ed), *Muslims in the UK: Policies for Engaged Citizens*, Open Society Institute, Budapest, 2005, pp 101-91.

Hamzah, M and Harrison, M, *Islamic Housing Values and Perspectives: Insights from Influentials in Malaysia*, "Race" and Public Policy Research Unit, University of Leeds, Leeds, 2005.

Hebert, D, "Islam, Identity and Globalisation: Reflections in the Wake of 11 September 2001", in S Coleman and P Collins (eds), *Religion, Identity and Change: Perspectives on Global Transformations*, Ashgate, Aldershot, 2004, pp 154-173.

Henley, A, *Caring for Muslims and their Families: Religious Aspects of Care*, National Extension College, Cambridge, 1982.

Hodgins, H, "Planning permission for mosques – the Birmingham experience", *Research Papers – Muslims in Europe*, No 9, 1981, pp 11-27.

Housing Association, The, "Muslim housing experiences", in *Sector Study 34*, Housing Association, London, 2004.

Islamic Foundation, *Islam: The Essentials*, Islamic Foundation, Leicester, 1974.

Jacobsen, J, "Religion and ethnicity: dual alternative sources of identity among young British Pakistanis", in *Ethnic and Racial Studies,* Volume 20, No 2, 1997, pp 238-256.

Jacobsen, J, *Islam in Transition: Religion and Identity among British Pakistani Youth*, Routledge, London, 1998.

Joly, D, "Making a place for Islam in British Society: Muslims in Birmingham", in T Gerholm and Y Lithman (eds), *The New Islamic Presence in Western Europe*, Mansell, London, 1990, pp 32-52.

Joly, D, *Making a Place for Islam in British Society: Muslims in Birmingham*, Research Papers in Ethnic Relations 4, Centre for Research in Ethnic Relations, University of Warwick, Coventry, 1987.

Joly, D, *Britain's Crescent: Making a Place for Muslims in British Society*, Avebury, Aldershot, 1995.

Joly, D and Imtiaz, K, "Muslims and citizenship in the United Kingdom", in R Leveau, K Mohsen-Finan and C Wihtol de Wenden (eds), *New European Identity and Citizenship*, Ashgate, Aldershot, 2002, pp 117-131.

Joly, D and Nielsen, J, *Muslims in Britain: An Annotated Bibliography, 1960-1984*, Centre for Research in Ethnic Relations, University of Warwick, Coventry, 1985.

Kahani-Hopkins, V and Hopkins, N, "'Representing' British Muslims: the strategic dimension to identity construction", in *Ethnic and Racial Studies*, Volume 25, No 2, 2002, pp 288-309.

Kamal, Z and Lowewnthal, K, "Suicide beliefs and behaviour among young Muslims and Hindus in the UK", in *Mental Health, Religion and Culture*, Volume 5, No 2, 2002, pp 111-118.

Khan, Z, "Muslim presence in Europe: the British dimension - identity, integration and community activism", in *Current Sociology*, Volume 48, No 4, 2000, pp 29-43.

King, J, "Tablighi Jamaat and the Deobandi Mosques in Britain", in S Vertovec and C Peach (eds), *Islam in Europe: The Politics of Religion and Community*, Macmillan Press, Basingstoke, 1997, pp 129-146.

Lawless, R, *From Ta'iz to Tyneside: An Arab Community in the North-East of England During the Early Twentieth Century*, University of Exeter Press, Exeter, 1995.

Leaman, O, *A Brief Introduction to Islamic Philosophy*, Polity Press, Oxford, 1999.

Lemu, A and Heeren, F, *Women in Islam*, Islamic Foundation, Leicester, 1978.

Lewis, P, *Islamic Britain: Religion, Politics and Identity Among British Muslims*, I B Tauris, London, 1994.

Lewis, P, "Being Muslim and Being British: The Dynamics of Islamic Reconstruction in Bradford", in R Ballard (ed), *Desh Pardesh: The South Asian Presence in Britain*, Hurst and Co, London, 1994, pp 58-87.

Lewis, P, *The Function, Education and Influence of the Ulama in Bradford's Muslim Communities*, Community Religions Project Monograph Series, Department of Theology and Religious Studies, University of Leeds, Leeds, 1996.

Lewis, P, "The Bradford Council for Mosques and the Search for Muslim Unity", in S Vertovec and C Peach (eds), *Islam in Europe: The Politics of Religion and Community*, Macmillan Press, Basingstoke, 1997, pp 103-128.

Lings, M, *What is Sufism?*, Unwin Paperbacks, London, 1975.

Macey, M, "Religion, male violence, and the control of women: Pakistani Muslim men in Bradford, UK", in *Gender and Development*, Volume 7, No 1, 1999, pp 48-55.

Malik, J (ed), *Muslim Minority Societies in Europe*, LIT Verlag, Munster, 2004.

Matar, N, *Islam in Britain: 1558-1685*, Cambridge University Press, Cambridge, 1998.

McDermott, M Y and Ahsan, M M, *TheMuslim Guide: For Teachers, Employers, Community Workers and Social Administrators in Britain*, Islamic Foundation, Leicester, 1992 (revised edition).

Matthews, R, Tlemsani, I and Siddiqui, A, *Islamic finance*, Centre for International Business Policy, Kingston Business School, nd.

Mawdudi, A, *Towards Understanding Islam*, Islamic Foundation, Leicester, 1981.

Mehasi, A and Ujra, S, *Barriers to Employment for Muslim Women in the East Midlands*, SEDI Ltd, Manchester, 2006.

Metcalf, B, *Islamic Revival in British India: Deoband 1860-1900*, Princeton University Press, Princeton, 1982.

Modood, T, "British Asian Muslims and the Rushdie Affair", in *Political Quarterly*, No 61, 1990, pp 143-160.

Modood, T, "Muslim views on religious identity and racial equality," in *New Community*, Volume 19, No 3, 1993, pp 513-519.

Modood, T, "The Place of Muslims in British Secular Multiculturalism", in N Ghanea (ed), *The Challenge of Religious Discrimination at the Dawn of the New Millennium*, Martinus Nijhoff Publishers, Leiden, 2003, pp 223-243.

Modood, T, "British Muslims and the politics of multi-culturalism", in T Modood A Traiandafyllidou and R Zapata-Barrero (eds), *Multiculturalism, Muslims and Citizenship: A European Approach*, Routledge, Abingdon, 2006, pp 37-56.

Momen, M, *An Introduction to Shi'i Islam*, Yale University Press, Yale, 1985.

Muslim Council of Britain, *Muslims and Housing*, Muslim Council of Britain, London, nd.

Naqshbandi, M, *Islam and Muslims in Britain: A Guide for Non-Muslims*, City of London Police, London, nd.

Nasr, S H, *Ideals and Realities of Islam*, George Allen and Unwin, London, 1966.

Nasr, S H, *Living Sufism*, Unwin Paperbacks, London, 1980.

Nasr, S H and Leaman, O (eds), *The History of Islamic Philosophy*, Routledge, London, 1995.

Naylor, S and Ryan, J, "The mosque in the suburbs: renegotiating religion and ethnicity in South London", in *Social and Cultural Geography*, Volume 3, 2002, pp 39-59.

Netton, I, *Sufi Ritual: The Parallel Universe*, Curzon Press, Richmond, 2000.

Netton, I (ed), *Encyclopaedia of Islamic Civilisation and Religion*, Routledge, London, 2007.

Nielsen, J, *A Survey of British Local Authority Response to Muslim Needs*, Research Papers on Muslims in Europe, No. 30/31, June/September, 1986.

Nielsen, J, "Muslims in Britain: searching for an identity", in *New Community*, Volume 13, No 3, Spring 1987, pp 384-394.

Nielsen, J, *Muslims in Western Europe*, Edinburgh University Press, Edinburgh, 1995 (2nd edition).

Nielsen, J, "Muslims in Britain: Ethnic Minorities, Community or Ummah?", in H Coward, J Hinnells and R Williams (eds), *The South Asian Religious Diaspora in Britain, Canada and the United States*, State University of New York Press, New York, 2000, pp 109-125.

Padwick, C, *Muslim Devotions*, SPCK, London, 1961.

Parker-Jenkins, M, *Children of Islam: Teacher's Guide to Meeting the Needs of Muslim Pupils*, Trentham Books, Stoke-on-Trent, 1995.

Peach, C, "The Muslim population of Great Britain", in *Ethnic and Racial Studies*, Volume 13, No 3, 1990, pp 415-419.

Peach, C and Glebe, G, "Muslim minorities in western Europe", in *Racial and Ethnic Studies*, Volume 18, 1995, pp 26-45.

Peach, C, "Britain's Muslim Population: an Overview", in T Abbas (ed), *Muslim Britain: Communities Under Pressure*, Zed Books, London, 2005, pp 18-30.

Peach, C, "Muslims in the 2001 census of England and Wales: gender and economic disadvantage", in *Ethnic and Racial Studies*, Volume 29, No 4, July 2006, pp 629-655.

Purdam, K, "Settler political participation: Muslim local councillors", in W Shadid and S Van Koningsveld (eds), *Political Participation and Identities of Muslims in Non-Muslim States*, Kok Pharos, Kampen, 1996, pp 129-143.

Purdam, K, "The political identities of Muslim local councillors in Britain", in *Local Government Studies*, Volume 26, No 1, 2000, pp 47-64.

Purdam, K, "Democracy in practice: Muslims and the Labour Party at the local level", in *Politics*, Volume 21, No 3, 2001, pp 147-157.

Rahman, F, *Islam*, University of Chicago Press, Chicago (2nd edition), 1979.

Rahman, T, *A Code of Muslim Personal Law*, Volumes I & II, Islamic Publishers, Karachi, 1978 and 1980.

Ramadan, T, *Islam, the West and Challenges of Modernity*, Islamic Foundation, Leicester, 2001.

Ramadan, T, *Western Muslims and the Future of Islam*, Oxford University Press, Oxford, 2004.

Raza, M S, *Islam in Britain: Past Present and Future*, Volcano Press Ltd, Leicester (2nd edition), 1992.

Rex, J, "The Urban Sociology of Religion and Islam in Birmingham", in T Gerholm and Y Lithman (eds), *The New Islamic Presence in Western Europe*, Mansell, London, 1990, pp 206-218.

Rex, J, "The Integration of Muslim Immigrants in Britain", in *Innovation*, Volume 5, No. 3, 1992, pp 65-74.

Robinson, F, *Varieties of South Asian Islam*, Research Paper No.8, Centre for Research in Ethnic Relations, University of Warwick, Coventry, 1988.

Runnymede Trust, The, *Islamophobia: A Challenge for Us All*, Runnymede Trust, London, 1997.

Runnymede Trust, The, *Islamophobia: Issues, Challenges and Action*, Trentham Books, Stoke-on-Trent, 2004.

Saeed, A and Saaed, H, *Freedom of Religion, Apostasy and Islam*, Ashgate, Aldershot, 2004.

Said, A and Sharify-Funk (eds), *Cultural Diversity and Islam*, University Press of America, Oxford, 2003.

Samad, Y, "Book burning and race relations: political mobilisation of Bradford Muslims", in *New Community*, Volume 18, No 4, 1992, pp 507-519.

Sanyal, U, *Devotional Islam and Politics in British India: Ahmad Riza Khan Barelwi and His Movement, 1870-1920*, Oxford University Press, Bombay, 1996.

Scantlebury, E, "Muslims in Manchester: the depiction of a religious community", in *New Community*, Volume 21, No 3, 1995, pp 425-435.

Schimmel, A, *Islamic Names*, Edinburgh University Press, Edinburgh, 1989.

Schnapper, D, "Conclusion: Muslim Communities, Ethnic Minorities and Citizens", in B Lewis and D Schnapper (eds), *Muslims in Europe*, Pinter, London, 1994, pp 148-160.

Sellick, P, *Muslim Housing Experiences*, Oxford Centre for Islamic Studies, Oxford, 2004.

Sharif, R, *Interviews with Young Muslim Women of Pakistani Origin*, Research Papers, Muslims in Europe, No. 27, 1985.

Shaykh Haeri, F, *The Elements of Sufism*, Element Books, Dorset, 1990.

Siddiqui, A, "Muslim Youth in Britain: Cultural and Religious Conflict in Perspective", in J Malik (ed), *Muslim Minority Societies in Europe*, LIT Verlag, Münster, 2004, pp 49-59.

Spalek, B, "British Muslims and the criminal justice system", in T Choudhary (ed), *Muslims in the UK: Policies for Engaged Citizens*, Open Society Institute, Budapest, 2005, pp 253-326.

Trimingham, J S, *The Sufi Orders in Islam*, Oxford University Press, Oxford, 1971.

UK Action Committee on Islamic Affairs, *Need for Reform: Muslims and the Law in Multi-Faith Britain*, UK Action Committee on Islamic Affairs, London, 1993.

Vertovec, S, *Annotated Bibliography of Academic Publications Regarding Islam and Muslims in the United Kingdom, 1985-1992*, Centre for Research in Ethnic Relations, University of Warwick, Coventry, 1993.

Vertovec, S, *Local Contexts and the Development of Muslim Communities in Britain: Observations in Keighley, West Yorkshire*, University of Warwick Centre for Research in Ethnic Relations, Coventry, nd.

Vertovec, S and Peach, C (eds), *Islam in Europe: The Politics of Religion and Community*, Macmillan Press, Basingstoke, 1997.

Wahab, I, *Muslims in Britain: Profile of a Community*, The Runnymede Trust, London, 1989.

Weller, P with Feldman, A and Purdam, K, "Muslims and Religious Discrimination in England and Wales", in J Malik (ed), *Muslim Minority Societies in Europe*, LIT Verlag, Münster, 2004, pp 115-144.

Werbner, P, "Islamic Radicalism and the Gulf War: Lay Preachers and Political Dissent Among British Pakistanis", in B Lewis and D Schnapper (eds), *Muslims in Europe*, Pinter, London, 1994, pp 98-115.

Werbner, P, "Divided loyalties? Empowered citizenship? Muslims in Britain", in *Citizenship Studies*, Volume 4, No. 3, 2000, pp 307-324.

Werbner, P, "Sufi Cults, Intimate Relations and National Pakistani Networking in Britain", in J Malik (ed), *Muslim Minority Societies in Europe*, LIT Verlag, Münster, 2004, pp 227-246.

Werbner, P., "Theorising complex diasporas: purity and hybridity in the South Asian public sphere in Britain", in *Journal of Ethnic and Migration Studies*, Volume 30, No 5, 2004, pp 895-911.

Werbner, P, "Islamophobia. Incitement to religious hatred – legislating for a new fear?", in *Anthropology Today*, Volume 21, No1, 2005, pp 5-9.

Wilson, R, "Islamic finance and ethical investment", in *International Journal of Social Economics*, Volume 24, No 11, 1997, pp 1325-1342.

Wolffe, J, "Fragmented Universality: Islam and Muslims", in G Parsons (ed), *The Growth of Religious Diversity: Britain from 1945, Volume 1: Traditions*, Routledge, London, 1993, pp 133-172.

Yawar, T, *Caring About Faith: Muslim Children and Young Persons in Care*, Islamic Foundation, Leicester, 1992.

Yip, A, "Negotiating space with family and kin in identity construction: the narratives of British non-heterosexual Muslims", in *The Sociological Review*, Volume 52, No 3, 2004, pp 336-350.

Zokaei, S and Phillips, D, "Altruism and intergenerational relations among Muslims in Britain", in *Current Sociology*, Volume 48, No 4, 2000, pp 45-58.

INTRODUCING SIKHS IN THE UK

SIKHS IN THE UK 247

ORIGINS AND DEVELOPMENT OF SIKHISM 248

SOURCES OF SIKH BELIEFS AND PRACTICES 249

KEY SIKH BELIEFS 250

TRADITIONS IN SIKHISM 252

SIKH LIFE 252

SIKH WORSHIP 256

SIKH PLACES OF WORSHIP 256

SIKH CALENDAR AND FESTIVALS 258

SIKH ORGANISATIONS 259

FURTHER READING 261

SIKHS IN THE UK

History in the UK

Over 80% of the world's Sikhs live in the Punjab, in the Indian subcontinent, but the Sikh population in the UK is the largest outside the Indian subcontinent. The older Punjab Province was partitioned in 1947 with the end of British rule in the sub-continent, when West Punjab became part of Pakistan and East Punjab part of India. Most Sikhs living in the UK are of Punjabi ethnic origin.

A fifteen year old Sikh prince, called Dalip Singh, the son of Maharaja Ranjit Singh, arrived in the UK as an exile in 1854 and was possibly one of the first Sikhs to reside here. He acquired the Elveden Estate in Norfolk and this place is now frequently visited by Sikhs marking their early connections with the UK.

Many Sikhs served in the British Indian armies in the First and Second World Wars and a number of ex-servicemen migrated to Britain, particularly after the Second World War. Although a number of Sikhs, mainly from the Bhatra (see below) community, settled in the UK between the 1920s and the 1940s, the vast majority of Sikh migrants arrived in the 1950s and 1960s.

Many Sikhs came directly to the UK from the Punjab, although a significant minority came from East Africa and other former British colonies to which members of their families had initially migrated.

Global and UK Populations

Worldwide, there are an estimated 24,000,000 Sikhs. The 2001 decennial Census questions on religion yielded 336,149 (or 0.6% of the total UK population) Sikh respondents. This is 0.7% of the population that identifies itself with any specific religion at all. Of these 336,149, a total of 327,343 were in England, 2,015 in

Wales, 6,572 in Scotland, and 219 in Northern Ireland.

As a proportion of the population in local authority areas, the 2001 Census shows that, in England, the greatest concentration of respondents identifying themselves as Sikhs is to be found in the London Boroughs of Slough (9.1%), Hounslow (8.6%) and in Ealing (8.5%); Wolverhampton (7.6%) and in Sandwell (6.9%).

Ethnicity in England and Wales

According to responses to the 2001 decennial census, 96.2% of the Sikh population of England and Wales gave their ethnicity as "Asian"; 2.1% as "White"; 0.8% as "Mixed"; 0.7% as "Chinese or Other Ethnic Group"; and 0.2% as "Black". Considered in terms of the ethnicity of respondents, 13.9% of all those recorded as "Asian" also identified as Sikh, along with 0.5% of "Chinese and Other Ethic Group", 0.4% of "Mixed", 0.1% of "Black or Black British", and 0.01% of those recorded as "White".

A very few Sikhs in the UK are converts, but conversion to the Sikh religion is not common since Sikhism does not aim to convert. Thus most Sikhs in the UK are of Punjabi background and speak Punjabi and English, with almost all *Gurdwaras* running Punjabi classes. *Gurmukhi* is the script of the Sikh Scriptures, which is also used for writing the modern Punjabi language.

Punjabi is held in great esteem and respect by Sikhs who have gone to great efforts to transmit it to second and third generation children. Punjabi, Urdu and Hindi are closely related.

ORIGINS AND DEVELOPMENT OF SIKHISM

The Ten Gurus

Sikhs understand the Sikh *dharam* (the Sikh way of life) or *Gurmat* to be an original, revealed religion. Some Sikhs may prefer the name of *Sikhi* to that of Sikhism, a term coined by non-Sikh Europeans.

Sikhism is based upon the teachings of the ten *Gurus* of Sikhism. The first *Guru*, honoured as founder of the faith, was *Guru* Nanak Dev (1469-1539). He was born in the Punjab at a place called Talwandi, renamed *Nankana Sahib* in his honour, and is now in Pakistan.

Sikhs believe that *Guru* Nanak Dev was born in an enlightened state. The *Janam Sakhis* (see below), accounts of his early life, illustrate that not only was he a precocious child, but that he also possessed divine charisma. When he was about thirty years old, he received the call to preach God's *Word* and over the next twenty-two years undertook four great journeys called *Udasis*.

Guru Nanak believed to have travelled extensively within and beyond the Indian subcontinent, as far as Assam in the east, Sri Lanka in the south, and the Middle East in the west, including Baghdad and the Muslim holy places of Makka and Madina.

His poetic compositions emphasise the oneness of God and the need to remain inwardly focused on God while fully involved in family life and in service to others. He taught that the worship of God, in whatever tradition one practised it, should be sincere and honest and not clouded by hypocrisy or ritualism. He eventually settled at Kartarpur in the Punjab and founded a community who became known as Sikhs (meaning *disciples*, or learners).

Guru Nanak Dev was succeeded by nine other *Gurus*: *Guru* Angad Dev (1504-1552); *Guru* Amar Das (1479-1574); *Guru* Ram Das (1534-1581); *Guru* Arjan Dev (1563-1606); *Guru* Hargobind (1595-1644); *Guru* Har Rai (1631-1661); *Guru* Har Krishan (1656-1664); *Guru* Tegh Bahadur (1621-1675); and *Guru* Gobind Singh (1666-1708). Sikhs believe that the *Gurus* who conveyed God's *Word* were all spiritually one.

In an Indian context, the word *guru* usually refers to a spiritual leader. But among the Sikhs, when applied to their ten *Gurus*, its significance is much greater. The Sikh *Gurus* are seen as special messengers of God and as exemplars who conveyed God's *Word*. They are not, however, objects of worship since the *Word* they convey is itself the *Guru*.

After the line of the ten *Gurus*, Sikhism acknowledges no more human *Gurus*. The tenth *Guru*, Guru Gobind Singh, vested spiritual authority in the *Guru Granth Sahib* (the Sikh sacred scripture) and temporal authority in the *Khalsa Panth*. Henceforth, the living *Guru*, the *Guru Granth Sahib*, was to be the eternal *Guru* embodying the Divine Word.

In 1699, Guru Gobind Singh instituted *Amrit Pahul* (see below) for both men and women, and in doing so completed the spiritual and temporal structure of the Sikh faith in the form of the *Khalsa Panth* (see also the section on "the Namdhari Sikhs" in the chapter on "Some Other Religious Traditions and Groups").

18th and 19th Century History of Sikhism

Sikhism has distinctive religious beliefs and institutions together with its own language, literature, tradition and conventions. During the eighteenth and nineteenth centuries, Sikhs faced considerable persecution in the Mughal Empire. However, in 1799 a forty year period of Sikh sovereignty in the Punjab began under Maharaja Ranjit Singh until the advent of the British Raj.

The Sikh *Gurus* founded several towns including Amritsar. The *Darbar Sahib* (known also as *Harmindir Sahib*, and among non-Sikhs as the *Golden Temple*) was developed by *Guru* Arjan Dev who installed the *Guru Granth Sahib* at its centre. *Guru* Hargobind built the *Akal Takhat* (Seat of the Immortal) in front of the *Darbar Sahib*, declaring it to be the seat of temporal authority. The Sikh sovereign,

Maharaja Ranjit Singh, who was generous in his donations to all faiths, also donated gold and other precious gifts to the *Darbar Sahib*, notably covering the exterior of the upper storey with gilded copper panels.

SOURCES OF SIKH BELIEFS AND PRACTICES

The Guru Granth Sahib

Sikhs believe that God has revealed himself continuously since before the advent of the ten *Gurus* and since their departure continues to do so by means of the scriptures. The *Guru Granth Sahib* is the supreme spiritual authority of the Sikhs. Revered as a living *Guru*, the scriptures are treated with great devotion and respect.

In academic usage, the *Guru Granth Sahib* is often called *Adi Granth*. *Adi Granth* is also the name of an earlier version of the present scriptures, compiled by *Guru* Arjan Dev and installed by him at Amritsar in 1604. *Ad* or *adi* means "first", in importance, and *Granth* means volume.

This original manuscript version of the *Adi Granth* is often referred to as the *Kartarpuri Bir* (*Bir* meaning "version"), after the place name of Kartarpur in the Punjab where it is kept. In this manuscript version there are 5551 *shabads* (hymns) set to 30 *rags* (musical compositions) laid out over 975 pages.

The *Adi Granth* contains the teaching of the first five *Gurus* and the Bhagat Bani, consisting of verses from Hindu and Muslim *saints* that were found to be compatible with the *Gurus'* teachings. Their inclusion was intended to underline the insight that divine truth could be perceived by anyone from any nation, creed or caste.

In 1706, at Damdama Sahib, *Guru* Gobind Singh added Guru Tegh Bahadur's *shabads*. In 1708, Guru Gobind Singh bestowed the status of *Guru* upon this *Damdama Bir*. The current *canonical* version of the *Guru Granth*

Sahib in its standard modern print version now contains 5817 *shabads* set to 31 *rags*, in 1430 pages.

The *Guru Granth Sahib* is written in the *Gurmukhi* (meaning, "from the mouth of the *Guru*") script that was newly created by the *Gurus* in order to record the compositions, while also including verses in Punjabi, Urdu, Persian or one of the many regional dialects. In doing this, the *Gurus* were intending to make the *Word of God* more accessible at a time when the ability to read sacred texts was often reserved to a priestly grouping.

Dasam Granth

The *Dasam Granth* contains some writings of *Guru* Gobind Singh, together with the work of some other poets. Both the *Guru Granth Sahib* and the *Dasam Granth* are written in the *Gurmukhi* script.

Rahit Nama

The *Rahit Nama* (*Code of Discipline*) consists of a set of principles according to which a Sikh's way of life should be conducted. They cover spiritual, moral and social discipline, and are reputed to be based on the injunctions of *Guru* Gobind Singh and compiled by various Sikh theologians from the late seventeenth to the late nineteenth century. However, the *Gurbani* (teaching of the *Gurus* - see further below) provides the fundamental guidelines and takes precedence in interpreting and following the *Rahit Nama*.

Rahit Maryada

Rahit Maryada is the *Sikh Code of Conduct* that is published by the Shiromani Gurdwara Parbandhak Committee (SGPC) in Amritsar, established in 1920 in the wake of the Gurdwara Reform Movement. Amongst the responsibilities of the SGPC are the organisation and administration (in accordance with Sikh tenets) of a large number of *Gurdwaras* in the Punjab, as well as hospitals and educational institutions. The

Sikh Code of Conduct was first drawn up in 1936, but was formally approved and adopted with some amendments in 1945.

Works of Bhai Gurdas and Bhai Nandlal

Although they do not have the same status as the *Guru Granth Sahib*, expositions by *Bhai* Gurdas and *Bhai* Nandlal are also highly regarded and are approved for reading and discourse in *Gurdwaras*.

Bhai Gurdas (1551-1637CE) was a Sikh scholar and theologian of distinction to whom the fifth *Guru*, Arjan Dev, dictated the *Adi Granth* when it was first compiled. His own thirty-nine *vars* (theological and historical expositions in verse form) were held in very high esteem by the fifth *Guru* who declared that these writings would be a key to the proper understanding of the *Guru Granth Sahib*. Bhai Nandlal (1633-1713) was an eminent scholar and poet who worked in the Mughal administration. He was a follower of *Guru* Gobind Singh and his writings, which were largely in the Persian language, were on Sikh philosophy.

KEY SIKH BELIEFS

Definitions

In the Guru *Granth Sahib*, it is said that one who calls himself a Sikh of the *Guru*, the *True Guru*, will rise in the early hours, bathe in the pool of Nectar, and meditate on the Lord's Name.

In the *Rahit Maryada* (see above) a Sikh is defined as one who believes in *Akal Purakh* (the one immortal God), the ten *Gurus*, the *Guru Granth Sahib* and the *Gurbani* (the teaching of the ten *Gurus* considered as a unity and incorporated in the *Guru Granth Sahib*).

The *Gurbani* is also known as *Gurshabad* (or word of the *Guru*) and is believed by Sikhs to be divine guidance.

A Sikh also believes in the *Amrit Pahul* (the Sikh form of initiation) of the tenth *Guru* and adheres to no other religion.

God

Sikhs are strictly *monotheistic* (believing in only One God). This One God is known among Sikhs by many names including Ram, Mohan, Gobind, Hari, Nirankar, and others. However, the two names traditionally used in worship, and these especially in *Nam Japna* (the recitation of God's name), are *Satnam* (*sat* meaning "true", "real" or "existential" and *nam* meaning "name" or "radiance of the Reality") and *Waheguru* (translated as "Wonderful Lord").

Sikhs believe that God is *nirgun* (transcendent) and also *sargun* (immanent) but that God never becomes incarnate. It is believed that God can be experienced but is beyond human comprehension. The *Mul Mantar*, the opening verse of the *Guru Granth Sahib* and the first prayer that Sikhs learn. It starts with the *Ik Onkar* that describes the attributes of God: "There is but One God, the Eternal Truth, the Creator, without fear, without enmity, timeless, immanent, beyond birth and death, self-existent: by the grace of the *Guru*, made known."

Sikhs believe that creation evolved slowly as a result of the creative will of God, developing from lower to higher forms of life: that from air came water, from water came the lower forms of life, leading to plants, birds and animals and culminating in humans as the supreme form of created life on earth. And the human form of life is believed by Sikhs to be the only opportunity one has for meeting becoming one with the Lord.

Goal of Life

Guru Nanak Dev taught that everything that exists or happens ultimately does so within God's will and that nothing exists or occurs outside of it. This concept of the divine order or will is known as *hukam*. The purpose of a human life, which is seen as the highest form of life on earth, is understood as being to seek its creator and to find union with God.

Since human beings are conscious of their actions and the consequences of them, a human life is therefore the time when the cycle of birth and death can potentially be broken. The *karam* (actions and their consequences) of this life partly determine whether a person will achieve union with God. Failure to do so leads to the cycle of *rebirth* that may include other forms of life than human. Liberation from rebirth is known as *mukti*.

Barriers to the liberation of the soul are believed to include *maya* which is seen as an illusory, materialistic view of the world, producing ignorance of one's own true nature and destiny and of God's will.

This results in *haumai* (self-centredness), giving rise to *kam* (lust), *karodh* (anger), *lobh* (greed), *moh* (worldly attachment/obsessions) and *hankar* (pride), all of which block union with God. One must therefore overcome these barriers, developing instead *santokh* (contentment), *dan* (charity), *daya* (kindness), *parsanta* (happiness) and *nimarta* (humility).

The path to union with God is seen as having five aspects: *Dharam Khand* (the region of realising one's social and spiritual duty), *Gian Khand* (region of divine knowledge), *Saram Khand* (region of wisdom and effort), *Karam Khand* (region of divine grace) and *Sach Khand* (region of truth or existential reality).

Khalsa Panth

Sikhs believe in the collective identity of the *Khalsa Panth* (the community of initiated Sikhs) as a society of equals irrespective of their background. Any person, male or female, who is a member of the *Khalsa*, has to strive to become a saint/soldier/guardian, dedicated to selfless service and self-sacrifice for the good of others.

The first five people to be initiated to the *Khalsa Panth* are known as the *Panj Pyare* (the five beloved ones). These five, from a variety of caste-groups, volunteered from the crowd of around 80,000 Sikhs who had been summoned by *Guru* Gobind Singh to Anandpur Sahib on 30th March 1699 when the *Guru* asked who would be prepared to die for their faith.

Prior to their initiation, the *Panj Pyare* had the original names of Daya Ram, Dharam Das, Mohkam Chand, Himmat Rai, and Sahib Chand. They were all given the name *Singh* as a substitute for their original caste names, in order to signify that Sikhism recognises no castes. *Guru* Gobind Singh knelt before the *Panj Pare* and requested them to give the *Amrit Pahul* to him thus emphasising the importance of the *Khalsa Panth*.

TRADITIONS IN SIKHISM

Unity and Diversity

Sikhs do not acknowledge internal groupings on the basis of doctrinal schools. Organisations do, however, exist within the *Panth* to cater for various interests or to reflect particular aspects of Sikh life. An example is that of the Sewa Panthis, a group devoted to the service of humanity founded in memory of Bhai Kanhaya. He was a Sikh who cared for the wounded without any discrimination whether they were the "enemies" or Sikh soldiers, and was highly praised for this by *Guru* Gobind Singh. When, in reply to a question, he stated that he saw no distinction between friend and foe but saw the *Guru* residing in all, the *Guru* warmly embraced him.

There are also groups whose origins can be found in the revivalist movements that have developed throughout Sikh history. These have generally been founded by Sikh individuals who are often given the honorific titles of *Sant*, *Bhai* or *Baba* on the basis of

their reputation for spiritual guidance and teaching. They are expounders of the *Gurbani* and may hold significant influence within particular *Gurdwaras* or Sikh organisations.

SIKH LIFE

Basic Orientations

Sikhs approach life with an attitude of *bhana manana* (accepting God's will). This is based on a conviction about the grace of God pervading the whole of life. It is not to be confused with fatalism, since Sikhism enjoins a very active spirituality embodied in the ideal of the Sikh as the "saint-soldier" working for the betterment of society as a whole, within the framework of a positive and constructive attitude of mind (*charhdi kala*), informed by prayerfulness.

Sikh Ethics

Sikhs believe that God should always be remembered in the course of everyday life. *Guru* Nanak Dev advocated that truth is above everything but that, while truth is high, truthful living is higher still than truth.

In Sikhism, men and women are encouraged to lead a truthful life of spiritual commitment amidst the day-to-day responsibilities of family and community life. There are certain ethical principles that are intrinsic to Sikh belief and practice. Foremost amongst these are: *nam japna* (reciting the name), *kirat karna* (earning a living by honest and approved means) and *vand chhakna* (sharing with the needy). Each of these are forms of *sewa* (service) to God.

Nam Japna

Nam Japna involves meditating on God and his attributes, reading and contemplating *bani* (passages) from the *Guru Granth Sahib*. It is said by Sikhs to result in being *gurmukh* (God-filled and God-centred) as opposed to being *manmukh* (self-centred). *Nam Japna* can be an individual or a group activity. In congregational worship it may be facilitated by *kirtan*, the singing of hymns from the *Guru Granth Sahib*. Although prayers can be said either individually or as a family, *sadh sangat* (congregational worship) is very important to Sikhs since it is believed that being in the company of enlightened souls helps purify one's own soul.

Kirat Kana (honest earnings)

Kirat Kana is based in the conviction that it is honestly earned money that helps families to flourish. This contrasts with financial dependency or wealth gained through corruption.

Vand Chhakna (sharing)

Sikhs also believe that sharing honestly earned money with the needy is a duty. It is recommended to share a tenth of one's income and all *Gurdwaras* are supported by the voluntary donations of devotees, including support for the *Langar*. Sikhs are required to donate *daswandh* (a tenth) of their wealth and time good causes and to carry out *Nishkam Sewa*.

Sewa (service)

A central Sikh teaching is about the importance of voluntary service to humankind being also service to God. Such service can include physical tasks like the preparation of food and cleaning in the *Langar*; monetary donations; professional services offered freely; and all other helpful activities that are offered without expectation of reward or recognition.

Equality

The concept of equality was of central importance to *Guru* Nanak Dev. He taught that all people are born with the opportunity to attain *mukti*, regardless of *caste* or creed and of whether they are rich or poor, male or female, educated or uneducated. What influences *mukti* is the *karam*, *maya* and *haumai* of individuals and the grace of the *Guru* in overcoming *haumai* and *maya*. The ten Sikh *Gurus* did not believe in any *caste* or professional distinctions and taught that every person is equal before God.

The Sikh concept of equality embraces women as well as men in all areas of life and was enjoined in the teachings and practices of the *Gurus* who exalted the status of women. Thus women have played a significant role in Sikhism. For instance at the first *Amrit Pahul* ceremony in Anandpur in 1699 in which *Guru* Gobind Singh's wife added sugar to the water.

Both women and men can be fully initiated into the Sikh religion and can act as a *granthi* (see section below) in a *Gurdwara*. Guru Nanak and the *Gurus* who followed him lifted up the status of women at a time when they were often considered to be an impediment to spiritual progress. However, in practice social and cultural conventions may influence gender roles.

Amrit Pahul

Amrit Pahul is the Sikh name for initiation into the *Khalsa Panth*. Amrit (the nectar of everlasting life or immortality) refers to the sweetened water used in *Amrit Pahul*. When coupled with adherence to the ethical principles of Sikhism this initiation is seen as the way to spiritual development and hence to the realisation of God's *grace*. The ceremony is for women as well as men and should take place at an age when the person can understand its significance.

The ceremony is called *Khande di Pahul* and commonly referred to as the *amrit sanchaar*. It can take place anywhere, providing that it is held in the presence of the *Guru Granth Sahib* and that five members of the *Khalsa Panth*, who have themselves been initiated by receipt of *amrit* are present. For this purpose, they constitute the *Panj Pyare*, are present to officiate. The ceremony follows the same practice as the original *amrit* ceremony carried out by *Guru* Gobind Singh in 1699.

Amrit is prepared by adding sugar sweets (*patasaer*) to water in an iron or steel bowl and stirring with a *khanda* (double-edged sword) while reciting five prayers: the *Japji*, *Jaap*, the ten *Swayas*, *Chaupai* and the *Anand*. The initiate is also inducted into the Sikh code of discipline, takes the vows of the *Khalsa* and is then offered *amrit* to drink and has some of it sprinkled five times onto the eyes and hair.

The receiving of *amrit* is an expression of commitment as a Sikh and a Sikh who has received *amrit* is known as an *Amritdhari* and becomes a member of the *Khalsa*, the community of initiated Sikhs.

Those who have not yet received *amrit* and who do not wear the long hair and other outward symbols of Sikhism are sometimes referred to as *Sahajdhari* (literally meaning "slow adopters"). They include those who believe in Sikhism but have deferred the commitment involved in taking *amrit* and those who have lapsed and would need to take *amrit* again if they were to return to the status of an *Amritdhari*.

The term *Keshdhari* is often used for those male Sikhs who keep a beard, uncut hair and turban whether or not they have taken *amrit*.

Panj Kakaars (Five Ks)

Many Sikhs expect to be initiated at some stage in their life. Belonging to the *Khalsa* involves taking *amrit* and wearing the five articles of faith that distinguish individual men and women as members of the *Khalsa*. These are the Panj Kakaars, commonly known as "the five Ks", because the Punjabi word for each begins with the sound of "k". The "five Ks" are:

Kesh (uncut hair)

Kesh refers to the uncut hair that is required of Sikhs as one of the outwardly distinctive signs of Sikh identity. Sikhs treat their hair as a gift from God and keep this gift as a source of spiritual power and faith. Men usually tie up and cover their hair with the *dastnar*, commonly known as the *turban*. Some

women may also choose to wear a *turban*. *Turbans* may be of any colour and tied in a variety of styles. Usually the style and colour of a *turban* signify personal preference only.

As well as the *"five Ks"*, the *turban* is seen as an essential and complementary adjunct to maintain the sanctity of the *kesh* and is treated by Sikhs with utmost respect. Historically, it is also a symbol of identity linked with royalty and responsibility. *Kesh* applies not only to the hair on the head and face: *Khalsa* Sikhs are enjoined not to cut or remove hair from any part of the body.

Kangha

A small wooden comb that should be worn in the hair. It is used to keep the hair clean and symbolises the importance of cleanliness.

Kara

A *kara* literally means a "link" or a "band". It is an iron or steel bracelet worn by Sikhs, which is understood as a reminder of the universality of God. It is a symbol of spiritual allegiance, as well as being a reminder of the covenant with the *Guru* to avoid wrong and to do good.

Kachhera

A *kachhera* is a special knee length garment, tailored in a special manner, and similar to long shorts. It is usually worn under other clothes. It represents modesty, dignity, moral restraint and fidelity.

Kirpan

A sword that may be full length or a symbolic shorter one is worn as a reminder of the dignity and self-respect that Sikhs are called upon to uphold. It represents a readiness to uphold justice and to fight for the protection of the weak and oppressed.

In short, the *"five ks"* have not only a moral and practical significance, but also a deep spiritual importance and the wearing of them is, for Sikhs, a sign of obedience to the will of God and of care for, and obedience to, the *Gurus* and their teachings.

Singh and Kaur

As instituted by *Guru* Gobind Singh, all Sikh men take the religious name *Singh* (meaning lion) and all Sikh women have *Kaur* (meaning princess) as their second name, for example, Paramjit Kaur (female), Mohinder Singh (male). This practice relates to *Guru* Gobind Singh's rejection of the *caste* distinctions and promotion of equality that was reflected in the surnames used by people.

It must, however, be noted that the name Singh does not necessarily mean that a person is a Sikh, since this name was common in India before the rise of Sikhism. In addition, in the UK, some Sikh wives use their husband's name of *Singh* as a surname following *Kaur*. Sikhs will also often have a third name which may be derived from a place or a *got* (patrilinear clan) name. Some Sikhs use this third name as a surname, whilst others use only *Singh* or *Kaur*.

Birth, Marriage and Death

Soon after the birth of a child, a naming ceremony may be held in the *Gurdwara*. After a prayer from the family, the name of the child is taken from the first letter of the *hukamnama vak* or "word/order of the day", which is a passage of the *Guru Granth Sahib* read after its random opening.

Sikh marriage is known as *Anand Karaj* (ceremony of bliss). It is not viewed simply as a social or civil contract, but is seen as a spiritual state since living in this world and discharging family duties are advocated as the Sikh way of life.

The marriage service involves the recitation and singing of four verses, called *lavan*, from the *Guru Granth Sahib*. As each *lav* is sung, the couple circle the *Guru Granth Sahib*. The ceremony concludes with *Gurmat*, advice on the institution of marriage and its importance and then, as is usual with all Sikh ceremonies, with *ardas*, a collective prayer said in the presence of relatives and friends.

At death, Sikhs normally cremate the body. At the crematorium the *granthi* leads the mourners in the reading of *Kirtan Sohila* from the *Guru Granth Sahib*, and this is then followed by a prayer.

The family and friends then return to the *gurdwara* where relevant passages are read and sung from the *Guru Granth Sahib* and, following *ardas*, *langar* is taken before all leave for home. The family may also have a *Sahaj Path* (a reading, with breaks, of the entire *Guru Granth Sahib* over several days) or an *Akhand Path* (a continuous reading for forty-eight hours) in memory of the departed soul as well as to console the immediate family and friends.

Diet

Sikhs are enjoined to avoid tobacco, alcohol and other intoxicants. Many Sikhs who have been initiated are vegetarians and will exclude fish, eggs and any food containing animal derivatives. Meat is only permitted for consumption if it is *jhatka*, where the animal is killed with only one stroke and instantaneously. Those Sikhs who eat meat must not eat *halal* meat (meat from animals killed according to Muslim law). Many Sikhs are, however, vegetarians and meat is never served in the *langar* (see below) in *gurdwara*s.

Pilgrimage

Although *pilgrimage* is not a religious duty for Sikhs, places associated with the Sikh *Gurus* are treated as places of *pilgrimage*. Many Sikhs going to the Punjab will visit the *Darbar Sahib* and some may also visit other sites, particularly Anandpur Sahib. A visit to the birthplace of *Guru* Nanak Dev at Nankana Sahib in Pakistan usually takes place in October/November each year when several hundred Sikhs from the UK join their fellow Sikhs from the Punjab in India and from other countries.

SIKH WORSHIP

Daily Prayers

A Sikh is called upon to rise early and after a bath or shower to meditate on one God. The daily prayer routine consists in the morning of the *Jap* or *Japji Sahib*, a prayer composed by *Guru* Nanak Dev, the *Jaap* and the ten *Swayas* (compositions of the tenth *Guru*), *Chaupai* and *Anand*. It is the custom of some Sikhs also to recite other additional prayers in the morning. In the evening, the *Sodar Rehras* is recited and, before retiring to bed, the *Sohila*. These are both compilations of verses by different *Guru*s.

Sadh Sangat

No single day of the week is considered especially holy for Sikhs. In the UK, for convenience, the *gurdwara* is usually visited for *sadh sangat* on a Saturday or Sunday. The *gurdwara* is usually open daily and some Sikhs visit it every morning and evening. *Diwan* usually lasts between two and four hours.

The main elements of worship in a *Gurdwara* are *path* (prayer by means of the recitation of scriptures), *simran* (chanting of God's name) and *kirtan* (singing of hymns). A typical Sikh religious service consists of *Gurbani kirtan* (hymn-singing), a discourse on the divine Name, followed by *Ardas* (a final corporate prayer).

The *Ardas* ends with the invocation of God's blessing on the whole of humanity and not just on the followers of the Sikh faith. Then follows the *Hukamnama*, a random reading of special significance from the *Guru Granth Sahib* understood as a spiritual message from the *Guru* to each individual member of the congregation. The service concludes by *Karah Prashad* (see below) and the sharing of *langar* (see below).

In the morning service *Asa di Var* is followed by *Anand Sahib* and by a collective prayer of the congregation. In the evening service, *Rehras* is usually followed by *Kirtan* and at the end of the service *Kirtan Sohila* is recited when the *Guru Granth Sahib* is laid to rest, usually in a separate room.

Path

A *path* is the liturgical reading of the *Guru Granth Sahib*. On special occasions it is read from cover to cover by relays of readers. Akhand Path is the uninterrupted recitation of the entire Guru Granth Sahib that takes forty-eight hours to complete. Devotees take it in turns to read, and visitors come, day and night, to listen. Akhand Paths are conducted to celebrate festivals and other special occasions.

Saptah Path is a form of *path* which is not continuous and which takes seven days. *Sahaj Path* is also not continuous, but is without time limit for the completion of reading.

While reading the *Guru Granth Sahib* in a *Gurdwara*, the reader or another person close by will wave over it a *chaur sahib* (a whisk made of white yaks' hair). Despite the historical origin of this practice, the *chaur* is not intended to serve as a fly-whisk or a fan, but is waved as a sign of respect for the *Guru Granth Sahib*.

SIKH PLACES OF WORSHIP

Gurdwara

The Sikh place of congregational worship is called the *gurdwara*, meaning "doorway of the *Guru*". The first *gurdwara* in the UK was opened in Shepherd's Bush in 1911 at the initiative of Sant Teja Singh, and with funding from Maharaja Bhupinder Singh of Patiala. As the size of the UK Sikh population grew, the number of *gurdwaras* increased.

The Registrar General's 2004 (which is the most recent year for which data is available) list of certified places of worship gives 187 *gurdwaras* in England, and 3 in Wales, while the CD-ROM accompanying this volume records around 194 *gurdwaras* in the UK, of which around 179 are in England, 9 in Scotland, 4 in Wales, and 2 in Northern Ireland.

The majority of *Gurdwaras* in the world, including in the UK, follow guidance from the Shiromani Gurdwara Parbandhak Committee (SGPC), Amritsar, which is based at the *Darbar Sahib* (Golden Temple) complex at Amritsar in the Punjab. A major municipal grouping of *gurdwaras* (Sikh places of worship) is the Council of Sikh Gurdwaras in Birmingham. Councils of *Gurdwaras* have also begun to emerge also in a number of other towns and cities.

The *Gurdwara* is not only a place for formal worship, but it is also a centre for religious education. Other activities also take place in *Gurdwaras*, such as Punjabi classes, social activities such as youth clubs, women's groups, welfare provision and elderly day centres. In keeping with the Sikh tradition of service, *Gurdwaras* often provide temporary accommodation for the needy.

A *gurdwara* is usually recognisable from the outside by the *Nishan Sahib* (*Nishan* meaning "flag" whilst *Sahib* is an honorific title of respect). This is a triangular saffron coloured flag with the *khanda* (*Khalsa* emblem) depicted in black. The emblem consists of a symbolic two-edged sword surrounded by a circle outside of which are two further swords, which symbolise the temporal and spiritual sovereignty of God.

Langar

Langar, which is the food served in the communal kitchen at the *gurdwara*, is provided free of charge to all who attend the *gurdwara*. The food provided, which has been blessed, is vegetarian and will not contain meat, fish or eggs or their by-products. Because the food served in the *langar* has been blessed, head covering is usually maintained in the *langar* hall. The *langar* is a meal to which outsiders are cordially welcomed. However, it is advisable to ask only for as much food as is actually wanted

rather than to accept too much and then have to leave some.

Both *Langar* and *Karah Prashad* (see below) symbolise universal fraternity and equality since it is intended that all should eat together regardless of their social position and that there are no strangers in the House of God.

Vistors to a Sikh Gurdwara

The clothing worn by both male and female visitors should be modest. For women it is advisable to wear a long skirt or trousers, while head covering is essential for both women and men. A large clean handkerchief is adequate for men, and women are expected to use scarves. The *gurdwara* will usually have some head coverings available for those who have not brought them, but not necessarily enough for a large group of visitors. Because shoes are removed before going into the *gurdwara* clean and presentable socks, stockings, or tights are therefore a good idea.

Tobacco, alcohol or drugs should never be taken into the buildings of a *gurdwara* (not just the prayer hall) and smokers should therefore remember to leave their tobacco or cigarettes outside. Shoes should be removed before entering the prayer hall and may also need to be left off before entering the *langar* hall. In addition to covering their heads, vistors may also be asked to wash their hands (which Sikhs do before entering to pray).

On entering, the visitor will see the *Guru Granth Sahib* (the Sikh sacred scripture) placed on a low platform, covered by a canopy. When Sikhs enter they touch the floor before this with their forehead and offer a gift such as food or money. Visitors may also bow in similar fashion as a mark of respect or, if they are uncomfortable with this for religious reasons, they may if they wish simply give a slight bow or stand for a few moments before the *Guru Granth Sahib* in silence as a mark of respect.

No gift would be expected from a visitor although, of course, it would be deeply appreciated. If making a gift, leave it with the others either in a wooden box, or on the floor in front of the *Guru Granth Sahib*.

Seating is on the floor (usually carpeted). Men and women usually sit in separate groupings. Seating should be in a position that avoids the feet being pointed toward the *Guru Granth Sahib*, or with the back being turned toward it since both these positions are considered disrespectful. A cross-legged meditational stance is the usual practice, but simply tucking one's legs in is acceptable.

If arriving during a time of worship, visitors will normally be expected to join the worshippers, but there is no obligation to participate in the worship itself. At the end of the worship visitors may be offered *Karah Prashad* (holy food). This is a sweet pudding that has been blessed during the service. It is given to all to signify that all are equal and united in their humanity and that there are no caste distinctions. The *Karah Prashad* is made of butter, flour, sugar and water. It is therefore buttery in texture and hands need wiping after it has been received. Often, paper napkins are distributed for this purpose.

If a visitor is, for religious reasons, uncomfortable about being given some of this sacred food to eat, then the person offering the food should be informed with a quiet "No thank you." If possible, it would be preferable in advance to explain to the hosts that this is because of personal religious position and not out of any disrespect. The same applies to *langar* (which is the food served in the communal kitchen at the *gurdwara*) since this has also been blessed.

Because the food served in the *langar* has been blessed, head covering is usually maintained in the *langar* hall. The *langar* is a meal to which outsiders are cordially welcomed. However, it is advisable to ask only for as much food as is actually wanted rather than to accept too much and then have to leave some.

SIKH CALENDAR AND FESTIVALS

Calendar

In 2003 a committee of the Shiromani Gurdwara Parbandhak Committee ruled that Sikh festivals should be calculated by the *Nanakshahi* calendar. In practice this means that the majority of the dates, which had previously been calculated by the *Vikrami* (in Punjabi also known as *Bikrami*) calendar used by Hindus in north India, now have a fixed date in relation to the *Gregorian*/secular calendar.

The exceptions, which are still calculated on *Vikrami* principles, are *Hola Mohalla*, *Bandi Chhor Divas* (*Divali*) and *Guru Nanak's Birthday*. At the same time, many Sikhs remain unaware of the changeover and some *Gurdwaras* still distribute calendars in which all the dates still follow the *Vikrami* system. It is also the case that, since in many *Gurdwaras* festivals are celebrated at the weekend, rather than on the day itself, the fact that the dates of festivals are now "fixed" in terms of the *Gregorian* calendar has made less practical difference than might be expected.

According to the *Nanakshahi* calendar the present era starts from the birth of *Guru Nanak Dev*. So, for example, 2007 is 538/539.

Gurpurbs and Melas

Sikh festivals are of two types: *Gurpurb* (i.e. an anniversary relating to the lives of the *Gurus*, including the scripture, the *Guru Granth Sahib*) and *mela* (literally a "fair"). *Vaisakhi* and *Divali* are both *melas* and are days in the Punjabi calendar on which Hindus had celebrated for centuries before the advent of Sikhism. *Gurpurbs* are simply marked by *akhand path*, *kirtan*, prayers, religious lectures, distribution of *karah prasad* and *langar*. Major

Gurpurbs include:

Guru Nanak's Birthday (November, but the date varies)

Martyrdom of Guru Tegh Bahadur (24th November)

Guru Gobind Singh's Birthday (5th January)

Martyrdom of Guru Arjan Dev (16th June)

Installation of Scriptures in Harmandir Sahib (1st September)

This took place at Amritsar in 1604.

Among the *Melas* are:

Vaisakhi (Baisakhi) (14th April)
This celebrates the day in 1699 when Guru Gobind Singh founded the order of the *Khalsa* by offering *amrit* to the *Panj Pyare,* in turn receiving *amrit* from them. Because this day was calculated on the basis of the solar rather than the lunar cycle its *Vikrami* date appeared to be almost constant (and during the 20th century often fell on 13th April) in relation to the *Gregorian* calendar. However, over a period of ten millennia, it would have moved from the Spring to the Autumn because of the twenty minute discrepancy between the *Vikrami* solar year and the *Gregorian* year.

By the *Nanakshahi* calendar, *Vaisakhi* always falls on 14th April, but many Punjabis, including many Sikhs, take for granted that it is on 13th April. On *Vaisakhi* day Sikhs usually replace the covering and pennant of the *Nishan Sahib* which flies outside *Gurdwaras* (see under section on *Gurdwara* below). There is often also a *nagar kirtan* (procession) in which the *Guru Granth Sahib* is carried through the streets, accompanied by *Panj Pyare.* Candidates are often initiated with *amrit* into the *Khalsa* early on *Vaisakhi.*

Divali (Bandhi Chhor Divas)
(October/November)
Although Sikhs have shared in celebrating *Divali,* the historical reason given for this distinguishes its celebration by Sikhs from that by Hindus. The name *Bandi Chhor Divas,*

by which the day is designated in the *Nanakshahi* calendar, refers to this historical background but is not in general usage. *Bandi Chhor Divas* means "Liberation of Prisoners Day". It commemorates the fact that when Guru Hargobind was released from imprisonment on *Divali* day by the Mughal Emperor, Jehangir, he brought with him fifty-two Hindu princes for whose freedom he had asked. On *Divali* day, Sikhs illuminate their *Gurdwaras* and set off fireworks.

Hola Mohalla (March, but the date varies)
This festival is traditionally held at Anandpur in the the Punjab, but can now also be found in *Gurdwaras* across the world. It was started by Guru Gobind Singh as a gathering for mock battles and the use of martial arts, reminding Sikhs of the importance of courage and of being prepared to stand against tryranny and on behalf of justice.

SIKH ORGANISATIONS

Organisational Listings

In the CD-ROM accompanying this volume, the organisations listed with their contact details include both the head offices of organisations with branches throughout the country and of other organisations that aspire to serve the Sikh community on a UK-wide basis. There are also contact details of a variety of forms of Sikh regional and local organisations, including *gurdwaras,* associations, centres, welfare and youth organisations.

Overall, the CD-ROM accompanying this publication records details of around 25 UK Sikh organisations operating at a UK level. It also records details of around 57 Sikh local organisations (of which around 42 are in England, 9 in Scotland, 4 in Wales, and 2 in Northern Ireland. Finally, it also includes details of around 4 Sikh organisations operating at a regional level in England, 1 in Scotland and 1 in Northern Ireland.

"Umbrella" Organisations and General Organisations

The Network of Sikh Organisations aspires to facilitate co-operation among Sikhs in the UK and is developing as a representative umbrella body, with more than ninety groups in membership. A range of other national groups and organizations also exist, such as the Sikh Missionary Society that has, for many years, published for free distribution an extensive range of materials on Sikhism, for both the Panth and for enquirers, as well as organising youth camps and classes. A number of groups see themselves in relation to the political demand for an independent Sikh homeland of Khalistan.

Other groups exist which serve the diverse needs of particular sections of the Sikh population, including literary, social, cultural or professional societies and associations, for example, the World Sikh Foundation and the Sikh Missionary Society.

Educational Organisations

In 1999, the Guru Nanak Primary school and Secondary school in Hayes, Middlesex, became the first state-funded Sikh schools in the UK. There are also many local supplementary schools which, outside of schools hours, teach Punjabi, as well as Sikh religion and culture.

Social Groupings

Sikhism teaches that there are no distinctions between people and rejects the concept of *caste* (or *Zaat*), which therefore has no religious significance for Sikhs. Many *gurdwaras* are named after one of the *Gurus* or the Sri Guru Singh Sabha, which was the name of the movement that helped to found the SGPC at the end of the nineteenth century.

Other terms that appear in the titles of some *Gurdwaras*, such as *Jat, Ramgarhia* and *Bhatra,* are historically related to economic categories and are rooted in the history of the forebears of the families concerned. They do not necessarily define any contemporary economic or social status or who is allowed to attend a *gurdwara*, although they may in practice indicate the background of those who do actually attend.

Historically, *Bhatras* were itinerant traders. Many settled in British ports before the Second World War. Therefore a number of the earliest *Gurdwaras* were founded by *Bhatras.* They retain their own organisations in order to maintain their specific traditions and way of life.

Ramgarhia is the preferred designation of those Sikhs whose ancestral roots and occupations cover carpentry, bricklaying, and masonry. These communities took their titles from their distinguished eighteenth century leader, Jassa Singh. He had renamed himself after the Ramgarh Fort, in Amritsar, which was named after *Guru Ram Das*. In order to defend the *Dashan Sahib* he rebuilt the fort, rebuilt his confidence and successfully led his *misal* (as association of military leaders).

The name *Ramgarhia* derives from the name of Guru Ram Das and the fort called Ramgarh, constructed to defend the *Darbar Sahib* by the *misal* (confederation) who thus became known as *Ramgarhias.*

The British encouraged groups of *Ramgarhias* to move to East Africa at the end of the nineteenth century in order to assist in the development of the transport network. As a result of the Africanisation policies of the newly independent East African states in the 1960s, many migrated from there to the UK or arrived as refugees.

Local Sikh organisations often serve several functions including the provision of youth and women's activities and education in addition to what are often understood to be more specifically religious functions.

Personnel

A Management Committee, which consists of honorary office bearers, president, secretary and treasurer, usually runs a *Gurdwara*. The people who serve on such committees are usually elected by the *congregation* every two years or so. Committees usually run for two years and change on *Vaisakhi Day*. There are also a number of *Gurdwaras* that are led by a *sant* (individual spiritual leader), for example, Guru Nanak Nishkam Sewak Jatha of the late Baba Puran Singh Karichowale in Birmingham.

Any adult male or female Sikh is permitted to perform religious ceremonies but many *gurdwaras* employ a *granthi*. A *granthi* is a professional reader of the *Guru Granth Sahib* and is usually also responsible for its care. Although the word "priest" is sometimes used by people outside of Sikhism, Sikhism recognises no priesthood and all Sikhs are of equal status in religious terms.

Sikh leaders may therefore be called *Bhai* (brother) or *Bhen* (sister). A *giani* is a learned and devout person who has meditated upon the *Guru Granth Sahib* and interprets its meaning to the congregation. There is often a regular group of *ragis* (singers and musicians) to help with diwan.

Other waged personnel may include a caretaker and sometimes, in the larger *Gurdwaras*, a community development worker.

FURTHER READING

Details follow of a number of useful general introductions to Sikhism together with some books and articles that provide some focus on Sikhs and Sikh organisations in the UK. The references are not comprehensive, but provide signposts to a range of relevant materials.

Babraa, D Kaur, *Visiting a Sikh Temple*, Lutterworth Educational, Guildford, 1981.

Ballard, R, "Differentiation and Disjunction Amongst Sikhs in Britain", in N Barrier and V Dusenbury, *The Sikh Diaspora: Migration and the Experience Beyond the Punjab*, Chanakya Publications, Delhi, 1989, pp 200–234.

Ballard, R, "Differentiation and Disjunction Among the Sikhs", in R Ballard (ed), *Desh Pardesh: The South Asian Presence in Britain*, Hurst, London, 1994, pp 88–116.

Ballard, R, "The Growth and Changing Character of the Sikh Presence in Britain", in H Coward, J Hinnells and R Williams, *The South Asian Religious Diaspora in Britain, Canada and the United States*, State University of New York Press, New York, 2000, pp 127–144.

Ballard R and Ballard R, "The Sikhs: The Development of South Asian Settlement in Britain", in J Watson (ed), *Between Two Cultures*, Basil Blackwell, Oxford, 1977.

Barrier, N and Dusenbury, V, *The Sikh Diaspora: Migration and the Experience Beyond the Punjab*, Chanakya Publications, Delhi, 1989.

Barrow, J, "Religious Authority and Influence in the Diaspora: Sant Jaswant Singh and Sikhs in West London", in P Singh and N Barrier (eds), *Sikh Identity: Continuity and Change*, Manohar, New Delhi, 1999, pp 335–348.

Beetham, D, *Transport and Turbans: A Comparative Study in Local Politics*, Open University Press, Milton Keynes, 1970.

Bhachu, P, *Twice Migrants: East African Sikh Settlers in Britain*, Tavistock, London, 1985.

Brown, K, *Sikh Art and Literature*, Routledge, London, 1999.

Chohan, S and Geaves, R, "The religious dimension in the struggle for Khalistan and its roots in Sikh history", in the *International Journal for Punjab Studies*, Volume 8, No 1, 2001, pp 29-96.

Cole, W O, *The Guru in Sikhism*, Darton, Longman and Todd, London, 1982.

Cole, W O, "Sikhs in Britain", in P Badham (ed), *Religion, State and Society in Modern Britain*, Edwin Mellen Press, Lampeter, 1989, pp 259-276.

Cole, W O, *Teach Yourself Sikhism*, Hodder, London, 1994.

Cole, W O, "Sikhs in Europe", in S Gill, G D'Costa and U King (eds), *Religion in Europe: Contemporary Perspectives*, Kok Pharos, Kampen, 2004, pp 105-119.

Cole, W O, *Sikhism*, Hodder and Stoughton, London, 2003.

Cole, W O, *Understanding Sikhs*, Dunedin Academic Press, Edinburgh.

Cole, W O and Sambhi, P Singh, *A Popular Dictionary of Sikhism*, London, 1990.

Cole, W O and Sambhi, P Singh, *The Sikhs: Their Religious Beliefs and Practices* (2nd edition), Sussex Academic Press, London, 1995.

Grewal, K S, "The Khalsa in Sikh tradition (Part I)", in *World Faiths Encounter*, No 23, July 1999, pp 5-16.

Grewal, K S, "The Khalsa in Sikh tradition (Part II)", in *World Faiths Encounter*, No 24, November 1999, pp 20-36.

Helweg, A W, *Sikhs in England: The Development of a Migrant Community*, Oxford University Press, Delhi, (2nd edition), 1986.

Henley, A, *Caring for Sikhs and Their Families: Religious Aspects of Care*, National Extension College, Cambridge, 1983.

James, A, *Sikh Children in Britain*, Oxford University Press, London, 1974.

Kalsi, S, *The Evolution of a Sikh Community in Britain*, Community Religions Project, University of Leeds, Leeds, 1992.

Kalsi, S, *A Simple Guide to Sikhism*, Global Books, Folkestone, 1999.

McLeod, W H (ed), *Textual Sources for the Study of Sikhism*, University of Chicago Press, Chicago, 1990.

McLeod, W H, *Sikhs and Sikhism*, Oxford University Press, New Delhi, 1999.

Madra, A S and Singh P, *Warrior Saints: Three Centuries of the Sikh Military Tradition*, Tauris and Co, London, 1999.

Mann, G, *Sikhism*, Prentice Hall, Upper Saddle Rivers, New Jersey, 2004.

Nesbitt, E, *Aspects of Sikh Tradition in Nottingham*, unpublished MPhil thesis, University of Nottingham, 1980.

Nesbitt, E, *The Religious Lives of Sikh Children in Coventry*, Community Religions Project, University of Leeds, 2000.

Nesbitt, E, "Young British Sikhs and Religious Devotion: Issues Arising From Ethnographic Research", in A King and J Brockington (eds), *Intimate Other: Love Divine in Indic Religions*, Orient Longman, New Delhi, 2004, pp 310-336.

Nesbitt, E, *Sikhism: A Very Short Introduction*, Oxford University Press, Oxford, 2005.

Nesbitt, E, "Festivals – Schools' Involvement in Tradition", in E Nesbitt (ed), *Intercultural Education: Ethnographic and Religious Approaches*, Sussex Academic Press, Brighton, 2004, pp 50-65.

Nesbitt, E, "Belief and Practice: God and Holy Work, in E Nesbitt (ed), *Intercultural Education: Ethnographic and Religious Approaches*, Sussex Academic Press, Brighton, 2004, pp 66-80.

Nesbitt, E and Singh Tatla, D, *Sikhs in Britain: An Annotated Bibliography", 2nd revised edition, No. 13, Bibliographies in Ethnic Relations*, Centre for Ethnic Relations, University of Warwick, Coventry, 1994.

Nesbitt E and Jackson, R, "Aspects of cultural transmission in a diaspora Sikh community", in *Journal of Sikh Studies*, Volume 10, No 1, 1994, pp 52-66.

Nesbitt, E and Kaur, G, *Guru Nanak*, Bayeux Arts, 1999.

Rait, S, *Sikh Women in England: Religious, Social and Cultural Beliefs*, Trentham Books, Stoke-on-Trent, 2005.

Shackle, C, *The Sikhs*, Minority Rights Group, London, 2nd edition, 1986.

Shiromani Gurdwara Parbandhak Committee, *Sikh Rehit Maryada* (translation), Shiromani Gurdwara Parbandhak Committee, Amritsar (available through the Sikh Missionary Society, London).

Sing, C, *The Wisdom of Sikhism*, Oneworld, Oxford, 2001.

Singh, G, *The Sikh Festivals*, Sikh Cultural Society of Great Britain, Edgware, 1982.

Singh, G and Tatla, D, *The Sikhs in Britain: The Making of a Community*, Zed Books, London, 2006.

Singh, K, *The Sikhs Today*, Orient Longman Ltd, Bombay, 1976.

Singh, P, *The Sikhs*, John Murray, London, 1999.

Singh, P and Barrier, N (eds), *Sikh Identity: Continuity and Change*, Manohar, New Delhi, 1999.

deSouza, A, *The Sikhs in Britain*, Batsford, London, 1986.

Strong, S (ed), *The Arts of the Sikh Kingdoms*, V & A Publications, London, 1999.

Takhar, O, *Sikh Identity: An Exploration of Groups Among Sikhs*, Ashgate, Aldershot, 2005.

Tatla, D Singh, "The Punjab Crisis and Sikh Mobilisation in Britain", in R Barot (ed), *Religion and Ethnicity: Minorities and Social Change in the Metropolis*, Kok Pharos, Kampen, 1993, pp 96-109.

Tatla, D Singh and Nesbitt, E, *Sikhs in Britain: An Annotated Bibliography*, University of Warwick Centre for Research in Ethnic Relations, Coventry, (revised edition) 1993.

Tatla, D Singh, *The Sikh Diaspora: The Search for Statehood*, UCL Press, London, 1999.

Thomas, T, "Old Allies, New Neighbours: Sikhs in Britain", in G Parsons (ed) *The Growth of Religious Diversity: Britain from 1945, Volume I: Traditions*, Routledge, London, 1993, pp 205-241.

Thomas, T and Ghuman, P, *A Survey of Social and Religious Attitudes Among Sikhs in Cardiff*, Open University, Cardiff, 1976.

Weller, P, "Hindus and Sikhs: Community Development and Religious Discrimination in England and Wales", in K Jacobsen and P Kumar (eds), *South Asians in the Diaspora: Histories and Religious Traditions*, Brill, Leiden, 2004, pp 454-497.

INTRODUCING ZOROASTRIANS IN THE UK

ZOROASTRIANS IN THE UK 265

ORIGINS AND DEVELOPMENT OF ZOROASTRIANISM 266

SOURCES OF ZOROASTRIAN BELIEFS AND PRACTICES 267

KEY ZOROASTRIAN BELIEFS 268

ZOROASTRIAN LIFE 273

TRADITIONS IN ZOROASTRIANISM 276

ZOROASTRIAN WORSHIP 277

ZOROASTRIAN PLACES OF WORSHIP 277

ZOROASTRIAN CALENDARS AND FESTIVALS 278

ZOROASTRIAN ORGANISATIONS 281

FURTHER READING 281

ZOROASTRIANS IN THE UK

History in the UK

Navroji Rustom Maneck Sett was the first Zoroastrian, and possibly the first Indian, known to have visited the United Kingdom and came in 1723. The first Indian firm to open for business in Britain was opened in 1855, was run by a *Parsi* (see section on *Parsis* below) family, and was called Cama and Company. The first community organisation, the Religious Funds of the Zarathushtrians of Europe was formally established in 1861. Today it is known as the Zoroastrian Trust Funds of Europe Incorporated (ZTFE Incorporated) and is the oldest community organisation of South Asian origin in the UK.

Zoroastrians thus form a long-established community in the UK. It was from its *Parsi* members, who made up the majority of the early Zoroastrian settlers, that the first three Asian Members of Parliament came. The first of these was the Liberal MP, Dadabhai Naoroji, elected in 1892. He was followed in 1895 by the Conservative MP, Sir Mancherjee Meherwanjee Bhownaggree, and then by Shapurji Dorabji Saklatvala for Labour in 1922 and for the Communist Party in 1929.

Other *Parsis* came from India in the 1950s, immediately following Indian independence and later, prior to the introduction in the 1960s of tighter immigration controls on migration from New Commonwealth countries. There were also Indian origin *Parsis* who came from Aden and from East Africa (mainly Zanzibar, Kenya and Uganda), after the introduction in the late 1960s and early 1970s of Arabisation and Africanisation policies in these newly independent states. Iranian Zoroastrians came to Britain from Iran largely after the downfall of the Pahlavi dynasty and the formation of the Islamic Republic in 1979.

Global and UK Populations

During much of the twentieth century, the global numbers of Zoroastrians was around 120,000-150,000. More recently, some estimates suggest that there are now around 2,544,000. They are located mainly in Iran, India (particularly Bombay, Pune and Gujarat state), Pakistan (particularly Karachi), Britain (particularly London and the South East), Canada, the USA, Australia and New Zealand.

In the UK, the 2001 decennial Census questions on religion did not offer to respondents the category of "Zoroastrian" or "Parsi" as a pre-set category of response. However, the specially commissioned Census Table M275 Religion (Most Detailed Categories) provides the breakdown of responses for England and Wales of respondents ticking the "Other Religions – please write in" box in the Census question on religious affiliation. From an analysis of this table, there were 3,355 Zoroastrian respondents in England and 383 in Wales. At the same time, the internal records of the Zoroastrian Trust Funds of Europe Incorporated indicate a population of over 5,000 Zoroastrians in the UK.

Ethnicity of Zoroastrians in the UK

Zoroastrians with family roots in India, whether directly from India or via East Africa, have Parsi Gujarati as their tongue of daily conversation. Zoroastrians with an Iranian family background, have Persian or Farsi as a mother tongue although most of them, including the young generation, are fluent in English. Zoroastrian prayers are said in the ancient Iranian languages of Avestan and Pazand.

ORIGINS AND DEVELOPMENT OF ZOROASTRIANISM

Zarathushtra

The term Zoroastrianism comes from the Greek form (Zoroaster) of the name Zarathushtra, who was the founder of the religion. The religion is also known as *Zarathushtrianism* from the Iranian form of the founder's name, or else as *Mazdayasni Zarthushti/Zartoshti* (*Mazdayasni* meaning worshipper of Mazda or Ahura Mazda, the Wise Lord or Lord of Wisdom and is the only Creator or God).

Among academics from outside of the community, there is considerable debate about the precise dates of Zarathushtra's life. Some Zoroastrians argue for a date as early as 6,000BCE, while other Zoroastrians and many external academics argue for a date around 1,700BCE to 1,200BCE. Whatever his precise date of birth, it is generally agreed that Zarathushtra lived in North Eastern Iran in ancient times, currently Afghanistan, Tajikistan and Iran.

Zoroastrian texts mention that, from infancy onwards, Zarathushtra's life was threatened by evil forces. At a young age he went to live a solitary life of meditation in the countryside and it is believed the religion was first revealed to Zarathushtra by Ahura Mazda at the age of thirty. Zarathushtra had further revelations which inspired him to infuse the traditional Iranian religion in which he functioned as a *zaotar* (head or leading ceremonial priest who invokes the prayers) with a personal and experiential dimension.

He spent the following forty-seven years of his life spreading a *prophet's* message in which he denounced the *daevas* (the former gods of some of the Indo-Iranians, which he saw as demonic spirits) and proclaimed the worship of Ahura Mazda (the only Creator and Wise Lord), was as the source of *Spenta Mainyu* (Holy or Bounteous Spirit), *Vohu Manah* (Good Mind), *Asha Vahishta* (Truth, Righteousness, Divine Law and Best Order, Justice), *Kshathra Vairya* (Divine Power and Strength, Sovereignty, Desirable Kingdom), *Spenta Armaiti* (Holy Devotion), *Haurvatat* (Perfection), *Ameretat* (Immortality, Everlasting Bliss). He called people to the threefold ethic of *humata* (good thoughts), *hukhta* (good words) and *hvarshta* (good deeds).

Zarathushtra's teaching was accepted by the then king Vishtaspa of the Kayanian dynasty, but he faced considerable opposition from supporters of the previously existing *polytheistic* religious structures.

History and Influence of Zoroastrianism

Zoroastrianism eventually became the imperial religion of four successive Iranian empires. Precisely how this occurred is uncertain, although during the Median dynasty the *Magi*, whom the historian Herodotus identifies as a *priestly* grouping of the Medes in the North West of Iran, seem to have adopted Zoroastrian beliefs and to have played a part in developing the religion's unifying role within the Empire.

In various forms of development Zoroastrianism became, successively, the religion of the Medes (700-559BCE) Achaemenids (559-331BCE), the Parthians (mid second century BCE -224CE) and the Sasanians (224-652CE). In various ways Zoroastrianism is thought to have had an influence on post-exilic Judaism, Christianity, Manichaeism, Gnosticism, Islam, Greek philosophers such as Plato, Pythagoras, Socrates and Aristotle, as well as *Mahayana* Buddhism and Hinduism in the East.

The Parsis in India and the Zoroastrians in Iran

In the 9th century CE some Zoroastrians from Khorasan, a province in Iran, left Iran following the Arab conquest, seeking religious and economic freedom. They settled at Sanjan in Gujarat, North West India, in 936CE after having been granted permission to stay by the local Hindu King Jadav Rana. This community became known as the *Parsis* or *Parsees*, a term given to them by the Indians meaning those who came from Parsa or Persia.

Over the next thousand years many more Zoroastrians emigrated to India due to their experience of religious persecution in Iran. Because of this, many Zoroastrians consider India as their adopted homeland, although a significant community also remained in Iran. The act of the Hindu King Jadav Rana in granting the Parsis refuge in India played a large part in ensuring that Zoroastrianism is still a living faith in the 21st century.

SOURCES OF ZOROASTRIAN BELIEFS AND PRACTICES

The Avesta

The main body of Zoroastrian scripture is known as the *Avesta*. It originally consisted of twenty-one books, the first group of seven on ceremonial and religious liturgies, including the *Gathas and Yasna*; the second group relating to legal matters including the *Vendidad*; and the third group relating to creation, cosmology and science.

The contents of the *Avesta* were for many centuries orally transmitted from generation to generation and then written down and canonised in the 5th or 6th century CE in a specially composed Avestan alphabet. However in the *Denkard* (*Acts of the Religion*), a ninth century Pahlavi (Middle Persian) text that contains a summary of the Zoroastrian religion, it is mentioned that the *Avesta* was written in gold ink on ox hides and it was known to be in existence until the end of the Achaemenid period.

The *Avesta* was looted together with the other Iranian treasures following the burning and ransacking of the imperial capital Persepolis by the Greeks upon the orders of Alexander (who, in the Pahlavi texts, is referred to as "the Accursed" rather than "the Great"). Due to the religious persecution of Zoroastrians that followed Arab invasion of Iran and which continued throughout the last millennium, only about one quarter of these texts survive in their original form. In its present form, the *Avesta* may be classified into five divisions:

Yasna and Gathas

The *Yasna* is concerned with acts of worship, praise, prayer, supplication and religious devotion. It is divided into seventy-two chapters, which include the seventeen *Gathas*.

The *Gathas* are *The Divine Hymns of Zarathushtra*. They are metrical compositions, similar to the *Rig Vedas*, but written in the ancient Gathic-Avestan language, a sister language to Sanskrit. They are difficult to translate today since some words in the *Gathas* appear now only in these sources and nowhere else. Sometimes, therefore, one can only gain an approximate sense of their meaning.

The Yashts (hymns)

The *Yashts* (*Yashti* meaning "homage" in Avestan) are prose and verse hymns of praise addressed to individual *Yazatas/Yazads* (meaning "adorable beings worthy of adoration"). Due to the destruction of Zoroastrian literature, there are in all, currently twenty-one *Yashts*, but more than twenty-one *Yazatas*. Some of these are thought to be very ancient and pre-Gathic in content and relate to the creation of *Airyana Vaeja* (the known limits of the Aryan or Indo Iranian world), to myths and to legendary history of ancient Iran and its people.

The Vendidad (or Videvdat)

The word *Vendidad* is the present form of the ancient Avestan word *Vidaeva-data*, meaning rules and regulations to oppose *daeva* or evil. It specifies in detail the laws of purity and also contains diverse material such as the account of creation; the geography of *Airyana Vaeja*; the legend of a golden age of King Jamsheed (being the Zoroastrian equivalent to Noah in the Biblical stories) who, after the last ice age, initiated the ancient Iranian New Year at the spring equinox.

Visperad

Visperad (meaning "Service of all the Masters") is a collection of materials that is supplementary to the *Yasna*. These are never recited independently, but are usually recited at the six religious festivals known as *gahambars* (see below). They contain invocations and offerings of homage to "All the Lords or Heavenly Powers" (*Vispe Ratavo*).

Khordeh Avesta

The *Khordeh Avesta* or *Minor Avesta* is a book of common or daily prayer which is a compilation of short extracts from the entire *Avesta*. It includes *Nyaishes*, which are litanies in praise to the elements - *Khorshed* (sun), *Mehr* (the heavenly light), *Mahabokhta* (the moon), *Avan* (the waters) and *Adar* (the holy fire). It also includes the *Afrinagan* and *Afrins*, which are blessings; the *Gahs*, which are prayers to the five parts into which a day is divided; and the *Sirozah*, which are invocations in honour of Ahura Mazda and the pantheon of Zoroastrian divinities, the *Amesha Spentas*, the *Yazatas*, and the *Fravashis* that form the thirty day month in the 12 monthly Zoroastrian calendar. Each of the invocations is addressed to Ahura Mazda or the divinity of the day.

Later Texts

In addition to the *Avesta* there are many texts written in Pahlavi (Middle Persian), mostly in the 9th century CE. The Middle Persian texts show the continuity of the religion through the ages. They form an important link with early Zoroastrian thought because they include some translations and summaries of otherwise lost ancient sources, while they also reflect the later growth of the religion and its encounter with Judaism, Christianity, Manichaeism, Islam and Buddhism.

KEY ZOROASTRIAN BELIEFS

Ahura Mazda

Zarathushtra taught that Ahura Mazda (the Wise Lord or the Lord of Truth, Wisdom and Light) is to be seen as the One Supreme, All-

Powerful, All-Knowing, All-Wise, uncreated, eternally Good and Perfect. Ahura Mazda's primary spiritual attributes are *Spenta Mainyu* (Holy and Bounteous Spirit), *Vohu Manah* (Good Mind), *Asha Vahishta* (Best Truth, Righteousness, Divine Law and Order, Justice), *Kshathra Vairya* (Divine Power and Strength, Sovereignty, Desirable Kingdom), *Spenta armaiti* (Holy Devotion), *Haurvatat* (Perfection), *Ameretat* (Immortality, Everlasting Bliss), collectively known in the *Younger Avesta* as the *Amesha Spentas*.

Ahura Mazda is present is all things good and holy but is not present in any thing bad and evil, because evil does not originate from Ahura Mazda. He is understood to be perfect and is therefore seen as a best friend to all, never to be feared by creation including human beings. According to the teaching of Zarathushtra, Ahura Mazda alone is worthy of absolute worship.

Zoroastrians believe that Zarathushtra identified, for the first time in human history, the importance of the *Vohu Manah* (Good Mind). His ethical *monotheism* taught human beings to think and reflect on the purpose of creation with a clear, rational mind, in order to dispel ignorance and blind faith.

Zoroastrians see this world as being in a state of constant warfare between the forces of good and the forces of evil. In this war Ahura Mazda is deemed to be extremely powerful, although currently in the world of conflict is temporarily non-omnipotent.

Zoroastrians believe that Ahura Mazda is *latently omnipotent* because if Ahura Mazda was currently omnipotent, then it would be the forces of evil would be prevented from attacking and afflicting the creation but this is not the case. However, that does not mean that Ahura Mazda is weak or powerless because in the Zoroastrian texts it is explicitly clear that Ahura Mazda is invincible and will be truly omnipotent and all-powerful at the end of time when evil is made impotent and will therefore be no

more. It is because of Ahura Mazda currently being temporarily non-omnipotent that chaos, misery, suffering, disease, death and all other negativities continue to exist in the world.

Ahura Mazda's power and greatest strength lies in his omniscience. It is because Ahura Mazda is believed to be omniscient that He knows that human beings, understood to be His finest creation, will make Him truly omnipotent. This, it is believed, will take place at the end of time when evil will be made totally impotent, through the cumulative power of the threefold ethic of *humata* (good thoughts), *hukhta* (good words) and *hvarshta* (good deeds).

Spenta Mainyu (The Holy and Bounteous Spirit) and Angra Mainyu (The Destructive Spirit)

The classical Zoroastrian teaching is that evil did not originate from Ahura Mazda as a perfect, All-Wise and Good God who, by definition could not be seen as creating evil or else would be deemed to be imperfect. If evil originated from Ahura Mazda then Ahura Mazda could not be worshipped as a perfectly good Being. By ceasing to be perfectly good it is believed that Ahura Mazda would cease to be God.

Because of this, evil is seen as coming into existence as a state of excess or deficiency in Ahura Mazda's otherwise perfect creations. It is state of moving away from Ahura Mazda, in the same way that darkness does not originate from light. Rather, evil is seen as the work of *Angra Mainyu* (the Destructive Spirit). The characteristics of *Angra Mainyu* are anger, greed, jealousy, death. *Angra Mainyu* cannot create and is, hence, destructive.

In this present world, the forces of evil attack and afflict Ahura Mazda's creations, adopting a kind of parasitic existence and eating away at the good creation, bringing chaos, violence, death and destruction in opposition to the force of *Spenta Mainyu* (the Holy and

Bounteous Spirit). Zoroastrians see human beings and the other six creations (created by Ahura Mazda who is perfect) as being like the other six creations that are created or born perfect. They are seen as *hamkar* (co-workers) with Ahura Mazda in bringing about the ultimate defeat of evil. While the spiritual origins of evil is debated among Zoroastrians, all Zoroastrians share the conviction that evil will be overcome by Ahura Mazda.

Zoroastrianism is a complex and living tradition that has evolved over the centuries. Its richness has therefore included differing emphases and accounts of how evil will be overcome. According to the *Bundahishn* (*Story of Creation*), a Pahlavi text of the 6th century, through His omniscience Ahura Mazda, created this world as a trap into which evil is ensnared from its spiritual existence into the physical world. In this physical world human beings as Ahura Mazda's finest creation will ensure that evil is ultimately destroyed using the threefold ethic of *humata* (good thoughts), *hukhta* (good words) and *hvarshta* (good deeds).

Following the total defeat and annihilation of evil by the forces of good, the physical resurrection of the body and the immortal soul will commence, and will be followed by the *Final Judgement* and *Frasho Keriti* (the "Making Wonderful" and paradise on earth as it is heaven). Some Zoroastrians, however, assign sole authority to the *Gathas* (see above) and in their interpretation of the *Gathas* they emphasise the absolute power of Ahura Mazda over evil.

The Seven Good Creations and Their Guardians

The seven primary physical creations that make up the world are believed by Zoroastrians to be (in chronological order) the spherical sky, waters, the disc shaped earth, plants, cattle, humans, and fire. Zoroastrians believe that prior to the physical creaton, the *Amesha Spentas* (Bounteous Immortals) were created. These are attributes of Ahura Mazda and who aided Him in fashioning this world.

Zoroastrian doctrine is based upon a hierarchical order with Ahura Mazda at the helm. Below but attached to Ahura Mazda are the *Amesha Spentas* followed by the *Yazatas* (see below). The *Yazatas* are not attached to Ahura Mazda, but are referred to as the "Adorable Ones", followed by the *Fravashis* (guardian spirits) of the departed, followed by living human beings and the other six physical creations.

Amesha Spentas

The *Amesha Spentas* fulfil a dual role. They are understood to be attached to Ahura Mazda in a way similar to the relationship between the sun's rays and the sun. Their virtues reflect the principal or primary attributes of Ahura Mazda and form the kernel of the ethical infrastructure of the Zoroastrian religion. They are, in addition, the guardians and protectors of the seven primary physical creations: sky, waters, earth, plants, cattle, humans and fire, although some Zoroastrians see them more as symbolic ideals. In either case, they are understood to set the ethical framework for humankind.

Since Zoroastrian doctrine is based upon a hierarchical order, the first *Amesha Spenta* is *Spenta Mainyu* (Holy Spirit of Ahura Mazda) the guardian of humankind; *Vohu Manah* (Good Mind) is the guardian of cattle; *Asha Vahishta* (Best Order/Truth and Righteousness) is the guardian of fire; *Kshathra Vairya* (Divine Kingdom/ Dominion) is the guardian of sky; *Spenta Armaiti* (Bounteous Devotion) is the guardian of earth; Haurvata (Perfection / Wholeness) is the guardian of water; *Ameretat* (Immortality) is the guardian of plants.

The *Amesha Spentas* all have Pahlavi (Middle Iranian) names, which are shorter than their Avestan or Old Iranian counterparts. Thus Spenta Mainyu is Spennag Menog Vohu Manah is known as Vahman or Bahman; Asha Vahishta as Ardvahisht or Ardibehesht; Kshathre Vairya as Shahrevar; Spenta armaiti as Spendarmad or Aspandarmad; Haurvatat as Hordad or Khordad; and Ameretat as Amardad.

Each of these forces is represented as a sample in important rituals and when invoked with devotion and purity they are believed to be powerfully present. For instance, during a *Jashan* ritual (thanks giving ceremony), the sky which the ancient Iranians saw as a metallic spherical enclosure, is represented by the metal utensils, the waters as water in a metal beaker; earth as the sacred demarcated space on which the *Jashan* is performed; plants by the fresh and dried fruits, nuts, fresh flowers and dried sandalwood in metal trays; animals by milk in a metal beaker; humans by the priests performing the *Jashan*; and fire by an oil lamp in a metal beaker.

All seven samples of the physical creation are linked by the metal trays and beakers touching each other (priests form the link by holding metal tongs or ladle). The *atash* (sacred fire) is lit in the *afarganyu* (fire vase) and during the *Jashan* the priests invoke the spirit of Ahura Mazda, the *Amesha Spentas*, the *Yazatas*, and the *Fravashis* of the departed, who descend through the sacred fire and consecrate the fruits, nuts and other sacred food, which in turn is consumed by the living after the *Jashan*.

Yazatas

Next in rank to the *Amesha Spentas* come the *Yazatas/Yazads* (or "adorable ones"). Unlike the *Amesha Spentas* (which are attributes Ahura Mazda), the *Yazatas* are separate from Ahura Mazda. The concept of *Yazatas* is a unique one in Zoroastrianism as they are seen as being neither as gods nor angels. In the earlier *polytheistic* religious structures prior to Zarathushtra's revelation some of the *Yazatas* were worshipped as divinities by the ancient Iranians. But after Zarathushtra's revelation those divinities which were not denounced as *daevas* were incorporated into the Zoroastrian pantheon and became known as *Yazatas*, thereby maintaining a continuity with all that was good in the earlier religious structures.

The *Yazatas* came to be understood as beings which assist the *Amesha Spentas* and further the well-being of the seven good creations of Ahura Mazda. Thus, for example, Asha Vahishta, the guardian of fire, is helped by Adar Yazad who is the *Yazata* for fire and Haurvatat, the guardian of the waters, is assisted by Tir Yazad who is the *Yazata* for the rains.

Each *Amesha Spenta* is assisted by three or four *Yazatas* and the *Yazatas* have a particular role in helping human beings to realise the inherent nature of Ahura Mazda and to achieve an all-embracing happiness rooted in recognising the nature of Wisdom.

Fravashi

Like the *Yazatas,* the concept of the *Fravashis* exisited in pre-Zoroastrian times, where it was believed that the spirits of the departed heroes lived with the gods in the underworld.

Therefore the spirits of the departed warriors came to be identified with the spiritual celestial world. The spirits were conceived to be powerful, winged and warlike beings to be worshipped and invoked by their living descendents in order they may be helped and protected by them.

In Zoroastrianism, it is believed every human being possesses a *Fravashi* (Guardian Spirit of Ahura Mazda). A *Fravashi* is depicted artistically as a half human – half bird winged figure with its right hand always pointed upwards (towards heaven) while its left hand holding the ring of divine kingship. Often it is erroneously described as an angel or Ahura Mazda. Initially, the *Fravashis* first existed in a spiritual form and aided Ahura Mazda to fashion the prototypes of the physical creations.

The *Fravashi* acts as an observer in one's life and does not interfere with the decision making process of humans unlike the *urvan* (soul). Hence it is not judged at the *Chinvat Peretu* (*Bridge of the Separator*) where the *urvan* is judged for its goodness in relation to its wickedness in order for it to pass into heaven or fall into a dark abyss of hell.

The *Fravashis* are seen to represent Ahura Mazda's essence within human beings. It is said in the *Bundahishn* (Story of Creation), that they are the "Wisdom of all knowledge", which links them to Ahura Mazda. They are also believed to be the spiritual protectors of humans who, when in difficulty, can invoke them.

The Role of Humanity

In Zoroastrian teaching, the first human was the hermaphrodite, Gayo maretan known in Pahlavi as Gayomard who had both male and female offspring. Of all the beings created by Ahura Mazda, humans are seen to be the most conscious creation and the most able to come to understand the Good Mind (*Vohu Manah*).

Therefore humans are Ahura Mazda's agents or soldiers in the combat against the forces of evil. They have also been given a *Fravashi* (guardian spirit of Ahura Mazda), and an *urvan* (soul) which is immortal and believed to operate on the basis of wisdom, innate reason, intellect and free will, all of which are understood to be filtered through conscience.

This immaterial essence and directing principle operates through wisdom, innate reason, intellect, will and conscience to enable them to make genuine choices between good and evil thoughts, words and deeds. Ahura Mazda has given humanity this freedom to choose between the forces of good and evil.

Human beings, therefore, are the makers of their own destiny according to the choices they make. Hence, at death their immortal *urvan* (soul) is responsible and is held accountable at the *Chinvat Peretu* (Bridge of the Separator) by the *Yazatas* delegated by Ahura Mazda to judge whether their for all their *urvan* should ascend to the *House of Song* (heaven) or fall from the bridge into the dark abyss – the *House of Deceit* (hell) where they will remain until the end of time.

The Concept of Death and Afterlife

In Zoroastrianism, death is seen as the negation of life. Therefore, death is deemed to be the work of evil, because it is only living human beings who, through their goodness, can bring about the final defeat of evil and make Ahura Mazda truly omnipotent. It is the inherent nature of evil to wreak havoc and destruction upon Ahura Mazda's good creations. Because evil is ignorant thus it attacks at random and death is seen as a random casualty of the cosmic battle against evil.

According to the Avesta upon death the *urvan* (soul) is separated from the *tanu* (body) and takes its seat near the head. As death is the work of evil, the *tanu* (body) should be disposed of as quickly as possible during daylight hours before sunset. On the dawn of the fourth morning after death, it is believed that the *urvan* (soul) commences its journey to be judged at the *Chinvat Peretu Bridge* (*Bridge of the Separator*). Its good thoughts, words and deeds are weighed in the balance against the evil and the *urvan* either ascends to the *House of Song* (heaven) or falls from the bridge into the dark abyss of the *House of Deceit* (hell) which, in Zoroastrian texts, is pictured as cold, damp and lonely place where every *urvan* feels alone.

Because Ahura Mazda is perfect and as there is no original sin, the soul of a child who dies during birth or before their *Navjote* (initiation ceremony) is not judged and directly ascends to heaven.

Saoshyant, End Time, Physical Resurrection, Last Judgement and Frasho-keriti

In classical Zoroastrian belief, the soul is immortal and is believed to continue to exist after death in heaven or hell until the end of time. It was believed that, at the end of time the forces of evil will be completely destroyed by the good. The *Saoshyant* (last human being or Saviour) will strike the final blow against evil. This will be followed by the *tan-i-pasen* (physical resurrection) where the *urvan* unites with its future body which is the prime age of a youth and the *Last Judgement* is initiated.

Heaven, earth and hell and all the resurrected bodies and souls in chronological order will be engulfed in "an ocean of molten metal" commencing with *Gayo maretan,* the first human being followed by the rest of humankind until the *Saoshyant* and also Zarathushtra. Those who are good, like Zarathushtra, will feel the "molten metal" as "cool milk", while the imperfect will be cleansed before joining the blessed.

Pairidaeza (paradise) as it is in heaven will exist on earth. Time will cease to exist and the world will return to its original perfect state of total goodness and harmony known to Zoroastrians as *Frasho-keriti* (Making Wonderful). Ahura Mazda will finally be truly omnipotent!

ZOROASTRIAN LIFE

Ethics

Asha (best truth/righteousness) is the central principle of Zoroastrian ethics. It is related to *Vohu Manah* (good mind) and includes within it all virtues.

Among the choices which confront human beings in the cosmic battle between good and evil are those between good thoughts, good words and good deeds and bad thoughts, bad words and bad deeds; between happiness and despair; between optimism and pessimism; between joy and misery; between moderation and deficiency or excess; between truth and falsehood; between order and chaos; between light and darkness; between generating money and wealth the honest way and by ill gotten means, between sharing excess wealth in charity and greed; between life and death.

Zoroastrians are urged to live life to the full, but in moderation and to enjoy the good creation. Zoroastrians, who believe that Ahura Mazda made the whole of the material world, including the sky, waters, earth, plants and animals, have always been very environmentally conscious. Fasting and celibacy are seen as weakening human beings and lessening their power to struggle against evil and as rejecting the divine gift of the good life. Moderation is encouraged and thus Zoroastrian ethics enjoin an active, industrious, honest and charitable life.

Initiation

Navjote (Gujarati for "new birth") or *Sedreh-Pushi* (Farsi for "wearing *sedreh*") is the initiation ceremony for the children of Zoroastrian parents. As there is no original sin in Zoroastrianism, the actions of a child born of Zoroastrian parents are held to be the responsibility of its parents until the child has undergone this ceremony. Although in earlier times the ceremony took place at the age of fifteen, it now usually takes place for both males and females between the ages of seven and eleven, before puberty.

Exceptionally, it can be held later on, with the permission of the officiating priest. Friends and relatives of the child attend the ceremony that combines prayer, ritual and celebration. Before the ceremony the initiate is given a *nahn* (ritual purificatory bath) and is then invested with the *sudreh* and *kushti* (see below) and recites the *Fravarane* which is a declaration of faith recited daily by Zoroastrians. The *Fravarane* begins with the words: "Come to my aid, O Mazda! I profess myself a worshipper of Mazda! I am a Zoroastrian worshipper of Mazda!" It praises good thoughts, good words and good deeds, and ends by ascribing all good things to Ahura Mazda.

Sudreh and Kusti/Koshti

The *sudreh* and *kushti* should be worn at all times by Zoroastrians. The *sudreh* is always worn next to the skin and is seen as "the garment of *Vohu Manah* (good mind)". It is a sacred vest made of muslin or cotton cloth and is always white. This symbolises purity of thought and so influences the mind to be good. At the bottom of its v-shaped neck there is a one inch square pocket which contains a slit. This pocket is known as the *gireban* or *kisseh-kerfeh* ("pocket of good deeds"). This reminds Zoroastrians that they should be filling up their lives with good deeds, but also that whatever good a person does, it is only one square inch compared to Ahura Mazda's goodness. There is also a large pouch (known as a *girdo*) at the back of the *sudreh* that represents a storehouse for future good deeds.

A small vertical dart, known as a *straight tiri*, comes out of the hem of the *sudreh*, the significance has varying interpretations, one of which is that it is the reminder of the existing imperfection in the physical world by evil. There is also a small *triangular tiri* on the opposite side of the *straight tiri* that symbolises the threefold Zoroastrian teaching of good thoughts, good words and good deeds.

The *sudreh* symbolises "the advantageous path" and the *kushti* indicates the proper direction finder for proceeding on that path. The *kushti* is a sacred cord that is worn over the *sudreh*. It is passed three times around the waist signifying good thoughts, good words and good deeds and reef knotted at the front and back.

The front reef knot is tied while reciting two *Ahunavars* (twenty-one word prayer) and reminds the initiate that Ahura Mazda is holy and matchless and that Zoroastrianism is the word of Ahura Mazda.

The rear reef knot is tied while reciting an *Ashem Vohu* (twelve word prayer) which is a symbolic confirmation of championing the cause of *Asha* (best truth/righteousness) for its own sake as it alone leads to everlasting happiness.

The *kushti* is woven from seventy-two threads of fine lambs' wool that symbolise the seventy-two chapters of the *Yasna* (Act of Worship). The *kushti* is sanctified by special prayers at every stage of the weaving. Both *sudreh* and *kushti* are seen as a protection against evil. The *sudreh- kushti* is commonly known as the spiritual armour and sword belt of the religion, worn in the battle against evil.

Gah/Geh

For devotional purposes the twenty-four hours in a day are divided into five *Gah* (times): *Havani* in Avestan *or Havan* in Pahlavi (from sunrise to noon); *Rapithwa* in Avestan or *Rapithwin* in Pahlavi (from noon till 3.00pm); *Uzayara* in Avestan or *Uzerin* in Pahlavi (from 3.00pm to sunset); *Aiwisruthra* in Avesta or *Aiwisruthrim* in Pahlavi (from sunset to midnight); *Ushah* in Avestan and *Ushahin* in Pahlavi (from midnight to sunrise).

Hence a Zoroastrian is enjoined to pray at least five times a day in order to remember Ahura Mazda, who through the *Amesha Spentas* and the *Yazatas* maintains a continuous vigil in the world. By communicating with Ahura Mazda through prayer a Zoroastrian learns to talk in a special way to Ahura Mazda, his Maker and Best Friend, resulting in an indefinable harmony.

To prepare for prayer Zoroastrians wash their hands, face and all uncovered parts of the body. However, Zoroastrians were, from ancient times, also encouraged to cover their feet with socks and not go bare footed because they picked up dirt which is linked to evil. Zoroastrians stand in either the east, west or south (never north) direction and commence praying. As they do so, they untie the *kusti*, holding the mid point in the left hand while the remaining length passes between the thumb and index finger of the right hand with the two ends hanging down loosely but not touching the floor. While doing this, they focus on the sun or fire (or artificial light if no natural light is available) as a symbol of *asha* (best truth). Prayers are then offered to Ahura Mazda and the *kusti* is retied.

Zoroastrian prayers and be roughly divided into five categories; Wisdom poetry such as Zarathushtra's *Gathas*; Meditative formulae such as the *Ashem Vohu* and *Ahunavar*; prayers of praise, propitiation and thanks-giving such as the *Yasna* and *Nyaishes*; prayers for boons and intercession such as *Yashts*; and prayers for ritual instruction such as the *Vendidad*.

The *Ashem Vohu* three line twelve word meditative prayer is the first prayer taught to all Zoroastrian children by their parents, usually by the age of three. It is also the last prayer to be recited just before death. If this is not possible then it is the duty of another Zoroastrian to softly recite it in the ear of the dying person. This meditative prayer is concerned with *Asha*, thus stressing to the child the importance of the best truth and being righteous for the sake of righteousness.

It is followed by the meditative twenty-one word *Ahunavar* or *Ahuna Vairya*, which in the Zoroastrian scriptures is said to have been recited by Ahura Mazda when He created the world. This is also deemed to be the most powerful instrument of prayer in warding off evil and it is stressed to the children that they should recite it whenever they are in difficulty or commencing a journey or leaving home in the morning.

Death Practices

Death is seen as the work of evil. A dead body represents the apparent triumph and presence of evil and is therefore seen as a *nasu* (corpse demon) and polluting. Because of this, it is believed that disposal should be carried out as quickly as possible and in a way which is least harmful to the living and the other good creations of Ahura Mazda.

Disposal into rivers or the sea is believed to pollute the water and disposal by burial could pollute the land while cremation would pollute the fire. Therefore, Zoroastrians traditionally exposed the dead body in the mountains to the natural elements and to birds and animals of prey. Later on a confined building was developed known as a *dakhma* (circular open roofed stone tower), colloquially known in the English language as a *Tower of Silence*, where the body was exposed to the hot sun and eaten by vultures.

Due to emphasis on burial that followed the Arab invasion and subsequent Islamisation of Iran, this traditional practice increasingly became extremely controversial. By the late twentieth century, burial had been adopted by the Zoroastrian minority in Iran. But instead of burying the body directly in the earth, the grave was lined with stone before burning the body, this being in line with ancient Zoroastrian belief that hard stone or strong metal will contain the *nasu*.

In India and Pakistan, the customary system of exposure of the body in a *dakhma* continues. However, since the nineteenth century the circular stone towers became more elaborate, and were designed and built using modern scientific and engineering principles and architectural plans including carbon filters and lime pits intended to provide further containment of the *nasu* (corpse demon).

In these *dakhma* the body is rapidly consumed by vultures. Bones dried by the hot sun are periodically swept into a deep pit and sprinkled with lime and destroyed by the *nasasalars* (professional corpse bearers) who also perform routine maintenance to ensure maximum efficiency. In accordance with purity laws anybody who enters the *dakhma* including the *nasasalars* must regularly undergo a ritual purification bath.

Only a small number of *dakhmas* are still in use in India and Pakistan, As the twentieth century progressed, and with it rapid urbanisation, there was increasing debate within the Zoroastrian community about whether to abandon this ancient practice, although it should be noted that the initial catalyst to adopt burial was not from the

Hindus, but from the British and European Christians during the British Raj. However, the Zoroastrians doggedly continued on the grounds that it was ecologically sound and egalitarian because the bodies of the dead, whether rich or poor, would undergo exposure in the same *dakhma*.

In the last years of the twentieth century, vultures in South Asia succumbed to *diclofenac*, a cheap non-steroidal anti-inflammatory drug in use by both humans and cattle and taken to reduce inflammation and pain. If cattle die and the carcass still contains *diclofenac* and the vulture eats the carcass, it becomes ill and quickly dies. Because of this, the over 95% of the vulture population in India and Pakistan has died within less then a decade.

Currently, the Royal Society for the Protection of Birds and other international agencies, together with the Bombay Natural History Society, have commenced a vulture breeding programme. However, at present there remains a dire shortage of vultures and this has once again ignited the debate in the Zoroastrian community about whether this ancient custom of exposure in the *dakhma* should continue or should be replaced by burial and cremation.

In the UK, there is no *dakhma* because there are no vultures. Thus, while occasionally the bodies are flown back to India to be exposed in the *dakhma* in Bombay, they are usually buried or cremated and the ashes interred at the Zoroastrian cemetery at Brookwood in Surrey, established in 1863.

Diet

Zoroastrians are, by tradition, not vegetarians. However, eating carnivores, humans and reptiles is prohibited. There are no dietary requirements for Zoroastrians when it comes to eating herbivores fish and seafood, although from personal choice or sometimes from deference to the wider religious population of Iran, Pakistan and India, many Zoroastrians abstain from pork and beef and some are vegetarian.

In the month of Vohu Manah or Bahman, which is the eleventh month in the twelve month Zoroastrian calendar, by tradition all Zoroastrians are vegetarian. This is because Bahman is mid January to mid February, which is when animals are pregnant and fish are full of roe.

Therefore, by consuming animals and fish in Bahman, the animal population would be depleted. In addition to the eleventh month of Bahman, there are four days in every 30 day month associated with the *Amesha Spenta, Vohu Manah,* or *Bahman* when traditional Zoroastrians are vegetarian. These are Bahman (2nd day), Mohor (11th day), Gosh (13th day) and Ram 20th day).

When a person dies, the family members and close relatives remain vegetarian until the fourth morning after death, when it is believed that the *urvan* commences its journey to be judged at the *Chinvat Peretu Bridge (Bridge of the Separator)*. By tradition the family of the departed must, on the fourth day known as *Charan*, consume meat as part of their main meal.

During a traditional wedding the festivities continue for about five to seven days prior to the actual marriage ceremony and on one of these days only vegetarian food is served.

TRADITIONS IN ZOROASTRIANISM

The main differences amongst Zoroastrians arise from the differing ancestral histories (see above) of the two main groups involved in the religion – the *Iranis* and the *Parsis*. These differences manifest themselves particularly in relation to the Zoroastrian calendar and some festivals (see below).

ZOROASTRIAN WORSHIP

Fire

Fire (*atar* or *adur/adar*) is used in virtually all Zoroastrian ceremonies and many individual Zoroastrians keep an oil lamp burning in their homes.

The centrality of this veneration of fire in Zoroastrian worship has often intrigued and puzzled non-Zoroastrians. It has led some people to describe Zoroastrians erroneously as "fire worshippers". This is, however, a misunderstanding and it is offensive to Zoroastrians. Zoroastrians do not worship fire, but worship Ahura Mazda. Zarathushtra was the bearer of an earlier Iranian tradition in which fire was associated with truth and order.

In the Gathas fire is linked with *Asha* and is considered a sacred force because it is a source of light and warmth as well as a symbol of truth and righteousness.

The consecrated sacred fire in a Zoroastrian *Fire Temple* is the focal point of worship, praise and propitiation. In its simplest form, fire is that which burns and gives out light. The burning fire may be likened to that which renders something pure, whilst its energy is understood to be the source of all other energies and of life itself throughout the universe.

The oldest consecrated sacred fires in Zoroastrianism have been continuously burning in Iran for over 2500 years and in India for over 1000 years, both being centres of Zoroastrian pilgrimage.

Standing before the consecrated sacred fire in a *Fire Temple*, Zoroastrians believe they are standing in the presence of spirit of Ahura Mazda. This philosophy lies behind the *atash Nyaish* (Litany of Fire).

ZOROASTRIAN PLACES OF WORSHIP

Places of Worship

Traditionally, Zoroastrian places of worship are known as *Fire Temples* because a consecrated fire burns perpetually inside them. While, a reverence for fire is found within the broader Aryan tradition that pre-dates Zarathushtra, the use of temples was introduced into Zoroastrianism during the times of the Achaemenid kings in around the fifth century BCE.

It is assumed that Zoroastrian men and women will have bathed at home prior to visiting the place of worship. Before entering the worship hall, Zoroastrian men and women must remove shoes, wash their hands and face, cover their heads when praying, and then perform the *kusti* ritual in the entrance to the place of worship.

There is a consecrated chamber where the fire is housed and into which only *priests* may enter. Zoroastrian worshippers may bow before the fire and take some cold ash to place on their forehead in order to receive the divine blessing.

Zoroastrian places of worship are not recorded as a separate category in the running totals of certified places of worship in England and Wales kept by the Registrar General. There are no traditional, formally consecrated, Zoroastrian *Fire Temples* in the United Kingdom. There is, however, a room for Zoroastrian worship at the new Zoroastrian Centre in Harrow.

Visitors to a Zoroastrian Place of Worship

Religious Education professionals and students, inter-faith groups and people from outside the Zoroastrian community may, on occasion, be invited to attend a *jashan* (thanksgiving festival). In these circumstances a general attitude of respectful presence is appropriate, along with appropriately modest clothing. During ceremonies visitors, just like Zoroastrians, must cover their head with a prayer cap or scarf.

During ceremonial occassions, out of respect for Zoroastrians who are praying, non-Zoroastrians are requested not to enter the prayer room, known as the *setayash gah* (place of worship) However, at other times they may enter providing they are accompanied with personnel from the Zoroastrian Centre.

ZOROASTRIAN CALENDARS AND FESTIVALS

Calendar

The Zoroastrian view of time is a linear one that has a specific end in view, known as *Frasho-Kereti* (Making Wonderful) when all things are restored to a state of wholeness and perfection. Therefore, reincarnation is rejected. When Iran was ruled by Zoroastrian monarchs, a new calendar commenced every time a new monarch was crowned.

Thus the current Zoroastrian dating system began with the date of the coronation of the last Zoroastrian monarch of Sasanian Iran, Yazdegird III, whose reign commenced in 631 CE. The letters "YZ" (Yazdegird Zoroastrian) are used to denote the year, making 2007 CE the Zoroastrian year 1376 YZ.

In ancient times the annual calendar was composed of twelve months with thirty days in each month. Since *No-Roz* or New Year's Day did not fall on the spring equinox, in 224 CE the first Sasanian king Ardashir I added five additional days, known as the *Gatha* days to the twelfth month, making a three hundred and sixty-five day annual calendar.

Traditionally the Zoroastrian calendar does not have a leap year day, but every one hundred and twenty years one month (thirteenth month) was added in order to synchronise this calendar with the solar calendar in order to ensure that the *No-Roz* or New Year's Day did fall on the spring equinox.

In the Zoroastrian calendar, the names of the months correspond with the names of the *Amesha Spentas* and the *Yazatas*. Therefore Zoroastrians view all days as holy and special, although there is also a cycle of annual festivals.

The *Shahenshahi* (monarchist) *Yazdegeri* calendar first adopted by the *Parsis* runs one month behind the Iranian *Kadmi* (ancient) *Yazdegerdi* calendar. This is because during the turbulent history of Zoroastrianism in the last millennium, the *Parsis* in India added the thirteenth month to the *Shahenshahi Yazdegeri* calendar in 498 YZ or 1129CE, while the Iranians did not, resulting in one month difference between the two calendars.

Subsequently both the *Parsis* in India and the Iranians did not add the thirteenth month. Therefore in neither the *Shahenshahi Yazdegeri* or *Kadmi Yazdegerdi No-Roz* or New Year's Day fall on the spring equinox.

Currently, *No-Roz* or New Year's Day is, according to the *Shahenshahi Yazdegeri,* is celebrated in August. In 1906 CE, a group of *Parsis* in India who were concerned that *No-Roz* was not falling on the spring equinox established the *Fasli* (solar) calendar by adding a leap year day every four years. Due to various reasons linked with traditional ceremonial practices the *Fasli* (solar) calendar failed to become popular in India but was adopted by some *Parsis* in the diaspora.

The *Fasli* calendar has dates that are fixed in alignment with the *Gregorian* calendar and is observed by the Iranian Zoroastrians instead of the *Kadmi Yazdegerdi* calendar. This is mainly because according to the current national Iranian calendar *No-Roz* commences with the spring equinox in March and also because the names of the twelve months of the current Iranian national calendar are the same as the Zoroastrian religious calendar.

However, due to the impact of anti-monarchist sentiments of the Iranian government following the Islamic Revolution, Zoroastrians residing in Iran have more recently stopped using the *Yazdegird* calendar and have adopted a new dating system commencing with era of Zarathushtra around 3500.

There are therefore three calendars that might be found in use amongst Zoroastrians. The vast majority of Zoroastrians in the UK, being *Parsis,* follow the *Shahenshahi Yazdegeri* calendar. However, it should be noted that, like most Zoroastrians in the UK and elsewhere in the world the Zoroastrian Centre in Harrow, tends to celebrate festivals such as New Year in all three Zoroastrian calendars, plus the Gregorian calendar, thus giving Zoroastrians reason for additional celebrations as happiness and joy are seen as being a part of Ahura Mazda's good creation.

Festivals

Religious festivals, of which there are various kinds, play a central role in the devotional life of Zoroastrians.

Gahambars (seasonal festivals)
These are a series of seven great festivals devoted to the seven *Amesha Spentas* and to the creation of sky, water, earth, plants, animals, humankind and fire. These festivals traditionally last for five days each. They are holy days of obligation during which prayers are recited. On the final day a communal feast is held.

The first *gahambar*, called *Maidyoizaremaya* or *Maidyu Zarem* (meaning "mid-Spring") is connected with the sky. The second, *Maidyoishema* or *Maidyu Shem* (meaning "mid-Summer") is linked with the waters. The third, *Paitish-hahya* or *Paiti Shahim* (meaning "bringing in the corn") is linked with the earth. The fourth, *Ayathrima* or *Ayathrem* (meaning "homecoming") is linked with plants. The fifth, *Maidhyairya* or *Maidyaryam* (meaning "mid-Winter") is linked with cattle. The sixth *gahambar*, *Hamaspathmaedaya* or *Hamas Pathmaidyam*, also known as *Fravashis or Fravahrs* (meaning "Feast of Heavenly Souls"), is a special festival in honour of humanity's creation.

The *gahambar* cycle is then completed by the observance of *No-Roz* (see below) that is the New Year festival. The dates of the *gahambars* vary according to which calendar is used and all vary in relation to the *Gregorian* calendar. The principal observance at the *gahambars* is the *Yasht-i-Visperad* which is a three-hours

long service commencing at sunrise, giving thanks for the creations and sanctifying them with rituals and sacred words.

No-Roz (New Year's Day – Spring Vernal Equinox) (20th/21st March)
This is the most important festival of the Zoroastrian year which is associated with the seventh creation fire, which in turn is linked to Asha (Best Truth). It is the last convivial occasion of the old year, but also signifies the imminent arrival of spring. According to traditional popular belief, it was founded by King Jamshed (Zoroastrian equivalent to Biblical Noah) of the ancient Pishdadian dynasty after the last ice age. It is marked by the wearing of new clothes, the holding of festivities, and the giving and receiving of presents. The *Shahenshahi No-Roz* is currently celebrated in the third week in August.

Khordad Sal (6th day after No-Roz)
Celebrates the birth of the Prophet Zarathushtra. Among Iranian Zoroastrians the festival is known as *Zad Rooz-e Ashoo Zartosht*.

Zarthosht no Diso (11th day, 10th month)
Marks the anniversary of Zarathushtra's death.

Muktad (26th day, 12th month)
This is the name given to the final ten days of the year observed in *Parsi* custom. Among Iranian Zoroastrians only the last five days (*Hamaspathmaedaya gahambar*), before *No-Roz* are observed. These days are in honour of the *Fravashis* of the departed and are usually marked by prayers and a ritual meal in honour of them. The last five days of *Muktad* are the five *Gatha* days and each day one of the five *Gathas* appropriate to that day are recited and ceremonies are performed in Zoroastrian homes and *Fire Temples*. Vases of flowers are put around homes and in *Fire Temples* to commemorate relatives who have died.

Prayers are recited in remembrance of them and for all human souls since it is believed that the souls, together with the *Fravardin* of the dead, of the dead pay visits at this time. The Iranian Zoroastrians also call the first five days of this period *Panje-kas* (the *Lesser Pentad*) and the last five days *Panje-mas* (the *Greater Pentad*).

Jashans

The names of the twelve months are also the names of twelve days of every month. Thus when the name of the *roz* or day coincides with name of the *mah* or months then that day is designated as a festival. Each *roz* and *mah* in the Zoroastrian calendar is dedicated to an *Amesha Spenta* or *Yazata*. The exception is *Fravardin* which is connected with the first month and the nineteenth day, known as *Farvardingan*, observed as a day of remembrance for departed souls. In addition to the obligatory days of observance outlined above there are other festival days when the particular days and months dedicated to the *Amesha Spentas* and the *Yazatas* coincide. Marking these days is not obligatory, but it is considered meritorious. The *Jashans* include:

Tirgan (on Tir roz / roj and, in Tir mah)
(13th day, 4th month)
A quarter year festival devoted to *Tir*, the *Yazata* of rain and fertility. The festival overlaps with the second seasonal *gahambar* and on this day, people throw water at each other in celebration of its significance.

Mehrgan (on Meher roz/roj, in Mehr mah)
(16th day, 7th month)
An autumnal half yearly festival, dedicated to the *Yazata Mehr*, who is associated with justice, keeper of contracts and promises and with the sun.

ava-roj Parab (on ava roz/roj in ava mah)
(10th day, 8th month)
Celebrated as the birthday of the waters. Special food offerings and prayers are made on this day in which Zoroastrians go to a river or to the seaside and give thanks for its purification and pray for the nourishment of the world.

adar-roj Parab (on adar roz/roj in adar mah)
(9th day, 9th month)
Celebrated as the birthday of fire on which, traditionally, food is not cooked in the house. Through this, fire is allowed to rest whilst Zoroastrians give thanks for the warmth and light that come from it throughout the year. Special prayers are offered in the presence of the house fire.

Sadeh (10th day, 11th month)
An open air mid-winter festival celebrated with bonfires and held fifty days before *No-Roz*. It celebrates the discovery of fire by Hoshang Shah, believed by Zoroastrians to have been an historical figure of the Pishdadian dynasty.

Jashan ceremonies include the representation of the sevenfold creation by means of the display of a variety of objects as explained in the section on the *Amesha Spentas* (see above). Each of these items is offered with specific prayers to their spiritual counterparts among the *Amesha Spentas* who are, in turn, by their powerful presence believed to bless the offerings that are then shared by those present.

ZOROASTRIAN ORGANISATIONS

Zoroastrian Organisational Listings

The Zoroastrian Trust Funds of Europe (Incorporated) and the World Zoroastrian Organisation are the two Zoroastrian organisations whose contact details are listed in the CD-ROM accompanying this volume. Whilst based in the UK and having a national role, they also have a role beyond the UK itself. Although there are small numbers of Zoroastrians elsewhere in Britain and Europe, the Zoroastrian Centre (which is the headquarters and centre of the Zoroastrian Trust Funds of Europe) in Harrow, Middlesex, is the central focal point for

Zoroastrian worship and community activity in the UK.

On a national level the first Zoroastrian organisation in the UK was established in 1861. It was known as the Religious Funds of the Zarathushtrians of Europe. Under the new name of the Incorporated Parsee Association of Europe it obtained rented premises for the conduct of Zoroastrian worship and, in 1929, it purchased a building in Kensington Olympia, London.

In 1969, and by then known as the Zoroastrian Association of Europe (Incorporated), it purchased another Zoroastrain House in West Hampstead, London. Since 1978, it has been known as the Zoroastrian Trust Funds of Europe (Incorporated) and in 2005 it shifted to the Zoroastrian Centre in Harrow, Middlesex which is a former grade 2★ heritage listed former art deco cinema. The World Zoroastrian Organisation is also based in London.

Since the Zoroastrian community in the United Kingdom is not very numerous, geographically widespread or structured into many local organisations, the CD-ROM accompanying this volume instead lists a range of contacts for local Zoroastrians.

Personnel

A *Dastur* (high priest) or a *Mobed* (authorised priest) officiates at Zoroastrian ceremonies and may be helped by *Ervad Sahebs* (assistants to the high priest). When officiating, Zoroastrian priests are dressed in white and wear the traditional *padan* (piece of white cloth) over their mouths, in order not to pollute the fire while praying.

The ceremony for initiation into the priesthood takes over a month and there are two grades of initiation. In the UK, the *Ervads* (priests) are members of priestly families who have been initiated in India and function here as priests on a part-time voluntary basis, as required.

FURTHER READING

Azargoshasb, A, *Festivals of Ancient Iran*, Tehran, 1970.

Boyce, M, *A History of Zoroastrianism*, Volume I, E J Brill, Leiden, 1976.

Boyce, M, *A Persian Stronghold of Zoroastrianism*, Clarendon Press, Oxford, 1977.

Boyce, M, *A History of Zoroastrianism*, Volume II, E J Brill, Leiden, 1980.

Boyce, M, *Textual Sources for the Study of Zoroastrianism*, Manchester University Press, Manchester, 1984.

Boyce, M, Zoroastrians: Their Religious Beliefs and Practices, Routledge and Kegan Paul, London, 1984.

Boyce, M, *Zoroastrianism: A Shadowy but Powerful Pressure in the Judaeo-Christian World*, Dr Willians Trust, London, 1987

Boyce, M, Grenet, F, and Beck, R, *A History of Zoroastrianism*, Volume III, E J Brill, Leiden, 1990.

Boyce, M, *Zoroastrianism: Its Antiquity and Constant Vigour*, 1985 Columbia University Iranian Lectures, 1992.

Clark, P, *Zoroastrianism: An Introduction to an Ancient Faith*, Brighton, 1998.

Dhalla, M N, *History of Zoroastrianism*, K R Cama Oriental Institute, Bombay, 1985.

Dhalla, M N, Zoroastrian Civilisation, K R Cama Oriental Institute, Bombay, 2000.

Dauond, P (trans), *The Holy Gathas*, D J Irani, Bombay, 1924.

Hinnells, J, *Zoroastrianism and the Parsis*, Ward Lock Educational, London, 1981.

Hinnells, J, "Parsi Zoroastrians in London", in Ballard, R (ed), *Desh Pardesh: The South Asian Presence in Britain*, Hurst and Company, London, 1994, pp 251-271.

Hinnells, J, "The Global Zoroastrian Diaspora", in Brown, J and Foot, R (eds),

Migration: The Asian Experience, Macmillan, London, 1994, pp. 56-82.

Hinnells, J, *Zoroastrians in Britain*, Oxford University Press, Oxford, 1996.

Hinnells, J, "Health and Suffering in Zoroastrianism", in Hinnells, J and Porter, R (eds), *Religion, Health and Suffering*, Kegan Paul, 1999, p. 1-22.

Hinnells, J, *Zoroastrian and Parsi Studies: The Selected Works of John R. Hinnells*, Ashgate, Aldershot, 2000.

Hinnells, J, *The Zoroastrian Diaspora: Religion and Migration*, Oxford University Press, Oxford, 2005.

Hinnells, J, Williams, A, *Parsis in India and the Diaspora*, Routledge, 2007.

Kanga, K E, *Khordeh Avesta: Transliterated and Translated into English*, Bombay Parsi Punchayet, Bombay, 1992.

Kanga, K E, *Gatha Ba Maani: Transliterated and Translated into English*, Bombay Parsi Punchayet, Bombay, 1997.

Kanga, K E, *Yasht Ba Maani: Transliterated and Translated into English*, Bombay Parsi Punchayet, Bombay, 2001.

Karaka, D F, *History of the Parsis, including their manner, customs, religion and present position in 2 volumes*, Cosmo Publications, New Delhi, 2002.

Kotwal, F, Boyd, J A, *A Guide to the Zoroastrian Religion*, Zoroastrian Studies, Bombay, 1995.

Kulke, E, *The Parsis in India: A Minority as Agent of Social Change*, Weltforum-Verlag, Munich, 1974.

Mehr, F, *The Zoroastrian Tradition: An Introduction to the Ancient Wisdom of Zarathustra*, Element Books, Dorset, 1991.

Menant, D, *The Parsis in 3 Volumes*, Jeroo Mango Books, Bombay, 1995.

Mistree, K, *Zoroastrianism: An Ethnic Perspective*, Zoroastrian Studies, Bombay, 1982.

Modi, J J, *Religious Ceremonies and Customs of the Parsis*, Bombay, 1986.

Shahzadi, F, *The Zarathushti Religion: A Basic Text*, Chicago, 1998.

Williams, C, "Deliverance and Human Destiny in Zoroastrianism", in Bowie, F (ed), *The Coming Deliverer: Millennial Themes in the World Religions*, University of Wales Press, Cardiff, 1997, pp 27-42.

Writer, R, *Contemporary Zoroastrians: An Unstructured Nation*, University Press of America, Maryland, 1994.

Writer, R, "Parsi Survival in India: the Role of Caste", in *World Faiths Encounter*, No. 10, March 1995, pp 38-47.

Zaehner, R, *The Teachings of the Magi*, Allen and Unwin, London, 1956.

Zaehner, R, *The Dawn and Twilight of Zoroastrianism*, Weidenfeld & Nicolson, London, 1961.

INTRODUCING SOME OTHER RELIGIOUS COMMUNITIES AND GROUPS

INTRODUCING SOME OTHER RELIGIOUS COMMUNITIES AND GROUPS 283

BRAHMA KUMARIS 287

CHRISTIAN SCIENTISTS 289

CHURCH OF JESUS CHRIST OF LATTER-DAY SAINTS 291

JEHOVAH S WITNESSES 293

NAMDHARI SIKH COMMUNITY 295

PAGANS 297

RASTAFARIANS 301

RAVIDASSIA 302

SANT NIRANKARIS 304

SATHYA SAI SERVICE ORGANISATION 305

VALMIKIS 306

INTRODUCTION

A Range of "Other Religious Groups"

This volume focuses primarily on nine world religious traditions that have substantial communities in the UK. There are, however, a range of other religious groups and forms of religious expression that either are not encompassed with these categories and/or groups. This chapter is an attempt to at least offer some supplementary information about a range of these forms of religious life. It offers a brief overview of each group covered and (generally speaking) a single contact print, although this should not be taken to imply that there might not be other useful points of contact.

These include groups that the reader may, in other contexts, see referred to as "New Religious Movements", although there are also many more groups that are beyond the scope of this directory, which might also be described by that name. For information on New Religious Movements, readers are referred to the specialist information service, INFORM (Information Network Focus on New Religious Movements, Tel: (020) 7955 7654, Email: inform@les.ac.uk, Internet at: http://www.inform.ac/uk), for which there is also a full page panel of information at the end of this chapter.

Some of the groups included in this chapter, such as the Sant Nirankaris and the Sathya Sai Service Organisation, have an understanding of themselves in universalistic terms as spiritual traditions that can include members of different religious traditions. At the same time groups who see themselves in more universalistic terms may be understood by others to be closely related to one of the nine world religious traditions which form the main focus of the directory.

Other groups may have some historical and/or doctrinal relationship with the nine traditions that form the directory's major subject matter.

At the same time, the precise nature of these relationships is often a disputed one, particularly from the perspective of the majority traditions covered in the earlier chapters. Placing details of such groups in this section is an acknowledgement of the existence of the issues involved. But the directory does not attempt to adjudicate on these disputes, resulting as they do from conflicting and often mutually exclusive self-understandings.

This chapter also includes information about Pagans who understands themselves as being entirely independent of the traditions covered in the earlier chapters. Some forms of Pagan organisation are relatively modern but Pagans in general understand themselves as in some way representing the older indigenous religious traditions of the UK. The Census Table M275 Religion (Most Detailed Categories) gives data on the variety of Pagan responses within the "Other religions – write in" category, and this data is included in the chapter's section on Pagans.

Other Religious Groups and the 2001 Census

In the Census this wider pattern of religious life was reflected in the category of response offered as "Other religions – write in". The total number of those in the UK responding to the Census question and using the option "Other religions - write in" was 178,837. This represents 0.3% of the total population and 0.4% of the population that identifies itself with any specific religion at all. Of these 178,837 a total of 143,811 were in England, 6,909 in Wales, 26,974 in Scotland, and 1,143 in Northern Ireland.

The Census did not offer a separate category of response for Bahá'ís, Jains and Zoroastrians, and it should therefore be noted that at least some respondents from these religions are likely to be included in the overall figures grouped by the Census results under the general category of "Other religions - write in". These figures are also likely to include some respondents from among traditions that have a contested relationship with one of the broad traditions where the Census offered a box to tick in response to the religious affiliation question.

As a proportion of the total population in local authority areas, the 2001 Census shows that, in England, the greatest concentration of respondents using the "Other religions – write in" option is to be found in the London Boroughs of Harrow (2.0%), Brent (1.1%), Barnet (1.0%); Brighton and Hove (0.8%), and the City of London (0.4%).

In relation to ethnicity, 78.4% of all those using the "Other religions – write in" option were also recorded as being "White", 13.7% as "Asian", 3.3% as "Black or Black British", 2.5% as "Mixed" and 2.0% as "Chinese or Other Ethnic Group". In addition, 0.9% of all those recorded in the Census as being "Asians" are also recorded as being of "other religions", as well as 0.7% of "Chinese and Other Ethnic Group", 0.6% of "Mixed", 0.4% of "Black or Black British" and 0.3% of those recorded as "White".

The Census Table M275 Religion (Most Detailed Categories) gives breakdowns for these religions and groups, but only for England and Wales. Many of these are recorded as having only very small numbers but the figures from this table can usefully be considered in relation to broad overall categories of respondents.

Christian–Related/Contested Groups in the 2001 Census

Respondents who are recorded under the category of "Other religions – write in" include some that have a disputed relationship with the wider Christian tradition, a number of which have specific sections giving further information on them within this chapter, while others do not.

Where respondents from these disputed groups did not use the category "Christian", but wrote the name of their group in under the "Other religions - write in" option, the following statistical breakdown can be found in the Office for National Statistics' Table M275 Religion (Most Detailed Categories).

Other than those which are included in sections in this chapter (Church of Jesus Christ of Latter-day Saints, Christian Scientists and Jehovah's Witnesses, the data for which is included in the relevant sections below), the Census write-in data includes British Israelites (30 in England and 0 in Wales); Christadelphians (2,123 in England and 245 in Wales), Christian Spiritualists (1,246 in England and 215 in Wales) and Unitarians (3,604 in England and 383 in Wales).

It should, however, be noted that Christian Research's *Religious Trends No. 4, 2003/4* gives higher 2001 estimates for some of these groups. This includes Christadelphians at 16,350 in England and 1,000 in Wales; and Unitarians and Free Christians at 4,350 in England and 1,000 in Wales.

Even allowing for the possibility that some of these figures may be over-estimates, the discrepancies with the data from the Census write-in responses would seem to indicate that significant numbers of respondents from these groups may well have simply ticked the box for Christian respondents rather using the option for "Other religions - write-in".

"New Religious Movements" in the 2001 Census

From Census Table M275 Religion (Most Detailed Categories), there is also data on a range of groups that are often described by the media and the general population in terms of the value-laden terminology of either *sects* or *cults*, but are generally described by academics in the study of religion by the more neutral terminology of as *New Religious Movements*. Among others, these groups include respondents attributed to Scientology (1,757 in England and 24 in Wales) and to the Unification Church (241 in England and 11 in Wales).

However, with regard to this latter group, it appears that respondents who used a write-in description of Unificationist were originally coded by the Office for National Statistics to the overall Christian data. But the Unification Church is listed here separately since it generally projects a more independent and universalist role than do the generally understood and accepted Christian *Churches*.

Hindu–Related Groups in the 2001 Census

The International Society for Krishna Consciousness (ISKCON) – often popularly known as "Hare Krishnas" after their chant - is an example of a movement that, having earlier often been seen as a "New Religious Movement", has now come to play a central part in the wider Hindu tradition and community in the UK.

It is therefore quite possible that the majority of people associated with ISKCON will have responded to the religion question using the tick box option of "Hindu", although Table M275 indicates that 612 respondents in England and 28 in Wales used the "Other religions – write in" option, giving the response "Hare Krishna".

There are also a number of other groups that have some relationship with the Hindu tradition, although quite a number of these understand their own identity and role in more universalist terms. Census Table M275 Religion (Most Detailed Categories) contains data on a number of groups that can be seen as in some way related to the Hindu tradition and/or aspects of it.

Other than those which are included in sections in this chapter (the Brahma Kumaris, the data for which is included in the relevant section below), these include the Divine Light Mission (18 in England and 3 in Wales); Eckankar (417 in England and 9 in Wales); and Raja Yoga (253 in England and 8 in Wales). Respondents giving Raja Yoga may be related to the Brahma Kumaris (see below) section.

Traditions Related to People of Chinese Descent in the 2001 Census

Many Chinese may have chosen to tick the pre-set option of Buddhist although the reality of Chinese religious life is often much more complex and multi-faceted than can be reflected in a single "tick-box" response. Census Table M275 Religion (Most Detailed Categories) also lists a number of groups that may be seen as in some way related to the religious life of people of Chinese descent (though it is likely that white, indigenous adopters of Taoism will be included in these figures). These include:

- Chinese Religions (141 in England and 7 in Wales)
- Confucianist (80 in England and 3 in Wales)
- Taoist (3,576 in England and 16 in Wales)
- Tin Tao (4 in England and 0 in Wales)

As noted in the section of this chapter on Paganism below, there were also 95 responses in England and 3 in Wales coded to Ancestor Worship that could relate to Chinese forms of religiosity and/or to Ancestor Worship in the context of Pagan-Related traditions.

Further "Other Religious Groups" in the 2001 Census

The Census Table M275 Religion (Most Detailed Categories) also includes data on a wide range of other respondents, from those indicating Satanism, through those indicating Rastafarianism, to followers of various New Age practices. The latter may have more or less to do with religion, depending on the individuals involved.

Thus Census Table M275 Religion (Most Detailed Categories) also lists a number of groups of these respondents which, excluding those which are covered in specific sections within this chapter include the following:

- Church of All Religion (60 in England and 10 in Wales)
- Deist (621 in England and 18 in Wales)
- Druze (260 in England and 0 in Wales)
- Mysticism (150 in England and 8 in Wales)
- New Age (869 in England and 36 in Wales)
- Occult (96 in England and 3 in Wales)
- Own Belief System (3,056 in England and 203 in Wales)
- Pantheism (1,516 in England and 87 in Wales)
- Sant Mat (53 in England and 0 in Wales)
- Santeri (21 in England and 0 in Wales)
- Spiritualist (30,124 in England and 2,280 in Wales)
- Theism (489 in England and 16 in Wales)
- Unitarian Universalist (30 in England and 0 in Wales)
- Universalist (914 in England and 57 in Wales)
- Vodun (208 in England and 5 in Wales).

Finally, in addition to all the above, there were 22,187 respondents in England and 610 in Wales whose responses to the "write-in" for "Other" have not been added to the specific coded groupings. There were also 17,894 respondents in England and 1,412 in Wales who indicated that they were of "Other" but without giving a specific "write-in" and who were therefore coded as "Other Religion (Not Described)".

BRAHMA KUMARIS

The Brahma Kumaris World Spiritual University (UK) is a movement based upon the teachings given earlier this century by a philanthropist from a Hindu religious background. He was born as Dada Lekhraj and later became known by the spiritual name of Prajapita Brahma. It is believed that Prajapita Brahma received a vision that the transformation of the world as we know it will be followed by the establishment of an earthly paradise of peace, happiness and abundance.

The movement believes in the soul as the eternal identity of the human being that uses the costume of the body to express itself. The human soul also goes through birth and rebirth, but always in human form. God is believed to be the Supreme of all souls, an unlimited source of light, love and peace.

The movement sees the universe in a cyclical process of creation, degeneration and re-creation, as in the Hindu framework of *yugas* or ages. The recreation of a paradise at the end of each cycle comes about through understanding and imbibing fundamental spiritual truths that are universal to most faiths.

The movement's world headquarters are in Mount Abu, Rajasthan, India. There are local Brahma Kumari Centres throughout India and in one hundred countries around the world. There are forty centres in the UK.

In the UK Census, where Brahma Kumaris used the "Other religions - write in" option provided in the religious affiliation questions, the Office for National Statistics' Table M275 Religion (Most Detailed Categories) indicates that 323 "write in" respondents in England and 8 in Wales responded in this way. At the same time, it should be noted from the same table that 253 respondents in England and 8 in Wales gave the response of Raja Yoga, of which it is likely that a substantial group could also be associated with the Brahma Kumaris. The Brahma Kumaris World Spiritual Assembly (UK) estimates that across the UK, there are around 200 Brahma Kumars (men) and Brahma Kumaris (women).

Students at the Brahma Kumari centres practice *Raja Yoga* meditation, the experience of the consciousness of the soul and the awareness of the eternal relationship with the Supreme Soul. Courses are offered in meditation and spiritual understanding. Other courses and activities include Positive Thinking, Stress Management, Anger Management, Self-Esteem and workshops on Inter-Personal Skills. Workshops and classes are also held in hospitals, prisons, in businesses, and for other interest groups.

Early morning meditation classes are held daily. On Thursday mornings, food is offered to God that is then shared with everyone who is present. Regular students of the Brahma Kumaris are vegetarian, abstain from tobacco and alcohol and are celibate.

Most centres outside India are run by people who are working and who devote their free time to teaching meditation. At larger centres, some full time teachers are required who lead a *"surrendered"* spiritual life. There is no membership, but people attend centres as regular students and also help with teaching and other duties, sometimes within a few months of studying.

On an international level, the Brahma Kumaris are a Non-Governmental Organisation affiliated to the United Nations and also have general consultative status with the United Nations Economic and Social Council and UNICEF. In this capacity they have organised international projects including the Million Minutes for Peace and Global Co-operation for a Better World Projects that reached 129 countries and "Sharing Our Values for a Better World", part of which is the publication, *Living Values: A Guidebook*, that has been in use as an educational tool in schools and community establishments in several countries. In the year 2000, the Brahma Kumaris were also major contributors to the United National International Year for the Culture of Peace.

Brahma Kumaris World Spiritual University (UK)

Global Co-operation House, 65 Pound Lane, London NW10 2HH

Tel: (020) 8727 3350 **Fax:** (020) 8727 3351

Contact: Sister Maureen

Position: Programme Director

Email: london@bkwsu.org

Bibliography

Hodgkinson, L, *Peace and Purity*, Random House, London, 1999.

Jayanti, BK, *God's Healing Power*, Penguin, London, 2002.

Kirpalani, J and Panjabi, M, *Living Values: A Guidebook,* Brahma Kumaris World Spiritual University, London, 1995.

O'Donnell, K, *Raja Yoga, New Beginnings*, Prajapita Brahma Kumaris World Spiritual University, Mount Abu, 1987.

Whaling, F, "The Brahma Kumaris", in *Journal of Contemporary Religion*, Volume 10, No. 1, 1995, pp 3-28.

CHRISTIAN SCIENTISTS

The Christian Science movement was founded by Mary Baker Eddy, who was born in New Hampshire, in the United States, in 1821.

The Church of Christ, Scientist, was incorporated with a charter in 1879. It sought to restore what it understood to be original Christianity and particularly the lost element of the healing ministry in contrast to reliance upon conventional medical treatment. In 1908, Mary Baker Eddy founded the daily international newspaper, *The Christian Science Monitor*, which has won seven Pulitzer prizes and is still published today.

Christian Science understands its authority to be drawn from the *Bible*. Its complete teachings are set out in the textbook entitled *Science and Health with Key to the Scriptures* by Mary Baker Eddy. A Christian Scientist's understanding of God and creation is based on the first chapter of the Book of Genesis where it is recorded that God made man (all men and women) in "his own image".

God, Spirit, is understood to be all-powerful, ever-present Mind, the source of all that is good. In absolute terms God's creation is seen as spiritual, entirely good and free from sin, suffering and death, although this ideal truth needs to be understood and proved by degrees in human experience.

Christian Scientists believe every individual can find physical healing and redemption from sin by understanding their God-given identity and by striving to adhere to the Bible's moral and spiritual guidance, including the *Ten Commandments* and *Christ's Sermon on the Mount*.

They seek to follow all the teachings and the example of Jesus Christ who is regarded as the *Saviour* of humankind. They understand Jesus as exemplifying the *Christ*, his God-given nature as the *Son of God*, and thereby revealing every individual's true spiritual nature. They accept Jesus' *virgin birth*, *crucifixion*, *resurrection* and *ascension*.

The Christian Science movement thus emerged from within the Christian community, and understands itself as within it, although this self-understanding would be disputed by many of the organisations referred to in the chapter on "Introducing the Christian Community", particularly on the basis of differences in understanding the person and role of Jesus.

The movement is organised in branch *churches* that hold Sunday worship services and Sunday School classes, host public talks on Christian Science, and are each expected to maintain a *Reading Room* in which Christian Science literature may be read, borrowed or bought.

On Wednesday evenings at Christian Science *churches Testimony Meetings* are held which include time for people to volunteer accounts of healings they have experienced.

The movement has *Christian Science Practitioners* who devote their lives full-time to the public practice of prayer-based healing.

In the UK Census, where Christian Scientists did not use the broad category of "Christian" for their response but wrote "Christian Scientist" under the "Other religions - write in" option provided in the religious affiliation questions, the Office for National Statistics' Table M275 Religion (Most Detailed Categories) indicates that there were 556 such Christian Scientist respondents in England and 22 in Wales.

However, it should be noted that Christian Research's *Religious Trends No. 4, 2003/4* figures for 2001 suggest a higher estimated figure of Christian Scientists in the UK, of 6,000 in England and 150 in Wales and, as noted above, many Christian Scientists may simply have ticked the Census option of "Christian" rather than using the "write in" option".

Church of Christ, Scientist

Christian Science Committee on Publication, Claridge House, 29 Barnes High Street, London, SW13 9LW

Tel: (020) 8282 1645 **Fax: (**020) 8487 1566

Contact: Mr Tony Lobl

Position: District Manager for Great Britain and Ireland

E-mail: londoncs@csps.com

Internet:
http://www.christianscience.com/

Bibliography

Christian Science Publishing Society, *The Healing Spiritually*, The Christian Science Publishing Society, 1996.

Eddy, Mary Baker, *Science and Health with Key to the Scriptures*, The First Church of Christ, Scientist, Boston, USA.

Von Fettweis and Warneck, *Mary Baker Eddy Christian Healer*, The Christian Science Publishing Society, 1998.

Gill, G, *Mary Baker Eddy*, Perseus Books, 1998.

Peel, R, *Spiritual Healing in a Scientific Age*, Harper and Row, Cambridge, 1988.

CHURCH OF JESUS CHRIST OF LATTER-DAY SAINTS

The *Mormons*, as they are often popularly known, are officially named The Church of Jesus Christ of Latter-day Saints. They claim to be a Christian *Church* and assert that there are three basic Christian positions.

The first is that of the *Churches* claiming an unbroken line of *Apostolic Succession*, such as the *Roman Catholic* and *Eastern Orthodox Churches*. The second is that of those *Churches* that claim a *Reformation* was necessary to restore the doctrinal integrity of the *Church*. The third is the position of The Church of Jesus Christ of Latter-day Saints which believes that apostasy has led to the need for a restoration of the true *Church*, believing that this restoration had to be divine not human.

Mormons claim that they are that *Restored Church* in these, the *Latter-days*. They use the term *saints* in the *New Testament* sense to indicate a believer (as distinct from someone who has been *canonised* as a *saint*).

Mormons differ from other Christian *Churches* in a number of other ways: they do not accept the teaching of the *Trinity* and affirm that the Godhead of Father, Son and Holy Ghost are three separate and distinct Beings. They also teach that the Father and the Son have physical bodies. They believe that their *Church President* is a *prophet* who receives continuing revelation from God.

The *Church* was founded in Fayette, New York, USA by Joseph Smith who became its first *President*. He claimed a mandate from God, through an event in 1820 that *Mormons* call the *First Vision* and which they believe consisted of the appearance of God the Father and His Son, Jesus Christ to the young Smith.

In 1827, Smith published *The Book of Mormon: Another Testament of Jesus Christ*. The *Church* uses this as scripture alongside the *Bible* in its King James version. Two other works are accepted as scripture: the *Doctrine and Covenants* and the *Pearl of Great Price*.

The *Church* formally came into existence in 1830. Its first foreign mission was to Britain, in 1837, and its oldest continuous branch anywhere in the world is in Preston, Lancashire. By the year 1996, its worldwide membership was 9,500,000, with 170,000 British members.

In the UK Census, where Mormons did not use the broad category of "Christian" for their response but wrote "Mormon/Church of Jesus Christ of Latter-day Saints" under the "Other religions - write in" option provided in the religious affiliation questions, the Office for National Statistics' Table M275 Religion (Most Detailed Categories) indicates that there were 11,673 such Mormon/Church of Jesus Christ of Latter-day Saints respondents in England and 1,049 in Wales.

At the same time, it should be noted that Christian Research's *Religious Trends No. 4, 2003/4* figures for 2001 suggest a higher estimated figure of Mormons in the UK, of 148,310 in England and 8,510 in Wales and, as noted above, many Mormons may singularly have ticked the census option of "Christian" rather than using the "write in option".

The worldwide governing body of the *Church* is the *First Presidency* (the *President* and two *Counsellors*). They are assisted by *The Council of the Twelve Apostles* and by *The Councils of the Seventy*. Worldwide, the *Church* is organised into *stakes* (the equivalent of a *diocese*), *wards* (organised local units), and *branches* (embryonic *wards*). Government is through *priesthood*, with two orders: the *Aaronic Priesthood* (for males aged twelve and upwards and judged worthy) and the *Melchizedek Priesthood* (a higher order for men aged eighteen and over).

The *Church* is well known for its *missionary work*. Many members (usually nineteen to twenty-one year old men) dedicate two years of their lives to serve as unpaid *missionaries* wherever they are sent. Members are encouraged to live by a health code known as *The Word of Wisdom*. This encourages healthy living and discourages the use of stimulants such as alcohol, tea and coffee.

The *Church* has *chapels* for regular public worship, but its *temples* are reserved for *sacred ordinances* and are entered only by members in good standing. *Temples* exist throughout the world, of which there are two in the UK. One of these is in Lingfield, Surrey and the other is in Chorley, Lancashire.

The family is viewed as of critical importance and its ultimate expression, it is believed, is to be found in *temple ordinances* for both the living and the dead. These *ordinances* include a course of instruction on the *gospel*. This course is known as an *endowment*. It is accompanied by a rite known as *sealing*, in which husbands and wives, who will previously have been married in a civil ceremony, extend their vows beyond this life to "time and all eternity".

In a similar ceremony parents are also *sealed* to their children and any existing children would be brought in, after the *sealing* of the couple, and *sealed* to them at that point. Any future children are automatically *sealed* to their parents and do not need to be *sealed* to them by an additional ceremony as they are deemed to be born "under the *covenant*".

Mormons believe that *temple* blessings may be offered to those of their family who have died. They practice *baptism* and, following genealogical research, they extend the offer of *baptism* through what they understand as *New Testament*-style proxy *baptisms* (I Corinthians 15 v 29). Proxy *sealings* are also performed. Throughout, though, the right to choose remains. Deceased ancestors have the full right to accept or reject *ordinances* performed on their behalf. Such *baptisms* are not recorded on membership records. Mormons refer to this as a "labour of love", offered freely, without compulsion.

The *Church* believes in good inter-faith relationships and it also co-operates with other *Churches* in worthwhile social and humanitarian projects designed to relieve suffering and uphold Christian values.

Because of what it perceives to be its unique position as the divinely-inspired restored *Church* it does not, however, participate in *ecumenical* councils, believing that *ecumenism* can lead to doctrinal compromise.

Church of Jesus Christ of Latter-Day Saints

751 Warwick Road, Solihull, West Midlands B91 3DQ

Tel: (0121) 711 2244, Ext 202

Fax: (0121) 709 0180

Contact: Mr Bryan J Grant

Position: Director of Public Affairs

Bibliography

Arrington, L J and Britton D, *The Mormon Experience: A History of the Latter-day Saints*, Allen and Unwin, London, 1979.

Davies, D, *The Mormon Culture of Salvation*, Ashgate, Aldershot, 2000.

Davies, D, *An Introduction to Mormonism*, Cambridge University Press, Cambridge, 2003.

Davies, D, "Mormonism", in J Hillerbrand (ed), *Encylopaedia of Protestantism*, Routledge, New York, 2004, pp 1313-1317.

Davies, D, "Time, Place and the Mormon Sense of Self", in S Coleman and P Collins (eds), *Religion, Identity and Change: Perspectives on Global Transformations*, Ashgate, Aldershot, 2004, pp 107-118.

Hinckley, G, *Truth Restored*, The Church of Jesus Christ of Latter-day Saints, 1979.

Ludlow, D (ed), *Encyclopaedia of Mormonism*, Macmillan, New York, 1992.

Smith, J, *Essentials in Church History*, Deseret News Press, Salt Lake City, 1942.

JEHOVAH'S WITNESSES

The Jehovah's Witness movement was founded by Charles Taze Russell, who was born into a Presbyterian Christian family in Pennsylvania, North America, in 1852. After a period of religious scepticism, between 1870 and 1875 he became deeply engaged in the study of the *Bible* with a group of six people. He issued a pamphlet entitled *The Object and Manner of the Lord's Return*, arguing for the spiritual nature of *Christ's* second coming.

In 1879, Russell founded *Zion's Watch Tower and Herald of Christ's Presence*. The Zion's Watch Tower Society was established in 1881 and, in 1884, the Society was granted a legal charter for "the dissemination of *Bible* truths in various languages" by means of publications.

Russell then produced a seven volume series of doctrinal works now known as *Studies in the Scriptures*. At a convention of the Society in 1931, a motion was adopted that the Society should from then on be known as Jehovah's Witnesses. The emphasis of the movement's activity moved increasingly towards witness in the streets and on the doorsteps of people's homes.

In seeking to share their faith with others, where the *New World* translation of the *Bible* is available in the language of the people concerned this is used in preference to other translations, since it is understood to be a literal translation from the original biblical languages of Hebrew, Aramaic and Greek.

The local units of the Jehovah's Witness organisation are the *congregations*, of which the Jehovah's Witnesses record there being 1,475 in Britain in 2002. These *congregations* meet in what are known as *Kingdom Halls* and are organised under the direction of a body of *elders*. The *congregations* are linked together into *circuits*. These, in turn, are grouped in *districts*. Globally, the work of the Jehovah's Witnesses is overseen by a small governing body.

In the UK Census, where Jehovah's Witnesses did not use the broad category of "Christian" for their response but wrote "Jehovah's Witnesses" under the "Other religions – write in" option provided in the religious affiliation questions, the Office for National Statistics' Table M275 Religion (Most Detailed Categories) indicates that there were 65,453 such Jehovah's Witness respondents in England and 5,198 in Wales.

At the same time it should be noted that Christian Research's *Religious Trends No. 4, 2003/4* figures for 2001 suggests a higher estimated figure of Jehovah's Witnesses in the UK, of 109,288 in England and 7,430 in Wales, while the Jehovah's Witnesses themselves, as of 2007, estimate a figure of 130,000 practising members (in other words those actively involved in public Bible educational work) in Britain. As noted above, many Jehovah's Witnesses may simply have ticked the census option of "Christian" rather than using the "write in option".

Jehovah's Witnesses base their religious authority upon an appeal to the *Bible*. For Jehovah's Witnesses, Jesus is viewed as God's Son, but not as "Jehovah God". He is seen as the first creation of Jehovah.

The holy spirit is seen as the active force of Jehovah and Jehovah's Witnesses therefore reject the doctrine of the *Trinity* held by the historic Christian *Churches*.

Jehovah's Witnesses view obedience to government authorities as part of their worship to God. They believe the *Bible* requires Christians to obey the law, pay taxes, show honour to government officials, and be willing to do good work in the community. They do not dictate what stand their fellow believers or others should take on issues regarding military service, political voting, or flag saluting. Such decisions are left to each individual Witness to resolve in harmony with the *Bible* and his or her *Bible*-trained conscience. However, when Witnesses choose not to enter the armed forces, they are free to perform alternative civilian duty if this is required and if their *Bible*-trained conscience so allows them.

This position of political neutrality is rooted in the belief that the only true government is that of Jehovah who rules in heaven alongside Jesus Christ and 144,000 individuals who were once earthly humans. Jehovah's Witnesses believe that, in the near future, Jehovah will replace all human government with his own. The earth will become again like Eden and the righteous of all the ages of the earth will be resurrected to live in harmony under Jehovah's rule.

To become a Jehovah's Witness involves a period of study of the *Bible* with other Jehovah's Witnesses. Then the person dedicates himself or herself formally to witnessing to, and serving, Jehovah God and is fully immersed in *baptismal* water to mark this new life of witness. Jehovah's Witnesses see witnessing to Jehovah's work and divine purpose as essential in their faith. Door to door witnessing is part of this.

Jehovah's Witnesses

IBSA House, The Ridegway, London NW7 1RN

Tel: (020) 8906 2211

Fax: (020) 8371 0051

EMail: pgillies@wtbts.org.uk

Bibliography

Beckford, J, *The Trumpet of Prophecy: A Sociological Study of Jehovah's Witnesses,* Basil Blackwell, Oxford, 1975.

Watchtower Bible and Tract Society, *Jehovah's Witnesses, Proclaimers of God's Kingdom,* Watchtower and Bible Tract Society, 1993.

Watchtower Bible and Tract Society of Pennsylvania, *Jehovah's Witnesses: Christians in the 21ˢᵗ Century,* Watchtower Bible and Tract Society of Pennsylvania, 2001.

NAMDHARI SIKH COMMUNITY

All Namdhari Sikhs are *Amritdhari* (initiated) and adhere strictly to the teachings of all the Sikh *Gurus* and believe in a continuing succession of living *Gurus* starting with the founder *Satguru* Nanak Dev. They believe with equal reverence in the Sikh scriptures of the *Adi Granth Sahib* and the *Dasam Granth Sahib*.

It is their fundamental belief that the tenth Guru, *Satguru* Gobind Singh did not pass away at Nander (Maharastra) in 1708 as Sikhs generally believed, but actually lived until 1812. The Namdharis further believe that the *Guruship* still continues with the successive living *Gurus* rather than that it has been conferred on the *Adi Granth*. For Namdharis, there has been no change in the status of the *Adi Granth* since the time of the fifth *Guru*, *Satguru* Guru Arjan Dev. In the understanding of Namdhari Sikhs the institution of scripture and of *Guruship* continue side by side, and do not coincide.

The Namdhari Sikhs believe that the eleventh Namdhari *Guru*, *Satguru* Balak Singh (1785-1862), was installed to *Guruship* by *Satguru* Gobind Singh. The twelfth Namdhari *Guru*, *Satguru* Ram Singh (born 1816 and exiled to Burma in 1872) was succeeded by *Satguru* Hari Singh (1819-1906) who, in turn, passed the *Guruship* to *Satguru* Partap Singh (1890-1959).

The present supreme spiritual head of over 2.5 million Namdhari Sikhs world-wide is His Divine Holiness Sri *Satguru* Jagjit Singh ji Maharaj who was born in 1920 and attained *Guruship* in 1959. It is this principle of a continuous succession and presence of a supreme spiritual authority forever in a living *Satguru* which distinguishes the Namdharis.

Satguru Ram Singh revived and reformed the Sikh principles laid down by earlier Sikh *Gurus* by challenging the distortions which many saw as having crept into the Sikh community over the years. As a sign of the restoration of the Sikh code of ethics and their social, moral, religious and political spirit, *Satguru* Ram Singh unfurled a white triangular Flag on the day of the *Baisakhi* Festival on 12 April 1857, symbolising freedom, truth, unity, love, purity, simplicity and peace. On this day the Namdhari *Panth* (*Sant Khalsa*) was inaugurated.

In India's political records, Namdharis are also known as *Kukas* ("shouters", in their state of mystical ecstasy). They were pioneers in the struggle for the freedom of India from the British Raj and hold an honourable place in the history of the independence of India. Today Namdharis are pacifists.

Namdharis are initiated by their living *Satguru* (True *Guru*) with the sacred *Nam* known as *Gurmantar* (God's Holy word), whispered into their ears secretly. The practice of *Nam* was originated by the *Satguru* Nanak and is used for silent recitation with meditation for the purpose of spiritual realisation, under the direct guidance and grace of their living *Satguru*.

Namdhari Sikhs are strict vegetarians and totally abstain from all intoxicating drinks containing drugs and any foods that contain animal products. They are also widely known for their very simple mass marriage ceremonies in the presence of their *Satguru* and they have an intense love for devotional and traditional Indian classical music. Namdharis can easily be recognised from their white turbans tied horizontally across their forehead and the white woollen *mala* or rosary (made with 108 knots) used in their meditation and prayer.

Namdharis are found in many countries around the world. Their international headquarters is at Sri Bhaini Sahib, Ludhiana District in Punjab, India. The 2001 Census did not yield seperate data on Namdharis, but it is estimated from within the community that there are around 10,000 Namdhari Sikhs in the UK.

National Organisation

Namdhari Sangat UK (The Sant Khalsa Spiritual Institute of the Namdhari Sikh Community in the UK)

Namdhari Sikh Gurdwaras and Community Centres in the UK

Gurdwara Namdhari Sangat

96 Upton Lane, Forest Gate,

London E7 9LW

Tel: (020) 8257 1460

Namdhari Sikh Community Centre

Unit 6, Balfour Buss Centre, Balfour Road,

Southall UB2 5BD

Tel: (020) 8893 6071

Website: www.kukasikhs.com

Gurdwara Namdhari Sangat and Namdhari Sikh Community Centre

1199 Coventry Road, Hay Mills,

Birmingham B25 8DF

Tel: (0121) 7530092

Website: www.namdharikhs.co.uk

Gurdwara Namdhari Sangat

61 Louis Street, Leeds LS7 4BP

Tel: (0113) 2625095

Bibliography

Achint, N D, *Sikh-Gurus Avtar*, Namdhari Darbar, Ludhiana, 1998.

Ahluwalia M, *Kukas: The Freedom Fighters of Punjab*, Allied Publishers, New Delhi, 1965.

Bali, Y and Bali, K, *The Warriors in White: Glimpses of Kooka History*, Har Anand Publications, New Delhi, 1995.

Cole, W and Singh Sambhi P, *The Sikhs: Their Religious Beliefs and Practices*, Routledge and Kegan Paul, London, 1978.

Grewel, G Singh, *Freedom Struggle of India and Sikhs in India* (2 volumes), Sant Isher Singh Rarewala Education Trust, Ludhiana, 1991.

Hanspal, H, *Namdharis Before and After Independence*, Punjabi Press, New Delhi, 1989.

Kaur B, *The Namdhari Sikhs*, Namdhari Sangat, UK, London, 1999.

MacLeod, W, *Textual Sources for the Study of Sikhism*, Manchester University Press, Manchester, 1984.

Singh Bhai N and Singh Bhai K, *Rebels Against the British Rule*, Atlantic Publishers and Distributors, New Delhi, 1989.

Singh, F, *Eminent Freedom Fighter of Punjab*, Punjabi University, Patiala, 1972.

Singh G, *Sant Khalsa*, Usha Institute of Religious Studies, Sirsa, 1978.

Singh, J, *Kuka Movement*, Atlantic Publishing, New Delhi, 1985.

Singh, K, *A History of the Sikhs* (*Volume II*), Oxford University Press, New Delhi, 1977.

Singh N, *Guru Ram Singh & Kuka Sikhs*, R K Printings (Vol 1, 2 and 3), New Delhi, 1966.

Singh N, *Enlighteners, Namdhari Sahi Parkashan*, Sri Jiwan Nagar, 1966.

McMullen, C (ed), *The Nature of Guruship*, Christian Institute for Sikh Studies, Batala, 1976.

Suri, V, *Ludhiana District Gazette, People - Namdhari*, Government of Punjab, Chandigarh, 1970.

Wells, S and Bhamrah, V, Singh, *Meeting the Namdhari Sikhs*, Wolverhampton Inter Faith Group, Wolverhampton, 1991.

PAGANS

Paganism is a religious outlook that is broadly characterised as nature-venerating and recognising many deities, both goddesses and gods. It is not a creedal system but finds expression in many theologies and practices, carried out by groups and by individuals.

Although many religious systems around the world could be called Pagan in this sense, most contemporary Pagans understand their religion as a revival and appropriate adaptation of practices and philosophies known, through archaeology and literature, from European antiquity. Explicitly Pagan worship was, however, until recent times made illegal under Christendom and in Islamic polities.

Meaning literally "local religion", Paganism retains its connection with the land. Modern Pagans readily acknowledge local deities known from ancient sources, but organised on-site worship of such deities (for example, Camulos in Colchester) is rare. Some Pagan deities are seen as embodying or protecting natural phenomena.

Unnamed spirits of place are venerated, together with universal guardians such as Pan or Hestia, as protectors of home and garden, and modern Pagans (like ancient ones), may worship deities identified with natural phenomena such as the wind, earth, sun and moon. Others connect Paganism more globally with the deep ecology movement and/or emphasis its role as a universal religion of Neopaganism.

Paganism is entirely distinct from *Satanism*, which exists in historical relationship to Christianity and/or Christian imagery rather than to Paganism. Thus *Satanists* may be concerned with a conscious and deliberate inversion of Christianity, and/or may utilise imagery from the Christian tradition as a focus for the celebration of personal power, pride and potential. From the 2001 Census Table M275 Religion (Most Detailed Categories) there were 1,459 respondents in England (and none in Wales) who stated that they were Satanists.

There are many forms of organised Pagan worship. Some Pagans follow their own inspirations. Others follow particular traditions, sometimes more than one. These traditions or "paths" include the *Craft* (or *Wicca*), *Druidry*, *Odinism* (*Asatru*), *Shamanism*, *Women's Traditions*, and *Men's Traditions*. There are significant differences between these groups, but all modern Pagans share in a sense of the organic vitality of the natural world and women's spirituality is respected in all traditions.

Since the divine world and the human world are thought to be in constant communication, *divination* and *magic* are accepted parts of life for many Pagans, from the folk traditions of herbalism to elaborate techniques of visualisation and high ritual drama. Trance work may be supplemented by mystical practices that aim at a radical transformation of consciousness.

The *Craft* or *Wicca* is a *Mystery* path aiming at communion with the powers of Nature and the human psyche and aims at self-transformation. Within these traditions men are initiated as *priests* and women as *priestesses*. In the UK, four main branches of the *Craft* can be found - *Gardnerian*, *Alexandrian*, *Traditionalist* and *Hereditary*.

Gardnerians claim lineage from Gerald Gardner who was central in the modern revival of the *Craft*; *Alexandrians* identify with Alex and Maxine Sanders who developed Gardner's ideas; *Traditionalists* claim their methods pre-date *Wicca's* modern revival and have been passed down to them; *Hereditaries* claim traditions passed on through relations of blood and marriage in particular families. Each *Craft* tradition is formed of many local independent groups, sometimes called *covens*, but an increasing numbers celebrate alone and are known as *solitaries*.

There are over twenty Pagan *Druid Orders*, of which the largest is the Order of Bards, Ovates and Druids (OBOD) and the British Druid Order (BDO). They see themselves as successors to the Celtic priesthood described by ancient authors and generally cultivate inspiration, poetry and song, tree lore and solar mysteries. Most use the *Druid's Prayer*, penned by Iolo Morgannwg, and some are teaching groups based upon correspondence courses.

Not all *Druid Orders* are Pagan. Some follow eighteenth century Deism and consider themselves Christian, while others cultivate Welsh Bardism, holding festivals of song called *Eisteddfodau*. Most *Druid Orders* recognise particular locations as sacred, including Stonehenge and Glastonbury.

The *Northern* tradition is found in many forms but is centred around the *Aesir*, which are culture deities and the *Vanir*, which are vitality and fertility deities. Both groups of deities are part of the pre-Christian traditions of Northern Europe. Some people within these north-west European traditions prefer the word *Ásatr?* (meaning "trust in deities"). Others, who have a particular affinity with the god Odin, use the name *Odinist*.

Shamanism is extremely diverse. Today *Shamanism* often refers to the tradition of Pagans who do not belong to *Druid*, *Heathen* or *Craft* groups and who meet in relatively unstructured and very participatory gatherings without belonging to identifiable traditions or groups within Paganism. Some *Shamans* describe themselves as *Wiccan*, *Druidic* or as *Women's Mystery Shamans*. Others, however, underline the specifically *Shamanistic* nature of their path which emphasises the reality of the spirit world and the *Shaman's* role as an intermediary with this world or as a guide through it.

All modern Pagan traditions have been influenced in some way by feminism, with which they share many concerns. Women's spirituality is therefore respected in all Pagan traditions and Women's Spirituality groups relate to the vision of goddesses or of the universal Goddess. Some Pagan women work within existing traditions whilst others have established their own traditions.

A few Men's groups have been formed to celebrate male spirituality by exploring male mysteries and initiatory cults, either ancient or modern.

From the 2001 Census Table M275 Religion (Most Detailed Categories) respondents linked with a named Pagan group could, when taken together, be seen as a total of 40,142 (37,905 in England and 2,237 in Wales). These include *Asatru* (90 in England and 3 in Wales), Celtic Pagan (460 in England and 48 in Wales), *Druidism* (1,568 in England and 89 in Wales), Pagan (28,943 in England and 1,714 in Wales) and *Wiccan* (6,844 in England and 383 in Wales).

In addition, 368 respondents in England and 38 in Wales were recorded under "Animism" which may also be seen as a branch of Paganism. Furthermore, there were 95 responses in England and 3 in Wales that were recorded as "Ancestor Worship" which could be a form of religion connected with people of Chinese descent and/or a Pagan-related tradition.

It should also be noted that 265 respondents in England and 13 in Wales were recorded as Heathens which is, of course, among the Pagan *Northern Traditions*, but whom it appears that the Office for National Statistics, perhaps following colloquial useage, coded among the figure for those of "no religion". Inclusion of all these responses into a total for Pagans in England and Wales would result in a total of 40,924 (including 38,633 in England and 2,291 in Wales).

Figures from the Census in Scotland, and obtained from the General Register Office for Scotland by the Scottish Pagan Federation as a 2001 Census Commissioned Table, give a total of at least 1,930 Pagans in Scotland, of which 1,140 gave write-in responses of

Pagan, 248 as *Wiccan*, 155 as *Wicca*, 133 as Pagan Other, 60 as Pantheist, 53 as *Druidism*, 28 as Animism, 27 as Pagan *Wiccan*, 19 as *Shaman*, 17 as Pagan *Wicca*, 15 as Celtic Pagan, 13 as Neo Pagan, 12 a *Heathen*, and 10 as Spiritual Pagan.

However, it should be noted that the Scottish Pagan Federation advised Pagans to respond to the write-in option with "Pagan" and it is therefore likely that these figures cannot be taken as an breakdown of the Scottish Pagan population by specific Pagan tradition. It is also possible that the 12 Discordianism, 10 Gaian, and 14 Nature responses can also appropriately be understood as Pagan, inclusion of which would bring the overall Pagan total for Scotland to 1,966, and an overall total for Britain of 42,890.

Finally, it should be noted that individual respondents recorded in the Census as Setians, New Age, Mysticism, Vodun, Occult and Santeri might consider themselves to be and/or be counted as Pagans, while Pagans can consider a range of other religions and traditions that are treated elsewhere in this directory, to be fundamentally Pagan, including Sant Mat, Confucianist, Chinese Religions, Raja Yoga, Brahma Kumaris, Hare Krishna, Taoist, Zurvanism, and Hindus.

Pagan Federation

BM Box 7097, London WC1N 3XX

President: Lindsey J. Heffern

Media enquiries: (0121) 476 0662

Email: Secretary@paganfed.org

Contact: Pam Gardner (Secretary) or Morgan Adams (Media Officer)

Internet: http://paganfed.org/pdawn

Bibliography

Aswynn, F, *Leaves of Yggdrasil: a Synthesis of Runes, Gods, Magic, Feminine Mysteries and Folklore*, Llewellyn, St. Paul, Minnesota, 1990.

Beth, R, *Hedgewitch: A Guide to Solitary Witchcraft*, Robert Hale Ltd, London, 1990.

Blain, J, *Wights and Ancestors: Heathenism in a Living Landscape*, Wyrd's Well, Devizes, 2000.

Blain, J, *Nine Worlds of Seid-Magic: Ecstasy and Neo-Shamanism in North European Paganism*, Routledge, London, 2001.

Carr-Gomm, P, *The Elements of the Druid Tradition*, Elements, Shaftsbury, 1993.

Carr-Gomm, P, *Druid Mysteries: Ancient Mysteries for the 21st Century*, Rider, London, 2002.

Cochrane, R, *The Robert Cochrane Letters: An Insight into Modern Traditional Witchcraft*, Cappall-Bann, Chieveley, 2002.

Crowley, V, *Wicca: A Comprehensive Guide to the Old Religion in the Modern World*, Aquarian Press, London, 1989.

Crowley, V, *The Phoenix From the Flame: Paganism in the New Age*, Thorsons, London, 1996.

Farrar, J & S, *The Witches Bible: The Complete Witches' Handbook*, Phoenix Publishing, 1996.

Hall, C, *Rites of Passage*, Cappall-Bann, Chieveley, 2000.

Hardman, C, and Harvey, G (eds), *Paganism Today*, Thorsons, London, 1996.

Harvey, G and Cliften, C (eds), *The Paganism Reader*, Routledge, London, 2005.

Harvey, G, Blain, J, and Ezzy, D (eds), *Researching Paganisms*, Altamira, New York, 2005.

Hutton, R, *The Triumph of the Moon: A History of Modern Pagan Witchcraft*, Blackwell, Oxford, 1999.

Hutton, R, *Shamans: Siberian Spirituality and the Western Imagination*, Hambledon and London, London, 2001.

House of the Goddess (ed), *The Pagan Index*, House of the Goddess, London, 1994.

Jennings, P, *Pagan Paths: A Guide to Wicca, Druidry, Asatru, Shamanism and Other Pagan Practices*, Rider, London, 2002.

Jones, P, "Contemporary paganism: an insider's analysis", in *Journal of Alternative and Spiritualities and New Age Studies*, Volume 2, 2006, pp 132-149.

Jones, P and Cochrane, R, *The Roebuck in the Thicket: An Anthology of the Robert Cochrane Tradition*, Cappall-Bann, Chieveley, 2001.

Jones, P and Pennick, N, *A History of Pagan Europe*, Routledge, London, 1995.

Jones, P, "A Goddess arrives, nineteenth century sources of the New Age Triple Moon Goddess", in *Culture and Cosmos*, Volume 9, No. 1, 2005, pp. 45-71.

Matthews, C, *Singing the Soul Back Home: Shamanism in Daily Life*, Connections Book Publishing, 2003.

Meadows, K, *Shamanic Experience: A Practical Guide to Contemporary Shamanism*, Element, Shaftsbury, 1991.

Pagan Federation, *Pagan Federation Information Pack*, Pagan Federation, London, (new edition), 2007 (packs are also available on *Druidry*, *Wicca*, and the *Northern Tradition*).

Pearson, J, Roberts, R and Samuel, G (eds), *Nature Religion Today: Paganism in the Modern World*, Edinburgh University Press, Edinburgh, 1998.

Pearson, J and Pike, S, "Wicca", in B Taylor (ed), *The Encyclopaedia of Religion and Nature*, Continuum, London, 2005, pp 1739-1742.

Pennick, N, *Practical Magic in the Northern Tradition*, Thoth, Northampton, 1994.

Rabinovitch, S and Lewis, S (eds), *The Encyclopaedia of Modern Witchcraft and Neo-Paganism*, Citadel, New York, 2002.

Restall-Orr, E, *Druidry*, Thorsons, London, 2000.

Restall-Orr, E, *Druid Priestess*, Thorsons, London, 2001.

Stone, A, *Explore Shamanism*, Heart of Albion, Loughborough, 2003.

Valiente, D, *Natural Magic*, Hale, London, 1975.

Wallis, R, *Shamans/Neo-Shamans: Ecstasies, Alternative Archaeologies and Contemporary Pagans*, Routledge, London, 2003.

RASTAFARIANS

The name Rastafarian derives from *Ras* (Prince) Tafari who, in 1930, became Emperor Haile Selassie I of Ethiopia, and is seen as being the 225th descendent in direct line of succession from King Solomon, having the titles *King of Kings, Lord of Lords* and *Conquering Lion of the Tribes of Judah*.

The origins of the contemporary Rastafarian movement are to be found in the experience of the dispossessed black people of a racially stratified Jamaica in the early twentieth century in which a variety of movements developed which sought to emphasise the dignity and pride of the black inheritance and promised the possibility of African independence.

One of those who was significant in this regard was Marcus Garvey, who prophesied the crowning of a black king. In studying the *Bible* in the light of contemporary events, groups of people came to see Haile Selassie as the *Lion of the Tribe of Judah* foretold in the *Book of Revelation* and what Rastafarians refer to as Ras Tafari Livity came into being.

The beliefs of Rastafarians can be quite varied. However, there is a general belief that, following what Rastafarians characterise as his physical "disappearance", the presence of Haile Selassie can still be accessed as *Jah*. Accordingly, Rastas use the terminology of "I and I" instead of referring to "me" or "you", and this indicates the indwelling of *Jah* within human beings.

Rastas also refer to the image of *Babylon* as a symbol of the totality of the godless system of the western world that is destined to collapse. Life outside Africa is experienced in terms of exile and suffering, but with the hope of an *Exodus* - a return to Ethiopia. As a symbol of continuous independence this stands for more than the present geographical boundaries of the modern state of Ethiopia.

Rastafarians often have a strong emphasis on living in harmony with the natural world and, accordingly, most are vegetarians and some are vegans. Many Rastafarians abstain from alcohol and tobacco, although the use of cannabis is seen as being sanctioned by the *Bible*. The *Bible* is seen as a divine Word, interpreted by Rastafarians through collective reading, study and debate, which is known among Rastafarians as *reasoning*.

Uncut, plaited hair, known as *dreadlocks*, are found amongst most male Rastafarians. The colours of black, red, green and gold (standing, respectively, for the black race; the memory of the blood of slavery; the promised land; and a golden future) are often found in combination in the clothing of Rastafarians.

In the UK Census, where Rastafarians used the "Other religions - write in" option provided in the religious affiliation questions to write in the name of "Rastafarian", the Office for National Statistics' Table M275 Religion (Most Detailed Categories) indicates that there were 4,592 such Rastafarian respondents in England and 100 in Wales.

Although some Rastafarians have rejected western Christianity as a white religion, some have been baptised as members of the Ethiopian Orthodox Church. Further information and advice on Rastafarians can be obtained from:

Rastafarian Society, The

290-296 Tottenham High Road, London N15 4AJ

Tel: (020) 8808 2185 **Fax:** (020) 8801 9815

Bibliography

Cashmore, E, *Rastaman: The Rastafarian Movement in England*, George Allen and Unwin, London, 1979.

Clarke, P, *Black Paradise: The Rastafarian Movement*, Aquarian Press, Wellingborough, 1986.

Plummer, J, *Movement of Jah People: The Growth of the Rastafarians*, Press Gang, Birmingham, 1978.

RAVIDASSIA

Ravidassia is the name of the community that takes its name from Guru Ravidass, who was born in Benares (Varanasi), the sacred city of the Hindu tradition, in northern India, in the first quarter of the fifteenth century CE. At this time, the religious situation in India was very complex and poor people felt greatly oppressed by the tyranny of high-*caste* society. Guru Ravidass was one of the prime exponents of a movement that pre-dated the emergence of Sikhism and which aimed to reform society through the preaching of *bhakti* (devotion) to God and the equality of humankind, and declared that God was accessible to all.

Against this background, Guru Ravidass struggled against the powerful in society in order to work for justice, equality and social freedom for all. Contemporary Ravidassia are inspired by his philosophy that encourages them to seek to create a classless society in which all may live with equal rights and freedom.

They follow the teachings and philosophy of Guru Ravidass and worship the holy book the *Sri Guru Granth Sahib*, within which forty-one hymns composed by Guru Ravidass are included. Ravidassia believe that these hymns were presented to Guru Nanak, the founder of the Sikh religion, at Benares and were later included the *Guru Granth Sahib*.

The Ravidassia community has its own identity, religious practice and symbols. They greet one another with the words "Jai Gurdev". Their *Jaikara* is "Jo Bole So Nirbhai....Guru Ravidass Maharaj Ji Ki Jai".

There are nineteen Guru Ravidass *sabhas* (associations) in the UK. Each *sabha* is a charity through its membership of the Sri Guru Ravidass Sabha UK which is registered with the Charity Commission. Each local *sabha* has its own *bhawan* (temple) but all are governed by the Supreme Council of the Sri Guru Ravidass Sabha UK, which operates from its head office at the Sri Guru Ravidass Bhawan in Handsworth, Birmingham. Also affiliated to this Supreme Council are Guru Ravidass *bhawans* in France, the USA and Canada. The identity of the Ravidassia Community is registered with relevant local authorities in the United Kingdom.

The *sabha*, a worship place for the community, also looks after its social, educational and cultural interests. The Supreme Council produces programmes to co-ordinate and organise activities which are designed to benefit the community in its leading of a peaceful and successful life in the UK.

Ravidassia celebrate Guru Ravidass's birthday as a major event and hold celebrations on the birthdays of the Sikh *Gurus* and other prominent *saints* who participated in the *Bhakti* movement to reform society. The Ravidassia are committed to peace but do not participate in any political activities.

Sri Guru Ravidass Sabha UK

Shri Guru Ravidass Sabha, Shri Guru Ravidass Bhawan, Union Row, Handsworth, Birmingham B21 9EN

Tel: (0121) 5548761 **Tel:** (07711) 701048 (mobile)

Email: brij_dhande@hotmail.com

Contact: Mr Brij Lal Dhande

Position: Assistant General Secretary

Bibliography

Cole, W O and Sambhi, P Singh, *A Popular Dictionary of Sikhism*, Curzon Press, London, 1990.

Juergensmeyer M, *Religion as Social Vision: The Movement Against Untouchability in 20th Century Punjab*, University of California Press, California, 1982.

Kalsi, S Singh, *The Evolution of a Sikh Community in Britain: Religious and Social Change Among the Sikhs of Leeds and Bradford*, Community Religions Project Monograph Series, University of Leeds Department of Theology and Religious Studies, Leeds, 1992.

Nesbitt, E, "Pitfalls in religious taxonomy: Hindus and Sikhs, Valmikis and Ravidasis," in *Religion Today*, Volume 6, No 1, 1990, pp 9-12.

Nesbitt, E, *My Dad's Hindu, My Mum's Side are Sikh: Issues in Religious Identity*, ACE Research and Curriculum Paper, Charlbury National Foundation for the Arts Education, Warwick, 1991.

Webster, C B, *Popular Religion in the Punjab Today*, ISPCK, Delhi, 1974.

SANT NIRANKARIS

The Sant Nirankari Mission (Universal Brotherhood) acts under the guidance of His Holiness Satguru Baba Hardev Ji with the aim of removing the barriers of difference created by ignorance. It does not profess to be a new religion, but rather a spiritual movement, the aim of which is to unite humankind.

Universal brotherhood does not subscribe to any form of casteism and believes in complete equality and responsible living in society. The Mission has a high regard for all religions and spiritual movements and is based on the teaching, set out by His Holiness Satguru Baba Hardev Ji that "True religion unites, never divides".

The Mission believes that spiritually enlightened beings realise the value of human life and recognise the presence of the formless God, Nirankar, in every individual. Through such enlightenment material, social and religious divisions melt away, and are replaced by the bridges of compassion, respect, and fellow feeling.

His Holiness Baba Ji does not seek to remove individuality. Rather, it is hoped that there can be unity in diversity that the movement believes is already turning into reality through devotees throughout the world who live together in peace and harmony. It is hoped that through such efforts, humankind will once again enjoy the peace and joy that it deserves.

The Mission's headquarters are based in Delhi, India, where it has its largest following, although it also has a significant presence in other parts of the world. In the United Kingdom, the Mission is a registered charity by the name of Sant Nirankari Mandal UK, under which there are currently twenty-two registered branches. It has been a leading member in promoting blood donation camps as well as having involvement in numerous charitable activities and emergency aid services.

Sant Nirankari Mandal UK

217-219 Cheshire Road, Smethwick BS67 6DJ

Contact: The General Secretary

Bibliography

Chadha, K, *Enlightening the World, Volumes I & II*, Sant Nirankari Mandal, Delhi, 1994.

Kalsi, S Singh, *The Evolution of a Sikh Community in Britain: Religious and Social Change Among the Sikhs of Leeds and Bradford*, Community Religions Project Monograph Series, University of Leeds Department of Theology and Religious Studies, Leeds, 1992.

Lal, K, *The Mission and the Missionaries*, Sant Nirankari Mandal, Delhi, 1987.

Sargar, K, *Understanding the Sant Nirankari Mission*, Sant Nirankari Mandal, Delhi, 1994.

Satyarthi, J, *Gurudev Hardev*, Sant Nirankari Mandal, Delhi, 1988.

Seekree, H, "The Sant Nirankaris", in C Webster, *Popular Religion in the Punjab Today*, ISPCK, Delhi, 1974, pp 26-29.

SATHYA SAI SERVICE ORGANISATION

Sai Baba was born in a tiny village called Puttaparthi in southern India in 1926 and began a mission at the age of fourteen. He teaches that basic human nature is divine and that the purpose of this life is the realisation of that divinity. He states that this will occur through leading a moral life, rendering selfless service to those in need, and developing love and respect for all life.

Sai Baba says that he has not come to disturb any religion but to confirm each in his own faith so that a Christian may become a better Christian, a Muslim a better Muslim, a Hindu a better Hindu. He teaches that love is the core of all religion and that this love crosses the boundaries of religion and embraces the whole of humanity.

Sai Baba has established elementary and secondary schools, colleges, a major university, clinics, hospitals and, more recently, a speciality hospital, all of which provide services without charge.

The Satya Sai organisation is global, being found in 137 countries. In the UK, there are over 145 centres and groups, consisting of people from all faiths and walks of life who practise Sai Baba's teachings through spiritual disciplines, education in human values and selfless service. The organisation understands itself as a spiritual organisation that embraces all faiths.

Sathya Sai Baba Organisation

19 Hay Lane, Kingsbury, London, NW9 0NH

Tel: (020) 8732 2886

website: www.srisathyasai.org.uk

email: info@srisathyasai.org.uk

Bibliography

Bowen, D, *The Sathya Sai Baba Community in Bradford: Its Origin and Development, Religious Beliefs and Practices*, Community Religions Project Monograph Series, University of Leeds, Leeds, 1988.

Hislop, J S, *Conversation with Bhagawan Sn Sathya Sai Baba*, Sri Sathya Sai Books and Publications Trust, Prashanti Nilayam, India.

Kasturi, N, *Sai Baba: Sathyam Sivam Sundaram*, Sri Sathya Sai Books and Publications Trust, Prashanti Nilayam, India, 1980.

Krystal, P, *Sai Baba: The Ultimate Experience*, Aura Books, Los Angeles, California, 1985.

Mason, P and Laing, R, *Sai Baba: The Embodiment of Love*, Gateway, London, 1999.

Murphet, H, *Sai Baba Avatar*, Frederick Muller Ltd, 1979.

Sandweiss, S, *Sai Baba The Holy Man and the Psychiatrist*, Birth Day Publishing Company, San Diego, California, 1940.

Sathya Sai Speaks Volumes 1 to 31, Sri Sathya Sai Books and Publications Trust, Prashanti Nilayam, India, 1981.

VALMIKIS

The Valmiki community derives its name from the *Maharishi* Valmiki, who is believed to have written the Hindu holy book, the *Ramayana*. Valmikis believe that they lived in India before the Aryan invasion and had a very rich and developed culture. The foundation of their social life was based upon the philosophy of *dharma*, *karma* and non-violence and the society was not divided into castes. Hence, Valmikis do not recognise the *caste* system as formulated in the later Hindu scriptures called the *Manusmriti*.

Valmikis focus upon the main themes of the Holy *Ramayana* as being: kingly obligations, parental authority, filial duty, wifely devotion, brotherly love, friendly loyalty, love and care for the environment and the whole creation. These are the values that are believed to reflect the spirit of the times and community to which the Holy *Ramayana* belonged. They also still form the basis of the Valmiki way of life here in the UK and all over the world.

Maharishi Valmik Sabha

Council of Valmiki Sabhas for the UK

Website: www.valmikisabhas.org.uk

Bibliography

Leslie, J, *Authority and Meaning on Indian Religions: Hinduism and the Case of Valmiki*, Ashgate, 2003.

Nesbitt, E, "Pitfalls in religious taxonomy: Hindus and Sikhs, Valmikis and Ravidasis," in *Religion Today*, Volume 6, No. 1, 1990, pp 9-12.

Nesbitt, E, "Religion and identity: The Valmiki community in Coventry", in *New Community*, Volume 16, No 2, pp 261-274.

Nesbitt, E, "Valmikis in Coventry: The Revival and Reconstruction of a Community", in R Ballard (ed), *Desh Pardesh: The South Asian Presence in Britain*, Hurst and Co, London, 1994, pp 117-141.

Nesbitt, E, "UK Valmikis and the Label 'Hindu' ", in J Leslie and M Clark (eds), *Creating a Dialogue: Text, Belief and Personal Identity (Proceedings of the Valmiki Studies Workshop, 2004)*, School of Oriental and African Studies, London, 2004, pp 25-31.

For information on new religious movements

INFORM

Information Network Focus on Religious Movements

Houghton Street
London WC2A 2AE

Tel: (020) 7955 7654
Fax: (020) 7955 7679

inform@lse.ac.uk
http://www.inform.ac

Office hours: Mon-Fri
10am - 4.30pm

- INFORM is a non-sectarian charity (Reg. 801729) which was founded in 1988 to help enquirers by providing information about minority religions ("new religious movements" "alternative religions" or "cults") which is as objective, balanced, and up-to-date as possible.

- Enquirers can contact INFORM by telephone, letter, email or fax or by making an appointment to visit the office, based at the London School of Economics in central London.

- INFORM's research covers the collection, analysis and dissemination of information about the whereabouts and diverse beliefs, practices, and organisation of new religious movements as well as about the effects that they can have on both their members and the rest of society.

- INFORM's international network of contacts includes scholars and organisations engaged in research, friends and relatives of members of the movements, current members and former members of the movements, and others, such as lawyers, doctors, counsellors, and NGOs with specialist knowledge in a wide variety of areas connected directly or indirectly with the subject.

- INFORM provides speakers for schools, universities, religious and other institutions. It also organises two day-long seminars each year, focusing on a particular aspect of new religions (e.g. children, law, media, conversion, leaving, finances, politics). International conferences are also held every six or seven years.

- Among those who contact INFORM are the friends and relatives of people who have joined one of the movements, former members, members of traditional religions and secular agencies, educational establishments, researchers, government departments, law-enforcement agencies, child protection agencies, the media, and members of the general public.

- INFORM receives funding from a variety of sources such as the Home Office

Department of Communities and Local Government and mainstream Churches. A number of foundations including the Smiths, J P Getty, Nuffield, Wates and the Jerusalem Trust have also given funding. INFORM has a policy of not accepting money from any of the new religious movements or any organisation that might wish to prejudice the outcome of its research.

Strict confidentiality is observed concerning individual enquirers.

RESOURCES FOR MAKING CONTACTS, ORGANISING EVENTS AND FINDING OUT MORE

INTRODUCTION 309

MAKING CONTACTS AND ORGANISING EVENTS 309

FINDING OUT MORE 316

GENERAL TEXTS ON RELIGIONS 318

DIRECTORIES ABOUT RELIGIOUS ORGANISATIONS 323

OTHER DIRECTORIES 326

INTRODUCTION

This chapter offers some resources for making contacts, organising events and finding out more and it is hoped that directory users will find this helpful in a practical way.

MAKING CONTACTS AND ORGANISING EVENTS

When making contact with religious groups, and/or organising events, projects or consultations that draw together members of different religious communities, there are no hard and fast guidelines as to how to do this successfully but this section of the chapter offers what may be found to be some useful ideas.

The CD-ROM accompanying this directory lists most of the key religious organisations and groups in the UK, while the present volume includes material about the basic aspects of each religion, especially as it is represented in the UK. Although much is held in common within individual religious communities, within most there are also various different traditions of interpretation and it is helpful to have a sense of these when planning to contact particular groups either for purposes of consultation and/or to visit their place of worship.

Knowing from which part of a religion a possible contact comes can help ensure balance and avoid later difficulties. For consultation purposes it can also be worth bearing in mind that within any given religious community, many ethnic and national backgrounds are likely to be represented. The introductory chapters on each of the religions in the UK contained in the directory are therefore designed to convey something of the diversity within each community, as well as an appreciation of its common beliefs and practices.

When planning a visit to a place of worship, the introductory materials on each religion contained in this volume give a description of what a visitor may see if visiting the places of worship of that religious tradition. Also included is a description of the personnel the visitor is likely to meet and explanations of some of the key concepts found in the religious tradition concerned. Usually people are delighted to show others their place of worship. It is a sharing of what they hold very dear. They will, however, hope that the visitor observes certain basic rules of conduct.

Before going to another's place of worship it is important that visitors give some thought to how they feel about such matters as joining in a service, or receiving food that has been offered to the deities of other religions and has been blessed. It is quite possible to visit others' places of worship without this kind of participation as long as reservations are explained courteously in advance.

The religious community being visited would not want visitors to feel ill at ease. Likewise, they would not wish to be made ill at ease themselves by criticisms of their ways of worship or of their religion. Questions are always welcomed but negative comparisons with the visitor's own customs are unlikely to promote a friendly relationship!

Whether visiting alone, or as a group, it is important to follow the guidelines for clothing and behaviour so as not to cause offence. For groups, it is important not to talk loudly, thus disturbing any who may be at prayer. If any group members have special needs, let the members of the place/centre that is being visited know about this in advance so that they can prepare to help.

For example, although the normal custom of the place of worship in question may be to sit on the floor or to stand for worship, chairs can often be provided for elderly, infirm or disabled visitors. It is wise to ask before taking any photographs as this is not always allowed.

Some Things to be Aware of When Making Contact

Contacts for the various religious organisations are generally happy to explain more about their community and to help with enquiries. However, this partly depends on the time they have available. If seeking information or organising an event, it is important to allow ample time for getting hold of the contact people and arranging a time to speak with them.

When inviting a speaker, it is often helpful to write to them first in order to give them some time to consider the invitation, and then to follow this up with a telephone call. Sometimes people who are not fluent in the enquirer's first language, and in whose first language the enquirer may not be fluent, will answer the telephone and it will be necessary to ring back later or ask for an alternative contact number.

It may be necessary to ring an organisation several times because contact people for the various religious communities are usually extremely busy and often work on a voluntary basis. *Imams*, *vicars*, temple secretaries, women's group leaders and others have hectic schedules and may have full-time employment in addition to voluntary work on behalf of their community.

Having made an arrangement for someone to speak or contribute to a consultation it is wise to check on the day before the event that the person is still planning to come or, if necessary, has found a suitable substitute.

Possible Areas of Sensitivity

Many people will be keen to respond positively to invitations. However, there are certain areas of sensitivity of which it is helpful to be aware when making contact. Sometimes, the previous experiences or the beliefs of the person being contacted may make them suspicious of, or even hostile towards, inter-faith encounter or multi-faith initiatives.

Where communities or their members have been the target of conversion campaigns by other religious groups, or have in the past found themselves drawn into some kind of syncretistic inter-faith encounter which has not honoured the integrity of the participating traditions, there may be particular wariness about inter-religious encounter. It is very important to explain the context of an enquiry or approach.

Avoiding Stereotypes

It is important, in sensitive ways, to ask religious community groups or individuals what they believe and consider important. Religion is not monolithic and it can be unhelpful and dangerous to operate with a stereotypical concept that is uncritically applied to all individuals who have some relationship with a particular religious tradition. Some people born into religious communities may not consider themselves any longer to be members of that community.

There are some atheists, agnostics and humanists who would find it unacceptable to be asked to say what constitutes their religious background. Likewise, there may be people who belong to a tradition by birth, and for whom religion is still important, but who do not set particular store by ceremonial or ritual observance and may also not observe the usual dietary regulations. In all cases, it is best to allow people to define their own religious identity. The following checklist may be helpful for organisers of events involving a number of religious traditions.

Avoiding Clashes with Religious Festivals

It is worth double-checking the date for the event so that it does not clash with one of the key festivals or special days of a group that is likely to be involved. The annual Shap Calendar of Festivals (available from the Shap Working Party on World Religions in Education, P O Box 38580, London, SW1P 3XF, Tel: (020) 7898 1494, Fax: (020) 7898 1493, Internet: http://www.shap.org/) is a vital resource for this. There is a full page panel at the end of this chapter on the resources provided by Shap.

Many commercial diaries now also include the main festival dates from a range of religions. If there is any doubt about the significance of the festival (in other words, whether it is one that means those observing it are unlikely to be able to attend other events), it is wise to contact the relevant community to double-check details.

Fridays are difficult for observant Muslims, and especially for *imams*, because of the importance of the Friday midday prayer. If possible, it is also important to avoid scheduling afternoon events during the period of *Ramadan* when practising Muslims *fast* from before dawn until sunset. From midday on Friday until sunset on Saturday can be problematic for observant Jews in relation to events involving travel and what could be construed as "work" (although interpretations of this vary within different parts of the community).

For *church*-going Christians, and for members of other religions who meet regularly on Sundays, that day can be difficult. However, because of the practical difficulty for many people of not being able to take time off during the working week, weekend events may prove necessary. If planning a weekend event, it is important to check with members of these religions how they personally feel about attending on these days or about their participation during particular parts of the event's timetable.

Allowing Plenty of Planning And Organising Time

Planning time of at least two to three months is advisable for local events. For national events, a lead in time of at least six, and preferably nine to twelve months will probably be needed. Good speakers and participants are obtainable from all religious communities, but are likely to have quite full diaries and need to be booked well in advance (except for response to political or social emergencies). Participant lists also take time to draw up and, if the event involves people needing to take time off work or to arrange childcare, adequate notice is needed.

Choosing an Appropriate Venue

It is important to use a venue in which participants feel at ease. For example, for a local inter-faith group just starting up and without a strong sense of each other's views and sensitivities, a meeting at a member's house or on "neutral" ground such as a local school or village hall might be the best way to begin, rather than meeting at one community's place of worship (even if such venues are later used).

If a meeting is to be held at the premises of a religious group it is important to discover where the "sacred" area of the religious building is. There may be other parts, such as a social meeting hall, which are not so imbued with religious and symbolic significance and which might therefore be more appropriate for inter-faith meetings.

This is because participants of different religions may feel more comfortable about meeting in these other areas (for example in the community centre attached to a *mandir*). They may not, however, feel comfortable about any visit which would involve them in entering the sacred space where they might feel obliged to offer gestures of respect to another's sacred symbols (or might be worried about causing offence in declining to do so for religious reasons).

In a *gurdwara*, *mandir* or a *mosque*, for example, the sacred area is clearly definable by the point beyond which visitors should not go without removing their shoes. In Christian *churches*, the matter may be less clear-cut because, particularly in modern and adapted

buildings, meetings without a specifically religious purpose sometimes take place even in what is the *church* itself, as distinct from its *church* hall. The introductory materials on each religious community and the sections on "Places of Worship" in each chapter provide background on sacred buildings, their contents, significance and the religious activities which take place within them.

Religious Observance During an Event

Members of all the different religious traditions may wish to retire for prayer or meditation at certain points during the day and time should be left within the schedule for this after consultation with members of the religious traditions involved. However, practising Muslims pray five times a day at specific times. For Muslims, it is important also to offer a room for prayer, showing the direction of Mecca, and to provide a sheet for covering the floor for prayer, as well as a bowl and jug of water and a towel for ablutions before prayer. If there is a toilet or bathroom nearby with washing facilities this is usually sufficient.

Shared Religious Observance During an Event

Any shared religious observance needs to be approached with great care. The least controversial option is a shared silent meditation or wordless prayer. If there is any doubt about the feelings of the participants it is wise to go for this choice. When spoken prayers or readings are used there is always the danger that people find themselves voluntarily or involuntarily joining in what appears to be a lowest common denominator activity, or which presupposes a particular view of the basic unity of all religions.

For example, participants may not be able to recognise in it worship of the deity to which they are themselves committed. Similarly, non-*theists* (such as Buddhists or Jains) can be put into an awkward situation by assumptions that all religions acknowledge a deity. For traditions where the divine is understood wholly or partly in feminine or impersonal terms, the exclusive use of masculine or personal terms may prove alienating. Given these possibilities of misunderstanding and offence, it is necessary to proceed with caution.

However, there are occasions when people may very much wish to meet together for prayer, or when civic life calls for communal celebration or mourning. In such contexts a widely used option is what is sometimes called "serial worship". In serial worship, members of different religions pray or offer a reading relevant to the theme to which others listen but in which they do not join. Rather, prayer is offered individually by members of the gathering in a way that respects the integrity of their own tradition.

Because the Church of England is the established Church in England, its *churches* and especially *cathedrals* have often been the venue for this kind of civic or communal worship. There are both opportunities and difficulties associated with this which are discussed in the booklet *Multi-Faith Worship?*, Church House Publishing, London, 1992 and in *All in Good Faith*, published by the World Congress of Faiths.

Catering for Multi-Faith Events

Many religious traditions have certain dietary requirements as a result of their beliefs. These are explained in more detail in the appropriate introductory material on each religion. Generally speaking, the easiest way to cater for a multi-faith event is to make it absolutely vegetarian. It is helpful to label food where its contents are not immediately apparent.

No animal fat should be used in any vegetarian cooking and when cheese is used it should be marked "vegetarian" on the packet indicating that it has not been made with rennet that is a meat product of cows. Puddings should not include gelatine (unless it is of a vegetarian variety). Cakes and biscuits should include no animal fat or gelatine. Some butter substitutes contain rendered beef fat, so labels need careful checking.

Within the vegetarian dishes, care should be taken to make sure that at least some contain no eggs or milk products like cheese, and also that some of these non-egg dishes also contain no garlic or onions (since all these may be unacceptable to some Hindus, observant Jains and also some other groupings). Observant Jains avoid eating all root vegetables that produce numerous sprouts from the skin (such as potatoes).

Within Judaism, the *kosher* rules are widely observed but with differing interpretations. Check in advance how any Jewish participants in the event interpret them. Normally, it is sufficient to provide vegetarian food and disposable plates, cups and cutlery. However, for the very *Orthodox*, it is necessary to provide separate meals which have been prepared in a *kosher* kitchen.

Kosher foods include *kosher* wine, bread and cheese as well as meats. Such food and drink is marked with a *hechsher* (seal) that certifies it to be *kosher*. A local *synagogue* can be asked for advice on vendors and also on any meals to be served during the festival of *Pesach/Passover* when special requirements apply.

Muslims will wish that, if possible, their food be prepared in a kitchen where the utensils (including knives) and contents have not been in contact with *haram* (forbidden) food. However, most Muslims are primarily concerned to ensure that any meat served is *halal* (permitted and slaughtered according to the *Shari'ah*), and are generally happy to eat vegetarian food that has no animal fat used in its production.

Buddhist *monks* frequently do not eat after midday. In an all day event it may therefore be important to provide substantial refreshments for them earlier in the morning. Some Christians fast on *Ash Wednesday* and limit the range of foods consumed during *Lent*. Some Jains do not eat after sunset. During *Ramadan*, most Muslims do not eat between dawn and sunset. Many Sikhs are vegetarian, but Sikhs who do eat meat are not permitted to eat *halal* or *kosher* meat.

Different traditions have varying approaches to the consumption of alcohol. In Islam it is considered *haram* (forbidden) to consume alcohol, even as an ingredient in cooked foods or sauces. Some Muslims may also consider socialising with those who are drinking alcohol to be prohibited. For Hindus and Jains it is considered undesirable. *Amritdhari* (initiated) Sikhs are also required to avoid alcohol.

For most Christians alcohol is not prohibited, although some groups advocate abstinence. Within Judaism there is likewise no prohibition and responsible use of alcohol is not frowned upon. Practice varies among Buddhists although alcohol is viewed as potentially dangerous in so far as it can hinder *mindfulness*. Bahá'ís are not allowed to consume alcohol, even as an ingredient in cooked foods or sauces.

Because of the diversity of practice within religions, alcohol is often not served at a specifically inter-faith event. If alcohol is provided at a function, it is wise to provide only wine and to set it at some distance from the non-alcoholic drinks. Fruit juices and mineral water should always be provided as an alternative. Being stimulants, coffee and tea are avoided by observant members of certain traditions. It is therefore important to provide fruit juice, water or herbal tea as alternatives to morning and afternoon coffee and tea.

Gender Relations

It is important to be aware of differing attitudes to the roles and relationships of men and women. These may vary even within one religious tradition according to how a group interprets that tradition as well as the cultural background in which their tradition is being practised.

For example, a *Chasidic* Jewish family will have a somewhat different dynamic from a *Reform* Jewish one, and Christians within various traditions may differ radically one from another concerning what they believe the *Bible* and tradition teaches about the roles of Christian men and women. Within Islam, interpretations of the *Qur'an* and *Shari'ah* by the different legal schools mean that there is a legitimate diversity of interpretation. However, modesty is an important concept in Islam for both women and men. Some interpret this to mean that single sex events should be the norm. Others interpret it to mean that a careful, formal and modest manner should characterise meetings between people of different sexes in public contexts.

Within almost every religious tradition there are those who believe that women should not exercise a public leadership role and there are those who believe they can do so. This can occasionally lead to some awkwardness when seeking women to participate in multi-faith events and panels. Generally speaking the best rule is to proceed with courtesy and care in requests for speakers and to try to accommodate requests for such things as hotel rooms in separate parts of the building for men and women, or perhaps to consider offering additional travel expenses to allow a person's husband, wife or family member to travel with them for reasons of propriety. Consideration of the provision of a crèche will support family participation.

When looking for contributions from different religious groups to consultation on particular issues, such as disability, inner city regeneration or sex education, there are some questions worth asking prior to setting up the consultation:

The Kind of Input That is Needed

Depending on the project, it might be most appropriate to bring together some or all of the following:

- Religious experts (including scholars or knowledgeable *clergy* or *laity*). Religious community leaders (who are not necessarily scholars or religious teachers themselves but can be official representatives).

- "Ordinary" members of particular faith communities (including women and young people).

- Members of religious communities with expertise on a particular topic.

Often a mixture of different kinds of participants is needed. For example, if a project or event is being set up to determine what different religions have to say about the care of the elderly, it might be good to include an expert who can give an overview of what the sacred texts and historical traditions have said. At the same time it could also be important to include members of religious groups who are themselves senior citizens and have thought about what their religion means in the context of their own ageing, as well as carers who are putting their faith into practice in caring for the elderly. There are many options and it is important to decide what it is hoped to gain from the encounter.

The Composition of Consultative Panels

The scope, timetable and financing of any project will clearly define some of the constraints. However, there are certain questions that it is important to ask at the outset:

- From which religions is an input sought?

- Should all the religions presented in the UK be represented, or just the larger groups?

- Are there occasions on which it is important to include smaller traditions within religions that are often perceived as being less "mainstream"? For example, including Jehovah's Witnesses or Christian Scientists, when health issues are being discussed.

- Should the panel or consultants reflect the national religious composition of the UK, or of the geographical areas in which particular religions are most involved? Jains, for example, might be a small grouping nationally but are particularly important in a city such as Leicester.

- Is input needed from: both men and women; people of varying ages; and lay people as well as *clergy*?

Questions such as these can only be answered in the context of a particular project or event. People often overlook the smaller religious communities, but if a project is working on an issue such as medical ethics its organisers may, for example, want to make a special effort to include a tradition which has a particular contribution to make to the discussion, even if that tradition is numerically not a large one in the UK.

For some purposes a "representative group" can be important. The diversity within and between most religious communities makes this difficult to achieve. It takes a while to establish who the key figures in a religious tradition are in a particular area of the country. It is also not always easy to find out who is genuinely representative and what their capacity is to relay information back to that community or to provide accurate information about what that community itself needs.

If seeking to involve religious "leaders", it will become apparent that the nature of these may vary very widely between traditions, as will the understanding of who or what is a religious leader. The role of an *imam*, for example, is not strictly comparable to that of a *vicar*. The job of a Sikh *granthi* is likewise very different. Different community structures have given rise to different types of religious personnel functions and roles.

Information on some of these roles can be found in the directory's introduction to the various communities. Care should be taken not to assume that religious leaders in other communities will conform to the pattern of the Christian *Churches*. With regard to all religious traditions, women and men under forty rarely appear in consultations where the membership draws solely upon religious leaderships.

Producing Guidelines and Information Packs

If basic information about different religions is needed, then many good resources exist already. It may not be necessary to arrange for consultants from different religions to produce an entirely new pack. At the same time, putting together such material can, in itself, be an important learning experience.

Some national religious organisations may have staff available to respond to written requests for information or invitations to participate in various events. Many do not, and this is also true at local level. If no reply is received to a request for help within a couple of weeks, it may be necessary to follow up the letter with a phone call.

If producing pamphlets or guidance for service providers working with people of a variety of religions, as noted earlier in this chapter, it is important to avoid stereotypes and in producing accessible materials, also to make clear that there can be a wide variety of interpretation, and degrees of strictness in observance.

Further Help

For further advice and information on the points discussed in this chapter or to be put in touch with individuals and organisations who can advise or assist, contact the publishers of this directory at the Multi-Faith

Centre at the University of Derby, Kedleston Road, Derby, DE22 1GB, Tel: (01332) 59285 or Email: mfc@derby.ac.uk).

A key UK source of information and advice on inter-faith initiatives, relations and dialogue, and on making contact with religious communities and their organisations is The Inter Faith Network for the UK. The Network is based at 8a Lower Grosvenor Place, London, SW1W 0EN, Tel: (020) 7931 7766; Fax: (020) 7931 7722; Email: ifnet@interfaith.org.uk.

The Inter Faith Network produces *Inter Faith Organisations in the UK: A Directory*, a 4th edition of which is due to be published soon after the present volume of *Religions in the UK*. This gives details of inter-faith and multi-faith bodies operating at local, regional, national and international level which are based in the UK.

The Network provides a range of helpful guidance documents on developing inter-faith initiatives which can be downloaded from its website at www.interfaith.org.uk and there is a full page panel at the end of this chapter which provides detailed contact information on the Network and some of the resources that it provides.

FINDING OUT MORE

There are many resources available for anyone who wants to find out more about any aspect of religion and/or inter-faith relations. Direct contact can be made with the faith community organisations included in the CD-ROM accompanying this directory. Some produce literature that they will be glad to send or they may have suggestions for where to go to get further information written by members of their tradition.

In addition, as a basic strategy the following sources of information can be used: *Whitaker's Books in Print*, which can be consulted at most bookshops, will indicate if the books you want are in print in the UK and can be ordered. The local library may also have the books available or else should be able to obtain them for you through an inter-library loan from another library in the UK.

Other useful resources are libraries of universities with a Department of Theology, Divinity or Religious Studies, and some university collections of materials on race and ethnic relations. Loans are rarely possible unless one is a student or a member of staff of the institution, although in some cases it is possible to register as an external user, often on the basis of the payment of an annual fee. There are also useful collections of resources in Religious Education Centres, which can be found in various parts of the UK.

Electronic subject, title and key word searches of CD-ROM and on-line book and journal bibliographies and library catalogues offer many suggestions for further reading. Computer search engines can also be useful.

The Internet provides a vast and growing resource for information and discussion about religions, including home pages on particular subjects, much of which is free to the user, although some is accessible only on a subscription basis. There are electronic discussion groups on the Internet, the number and scope of which is constantly changing.

Complete texts are accessible on the Internet and can be downloaded to PC and disc including, for example, parallel versions of some scriptures in different languages. However, when using the Internet, it is important to be aware that while there is much that will be of value, there is also a lot of material of questionable worth and also some of questionable accuracy. It is therefore a resource that should be used with discernment.

With regard to electronic resources on the Christian Churches, ChurchNet UK http://www.churchnet.org.uk/ provides a valuable electronic gateway into relevant information, and for Religious Education resources, there is RE-XS (see: http://re-xs.ucsm.ac.uk/. *MultiFaithNet* is a self-access Internet service, offered through the Multi-Faith Centre at the University of Derby's website, to be found at http://www.multifaithcentre.org. It includes resources on religious traditions and communities, and on inter-faith initiatives, together with the possibility to post questions, notices and engage in on-line dialogues.

Increasingly, publishers are offering collated on-line resources, such as the Routledge Reference Resources Online (found at http://www.reference.routledge.com) which gives on-line access to a range of Routledge's reference titles through a seachable and cross-referenced resource.

Overviews of Religions

Encyclopaedias such as the *Encyclopaedia Britannica,* or one of the encyclopaedias specifically dedicated to religion, such as the *Macmillan Encyclopaedia of Religion* offer overview articles of various kinds.

Other possibilities include consulting relevant chapters in readily available general introductory books on world religions (see sub-section on "World Religions: Overview" in the section on "General Texts on Religions" below). It is, however, important to bear in mind that interpretations of a given tradition's history, beliefs and practices can vary widely, and that beyond basic facts there may be many different ways of describing the tradition in question.

Special Topics

The sub-section on "World Religions: Special Topics" in the section on "General Texts on Religions" below provide an opportunity to explore a given topic or topics across all the religions, while the "Further Reading" sections at the end of most of the other chapters in this directory or to find out more about a particular religion and those who identify with it.

An electronic keyword search of the Internet, on CD-ROM bibliographies (such as *Religion Index I*, see below) or of library catalogues can provide a mine of information to follow up on particular topics.

The further reading on each religious community in this directory includes some translations or interpretations of sacred texts (among Muslims, it is understood that the Qu'ran cannot be adequately "translated" from the original Arabic, but only "interpreted" into other languages). In the section on "General Texts on Religions" below, there are suggestions of publications that bring together selections from the sacred texts of various traditions.

GENERAL TEXTS ON RELIGIONS

This section lists a selection of the large number of useful general overviews of religious traditions. Some of these provide an overview of a variety of world religious traditions. Others cover particular topics across a number of religions, such as women or prayer. Still others are bibliographical in nature. Finally, there is a section that covers books that include a variety of scriptural texts from different religions. In addition to texts on the world religious traditions, there is also a selection of texts that provide an overview of the forms of organised religious life known as "New Religious Movements".

World Religions: Overviews

Al-Faruqi, I (ed), *Historical Atlas of the Religions of the World*, Macmillan, New York, 1974.

Beckerlegge, G (ed), *The World Religions Reader*, Routledge, London, 1998.

Bishop, P (ed), *The Encyclopaedia of World Faiths*, Orbis, New York, 1987.

Bowker, J, *The Oxford Dictionary of Religions*, OUP, Oxford, 1997.

Bowker, J, *World Religions*, Dorling Kindersley, London, 1997.

Bowker, J (ed), *The Oxford Dictionary of World Religions*, Oxford University Press, Oxford, 1997.

Cantwell Smith, W, *The Meaning and End of Religion: A Revolutionary Approach to the Great Religious Traditions*, SPCK, London, 1978.

Cole, W O and Morgan, P, *Six Religions in the Twentieth Century*, Hulton Educational, London, 1984.

Eliade, M (ed), *The Encyclopaedia of Religion* (sixteen volumes), Collier Macmillan, London, 1986.

Geaves, R, *Continuum Glossary of Religious Terms*, Pinter, London, 2000.

Glazier, S (ed), *Encyclopaedia of African and African-American Religions*, Routledge, London, 2001.

Hardy, F (ed), *The World's Religions: The Religions of Asia*, Routledge, London, 1988.

Harris, I, Mews, S, Morris, P and Shepherd, J, *Contemporary Religions: A World Guide*, Longman, London, 1993.

Harvey, G (ed), *Readings in Indigenous Religions*, Continuum, London, 2002.

Hinnells, J (ed), *A New Dictionary of Religions*, Blackwells, Oxford, 1995.

Hinnells, J (ed), *A New Handbook of Living Religions*, 2nd edition, Blackwells, Oxford, 1996.

Hinnells, J (ed), *The Routledge Companion to the Study of Religion*, Routledge, London, 2005.

Lewis, J (ed), *The Encyclopaedic Sourcebook of New Age Religions*, Prometheus Books, Amherst, New York, 2004.

Linzey, A, *Dictionary of Ethics, Theology and Society*, Cassell, London, 1997.

Lurker, M, *Dictionary of Gods and Goddesses, Devils and Demons*, Routledge and Kegan Paul, London, 1987.

Melton, G and Bauman, M (eds), *Religions of the World: A Comprehensive Encyclopaedia of Beliefs and Practices*, ABC-CLIO, Santa Barbara, 2002.

Rausch, D and Voss, C, *World Religions: A Simple Guide*, SCM Press, London, 1994.

Schumacher, S and Woerner, G (eds), *The Rider Encyclopaedia of Eastern Philosophy and Religion: Buddhism, Hinduism, Taoism, Zen*, Rider, London, 1989.

Seagal, R (ed), *The Blackwell Companion to the Study of Religion*, Blackwell, Oxford, 2005.

Smart, N, *The World's Religions: Old Traditions and Modern Transformations*, Cambridge University Press, Cambridge, 1989.

Smart, N (ed) *Atlas of the World Religions*, Oxford University Press, Oxford, 1999.

Smith, H, *The World's Religions*, Harper Collins, San Francisco, 1991.

Suffolk Inter-Faith Resource and the Festival Shop, *A Handbook of Faiths: The Beliefs and Practices of Different Faiths and Cultures*, Suffolk Inter-Faith Resource and the Festival Shop Ltd., Birmingham, 2005.

Swatos, W, Jnr (ed), *Encyclopedia of Religion and Society*, Sage, London, 1998.

Woodhead, L; Fletcher, P; Kawanami, H and Smith, D (eds), *Religion in the Modern World: Traditions and Transformations*, Routledge, London, 2002.

World Religions: Special Topics

Barzilai, G (ed), *Law and Religion*, Ashgate, Basingstoke, 2007.

Boyle, K and Sheen, J (eds), *Freedom of Religion and Belief: A World Report*, Routledge, London, 1997.

Bowie, F (ed), *The Coming Deliverer: Millennial Themes in the World Religions*, University of Wales Press, Cardiff, 1997.

Brasher, B (ed), *Encyclopaedia of Fundamentalism*, Abingdon, London, 2001.

Brosse, J, *Religious Leaders*, W & R Chambers, Edinburgh, 1991.

Carmody, D and J, *Prayer in World Religions*, Orbis, New York, 1990.

Coakley, S (ed), *Religion and the Body: Comparative Perspectives on Devotional Practices*, Cambridge University Press, Cambridge, 1997.

Cohn-Sherbok, D (ed), *World Religions and Human Liberation*, Orbis, New York, 1992.

Cooey, P, Eakin, W and McDaniel, J (eds), *After Patriarchy: Feminist Transformations of the World Religions*, Orbis, New York, 1991.

Cookson, C (ed), *Encyclopaedia of Religious Freedom*, Abingdon, London, 2003.

Edge, P, *Religion and Law: An Introduction*, Ashgate, Basingstoke, 2006.

Fawcett, L (ed), *Religion, Ethnicity and Social Change*, Macmillan, Basingstoke, 2000.

Forward, M (ed), *Ultimate Visions: Reflections on the Religions We Choose*, Oneworld, Oxford, 1995.

Harvey, G (ed), *Ritual and Religious Belief: A Reader*, Equinox, London, 2005.

Hinnells, J (ed), *Who's Who of World Religions*, Macmillan, London, 1991.

Holm, J and Bowker, J (eds), *Worship*, Pinter, London, 1994.

Holm, J and Bowker, J (eds), *Making Moral Decisions*, Pinter, London, 1994.

Holm, J and Bowker, J (eds), *Myth and History*, Pinter, London, 1994.

Holm, J and Bowker, J (eds), *Attitudes to Nature*, Pinter, London, 1994.

Holm, J and Bowker, J (eds), *Human Nature and Destiny*, Pinter, London, 1994.

Holm, J and Bowker, J (eds), *Sacred Writings*, Pinter, London, 1994.

Holm, J and Bowker, J (eds), *Picturing God*, Pinter, London, 1994.

Holm, J and Bowker, J (eds), *Rites of Passage*, Pinter, London, 1994.

Holm, J and Bowker, J (eds), *Sacred Place*, Pinter, London, 1994.

Holm, J and Bowker, J (eds), *Women in Religion*, Pinter, London, 1994.

Hutton, R, *The Stations of the Sun: A History of the Ritual Year in Britain*, Oxford University Press, Oxford, 1996.

Jelen, T and Wilcox, C (eds), *Religion and Politics in Comparative Perspective*, Cambridge University Press, Cambridge, 2002.

Jensen, T and Rothstein, M (eds), *Secular Theories on Religion: Current Perspectives*, Museum Tusculanum Press, University of Copenhagen, Copenhagen, 2000.

King, R, *Orientalism and Religion*, Routledge, London, 1999.

King, R, *Indian Philosophy*, Edinburgh University Press, Edinburgh, 1999.

King, U, *Women in the World's Religions*, Paragon, New York, 1987.

King, U, *Religion and Gender*, Blackwell, Oxford, 1995.

King, U and Beattie, T (eds), *Gender, Religion and Diversity: Cross-Cultural Perspectives*, Continuum, London, 2004.

Landes, R (ed), *Encyclopaedia of Millenialism and Millenial Movements*, Routledge, Abingdon, 2000.

Leaman, O (ed), *Eastern Philosophy: Key Readings*, Routledge, London, 2000.

Magida, A, *How to be a Perfect Stranger: A Guide to Etiquette in Other People's Ceremonies*, Jewish Light Publishing, Woodstock, Vermont, 1996.

Morgan, P and Lawton, C (ed), *Ethical Issues in Six Religious Traditions*, Edinburgh University Press, Edinburgh, 1996.

Palmer-Fernandez, G (ed), *Encyclopaedia of Religion and War*, Routledge, Abingdon, 2003.

Park, C, *Sacred Worlds: An Introduction to The Geography of Religion*, Routledge, London, 1994.

Parrinder, G, *Sexual Morality in World's Religions*, Oneworld, Oxford, 1996.

Partridge, C and Reid, H (eds), *Finding and Losing Faith: Studies in Conversion*, Paternoster, 2005.

Percy, M (ed), *Previous Convictions*, SPCK, London, 2000.

Prickett, J (ed), *Living Faiths: Initiation Rites*, Lutterworth, Press, London, 1978.

Prickett, J (ed), *Living Faiths: Death*, Lutterworth Press, London, 1980.

Prickett, J (ed), *Living Faiths: Marriage and the Family*, Lutterworth Press, London, 1985.

Rambo, L, *Understanding Religious Conversion*, Yale University Press, London, 1993.

Salamone, F (ed), *Encyclopaedia of Religious Rites, Rituals and Festivals*, Routledge, Abingdon, 2004.

Schmidt-Leukel, P, *War and Peace in World Religions*, SCM Press, London, 2004.

Segal, R, *Myth: A Very Short Introduction*, Oxford University Press, Oxford, 2004.

Sorbaji, R and Rodin, D (ed), *The Ethics of War: Shared Problems in Different Traditions*, Ashgate, Aldershot, 2006.

Stout, D (ed), *Encyclopaedia of Religion, Communication and Media*, Routledge, Abingdon, 2006.

Sutcliffe, S (ed), *Religion: Empirical Studies*, Ashgate, Aldershot, 2004.

Williams, C (ed), *Contemporary Conceptions of God: Interdisciplinary Essays*, Edwin Mellen, Lampeter, 2003.

Woodhead, L; Davies, G; and Heelas, P (eds), *Predicting Religion: Christian, Secular and Alternative Futures*, Ashgate, Aldershot, 2003.

Woodward, P, *Festivals in World Religions*, Religious and Moral Education Press, Norwich, 1998.

World Religions: Bibliographical Resources

American Theological Library Association, *Index to Book Reviews in Religion: An Author, Title, Reviewer, Series and Annual Classified Index to Reviews of Books Published in and of Interest to the Field of Religion*, American Theological Library Association, Evanston, Illinois, annual (since 1989 and now available on a single Religion Index CD-Rom).

American Theological Library Association, *Religion Index One: Periodicals*, American Theological Library Association, Evanston, Illinois, semi-annual (since 1949 and now available on a single Religion Index CD-Rom).

American Theological Library Association, *Religion Index Two: Multi-Author Works*, American Theological Library Association, Evanston, Illinois, annual (since 1976 and now available on a single Religion Index CD-Rom).

Arweck, E and Clarke, P, *New Religious Movements in Western Europe: An Annotated Bibliography*, Greenwood Press, London, 1997.

Barley, L, Field, C, Kosmin, B and Nielsen, J, *Reviews of United Kingdom Statistical Sources, Volume XX, Religion: Recurrent Christian Sources, Non-Recurrent Christian Data, Judaism, Other Religions*, Pergamon Press, Oxford, 1987.

Daniels, T, *Millennialism: An International Bibliography*, New York, Garland, 1992.

Carman, J and Juergensmeyer, M (eds), *A Bibliographic Guide to the Comparative Study of Ethics*, Cambridge University Press, Cambridge, 1991.

Holm, J, *Keyguide to Information Sources on World Religions*, Mansell, London, 1991.

Lea, E and Jesson A (compilers), *A Guide to the Theological Libraries of Great Britain and Ireland*, Association of British Theological and Philosophical Libraries, London, 1986.

Whitaker, *Religious Books in Print: A Reference Catalogue*, Whitaker, London, annual (since 1984).

World Religions: Texts

Burke, T, *The Major Religions: An Introduction with Texts*, Blackwell, Oxford, 1996.

Comte, F, *Sacred Writings of World Religions*, W & R Chambers, Edinburgh, 1992.

Coward, H, *Sacred Word and Sacred Text: Scriptures in World Religions*, Orbis, New York, 1991.

Markham, I (ed), *A World Religions Reader*, Blackwell, Oxford, 1996.

Smart, N and Hecht, R (eds), *Sacred Texts of the World: A Universal Anthology*, Macmillan, London, 1982.

New Religious Movements: Bibliographical Resources

Arweck, E and Clarke P B, *New Religious Movements in Western Europe: An Annotated Bibliography*, Greenwood Press, London, 1997.

Barker, E, *New Religious Movements: A Practical Introduction*, HMSO, London, 1989.

Barker, E, "New Religious Movements in Britain", in H Meldegaard and J Aagaard (eds), *New Religious Movements in Europe*, Aarhus University Press, Aarhus, 1997, pp 99–123.

Barrett, David V, *Sects 'Cults' and Alternative Religions: A World Survey and Sourcebook*, Cassell, London, 1998.

Barrett, David V, *The New Believers: Sects, 'Cults' and Alternative Religions*, Cassell, London, 2001.

Beckford, J, *Cult Controversies: The Societal Response to the New Religious Movements*, Tavistock, London, 1985.

Beckford, J, (ed) *New Religious Movements and Rapid Social Change*, Sage, London, 1986.

Bhatt, C, *Liberation and Purity: Race, New Religious Movements and the Ethics of Postmodernity*, UCL Press, London, 1997.

Chryssides, G, *Exploring New Religions*, Cassell, London, 1999.

Chryssides, G and Wilkins, M (eds), *A Reader in New Religious Movements*, Continuum, London, 2006.

Clarke, P (ed), *The New Evangelists: Recruitment, Methods and Aims of New Religious Movements*, Ethnographica, London, 1987.

Clarke, P and Somers, J (eds), *Japanese New Religions in the West*, Curzon Press, London, 1994.

Dyson, A and Barker, E (eds), *Sects and New Religious Movements*, Bulletin of the John Rylands University Library of Manchester, Manchester, 1988.

Faivre, A et al, (eds), *Brill Dictionary of Gnosis and Western Esotericism*, Brill, Leiden, 2005.

Lewis, J (ed), *The Encyclopaedic Sourcebook of New Age Religions*, Prometheus Books, Amhurst, New York, 2004.

Meldegaard, H and Aagaard, J (eds), *New Religious Movements in Europe*, Aarhus University Press, Aarhus, 1997.

Melton, G (ed), *New Age Encyclopaedia*, Gale, Detroit, 1990.

Melton, G (ed), *Cults, Religion and Violence*, Cambridge University Press, Cambridge, 2002.

Needleman, J and Baker, G, *Understanding the New Religions*, The Seabury Press, New York, 1978.

Sutclfiffe, S, "Some notes on a sociology of New Age and related counter-cultural religiosity in Scotland", in *Journal of Contemporary Religion*, Volume 10, No. 2, 1995, pp 181-184.

Sutcliffe, S, "Seekers, networks and 'New Age'", in *Scottish Journal of Religious Studies*, Volume 18, No, 2, 1997, pp 97-114.

Sutcliffe, S, *Children of the New Age: A History of Spiritual Practices*, Routledge, London, 2003.

Sutcliffe, S and Bowman, M (eds), *Beyond New Age: Exploring Alternative Spiritualities*, Edinburgh University Press, Edinburgh, 2000.

Traer, R, "New Religious Movements – some problems of definition", in *Diskus*, Volume 2, No. 2, 1994.

Wallace, R, *The Elementary Forms of New Religious Life*, Routledge, London, 1984.

Wilson, B, *The Social Dimensions of Sectarianism: Sects and New Religious Movements in Contemporary Society*, Clarendon Press, Oxford, 1990.

Wilson, B and Creswell, J (eds), *New Religious Movements: Challenge and Response*, Routledge, London, 1999.

Special Topics: Bibliographical Resources

There is a range of publications that provide details on a multi-faith basis, about particular topics or themes. An example is included below of publications on health, health and social care, dying, death and disposal.

Amin, K, "Religious Faith and Communities: Directory and Select Bibliographies for Social Workers", in N Patel, D Naik, and B Humphries (eds), *Visions of Reality: Religion and Ethnicity in Social Work*, Central Council for Education and Training in Social Work, London, 1998, pp 120-155.

Badham, P and Badham, L (eds), *Death and Immortality in the Religions of the World*, New York, Paragon House, 1986.

Beit-Hallahmi, B and Argyle, M, *The Psychology of Religious Behaviour, Belief and Experience*, Routledge, London, 1997.

Berger, A, Badham, P, Kutscher, A H, Berger, Perry, Michael and Berloff, J (eds), *Perspectives of Death and Dying: Cross Cultural and Multidisciplinary Viewpoints*, T Charles Press Publishing, Philadelphia, 1990.

Bhugra, D (ed), *Psychiatry and Religion*, Routledge, London, 1996.

Bowker, J, *The Meanings of Death*, Cambridge University Press, Cambridge, 1991.

Cobb, M, *The Dying Soul*, Open University Press, Milton Keynes, 2001.

Davies, D, *Death, Ritual and Belief*, Continuum, London, 2002.

Dickenson, D and Johnson, M (eds), *Death, Dying and Bereavement*, Sage, London, 1993.

Green, J and Green, M, *Dealing with Death: Practices and Procedures*, Chapman Hall, 1992.

Henley, A and Schott, J, *Culture Religion and Patient Care in a Multi-Ethnic Society: A Handbook for Professionals*, Age Concern, London, 1999.

Hinnells, J R and Porter, Roy, (eds) *Religion, Health and Suffering*, Kegan Paul International, London, 1999.

Irish, P D, Lundquist, K and Jenkins, V, *Ethnic Variations in Dying, Death and Grief*, Taylor and Francis, 1993.

Jewell, A (ed), *Spirituality and Ageing*, Jessica Kingsley Publishers, London, 1998.

Johnson, C J and McGee, M G, *How Different Religions View Death and Afterlife*, Charles Press Publications, Philadelphia, 1998.

Kirkwood, Neville A, *A Hospital Handbook on Multiculturalism and Religion*, Morehouse, Harrisburg, 1994.

Koenig, Harold, G. *Handbook of Religion and Mental Health*, Academic Press, London, 1998.

Miles, M, "Disability in an eastern religious context: historical perspectives", in *Disability and Society*, Volume 10, No. 1, 1995 pp 45-69.

Mondragon, D (ed), *Religious Values of the Terminally Ill: A Handbook for Health Professionals*, University of Scranton Press, 1997.

Neuberger, J *Caring for Dying Patients of Different Faiths*, Mosby, London, 1994.

Patel, N, Naik, D, and Humphries, B (eds) *Visions of Reality: Religion and Ethnicity in Social Work*, Central Council for Education and Training in Social Work, London, 1998.

Sanzenach, P, with responses from Canda, E, and Vincentia, J, "Religion and Social Work: It's Not That Simple!", in N Patel, D Naik and B Humphries (eds), *Visions of Reality: Religion and Ethnicity in Social Work*, Central Council for Education and Training in Social Work, London, 1998, pp 84-96.

Schott, J and Henley, A, *Culture, Religion and Childbearing in a Multiracial Society*, Butterworth-Heinemann, Oxford, 1996.

Spiro, H; McCrea, C; Mary G; and Palmer Wandel, L (eds), *Facing Death*, Yale University Press, New Haven and London, 1996.

DIRECTORIES ABOUT RELIGIOUS ORGANISATIONS

This section includes details of relevant directories and handbooks on the religions covered in the directory. Some of these give less detail on particular organisations than can be found in this directory and some give more. A number are produced annually and others every few years, some on a regular and others on an irregular basis. Some of the religious community directories are now quite old, but where they have not been superseded by later editions they are included here as an historical record of the development of these communities.

Bahá'í Directories

There is no generally available publication giving details of Bahá'í groups in the UK. However, the Bahá'í Community of the UK, Tel: (020) 7584 2566, Email: nsa@bahai.org.uk, Internet site: http://www.bahai.org.uk, maintains up-to-date listings of all Spiritual Assemblies and Local Groups.

Buddhist Directories

In addition to the publications listed below, there is an on-line directory, provided by BuddhaNet, and called the World Buddhist Directory, which is a searchable database. This can be found at: http://www.buddhanet.net/wbd/. In addition, in hard copy format there is:

Looie, P and Fookes, J (eds), *The Buddhist Directory: A Unique Reference to Europe's and the Rest of the World's Buddhist Centres*, Newleaf, London, 1996.

The Buddhist Society, *The Buddhist Directory: 2004-6 Edition*, 9th edition, Buddhist Society Publications, London, 2004.

Christian Directories

Most of the Christian *Churches* and some of the organisations listed in this directory have their own national and regional level directories or handbooks and most now also have on-line databases of searchable contact information. The directories listed here are only those that cover a number of *Churches* or types of Christian group. For directory information on individual *Churches* and Christian organisations, a search engine can be used to go to the *Church* or organisation's home page.

Other directories are also increasingly becoming accessible in electronic formats. Thus Eden.co.uk has a partnership with Christian Research to provide the UK Christian Handbook On-Line, at: http://www.eden.co.uk/directory/, while Church Net UK has an electronic directory at: http://www.churchnet.org.uk/directory/

At a local level many Churches Together ecumenical bodies produce directories of their member *Churches* and organisations. Some of these are also available electronically. In addition to these and other electronic resources, there are the following directories in hard copy format:

Brierley, P (ed), *UK Christian Handbook Religious Trends No 6, 2006/2007*, Christian Research Association, London, 2006. Internet site at: www.christian-research.org.uk

Centre for Black and White Christian Partnership, *Black Majority Churches UK: Directory 2000*, Centre for Black and White Christian Partnership, African and Caribbean Evangelical Alliance, Birmingham, 2000.

Churches Together in Britain and Ireland, *Directory of Black Majority Churches UK, 2003/4*, Churches Together in Britain and Ireland, London, 2004.

Hindu Directories

There is no generally available Hindu publication listing Hindu religious groups nationally. There is a range of handbooks pertaining to specific *caste* organisations, but these are not generally publicly available. However, the National Council of Hindu Temples, UK (NCHT) and ISCKON jointly maintain a database of Hindu *mandirs* that have installed deities and this now been published by the NCHT as the first directory of Hindu Temples in the UK (see further below). Some of the temple contact details published in the hard copy directory are also accessible on the internet through the NCHT website at: http://www.nchtuk.org/content.php?id=79.

National Council of Hindu Temples, *Directory of Hindu Temples in the UK, 2004-6*, National Council of Hindu Temples, Leicester, 2004.

Jain Directories

There are no publicly available Jain directories or handbooks. However, the Institute of Jainology (Internet at: http://www.jainology.org/) maintains an up-to-date database of Jain groups and Jain temples. The Institute of Jainology's list of Jain Temples can be accessed at: http://www.jainology.org/viewindex.asp?article_id=Resources%5FJaintemplesuk

Jewish Directories

Many local/regional Jewish Representative Councils produce their own directories of member organisations and synagogues. The most comprehensive overall Jewish directory is annual and the current edition is:

Massil, S (ed), *The Jewish Year Book*, Vallentine Mitchell, London, 2006.

Muslim Directories

In common with directories covering other religions, there are now on-line as well as hard copy directory resources about Muslim mosques and organisations. Thus, the now well-established Muslim Directory is available as a searchable database, at: http://www.muslimdirectory.co.uk/

Sikh Directories

There is no generally available up-to-date Sikh directory or handbook. However, there are some electronically available listings of Sikh Gurdwaras in Britain, including those maintained within a global database by Gurdwara Net at:

http://www.gurudwara.net/gurudwaranet/s ubcat.aspx?tab=1&catid=35

Zoroastrian Directories

There is no generally available Zoroastrian directory or handbook. However, the Zoroastrian Trust Funds of Europe, Tel: 020-8866-0765, Email: secretary@ztfe.com, and Internet at: http://www.ztfe.com/) maintains details of the Zoroastrian community in the UK.

Directories on New Religious Movements

INFORM (The Information Network Focus on New Religious Movements, Tel: (020) 79557654, Email: inform@les.ac.uk, and Internet at: http://www.inform.ac.uk) maintains a database of details, including contact information, on New Religious Movements in the UK. There is a full page panel about INFORM and its work that can be found at the end of the previous chapter on "Some Other Religious Communities and Groups".

Local and Regional Religious Directories

Many local and regional directories and listings exist, as well as reports that deal with the interface between local religious groups and the wider community in terms of social and community action. Details of these can often be obtained through local Racial Equality Councils, local Councils for Voluntary Service, or local libraries (which sometimes also have computerised listings).

Since the 2001 edition of the directory, an increasing amount of mapping of religious communities and groups has been undertaken on a county and regional level. This has often been linked with to the development of regional inter-faith fora that relate to the structures for regional governance in England. A sample of this work conducted at a regional level includes the following:

Bates, J and Collishaw, S, *FaithinDerbyshire: Working Towards a Better Derbyshire: Faith Based Contribution*, Diocesan Council for Social Responsibility, Derby, 2006.

Beattie, A, Mortimore, C, and Pencavel, H, *Faith in Action in the South West: A Survey of Social and Community Action by Faith Groups in the South West of England*, Faithnetsouthwest, Bristol and Newton Abbot, 2006.

Churches Together in Dorset, *Church Based Social and Community Action in the Market Towns of Dorset*, Churches Together in Dorset, 2003.

Churches Regional Commission for Yorkshire and the Humber, *Angels or Advocates: Church Social Action in Yorkshire and the Humber*, Churches Regional Commission for Yorkshire and the Humber, Leeds, 2002.

Jackson, M and Kimberlee, R, *Daily Service: How Faith Communities Contribute to Neighbourhood Renewal and Regeneration in the South West of England. Final Report*, Government Office for the South West, Bristol, 2004.

Jackson, M and Kimberlee, R, *Daily Service: How Faith Communities Contribute to Neighbourhood Renewal and Regeneration in the South West of England. Case Studies*, Government Office for the South West, Bristol, 2004.

Lewis, S, Beyond Belief? *Faith at Work in the Community. A Report by South East of England Faith Forum About Faith based Regeneration Activities*, South East England Faith Forum, 2004.

London Churches Group for Social Action and Greater London Enterprise, *Neighbourhood Renewal in London: The Role of Faith Communities*, London Churches Group for Social Action and Greater London Enterprise, 2002.

London Church Leaders and the Evangelical Alliance, *Faith, Work and the City: A Christian Contribution to the Mayor of London Election*, London Churches Group for Social Action and the Evangelical Alliance, London, 2004.

London Churches Group for Social Action and Greater London Enterprise, *Regenerating London: Faith Communities and Social Action*, London Churches Group for Social Action and Greater London Enterprise, 2002.

Lovatt, R, Lyall-Grant, F, Morris, Z, and Whitehead, C, *Faith in Action: A Report on Faith Communities and Social Capital in the East of England for the East of England Faiths Leadership Conference*, East of England Development Agency, East of England Faiths Council, and University of Cambridge, 2003.

Northwest Development Agency, *Faith in England's Northwest: The Contribution Made by Faith Communities to Civil Society in the Region*, Northwest Development Agency, Warrington, 2003.

Northwest Regional Development Agency, *Faith in England's Northwest: Economic Impact Assessment*, Northwest Regional Development Agency, Warrington, 2005.

Yorkshire and Humber Assembly, *Religious Literacy: A Practical Guide for the Region's Faith Communities*, Yorkshire and Humber Assembly, 2002.

Weller, P and Beale, D, *Multi-Faith Infrastructure Support in the East Midlands: An Investigation into Activity and Needs in the East Midlands*, University of Derby, Derby, 2004.

West Midlands Faiths Forum, *Believing in the West Midlands: Report of the First Conference of the West Midlands Faith Forum*, West Midlands Faiths Forum, Birmingham, 2005.

OTHER DIRECTORIES

There are a range of other directories – for example of voluntary and community sector groups and minority ethnic organisations, that are not primarily concerned to cover religious groups but do, in fact, provide useful contact information for them.

At local level there are many such directories and listings, the details of which can often be obtained through bodies such as local Councils for Voluntary Service (for details contact National Council for Voluntary Organisations (NCVO), Tel: (020) 7713 6161, Email: ncvo@ncvo-vol.org.uk, and Internet at: http://www.ncvo-vol.org.uk/) or local libraries.

THE INTER FAITH NETWORK FOR THE UK

Building good relations between the UK's faith communities:

www.interfaith.org.uk

Check out the Network's site for contact details for regional and local inter faith bodies in your area.

The Network also has a helpline for queries on inter faith issues: (020) 7931 7766

The Local Inter Faith Guide: Faith Community Cooperation in Action

A guide to setting up and running a local inter faith initiative. Published in 2005 by the Inter Faith Network for the UK. ISBN 1 902906 1 95.

Price £8.70 plus £1.75 postage and packing

Inter Faith Organisations in the UK: A Directory

A directory listing contact details and giving detailed information about the work of over 250 organisations working to promote good inter faith relations at UK-wide, national, regional and local level. Third Edition Published by the Inter Faith Network for the UK 2007 ISBN 1 902906 31 4 Price £8.95 plus £2.05 postage and packing

Available from the Inter Faith Network Office:
8A Lower Grosvenor Place,
London
SW1 0EN

Email: ifnet@interfaith.org.uk

Registered charity no. 1068934 company limited by guarantee no. 3443823 registered in England

THE SHAP WORKING PARTY ON WORLD RELIGIONS IN EDUCATION

For over 35 years the **Shap Working Party** has promoted good practice in the teaching of world religions.

Shap is committed to:

- Promoting excellence in the study of religions at all levels
- Supporting those who, in their professional lives, work with different religious communities
- Providing an accurate understanding of religious beliefs and practices

Shap provides:

- **An annual Calendar of Religious Festivals** appearing each year in September, covering a period of 16 months which includes a booklet that explains the festivals in the 12 major religions
- **A colour coded wall chart** of the festivals
- **A laminated festivals mini-chart** to fit an A5 desk diary or personal organizer
- **An annual Journal** on a different theme each year
- **A Pictorial Calendar** for the year January to December
- A revised edition of **'Festivals in World Religions'** (RMEP, 1998);

*Further details of **Shap publications** and subscriptions to the Journal and/or the Calendar can be obtained from:

The Administrator,
The Shap Working Party,
P.O. Box 38580
London
SW1P 3XF
Tel: (020) 7898 1494 Fax: (020) 7898 1493
Email: shap@natsoc.c-of-e.org.uk

ACKNOWLEDGEMENTS

INTRODUCTION

The Multi-Faith Directory Research Project that has led to this 2007 edition originated in a joint initiative between The Inter Faith Network for the United Kingdom and the University of Derby. This resulted in earlier editions of the directory being published in 1993, 1997, and 2001. By the time of the latter edition – which, very pleasingly, won the Shap Working Party on World Religions in Education 2001 prize for an outstanding contribution to the teaching of world religions - the Derby based ownership of the directory project transferred from the University of Derby to the new Multi-Faith Centre at the University of Derby.

More recently, having facilitated the inception and initial development of the project, in 2006 the Inter Faith Network for the UK transferred its share in the intellectual property in the project to Multi-Faith Centre. The Centre has, in turn, again shared this with the University of Derby in the light of further recent investment in the project made by the University's Faculty of Education, Health and Sciences.

For a period, changes in funding and in accounting methods had meant that it was not clear how, if at all, the project might continue to this further edition. However, in 2005, the Home Office provided funding through the Office for National Statistics' Neighbourhood Statistics Services, for the Multi-Faith Centre to develop the Multi-Faith Directory Project's database of religious organisations, thus providing a vital injection of funds at a critical point.

As well as facilitating the updating of the organisational listings covered in the 2001 edition of the directory, the work undertaken for the Office for National Statistics allowed the extension of the organisational coverage to include also the collection, for the first time by the project, of some basic contact information on Christian organisations in England, Wales and Scotland that had not been included in the 2001 edition due to both resource constraints and the limitations of space imposed by the printed format.

This extension of the scope of the organisational listings, coupled with the desirability of enabling a more regular update to the contact data than was available through hard copy editions published several years apart, has led to the current edition of the directory separating the organisational listings off into the CD-ROM format accompanying this edition, and to the provision of an on-line database through the Multi-Faith Centre's website at: http://www.multifaith centre.org.

The updating and development of the textual materials in this edition was then made possible by the re-engagement in the project of the University of Derby, now in partnership with the Multi-Faith Centre. Since the Centre is a legally independent charitable Trust, the University's Faculty of Education, Health and Sciences was able, in partnership with the Centre, to deploy some of the development funds made available to it by the University's Higher Education Innovation Fund allocation for investment in University, business and community partnerships, in order to underpin the revision, updating, printing and publication of these materials.

Over the years, as well as the organisations named above, it is also the case that many individuals and other groups have offered assistance to the project. However, of all the acknowledgements that should be made to individuals, the most significant must be to **Mrs Eileen Fry** and to **Mrs Michele Wolf**e.

Eileen Fry began work on the phase of the project that led to its 1997 edition, by working as a Research Assistant. By the time of the 2001 edition, she had become Project

Manager, a role that she has continued in work towards the present edition, but now in the wider context of her role as Director of the Multi-Faith Centre. Her dedication has been the bedrock of the project, while her careful financial management has conserved and maximised the use of the project's resources.

Over her years of working on the project, Eileen has built up an extensive network of relationships and trust. This has included the consultants whose role within the project is so important; the representatives of many of the organisations listed in the directory; and a wide range of people and organisations who find the directory to be of considerable value to them. Eileen has also commented on the directory's draft texts.

Throughout most of the period leading to the current edition, Michele Wolfe contributed to the project in a variety of capacities that underline the commitment that she brought to her work on it. Initially she worked for the project on a voluntary basis. For a period leading up to the 2001 edition she was employed as Research Assistant to then Project Director, with a proportion of her time allocated to the directory project, while for the final year before that edition she was fractionally employed as a Research Assistant specifically for the directory project.

During 2005-6 Michelle was again engaged with the project as Project Researcher for the electronic database development. During all of this time, she continued to offer a voluntary contribution, considerably above and beyond any contractual obligations.

The current edition of the directory builds upon the previous 1993, 1997 and 2001 editions. Although the project is no longer formally a partnership with the Inter Faith Network for the UK, acknowledgements are due to the Network for its flexibility in being prepared to support the continuation of the project by transfer to the Multi-Faith Centre

of its share in the intellectual property rights, and to the staff of the Inter Faith Network for their many contributions during work on the first three editions of the directory – and especially to **Mr Brian Pearce**, the Network's Director, and to **Dr Harriet Crabtree**, its Deputy Director. At the same time, the Network should not be held responsible for the contents of the present edition in which it has not been a partner.

CONSULTATION PROCESSES AND THE 2007 EDITION

For the 1993 and 1997 editions of the directory, panels of consultants were convened that included both individuals from within each of the religious traditions concerned and a number of individuals with particular academic expertise from outside of the traditions.

These panels of consultants include the individuals and organisations listed below who offered their time and expertise in commenting upon and contributing to drafts of the texts for each religious community.

The materials on "Inter-Faith Activity in the UK" that originally appeared in a separate chapter of the directory are now partially incorporated in the "Religious Landscape of the UK" chapter. Materials from the chapters on "Visiting Places of Worship and Hosting Visits" and on "Making Contact, Organising Events and Consultations" are now incorporated, respectively, in the introductory chapters to the individual religions, and in the chapter on "Resources for Making Contacts, Organising Events and Finding Out More".

A number of the consultants to the directory also commented helpfully on the categories of "traditions", "movements", "languages": which were used in seeking information from organisations and places of worship for use in the data fields that give contact information on religious organisations. They also contributed to the checking of organisational data for national organisations within their religions.

The 1993 edition established basic texts that were recognised and affirmed by consultants both from within and from outside the religions covered in the directory as providing an accurate portrayal of the traditions and communities concerned. The 1997 edition updated and, where necessary, provided additional balance to the written texts so that, based upon six years of consultative and editorial processes, they could be regarded as being as reliable a portrayal as possible.

The 2001 edition, by and large, only carried out amendment of the texts of 1997 edition where this was necessary in order to be up to date and accurate, and this is also the case with the current, 2007, edition. Therefore, the textual parts of the present edition of the directory in significant measure still reflect the contributions to the drafting process made by the consultants to the 1997 and 2001 editions of the directory.

Those consultants cannot, of course, be held responsible for any errors that may be contained in the present amended texts, as they have not been directly consulted on these. However, since they contributed to the preparation of the texts in the previous editions, upon which the present edition has built in an organic way, it is appropriate to acknowledge again their earlier contributions as consultants to the project. Therefore, in recognition of this, they are listed at the end of this "Acknowledgements" chapter.

For the present edition, the most extensive rewriting has been of the chapter on "The Religious Landscape of the UK". In this case, the vast majority of the changes have been concerned with reflecting the developments that have occurred since the publication of the 2001 edition. Some of the text in this chapter has been updated by drawing upon material from the chapter on, "The Changing Religious Landscape", in the editor's authored book, *Time for a Change: Reconfiguring Religion, State and Society.* Acknowledgements are therefore due to T & T Clark, the publishers of that book.

Other material on the demography and economic profiles of religious groups that is included in the chapter on the "The Religious Landscape of the UK" draws upon material that was originally published in a 2006 report for the Office of the Deputy Prime Minister (ODPM) on *Review of the Evidence Base on Faith Communities.*

This was based on research undertaken by the author working together with Professor Jim Beckford (University of Warwick), Dr Richard Gale (University of Birmingham), Dr David Owen (University of Warwick), and Professor Ceri Peach (University of Oxford).

The report examined the evidence base with special reference to Hindu, Muslim and Sikh populations in relation to ODPM policy areas and strategic priorities. Acknowledgements are therefore due to the co-authors of the report and to the University of Warwick, for permission to draw upon that material in this context.

Acknowledgements are also due to the Office for National Statistics for use of numerical data on religious affiliation taken from the results of 2001 decennial census and that are sourced from National Statistics (www.statistics.gov.uk). This data has been used as a basis for percentage calculations and discussion developed by the editor, the responsibility for which remains with the editor.

The chapter also uses data from Table M275: Religion (Most Detailed Categories). In both cases the material is Crown Copyright and is reproduced with the permission of the Controller of HMSO via the click-use licence.

CONSULTANTS TO THE 2007 EDITION

Consultants on the Introductions to Individual Religions in the UK

Thanks are due for their comments on the revised materials for their own religion to those who were, at the time of the preparations for the 2007 edition, faith community members of the Board of Trustees of the Multi-Faith Centre at the University of Derby, including, as follows:

Dr Manazir Ahsan (Muslim); *Mr Raj Kumar Bali* (Hindu); *Revd Dr Inderjit Bhogal* (Christian); *Mr Jogindar Singh Johal* (Sikh); *Dr Wendi Momen* (Bahá'í); and *Revd Malcolm Wiseman OBE* (Jewish). *Revd Dr Nick Watson* (Christian) commented on the text on behalf of *Rt Revd Dr Alastair Redfern* (Christian), the Chair of Trustees of the Multi-Faith Centre. In addition, one member of the Trustees asked for assistance from another person in commenting on the draft text. Such assistance was received from: *Dr Moojan Momen*, in relation to the Bahá'í text. Also, a former Vice-Chair of the Trustees, *Emeritus Professor Jonathan Powers*, commented on drafts of the Buddhist material.

Thanks are also due to those who were, at that time, faith community members of the Programme Committee of the Multi-Faith Centre at the University of Derby, and also commented on the draft texts relating to their own religions including, as follows:

Ms Jo Hale (Buddhist); *Mr Phil Henry* (Buddhist); *Revd Donald MacDonald* (Christian); and *Mr Aslam Siddiqi* (Muslim). In addition, another member of the Centre's Programme Committee asked for assistance in commenting on the draft text. Such assistance was received from: *Rabbi Amanda Golby*, in relation to the Jewish text.

Special thanks are also due to the Director and Deputy Director of the Inter Faith Network and members of the Network's Executive Committee. Although the directory project is no longer a joint project directly involving the Inter Faith Network, as part of the agreements around taking the project forward under its new publication arrangements, members of the Executive Committee of the Network kindly consented to be approached to comment on the draft texts relating to their particular faith traditions. Those who provided such comments did so in their individual capacities as people of national standing in their religious traditions and included, as follows:

Dr Fatma Amer (Muslim); *Ven Tawalama Bandula* (Buddhist); *Dr Elizabeth Harris* (Christian); *Hon Barnabas Leith* (Bahá'í); *Mr Yann Lovelock* (Buddhist); *Rabbi Rachel Montagu* (Jewish); *Mr Neville Nagler* (Jewish); *Mrs Ravinder Kaur Nijjar* (Sikh); *The Revd Daniel Otieno-Ndale* (Christian); *Ms Anuja Prasha* (Hindu); *Dr Nawal Kant Prinja* (Hindu); *Mr Resham Singh Sandhu MBE* (Sikh); *Dr Natubhai Shah* (Jain); *Dr Indarjit Singh OBE* (Sikh); *Mr Jagjiwan Singh* (Sikh); *Rabbi Jacqueline Tabick* (Jewish); and *Revd Guy Wilkinson* (Christian).

In addition, in some instances, members of the Network's Executive Committee asked for assistance from others in commenting on the draft text on the individual faith community chapters. Such assistance was received from: *Mr Malcolm Deboo*, in relation to the Zoroastrian text; and *Dr Girdhari Bhan*, in relation to the Hindu text.

A number of academics were also consulted on the text of the individual chapters on specific faith communities, as appropriate to their expertise. These included: *Professor Richard Gombrich* (University of Oxford), *Ms Peggy Morgan* (University of Oxford), and *Dr John Peacock* (University of Bristol), in relation to the text on Buddhists in the UK; *Professor Kim Knott* (University of Leeds), in relation to the text of Hindus in the UK; *Dr Eleanor Nesbitt* (University of Warwick) and *Professor Christopher Shackle* (School of Oriental and African Studies,

University of London) in relation to the text on Sikhs in the UK; and **Rabbi Dr Norman Solomon** (University of Oxford), in relation to the text on Jews in the UK.

The project has, however, also greatly benefitted from the voluntary contributions of a number of academics and others offering feedback and comment on the materials in the directory's chapter on the "Religious Landscape of the UK". These included the following:

Consultants on the Chapter on Religious Landscape of the UK

Dr Elizabeth Arweck (University of Warwick); **Dr Peter Brierley** (Christian Research Association); **Professor Grace Davie** (University of Exeter); **Dr Adam Dinham**, (Anglia Ruskin University); **Professor Leslie Francis** (University of Wales, Bangor); **Dr Richard Gale** (University of Birmingham); **Dr Sophie Gilliat-Ray** (University of Cardiff); **Professor Kim Knott** (University of Leeds); **Dr Vivien Lowndes** (de Montfort University, Leicester); **Dr Eleanor Nesbitt** (University of Warwick); **Dr David Owen** (University of Warwick); and **Dr Gerald Parsons** (The Open University).

In relation to the sections on education and religion, in addition to comments from the consultants listed above, specific input on education and religion in England was made by **Dr David Lankshear** (University of Wales, Bangor); on Northern Ireland by **Dr Philip Barnes** (King's College, University of London); on Scotland by **Mr Stephen McKinney** (University of Glasgow); and on Wales by **Ms Tania Ap Sion** (University of Wales, Bangor).

Mr Brian Peace, the Director of the Inter-Faith Network for UK and **Dr Harriet Crabtree**, Deputy Director of the Network also kindly, in a personal capacity, offered comment on this chapter.

Also, acknowledged in relation to data from the *Classification of Denominations and Production of Annual Statistics*, included in the section on places of worship in the "Religious Landscape" chapter, as well as feedback on drafts of the directory's description of the procedures for recognition of places of worship, is **Ms Marion Fazackerley** and **Mr Selwyn Hughes** of the General Register Office.

Finally, acknowledgement is recorded to the Controller of HMSO for use of crown copyright material as taken from the Census results on religious affiliation recorded in National Statistics, www.statistics.gov.uk and from the commissioned Table M275: Religion (Most Detailed Categories) covering England and Wales, as well as a commissioned Table on Pagans in Scotland from the General Register Office for Scotland.

CONSULTANTS ON THE CHAPTER ON SOME OTHER RELIGIOUS COMMUNITIES AND GROUPS

For the chapter on "Some Other Religious Communities and Groups", the following representatives of the communities and groups that are covered were consulted and offered feedback: On the Brahma Kumaris, **Sister Maureen** of the Brahma Kumaris World Spiritual University; on the Christian Scientists, **Tony Lobl** of the UK and Republic of Ireland Christian Science Committees on Publication; on the Jehovah's Witnesses, **Paul Gillies,** Office of Public Information of the Watch Tower Bible and Tract Society of Britain; and, on Pagans, **Dr Prudence Jones** of the Pagan Federation.

COLLECTION AND VERIFICATION OF ORGANISATIONAL DATA

To compile the original contact lists that form the basis of the organisational data in the CD-ROM accompanying this publication, the project contacted all the organisations and places of worship contained in the 2001 edition.

It supplemented information gained in this way with further research aimed at including organisations that were not uncovered by the research for the 2001 edition or else did not yet exist at that time.

In its research, the project acknowledges the co-operation and contributions of many individuals and organisations that have provided it with information. This includes many national religious organisations; local **Race Equality Councils**; local **Councils for Voluntary Service**; **Local Education Authority Religious Education Advisers**; **Local Authority Planning Departments**; and **Local Authority Library Services**. Not all from these organisations who assisted can be named individually here but they provided valuable information about organisations in putting together the information grid that the project used to identify organisations for possible inclusion.

Acknowledgements should also be recorded to the editors and publishers of existing handbooks and directories of religious organisations and groups, which this directory is not intended to replace, but rather to complement. The project referred to these during the process of preparing (in the case of the other than Christian data) to make its own direct contact with the organisations listed in this edition which had not previously been in existence or had not been uncovered by the research for the 2001 edition. Details of many of these handbooks and directories are to be found in this volume's chapter on "Resources for Making Contacts, Organising Events and Finding out More".

CONSULTANTS TO THE 1997 AND 2001 EDITIONS

The chapters on different religions in the UK have, in general, not substantially altered from those included in the 1997 and 2001 editions except by the inclusion of material on visiting places of worship in the religions concerned; the addition of 2001 Census data; and general updating of community and organisational developments, as well as the bibliographies. Therefore the following is a list of those consultants to the 1997 and 2001 editions who have not also been consultants on the 2007 edition is also included here in recognition of their previous contributions to the original version of the present texts. At the same time, those listed bear no responsibility for the present form of the texts.

Those who are listed below as being members of the Inter Faith Network Executive Committee were consulted in that capacity for the 2001 edition. Others who are listed are listed in the capacities they had in 1997 when they were consulted on the text.

It should be noted that, since the 2001 edition, some names, titles and awards will have changed for some of these individuals and that it should also be noted that since the time they were consulted, some individuals are now deceased.

However, in the following lists, their names, titles and awards are listed as they were, respectively, in 1997 or 2001. They remain listed here in acknowledgement of their consultative contributions.

Bahá'ís in the UK

Mr Hugh Adamson, Bahá'í Community of the United Kingdom; **Dr Novin Doostar**, Inter Faith Network for the UK, Executive Committee.

Buddhists in the UK

Mr Stephen Batchelor, Sharpham; **Mr Anil Goonewardene**, Buddhist Society; **Venerable Rathna Jothi**, East Midlands Buddhist Association; **Dharmachari Kulananda**, Friends of the Western Buddhist Order; **Mr Ron Maddox**, The Buddhist Society; **Revd Myokyo-ni**, The Zen Centre, London; **Dr Akong Tulku Rinpoche**, Kagyu Samye

Ling; **Mr Paul Seto**, Inter Faith Network for the UK, Executive Committee; **Ms Dal Strutt**, The Buddhist Society; **Most Venerable Dr Medagama Vajiragnana,** Inter Faith Network for the UK, Executive Committee; **Ms Georgina Black**, Network of Buddhist Organisations (UK) who co-ordinated wider consultation with a number of the Network of Buddhist Organisations' member organisations. **Dr Paul Williams**, University of Bristol.

Christians in the UK

Most Revd Father Olu Abiola, Council of African and Afro-Caribbean Churches (UK); **Mr John Adegoke**, Centre for Black and White Christian Partnership, Birmingham; **Canon David Atkinson**, Archdeacon of Lewisham; **Father Michael Barnes**, Westminster Interfaith Programme; **Ms Vida Barnett**, Shap Working Party on World Religions in Education; **Revd Esme Beswick**, Joint Council for Anglo-Caribbean Churches; **Revd Marcus Braybrooke**, World Congress of Faiths; **Revd Eric Brown**, Afro-West Indian United Council of Churches; **Rt Revd Tom Butler**, Inter Faith Network for the UK Executive Committee; **Mrs Jenny Carpenter**, Churches Together in England; **Revd Canon Dr Tony Chesterman**, University of Derby, Religious Resource and Research Centre Steering Committee; **Revd Maxwell Craig**, Action of Churches Together in Scotland; **Revd Dr Colin Davey**, Council of Churches for Britain and Ireland; **Revd Noel Davies**, Churches Together in Wales; **Revd S M Douglas**, International Ministerial Council of Great Britain; **Canon Michael Evans**, Tunbridge Wells; **Venerable Ian Gatford**, University of Derby, Religious Resource and Research Centre Steering Committee; **Mrs Ivy Gutridge, MBE**, Wolverhampton Inter-Faith Group; **Revd Basil Hazledine**, Epsom; **Rt Revd Charles J Henderson**, Inter Faith Network for the UK Executive Committee; **Revd David Heslop**, University of Derby, Religious Resource and Research Centre; **Revd Canon Dr Michael Ipgrave**, Inter Faith Network for the UK Executive Committee; **Mrs Angela Jagger**, Inter Faith Network for the UK Executive Committee; **Revd Carmel Jones**, New Assembly of Churches; **Revd Canon Dr Christopher Lamb**, Churches'

Commission for Inter Faith Relations, Council of Churches for Britain and Ireland; **Revd Anne McClelland**, Richmond Inter-Faith Group; **Mrs Jean Potter**, Inter Faith Network for the UK Executive Committee; **Revd Paul Quilter**, University of Derby, Religious Resource and Research Centre Steering Committee; **Revd. Simon Reynolds**, Inter Faith Network for the UK Executive Committee; **Revd Geoffrey Roper**, General Secretary of the Free Church Federal Council; **Sister Margaret Shephard, nds**, Inter Faith Network for the UK Executive Committee; **Sister Isobel Smyth**, Inter Faith Network for the UK Executive Committee; **Revd David Staple OBE**, former General Secretary of the Free Church Federal Council; **Dr David Stevens**, Irish Council of Churches; **Rt Revd Roy Williamson**, former Church of England Bishop of Southwark; **Ms. Gillian Wood**, Inter Faith Network for the UK Executive Committee.

Hindus in the UK

Mr Rameshbhai Acharya, Leicester; **Mr Vipin Aery**, National Council of Hindu Temples; **Sri Akhandadi das**, International Society for Krishna Consciousness; **Mr Raj Bali**, University of Derby, Religious Resource and Research Centre Steering Committee; **Professor Bharadwaj**, Arya Pratinidhi Sabha; **Mrs Saraswati Dave**, Inter Faith Network for the UK Executive Committee; **Mr A Daxini**, Shree Sanatan Mandir, Leicester; **Mrs Saroj Lal** (Inter Faith Network for the UK Executive Committee); **Mr Deepak Naik**, National Council of Hindu Temples; **Dr Nandakumara**, Bharatiya Vidya Bhavan; **Mr Nitin Palan**, Inter Faith Network for the UK Executive Committee; **Mr Jitubhai Pancholi**, Swaminarayan Hindu Mission; **Mr D B Patel**, Shree Sanatan Mandir, Leicester; **Mr Navin Patel**, Swaminarayan Hindu Mission; **Rasamandala das**, ISKCON Education Service; **Dr H V Satyanarayana Shastry**, Bharatiya Vidya Bhavan; **Dr Ramanbhai Shah**, Swaminarayan Hindu Mission; **Mr Om Parkash Sharma**, MBE, Inter Faith Network Executive Committee; Also consulted were **Dr Dermot Killingley**, University of Newcastle upon Tyne; and **Dr Malory Nye**, University of Stirling.

Jains in the UK

Mr Nemu Chandaria, Institute of Jainology; *Professor Padminabh Jaini*, University of California, Berkeley, USA and Institute of Jainology Trustee; *Mr Vinod Kapashi*, Federation of Jain Organisations in the UK; *Mr Bipin Mehta*, Inter Faith Network for the UK Executive Committee. Also consulted were: *Dr Paul Marett*, Jain Academy; *Ms Kristi Wiley*, University of California, Berkeley, USA.

Jews in the UK

Rabbi David Goldberg, London Society of Jews and Christians; *Revd Jonathan Gorsky*, Council of Christians and Jews; the late *Rabbi Hugo Gryn CBE*, West London Synagogue of British Jews; *Rabbi Dr Julian Jacobs*, Chief Rabbi's Representative on Inter-Faith Affairs; *Mr Paul Mendel*, Council of Christians and Jews; *Professor Eric Moonman OBE*, London; *Rabbi Alan Plancey*, Inter Faith Network for the UK Executive Committee; *Mrs Rosalind Preston OBE*, Inter Faith Network for the UK Executive Committee; and *Mr Ramesh Shah*, Inter Faith Network for the UK Executive Committee; *Mr Robert Rabinowitz*, Jewish Continuity; *Mr Laurie Rosenberg*, Board of Deputies of British Jews; *Ms Marlena Schmool*, Board of Deputies of British Jews.

Muslims in the UK

Dr Manazir Ahsan, Inter Faith Network for the UK Executive Committee; *Dr Bahadur Dalal*, World Ahl ul-Bayt (AS) Islamic League; *Mr Gai Eaton*, Islamic Cultural Centre, Regent's Park Mosque, London; *Mr Mohsin Jaffer*, Islamic Education Board; *Mr Ayub Laher*, Inter Faith Network for the UK Executive Committee; *Mrs Ummul Banin S Merali*, World Ahl ul-Bayt (AS) Islamic League; *Mr Abdul Hamid Qureshi*, Lancashire Council of Mosques; *Maulana Mohammad Shahid Raza*, Imams and Mosques Council, UK; *Mr Iqbal Sacranie*, UK Action Committee on Islamic Affairs; *Mr Aslam Siddiqi*, University of Derby, Religious Resource and Research Centre Steering Committee; *Dr Ataullah Siddiqui*, Islamic Foundation; *Mr Syed*

Syediau, World Islamic Mission (UK). Also consulted were *Dr Jorgen Nielsen*, Centre for the Study of Islam and Christian-Muslim Relations, Selly Oak Colleges, Birmingham and *Mr Ahmed Andrews*, University of Derby.

Sikhs in the UK

Mr Surinder Singh Attariwala, Network of Sikh Organisations (UK); *Mrs Bhupinder Kaur Bagga*, Inter Faith Network for the UK Executive Committee; *Mr Mohinder Singh Chana*, Bradford; *Dr Hardial Singh Dhillon*, University of Derby, Religious Resource and Research Centre; *Mr Jaswant Singh Heera*, Inter Faith Network for the UK Executive Committee; *Mr Surjit Singh Kalra*, Birmingham; *Mr Teja Singh Manget*, Sikh Missionary Society; *Mrs Satwant Kaur Rait*, Leeds; *Mr Gurpal Singh*, Bhatra Sikh Centre, Cardiff; *Dr Kartar Surinder Singh*, Sikh Council for Inter Faith Relations; *Mr Darshan Singh Tatla*, Birmingham.

Zoroastrians in the UK

Mr Jehangir Sarosh, Inter Faith Network for the UK Executive Committee; *Mr Shahrokh Shahrokh*, London; *Dr Rashna Writer*, Birkbeck College, London. Also consulted was *Professor John Hinnells*, School of Oriental and African Studies, University of London and Professor of Comparative Religion, University of Derby.

Religious Landscape of the UK

In 2001, for the chapter on "The Religious Landscape of the UK", members of the Inter Faith Network Executive Committee at the time (as included in the above list) were consulted, as also were the following individuals with specific relevant expertise on religions in the UK, listed according to their institutional affiliations, names, titles and awards at the time they were consulted.

Dr Roger Ballard, University of Manchester; *Dr Rohit Barot*, University of Bristol; *Professor Steve Bruce*, University of Aberdeen; *Ms Mandy Clough*, Office for National Statistics; *Revd J G Harris and Mr Hywell Evans*, Welsh National Association of

Standing Advisory Councils on Religious Education; **Dr Sewa Singh Kalsi**, University of Leeds; **Professor Kim Knott**, University of Leeds; **Mr John Leigh**, Churches and Chapels Section, Office for National Statistics; **Revd Dr Stephen Orchard**, Religious Education Council; **Professor Ceri Peach**, University of Oxford; **Mr David Rayner**, Inner Cities' Religious Council, Department for the Environment, Transport and the Regions; **Revd Maurice Ryan**, Stranmillis College, Belfast; **Ms Marlena Schmool**, Board of British Deputies of British Jews; **Mr Greg Smith**, University of East London; **Revd John Stevenson**, Church of Scotland; **Dr Steve Vertovec**, University of Oxford.

Where there was some special need to check out some particular aspects of a chapter, consultation arrangements were established with some individuals from beyond the Officers and membership of the Network's Executive Committee of 2001. These consultants included: **Revd John C Clifford** (Unitarian and Free Christian Christian tradition); **Canon Michael Evans** (*Roman Catholic* Christian tradition); **Chas Raws** (Quakers/Society of Friends tradition).

Inter-Faith Activity in the UK

For what was originally in the 1997 and 2001 edition a separate chapter on "Inter-Faith Activity in the UK" (materials from which are now reflected in an abbreviated and also developed way in the present edition), the 1997 and 2001 members of the Inter Faith Network Executive Committee (listed above) were consulted, as also were a large number of individuals associated with local, national and international inter-faith organisations based in the UK. These are all named in the Acknowledgements section of previous editions of the directory, but not also listed here due to the substantial change and shortening that the text has undergone through its incorporation into "the Religious Landscape" chapter.

Some Other Religious Communities and Groups

For the chapter on "Some Other Religious Communities and Groups", this included consultation, as follows:

On the Church of Christ, Scientist, with **Mr Alan Grayson** of the Christian Science Committee on Publication for Great Britain and Ireland; on the Church of Jesus Christ of Latter-day Saints, **Mr Bryan Grant** of the Public Affairs Office of the Church of Jesus Christ of Latter-day Saints, Europe North area; on the Namdharis, **Mr Vasdev Singh Bhamrah** of the Namdhari Sangat UK; on the Sant Nirankaris, **Mr Jagjit Khambe** of the Sant Nirankari Mission; on Pagans, **Dr Graham Harvey** of King Alfred's College of Higher Education, Winchester and **Dr Ronald Hutton**, University of Bristol; on the Rastafarians, **Mr Henry Nicholson** of the Rastafarian Society, London; on the Ravidassia, **Mr Brij Lal Dande** of the Sri Guru Ravidass Sabha UK; on the Sri Sathya Sai Service Organisation, **Mr Ishver Patel** of the Central Council of the United Kingdom; on the Valmikis, **Dr Davinder Prasad** of the Maharishi Valmik Sabha, Coventry.

OTHER ACKNOWLEDGEMENTS

The participation and support of the consultants to the 1997, 2001 and the present, 2007 editions, saved the project from making a number of avoidable errors and has ensured that the directory is the product of a truly co-operative process of partnership and what might be called an attempt at "dialogical scholarship".

The present edition of the directory has benefited greatly from feedback on earlier drafts that has been offered by those who are listed as having been consultants for this edition. At the same time, none of the consultants for 1997, 2001 or the present, 2007 edition, should be held responsible for any inaccuracies or imbalances that may remain in what has been finally published and for which, as editor, I take full responsibility.

The contribution of others, who have contributed in different ways from inception of the original project through to the actual production of the present edition, should also be acknowledged. It is difficult to list all those who have contributed and I apologise for any whose names I have left out in error.

Acknowledgement is due to **Ms Jo Thornewill** and **Ms Emma Mottram** of the Multi-Faith Centre staff, for administrative assistance to the processes of consultation leading to the present edition, as well as Ms **Georgina Wild** for help in proof reading.

The support of past and present University of Derby staff has also been crucial to the project. For their initial support to getting the project that led to the first edition off the ground in 1990, thanks remain due to **Mr David Udall**, former Deputy Director (Academic); **Mr Trevor Easingwood**, former Deputy Director (Resources); and **Mr Michael Hall**, former Deputy Vice-Chancellor.

Special thanks are also due to **Professor Emeritus Jonathan Powers**, former Pro Vice Chancellor of the University of Derby, and until recently Vice Chair of the Multi-Faith Centre at the University of Derby, who effected the transfer of the project to the Multi-Faith Centre in 2001 at a time when it could no longer be sustained in the University context. For this edition thanks are due to **Ms Louise Spry**, the Business Development Manager of the University's Faculty of Education, Health and Sciences.

Derby University Enterprises Ltd provided support for the original development of the *MultiFaithNet* website (developed by the technical expertise of **Dr Klaus Stoll** and **Mr Kay Stecher** and taken forward later by **Dr Paul Trafford**) that gave a platform for the electronic version of the directory, *Religions in the UK: On-Line*. Acknowledgements are due for the further development of this, and also for the creation of the CD-ROM accompanying this directory to the University of Derby's I4L service and specifically to **Mr Charles Shields** and **Mr Frank Salvador**.

Special thanks are due to **Ms Debbie Walkington** and **Mr David Bush** of the University Print Unit for their professionalism, patience and collaborative working with project staff on production of this hard copy. Thanks are also due to **Mr Simon Redfern** in the University of Derby Press Office for organising publicity around the public launch of this edition.

As in previous editions, a final word of thanks is due to my wife **Mrs Greta Preisler-Weller** who, together with her patience with my commitment to this project, was also a contributor to the project in her own right by designing the directory's cover used in this and all previous editions of the directory and also helpful in proof-reading for this edition; as to my parents, **Revd Denis** and **Mrs Rhoda Weller**, for their support to me in and through the educational opportunities and professional developments which lie behind and inform my work in this project; and finally to my children **David**, **Lisa** and **Katrina Weller**.

Katrina was one of a group of fourteen children, boys and girls from seven religious traditions, who, in December 2003, shared in laying the foundation stone for the Multi-Faith Centre. It is my hope that, together with the future of the Multi-Faith Centre, this new edition of the directory will contribute towards the creation of a society in which prejudicial, inaccurate and unbalanced portrayals of the beliefs, values, commitments and perspectives of people of diverse religions can be left behind – a future in which the diverse religions and their communities can be properly valued for the contribution that they can make to the development of an equitable and religiously inclusive UK, Europe, and world.

Paul Weller

Professor of Inter-Religious Relations, University of Derby and Visiting Fellow, Centre for Christianity and Culture Regent's Park College, University of Oxford.

TOPIC INDEX

The "Topic Index" lists the page references within the general introductory chapters and the introductions to each religious community where you can find paragraphs of material on particular items. The items appearing in bold are the standard main section titles that appear in the introductions to each religion. The items in normal type are the sub-sections particular to the religion concerned, and the sections in italics are more detailed and specific paragraphs within these sub-sections.

If something that you are looking for does not appear in this index, you can also search for it in the "Significant Word Index" which gives individual page references for each word which is italicised in the text (generally, these are Romanisations of words in languages other than English, or are English language words with a specific meaning within the religion concerned) and also for a number of other significant words including titles of religious personalities and leaders etc.

USER S GUIDE

Accuracy: 19
Apparent Omissions: 19
Calendar and Festivals: 14
Calendars and Festivals: 14
Christian Organisational Data: 15
Contact Details: 15
Further Reading: 14
Further Reading and Help: 20
How the Organisational Data was Compiled: 18
In the UK: 14
Indexes: 20
Introduction: 13
Introductions to the Religions in the UK: 13
Key Beliefs: 14
Life: 14
Organisation: 14
Origins and Development: 14
Places of Worship: 14
Religions Covered by the Directory: 13
Resources for Making Contact, Organising Events and Finding Out More: 20
Sources of Beliefs and Practices: 14
Traditions: 14
Transliteration, Translation and Diacritical Markings: 15
Understanding the Organisational Data: 16
Using the Organisational Data on the Accompanying CD-ROM: 15
Worship: 14

RELIGIOUS LANDSCAPE OF THE UK

Belief and Practice: 36
Beyond Christian Diversity: 23
Chaplaincy and Pastoral Care: 55
Collective Worship in England and Wales: 66
Counting Religion: Christian, Plural and Secular: 26
Demography: 32
Discrimination in Employment: Religion and Belief: 59
Equalities and Human Rights: An Emerging Unified Approach: 60
European Contexts: 70
Further Reading: 73
Geography of Religions in the UK: 29
Higher Education and Religious Identity: 69
History of Christians in the UK: 22
Immigration Regulations and Ministers of Religion: 69
Incitement to Religious Hatred: 61
Inheritance and Change: 21
Inter-Faith Initiatives at a National Level: 45
Local Inter-Faith Initiatives: 46
Media and Advertising: 55
Origins and Early Developments of Inter-Faith Initiatives: 44
Patterns of Public Consultation with Religious Bodies: 52
People of "No Religion" in the 2001 Census: 35
Places of Worship: 38
Questions About Religious Affiliation: 27

Recognition and the Legal Protection of Religious Identity: Developments: 57

Recognition and the Legal Protection of Religious Identity: History: 56

"Registered" Places of Worship in England and Wales: 39Religion and Belief in the European Union: 70

Religion and Education in Northern Ireland: 67

Religion and Education in Scotland: 66

Religion and the Wider Europe: 70

Religion, Belief and Human Rights: New Developments: 58

Religion, Belief and the Law: 56

Religion, Belief, Humanism and Atheism: 34

Religion, Education and the Four Nations of the UK: 62

Religion, Ethnicity and Language: 30

Religion, State and Society in England: 48

Religion, State and Society in Northern Ireland and the Republic of Ireland: 50

Religion, State and Society in Scotland: 49

Religion, State and Society in the UK: 48

Religion, State and Society in Wales: 50

Religions and Inter-Faith Relations: 44

Religions in Public Life: Evolving Inclusivity: 50

Religions in Public Life: the Christian Inheritance: 48

Religions, Belief and the Legal Systems of the UK: 56

Religious and Civil Belonging: 48

Religious Communities and Education: 62

Religious Discrimination: Evidence and Policy Options: 58

Religious Diversification After the Second World War: 24

Religious Diversity and Change: 50

Religious Education in England and Wales: 64

Religiously Based Schools in England and Wales: 62

Secularisation: 34

Socio-Economic Profiles: 33

State Occasions and Religious Observances: 51

Table 1: Religion Responses in the 2001 Census: 28

Table 2: Percentages of "Religion by Ethnicity" Among 2001 Census Respondents in England and Wales:: 31

Table 3: Percentages of "Ethnicity by Religion" of the 2001 Census Respondents in England and Wales: 33

The 2001 Census Picture of Religions in the UK: 26

The Challenges of Terrorism and Social Cohesion: 72

The Challenges of the Future: 71

The Development of a Religiously Plural Country: 22

The Geography and Ethnicity of Religions in the UK: 29

The Variety of Religions: 21

Whither "Multi-Culturalism"?: 71

BAH ŒS IN THE UK:

'Abdu'l-Bahá: 92

A Summary: 93

Bahá'í Calendar and Festivals: 98

Bahá'í Collective Worship: 97

Bahá'í Life: 94

Bahá'í Organisations: 99

Bahá'í Places of Worship: 97

Bahá'í Scriptures: 93

Bahá'í Worship: 96

Bahá'u'lláh: 92

Buildings: 97

Calendar: 98

Core Activities: 95

Diet: 96

Education and Spirituality: 94

Ethics and Spirituality: 94

Ethnicity: 91

Festivals: 98

Further Reading: 101

History in the UK: 91

Houses of Worship: 97

Individual Daily Prayers: 96

International Level: 100

Joining the Community: 94

Key Bahá'í Beliefs: 93

Local Groups: 100

Local Spiritual Assemblies: 99

National Spiritual Assemblies: 100

Nature and Goal of Human Life: 94

Oneness of Humankind: 93

Organisational Listings: 99

Origins and Development of the Bahá'í Faith: 92

Personnel: 101

Populations: 91
Progressive Revelation: 93
Recent Decades: 92
Regional Level: 100
Shoghi Effendi: 92
Sources of Bahá'í Beliefs and Practices: 93
Teaching and Pioneering: 95
The Báb: 92
The Consultative Principle: 101
The Covenant: 95
Traditions in the Bahá'í Faith: 96
Universal House of Justice: 92
Visitors to Bahá'í Worship: 98
Voluntary Sharing: 96
Women and Men: 96

BUDDHISTS IN THE UK

Bodhi: 110
Buddhist Calendar and Festivals: 118
Buddhist Life: 114
Buddhist Organisational Listings: 119
Buddhist Organisations: 119
Buddhist Places of Worship: 116
Buddhist Worship: 116
Buildings for Devotional Practice: 116
Calendar: 118
Ch'an, Zen, Thien and Son Buddhism: 113
Devotional Practice: 116
Duhkha (Suffering Or Unsatisfactoriness): 108
Ethnicity in England and Wales: 104
Festivals: 118
Four Noble Truths: 108
Further Reading: 124
Gautama Buddha/Gotama Buddha: 104
Global and UK Populations: 104
History in the UK: 103
Introducing Buddhists in the UK: 103
Jataka Stories: 108
Karma and Vipaka: 109
Key Buddhist Beliefs: 108
Mahayana: 111
Mahayana Organisations: 120
Main Branches: 110
Marga (The Way): 109
Meditation: 115
Nichiren Buddhism: 114
Nirvana (Cessation of Duhkha): 109
Noble Eightfold Path: 114
Non-Aligned Buddhist Groups: 122

Origins and Development of Buddhism: 104
Paramita: 115
Paticca Samuppada/Pratitya Samutpada (Dependent Origination): 109
Personnel: 122
Political and Social Engagement: 122
Pure Land Buddhism: 113
Samsara: 109
Samudaya (Origin of Suffering Or Unsatisfactoriness): 108
Shrines and Buddharupas: 117
Shunyata/Suññata: 110
Sources of Buddhist Beliefs and Practices: 106
The Buddha: 106
The Five Precepts: 114
The Mahayana Canon: 107
The Pali Canon: 107
The Three Refuges: 106
Theravada: 111
Theravada Organisations: 120
Tibetan Buddhism: 111
Traditions in Buddhism: 110
Transmission: 105
"Umbrella" Organisations: 120
Vegetarianism: 116
Visitors to a Buddhist Temple: 117

CHRISTIANS IN THE UK

Anglican: 138
Anglican Churches: 156
Christian Calendar and Festivals: 148
Christian Life: 141
Christian Organisations: 152
Christian Places of Worship: 146
Christian Traditions and Churches in the UK: 153
Christian Witness: 143
Christian Worship: 144
Christians in the UK: 127
Church Buildings: 146
Churchmanship: 140
Confirmation and Membership: 142
Dietary Issues: 143
Early Years: 130
Eastern and Western Christendom and Protestant Reformation: 131
Ecumenical Structures: 162
Ethics and Discipleship: 143
Ethnicity Among Christians in the UK: 129

Eucharistic Worship: 144
Fasting: 143
Further Reading: 165
Global and UK Populations: 128
God, Incarnation and Revelation: 134
History in the UK: 127
Jesus: 133
Judgement and Eternal Life: 135
Key Christian Beliefs: 133
Main Branches: 137
Monks, Nuns and Religious: 144
Organisational Listings: 152
**Origins and Development of
   Christianity: 130**
Orthodox: 137
Orthodox Churches: 158
Other Christian Organisations: 163
Other Interdenominational Networks: 163
Pentecostal: 139
Personnel: 163
Prayer: 144
Preaching: 146
Protestant: 138
Protestant Churches: 158
Protestant Reformation: 128
Quakers and Unitarians: 140
Reason, Conscience and Experience: 133
Restorationist and House Church
   Movements: 139
Roman Catholic: 137
Roman Catholic Church: 157
Salvation: 135
Scriptures: 131
**Sources of Christian Beliefs and
   Practices: 131**
Sunday: 148
The Christian Calendar: 148
The Church: 133
The Church Year and Festivals: 149
The Creeds: 132
The Ecumenical Movement: 141
The Holy Trinity: 135
The Pattern of Jesus: 141
The Protestant Reformation and the
   Missionary Movement: 131
The Saints: 136
The Virgin Mary: 136
Tradition: 132
Traditions in Christianity: 137
Traditions in the UK: 129
Visitors to a Christian Church: 147

HINDUS IN THE UK

Arti Ceremony: 181
Ashramas: 180
Atman: 174
Calendar: 184
Commonality and Variety: 171
Corporate Devotional Activity: 181
Dharma: 175
Domestic Worship: 181
Educational Organisations: 188
Ethnicity in England and Wales: 170
Fasting: 181
Festivals: 184
Further Reading: 189
Gender Roles: 180
Global and UK Hindu Populations: 169
Guru-Disciple Relationship: 180
Havan: 181
Hindu Calendar and Festivals: 184
Hindu Life: 178
Hindu Organisational Listings: 185
Hindu Organisations: 185
Hindu Places of Worship: 182
Hindu Worship: 181
Hindus in the UK: 169
History in the UK: 169
Jati (Community) Associations: 186
Karma: 175
Key Hindu Beliefs: 173
Mandirs: 182
Maya: 175
Moksha: 174
Murtis: 182
One and Many: 173
Origins: 170
**Origins and Development of the
   Hindu Tradition: 170**
Other Temple Features: 183
Personnel: 188
Pilgrimages: 185
Regional/Linguistic Groups: 188
Representative Groups: 186
Sacred Texts: 171
Sampradaya: 177
Shruti: 171
Smriti: 172
**Sources of Hindu Beliefs and
   Practices: 171**
Spiritual Movements: 187
The Four Aims: 178
The Four Varnas: 179
The Four Vedas: 172

The Six Darshanas: 175
Traditions in Hinduism: 175
Vaishnavas, Shaivas and Shaktas: 177
Values: 178
Varnashrama Dharma: 178
Vedanta: Dvaita and Advaita: 176
Vegetarianism: 181
Visitors to a Hindu Mandir: 183
Yuga: 175

JAINS IN THE UK

Ahimsa: 195
Angabahya: 195
Angas: 194
Anuvratas: 198
Calendar: 200
Digambara: 197
Festivals: 200
Further Reading: 202
Global and UK Populations: 193
History in the UK: 193
Jain Calendar and Festivals: 200
Jain Life: 198
Jain Organisational Listings: 201
Jain Organisations: 201
Jain Path to Moksha: 196
Jain Places of Worship: 199
Jain Worship: 198
Jainism in India: 194
Jains in the UK: 193
Karma: 196
Key Jain Beliefs: 195
Mahavira: 194
Mahavratas: 198
Main Branches: 197
Mandirs: 199
Origins and Development of Jainism: 193
Other Texts: 195
Personal Puja: 198
Personnel: 201
Purvas: 194
Reality in Jain Perspective: 195
Scriptures: 194
Sentient Beings: 195
Shvetambara: 197
Sources of Jain Beliefs and Practices: 194
The Tirthankaras: 193
Traditions in Jainism: 197
Visitors to a Jain Temple: 200

JEWS IN THE UK

Barmitzvah and Batmitzvah: 209
Calendar: 215
Circumcision: 209
Clothing and Prayer: 212
Diaspora, Holocaust and Israel: 205
Eretz Yisrael, Zionism and Attitudes Towards Israel: 207
Ethnicity in England and Wales: 204
Festivals: 215
Further Reading: 219
General National Organisations: 218
Global and UK Populations: 203
Halakhah: 206
Haredim: 208
Hasidic: 208
History in the UK: 203
Humanity: 207
Independent Synagogues: 219
Israel: 211
Jewish Calendar and Festivals: 215
Jewish Life: 209
Jewish Organisations: 217
Jewish Places of Worship: 213
Jewish Worship: 212
Jewishness: 209
Jews in the UK: 203
Kashrut: 210
Keeping the Commandments: 212
Key Jewish Beliefs: 207
Kingdom of God: 207
Kingdoms and Exile: 205
Main Branches: 208
Masorti: 219
Masorti (Conservative): 209
Midrash: 206
Minor Festivals and Additional Fast Days: 216
Moses and the Israelites: 205
Organisational Listings: 217
Origins and Development of Judaism: 204
Orthodox: 208
Orthodox Organisations: 218
Other Communal Worship: 213
Patriarchs: 204
Personnel: 219
Progressive: 209
Reform and Liberal Organisations: 218
Representative Organisations: 217
Sephardi and Ashkenazi: 203
Shabbat: 210

Shabbat Worship: 212
Shema: 207
Sources of Jewish Beliefs and Practices: 205
Synagogues: 213
Talmud: 206
Tenakh: 205
The Shalosh Regalim: 215
The Yamim Noraim: 215
Torah and Mitzvot: 207
Traditions in Judaism: 208
Visitors to a Jewish Synagogue: 214
Women: 211

MUSLIMS IN THE UK

Becoming a Muslim: 230
Calendar: 233
Community Groups: 238
Dawah Organisations: 237
Development and Diversity: 225
Educational Organisations: 237
Ethnicity in England and Wales: 224
Further Reading: 238
Gender and Family: 231
Global and UK Populations: 223
Goal and Purpose of Human Life: 228
Halal: 230
History in the UK: 223
International Organisations: 238
Introducing Muslims in the UK: 223
Jihad: 230
Key Muslim Beliefs: 227
Main Branches: 228
Media Organisations: 238
Monotheism: 227
Mosques: 232
Movements: 236
Muslim Calendar and Festivals: 233
Muslim Life: 230
Muslim Organisations: 235
Muslim Places of Worship: 232
Muslim Worship: 231
Muslims in the UK: 223
Organisational Listings: 235
Origins and Development of Islam: 224
Other National Organisations: 237
Personnel: 238
Political Organisations: 238
Qur'an: 226
Radical Groups: 237

Revelation: 224
Salah: 231
Schools: 227
Shari'ah: 230
Shari'ah: 226
Sources of Muslim Beliefs and Practices: 226
Sunni: 228
Tasawwuf: 230
The Key Beliefs and Five Pillars of Islam: 227
The Prophet Muhammad and the 'Ummah: 224
Traditions in Islam: 228
"Umbrella" Organisations: 235
Visitors to a Mosque: 233
Women's Groups: 238
Youth Groups: 237

SIKHS IN THE UK

18th and 19th Century History of Sikhism: 249
Amrit Pahul: 253
Basic Orientations: 252
Birth, Marriage and Death: 255
Calendar: 258
Daily Prayers: 256
Dasam Granth: 250
Definitions: 250
Diet: 255
Educational Organisations: 260
Equality: 253
Ethnicity in England and Wales: 248
Further Reading: 261
Global and UK Populations: 247
Goal of Life: 251
God: 251
Gurdwara: 256
History in the UK: 247
Key Sikh Beliefs: 250
Khalsa Panth: 251
Langar: 257
Organisational Listings: 259
Origins and Development of Sikhism: 248
Path: 256
Personnel: 260
Pilgrimage: 255
Rahit Maryada: 250
Rahit Nama: 250

Sadh Sangat: 256
Sikh Calendar and Festivals: 258
Sikh Ethics: 252
Sikh Life: 252
Sikh Organisations: 259
Sikh Places of Worship: 256
Sikh Worship: 256
Sikhs in the UK: 247
Singh and Kaur: 255
Social Groupings: 260
Sources of Sikh Beliefs and Practices: 249
The Guru Granth Sahib: 249
The Ten Gurus: 248
Traditions in Sikhism: 252
"Umbrella" Organisations and General Organisations: 260
Unity and Diversity: 252
Vistors to a Sikh Gurdwara: 257
Works of Bhai Gurdas and Bhai Nandlal: 250

ZOROASTRIANS IN THE UK

Ahura Mazda: 268
Calendar: 278
Death Practices: 275
Diet: 276
Ethics: 273
Ethnicity of Zoroastrians in the UK: 266
Festivals: 279
Fire: 277
Further Reading: 281
Gah/Geh: 274
Global and UK Populations: 266
History and Influence of Zoroastrianism: 267
History in the UK: 265
Initiation: 273
Key Zoroastrian Beliefs: 268
Origins and Development of Zoroastrianism: 266
Personnel: 281
Places of Worship: 277
Saoshyant, End Time, Physical Resurrection, Last Judgement and Frasho-Keriti: 272
Sources of Zoroastrian Beliefs and Practices: 267
Spenta Mainyu (The Holy and Bounteous Spirit) and Angra Mainyu (The Destructive Spirit): 269
Sudreh and Kùstì/Koshti: 273
The Avesta: 267
The Concept of Death and Afterlife: 272
The Parsis in India and the Zoroastrians in Iran: 267
The Role of Humanity: 272
The Seven Good Creations and their Guardians: 270
Traditions in Zoroastrianism: 276
Visitors to a Zoroastrian Place of Worship: 277
Zarathushtra: 266
Zoroastrian Calendars and Festivals: 278
Zoroastrian Life: 273
Zoroastrian Organisational Listings: 280
Zoroastrian Organisations: 280
Zoroastrian Places of Worship: 277
Zoroastrian Worship: 277

SOME OTHER RELIGIOUS COMMUNITIES AND GROUPS

A Range of "Other Religious Groups": 283
Brahma Kumaris: 287
Christian Scientists: 289
Christian-Related/Contested Groups in the 2001 Census: 284
Church of Jesus Christ of Latter-Day Saints: 291
Further "Other Religious Groups" in the 2001 Census: 286
Hindu-Related Groups in the 2001 Census: 285
Introducing Some Other Religious Communities and Groups: 283
Introduction: 283
Jehovah's Witnesses: 293
Namdhari Sikh Community: 295
"New Religious Movements" in the 2001 Census: 285
Other Religious Groups and the 2001 Census: 284
Pagans: 297
Rastafarians: 301
Ravidassia: 302
Sant Nirankaris: 304
Sathya Sai Service Organisation: 305
Traditions Related to people of Chinese Descent in the 2001 Census: 286
Valmikis: 306

RESOURCES FOR MAKING CONTACTS, ORGANISING EVENTS AND FINDING OUT MORE

Allowing Plenty of Planning and Organising Time: 311

Avoiding Clashes with Religious Festivals: 311

Avoiding Stereotypes: 311

Bahá'í Directories: 323

Buddhist Directories: 324

Catering for Multi-Faith Events: 313

Choosing An Appropriate Venue: 312

Christian Directories: 324

Directories About Religious Organisations: 323

Directories on New Religious Movements: 325

Finding Out More: 316

Further Help: 316

Gender Relations: 314

General Texts on Religions: 318

Hindu Directories: 324

Introduction: 309

Jain Directories: 324

Jewish Directories: 325

Local and Regional Religious Directories: 325

Making Contacts and Organising Events: 309

Muslim Directories: 325

New Religious Movements: Bibliographical Resources: 321

Other Directories: 326

Overviews of Religions: 317

Possible Areas of Sensitivity: 310

Producing Guidelines and Information Packs: 316

Religious Observance During An Event: 312

Shared Religious Observance During An Event: 312

Sikh Directories: 325

Some Things to Be Aware of When Making Contact: 310

Special Topics: 317

Special Topics: Bibliographical Resources: 322

The Composition of Consultative Panels: 315

The Kind of Input That Is Needed: 315

World Religions: Bibliographical Resources: 321

World Religions: Overviews: 318

World Religions: Special Topics: 319

World Religions: Texts: 321

Zoroastrian Directories: 325

ACKNOWLEDGEMENTS

Bahá'ís in the UK: 334

Buddhists in the UK: 334

Christians in the UK: 335

Collection and Verification of Organisational Data: 333

Consultants on the Chapter on Religious Landscape of the UK: 333

Consultants on the Chapter on Some Other Religious Communities and Groups: 333

Consultants to the 1997 and 2001 Editions: 334

Consultants to the 2007 Edition: 332

Consultation Processes and the 2007 Edition: 330

Hindus in the UK: 335

Inter-Faith Activity in the UK: 337

Introduction: 329

Jains in the UK: 336

Jews in the UK: 336

Muslims in the UK: 336

Other Acknowledgements: 337

Religious Landscape of the UK: 336

Sikhs in the UK: 336

Some Other Religious Communities and Groups: 337

Zoroastrians in the UK: 336

SIGNIFICANT WORD INDEX

This index lists all the significant words appearing in the directory's textual materials but not in the listings. These significant words include all the words appearing within the text in italics (generally these are Romanisations of words in languages other than English or are English language words with a specific meaning within the religion concerned). But a number of other significant words are also given including names of various scriptures and titles of religious personalities and leaders, etc. While an attempt has been made to be consistent within the directory's textual materials, words that appear in other than English and non-European languages can be found in English in a variety of Romanisations so it is always worth

checking the index for other possible renderings of the word which you want to find. Therefore once you have looked up a word initially if other renderings are noted it would also be worth checking if there are references for these within this index.

The singular form of English words in the index covers page references for both the singular and plural forms of the word. Not every single instance of a word within the directory is given but a range are included that will help users to unlock the meaning of the word or to set it in a wider context. General thematic references are not included in this index. For these such as worship festivals etc in the various religions the reader should consult the directory's Topic Index that sets out the pages on which these topics are dealt with in respect of each religion and also more general topics such as religious education, and religion and the law.

A

Aaronic Priesthood, 291
Abbots, 124
Abdu'l-Bahá, 91-96, 99
Abdu'l-Bahá's Will, 92
Abedkarites, 120
Abhidhamma, 107
Abhidhamma-pitaka, 107
Acharanga Sutr, 194
Acharyas, 199
Act of Supremacy, 153, 155
Act of Uniformity, 154
Acts of the Apostles, 134, 139
Adar, 268
Adharma, 195
Adi Granth, 249, 250, 295
Administrative Order, 95
Adur/Adar, 277
Advaita, 174, 176, 178, 185, 187
Advaitins, 176
Advent, 149
Aesir, 298
Afarganyu, 271
African Churches, 163
African Independent Churches, 23

Afrin, 268
Afrinagan, 268
Aga Khan, 229
Agama, 107, 194
Agape, 134, 141
Agencies, 162
Aggadah, 206
Agha Khanis, 229
Ahimsa, 178, 181, 184, 195, 198
Ahl-e-Hadith, 229
Ahuna Vairya, 275
Ahunavar, 275
Ahunavars, 274
Airyana Vaeja, 268
Aiwisruthrim, 274
Aiwisruthra, 274
Ajiva, 195
Akal Purakh, 250
Akal Takhat, 249
Akasha, 195
Akya, 112, 121
Alaya, 199
Alexandrian, 297
Al-khulafa ar-rashidun, 225
All Saints, 152

Allah, 227
Altar, 147, 148, 151
Ambedkarite, 104, 106
Ameretat, 266, 270
Amesha Spenta, 270
Amgarhia, 260, 261
Amir, 225, 226
Amrit, 253, 254, 259
Amrit Pahul, 249, 251-253
Amrit sanchaar, 253
Amritdhari, 254, 295
Amsterdam Treaty, 71
Anatman, 108, 110
Anatta, 108
Anavil Brahmins, 179
Anavil jati, 186
Anekantavada, 195
Angabahya, 194, 195
Angas, 194, 195
Anglican, 22-23, 40, 43, 49, 50, 56, 60, 63, 131-132, 136-142, 144-147, 149, 150-152, 153, 156-157, 164, 165, 167
Anglo-Catholic, 136, 139, 140, 145-147, 149, 151

Angra Mainyu, 269
Anjali, 118
Anno Domini, 148
Annual Register of Statistics, 39, 40
Anointed One, 133, 207
Anti-Terrorism, Crime and Security Act, 61, 62
Anuvratas, 198
Aparigraha, 198
Apocrypha, 132
Apostle, 134, 137, 149, 164
Apostles' Creed, 132
Apostolic, 137
Apostolic succession, 139, 291
Apostolicity, 137
Apostoloi, 134
Aql, 226
Arahat, 111
Aranyakas, 172
Arati, 199
Aravot, 216
Arba Kanfot, 212
Archbishop of Canterbury, 127, 138
Archbishop, 48, 138, 157, 158, 165
Archdioceses, 158
Ardas, 255, 256
Area Superintendent, 165
Arhat, 197-198
Aron Kodesh, 214
Aroras, 179
Artha, 178
Artharva Veda, 172
Arthaveda, 172
Arti, 181, 183, 184
Aruna, 110, 114
Asalaam-u-'alaikum, 233
Asatru, 297, 298
Ascended, 134
Ascension, 99, 151, 289
Ascension Day, 151
Ascetics, 105, 194, 198, 199, 201, 230
Ash Wednesday, 150
Asha, 273-277
Asha Vahishta, 266, 269, 270
Ashan Sahib, 261
Ashem Vohu, 274, 275

Ashkenazi, 24, 203, 204, 213
Ashram, 180
Ashrama, 178, 180
Asr, 232
Assembly, 95, 100, 160
Association, 159
Assumed, 152
Assumption of the Blessed Virgin Mary, 136
Asteya, 198
Astnar, 254
Atar, 277
Atash Nyàish, 277
Atash, 271
Atharva Veda, 172
Atman, 172, 174, 176, 177
Atmas, 195
Atoned, 135
Atonement, 145
AUM, 183
Autocephalous, 138
Auxiliary Board, 101
Avan, 255, 268
Avatamsaka Sutra, 107
Avataras, 176
Avesta, 267, 268
Avot, 204
Awakened, 106
Ayah, 24
Ayathrem, 279
Ayathrima, 279
Ayurveda, 172

B

Báb, 92, 93, 98, 99, 102
Baba, 252
Bábi, 92
Babylon, 301
Bahá'í International Community, 101
Bahá'u'lláh, 91-100
Bahá'u'lláh's Declaration, 98
Bahá'u'lláh's Hidden Words, 93
Bahá'u'lláh's Will, 92
Baisakhi, 295
Balmikis, 179
Bandha, 196
Bandi Chhor Divas, 259, 260
Bani, 252
Baptise, 164

Baptised, 142, 150-152, 159, 160
Baptism, 142, 151, 292
Baptism in the Spirit, 139, 140
Baptismal, 142, 151, 294
Baptismal font, 142
Baptisms, 292
Baptist, 22, 130, 132, 142, 147, 153, 154, 156, 159, 160, 164, 165
Baptistries, 142
Bar Mitzvah, 209, 210
Barelwi, 228, 229, 234, 236
Basket of [Monastic] Discipline, 107
Basket of Discourses, 107
Basket of Further Teachings, 107
Bat Hayil, 210
Bat Mitzvah, 210
Beatitudes, 143
Benedictines, 144
Beth Din, 206, 211, 220, 221
Bhagavad Gita, 172, 173, 179
Bhagavata Purana, 171, 173
Bhagavati Sutra, 194
Bhai, 250, 252, 261
Bhajan, 181, 185
Bhakti, 178, 302
Bhakti yoga, 176
Bhana manana, 252
Bharat desha, 171
Bhatras, 260
Bhava, 195, 199
Bhawan, 302
Bible, 131, 138, 143, 155, 204, 206, 208, 289,, 291, 293, 294, 301
Biblical, 205, 211
Bimah, 214
Bishop, 48, 131, 137-139, 142, 143, 146, 147, 155, 157, 164, 165
Bishop of Rome, 127, 131, 137, 165
Bishops' Conference, 157
bKa'gyur, 108
Black-majority, 161
Blasphemy, 57, 58
Blessing, 148, 215

Boddhisattivas, 111
Bodhi Tree, 105, 106, 110, 119
Bodhicitta, 112
Bodhisatta, 111, 112
Bodhisattva, 110-112, 115-117,
    119, 123
Bodhisattva-Mahasattvas, 111
Bodhisattvayana, 110
Bohras, 230
Book of Common Prayer, 154,
    155, 160
Book of Esther, 217
Book of Genesis, 210
Book of His Covenant, 95
Book of Mormon: Another
    Testament of Jesus Christ, 291
Book of Revelation, 132, 135, 301
Book of Ruth, 217
Book of the Acts of the Apostles,
    132, 133
Book of the Covenant, 92
Brahmacharin, 180
Brahmacharya, 198
Brahman, 174, 176
Brahmanas, 172
Brahmin, 180, 187, 188
Branches, 291
Brdo Retreat, 112
Brdo Thodol, 112
Breaking of Bread, 145
Brethren, 161
Brihaspati Agama, 170
Brit, 204
Brit Milah, 209
Britain Yearly Meeting, 162
Broad Church, 139
Broadcasting Act, 55
bsTan'gyur, 108
Buddha, 93, 103, 105-111, 113-
    119, 123-125, 171
Buddha Day, 118
Buddha Jayanti, 118
Buddha's "Enjoyment Body", 112
Buddha's Way, 125
Buddha-nature, 106, 107
Buddharupa, 117
Bundahishn, 270, 272

C

Caliph, 225, 228
Caliphate, 225

Calvinism, 155
Calvinist, 128, 155
Canon, 107, 132, 195
Canon law, 51, 128
Canonical, 249
Canonised, 291
Cardinals, 165
Carmelites, 144
Caste, 31, 39, 120, 179, 186, 201,
    253, 255, 260, 302, 306
Catechism of the Catholic
    Church, 166
Cathedral choirs, 147
Cathedral, 51, 147
Catholic, 48, 50, 68, 127, 128, 130,
    135, 137-140, 147, 148, 150-
    154, 157, 165
Catholicism, 167
Catholicity, 137
Catholic-Protestant, 68
Catur Aryasatya/Cattari
    Ariyasaccani, 108
Celestial Buddhas, 106
Ch'an, 111, 113, 121
Ch'an-na, 113
Chabad, 220
Chair, 159
Chandas, 173
Chapel, 146, 292
Charhdi kala, 252
Charismatic, 139, 140
Charnamrita, 183
Charraka, 176
Chaupai, 256
Chaur, 256
Chaur sahib, 257
Chazzan, 214
Cheder, 204
Chief Stewards of the Faith, 92
Chinese Buddhism, 114
Chinese canon, 107
Chinese Zen, 116
Chinvat Peretu, 271, 272, 276
Chishti, 230
Choirs, 147
Chrism, 142
Chrismated, 142
Chrismation, 142
Christ, 93, 133, 144, 145, 149,
    150, 289, 293
Christendom, 128

Christening, 142
Christian Brethren, 130, 161,
    164
Christian Science Monitor, 289
Christian Science, 289
Christmas, 21, 149, 150
Christological, 162
Christos, 133
Church, 15, 16, 22, 23, 38-40, 43,
    48, 50, 51, 63, 65, 68, 128,
    130- 133, 136-165, 232, 285,
    289, 291-293
Church Fathers, 132
Church President, 291
Church's Apostolicity, 137
Churches of Christ, 158
Churches Testimony Meetings,
    289
Churches Together, 163
Churchmanship, 140, 163
Circuit, 159, 293
Circumcise, 209, 219
Citizenship Studies, 245
Clergy, 154, 155, 157, 165
Cluster Co-Ordinators, 98
Clusters, 160
College of Bishops, 137
College of Cardinals, 165
Commandments, 209
Common Era, 215
Commonwealth Immigrants Act,
    25
Communicant, 148
Communications Act, 55
Communion, 137, 142, 144, 145,
    148
Communion of Saints, 152
Conference, 159
Confirmation, 142
Congregation, 144, 145, 147, 156,
    160, 164, 165, 212, 213, 261,
    293
Congregational, 149, 156, 158,
    160, 214
Congregationalism, 160
Congregationalist, 22, 154, 130,
    160
Consecrated mandirs, 199
Consecrated, 146, 198, 199
Conservative Judaism, 209

Continental Boards of Counsellors, 101
Convention, 58
Conversion, 138
Core Activities, 98
Corp, 160
Council of the Twelve Apostles, 291
Councils of the Seventy, 291
Counsellor, 291
Covenant, 95, 96, 131, 209, 204, 292
Covenant naming, 209
Covenantal, 204
Covenant-breakers, 96
Covens, 297
Craft, 297, 298
Creator, 134
Credal, 132, 134, 140
Creeds, 132-134, 138, 162
Cross, 134, 147, 151
Crucifixion, 134, 135, 145, 151, 289
Cults, 285
Cymdeithas yr Iaith Gymraeg, 50

D

Da'wah, 230
Daeva, 266, 268, 271
Dakhma, 275, 276
Dalai Lama, 104, 113, 121
Dalit, 106, 180
Damdama Bir, 249
Dan, 251
Darbar Sahib, 249, 257
Darshan, 183
Darshana Shashtras, 175
Darul'ulum, 228
Dar-ul-uloom, 241
Dasam Granth, 250, 295
Dasha-lakshana-parva, 200
Dastur, 281
Daswandh, 253
Dawah, 237
Dawat-ul-Islam, 236
Dawning Place of God's Praise, 97
Day of Judgement, 227, 228
Daya, 251
Dayan, 221
Dayanim, 221
Deacons, 137, 145, 146, 152,

Deanery, 157
Decalogue, 143
Declaration, 98
Defender of Faith, 49
Defender of The Faith, 49
Denkard, 267
Denomination, 133, 139, 146
Deobandi, 228, 229, 236
Deuteronomy, 205
Dev Vak, 172
Devas, 173, 174, 176
Dhammachakka, 119
Dhanurveda, 172
Dharam, 248
Dharam Khand, 251
Dharma, 106, 107, 113, 114, 117, 118, 122, 170-175, 178, 179, 195, 306
Dharma Shastra, 172, 173
Dharma/dhamma, 106
Dharmacharinis, 124
Dharmacharis, 124
Dhr, 175
Dhyana, 197
Diaconal, 164
Diaconate, 164
Diakonos, 164
Diaspora, 204, 205, 208, 216
Diclofenac, 276
Digambara, 194, 195, 197-201
Digambara mandirs, 199
Digambara monks, 198
Digambara nuns, 198
Diksha, 198, 201
Diocesan, 157
Diocese, 147, 158, 157, 165, 291
Dipas, 185
Disciples, 134, 143, 144, 151, 164, 248
Discipleship, 143
Discourse on the Turning of the Wheel of the Dharma, 119
Disestablished, 50
Disestablishment, 50, 157
District, 159-161, 293
District Chair, 165
Divali, 259, 260, 259
Divas, 185
Divination, 297
Divine Hymns of Zarathushtra, 268

Divine Light, 228
Divine Liturgy, 145
Divisions, 160
Diwali, 185, 201
Diwan, 256
Doctrine and Covenants, 291
Dominicans, 144
Door, 92
Dormition, 152
Dravya, 195
Drbar Sahib, 255, 257, 261
Dreadlock, 301
Druid Orders, 298
Druid Priestess, 300
Druid, 298
Druid's Prayer, 298
Druidic, 298
Druidism, 299
Druidry, 297, 300
Dualism, 177
Dualistic, 176
Duhkha, 108, 109, 114, 115, 175
Dussehra, 185
Dvaita, 174, 176, 178
Dvaitins, 176
Dwarpa, 175

E

Easter, 135, 149-152
Easter Vigil, 151
Eastern, 130, 137
Eastern Catholic Churches, 148
Eastern Christendom, 131
Eastern Orthodox, 129
Eastern Orthodox Churches, 291
Eastern Orthodoxy, 130
Ecclesia, 123, 153
Ecclesiastical, 49, 137, 153
Ecumenical, 39, 51, 131, 143, 144, 162, 163, 292
Ecumenical Council, 137, 138
Ecumenical Instrument, 15, 16, 163
Ecumenical Movement, 141
Ecumenical Officer, 163
Ecumenical Patriarch, 138
Ecumenism, 292
Education (Scotland) Act, 67
Education Act, 63, 64, 66, 67
Education Reform Act, 64, 66
Eisteddfodau, 298

Ekklesia, 133
Elder, 155, 158, 293
Employment Act, 57
Employment Equality (Religion or Belief) Regulations, 59
Encyclicals, 143
Endowment, 292
Enlightened, 106, 109
Enlightenment, 105, 106, 110-112, 118
Eostre, 151
Epiphany, 149, 150
Episcope, 155
Episcopal, 50, 139, 157, 161
Episcopal Church, 142
Episcopalian, 155, 156
Epistle, 131, 132, 134
Epistole, 134
Equality Act, 60
Ervad Sahebs, 281
Esoteric, 22, 230
Essentials in Church History, 292
Established, 40, 48-50, 56, 66, 128, 155, 165
Established Churches, 51, 153, 157
Establishment, 49, 55
Esther, 206
Etrog, 216
Euangelion, 143
Euangelizo, 140
Eucharist, 137, 145, 147, 149, 151-152, 160, 164
Eucharist/Mass/Communion, 148
Eucharistia, 145
Eucharistic, 145
European Convention on Human Rights and Fundamental Freedoms, 58, 59, 70
Evangelical, 135, 139, 140, 143, 160, 161, 163
Evangelical Revival, 131, 140, 146, 159
Exclusive Brethren, 161
Exegesis, 206
Exodus, 205, 216, 301
Ezekiel, 206

F

Fair Employment Act, 60
Faith in the City, 52

Faith, 141
Fajr, 232
Far Eastern, 110, 118, 123
Farvardingan, 280
Fasli, 278,
Fast, 99, 144, 216, 234
Fast of Esther, 217
Fasting, 150, 151, 181, 184, 200, 234
Father, 134-136, 138, 152
Fatiha, 226
Feast, 97
Feast of Heavenly Souls, 279
Feast of Weeks, 152
Festival of Sacrifice, 235
Filioque, 138
Fire Temple, 41, 277, 280
Fireside, 97, 98
First Communion, 145
First Presidency, 291
First Temple, 217
First Vision, 291
Five Ks, 254
Five Pillars of Islam, 227
Five Precepts, 107, 114, 115, 123
Foot Washing, 151
Ford-Makers, 194
Four Noble Truths, 107, 114, 115
Franciscans, 144
Frasho Keriti, 270, 273
Fravarane, 273, 273
Fravashi, 268, 270-272, 279-280
Fravahrs, 279
Free Church, 22, 23, 43, 50, 56, 138, 146, 153, 154, 156, 159, 161
Fuqaha, 238

G

Gah, 268, 274
Gahambar, 194, 268, 279, 280
Gandharvaveda, 172
Garbha-griha, 183
Gardnerian, 297
Gate, 92
Gatha, 268, 270, 275, 278, 280, 282
Gathas and Yasna, 267
Gayo Maretan, 273
Gelug, 112, 113

Gelugpa, 121
Gelugpa nuns, 123
Gemara, 206
General Assembly, 49
General Secretaries, 165
General Synod, 157
Genesis, 205
Gentile, 130, 150
Get, 211
Ghar mandir, 181
Ghayr muqallidun, 229
Gian Khand, 251
Girdo, 274
Gireban, 274
Glory of God, 92
Glossolalia, 139
God's Healing Power, 288
Godparent, 142
Godspell, 132
Gohonzon, 122
Golden Temple, 249
Good News, 132, 140, 143
Good Shepherd, 133
Gopi, 182
Gospel, 131-135, 150, 159, 224, 228, 292
Gospel According to Luke, 132
Gospel According to Matthew, 143
Gospel choirs, 147
Gospel of Barnabas, 132
Gospel of John, 151
Grace, 135, 136, 141, 178, 253
Granth Sahib, 249-250
Granthi, 253, 255, 261
Great Fast, 150
Great Scripture Store, 107
Great Vehicle, 110
Great, 130
Greater Pentad, 280
Gregorian, 149, 150, 184, 215, 258, 278, 279
Grihastha, 180
Grihini, 180
Grihya Sutra, 172, 173
Guardian of the Faith, 92, 95
Guided One, 229
Gunas, 174
Gur, 250, 295
Gurbani, 250, 252

Gurbani kirtan, 256
Gurdwara, 25, 38, 43, 44, 248, 250-253, 255-261
Gurmantar, 295
Gurmat, 248, 255
Gurmukh, 252
Gurmukhi, 248, 250
Gurpurb, 259
Guru, 112, 123, 177, 180, 181, 188, 248-257, 295, 302
Guru Granth Sahib, 249-253, 256-261, 302
Guru Nanak, 263
Guru Nanak's Birthday, 259
Guru Ram Das, 261
Guru Ram Singh, 296
Guru Shishya, 180
Gurudev Hardev, 304
Guru-pancami, 200
Guruship, 295

H
Hadassim, 216
Hadith, 226-229
Haftarah, 212
Haggadah, 216
Hajj, 227, 235
Halakhah, 206, 209, 211
Halal, 230, 231, 255
Haldi, 183
Hamas Pathmaidyam, 279
Hamaspathmaedaya, 279
Hamaspathmaedaya gahambar, 280
Hamkar, 270
Hanafi, 227-229
Hanbali, 227
Hands of the Cause of God, 92
Hankar, 251
Hanukah, 217
Hanukiyyot, 217
Haram, 230
Haredim, 204, 208
Harijans, 180
Harminder Sahib, 249
Harvest, 152, 216
Hasid, 208
Hasidic, 208, 220, 221
Hatha Yoga, 188
Haurvatat, 266, 269
Havan, 181, 274

Havana, 115, 116
Havani, 274
Havdalah, 210
HazIratu'l-Quds, 100
Hazzan, 221
Hazzanim, 221
Head of the Church, 153
Heathen, 298, 299
Hebrew Scriptures, 131
Heder, 213
Herald of Christ's Presence, 293
Hereditaries, 297
Hereditary, 297
Hevra Kaddisha, 221
High Church, 139
High Holy Days, 207, 213
High Priest, 207, 217
Hijab, 231, 240
Hijra, 225, 233
Hikantaza, 113
Hikshu/bhikkhus, 122
Hikshuni/bhikkhunis, 122-123
Himsa, 114
Hola Mohalla, 258
Holi, 184
Holiness, 129, 161
Holocaust, 205
Holocaust Remembrance Day, 217
Holy Communion, 142, 144-146, 147, 152
Holy Father, 165
Holy Roman Emperor, 131
Holy Spirit, 134-136, 138, 140, 142, 149, 152
Holy Week, 151
House Church, 139, 146, 162, 164
House of Deceit, 272
House of God, 227
House of Justice, 100, 101
House of Song, 272
House of Worship, 41, 97
Huguenots, 129
Hujjah, 229
Hukam, 251
Hukamnama vak, 255, 256
Hukhta, 266, 269, 270
Human Rights Act, 58, 70
Humash, 205, 208
Humata, 266, 269, 270
Hunyata, 110, 111

Hvarshta, 266, 269, 270
Hyana, 113
Hymns, 159
Hypostases, 136
Hypostasis, 136

I
Ibadah, 231
Icon, 147-148
Iconographic, 147
Iconostasis, 147
Ijma, 226-228
Ijtihad, 226, 227
Ik Onkar, 251
Imam, 229, 232-233, 234-237, 238
Imamate, 225, 230
Immaculate Conception, 136
Imran, 256
Inaya, 123
Inayana, 110
Incarnation, 134, 136, 148, 149
Independent, 43, 130, 155-156
Injil, 121, 224, 228
Inter Faith Network for the UK, 8, 46, 81, 87
Inter-Church Process, 162
Inter-denominational, 163
Intermediate Bodies, 163
International Counsellors, 101
International Teaching Centre, 101
Interpreter of Scripture, 24, 92
Irani Zardushtis, 31
Iranis, 31, 276
Isaiah, 206
Ishta-deva, 177
Islamophobia, 59
Isma'ilis, 229
Ithna Asherite, 229
Itihasa, 172

J
Ja'fari, 227
Jap, 256
Jah, 301
Jaikara, 302
Jain, 193
Jamaat-i-Islami, 229, 236
Jami, 232
Janam Sakhis, 248
Janma, 175

Japa, 181
Japanese, 107, 113, 124
Japanese Zen, 116
Japji, 254, 256
Japtah Path, 257
Jashan, 271, 277, 280
Jat, 260
Jataka, 108, 111, 115
Jati, 31, 179, 186, 187
Jeremiah, 206
Jesuit, 144
Jesus Prayer, 144
Jhatka, 255
Jihad, 230
Jinas, 193, 194, 197, 199
Jiva, 176, 177, 195
Jnana, 196
Jnana yoga, 176
Jnana-pancami, 200
Jodo Shinshu, 114
Joshua, 206
Judges, 206
Julian, 149
Jyotisha, 173

K

Ka'bah, 227
Kabbalah, 208
Kabbalat Shabbat, 212
Kabbalat Torah, 210
Kabbalistic, 208
Kachhera, 254
Kadampa, 112
Kadmi, 278
Kadmi Yazdegerdi, 278
Kagyu, 112, 113
Kagyupa, 121
Kala, 195
Kalasha, 183
Kali Yuga, 172-173, 175, 179, 185
Kali, 175
Kalpa Sutra, 195, 200
Kalpa, 173
Kama, 178
Kammic, 109
Kandhas/khandhas, 108
Kara, 254
Karah Prashad, 257
Karam Khand, 251
Karam, 251, 253

Kararah Prashad, 256, 258, 259
Karma, 109, 112, 114, 172, 174, 175, 196, 197, 306
Karma Kagyu, 112
Karma yoga, 176
Karma/Kamma, 109
Karmapa, 112, 113
Karmic, 196, 197
Karmically, 109
Karodh, 251
Kartarpuri Bir, 249
Kashered, 211
Kashrut, 210
Katholo, 137
Kaur, 255
Kegon, 111
Kenna, 113
Kensho, 113
Kesh, 254
Keshdare, 254
Ketuvim, 205, 206
Kevalajnana, 193, 194
Kevalin, 197
Khalifa, 225
Khalsa, 251, 254, 259
Khalsa Panth, 249, 251-253
Khand Path, 255, 259
Khanda, 254, 257
Khande di Pahul, 253
Khattris, 179
Khilafa, 228
Khordeh Avesta, 268
Khorshed, 268
Kiddush, 210, 213, 215
Kihism, 262
King of Kings, 301
Kingdom Halls, 293
Kingdom of God, 135, 207
Kings, 206
Kippah, 212
Kirat Kana, 252, 253
Kirk, 49
Kirtan, 256, 259
Kirtan Sohila, 255, 257
Kirtan, 181, 253
Kirth, 118
Kisseh-kerfeh, 274
Kitáb-i Iqán, 93
Kitáb-i-Ahd, 95
Kitáb-i-Aqdas, 93

Koan, 113, 124
Kodashim, 206
Kosher, 210, 211, 213, 219, 231
Koti, 173
Krishna-Janmashtami, 187
Kshathra Vairya, 266, 269, 270
Kshatriya, 180, 194
Kshetra, 195
Kukas, 295-296
Kumkum, 183
Kuriakon, 133
Kushti, 273-275, 277
Kusti, 274

L

Laity, 157, 163
Lam Rim, 121
Lama, 112, 113, 121, 123
Lamas, 107
Langar, 253, 255- 259
Lao, 163
Last Judgement, 135, 143
Last Supper, 144, 145, 151
Latently Omnipotent, 269
Latter-day, 291
Lav, 255
Law of Manu, 173, 180
Lay, 159, 165
Lay Local Preachers, 159
Lay ministers, 124
Lay Preachers, 146, 164
Laying-on of hands, 142
Lectern, 147
Leitourgia, 145
Lent, 143, 149-151
Lesser Pentad, 280
Leva Patel, 187
Leviticus, 205
Liberal, 139, 141, 209, 215, 220
Liberal synagogues, 213
Lilas, 172
Lineages, 112
Linga, 184
Liturgical, 139, 149
Liturgy, 138
Local Assembly, 98, 100
Local Ecumenical Partnerships, 163
Local Ecumenical Projects, 163
Local Inter Faith Organisations, 53

Local Spiritual Assemblies, 95, 98-101
Lohana, 179, 186, 187
Loka, 195
Lord of Feast, 98
Lord of Lords, 301
Lord Swaminarayan, 185
Lord, 133, 149
Lord's Prayer, 144
Lotus of the True Dharma, 107
Lotus Sutra, 114, 122
Lotus, 183
Lotus-Born, 111
Low Church, 139
Lubavich, 220
Luke, 132
Lulav, 216
Lutheran, 130, 160, 161

M

Maariv, 212, 213
Madhahib, 227
Madhhabs, 227
Madrassahs, 237
Magen David, 214
Magga, 108
Maghrib, 232
Magi, 150, 267
Magic, 297
Magisterium, 137
Mah, 280
Maha, 110
Maha Yuga, 175
Mahabharata, 170-173, 175
Mahabokhta, 268
Mahamudra, 112
Maharaj, 188
Maharishi, 306
Mahatma, 180, 199
Mahavairocara (Great Sun) Sutra, 121
Mahavira, 194, 195, 200, 201
Mahavratas, 198, 201
Mahayana, 104, 106-112, 115, 116, 119-121, 123, 267
Mahayana canon, 107
Mahayana Parinirvana Sutra, 107
Mahayana sutras, 107
Mahayanists, 106
Mahdi, 229
Mahzorim, 213

Maidhyairya, 279
Maidyaryam, 279
Maidyoishema, 279
Maidyoizaremaya, 279
Maidyu Shem, 279
Maidyu Zarem, 279
Maliki, 227
Mandal, 201
Mandalas, 116
Mandatum novum, 151
Mandir, 25, 38, 181-184, 186, 188, 199-201
Manifestation of God, 93, 94, 95
Manmukh, 252
Mantra, 114, 116, 122, 172, 181, 198, 199, 200
Manusmriti, 173, 180, 306
Mardi Gras, 150
Marga, 108
Mark, 132
Martyrs, 149
Mas, 146
Mashiach, 133, 207
Mashriqu'l-Adhkar, 97
Masjid, 232
Masorti, 209, 213, 215, 220
Mass, 137, 145
Maste, 92
Mata, 174
Matthew, 132
Matzah, 216
Maulana, 229
Maundy Thursday, 151, 152
Maya, 175-177, 251, 253
Mazdayasni Zarthushti/Zartoshti, 266
Meeting Houses, 146
Mehr, 268
Mela, 258
Melchizedek Priesthood, 291
Men's Traditions, 297
Mendicant, 105, 196-199
Menorah, 214, 217
Meretat, 269
Messenger, 92, 93, 134, 230
Messiah, 133, 207
Messianic, 207
Methodism, 138, 159, 164
Methodist, 22, 63, 68, 130,133, 142, 147, 156, 159, 164
Mezuzah, 212

Mezuzot, 221
Micchami dukkadam, 201
Michaelmas, 152
Mida Buddha, 114
Middle Way, 109
Midrash, 206
Midrashic, 216
Mihrab, 232
Mikveh, 211
Milad, 228
Millennium, 148
Mimamsa, 175
Minbar, 232
Mindfulness, 115
Minhah, 213
Minister, 124, 142, 164
Ministry, 164
Minor Avesta, 268
Minyan, 211, 213
Mishnah, 205, 206
Missa est, 145
Mission, 160
Missionaries, 131, 292
Missionary, 127, 131, 143, 237
Missionary societies, 131
Missionary work, 291
Missions, 131
Mitzvot, 207, 209
Mo'ed, 206
Mobed, 281
Mochis, 179, 186
Moderator of the General Assembly, 165
Moh, 251
Mohel, 209
Moksha, 172, 174-176, 178, 194, 196, 197, 201
Monastery, 103-104, 116-119, 124
Monastic, 107, 123, 197
Monism, 174, 176, 177
Monk, 55, 104, 107, 117-124, 144, 165, 194, 197, 198, 200, 201
Monogamy, 231
Monotheism, 207, 269
Monotheistic, 134, 174, 227, 251
Moonies, 26
Moravian, 130, 161
Mormons, 26, 291
Mosque, 25, 38, 43, 232, 233, 235, 237, 238
Mother Church, 150

Mother of God, 136, 149, 152
Mother Temple of the West, 97
Mother's Day, 150
Motor-Cycle Crash Helmets (Religious Exemption) Act, 57
Mudras, 116
Mufti, 228
Muhpatti, 197
Muktad, 280
Mukti, 251, 253
Mul Mantar, 251
Murti, 181-183, 187
Musaf, 212
Musta'lian Ismailis, 230
Mystery, 135, 297

N

Nagar Kirtan, 259
Nam, 251, 295
Nam Japna, 251, 252
Namaz, 231, 233
Namdhari Sikhs, 296
Nam-myoho-renge-kyo, 114, 122
Namu-Amida-butsu, 114
Nanakshahi, 258
Nand Karaj, 255
Nand Sahib, 256
Nand, 254, 256
Nankana Sahib, 248
Naqshbandi, 230
Nasasalars, 275
Nashim, 206
Nasu, 275
National Assembly, 100
National Spiritual Assemblies, 99-101
Nationality Act, 25
Natural Magic, 300
Nature of Guruship, 296
Navaratri, 185
Navi, 206
Navjote, 272, 273
Navnat, 201
Naya, 195
Nekhamma, 114
Ner Tamid, 214
Nevi'im, 205, 206, 213
New Age, 22
New Church, 23, 43, 130, 162
New Kadampa, 113, 121

New Religious Movements, 22, 285
New Testament, 128, 131-133, 145, 161, 291, 292
New World, 293
New Year, 119
Nezikin, 206
Nibbana, 105
Nicene Creed, 132
Nichiren, 114, 117, 122
Nichiren Shoshu, 121
Nimarta, 251
Nineteen Day Feast, 95-99
Nirgun, 251
Nirjara, 197
Nirodha, 108
Nirukti, 173
Nirvana, 105, 109, 112, 194, 201
Nisham, 257, 259
Nishkam Sewa, 253
Nitya/anicca, 108
Nizari, 226, 230
Noble Eightfold Path, 114, 115
Noble Truths, 109
Nonconformist, 48, 128, 146, 154
Non-consecrated, 199
Non-dualism, 177
Non-dualist Vedanta, 176
Non-statutory National Framework for Religious Education, 65
Non-Trinitarian, 43
No-Roz, 278-280
Northern Buddhism, 123
Northern Ireland Act, 50, 69, 156
Northern Tradition, 298, 300
Northern Transmission, 106
Novice, 123
Nun, 107, 116-120, 122-124, 144, 194, 197, 198, 200, 201
Nyaishe, 268
Nyaishes, 275
Nyaya, 175, 176

O

Odinism, 297
Odinist, 298
Oikumene, 141
Old Testament, 131, 132, 143, 205
OM, 183

One Whom God Shall Make Manifest, 92
Ordained, 114, 124, 146, 162-164
Order, 123, 128, 144, 236
Ordinances, 292
Ordinary Time, 149
Ordination, 123, 152, 164, 165
Oriental Orthodox, 158
Original sin, 136, 150
Orthodox, 22, 25, 130, 132, 136-138, 141, 142, 144, 145, 147-152, 158, 164, 165, 206, 208-215, 219-221
Orthodox Ashkenazi, 220
Orthodox Beth Din, 221
Orthodox church, 132, 138, 141, 142, 145, 147, 148-150, 152, 153, 158, 165
Orthodox Dioceses, 147
Orthodox priests, 165
Orthodox rabbis, 220
Orthodox synagogue, 211-216, 220, 221
Orthodoxy, 137, 138, 208
Oshwal, 201
Outcastes, 179

P

Padan, 281
Padmasambhava Day, 119
Pagan, 131
Pairidaeza, 273
Paiti Shahim, 279
Paitish-hahya, 279
Pali, 104
Pali canon, 107, 108, 111
Panca Silani, 114
Pancami, 200
Panca-namaskara-mantra, 198
Pancha Mahabhuta, 183
Panchang, 184
Panchen Lama, 113
Pandit, 188
Panj Pyare, 252, 253, 257, 259
Panje-kas, 280
Panje-mas, 280
Panth, 252, 295
Papacy, 128, 154
Papal, 131, 157
Paramita, 115

Parampara, 180
Parashah, 212
Parinirvana, 105
Parish, 139, 146, 157, 163, 165
Parochet, 214
Parochial, 139
Parinibbana, 105
Parsanta, 251
Parsee, 24, 31, 267
Parsi, 24, 31, 265, 267, 276, 278, 279
Parve, 210
Paryayas, 195
Paryushana-parva, 200
Paschal, 151
Passion, 149, 151
Passover, 216
Pastors, 164
Patasaer, 254
Path, 256, 257
Patidar, 179, 187
Patriarch, 138, 165
Patriarch of Constantinople, 138
Patristic, 132
Peace and Purity, 288
Pearl of Great Price, 291
Pentecost, 149, 151, 152
Pentecostal, 43, 129, 130, 137, 139, 140, 142, 147, 153, 161, 164
Perfection of Wisdom, 107
Personalist monotheism, 176
Persons, 136
Pesach, 216
Petertide, 152
Pews, 148
Phylacteries, 212
Pilgrim Festivals, 213
Pilgrimage, 255
Pioneering, 95
Pirs, 228-230, 238
Places of Worship Registration Act, 40
Polyandry, 231
Polygamous, 231
Polygamy, 231
Polytheistic, 173, 267, 271
Pope, 127, 131, 137, 143, 165
Poson, 118
Postulants, 124
Practitioners, 289

Prajna, 110
Prajna-paramita sutras, 107
Prakriti, 174, 176, 177
Prasad, 183
Prasada, 184
Prasadam, 183
Prasthana Vakya, 172, 173
Pratikramana, 199
Pravachan, 181
Preach, 164
Preacher, 147
Preaching, 138, 146, 165
Precepts, 116
Prema, 178
Presbuteros, 155, 158
Presbyter, 155, 159
Presbyteral, 164
Presbyterian, 22, 23, 49, 50, 66, 68, 128, 155, 156, 158-160
Presbyterianism, 128, 158
Presbyters, 164
Presbytery, 49, 155
President, 159, 165, 291
President of the Conference, 165
Prevention of Incitement to Hatred Act (Northern Ireland), 61
Priest, 107, 122, 145, 147, 148, 150, 164, 165, 183, 188
Priestesses, 297
Priesthood, 164, 291
Priestly, 267
Primordial Buddha., 112
Principles of Bahá'í Administration, 102
Prinirvana, 118
Progressive, 207, 209-213, 215-216, 219-221
Progressive synagogues, 208, 212, 221
Prophet, 93, 224, 226-228, 230, 234, 266, 291
Protestant, 50, 68
Protestant Churches, 22
Psalms, 206, 210
Public Order (Northern Ireland) Order, 61
Public Order Act, 1986, 61, 62
Pudgalas, 195
Puja, 116-117, 181, 183, 185, 188, 198

Pujari, 188, 201
Pujaris, 188
Pulpit, 232
Puranas, 171-173. 187
Purdah, 231
Pure Land, 107, 111, 113, 114, 121, 123
Purim, 217
Purohit, 188
Purusha Sukta, 179
Purusharthas, 178
Purva Mimamsa, 175, 176
Purvas, 194
Pushtimarg, 187
Qadiri, 228, 230
Qiblah, 232
Qiyas, 226, 228
Qur'an, 224, 226, 228, 229, 230, 231, 234, 237, 238
Qur'anic, 227, 237

R
Rabbi, 206, 212, 213, 219-221
Rabbinate, 219
Rabbinic, 205, 206, 208, 217, 221
Rabbinical, 208
Rabbis, 205, 220, 221
Race Relations Act, 58
Racial and Religious Hatred Bill, 62
Racist Incident Monitoring Annual Report, 62
Rag, 249, 250, 261
Rahit Maryada, 250
Rahit Nama, 250
Rains Retreat, 119
Raja yoga, 176, 188, 287
Rajas, 174
Rajoharana, 197
Rakhi, 178
Rama Rajya, 173
Ramadan, 171-173, 227, 234, 234, 306
Ramayana, 306
Rapithwa, 274
Rapithwin, 274
Rarhi Brahmins, 179
Ras, 301
Ravidasis, 179
Reading Room, 289

Reasoning., 301
Rebbe, 221
Rebecoming, 109
Rebirth, 108-109, 112, 123, 177, 251
Redemption, 216
Reform, 209, 211, 213, 215, 220
Reform Beth Din, 221
Reform synagogue, 220
Reformation, 48, 49, 66, 291
Regional Bahá'í Councils, 100, 101
Rehras, 256
Reincarnation, 109, 112, 113
Religious Offences Bill, 62
Restorationist, 23
Restored Church, 291
Resurrection, 207, 289
Reverend, 221
Rig Veda, 172, 268
Rimé, 112
Rinzai Zen, 113, 121, 124
Rishis, 172
Rites of Passage, 299
Rituals in Babism and Baha'ism, 102
Road Traffic Act, 57
Roman Catholic, 22, 23, 43, 48, 50, 56, 57, 63, 67, 68, 291
Rosh Hashanah, 215, 216
Roz, 280
Rupa, 108, 115
Ruth, 206

S

Sabbath, 206, 209, 210, 215
Sabha, 302
Sach Khand, 251
Sacred Fold, 100
Sacred ordinances, 292
Sadaqa ul-Fitr, 227
Saddharma-pundarika, 107
Sadh sangat, 253, 256
Sadhus, 194, 198, 199, 201
Sadhvis, 194, 198, 201
Sahaj Path, 255, 257
Sahajdhari, 254
Sahib, 257
Sai Baba, 305
Saint, 249, 291, 302
Salah, 226, 231, 233

Salat al-Jum'ah, 232
Sama Veda, 172
Samaj, 201
Samanas, 197
Samanera precepts, 124
Samanis, 197
Samhitas, 172
Samjna, 108
Samkhya, 175
Sampradaya, 177, 182, 187, 189
Samsara, 109, 110, 115, 174, 194
Samskaras, 108
Samudaya, 108
Samuel, 206
Samvatsari-pratikramana, 200
Samyagajiva/samma ajiva, 115
Samyagdrishti/samma ditthi, 114
Samyagvac/samma vaca, 115
Samyagvyayama/samma vayama, 115
Samyak-caritra, 197
Samyak-darshana, 197
Samyak-jnana, 197
Samyakkarmanta/samma kammanta, 114, 115
Samyaksamadhi/samma samadhi, 115
Samyaksamkalpa/samma sankappa, 114
Samyaksmriti/samma sati, 115
Sanatana Dharma, 170, 170, 175, 178, 185
Sanctification, 215
Sangh, 201
Sangha, 105-107, 122-123
Sankharas, 108
Sañña, 108
Sannyasa, 180
Sannyasin, 180, 187
Sant Khalsa, 296
Sant, 252, 261
Santokh, 251
Saoshyant, 273-273
Saram Khand, 251
Sargun, 251
Satanic Verses, 237
Satanism, 297
Satanists, 297
Satguru, 295
Satnam, 251
Sattva, 174, 181, 198

Satya, 175
Saviour, 289
Sawm, 227
Sayyids, 228
Scheduled castes, 106, 180
School Standards and Framework Act, 63
Science and Health with Key to the Scriptures, 289, 290
Sealed, 292
Sealing, 292
Second Review of the Race Relations Act 1976, 58
Second Temple, 217
Sector Study 34, 241
Sects, 285
Sedarim, 206
Seder, 216
Sedreh, 273
Sedreh-Pushi, 273
Sefer Torah, 214
Sephardi, 203, 204, 220, 213
Serious Organised Crime and Police Bill, 62
Sermon on the Mount, 289
Servant of the Glory, 92
Setayash gah, 278
Seva, 182
Seveners, 229
Sewa, 252
Shabads, 249, 250
Shabbat, 206, 207, 209, 210, 212, 213, 216
Shafi'i, 227
Shahada, 230
Shaharit, 212, 213
Shahenshahi, 278
Shahenshahi No-Roz, 279
Shahenshahi Yazdegerdi, 278, 279
Shaivas, 177, 178
Shakyamuni, 105-106, 112, 118
Sakyamuni, 106
Satori, 113
Shalivan, 185
Shalivana, 184
Shalosh Regalim, 215
Shaman, 298, 299
Shamanism, 297, 298
Shamanistic, 298
Shamatha, 115
Samatha, 115

Shametz, 216
Shar'iah, 227, 226, 229-231
Shat Khanda-Agama, 194
Shavuot, 217, 230, 238
Shechita, 219, 231
Shechitah, 211
Sheitel, 212
Shema, 207, 212
Shi'a, 92, 225, 227-230, 234, 236
Shi'a Ithna 'Asherite, 231
Shi'ite, 225
Shiat 'Ali, 225
Shiksa, 173
Shilpaveda, 172
Shingon, 111, 121
Shochet, 211
Shofar, 216
Shoghi Effendi, 95, 99
Shraddha/saddha, 116
Shramanera, 123
Shravakas, 194, 201
Shravakayana, 110
Shrimad Bhagavatam, 171
Shrine room, 117, 118
Shruta, 194
Shruti, 171
Shtetls, 208
Shul, 213
Shulhan Arukh, 206
Shvetambara, 194, 195, 197, 199-
    201
Shvetambara monks, 197
Shvetambara nuns, 197
Siddha, 197
Siddhanta, 194
Siddhas, 199
Siddur, 213
Sidrah, 212
Sikh Code of Conduct, 250
Sikhi, 248
Silsilahs, 230
Simchat Torah, 214, 216
Singh, 252, 255
Sins, 207
Sirozah, 268
Sitting Shivah, 213
Smriti, 171, 172
Sodar Rehras, 256
Sofer, 221
Sohila, 256

Soka Gakkai, 121, 122
Solitaries, 297
Son of God, 289
Song of Songs, 206
Song of the Blessed Lord, 173
Sorthern Transmission, 110, 111,
    119
Soto Zen, 113, 121
Soul, 196, 197
Southern Canon, 104
Southern Transmission, 107, 110,
    111
Spenta Armaiti, 266, 269, 270
Spenta Mainyu, 266, 269, 270
Spiritual Assembly, 30, 99
Splendour, 98
Sravaka, 111
Sri Guru Granth Sahib, 302
Stakes, 291
Star Wars, 35
Sthanakvasi upashraya, 199
Sthanakvasi, 197, 199
Straight tiri, 274
Studies in the Scriptures, 293
Study Circles, 97
Sub-castes, 179
Sudras, 180
Sudreh, 273, 274
Sudreh-kushti, 274
Suf, 230
Sufi, 229, 236, 238
Sufi Orders, 230, 236
Sufism, 228, 230
Suhrawardi, 230
Sukha, 196
Sukkot, 216
Sunna, 225, 226, 228
Sunni, 225, 227-230, 231, 234, 236
Supreme Governor, 49
Surah, 226
Surrendered, 287
Sutra, 107, 111, 114, 119
Sutra/sutta, 107
Sutta-pitaka, 107, 108
Sva-dharma, 178
Swami, 183, 188
Swaminarayan, 177, 187
Swastika, 183, 199
Swayas, 256
Syadvada, 195

Syat, 195
Synagogal, 211
Synagogue, 38, 43, 209, 210-221
Synagogue minister, 221

T

Tabernacles, 216
Tablets, 93
Tablighi Jamaat, 229, 236
Taizokyo, 108
Tallit, 212
Tallitot, 212
Talmud, 205, 206, 208
Talmudic, 219
Tamas, 174
Tanach, 204, 205
Tan-i-pasen, 273
Tantras, 173, 187
Tantric, 110-112
Tanu, 272
Tapas, 197
Tasawwuf, 230
Ta-ts'ang-ching, 107
Tattvartha Sutra, 195
Teaching, 95
Teachings of the Magi, 282
Temple, 119, 205-207, 214, 216,
    292
Temple Ordinances, 292
Ten Commandments, 289
Tenakh, 206
Tephilin, 212, 221
Terapanthi, 197, 199
Terephah, 210
Test Acts, 56
Thang-ka, 116
Theravada, 104-108, 110, 111, 115-
    118, 120, 123
Theravada Buddhism, 118
Theravada monastic, 119, 124
Theravada sangha, 123
Theravadins, 115, 119
Thien, 113, 121
Three Jewels, 122
Three Jewels of Jainism, 197
Three Refuges, 118
Three Signs of Being, 108, 115
Tibetan, 110, 112, 113, 116-119,
    121, 123
Tibetan Book of the Dead, 112

Tibetan Buddhist, 121
Tibetan canon, 108
Tipitak, 107
Tir, 280
Tiri, 274
Tirthankara, 194, 195, 198-200
Tohorot, 206
Torah, 205, 207-210, 212-217, 221, 224, 228
Tower of Silence, 275
Traditionalist, 297
Tranquillity meditation, 115
Translated Treatises, 108
Translated Words of the Buddha, 108
Transmigration, 109
Treat, 175
Treif, 210
Trimurti, 174
Trinity, 291, 293
Triratna/tiratana, 106
Trishna, 109
Trishna/tanha, 108
Trishul, 183
True Guru, 250
Truth Restored, 292
Tulku, 112, 113
Tupa/thupa, 117
Tupas, 117
Turban, 254
Twelvers, 227, 229
Tzitzit, 212

U

Udasis, 248
Ulama, 238
Ultra-Orthodox, 208
Unity Feast, 97, 98
Universal House of Justice, 92, 95, 96, 100, 101
Untouchability, 180
Untouchables, 106, 180
Upadhyayas, 199
Upanishads, 172, 176
Upas, 106
Upasaka, 107
Upasampada, 123
Upashraya, 199
Upasika, 107
Upavedas, 172

Uposatha Days, 118
Urvan, 271, 272, 276
Ushah, 274
Ushahin, 274
Usul al-fiqh, 227
Uttara Mimamsa, 175
Uzayara, 274
Uzerin, 274

V

Vahana, 183
Vaidyas, 179
Vaisakha Puja, 118
Vaisakhi, 259, 261
Vaisesika, 175
Vaisheshika, 175
Vaishnava, 171, 177-178, 185
Vaishnava sampradayas, 178
Vaishyas, 180
Vajradhara, 112
Vajrayana, 110, 112
Vallabha sampradaya, 187
Vanaprastha, 180
Vand chhakna, 252
Vanir, 298
Varna, 178, 179, 188
Vars, 250
Vassa, 119
Veda, 171, 172
Vedanga, 172
Vedangas, 173
Vedanta, 175, 176
Vedanta-Sutras, 173
Vedas, 187, 170-173, 179, 187
Vendidad, 267, 268, 275
Vidaeva-data, 268
Vietnamese Buddhism, 114
Vihara, 117, 119, 120
Vijayadashami, 185
Vikram, 184
Vikram Samvat, 184
Vikramasamvat, 200
Vinaya-pitaka, 107
Vipaka, 109
Vipashyana/ vipassana, 115
Vipassana, 115
Vira-nirvana-samvat, 200
Virgin birth, 289
Vispe Ratavo, 268
Visperad, 268

Visualisation, 111
Vohu Manah, 266, 269, 270, 273, 274
Vrats, 181
Vyakarana, 173
Vyasasanas, 183

W

Wa 'alaikum-us-salaam, 233
Waheguru, 251
Ward, 291
Way of the Elders, 110
Wayas, 256
Wayas, Chaupai, 254
Wesak, 118
Wicca, 297-300
Will and Testament, 95
Wills, 96
Women's Mystery Shaman, 298
Women's Traditions, 297
Word, 248, 249
Word of God, 250
Writings, 93
Wudu, 232, 233

Y

Yad, 214
Yajur Veda, 172
Yalwa Karmapa, 112
Yamim Noraim, 215
Yana, 110
Yarmulkah, 212
Yasht, 268
Yasht-i-Visperad, 279
Yasna, 267-268, 271, 274, 275, 280
Yazata Mehr, 280
Yazatas, 268, 270-272, 274, 278, 280
Yazatas/Yazads, 268, 271
Yazdegerdi, 278
Yazdegird, 279
Yeshiv, 219
Yeshivot, 218, 219
Yingma, 112
Yoga, 175, 176, 188
Yom Kippur, 216
Younger Avesta, 269
Yuga, 171, 172
Yugabda, 184
Yugas, 287

Z

Zaat, 260
Zad Rooz-e Ashoo Zartosht, 279
Zakat, 233
Zaotar, 266
Zarathushtrianism, 266
Zazen, 113
Zen Way,, 125
Zera'im, 206
Zion's Watch Tower, 293
Zionism, 208
Zionist, 208, 219
Zohar, 208
Zuhr, 232